THE NEIGHBORS RESPOND

THE NEIGHBORS RESPOND

THE CONTROVERSY OVER THE
JEDWABNE MASSACRE IN POLAND

Edited by Antony Polonsky
and Joanna B. Michlic

PRINCETON UNIVERSITY PRESS

PRINCETON AND OXFORD

LIBRARY OF CONGRESS CATALOGING-IN-PUBLICATION DATA

THE NEIGHBORS RESPOND : THE CONTROVERSY OVER THE JEDWABNE MASSACRE

IN POLAND / EDITED BY ANTONY POLONSKY AND JOANNA B. MICHLIC.

P.   CM.

INCLUDES BIBLIOGRAPHICAL REFERENCES AND INDEX.

ISBN 0-691-11643-1 (ALK. PAPER) — ISBN 0-691-11306-8 (PBK. : ALK. PAPER)

1. JEWS—PERSECUTIONS—POLAND—JEDWABNE. 2. HOLOCAUST, JEWISH (1939–1945)—

POLAND—JEDWABNE—MORAL AND ETHICAL ASPECTS. 3. ANTISEMITISM—

POLAND—JEDWABNE—HISTORY—20TH CENTURY. 4. JEDWABNE (POLAND)—

ETHNIC RELATIONS. 5. GROSS, JAN TOMASZ. SĄSIEDZI. I. POLONSKY, ANTONY.

II. MICHLIC, JOANNA B.

DS135.P62J4458   2004

940.53′18′09438—dc21   2003043366

BRITISH LIBRARY CATALOGING-IN-PUBLICATION DATA IS AVAILABLE.

THIS BOOK HAS BEEN COMPOSED IN PALATINO

PRINTED ON ACID-FREE PAPER. ∞

WWW.PUPRESS.PRINCETON.EDU

PRINTED IN THE UNITED STATES OF AMERICA

1   3   5   7   9   10   8   6   4   2

The Institute for National Memory has been attacked because it has investigated crimes committed by Poles and not against Poles. I should like to underline what Professor Kieres has repeatedly emphasized, speaking about Jedwabne, and remind you that "those who died there were also citizens of Poland—of a different faith, with different customs and traditions. The Jews of Jedwabne were Poles. . . ." This is simple and obvious, yet at the same time how difficult it is for us to comprehend it.

—*Father Adam Boniecki*

CONTENTS

PREFACE

THE DEBATE provoked by the publication of Jan Gross's book *Sąsiedzi: Historia zagłady żydowskiego miasteczka* (Sejny, 2000) and its English translation *Neighbors: The Destruction of the Jewish Community in Jedwabne, Poland* (Princeton, 2001) has been the most prolonged and far-reaching of any discussion of the Jewish issue in Poland since the Second World War. It is also probably the most profound examination of any social issue since the end of the Communist regime in 1989 and the establishment of a pluralistic and democratic political system. The number of articles on the topic runs into the hundreds, not to mention the large number of Web sites on which the issues it raises have been aired. In this volume it has been our goal to enable a non-Polish reader to understand the issues in the debate and the positions adopted by the various participants. Poland's complex and painful past, with its long struggle to regain its lost independence and the traumas the country experienced in the twentieth century, has often made it seem to outsiders that Polish culture is hermetic and difficult to grasp. We do not believe this to be the case. The issues raised by the controversy over the Jedwabne massacre are echoed in many other European countries and have a wide significance in a world in which large numbers of national groups and states are struggling to come to terms with the difficult aspects of their past.

We have tried to orient the reader by providing an introduction and explanatory notes, both in individual articles and at the end of the volume. We have divided the book into seven parts. The first deals with the initial reporting of the issue, both before and after the publication of *Neighbors*. The second examines the response of the Polish intelligentsia, which still sees itself as charged with the heavy responsibility of articulating the national stance in the face of disturbing and complex issues. The third investigates the way the official organs of Polish society have reacted to the crisis, and the fourth looks at the divisions that have arisen over the issue in the Roman Catholic Church in Poland. The fifth outlines the way the inhabitants of the town of Jedwabne itself have attempted to deal with their painful past. The largest section, the sixth, deals with the historical debate. This is because we firmly believe that the way forward must lie above all in a thorough and careful analysis of the past, which will go beyond the necessary moral reckonings and will lead to a degree of agreement and understanding about what occurred. Even if we cannot change the past, we can at least come to accept the tragic events of which it is composed. The final section briefly examines the debate outside Poland.

We believe that the debate, acrimonious and bad-tempered as it has sometimes been, is a necessary stage in the creation of a democratic and pluralistic Poland. It is part of a reckoning with the past long delayed by the negative impact of communist censorship and taboos. It is our hope that this volume will be a part of this process and will also make it more widely known and understood outside Poland.

We would like to express our gratitude to all those who have given their permission to have their views reproduced here. In particular we are obliged to Zbigniew Nosowski, chief editor of *Więź*, and to the staff of the periodical, to whose publication *Thou Shalt Not Kill: Poles on Jedwabne* (Warsaw, 2001) we are especially indebted. There are many articles that we would like to have included but were unable to do so because of the constraints of space. We apologize to their authors and encourage the reader to see this volume as only a small part of a much larger debate. In addition, we should like to express our appreciation to the David and Barbara B. Hirschorn Foundation for a grant toward the cost of translating and editing the texts in this volume.

Translations, unless otherwise noted, are by Claire Rosenson, for whose assistance we are very grateful.

INTRODUCTION

"We were taught as children"—I was told by a seventy-
year-old Pole—"that we Poles never harmed anyone. A
partial abandonment of this morally comfortable position
is very, very difficult for me."
—Helga Hirsch, a German journalist, in
Polityka, 24 February 2001

T HE COMPLEX and often acrimonious debate about the character and significance of the massacre of the Jewish population of
the small Polish town of Jedwabne in the summer of 1941—a
debate provoked by the publication of Jan Gross's *Sąsiedzi: Historia zagłady żydowskiego miasteczka* (Sejny, 2000) and its English translation
Neighbors: The Destruction of the Jewish Community in Jedwabne, Poland
(Princeton, 2001)—is part of a much wider argument about the totalitarian experience of Europe in the twentieth century. This controversy
reflects the growing preoccupation with the issue of collective memory,
which Henri Rousso has characterized as a central "value" reflecting
the spirit of our time.[1] One key element in the understanding of collective memory is the "dark past" of nations—those aspects of the national past that provoke shame, guilt, and regret; this past needs to be
integrated into the national collective identity, which itself is continually being reformulated.[2] In this sense, memory has to be understood
as a public discourse that helps to build group identity and is inevitably entangled in a relationship of mutual dependence with other iden-
tity-building processes. As John Gillis has written, "The core meaning
of any individual or group identity, namely, a sense of sameness over
time and space, is sustained by remembering; and what is remembered
is defined by the assumed identity."[3] Consequently, memory cannot be
seen as static and unchanging. Rather, it is a representation of past reality, revised and modified according to the changing demands of present-day identity, something that is itself subject to modification.[4]

[1] Henry Rousso, *La hantise du passé: Entretien avec Phillipe Petit* (Paris, 1998), 14. English translation: *The Haunting Past: History, Memory and Justice in Contemporary France*
(Philadelphia, 2002).
[2] The "dark past" is a commonly used term in studies of collective memory. Similar
recurrent locutions are the "difficult past" and the "troubling past."
[3] John R. Gillis, "Memory and Identity: The History of a Relationship," in *Commemorations: The Politics of National Identity,* ed. John R. Gillis (Princeton, 1994), 3.
[4] Ibid.

The retrieval of the "dark past" is further complicated by a problem that has been highlighted in the work of Franklin Ankersmit,[5] who maintains that the only point when the past truly exposes itself to us is at the moment of trauma, which causes shock and pain. Trauma causes our convictions, categories, and expectations to shatter, and history is composed of traumatic collective experiences. The "traumatic past" is a record not of past events but rather of the impact of experiences that cannot be assimilated or accepted. It has a paradoxical character because it can be neither forgotten nor remembered. "Normal" history can be acquired, adopted, domesticated—traumatic history cannot. The traumatic past, whether private or national, exists within us like a foreign body of which we cannot rid ourselves. Yet, at the same time, there is a marked disinclination to confront these painful memories. Ankersmit argues that the only way to cope with such traumas is to accept that there is a conflict among different memories of the past. The discourse of the historian, which, he claims, merely examines the past but does not try to explore or penetrate it, must be replaced by that of traumatic memory.

Central to the recovery and understanding of the "dark past" have been the debates that have taken place in many countries in Europe about the origins and character of the genocide which the Nazis attempted to inflict on the Jewish people during the Second World War. These debates have been possible only in situations where the political culture has permitted a public reckoning with the more dubious aspects of the national past, and where there is a high level of acceptance of the practice of national self-criticism.[6] Not surprisingly, they have gone furthest in Germany, first in the Federal Republic and subsequently in the united Germany that was established in 1989. Starting with the controversy over Germany's responsibility for the outbreak of the First World War, aroused by the publication of Fritz Fischer's *Griff nach der Weltmacht* in 1961, German historians have undertaken a thorough and complex reexamination of their country's past, which culminated in the *Historikerstreit* of the 1980s and the debate over Daniel Goldhagen's *Hitler's Willing Executioners*. This has greatly clarified the problems of how the Nazis came to power, the nature of the regime they established, and how they came to adopt and implement their anti-Jewish genocide. A similar wide-ranging debate has also devel-

[5] F. Ankersmit, "Remembering the Holocaust: Mourning and Melancholia," in *Reclaiming Memory: American Representations of the Holocaust*, ed. P. Ahokas and M. Chard-Hutchinson (Turku, 1997).

[6] The importance of the practice of self-criticism for the process of reckoning with the "dark past" is raised by Iwona Irwin-Zarecka, *Frames of Remembrance* (New Brunswick and London, 1994).

oped in France, although it started somewhat later, over the character of the Vichy regime, the nature of the antisemitic policies it implemented, and its responsibility for the deaths of perhaps a quarter of French Jews in the Holocaust. Analogous attempts to "overcome the past" have been undertaken in Austria, Switzerland, and elsewhere in Western and Central Europe, although the extent to which they have modified attitudes is debatable.

The question of local populations' responsibility for the fate of the Jews in the Nazi genocide in East-central Europe began to be seriously discussed only after the collapse of communism in the area in 1989–1991. This was the case both in the states that were allied with the Nazis during the Second World War and in those occupied areas where no state-level collaborationist regimes were established by the Nazis, as in Lithuania, Belarus, and Ukraine. Since then there has been considerable dispute in Romania about the role of General Ion Antonescu, and in Slovakia of Father Tiso, and of the conduct of the Nazi satellite regimes in Hungary and Croatia. There has also been a good deal of debate in Lithuania and Latvia, and rather less in Ukraine, about the participation of local militias in the mass murder of Jews.

The debate in Poland goes back somewhat further than in its neighboring countries. Poland, home of the largest Jewish community in Europe in 1939, was one of the principal areas where the Nazis attempted to carry out their planned genocide of European Jewry. It was here that the principal death camps were established, and that Jews were brought from all over Nazi-occupied Europe to be gassed, above all in Auschwitz, where probably one million lost their lives in this way. Over 90 percent of Polish Jews perished in the Holocaust, a death rate exceeded only in the Baltic states. Most of them died in the period before the end of 1942, when Nazi power was at its height, when there was little possibility either within Axis-occupied Europe or outside of halting their genocidal activities. But this has not stilled criticism of the response of Polish society. To the small group of Jews who survived in Poland or who returned from the USSR, Polish behavior during the war seemed to have confirmed their worst suspicions. It was clear to them that they were not wanted on Polish soil, and even that it was dangerous for them to remain in Poland. In their eyes, the Poles had stood aside while the Nazis had implemented their murderous plans. The small amount of assistance provided was, in their eyes, outweighed by the activities of the denouncers and blackmailers, while the attitude of the majority was, at best, indifferent. This feeling of alienation was strengthened by the postwar insecurity and the outbreaks of anti-Jewish violence that culminated in the Kielce pogrom of July 1946, in which at least forty Jews were murdered.

Under these circumstances, it is perhaps not surprising that the assessment by the surviving Jews of the behavior of Polish society during the Holocaust should have been negative. According to Mordekhai Tenenbaum, commander of the Jewish Fighting Organization in the Białystok ghetto, whose memoirs were published shortly after the war:

> If it had not been for the Poles, for their aid—passive and active— in the "solution" of the Jewish problem in Poland, the Germans would never have dared to do what they did. It was they, the Poles, who called out "Yid" at every Jew who escaped from the train transporting him; it was they who caught the unfortunate wretches, who rejoiced at every Jewish misfortune—they were vile and contemptible.[7]

A somewhat more moderate but still strongly critical view was expressed by Emanuel Ringelblum in his *Polish-Jewish Relations during the Second World War*, written in hiding on the "Aryan" side in 1944:

> The Polish people and the Government of the Republic of Poland were incapable of deflecting the Nazi steam-roller from its anti-Jewish course. But the question is permissible whether the attitude of the Polish people befitted the enormity of the calamities that befell the country's citizens. Was it inevitable that the Jews, looking their last on this world as they rode in the death trains speeding from different parts of the country to Treblinka or other places of slaughter, should have had to witness indifference or even joy on the faces of their neighbors? In the summer of 1942, when carts packed with captive Jewish men, women and children moved through the streets of the capital, did there really need to be laughter from the wild mobs resounding from the other side of the ghetto walls, did there really have to prevail such blank indifference in the face of the greatest tragedy of all time?[8]

These views are echoed in the most important scholarly investigation of the problem, that by Yisrael Gutman and Shmuel Krakowski,[9] and are shared by the doyen of Holocaust historians, Yehuda Bauer. He has written:

---

[7] Mordekhai Tenenbaum, *Dapim min hadelekah* (Bet lohamei hageta'ot, hakibbuts hameuhad, 1947), 49–50.

[8] Emanuel Ringelblum, *Polish-Jewish Relations during the Second World War*, ed. Joseph Kermish and Shmuel Krakowski (Evanston, Ill., 1992), 7–8.

[9] Yisrael Gutman and Shmuel Krakowski, *Unequal Victims: Poles and Jews during World War Two* (New York, 1968).

The picture that finally emerges is not a very pleasant one. There were some Poles who helped; there were groups of Poles who helped, too . . . [b]ut the majority, and that included the official underground linked to the Government-in-Exile in London and its armed forces, were either indifferent or actively hostile.[10]

Until recently, most Poles have rejected these charges and have attempted to explain the conditions that determined Polish behavior, and to assert that in no way could more assistance have been provided to the Jews. This response soon became an integral part of the wider process by which the postwar Communist regime attempted to transform all aspects of Polish society. During the Communist era, the memory of the Holocaust was subordinated to a far-reaching process of reworking and manipulation, which served the authorities' political and ideological needs. As a result, a specific representation of the Holocaust was constructed that became the paradigm for remembering this event in the Polish collective memory, and that was expressed and cultivated in a strictly controlled cultural scene, commemorative sites, official speeches, and historical narratives.

The process of reworking the memory of the Holocaust started during the Stalinist period (1948–1953). At this time, the genocide came to be perceived as an inconvenient subject for the newly established Communist regime, as well as for other Eastern European communist states such as East Germany. It could not easily be fitted into the obligatory Soviet narratives of the antifascist front of the working class and of the "Great Patriotic War." Stalin's growing obsession with Jewish matters, which culminated in the liquidation of Soviet Yiddish culture and the execution of the main Jewish cultural figures in the USSR, along with attempts to provide the Communist regime in Poland with a degree of national legitimation, also played a role in the official evaluation and presentation of the fate of the Jews during the Second World War. As a result, as Michael Steinlauf has described in the classic work on the subject, *Bondage to the Dead: Poland and the Memory of the Holocaust*, the Holocaust became marginalized and was repressed in public memory.[11] An illustration of this marginalization was the fate of the sites of Holocaust commemoration, such as the monument to the Warsaw ghetto fighters designed by Nathan Rappaport, which was unveiled in Warsaw in 1948.[12] Commemorations staged at that site were

[10] Introduction to ibid., iii.

[11] Michael C. Steinlauf, *Bondage to the Dead: Poland and the Memory of the Holocaust* (Syracuse, 1997), 63–74.

[12] See, for example, Marcin Zaremba, "Urząd zapomnienia," *Polityka*, no. 41 (13 October 2001): 72.

designed not to emphasize its Jewish character and meaning. Indeed, one could argue that from its inception the site was transformed from a place of collective remembrance to one of ritual forgetting, a "collective amnesia" that was to be its chief characteristic until the 1980s.

The regime's attitude toward the discussion of this aspect of Poland's "dark past" also reflected the widespread conviction of its ideologues that "one should not stress Jewish matters." The questioning of Polish attitudes and behavior toward Jews during the war was no longer allowed, and the postwar debate of 1945–1947 on Polish-Jewish relations and Polish antisemitism, which had been begun by a small group of intellectuals, was abruptly silenced in 1948.[13] The discussion of these issues in literary and historical works also became taboo.

The reworking of the memory of the Jewish genocide was completed in the second half of the fifties and throughout the sixties when Władysław Gomułka was first secretary of the Polish United Workers' Party (PZPR). It was part of the gradual process of the ethnonationalization of communism, in accordance with the frequently observed phenomenon that "all communism tends to become national communism," and of the resurfacing of the "Jewish question" within the Party itself.[14] This was also the period in which communist narratives became increasingly acceptable to and accepted by the general public. Michael Steinlauf has convincingly argued that this acceptance was possible only because "the official way of dealing with the memory of the Holocaust reflected, after all, a popular need."[15]

As in the previous Stalinist period, the specific features of the Holocaust were subsumed by the "internationalization" of its victims. This was nowhere more apparent than in the commemorative rituals at the Auschwitz-Birkenau memorial site, where the word "Jew" was hardly mentioned and the Jewish victims were encompassed in the nationality of the countries from which they came. At the same time, the Holocaust was integrated into the specific national framework of the Polish collective memory of the war. The genocide of Polish Jews was usually presented as an integral part of the ethnic Polish tragedy, as in the statement that "six million Poles died during the war," which also strengthened the popular belief that the Poles had suffered more than

[13] On the first postwar debate on the "dark past" in Polish-Jewish relations, see, for example, Joanna Michlic, "The Holocaust and Its Aftermath As Perceived in Poland: Voices of Polish Intellectuals, 1945–1947," in *The Return of Jews to Europe, 1945–49*, ed. David Bankier (forthcoming Jerusalem, 2004).

[14] On the development of the patterns of remembering the Holocaust during the communist era, see, for example, Lucy Davidowicz, *The Holocaust and the Historians* (Cambridge, Mass., 1981), 88–124; and Steinlauf, *Bondage*, 62–88.

[15] Steinlauf, *Bondage*, 74.

any other nation during this period.[16] This, in turn, led to the presentation of the Holocaust as an event somehow parallel to the ethnic Polish tragedy of the war: Jewish deaths were described as numerically ✗ equivalent to ethnic Polish deaths, and the distinction between the fate of Poles and Jews was blurred.

In addition, the memory of the Polish "dark past" continued to be neutralized and silenced in the public sphere. If negative Polish behavior was mentioned at all, as in the case of the blackmailers who preyed on Jews attempting to hide on the "Aryan side," this was presented as a marginal social problem, limited to a small and unrepresentative group, a phenomenon that was paralleled in other European countries. Discussion of such issues was also generally confined to a small number of publications, usually of the Jewish Historical Institute (ŻIH) in Warsaw, which were not intended for mass circulation. Official history emphasized the solidarity of Polish society with the Jews and the widespread support for attempts to rescue and hide Jews. It clearly served the Party's attempt to present itself as a national body representing the interests of the Polish people. This was part of a process, which was particularly marked in the Gierek years (1970–1980), of stressing the "moral and political unity of the nation" and avoiding controversial topics or issues that could highlight negative aspects of its citizens' behavior. It evoked a largely positive response, since it catered to the universal human desire to avoid confrontations with the less creditable aspects of the past.

It should be stressed that these narratives were not constructed by the Polish United Workers' Party but appropriated from the anticommunist opposition. During the war, as David Engel has demonstrated, the Polish government-in-exile, embarrassed to learn of antisemitic views among Poles under Nazi occupation, attempted to protect the country's "good name" by promoting such conceptions.[17] This response can be seen even earlier. For instance, when accounts of anti-Jewish violence after the First World War emerged in the West, many Poles reacted defensively, convinced that Poland's "honor" and "reputation" were being attacked by unnamed forces who wished to under-

---

✗ [16] Polish studies carried out since the fall of communism have established that a maximum of 2 million Polish Christians were killed during the war. These studies have corroborated the figure of 3 million Polish Jews killed. The studies, by Prof. Krystyna Kersten and others, were published in 1994 in the Warsaw journal *Dzieje Najnowsze* 26, no. 2. Estimates of Polish casualties at Soviet hands have also recently decreased and are probably around 200,000.

[17] See D. Engel, *In the Shadow of Auschwitz: The Polish Government-in-Exile and the Jews, 1939–1942* (Chapel Hill, N.C., 1987) and *Facing a Holocaust: The Polish Government-in-Exile and the Jews, 1943–1945* (Chapel Hill, N.C., 1993), passim.

mine the country's newly won independence. In the fifties and sixties, such views were also frequently disseminated in Polish émigré circles and by individuals in Poland who had themselves been victims of Stalinist repression. "Official history" narratives have also been a feature of the debate about *Neighbors*.

In the late sixties, the "Partisan" faction within the Party, led by General Mieczysław Moczar, undertook a further tendentious reworking of the memory of the Holocaust, which resulted in the construction of a radical version of the dominant paradigm embodying strongly anti-Jewish elements.[18] This version became an integral part of the official antisemitic campaign, which culminated in the "anti-Zionist" purge of 1968.

The Partisans represented the ethnonationalist faction within the Party, and their ideological position was an eerie reincarnation of the views of the prewar National Democratic Party (Endecja), which had seen in "the Jew" a major threat to Poland and its people.[19] Indeed, they even at times exploited the traditional stereotype of Judeo-communism (Żydokomuna). The Partisans' acceptance of this antisemitic stereotype inevitably led to a mind-set that saw the Holocaust, with its specifically Jewish character, as a threat to their emphasis on Polish wartime martyrdom and suffering, as well as to their use of their own partisan past to establish a degree of legitimacy for the unpopular communist regime. In turn, this led to the replacement of the previous official narrative of the "parallel" fates of Jews and Poles during the war with a more radical version that *equated* the fates of Jews and Poles, stressing that the two groups were similarly persecuted by the Nazis. A good illustration of this shift was the revision in 1968 of the entry "Nazi concentration camps" in volume 8 of the 1966 *Wielka Encyklopedia Powszechna* (Great universal encyclopedia). The editors of the original article had distinguished between the annihilation camps, in which almost all the victims were Jews, and the concentration camps, in which many of the prisoners were ethnic Poles. In the Partisans' amended version this distinction was explicitly repudiated, and the

---

[18] Mieczysław Moczar was a leading figure in the communist underground in Poland during the war. Demoted together with Gomułka in 1948, he returned to office after 1956, first as deputy minister of the interior and then as minister of the interior. As leader of the "Partisans' Group" within the PZPR, he hoped to establish a firmer base for communism in Poland by making it more nationalistic and populist.

[19] The Endecja, the commonly used acronym for the National Democratic Party, was a prewar nationalist movement that enjoyed wide public support. Its leader Roman Dmowski is known as the father of Polish ethnic nationalism. The Endecja was characterized by various anti-Jewish views and practices.

editor responsible for the original article, who was of Jewish origin, was dismissed.

The Partisans' concept of the equal fate of Poles and Jews under Nazi occupation can be viewed as a manifestation of the peculiar and distasteful competition over "who suffered most," a competition that has remained an integral element of the Polish apologetic position and has been a feature of the debate over Jan Gross's *Neighbors*. It has a "non-suffering" variant, which claims that whatever wrongs the Poles may have committed against the Jews, these are equaled, if not outweighed, by the wrongs that the Jews committed against the Poles. In his diary in 1970, the historian Witold Kuła commented acidly, "In the past the Jews were envied because of their money, qualifications, positions, and international contacts—today they are envied because of the crematoria in which they were burned."[20]

Alongside this concept of the equal fate shared by Poles and Jews, the Partisans developed another theme that has since become firmly established in the apologetic arsenal, the argument that, in the West, Polish martyrdom was being downplayed, because of Jewish "antipolonism," a prejudice similar to antisemitism. This idea developed at a time when critical accounts of Polish behavior toward the Jews during the war appeared in the West. The Partisans seized on simpleminded presentations that described the Poles as "eternal antisemites" and accomplices to the Nazi genocide. Given that Polish-Jewish relations were often presented in Western Europe, North America, and Israel in a highly superficial and biased manner, this struck a chord. The Partisans exploited resentment of these stereotypical images among Poles both in the country and in émigré circles to advance their political ends, hoping to portray the West as "anti-Polish" and themselves as the defenders of Polish national honor. Any investigation into the negative aspects of the Polish past was also labeled "anti-Polish," and anyone undertaking such an investigation was seen as a tool of "antipolonism."

Along with the sanitized version of the Polish past that they promoted, the Partisans also highlighted negative aspects of Jewish behavior with the aim of presenting Polish treatment of the Jews in a more favorable light. They stressed the "lack of gratitude" on the part of Polish Jews toward Poles who had assisted them, their "anti-Polish" behavior during the war, their passivity in the face of the genocide, and the collaboration of the Jewish Councils and Jewish Police with the Nazis. In this last area, they frequently cited the work of

[20] Witold Kula, *Rozdziałki* (Warsaw, 1996), 213.

Hannah Arendt. These motifs have also been elaborated upon during recent years.

Given the fact that by the late sixties the Partisans had managed to obtain control of a large segment of the national mass media as well as institutions of national heritage and education, their version of the Holocaust cannot be regarded as insignificant. As Michael Steinlauf has pointed out, it was at this time that the memory of the Holocaust was expelled from public consciousness.[21] The Partisans also succeeded in sweeping the issue of the "dark Polish past" completely under the carpet. Moreover, their version of Holocaust memory was to become the basis for the "radical apologetic" position with its anti-Jewish elements, a point of view that has been held in the past two decades not only by former national communists but also by a variety of right-wing ethnonationalists. This was apparent in the acrimonious debate over the future of the Carmelite convent in the Auschwitz concentration camp, and its legacy is clearly to be seen in the debate over *Neighbors*.[22]

Indeed, it is striking that one of the most characteristic articulations of the apologetic point of view on the Polish-Jewish past should have been set out, not by one of the national communists, but by the late Władysław Siła-Nowicki, a prominent opposition lawyer and former resistance fighter. In a 1987 article he attacked those who voiced a harsh assessment of the Polish record during the Second World War in relation to the Jews, arguing that such views played into the hands of Poland's enemies and lent credibility to "anti-Polish propaganda." He then rehearsed the arguments already described as characteristic of the apologetic position. For centuries, he asserted, when they were expelled elsewhere, Jews were able to settle in Poland and their numbers increased remarkably. The hostility they aroused before 1939 was moderate considering their privileged position. They "dominated" certain professions and controlled a "disproportionate part" of wealth in Poland. The prewar quota on university admissions (the *numerus clausus*) for Jews was justified since "it is natural for a society to defend itself against the numerical domination of its intelligentsia." During the war, no European nation did more to assist Jews than Poland, where the risk of such assistance was the greatest, the normal penalty being death—and death not only of the individual but of his or her family as well. Polish suffering during the occupation was enormous, second only to that of the Jews. There were, he argued, no quislings in Poland, and the Polish underground sentenced to death those who betrayed

[21] Steinlauf, *Bondage*, 75–88.
[22] See Władysław T. Bartoszewski, *The Convent at Auschwitz* (London, 1990).

Jews to the Nazis. It was the passivity of the Jews, more than anything else, that led to their destruction. Habits of accommodation, presumably different from those of the rebellious, insurrectionary Poles, caused them to go to their deaths without offering resistance. He concluded defiantly (and inconsistently):

> I am proud of my nation's stance in every respect during the period of occupation, and in this I include the attitude toward the tragedy of the Jewish nation. Obviously, attitudes toward the Jews during that period do not give us a particular reason to be proud, but neither are they any grounds for shame, and even less for ignominy. Simply, we could have done relatively little more than we actually did.[23]

There was, however, a persistent minority position that took a much more critical view of the Polish-Jewish past and of Polish behavior during the Holocaust. In the immediate postwar period, before the imposition of a rigidly Stalinist and Soviet-dominated regime, there were several efforts to come to terms with these issues. It was at this time that Michał Borwicz and his colleagues at the newly established Jewish Historical Commission (the precursor of the Jewish Historical Institute) initiated a very valuable attempt to document the events of the Shoah and to preserve the testimony of the survivors. Several courageous Polish voices also castigated the evil of antisemitism. They included the writer Jerzy Andrzejewski who observed in 1947:

> For all honest Poles, the fate of the perishing Jews must have been exceedingly painful, for the dying were people whom our people could not look straight in the face, with a clear conscience. The Polish people could look straight in the face of Polish men and women who were dying for freedom, not in the face of the Jews dying in the burning ghettos.[24]

The Kielce pogrom provoked the sociologist Stanisław Ossowski to write:

> A more far-sighted, cynical or wily person, or someone with greater historical knowledge, might have recalled that sympathy is not the only reaction to the misfortune of others; that those whom the gods have singled out for extinction easily become re-

---

[23] Władysław Siła-Nowicki, "Jan Błoński w odpowiedzi," *Tygodnik Powszechny*, 22 February 1987. For an English translation, see Antony Polonsky, ed., *'My Brother's Keeper?' Recent Polish Debates on the Holocaust* (London, 1990), 59–68.

[24] J. Andrzejewski, "Zagadnienia Polskiego Antysemitizmu" (The problem of Polish antisemitism), in *Martwa fala* (The dead wave) (Warsaw, 1947).

pugnant to others and are even removed from inter-human relations. He might also recall that if one person's tragedy gives someone else an advantage, it often happens that people want to
convince themselves and others that the tragedy was morally justified. Such persons as the owners of former Jewish shops or those
who harass their Jewish competitors can be included in this group.
And perhaps by citing a whole array of historical examples, I
could express my doubt as to whether the reaction against the
Nazi achievements will, in the short run, root out the influences
of the Nazi spirit which, within the course of a few years, attained
so much and which led human awareness to become inured, because of their frequent repetition, to certain offensive slogans.[25]

However, the political climate exercised a baleful effect on these attempts to "overcome the past," and it was only in the late 1970s and
the 1980s that a new willingness began to develop to look again at
the thorny and difficult problem of Polish-Jewish relations during the
Second World War. This was an inevitable consequence of the growth
of interest in the Polish-Jewish past that was a feature of those years.
It was increasingly realized in Polish oppositional circles that Poland
had been for nearly seven hundred years one of the main centers of
the Jewish Diaspora, and from the early 1980s, the importance of the
development of this community for Polish life was widely recognized.
Departments of Jewish history were created at the Jagiellonian University in Kraków, the University of Warsaw, the University of Lublin, and
a number of other centers. Interest in the Jewish past became widespread. Books on Jewish subjects disappeared rapidly from the shops,
plays on Jewish themes were sold out, and performances of visiting
Israeli dance companies or orchestras were greeted with rapturous applause. Jewish history and culture were also among the subjects studied by the underground "flying university" in the late 1970s. Similarly,
at that time the Catholic Church and the opposition began to sponsor
"Weeks of Jewish Culture" in a number of cities, during which school-
children and university students attended lectures on Jewish topics
and participated in the restoration of Jewish cemeteries. Catholic
monthlies like *Znak* and *Więź* devoted entire issues to Jewish topics, a
phenomenon that has continued since the end of communism in 1989.
One of its most striking manifestations has been the enormously popular annual Festival of Jewish Culture in Kraków.

This interest is partly nostalgic in character. Poland today is practically monoethnic and monoreligious (although this homogeneity

[25] Quoted by Yisrael Gutman in "Ethical Problems of the Holocaust in Poland," in
Polonsky, *'My Brother's Keeper?'*, 205.

should not be exaggerated), and there is a genuine sense of loss at the disappearance of the more colorful Poland of the past, with its mixture of religions and nationalities. It does, however, have a deeper character. The experiences of the Solidarity years also gave the Poles a greater sense of self-esteem. In sharp contrast with the traditional stereotype of the Poles as quixotic and impractical political dreamers, in these years Poland astonished the world by its political maturity. A nonviolent movement challenged the might of the Soviet Empire for nearly a year and a half, and though it was finally crushed, it paved the way for the negotiated end of communism less than ten years later. Under these conditions, there was a greater willingness to look at the more controversial aspects of the Polish past and to consider again more critically how the Poles had treated the other peoples alongside whom they had lived, above all the Jews and the Ukrainians.

Increasingly, too, particularly among the younger generation, there was a growing feeling of shame over the events of 1968. At the time, the prevailing mood had it that this was merely a settling of accounts among the communist elite, and that all the Party factions fighting for power were equally tainted. By the late 1970s, however, the realization emerged that one of the consequences of those years had been to deprive Poland of most of what remained of its Jewish intelligentsia, and that society had allowed itself to be manipulated by the crude use of antisemitic slogans; this led to an increasing feeling of anger. The role of the 1968 crisis in depriving the communist regime of political legitimacy has, in general, been greatly underestimated.

A further factor stimulating a more critical look at the Polish-Jewish past and, in particular, at Polish-Jewish relations during the Holocaust was the series of Polish-Jewish historical conferences that began at Columbia University in spring 1983 and culminated in the conference in Jerusalem in February 1988. All points at issue between Poles and Jews were extensively aired, and the discussions were often acrimonious, painful, and difficult. Of one such discussion at Oxford in September 1984, the literary critic Jan Błoński wrote:

> I recall one moving speech at the Oxford conference, in which the speaker started by comparing the Jewish attitude to Poland to an unrequited love. Despite the suffering and all the problems which beset our mutual relations, he continued, the Jewish community had a genuine attachment to their adopted country. Here they found a home and a sense of security. There was, conscious or unconscious, an expectation that their fate would improve, the burden of humiliation would lighten, that the future would gradually become brighter. What actually happened was exactly the oppo-

site. "Nothing can ever change now," he concluded. "Jews do not
have and cannot have any future in Poland. Do tell us, though",
he finally demanded, "that what has happened to us was not our
fault. We do not ask for anything else. But we do hope for such
an acknowledgement". [26]

Błoński correctly understood this to be a call for Poles to accept some
responsibility for the fate of the Jews during the war, and it was one
of the spurs that led him to write his pathbreaking article, "The Poor
Poles Look at the Ghetto," from which this quotation is taken.

A final factor in provoking discussion of these thorny issues was
Claude Lanzmann's film *Shoah*. When it was first shown in Paris, it
was bitterly attacked by the official Polish press as an anti-Polish provocation, and the Polish government even delivered a note of protest to
the French government, which had partly financed the film. When
Shoah was finally shown in Poland, as a result of a change of heart on
the part of the authorities, reactions were more complex. Most Poles
rejected Lanzmann's division of European society during the Holocaust (particularly in Poland) into the murderers, their victims, and the
bystanders, largely unsympathetic to the fate of the Jews. Yet many
were shocked by his interviews with Polish peasants living in the vicinity of the death camps, which revealed the persistence of crude antisemitic stereotypes in the Polish countryside. For Catholics, which of
course meant the overwhelming majority of Poles, Lanzmann's argument that Nazi antisemitism was the logical culmination of Christian
antisemitism was also unacceptable. But it, too, forced a reexamination
of many strongly held attitudes.

The most characteristic expression of the more critical attitude toward the Polish-Jewish past was set out by Jan Błoński in the article
referred to above. In it, he observed that any attempt by Poles to discuss Polish reactions to the Nazi anti-Jewish genocide, whether with
Jews or with other people, very quickly degenerates into apologetics
and efforts to justify Polish conduct. The reason for this, he claimed,
was the Poles' fear, conscious or unconscious, of being accused either
of participation in this genocide or, at best, of observing it with acquiescence. This fear cannot be easily evaded, even if it is shared by the
Poles with the rest of Europe. The only way to deal with it, he asserted,
was for the Poles to "stop haggling, trying to defend and justify ourselves. To stop arguing about the things that were beyond our power
to do, during the occupation and beforehand. Nor to place blame on

---

[26] Jan Błoński, "Biedni Polacy patrzą na ghetto," *Tygodnik Powszechny*, 11 January 1987.
Taken from the English translation in Polonsky, *'My Brother's Keeper?'*, 45.

political, social and economic conditions. But to say first of all, 'Yes, we are guilty'."

This guilt did not consist, in his view, of involvement in the mass murder of the Jews, in which he claimed the Poles did not participate significantly. It had two aspects. First, there was the Poles' "insufficient effort to resist," their "holding back" from offering help to the Jews. This was the consequence of the second aspect, that the Poles had not in the nineteenth and early twentieth centuries created conditions in which the Jews could be integrated into the Polish national community.

> If only we had behaved more humanely in the past, had been wiser, more generous, then genocide would perhaps have been "less imaginable", would probably have been considerably more difficult to carry out, and almost certainly would have met with much greater resistance than it did. To put it differently, it would not have met with the indifference and moral turpitude of the society in whose full view it took place.[27]

These Jewish "accusations" and Polish "apologetics" and "apologies" are, above all, concerned with how one should respond to the past and deal with a shared but divisive memory. This divided memory is very difficult to overcome. For both Poles and Jews, memory is a key element in the public discourse that helps to build group identity. Thus it is not surprising that Father Edward Orłowski, the Catholic priest in Jedwabne, should say without any sense of embarrassment, "The Jews have their memory [of the massacre that took place in the town] and we have ours."

The controversy over Błoński's article revealed that the desire to come to terms with the more problematic aspects of the Polish-Jewish past was to be found only within a minority of the Polish intelligentsia and was certainly not shared by the society as a whole. Błoński's position was rejected by most of the two hundred individuals who participated in the debate. Characteristically similar criticism was voiced by people with very different ideological backgrounds ranging from Communist official circles to the right wing of Solidarity. Many accused Błoński and the editors of *Tygodnik Powszechny* of playing into the hands of Poland's enemies and of endorsing anti-Polish propaganda, and some even called for Błoński to be prosecuted under the Polish criminal code for "slandering the Polish nation." These reactions were a clear indication of how little public acceptance there was of the

---

[27] Jan Błoński, "Biedni Polacy patrzą na ghetto," *Tygodnik Powszechny*, 11 January 1987. Taken from the English translation in Polonsky, *'My Brother's Keeper?'*, 34–52.

need to come to terms with the Polish "dark past" or to reevaluate the memory of the Holocaust.

The years since the negotiated end of communism in Poland in 1989 have been followed by a series of set-piece debates similar to that aroused by Błoński's article. The first of these was the controversy initiated by the publication in *Gazeta Wyborcza* on 29–30 January 1994 of an article by a young (non-Jewish) journalist, Michał Cichy, entitled "Poles and Jews: Black Pages in the Annals of the Warsaw Uprising." In it, Cichy discussed anti-Jewish attitudes and actions on the part of Polish military organizations and the civilian population during the sixty-three-day Warsaw Uprising launched against the Germans on 1 August 1944. In particular, he described individual and group murders of several scores of Jews, by the National Armed Forces (Narodowe Siły Zbrojne), and by some units of the Home Army (Armia Krajowa [AK]). Although Cichy's revelations were confirmed by three leading historians of the Second World War in Poland—Andrzej Paczkowski, Andrzej Friszke, and Teresa Prekerowa—a majority of discussants (including Tomasz Strzembosz, who has played a large role in the discussion of *Neighbors*) refused to accept them. In addition, groups of ex-soldiers of the Home Army and "representatives of the Polish intelligentsia" signed protests objecting to the publication of the article and accusing *Gazeta Wyborcza* of "anti-Polish" and "anti-goyish" prejudice (this latter remark was an antisemitic reference to the Jewish origin of the paper's principal editor, Adam Michnik). The controversy also brought to the surface old claims that communism was a Jewish phenomenon (*Żydokomuna* or Judeo-communism), and that the Jews had been responsible for the vicious postwar propaganda campaign against the AK and had played a key role in the security establishment of the postwar communist regime. Cichy's assertions, it was argued, were merely a repetition of discredited Stalinist propaganda against the Home Army. One could not understand attitudes toward the Jews if one did not take into account Jewish "collaboration" with the Soviets in eastern Poland between 1939 and 1941. When talking about alleged Polish crimes against the Jews, one needed also to remember the role of Jewish communists in the post-1944 regime and the crimes they had committed against Poland.[28]

---

[28] The debate, including publication of letters and phone calls received by *Gazeta Wyborcza*, was published on 2, 3, 7, 11, and 12–13 February 1994. The responses by the historians Andrzej Friszke, Andrzej Paczkowski, and Teresa Prekerowa, and Włodzimierz Borodziej and Tomasz Strzembosz, were published in the issue dated 5–6 February. See *Intelligence Report—Article on Warsaw Uprising Touches Raw Nerve in Polish-Jewish Relations*, no. 8 (April 1994), 1–2, published by the Institute of Jewish Affairs (London, 1994),

On this question, Andrzej Paczkowski of Warsaw is conducting pioneering research. He and Lech Głuchowski have assessed the nationality of functionaries in the Urząd Bezpieczeństwo (UB), the political police in Stalinist Poland, making use of a confidential study prepared by the Ministry of Internal Affairs in 1978. According to this study, between 1944 and 1945, 287 individuals held leadership positions in the UB. The number of those listed as having "Jewish nationality" totaled 75. This meant that Jews made up 26.3 percent of the UB leadership, while the figure for Poles was 66.9 percent. The remaining 6.8 percent were Russians, Belarusians, and Ukrainians. The proportion of Jews at lower levels of the organization was considerably less. In another document, Stanisław Radkiewicz informed Bolesław Bierut that in November 1945 the Security Office employed 25,600 personnel, and that 438 (1.7 percent) of them were Jews. Furthermore, the rapid increase in the number of UB functionaries in 1945 occurred in a political framework that placed the political orientation and class origins of the candidate above almost all other considerations. To quote Paczkowski and Głuchowski:

> The great majority of candidates actually consisted of young—and very young—political transients, with no professional experience and mixed reasons, if not questionable motives, for joining the UB. There was a constant movement of lower-level cadres in and out of the UB between 1945 and 1946. At this time, approximately 25,000 employees left the UB: about the same number that were employed by the UB at the end of 1946. The majority had been released from the UB for drunkenness, theft, abuse, or for a lack of discipline.[29]

Similar debates were provoked by the exchange in the pages of *Tygodnik Powszechny* in late 1997 between Fathers Stanisław Musiał and Waldemar Chrostowski on the reaction of the Polish hierarchy to the antisemitic utterances of Father Henryk Jankowski,[30] and by the article "The Disgrace of Indifference" ("Hańba obojętności") by the sociologist Hanna Świda-Ziemba, which appeared in *Gazeta Wyborcza* on 17 August 1998 and which repeated in sharper form the arguments set out by Błoński.

---

and J. Michlic, "The Troubling Past: Polish Collective Memory of the Holocaust," *East European Jewish Affairs* 29, nos. 1–2 (1999): 79–80.

[29] Letter to the *Times Literary Supplement*, 29 March 1997. See also Paczkowski's article in *POLIN: Studies in Polish Jewry* 16 (2003): 453–64.

[30] This debate was translated into English in *POLIN: Studies in Polish Jewry* 13 (2000): 303–28.

What is striking about these debates is their moral character. It is no accident that several of them took place in a progressive Catholic periodical. They have mostly been conducted by theologians, philosophers, and literary critics (the Cichy debate constitutes something of an exception, although the responses to his very specific analysis were also characterized by the retreat into vague generalizations). However, as was pointed out by Jerzy Turowicz, the veteran editor of *Tygodnik Powszechny* who died in 1998, the argument between the two sides was "conducted on totally different planes."[31] What was at issue here, according to the Polish-Jewish sociologist Zygmunt Bauman, who was forced to leave Poland in 1968, is what he describes as the "rationality of evil." The process of mass murder rested on persuading all involved, both victims and bystanders, that it was more sensible to cooperate than to resist, whether by false claims that what was occurring was merely resettlement, by holding out the hope that some would survive, or by stressing the penalties for noncooperation:

> Siła-Nowicki and Błoński do not argue with, but past, each other. Błoński wrote of the moral significance of the Holocaust, Siła-Nowicki responded with an investigation of the rationality of self-preservation. What he failed to notice was the ethical meaning of the very form such rationality took (or, rather, was forced to assume): the very fact that the Nazi regime set the logic of survival against the moral duty (as a value superior to ethics) was simultaneously the secret of the technical success of the mass murder, one of the most sinister horrors of the event called the 'Holocaust', and the most venomous of its consequences . . .[32]

In fact, as Bauman correctly states,

> . . . the issue is not whether the Poles should feel ashamed or whether they should feel proud of themselves. The issue is that only the liberating feeling of shame—the recovery of the moral significance of the joint historical experience—may once and for all exorcise the specter of the Holocaust, which continues to haunt not only Polish-Jewish relations, but also the ethical self-identity of the Poles and the Jews alike, to this very day. The choice is not between shame and pride. The choice is between the pride of morally purifying shame, and the shame of morally devastating pride.[33]

[31] Jerzy Turowicz, "Polish Reasons and Jewish Reasons," in Polonsky, *'My Brother's Keeper?'*, 138.

[32] Z. Bauman, "On Immoral Reason and Illogical Morality," *POLIN: A Journal of Polish-Jewish Studies* 3 (1988): 296–97.

[33] Ibid., 298.

A cynic might argue that what has also been characteristic of these debates is that the apologies have been made by those who have had no need to apologize, while those who need to reexamine their attitudes have adopted an intransigent stance, which has often had antisemitic overtones. Unquestionably such exchanges are necessary and have done something to change attitudes. But it must be doubted whether they have had a large resonance outside the Polish intelligentsia, where debate about moral dilemmas has long been a major preoccupation. One is reminded here of the eponymous hero of Joseph Conrad's very Polish *Lord Jim*, whose whole life is an attempt to atone for a single moral lapse at a critical time.

There have also been a number of other developments since the end of communism that have stimulated a more open approach to the "dark past" and have attempted to dispel antisemitic and xenophobic stereotypes in Poland. As demonstrated by controversies such as that provoked by the "Papal Cross" in Auschwitz or that over *Neighbors*, these sentiments are easily aroused. One important development is the increased commitment of the church to taking a stand against the manifestations of antisemitism. Of key significance here was the pastoral letter of the Polish bishops of 20 January 1991.[34] This was the first unequivocal condemnation of antisemitism by the clerical hierarchy, and it was read in every one of Poland's twenty thousand parishes. It began by affirming:

With the Jewish nation, we Poles are linked with special ties, and since as early as the first centuries of our history Poland became another homeland for many Jews—the majority of Jews living all over the world at present derive from the territories of the former and present Republic of Poland. Unfortunately it is exactly this land that became the grave of several million Jews in our century, not by our will nor by our hand. This is what, not long ago, on 26 September 1990, the pope, the Holy Father, said about our common history: "There is one more nation, one more special people, the people of the patriarchs, Moses, and the prophets, the legacy of the faith of Abraham. These people lived with us for generations, shoulder to shoulder on the same land, which somehow became the new land of the Diaspora. Horrible death was inflicted on millions of sons and daughters of this nation: first they were branded with a special stigma; then they were pushed into ghettos and separated districts; next they were transported to gas chambers and killed only because they were children of this nation. The murderers did this on our soil perhaps in order to defile it." But earth

[34] *Gazeta Wyborcza*, 26 January 1991.

cannot be defiled by the blood of innocent victims; earth becomes a holy relic owing to such deaths.

Many Poles, according to the bishops' letter, saved Jewish lives during the war, and they go on to rehearse the number of Polish trees in the Avenue of the Righteous at Yad Vashem. Nevertheless they continue:

> Despite such a large number of examples of heroic assistance on the part of Christian Poles, there were also people who remained indifferent to that inconceivable tragedy. We particularly suffer because of those Catholics who were in any way instrumental in causing the death of Jews; they will forever remain a pang of conscience for us, also a blot on our society. If there was only one Christian who could have helped a Jew in danger but did not give him a helping hand or had a share in his death, we must ask our Jewish brothers and sisters for forgiveness.
>
> We are aware that many of our compatriots still nurse in their memory the harm and injustice inflicted by postwar communist rule, in which people of Jewish origin participated as well. But we must admit that the source of inspiration for their actions cannot be seen in their Jewish origin or in their religion but came from the communist ideology from which Jews, too, suffered much injustice. We also express our sincere regret for all cases of antisemitism that have occurred on Polish soil. We do this because we are deeply convinced that all signs of antisemitism are contrary to the spirit of the gospel and, as Pope John Paul II has recently underlined, will remain totally contrary to the Christian vision of human dignity . . .
>
> We Christians and Jews are united by the belief in one God, the Creator and the Lord of the whole universe who created man in his own image; we are united by the ethical principles that are embodied in the Decalogue, which may be reduced to the commandment of the love of God and the love of one's fellow man. We are united by our veneration for the Old Testament as the Holy Scripture and our common traditions of prayer. And we are united by the hope for the final coming of the Kingdom of God. We wait together for the savior, the Messiah, although we believe that he is Jesus of Nazareth and we await not his first but his second coming in might and glory . . .

There have also been attempts to introduce in Polish schools more satisfactory textbooks dealing with Polish-Jewish relations in the twentieth century. An analysis of history textbooks for primary and secondary schools conducted by the Jewish Historical Institute in Warsaw in May 1997 demonstrated that the dominant paradigm for remembering the Holocaust, which developed prior to the political transformation of Poland, continued to prevail in the postcommunist educational system.[35] For the most part, there was still little in the current textbooks on the Holocaust, although individual teachers had begun to introduce the subject separately from the "World War II" unit that has always been included. A Polish-Israeli commission to remove negative stereotypes from textbooks was also set up and reported in 1995.[36] Since then some progress has been made, though it is painfully slow. On 27 January 2000 the Polish government signed the Stockholm Declaration, by which it committed itself to teaching the subject of the Holocaust in schools. This was followed by the preparation by Robert Szuchta in Warsaw and Piotr Trojański in Kraków of a curriculum guide for teachers on how to teach the Holocaust, which appeared in the summer of 2000. They are at present, at the behest of the Ministry of National Education (MEN), working on a textbook to go with it. The eminent historian Jerzy Jedlicki is also preparing a short text for schools on Polish-Jewish relations, in which the Holocaust will assume a central place.

However, the most important developments stimulating a rethinking of attitudes toward Jews and the "Jewish Question" in the last decade have been neither the big set-piece debates nor the attempts to deal frontally with the problem of antisemitism in Poland. They are, rather, first, the large mass of new historical material that has provided a much fuller picture of Polish-Jewish relations in the twentieth century, and, second, the emergence of a new generation of Polish-Jewish writers who have brought a new and unique voice to the debate.

Let us start by saying something about recent historical scholarship. We must consider four periods here, that before the First World War, the years between 1918 and 1939, the years of the occupation, and the postwar period; what follows can only be fragmentary and highly selective. For the period before 1914, we have Jerzy Jedlicki's very important work on the pervasiveness of antisemitism in the last years before the First World War and on the poisonous effect of Dmowski's exploitation of the nationalist issue in the 1912 election to the Duma in Warsaw; Stephen Corrsin's work on ethnic conflicts in Warsaw before

[35] Important articles on the representation of the Holocaust in history textbooks in Polish schools of the 1990s were published in the *Biuletyn Żydowskiego Instytutu Historycznego*, nos. 3–4 (1997). See also Hanna Węgrzynek, *The Treatment of Jewish Themes in Polish Schools* (New York, 1998).

[36] See Shevach Eden, "Attempts to Use Historical and Literary Textbooks in Poland and Israel to Foster Mutual Understanding," *POLIN: Studies in Polish Jewry* 14 (2001): 306–14.

the First World War; the important monograph by Brian Porter on the
protofascist character of the Endecja; and the work of Robert Blobaum,
Ted Weeks, and Tadeusz Stegner on the development of antisemitism
at this time.[37] For the interwar years, there are works in Polish by Jan
Józef Lipski and Anna Landau-Czajka and in English by Ron Modras
on the increasing dominance of anti-Jewish views in the Catholic
Church.[38] Monika Natkowska has documented the desire of the nationalist right to exclude the Jews from universities, and Olaf Bergmann
has given a not wholly satisfactory account of the Endecja in the
1920s.[39] Szymon Rudnicki has given us a devastating picture of one of
the more extreme fascist offshoots of the Endecja in the 1930s, while
Jolanta Żyndul has thoroughly documented anti-Jewish violence in
1936 and 1937.[40] Czesław Miłosz's *Wyprawa w Dwudziestolecie* (Kraków,
1999) documents the increasing strength in Poland in the 1930s of
chauvinistic and near-fascist attitudes. There is a mass of material on
the war, which includes Tomasz Szarota's work on anti-Jewish violence
perpetrated by "bystanders" in the first stages of the war, the examination of the policies and attitudes toward Jewish issues of the Polish
government-in-exile by David Engel and Dariusz Stola, and the very
important work by Jan Gross.[41] For the postwar period, we have a

[37] J. Jedlicki, "The End of Dialogue: Warsaw 1907–1912," in *The Jews in Poland* (Kraków,
1999), 2:111–24; S. Corrsin, *Warsaw before the First World War: Poles and Jews in the Third
City of the Russian Empire, 1880–1914* (Boulder, Colo., 1989); B. Porter, *When Nationalism
Began to Hate: Imagining Modern Politics in Nineteenth Century Poland* (New York, 2000);
Theodore R. Weeks, "Fanning the Flames: Jews in the Warsaw Press, 1905–1912," *East
European Jewish Affairs* 28, 2 (Winter 1998–1999): 63–81 Tadeusz Stegner, "Liberałowie
Królestwa Polskiego wobec kwestii żydowskiej na początku XX wieku," *Przegląd Historyczny* 80, 1 (1989): 69–88; Theodore R. Weeks, "Polish 'Progressive Antisemitism,' 1905–
1914," *East European Jewish Affairs* 25, 2 (1995): 49–68; Robert Blobaum, "The Politics of
Antisemitism in Fin-de-Siècle Warsaw," *Journal of Modern History* 73, 2 (June 2001): 275–
306, and "Criminalizing the 'Other': Crime, Ethnicity and Antisemitism in Early Twentieth-Century Poland" (unpublished).
[38] J. J. Lipski, *Katolickie Państwo narodu polskiego* (Warsaw, 1994): A. Landau-Czajka, *W
jednym stali domu . . . Koncepcje rozwiązania kwestii żydowskiej w publicystice katolickiej lat
1933–39* (Warsaw, 1998); R. Modras, *The Catholic Church and Antisemitism—Poland, 1933–
1939* (Chur, Switzerland, 1994).
[39] M. Natkowska, *"Numerus clausus", "ghetto ławkowe", "numerus nullus": Antisemityzm
na uniwersytecie Warszawskim 1931–39* (Warsaw, 1999); O. Bergmann, *Narodowa Demokracja wobec problematyki żydowskiej w latach 1918–1929* (Poznań, 1998).
[40] S. Rudnicki, "ONR czyli antysemitzm totalny," *Biuletyn ŻIH*, no. 3 (1991): 29–57;
J. Żyndul, *Zajścia antyżydowskie w Polsce w latach 1935–1937* (Warsaw, 1994).
[41] T. Szarota, *U progu zagłady: zajścia antyżydowskie i pogromy w okupowanej Europie*
(Warsaw, 2000); Engel, *In the Shadow of Auschwitz*; idem, *Facing a Holocaust*; Dariusz Stola,
*Nadzieja i zagłada: Ignacy Schwarzbart—żydowski przedstawiciel w Radzie Narodowej RP
1940–1945* (Warsaw, 1995); Dariusz Libionka, "Kościół w Polsce wobec zagłady w świetle
polskiej publicystyki i historiografii," *Biuletyn ŻIH*, no. 3 (2000): 329–41, and idem, "Pol-

much clearer picture of the difficult position of Jewish survivors and their ambiguous relationship with the communist regime from the work of Krystyna Kersten, Bożena Szaynok, Anna Cichopek, Andrzej Paczkowski, and Jaff Schatz.[42] On 1968, there are important new books by Jerzy Eisler and Dariusz Stola.[43]

This is not a complete list, and much other notable research is being undertaken, but a clear and unambiguous picture is emerging. This was set out in an important review article by Maria Janion in *Tygodnik Powszechny* on 22 October 2000. She points out that although Goldhagen's work *Hitler's Willing Executioners* has many flaws, his concept of "eliminationist antisemitism" is a useful analytical tool. She argues that there are several stages before a society adopts such a stance. Jews are first seen as undesirable and to be denied some rights. Then comes a demand for the voluntary or compulsory removal of most Jews from the society, Only then does the move to mass murder occur. Janion argues persuasively that the majority of Polish citizens and of Polish political parties had come by the 1930s to the position that the "solution" of the "Jewish problem" was the voluntary or compulsory removal of most Jews from Poland by emigration. This view had earlier been articulated by Jerzy Tomaszewski, who, after pointing out that this was not a feasible course in the late 1930s, makes the following observation:

> A lasting solution of the social and economic problems of the Jews had thus to be sought in Poland, in close association with the whole range of problems faced by the country. It is difficult today to reach a conclusion on the chances of finding such a solution, because the outbreak of the war made a breach in the normal evolution of the country. If one takes into account the situation that prevailed at the end of the 1930s, the prospects for lasting solutions must seem doubtful.[44]

---

skie duchowieństwo katolickie wobec eksterminacji i zagłady Żydów" (unpublished); Jan Gross, *Upiorna dekada. Trzy eseje o stereotypach na temat Żydów, Polaków, Niemców i Komunistów 1939–1948* (Kraków, 1998) and *Sąsiedzi: Historia zagłady żydowskiego miasteczka* (Sejny, 2000).

[42] K. Kersten, *Polacy, Żydzi, komunizm. Anatomia półprawd 1939–68* (Warsaw, 1992); B. Szaynok, *Pogrom Żydów w Kielcach 4 lipca 1946* (Wrocław, 1992); Anna Cichopek, *Pogrom Żydów w Krakowie* (Warsaw, 2000); Andrzej Paczkowski, "Wstęp do 'Raporty o Pogromie'," *Puls* 50, 3 (1991): 103–10; idem, "Żydzi w UB: próba weryfikacji stereotypu," in *Komunizm. Ideologia, system, ludzie*, ed. T. Szarota (Warsaw, 2001); J. Schatz, *The Generation: The Rise and Fall of Jewish Communists of Poland* (Berkeley, 1991).

[43] Jerzy Eisler, *Marzec 1968. Geneza, przebieg, konsekwencje* (Warsaw, 1991); Dariusz Stola, *Kampania antysyjonistyczna w Polsce 1967–1968* (Warsaw, 2000) and "Fighting against the Shadows: The Anti-Zionist Campaign of 1968" (unpublished).

[44] *Najnowsze Dzieje Żydów w Polsce* (Warsaw, 1993), 215.

These are conclusions that it is hard for Poles to accept. However, we are faced here not with moral imperatives but with hard facts, which, one hopes, will in the long run prove much more convincing. These are tragic developments that are part of the more general tragedy of the twentieth century. They cannot be changed—accepting them will be a sign of political and social maturity. As the eighteenth-century French writer Alain-René Lesage put it, "Facts are stubborn things."

A second important development was the emergence in the 1990s of a new group of Polish-Jewish writers and the more widespread distribution in Poland of the works of already established Polish-Jewish authors. It is a paradoxical fact that the waning of Poland after 1939 as one of the great centers of the Jewish world has been accompanied by a flourishing of what has been described as a "Jewish School of Polish Literature,"[45] a group of writers who have explored the key dilemmas faced by Polish Jewry, above all how to record and memorialize the Holocaust, and how to go on living in a country where it took place and where the attitude of the majority of the population to the genocide raised serious and difficult questions. The word "school" perhaps overstates the unity of this group, which falls into two divisions: an older generation, of whom the most important members were Julian Stryjkowski, Adolf Rudnicki, and Stanisław Wygodzki, who came to maturity before the war; and a younger group, of whom the most notable are Ida Fink, Henryk Grynberg, Bogdan Wojdowski, and Hanna Krall, who grew up during the war.

These Polish-Jewish writers have great significance in the shaping of Polish attitudes. Polish-Jewish dialogue initially began to make progress, as was pointed out by the former Polish foreign minister Władysław Bartoszewski, himself one of the founders of the wartime Council for Aid to the Jews (Rada Pomocy Żydom, cryptonym Żegota), when Poles started to criticize Polish behavior and Jews to criticize Jewish behavior. Yet there is no doubt that the testimony of Jews on how they experienced Poles and Poland is crucial if there is to be an advance beyond worthy moral platitudes. Many Poles have been resistant to Jewish testimony, seeing it as one-sided and excessively subjective. For example, Wojciech Wierzewski, in his review of Michael Steinlauf's *Bondage to the Dead* in the pages of *Nowy Dziennik*, the principal Polish daily in the United States, after perfunctorily praising the author, went on to ask why a Jew was writing about Polish reactions to the Holocaust, rather than focusing on the reactions of Jews—partic-

[45] Jan Błoński, "Is There a Jewish School of Polish Literature?" *POLIN: A Journal of Polish-Jewish Studies* 1 (1986): 196–211.

ularly of those in the United States, who, in his view, did not speak out strongly enough against the mass murder. In his view, Steinlauf should have observed the principles of "fair play" and "displayed his cards" only after a "reliable and competent Polish author" had dealt with the subject.

It is much more difficult to make such tendentious arguments against Jews writing in Polish. The nineties were marked by a new explosion of creativity by authors such as Hanna Krall and Henryk Grynberg and also saw the emergence of important new writers, such as Wilhelm Dichter, and the publication of new works by authors like Michał Głowiński, in which they dealt extensively with their previously concealed Jewish backgrounds. All had a common background in that they had experienced the war as children hidden on the "Aryan" side and grew up in the complex postwar years. Their work gave a graphic and largely negative picture of what it was like to be a Jew in a hostile environment both during the war and under communism.[46]

Although he comes from a different generation and a somewhat different background, Jan Gross can also be considered part of this group. Indeed, he can be seen both as a Polish-Jewish writer and as one of the historians whose work has helped to reshape our understanding of the Polish-Jewish past since 1989. He was born after the war—his grandfather was a well-known Jewish liberal in Kraków and deputy in the Austrian Reichsrat of the Klub Niezawisłych Żydów (Club of Independent Jews), and his father headed a prominent legal practice. His mother was not Jewish, and the family was thoroughly assimilated. He became caught up in the Polish student unrest of 1968 and after a brief imprisonment was forced to leave the country and settle in the United States. Here he established himself as one of the leading historians of recent Poland and of the complicated ethnic relations in that country since 1939. His *Polish Society under German Occupation: The Generalgouv-*

---

[46] Henryk Grynberg made his reputation with a lightly fictionalized version of his own life. Among his recent works are *Drohobycz, Drohobycz* (Warsaw, 1997) and *Memorbuch* (Warsaw, 2000), which deals with the vexed question of the Jewish relationship with communism in the form of a lightly fictionalized biography of a Jewish communist, Adam Bromberg. Wilhelm Dichter's first novel, *Koń Pana Boga* (God's donkey) (Kraków, 1996) describes his wartime experiences, while the second, *Szkoła bezbożników* (The school for atheists) (Kraków, 1999), describes his adolescence in the Warsaw of the late 1940s and early 1950s. Michał Głowiński is one of Poland's leading literary scholars and has written extensively both in *Tygodnik Powszechny* and various literary periodicals, including those of the "alternative" press (*drugiego obiegu*). Yet it was only in his memoir *Black Seasons* (*Czarne sezony* [Warsaw, 1998]) that he revealed his Jewish background.

ernement, 1939–1944 (Princeton, 1979) is certainly the best account in English of the complex questions raised by the Nazi occupation of Poland. In *Revolution from Abroad: The Soviet Conquest of Poland's Western Ukraine and Western Belorussia* (Princeton, 1988) he shed much light on one of the most important "blank spots" in twentieth-century Polish history and showed the falsity of some of the stereotypes that had been current in communist Poland in connection with the Soviet annexations of 1939. In recent years, he has begun to address Holocaust issues directly and in Polish. His *Upiorna dekada. Trzy eseje o stereotypach na temat Żydów, Polaków, Niemców i Komunistów 1939–1948* (Cursed decade: Three essays on stereotypes about Jews, Poles, and Communists) (Kraków, 1998) is a major contribution to our understanding of the events of the Holocaust and the immediate postwar period in Poland.

Even more important has been his *Neighbors*, the subject of this volume, which is unquestionably one of the most important books of the last decade both on the general question of the mass murder of the Jews during the Second World War and on the more specific problem of the reaction of some segments of Polish society to that genocide. From the point of view of larger Holocaust historiography, the massacre in Jedwabne raises significant questions about the wave of anti-Jewish violence that accompanied the first weeks of the Nazi invasion of the Soviet Union. General Walter Stahlecker, commander of *Einsatzgruppe* A, reported at the time that Lithuanians had killed as many as 1,500 Jews in one night in Kaunas at the end of June 1941.[47] Other sources estimate that in the Kaunas massacre as many as 10,000 Jews were murdered, and that pogroms broke out in at least forty Lithuanian towns.[48] A recent study of western Ukraine by Marco Carynnyk has described how pogroms erupted in as many as thirty-five places after the Nazi invasion of the Soviet Union and resulted in the deaths of between 28,000 and 35,000 victims.[49] A more cautious figure has put the death toll at 12,000.[50] Within the ethnically Polish area, there were fewer such incidents. Such evidence as we have, both Polish and Jewish, suggests that the Łomża region in northeastern Poland where Jedwabne is located, an area that had long been a stronghold of the extreme right, was the only area in which collective massacres of Jews

[47] Tomasz Szarota, *U progu zagłady: Zajścia antyżydowskie i pogromy w okupowanej Europie* (Warsaw, 2000), 239.
[48] Dov Levin, "Kovno," in *Encyclopedia of the Holocaust*, ed. Israel Gutman, vol. 1 (New York, 1990), 825: Marek Wierzbicki, *Polacy i Żydzi w zaborze sowieckim* (Warsaw, 2000), 198.
[49] Marco Carynnyk, "Furious Angels: Ukrainians, Jews and Poles in the Summer of 1941" (unpublished), 5.
[50] Wierzbicki, *Polacy i Żydzi w zaborze sowieckim*, 198.

by civilian Poles took place in the summer of 1941—when the region, previously occupied by the Soviet Union, was reoccupied by Nazi Germany. Massacres of the Jewish population by ethnic Poles also took place at the beginning of July 1941 in Radziłów and Wąsosz. Other places where ethnic Poles were involved in killings of the Jewish communities are Goniądz, Kolno, Knyszyn, Stawiska, Szczuczyn, and Suchowoła. Information about these latter crimes first appeared in Szymon Datner's "Eksterminacja Żydow Okręgu Bialostockiego," *Biuletyn Żydowskiego Instytutu Historycznego* 60 (October–December 1966): 1–29. Datner referred to these cases as massacres conducted by the local population ("miejscowa ludność"), and not explicitly by ethnic Poles. The terminology was undoubtedly dictated by communist censorship.

Massacres were also committed by the Romanians.[51] These were somewhat different in that there was a Romanian state that was allied with the Germans and took part in the invasion of the Soviet Union. The first massacre took place in Jassy, three days after the invasion of the USSR. The Jews were accused (falsely) of aiding the Red Army, and in a series of massacres that took place over several days, thousands of Jews died at Romanian hands. German diplomats estimated the number of victims at 4,000, a figure accepted by Raul Hilberg. The Italian writer Curzio Malaparte, who was in Romania during the war, gives a figure of 7,000 dead. Perhaps the most reliable figures are those collected by the Romanian Ministry of the Interior, which numbered the dead at 8,000. These killings were followed by a series of "spontaneous attacks on Jews by the local population after the departure of the Soviets and before the entry of the German or Romanian forces."[52]

A major role in subsequent atrocities was taken by the Romanian army, which was instructed by General Antonescu to assist the gendarmes and police in "cleansing the land of its 'Yids.' " In particular, he was eager to expel the Jews from the areas of Bessarabia and Bukovina reconquered from the Soviet Union. As Antonescu put it:

> I am in favor of expelling the Jews from Bessarabia and Bukovina to the other side of the border . . . There is nothing for them to do here and I don't mind if we appear in history as barbarians . . .

---

[51] See Randolph Braham, ed., *The Tragedy of Romanian Jewry* (New York, 1994). Ilya Ehrenburg and Vassili Grossman, eds., *The Black Book of Soviet Jewry* (New York, 1981), 77–91; Dora Litani, "The Destruction of the Jews of Odessa in the Light of Romanian Documents," *Yad Vashem Studies* 6 (1967): 135–54, and Radu Ioanid, *The Holocaust in Romania: The Destruction of Jews and Gypsies under the Antonescu Regime, 1940–1944* (Chicago, 2000).

[52] See Jean Ancel, "The Romanian Way of Solving the 'Jewish Problem' in Bessarabia and Bukovina, June–July 1941," *Yad Vashem Studies* 19 (1988): 187–232.

There has never been a more suitable time in our history to get rid of the Jews, and if necessary, you are to make use of machine guns against them.[53]

In the resultant massacres more than 300,000 Jews died at Romanian hands.

None of these massacres was carried out by the Germans, although they certainly encouraged such actions and, in some cases, may have coordinated them. This raises important questions about the thin line between the desire to expel an unwanted minority and a small-scale genocidal project under sanctioned conditions. Further investigation is needed not only to investigate what actually happened but to contextualize it within the evolution of Nazi policy toward the Jews. There has been a great deal of argument in recent years on when the Nazis actually initiated the policy of genocide against the Jews. Most scholars accept that the move to mass murder was part of the radicalization of Nazi policy that accompanied Operation Barbarossa. The majority view is that its final adoption accompanied the euphoria of victory in September and October 1941. A minority hold the opinion, most recently advanced by Arno Mayer and the Swiss historian Philippe Burrin, and earlier by Uwe Adam, Martin Broszat, and Wolfgang Mommsen, that it was a response to the first check to the Blitzkrieg and the consequence of the view that the Jews should be punished for the failure of the Nazi war effort. They still disagree as to whether a policy of mass murder had been adopted before the invasion of the Soviet Union or was the consequence of the progressive radicalization of Nazi policy during Operation Barbarossa.[54]

The policy may have been decided upon somewhat earlier, as there was inevitably a time lag between its adoption and implementation, caused both by technical problems inherent in carrying it out and by efforts to ensure that it would achieve its objectives. The view that it was adopted earlier is held by the biographer of Heinrich Himmler, Richard Breitmann. It is clear, for instance, that there were considerable doubts within the Nazi leadership as to whether genocide was feasible, and that this accounts for the many arguments as to how it should be implemented.[55]

During the first phase of the genocide, the SS, the body entrusted with carrying out policy toward the Jews, was not sure how to pro-

[53] Avigdor Shachan, *Burning Ice: The Ghettos of Transnistria* (New York, 1996), 51.

[54] For a description of this process, see C. Browning, "Hitler and the Euphoria of Victory: The Path to the Final Solution," in *The Final Solution: Origins and Implementation*, ed. David Cesarani (London, 1994), 137–47.

[55] There is a useful summary of these issues in Cesarani, *The Final Solution*.

ceed. They had had a number of failures, most notably the scheme for
a Jewish reservation around Nisko, between Lublin and Rzeszów, and
the project to send Jews to Madagascar, to which a great deal of effort
had been devoted. They were eager to exploit anti-Jewish resentments
among the local population and to see whether these could be harnessed to their purposes. Thus Reinhard Heydrich, a key figure in the
SS, instructed the commanders of the *Einsatzgruppen* after the invasion
of the Soviet Union to "trigger" pogroms by the local population
against communists and Jews, and to "intensify them if necessary and
channel them properly . . . without leaving any trace" and without giving the perpetrators any opportunity to plead later that they were following instructions.[56]

Dr. Walter Stahlecker, one of the commanders of the *Einsatzgruppen*,
reported in October 1941:

> It was unwelcome that the *Sicherheitspolizei* should be seen to be
> involved with actions which were in fact exceptionally harsh and
> which were bound to create shock in German circles. It was neces-
> sary to demonstrate that the indigenous population had taken the
> first measures on its own initiative as a national reaction to de-
> cades of Jewish oppression and communist terror.[57]

The wider context of the Jedwabne massacre has not so far figured
prominently in the discussion of *Neighbors*. One of the important future
tasks of historians, not only in Poland, will be to investigate, using
newly available Soviet and other documents, this wave of anti-Jewish
violence and its relation to the larger issue of the way the Nazi genocide was initiated and implemented.

The Polish debate has concentrated rather on the question of Polish
participation in the massacre in which the great majority of the Jewish
population of Jedwabne were murdered by their Polish neighbors. This
event remains appalling even if there are disputes as to how much German incitement there was, how many of the inhabitants of Jedwabne
actually participated in the murder, and how many victims there were.
The murder is graphically described in *Neighbors* on the basis of testimony, given shortly after the war, that is almost unbearable to read. In
addition, Gross draws important and controversial conclusions from
the event, relating it to a number of other key issues in the history of

[56] Heydrich's operation orders of 29 June, 1 July, and 2 July 1941: Bundesarchiv R 70
SU/32. Quoted in Christian Streit, "*Wehrmacht, Einsatzgruppen* and Anti-Bolshevism," in
Cesarani, *The Final Solution*, 104.
[57] Nuremberg Documents, 180-L, IMG, vol. 37, 672. Quoted in Streit, "*Wehrmacht, Einsatzgruppen* and Anti-Bolshevism," 104–5.

twentieth-century Poland: the reception of the Soviets who occupied the eastern part of Poland in September 1939 and the vexed question of Jewish "collaboration" with this occupation, the way Polish society responded to the Nazi attack on the USSR in July 1941, and the mechanics and character of the Communist takeover in 1944. He thus directly confronts the Poles' image of themselves during the Second World War as "victims and heroes."

The debate about Jedwabne is probably the most profound on any historical issue in Poland since 1989. As the historian Marcin Kula has observed, even the assessment of the legacy of communism has not evoked such intense interest.[58] It has also had considerable resonance in Western Europe, Israel, and North America. To borrow a term from the French historian Pierre Nora, the arguments set out in *Neighbors* represent a clear "counter-memory" to the canonical Polish memory of the Holocaust and Polish-Jewish relations, the most articulate expression of the "self-critical" view of the Polish past.[59] Far more than earlier exponents of this point of view like Błoński, Gross does seem to have forced significant elements within the political and cultural elite, as well as parts of the wider society, to rethink their views on these topics. The debate has also stimulated a reconsideration of other questionable aspects of the Polish past, such as the forced resettlement after 1945 of the Ukrainian population of southeastern Poland to the west of the country in "Operation Wisła" and the abuses that accompanied the expulsion of the Germans from what is today western Poland. At the same time, it has stimulated a powerful restatement of the "apologetic" view of the Polish past. Indeed, the debate over *Neighbors* can be viewed as a battle over memory, a battle to establish a more accurate understanding of Polish-Jewish relations in the twentieth century and especially during the wartime period. This is a battle in which the "counter-memory" of the Holocaust has confronted the prevailing Polish orthodoxy in the most confident and sharpest way, exposing its distortions, omissions, and internal inconsistencies.[60]

[58] Marcin Kula, "Refleksje na marginesie dyskusji o Jedwabnem" (unpublished), 1. We would like to express our thanks to Prof. Kula for making this article available to us. Kula has also made a contribution to the debate in the article "Ludzie Ludziom," published in *Rzeczpospolita*, 17 March 2001, A5.

[59] For reflections on history, memory, and counter-memory see Pierre Nora, "General Introduction: Between Memory and History," in the English translation *Realms of Memory: The Construction of the French Past*, vol. 1, *Conflicts and Divisions*, ed. Laurence D. Kritzman (New York, 1997). This article first appeared in English translation as "Between Memory and History: Les Lieux de Memoire," *Representations* 26 (Spring 1989): 13–25.

[60] In this introduction, the Jewish reactions to the massacre at Jedwabne and to Gross's book are not discussed. For interesting reflections on this subject, see Laurence Wein-

Neighbors challenges the widely accepted view that during the Holocaust the Poles were, at worst, mostly hostile bystanders, unwilling or unable to assist their Jewish neighbors and profiting materially from their destruction: Gross provides a concrete case of active Polish involvement in the process of mass murder, even if it is on a lesser scale than similar occurrences in Ukraine, Lithuania, and Romania. The controversy also differs from the earlier debates in a number of ways. Whereas they all lasted for only a few months, the argument over *Neighbors* has continued at varying levels of intensity for nearly two years and shows no signs of abating. Unlike earlier debates, that over *Neighbors* has been conducted in a wide range of national and local papers. It has also reached other mass media—television, radio, and the Internet; it has been accompanied by the broadcasting on Polish television of Agnieszka Arnold's documentary film *Neighbors* and various commemorative events, including the Day of Repentance and Mourning conducted by the Catholic hierarchy on 27 May 2001 for the Jewish victims of the massacre and the unveiling of a new monument outside the town on its sixtieth anniversary.

This is also the first debate in which political figures have taken an active role, and in which some, notably the president of Poland, Aleksander Kwaśniewski, have given support to the "self-critical" image of the Polish-Jewish past.[61] The "counter-memory" has also been effectively expressed by a large number of influential cultural figures and is now much more widely dispersed. Certainly, one main consequence of the debate has been a significant undermining of the previously dominant mode of remembering the Holocaust.

The debate has undoubtedly brought the subject of the Holocaust to the center of public attention and has led, among a significant sector of society, to its regaining its significance as one of the key events of the twentieth century with both particular and universal messages for humanity.[62] In these circles, the genocide of Polish Jews is being inte-

baum, *The Struggle for Memory in Poland: Auschwitz, Jedwabne and Beyond* (Jerusalem, 2001), 35–38.

[61] See, for example, Aleksander Kwaśniewski, "Polska szlachetność i polska hańba. Z prezydentem Aleksandrem Kwaśniewskim rozmawiają ks. Adam Boniecki i Krzysztof Burnetko," *Tygodnik Powszechny*, 15 April 2001, 8–9; and Aleksander Kwaśniewski, "Co to znaczy przepraszam," *Polityka*, no. 28 (14 July 2001): 13.

[62] The debate certainly exposed the absence of appropriate educational tools for an unbiased presentation of the subject of the Holocaust in schools. Its timing coincided with the discussion of the first unbiased Polish Holocaust textbook, which is being written by Robert Szuchta and Piotr Trojański. It is possible that the debate helped to speed up the process by which the textbook was accepted by the educational authorities. One of the events that accompanied the controversy was a seminar on the Holocaust for thirty schoolteachers from the province of Podlasie, organized by the Institute of Na-

grated into the narrative of Polish history. This is an important development involving the inclusion of the Polish-Jewish past in the postwar Polish collective memory, which for the last fifty years has been largely concerned with the Polish ethnic collectivity. The degree to which Polish memory of the Second World War has been polonocentric has emerged strikingly in studies by Barbara Engelking and Anita Shapiro, although it should be mentioned that the Poles are hardly unique in this respect.[63]

The dispute has also raised the vexed question of the emotional and moral remoteness of Polish society from the Jewish genocide. Thus Archbishop Józef Życiński of Lublin in his article "The Banalization of Barbarity" called for an expression of mourning and grief for the Jewish victims, asserting, "[T]oday, we need to pray for the victims of the massacre, displaying the spiritual solidarity that was missing at the hour when they departed from the land of their fathers."[64]

One can tentatively argue that this long-awaited mourning has to some degree begun to occur with the various commemorative events dedicated to the victims of the Jedwabne massacre. Unfortunately this grief has proved to be only partial, since the local population of Jedwabne, guided by its parish priest, Father Edward Orłowski, refused to take part in the official commemoration staged in Jedwabne on 10 July 2001. They seem unable at present to come to terms with the town's "dark past" and cling to the "apologetic" version of Polish history, often in its radical form.[65]

In an article that appeared in late April 2001 in the newspaper *Rzeczpospolita*, the historian Andrzej Paczkowski set out a tentative typology of the discussion, which, as he rightly observed, is concerned less with the massacre as such than with the "range, intensity, and nature of Polish antisemitism."[66] He identified four categories: first, the "affir-

tional Memory. See Adam Szostkiewicz, "Powiedzcie to synom," and Piotr Pytlakowski, "Historia pewnego podręcznika," both published in *Polityka*, no. 16 (21 April 2001).

[63] Barbara Engelking, *Zagłada i Pamięć. Doświadczenia Holocaustu i jego konsekwencje opisane na podstawie relacji autobiograficznych* (Warsaw, 1994); and Anita Shapiro, "Holocaust: Private Memories, Public Memory," *Jewish Social Studies* 4, 2 (1998): 40–58.

[64] Jozef Zyciński, "The Banalization of Barbarity," in *Thou Shalt Not Kill: Poles on Jedwabne* (Warsaw, 2001), 257.

[65] On the responses of the local population of Jedwabne to the news about the 10 July 1941 massacre of Jedwabne Jews and to Gross's book, see a number of important articles by Anna Bikont, "My z Jedwabnego," *Gazeta Wyborcza*, 23 March 2001, 10–15; "Proszę tu więcej nie przychodzić," *Gazeta Wyborcza*, 31 March–1 April 2001, 10–12; and "Mieli wódkę, broń i nienawiść," *Gazeta Wyborcza*, 15 June 2001, 10–14. See also Jaroslaw Lipszyc, "Sąsiedzi i ich wnuki," *Midrasz*, no. 6 (June 2000): 41–44; Stanisław Przechodzki, "Szatan wstąpił do Jedwabnego," *Gazeta Wyborcza*, 5 April 2001, 18; and Adam Wilma, "Broda mojego syna," *Gazeta Pomorska*, 4 August 2000.

[66] See Andrzej Paczkowski, "Debata wokół 'Sąsiadów': próba wstępnej typologii," *Rzeczpospolita*, 24 March 2001.

mative," which upholds Gross's basic premises and is particularly concerned about their moral ramifications; second, the "defensive open" genre, which accepts some of Gross's conclusions but raises questions about his research priorities and methods and stresses, in particular, the issue of German participation in the atrocity; third, the "defensive closed" position, which argues that the murder was the work of, at the worst, a small number of the Polish inhabitants of Jedwabne who were unwitting dupes of the Nazis, and who were largely motivated by a desire to retaliate for the wrongs perpetrated against them by the Jews who worked for the Soviet authorities between 1939 and 1941; finally, there are those who reject the arguments of Gross's book *tout court*, in the process often resorting to stereotyₚical accusations, from Jewish deicide to Jews' having mounted perfidious conspiracies against Poland.

This is a helpful analysis, although the terms "self-critical" for the first category, "moderate apologetic" for the second, and "radical apologetic" for the third and fourth might be preferable. It should also be stressed that there are legitimate points of debate raised by Gross's book, and the term "moderate apologetic" should not be taken to mean that the views expressed by people in this group are not worthy of careful consideration. In the debate, the "self-critical" position has mainly been presented in the national dailies *Gazeta Wyborcza* and *Rzeczpospolita*, and the progressive Catholic journals, the weekly *Tygodnik Powszechny* and the monthly *Więź*. The "radical apologetic" position is mainly to be found in *Myśl Polska*, *Nasz Dziennik*, *Niedziela*, *Najwyższy Czas*, *Tygodnik "Solidarność"*, *Głos*, and *Życie*.[67]

If the viewpoints of the two sides are examined in more detail, it can be argued that Gross's analysis of the Jedwabne massacre had as one of its aims the deconstruction of the cherished Polish self-image as heroes and victims. The lack of any significant response to his *Upiorna dekada* may have led him to the view that a more frontal assault on Polish complacency was necessary. He certainly believes that the deconstruction of what he sees as the distorted and partial self-image that is common in Poland is necessary for healthy political evolution, since the country has long swept its "dark past" under the carpet and fostered a sanitized view of its history. This has, in turn, led to pathological reactions when the image is challenged: Poles have been quick to defend Poland's "good name" and blame "others" for any attempts to

---

[67] We have probably underrepresented in our selection articles that deny or justify the massacre. We make no apology for this—the deniers offer little nuance or subtlety in their arguments. For a fuller account of their views, see Joanna Michlic, "Coming to Terms with the 'Difficult Past': The Polish Debate about the Jedwabne Massacre," *Acta*, no. 21, Vidal Sassoon Centre for the Study of Antisemitism, the Hebrew University of Jerusalem, Jerusalem, 2002.

tarnish it. Gross is well aware that this form of collective defense is not peculiar to Poland. He calls for it to be overcome through the rewriting of Polish history in a more balanced and truthful manner, arguing that "like several other nations, in order to reclaim its own past, Poland will have to tell its past to itself anew."[68]

Gross's call for a "counter-memory" of the collective past has been accepted in the self-critical camp. Many voices within the intelligentsia have called for a new Polish self-image, which would include not only the heroic and suffering past but also the darker side of the national story. Thus a leading figure of the progressive Catholic intelligentsia, Jarosław Gowin, in his article "Naród—ostatni węzeł?" (The nation—the last knot) argued that "[w]e have the responsibility to pass on our heritage to future generations: transmitting the memory of ourselves as heroes is our duty; transmitting the memory of Polish crimes against others should constitute a warning for the future."[69]

In her article "Zbiorowa wyobraźnia, wspólna wina" (Collective imagination, common guilt), the psychologist Krystyna Skarzyska has described the psychological roots of the inability to come to terms with the "dark past" and its negative consequences. Like Gross, she calls for the deconstruction of the dominant collective self-image:

It is understandable that we feel psychological discomfort when our own community is blamed for serious sins. The inclusion of cruelty toward others in national collective memory is completely at odds with our self-image. Its acceptance is almost impossible for people who are convinced that they have usually been victims and solely victims . . . What is urgently required is a debate about our collective memory and social identity and an attempt to deconstruct our past self-image.[70]

Individual voices within the Catholic Church and within some political parties, such as the Union of Freedom (Unia Wolności), have also embraced this call.[71] In the case of the postcommunist Social Democratic

---

[68] Citation from the English translation, Gross, *Neighbors*, 169.

[69] Jarosław Gowin, "Naród-ostatni węzeł?" *Rzeczpospolita*, 18 January 2001.

[70] Krystyna Skarzyska, "Zbiorowa wyobraźnia, wspólna wina," *Gazeta Wyborcza*, 25–26 November 2000.

[71] Examples of the representatives of the liberal wing of the Polish Catholic Church are Rev. Michał Czajkowski, "Czysta Nierządnica. Dlaczego należy przepraszaća Jedwabne," *Tygodnik Powszechny*, 27 May 2001, 1, 5; Rev. Adam Boniecki, "Bronię księdza Michała," *Tygodnik Powszechny*, 27 May 2001, 4; Rev. Wojciech Lemański, "Chrystus w zgliszczach stodoły," *Więź*, June 2001, 78–85; Father Stanisław Musiał, "Jedwabne to nowe imię Holokaustu," *Rzeczpospolita*, 10 July 2001; Bishop Henryk Muszyński, "Biedny chrześcijanin patrzy na Jedwabne," *Tygodnik Powszechny*, Kontrapunkt, nos. 1–2, 25 March 2001, 13; Bishop Tadeusz Pieronek, "Prawda Jedwabnego," *Wprost*, 13 May

Alliance (SLD), its General Council, in March 2001, issued a letter to its members and supporters with the telling title "We Are Not Inheritors of Glory Alone" ("Dziedziczymy nie tylko chwałę"). President Kwaśniewski has also accepted the need for a more critical attitude toward the recent Polish past, most strikingly in the speech he delivered at the ceremony on the sixtieth anniversary of the Jedwabne massacre on 10 July 2001:

> Thanks to the great national debate around this crime of the year 1941, much has changed in our lives in this year 2001, the first of the new millennium . . . We have come to realize that we are responsible for our attitude toward the black pages of history. We have understood that those who counsel the nation to deny this past serve the nation ill. Such an attitude leads to moral self-destruction . . . We express our pain and shame; we give expression to our determination in seeking to learn the truth, our courage in overcoming an evil past, our unbending will for understanding and harmony.[72]

The challenge to the one-sided Polish self-image has also undermined some other popular myths, including the view that Poland was always tolerant and hospitable toward the other religious and national groups that once dwelled within its borders.[73] Its main emphasis has inevitably been on the events of the Second World War. Here Gross and other representatives of the self-critical position have attempted to show the complexity of events and the need to reject the one-sided view of the solidarity of the majority of Poles with their Jewish co-citizens.[74] *Neighbors* is only part of this attempt, which is also one of the main objectives of Gross's *Upiorna dekada*.

At the same time, the debate has stimulated a strong response from the adherents of the "apologetic" position, frequently in its more radical manifestations. In these circles, from the start, the massacre was

---

2001, 8. Among the members of Unia Wolności, who participated in the debate, were Jacek Kuroń and Henryk Wujec. Kuroń and Wujec, together with Rev. Michał Czajkowski and Jan Nowak-Jeziorański, issued an appeal calling for active participation in repentance prayers in Jedwabne on 10 July. The appeal was published in *Tygodnik Powszechny*, 22 April 2001, 5.

[72] Excerpt from the official speech of Aleksander Kwaśniewski of 10 July 2001 at the commemorative ceremony in Jedwabne. The speech was published in *Gazeta Wyborcza* on 10 July 2001.

[73] See, for example, Janusz A. Majcherek, "Ciemne karty polskiej historii," *Tygodnik Powszechny*, Kontrapunkt, nos. 1–2, 25 March 2001, 16.

[74] See, for example, Joanna Tokarska-Bakir, "Obsesja niewinności," *Gazeta Wyborcza*, 13–14 January 2001, 22–23; and idem, "Nasz człowiek w Pieczarach. Jedwabne: pamięć nieodzyskana," *Tygodnik Powszechny*, 31 March 2002, 1, 4.

understood as a crime committed by the Germans and not by the Poles. This "radical apologetic" position has widespread support in the right wing of Polish politics and is also well represented in the conservative part of the Polish Catholic Church.[75] In their view, the stress on Jewish suffering during the Second World War is unbalanced—a quest by the Jews for "ultimate victimization"—and is a means of devaluing Polish suffering. Radical apologists frequently cite the Polish version of Norman Finkelstein's *The Holocaust Industry* as confirmation of the correctness of their views, which are here upheld by a "leading Jewish-American scholar."[76] The term "the Holocaust business" ("the Holocaust *gesheft*") which in Poland has clearly antisemitic connotations, has been incorporated into the narratives defending the canonical memory of the Holocaust and criticizing *Neighbors*.[77]

Various snippets of information about the investigation into the massacre that is being conducted by the Institute of National Memory (Instytut Pamięci Narodowej) have been seized upon as "proof" of direct German participation. For example, the news of the discovery of German bullets in the barn where the Jews were burned and where a partial exhumation of bodies was carried out in late May–early June 2001 was presented as definitive evidence of German responsibility. Subsequent forensic analysis of the bullets showed that they came from completely different periods of time.[78] Jewish support for the Soviet regime between September 1939 and 1941, as well as during the postwar period, is stressed to minimize the criminal nature of the massacre. Some "radical apologists" have fused the concept of German responsibility with the idea of "Judeo-communism," arguing that the genocide was part of an anti-Bolshevik crusade. Thus both Father Orłowski and the Łomża senator Jadwiga Stokarska have asserted that the Germans

<hr>

[75] See, for example, Antoni Macierewicz, "Oskarżam Aleksandra Kwaśniewskiego," *Tygodnik Głos*, no. 14 (17 April 2001); Klub Konserwatywny w Łodzi, "Stanowisko w związku ze sprawą Jedwabnego," *Tygodnik Głos*, 7 July 2001; Rev. Jerzy Bajda, "Przepraszać? Kto kogo?" *Nasz Dziennik*, 14 March 2001; Rev. Prof. Waldemar Chrostowski, "Kto utrudnia dialog? Rozmowa Pawla Paliwody," *Życie*, 10 April 2001.

[76] For critical analysis of Norman Finkelstein's *The Holocaust Industry* (London, 2001), see David Cesarani, "Is There, and Has There Ever Been, a 'Holocaust Industry?' " in *The Issues of the Holocaust Research in Latvia* (Riga, 2001), 83–100. See also Jerzy Sławomir Mac, "Czerwona podszewka. 'Przedsiębiorstwo Holocaust' to połączenie nazistowskiej i komunistycznej propagandy," *Wprost*, 23 September 2001, 78–79.

[77] For example, the bishop of Łomża Stanisław Stefanek, Bishop Józef Michalik, and Rev. Edward Orłowski of the Jedwabne parish have used the term in their sermons and comments. The right-wing journalist Henryk Pająk has published a book entitled *Jedwabne Geszefty* (Lublin, 2001), 2d ed.

[78] See the report "New Evidence on Polish Massacre," *BBC News*, 19 December 2001. The bullets came from the First World War and from after 1942.

killed the Jews because they were Communists and fought against the Germans on behalf of the Soviet Union.[79]

In the "radical apologetic" camp, Gross's book has been dismissed as a "lie aiming to slander the good name of Poland." It has also been categorized as another Jewish or Jewish-American conspiracy against Poland and as confirmation of the "truth" that "the Jew" always wants to harm "the Pole."[80] At the same time, this group stresses both the large amount of assistance provided by Polish society to the Jews during the war and Jewish "ingratitude" for these sacrifices.

An assessment of the "moderate apologetic" position is more complex. Gross's book is clearly not the last word on the subject, and there are many issues that are the subject of legitimate debate, including the strength of Polish antisemitism before the war, the impact of the Soviet occupation in widening the gap between Poles and Jews between 1939 and 1941, and the actual character of German involvement in the massacre. Certainly dispassionate historical investigation is a better way forward than well-intentioned moral statements and apologies. But the actual historical debate about the Jedwabne massacre has thus far been a disappointment. Many of those who have espoused what Andrzej Paczkowski describes as a "defensive open" stance in the controversy have come to adopt quite extreme positions, as has been the case, for instance, with Tomasz Strzembosz. They seem to have great difficulty in abandoning the self-image of the Poles as heroes and victims and often use strongly apologetic arguments. To a number of them, the imperative of defending national honor, Poland's "good name," also appears to play a large role.[81] These factors seem to make it difficult for them to analyze the national self-image in a detached, objective, and critical manner. This has often led to a blurring of the line between legitimate criticism of Gross's book and the "radical apologetic" position, with its clearly antisemitic overtones.[82]

---

[79] Jadwiga Stokarska, "Kampania oszczerstw," *Nasz Dziennik*, 19 March 2001, and Edward Orłowski "Niech zwycięży prawda. Conversation of Rev. Pawel Bejger with Rev. Orłowski," *Tygodnik Mlodzieży Katolickiej "Droga"*, 13 March 2001.

[80] See, for example, Leon Kalewski, "Opowieści niesamowite. Part 1 and 2," *Nasza Polska*, 21 November 2000 and 19 December 2000; Jerzy Robert Nowak, "Kto fałszuje historię," *Nasz Dziennik*, 13 May 2000; Piotr Gontarczyk, "Gross kontra fakty," *Życie*, 28 February 2001; and Jan Engelgard, "Antynarodowa histeria," *Myśl Polska*, 30 March 2001.

[81] On the positive correlation between national honor and reputation and absence of self-criticism in collective cultures, see Irwin-Zarecka, *Frames*, 8–82. See also Michlic, "The Troubling Past," 81–82.

[82] In his short typology of different positions within the debate, Andrzej Paczkowski was the first to indicate that in some cases the borders between the positions are not clearly defined.

Why is the self-image of Poles as heroes and victims so powerful in collective memory? This is a complex question and can be understood only in the context of Poland's tragic history in the last two centuries. It became established in Polish collective self-awareness in the first half of the nineteenth century, when it was rooted in the romantic national myth of the Poles fighting "for your freedom and ours" (*Za waszą i naszą wolność*), and was an important element in shaping the modern Polish national consciousness throughout the nineteenth century and the first two decades of the twentieth—the long era of the partitions and struggle for independence. During the Second World War it again became a powerful myth in the Sorelian sense, enabling the Polish people to resist both Soviet and Nazi attempts to destroy their national existence. The experience of this war strongly reinforced the Polish consciousness of being solely heroes and victims. Certainly Poles have much to be proud of in their participation in the Allied war effort and in their record of resistance in occupied Poland. The Polish armed resistance movement was the second largest in Europe after Tito's partisans, while Poland was the only occupied country in Europe that had an organized underground civilian administration, as well as an underground education system and an extensive underground press. The Poles also suffered appalling losses—Nazi terror was much more brutal here than in Western Europe, and it has been estimated that nearly 10 percent of the ethnic Polish population died as the result of the war.

The war itself was widely perceived as an embodiment of Polish collective martyrdom and heroism, and this made any meaningful discussion of the black pages of Polish attitudes and behavior toward the Polish-Jewish minority seem out of place. This view of the war continued to exert a powerful hold on the collective self-image under communism, and it was intensified during the Solidarity period and particularly in the period of martial law after the crushing of the first Solidarity. It was at this time that the wartime image of "fighting Poland" (*Polska walcząca*) resisting the Nazis was transformed into the image of "fighting Solidarity" (*Solidarność walcząca*) resisting the communist regime.[83] Under these conditions one can fully understand why it is so hard, even at present, for many Poles to accept the "dark past" as an integral part of the Polish self-image.

Has the debate changed attitudes in Poland significantly? Judging by the opinions expressed in letters and Internet group discussions

---

[83] On the perception of the Second World War in public memory of the 1980s and 1990s, see Tomasz Szarota, "Wojna na dobre samopoczucie," *Gazeta Wyborcza*, 6 September 1996.

published in *Gazeta Wyborcza, Polityka, Tygodnik Powszechny,* and *Wprost,* the "self-critical" version of Polish-Jewish relations is now more widely accepted, particularly by young people. But it has not gone unchallenged. Public opinion polls show widespread confusion on the subject and difficulty in reaching firm conclusions.[84] Thus in a poll held in early April 2001, 48 percent of those surveyed did not believe that Poles should apologize to the "Jewish nation" for the crime of Jedwabne, while 30 percent were in favor of an apology. Eighty percent did not feel—as Poles—any moral responsibility for Jedwabne, while only 13 percent felt such a responsibility; 34 percent believed that the Germans were solely responsible for the crime, 14 percent that Germans and Poles were jointly responsible, and 7 percent that Poles were solely responsible.[85]

An opinion poll conducted in August 2001, after the memorial service and the extensive television coverage of the massacre, showed only small changes in attitude: 28 percent of respondents still believed that the Germans/Nazis were solely responsible for the massacre of Jedwabne Jews; 12 percent claimed that a few Poles together with the Germans participated in the massacre; 4 percent stated that Poles forced by the Germans committed the massacre; 8 percent stated that Poles alone were responsible for the massacre. Thirty percent were not able to say who was responsible for the murders. What is clear is that knowledge of what happened in Jedwabne is now widely disseminated in Poland.

Even after the publication of the report of the Institute of National Memory in October 2002, 50 percent of those polled were unable to say who was responsible for the massacre. This answer was most frequently given by people without higher education, among those who lived in the countryside or who declared they had no interest in politics. Three percent held that the murders had been committed by the local Polish population without the participation of the Germans; 17 percent held that those responsible were the local Poles incited by Germans; 28 percent by Germans with the help of Poles; 34 percent by Poles compelled to do so by Germans; and 18 percent by Germans without Polish help. Asked what sort of Poles participated in the mas-

---

[84] Opinion poll, conducted by Centrum Badania Opinii Społecznej (CBOS) on 28 August 2001, *Report of CBOS,* Warsaw, September 2001.

[85] According to opinion polls conducted by Pentor, one of the leading Polish survey organizations, 23.3 percent of Poles between the ages of 15 and 25 stated that they felt "satisfaction that the truth about the massacre of Jedwabne Jews had been revealed and that the victims were honorably commemorated." On the whole, 68 percent of the respondents felt that the revelation of the participation of Poles in the murders was an important event. This opinion poll was published in *Wprost,* 22 July 2001, 26.

sacre, 50 percent responded "ordinary people, like everyone else," while 32 percent believed that they were "marginal people." Eighty-three percent held that it was good that the crime at Jedwabne had been brought to light. Forty percent approved of the president's apology; 35 percent disapproved. Forty-four percent thought such an apology necessary against 35 percent who did not. The body that carried out this poll (OBOP) concluded, "Those who refuse to acknowledge guilt for Jedwabne are primarily older people, those with less education, who live in the countryside and in small towns. Those who are in favor of such an acknowledgment are mostly younger, more educated, and town-dwellers." It may be that, as in Germany, the long-term impact of the controversy will be very different from its first reception, as is suggested by this last poll.[86]

How is one to interpret the significance of the debate? Those who have attempted to do so can be categorized either as optimists or as pessimists. The optimists have paid particular attention to the development of the "self-critical" aspect of the debate. They see it as a cathartic discussion that will transform the Poles' way of remembering the Holocaust, Polish-Jewish relations, and their own wartime self-image.[87] In their opinion, the debate has broken the taboo on discussing the more painful aspects of Polish-Jewish relations. The pessimists have stressed rather the strength of the "radical apologetic" position that has attacked Gross's book as an "anti-Polish lie aiming at the extortion of billions of dollars from hapless Poles." They also take a critical view of the "moderate apologists" and have underlined the common ground between them and the radicals. Their conclusion is that the debate has confirmed the firm grip of the past on the present and the inability of Polish society to undergo a process that would lead to the "modernization of its mentality." In their opinion, the shock of Jedwabne will "soon be forgotten" by the public and "antisemitism will become a part of the daily norm of life."[88]

However, these interpretations reflect primarily the position of the observer rather than the debate itself. It seems more sensible to view it as a reflection of the inevitable process of democratization of political and social life in Poland that has been possible only since 1989.[89] It is

[86] Public opinion survey conducted by CBOS on 6–9 April on 1,036 persons, Polska Agencja Prasowa (PAP), 1 May 2001, CBOS, 23–25 November 2002 on 1,008 persons.

[87] See, for example, Krzysztof Darewicz, "Debata o Jedwabnem zmieni Polaków," *Rzeczpospolita*, 2–3 May 2001, 3; and opinion of Marian Turski cited by Tony Wesolowski in "Jedwabne, Poland," *Christian Science Monitor*, April 2001.

[88] See the opinions of the editors of the journal, Marcin Król, Paweł Śpiewak, and Marek Zaleski, in the discussion in *NowaResPublica*, no. 7 (July 2001).

[89] Ewa K. Czaczkowska, "Byłem sam, będą nas setki," *Rzeczpospolita*, 10 July 2001.

also a product of the emergence of a pluralistic culture in which two competing visions of Poland, harking back in a strange way to the earlier conflict between Piłsudski and Dmowski, are competing for dominance.[90] The first concept of Poland is based on the civic pluralistic model—it is inclusive of the memory of "others" and acknowledges the wrongs done to them. The second is the ethnic nationalist model— it is not interested in the memory of "the other" and seeks to foster a vision of the past that stresses Polish suffering and the wrongs done to the Poles. These points of view also differ about how the country should develop in the future and whether its identity is threatened by globalization and entry into the European Union. Although the outward-looking and pluralistic vision of the Polish future still seems dominant and is represented both in the postcommunist and parts of the post-Solidarity camps, the integral nationalist and populist camp seems to be growing in strength, as was demonstrated by the strong showing of groups like the League of Polish Families (Liga Polskich Rodziń) and Self-defense (Samoobrona) in the parliamentary elections of September 2001.[91]

These two broad groups use very different language to address Jewish issues. Those who espouse a civic and pluralistic vision of Poland generally talk of "the Polish Jews," "our co-citizens," and "co-stewards of this land" (*współgospodarze*—the term used on the new monument in Jedwabne), language that reflects their rejection of ethnonationalism.[92] In contrast, for those who favor an integral nationalist view of Poland, the Jew is still referred to as a Jew (*Żyd*, sometimes lowercased, *żyd*), a term that demarcates the Jews from Poles and that in present-day Poland has a pejorative tone (except when used by Jews).[93] This

[90] This has been, for instance, the view of the late Jerzy Giedroyć, the long-standing editor of *Kultura*.

[91] The Liga Polskich Rodzin, which was founded just before these elections, adopts a conservative nationalist position. Its leader, Roman Giertych, comes from a prominent National Democratic family, and it has the support of a significant part of the conservative element within the Polish Catholic Church, most notably Father Tadeusz Rydzyk of Radio Maryja. It is strongly opposed to Polish entry into the European Union. So, too, is the Przymierze Samoobrona, which was created in 1992 as the militant political representative of the radical farmers' trade union of the same name. Its leader, Andrzej Lepper, is notorious for his aggressive and xenophobic statements.

[92] The former prime minister Jerzy Buzek, president of Poland Aleksander Kwaśniewski, and chairman of Instytut Pamięci Narodowej (IPN) Leon Kieres have used such terms. For example, in an interview for *Dziennik Bałtycki*, 15 June 2001, Kieres stated, "I treat 'Polishness' as a civic category and thus treat the Jews of Jedwabne as my compatriots." Cited in *Polityka*, no. 26 (30 June 2001): 88.

[93] It should be mentioned that prewar integrationists and assimilationists lowercased żyd to stress that the Jews were a religious and not a national group. Today, however, this usage is clearly antisemitic.

linguistic difference is indicative of the former group's willingness to
adopt a critical stance in relation to the history of Polish-Jewish relations and reflects their desire to integrate the Jews posthumously into
the community of Poland and into the Polish consciousness, a desire
that is clearly lacking in the second group. In this sense, the debate
should be seen as part of the struggle between two concepts of Poland
that entail significantly different and conflicting memories of the Holocaust and constructions of the Polish self-image.[94]

The conflict between these two visions of Poland is not yet decided,
and its outcome will have major implications for the country's future.
The debate about Jedwabne is only a part of this conflict, but it is a
significant part. Writing about developments in Poland between 1989
and 1995, Michael Steinlauf observed that it was still not possible to
foresee what Poles would do with the memory of the Holocaust, and
how it would shape Polish history and consciousness.[95] He expressed
the hope that this memory "would be used in the service of renewal
rather than repression." The dynamics of the debate over *Neighbors*
suggests that renewal has definitely taken place, but that it is accompanied by repression. Time will tell whether this repression is a significant or a marginal phenomenon. Jews, both in Poland and outside,
clearly have some role to play in affecting the outcome of this process.
Popular Jewish perceptions of the Poles are preponderantly negative
and underplay Polish resistance to the Nazis (and Soviets). Some recognition on the Jewish side of the level of Polish resistance and suffering would clearly strengthen those in Poland who are struggling to
come to terms with the negative aspects of Polish-Jewish relations.

At the same time, although the debate among historians has so far
been both acrimonious and disappointing in its results, it is this debate
that seems to offer the best chance of forward movement. In this context, the debate about *Neighbors* is part of a general process, which has
only really begun since the end of the communist system, of coming
to terms with many neglected and taboo aspects of the Polish past.
Among these are the history of Poles beyond the borders of present-
day Poland, above all in the former Soviet Union, and relations between Poles and Ukrainians, Lithuanians, Germans, and Russians. For
too long, these topics have been the subject of much mythologization.
The first approach to such issues has to be from a moral point of

---

[94] We borrow the concept "transmission of memory" from the leading sociologist of
memory, Maurice Halbwachs. Halbwachs originated the contention that memory is an
activity deeply affected by its medium of transmission. See Maurice Halbwachs, *The Collective Memory* (New York, 1980).

[95] Steinlauf, *Bondage*, 144.

view—a settlement of long-overdue accounts. In the case of Polish-Jewish relations, we are now beginning to enter a second stage, where apologies and apologetics will increasingly be replaced by careful and detailed research and reliable and nuanced firsthand testimony.[96] Franklin Ankersmit has argued that since what we are dealing with here is not "normal" but "traumatic" history, this Polish-Jewish past is not susceptible to the discourse of the historian, which in his view merely examines the past but does not try to explore or penetrate it. This is too pessimistic. It should be possible to move beyond strongly held, competing, and incompatible narratives of the past and to reach some consensus that will be acceptable to all people of goodwill and will bring about a degree of normalization both in Poles' attitudes toward the past and in Polish-Jewish relations, while also increasing awareness in the Jewish world of the complexity of the Polish situation between 1939 and 1945. Some have questioned whether normalization is a desirable or realizable goal. The past is too near and painful for that. Perhaps the aim should be for both Poles and Jews (insofar as these are mutually exclusive categories) to strive for a "tragic acceptance" of those events which have united and, so often, divided them in the past century. That, at least, is owed to the millions of victims of the totalitarian systems of the last century.

[96] Indeed, the debate about *Neighbors* does seem to have facilitated a serious debate about relations between Poles and Ukrainians. In a recent issue of *Więź* (April 2002) entitled *Z Ukraińcami po Jedwabnem* (With the Ukrainians after Jedwabne), there is an extended discussion of Ukrainian ethnic cleansing directed against Poles in Volynia during the Second World War and the postwar "Operation Wisła" in which the Ukrainian population of southeastern Poland was forcibly resettled in the north and west of the country.

PART I

THE INITIAL REPORTING

INTRODUCTION

> Many citizens of Jedwabne refused to talk, and yet without
> great difficulty I obtained general confirmation of the Jew-
> ish accounts of the perpetrators of the extermination. It
> was not just older people who had lived in the town
> throughout the war who knew and stated that Poles com-
> mitted the murderous acts, but also young people who
> knew the truth only through family stories.
> —Andrzej Kaczyński, *Rzeczpospolita*, 5 May 2000

E VEN DURING the Communist period Poland had a well-estab-
lished tradition of investigative journalism. Thus it is not surprising that journalists, both local and national, should have
played an important role in researching and making public the massacre in Jedwabne. As early as July 1988, two local journalists, Danuta
and Alexander Wroniszewski, wrote an extensive account of the Jedwabne massacre in the Łomża weekly *Kontakty*.[1] They underscored the
poverty and isolation of the town, and pointed out that in the 1930s
the local priest had been a "supporter of the 'Nationalists,'" a strong
advocate of the boycott of Jewish shops, and a proponent of "new
ideas imported directly from Nazi Germany." The local Jews, though
impoverished, were better off than the remainder of the population
and occupied most of the houses around the market square and in the
center of the town. They were a clear majority of the population, and
"in order for a Pole to be elected mayor of a Polish town, it was necessary to gerrymander three hamlets into the boundaries of the town."

They describe the monument erected in the late 1960s by the Union
of Fighters for Freedom and Democracy (ZboWiD—the main organization created by the partisan faction in the Polish United Workers'
Party), with its notorious inscription: "Site of the Suffering of the Jewish Population. The Gestapo and the Nazi gendarmerie burned 1,600
people alive, 10 July 1941." They also interviewed a number of inhabitants of the town who maintained that the German occupiers were
solely responsible. They reprinted in full the account that Szmul Wasersztajn had written on 5 April 1945, and found locals who confirmed
some aspects of his story. Among them were some who claimed that
the massacre was the work of "farmhands and stable boys" from the

[1] *Kontakty*, 10 July 1988.

surrounding countryside, and others who held that it was the responsibility of those living in the town. In addition they interviewed the enigmatic figure of Waldemar Monkiewicz, a member of the Białystok Regional Commission for the Investigation of Nazi Crimes, who wrote in an article in *Studia Podlaskie* in 1989:

> In early July 1941, 200 men from the 309th and 316th [German] police battalions were detached to form a special unit, called Kommando Białystok, under the command of Wolfgang Birkner, who was seconded from the Warsaw Gestapo. On 10 July, this unit arrived in Jedwabne by truck. Both the gendarmerie and the auxiliary police were engaged in the operation carried out against the Jews. The auxiliary police were involved only in leading the victims to the square and escorting them out of town.[2]

Speaking to the Wroniszewskis, he asserted again that the massacre was the work of the "Birkner *Kommando*," which he described as made up of local people, part of a volunteer police force created after the collapse of Soviet authority. "When the Germans arrived, some of these people in the police resigned, while others resolved to collaborate with the Germans." They consisted of "some two hundred ruffians, people devoid of all scruples. They drifted from one locality to another, carrying out a new pogrom every other day." He also repudiated his alleged role as a prosecutor in the postwar trials of Poles accused of carrying out the massacre. "Those people ... had to be convicted regardless of the extent of their guilt. After all, that was the time of Jakub Berman and people like him."[3]

This section includes two accounts by local journalists. The first is by Gabriela Szczęsna and, like the Wroniszewskis' article, was published in the Łomża-based weekly *Kontakty*. The result of many local interviews, it relates the views of both those who deny and those who admit substantial Polish involvement. Maria Kaczyńska lives in Łomża and writes for the local paper *Gazeta Współczesna*. She has produced a number of pieces on Jedwabne. In her article "In Memory and Admonition," she describes how she found many people prepared to confirm that Poles were primarily responsible for the massacre, although she also remarks on the general climate of intimidation in the town.

The Jedwabne massacre has also attracted the attention of the national press. On 5 May 2000, three weeks before the publication of the

[2] *Studia Podlaskie* 2 (1989): 345–46.
[3] A reference to Jakub Berman, a key figure in Poland during the Stalinist period who between 1949 and 1954 was a member of the Commission of Security Matters of the Central Committee of the Polish United Workers' Party. His Jewish origin was often commented on.

Polish edition of *Neighbors*, the seasoned investigative journalist Andrzej Kaczyński published a long and well-documented article entitled
"Burnt Offering" in *Rzeczpospolita*, one of the leading Polish dailies.[4]
Kaczyński learned about the massacre from Jan Gross's article in the
festschrift for Tomasz Strzembosz, *Europa Nieprowincjonalna* (Warsaw,
2000), in which Gross reproduced Szmul Wasersztajn's testimony, and
from the *Yizkerbukh* compiled by the surviving Jedwabne Jews, which
was published in 1980 and has been posted on the Internet. His conclusions are unequivocal: "Local Poles carried out the death sentence. Recently revealed eyewitness accounts by Jews who survived the Holocaust confirm this. Nor do Polish residents of Jedwabne who witnessed
the tragedy deny it."

---

[4] *Rzeczpospolita* was first published in the interwar period as a paper representing the
voice of the right-wing Christian-National Union (Stronnictwo Chrześcijansko-Naro-
dowe). The paper became the chief organ of the new government in 1944 but was closed
down in 1950. In 1980 *Rzeczpospolita* reappeared as a daily representing the voice of the
government, but in 1989 it was transformed into a social and political daily open to various ideological and political ideas. It is generally regarded as center-right in its political
orientation. Its average national circulation is 264,000 copies, and its chief editor is Maciej Łukasiewicz.

Andrzej Kaczyński

BURNT OFFERING

RZECZPOSPOLITA, 5 MAY 2000

I N JEDWABNE, the German extermination of the Jews was carried out by Polish hands.

On 10 July 1941 in Jedwabne, in the Łomża region, the Germans ordered that the entire Jewish community of the small town be exterminated. Local Poles carried out the death sentence. Recently revealed eyewitness accounts by Jews who survived the Holocaust confirm this. Nor do Polish residents of Jedwabne who witnessed the tragedy deny it. From these same sources, it is also known that the Germans used Polish hands to commit similar massacres of Jews in Wąsosz, Wizna, and Radziłów. Many of these documented testimonies were previously known to Polish scholars. These scholars did not, however, contribute to exposing the shocking truth about Polish involvement in the Nazi extermination of the Jews. This knowledge has reached us from abroad.

One Tragedy, Two Histories

A boulder with a memorial tablet is the only trace of more than two hundred years of Jewish presence in Jedwabne, near Łomża. But the inscription on it accusing the Nazis alone of carrying out the destruction of the Jewish residents of the town does not tell the entire truth. Nor did historians living in Poland reveal that truth. Only recently, Prof. Jan Tomasz Gross of New York published Szmul Wasersztajn's account describing the general participation of local Poles in the murder of Jedwabne's Jews. This document, written in 1945 and preserved in the archives of the Jewish Historical Institute in Warsaw, had been known to, or at least referred to, by Polish historians who nevertheless concealed its true significance. A collection of later Jewish testimonies, which also accuses a certain number of Poles from Jedwabne and the nearby villages of involvement in the crime (it accuses them by name, and there are at least thirty names), has recently been placed on the Internet in the United States.

A discussion on the subject of the murder of Jedwabne's Jews has developed on the Internet, based on this documentation as well as on a lecture by Prof. Jan Tomasz Gross at an American university. One posting, from a month or so ago, reads in part: "The Germans entered Jedwabne. The Poles asked them to leave town for eight hours. Eight hours later, there were 1,100 fewer Jews." The author got her distorted information secondhand, or she heard it inaccurately. Another author confuses the dates and informs the world that [in Jedwabne] the Poles murdered Jews who had survived the Nazi Holocaust. "Kielce [the 3 July 1946 pogrom] was peanuts by comparison," he adds. Both authors display considerable curiosity about, and a degree of familiarity with, Polish affairs. These are the results of the truth's having been covered up. The reaction of Internet readers who know little or nothing about Poland is something that it is better not even to think about.

I checked to see what Polish researchers of the Shoah had written on the subject. It turns out that there are two different and even contradictory versions of the destruction of the Jedwabne Jews. Polish sources attribute responsibility for the massacre exclusively, or almost exclusively, to the Germans—the Nazi gendarmerie and police. The Polish role in it is downplayed, silenced, or denied outright.

Will They Take Back Formerly Jewish Property?

Many citizens of Jedwabne refused to talk, and yet without great difficulty I obtained general confirmation of the Jewish accounts of the perpetrators of the extermination. It was not just older people who had lived in the town throughout the war who knew and stated that Poles committed the murderous acts, but also young people who knew the truth only through family stories. "None of the murderers is still alive," they assured me. Yet almost all of them demanded anonymity. When our photographer approached some youngsters gathered in the town square and asked them to point out any mementos of the Jedwabne Jews, or the monument to them, they first asked with a hint of sarcasm whether he had come to take back the property that formerly belonged to the Jews.

Only one Jewish apartment house remains in Jedwabne. The author of one of the accounts placed on the Internet visited the town some twenty years ago and lamented that he had seen hardly any Jewish buildings left.

About 75 percent of the town was destroyed during the First World War. A few years before World War II, the church and synagogue were rebuilt. The Germans burned down the splendid new synagogue, the pride of the Jedwabne Jews, in September 1939.

On 28 September 1939, the two invaders, the Third Reich and the Soviet Union, agreed on their division of Poland. For twenty months, Jedwabne was under Soviet occupation. The Germans again entered the town on 23 June 1941, the second day of their attack on the USSR. Eighteen days later, almost all the Jedwabne Jews were burned alive.

The Jewish Version

The few Jews who survived the burning or who heard about it from eyewitnesses accuse Poles, their neighbors and fellow townspeople, from Jedwabne and from other nearby villages, of the crime. According to their accounts, Poles were the sole perpetrators of this crime. Germans may have issued the orders or incited the pogrom, but it is not certain whether they were in town at the time, and they may have even tried to moderate or limit the extermination.

The first source is two depositions that Szmul Wasersztajn, an eyewitness to the tragic events in Jedwabne on 10 July 1941, presented to the Jewish Historical Committee in Białystok in 1945. These statements are preserved in the archives of the Jewish Historical Institute in Warsaw. The JHI archives also contain depositions on the events in Jedwabne and the vicinity from, among others, Menachem Finkelsztejn, Abraham Śmiałowicz, and A. Belawicki. All of them accuse the Poles. These documents have been known to scholars for a dozen years or more, or at least have been cited by all Polish scholars in their lists of sources. Jan Tomasz Gross was the first to publish one of Szmul Wasersztajn's two depositions (the longer one) in its entirety (in a festschrift for Prof. Tomasz Strzembosz titled *Europa nieprowincjonalna* [Nonprovincial Europe], (Warsaw, 2000). While indicating that he found several discrepancies between Wasersztajn's two depositions, Gross did not engage in any basic criticism of them as sources (no doubt regarding them as basically credible). He also outlined plans for further research on Polish attitudes toward the extermination of the Jews in the eastern territories of Poland occupied by the Germans after their attack on the Soviet Union.

Among the testimonies on the Internet (http://www.jewishgen. org/Yizkor/jedwabne/) are those of three eyewitnesses: Herszel Piekarz-Baker, Rywka Fogel, and Icchak (Janek) Neumark.

Wasersztajn claims that on the third day of the German occupation of Jedwabne, 25 June 1941, "local Polish bandits" started stealing Jew-

ANDRZEJ KACZYŃSKI   53

ish property and brutally beating and even killing Jews. With his own eyes he saw three people murdered. "Jakub Kac was stoned with bricks; Eliasz Krawiecki was stabbed repeatedly with knives, then his eyes were gouged out and his tongue was cut off. He suffered inhumanly for twelve hours before drawing his last breath." Rywka Fogel names four other victims of the massacre.

Wasersztajn continues: "That same day I observed a horrible scene. Chaja Kubrzańska, twenty-eight years old, and Basia Binsztejn, twenty-six years old, both holding newborn babies, when they saw what was going on, went to the pond to drown themselves with the children rather than fall into the hands of bandits. They put their children in the water and drowned them with their own hands: then Baśka Binsztejn jumped in and immediately went to the bottom, while Chaja Kubrzańska suffered for a couple of hours." Rywka Fogel offered slightly different details. The two women exchanged babies. They slashed their own veins before throwing themselves into the pond. According to Wasersztajn, the hooligans treated the tragedy as a spectacle. Fogel claimed some Poles rescued the women the first time they attempted suicide. Their husbands, communist activists, had escaped with the Russians.

The pogrom lasted one day. Wasersztajn stated that it was stopped by the priest, who explained "that the German authorities would take care of things by themselves."

On 7 and 8 July, Jewish refugees from pogroms in Wizna and Radziłów had sought shelter in Jedwabne. About a thousand Jews lived in Jedwabne, and it is not known how many fled with the Russians. Some place the number of fugitives as high as seven hundred. Some hid outside of the town, anticipating a catastrophe; the Nazis had been organizing a pogrom in a different locality each day.

Early in the morning of 10 July, the people in hiding watched as many peasants from the outlying hamlets arrived in town by cart. Just as on a market day. Germans also arrived. Eight Gestapo functionaries held a meeting with representatives of the town's Polish authorities. According to Wasersztajn, the Germans wanted to kill most of the Jews while sparing skilled craftsmen who would be useful to them, while the Poles demanded that none of the Jews be left alive, because there were enough skilled Christian craftsmen to do any work. Other Jewish reports give a similar account of the meeting. Some Polish witnesses also overheard the locals taking just such a stance in the negotiations with the Gestapo.

The Jews were ordered to gather in the town square. "Local hooligans armed themselves with axes, special clubs studded with nails, and other instruments of torture and destruction and chased all the Jews into the street," testified Wasersztajn. They forced the Jews to weed and clean the square. A statue of Lenin was toppled from its pedestal, and young Jews were ordered to carry it around the square while singing Soviet songs and chanting: "This war is our doing." According to some accounts, the Poles selected dozens of strong young men and ordered them to carry Lenin's statue to the Jewish cemetery outside of town. There, they forced them to dig a large pit and bury the statue in it. After that, they murdered all these men and threw their bodies into the same pit. The rest of the Jews were kept in the town square all day under the scorching sun, without a drop of water. They were insulted and beaten. Polish hoodlums tormented the gray-haired rabbi, Awigdor Białostocki, and did not spare the women and the children. In the evening they marched all the Jews, in rows of four, toward the Jewish cemetery. According to some accounts, the rabbi was ordered to march in the front rank carrying a red banner. Everyone was forced into a barn. The barn was doused with a flammable liquid and set alight. Icchak Neumark, a former citizen of Jedwabne, testified that a Pole whom he recognized stood guarding the barn door, ax in hand. "He was ready to kill anyone who tried to get out. My family and I were standing near the door because, fortunately, we were among the last to be pushed into the barn. Suddenly, the barn door fell apart in the flames. The one guarding the door raised his ax to strike me, but fortunately I managed to knock it away. My sister, her five-year-old daughter, and I managed to escape to the cemetery. I saw how my father collapsed in flames on the floor of the barn."

Those who were not burned alive in the barn were beaten to death wherever the Polish perpetrators found them. Rywka Fogel heard the terrible screams of Józef Lewin, a boy whom the bandits clubbed to death. "The goys grabbed little Judka Nadolna, cut off her head, and played with it like a soccer ball," testified Fogel. Icchak Neumark said that one woman, nine months pregnant, had her abdomen ripped open by her father-in-law's farmhand. "I saw with my own eyes how Aron lay dead in the street with a cross carved into his chest. Three-year-old Chana hid in a chicken coop. The goys found her and threw her into the fire like a piece of wood," said Neumark.

"Not even one German participated in the killing that day. On the contrary, two officers came to the barn of destruction to save at least the craftsmen, tailors, cobblers, blacksmiths, and carpenters, whose labor the Germans required. But the goys told them: 'Not one Jew can remain alive. There are enough skilled craftsmen among the Christians,' " Neumark reported. "Even though the Germans gave the order, it was Polish hooligans who took it up and carried it out, using the most horrible methods," said Szmul Wasersztajn. "The Poles decided to kill all the Jews and they did so. The Germans looked with disdain upon the overt bestiality of the Poles," testified Herszel Piekarz-Baker, the author of one of the accounts published on the Internet.

The Polish Version

In a 1966 article in *Biuletyn Żydowskiego Instytutu Historycznego* (Bulletin of the Jewish Historical Institute), Szymon Datner charged the special operational groups of the German police with the crimes committed on a mass scale against the Jewish population of the Białystok region after the attack on the USSR by the Third Reich. "Those units were supported by 'native' police formations consisting of traitors, fascists, degenerates, and criminals. Often playing on the lowest instincts of these people, the [German] units organized outbursts" of popular fury, "supplying arms and giving instructions without themselves taking part in the slaughter. As a rule, they photographed the scenes that were played out as evidence that the Jews were hated not only by the Germans." Datner goes on to write about the Łomża region: "The Germans dragged the dregs of the local community, as well as the so-called Blue Police into these crimes. This was a phenomenon that was relatively rare in occupied Poland, as well as in the rest of the Białystok area, where the local population—Polish and Belarusian alike—refused to be hoodwinked by German provocation . . . In a few cases, the local scum and criminal elements allowed themselves to be used as henchmen by the Germans. However, the majority" of the work "was done by German hands." Szymon Datner did not say unequivocally who perpetrated the crime in Jedwabne.

The most detailed Polish account of the events in Jedwabne was presented in 1989 by Waldemar Monkiewicz, a public prosecutor and member of the Białystok Regional Commission for the Investigation of Nazi Crimes in Poland, in the University of Białystok's *Studia Podlaskie* [Podlasie studies]. "In early July 1941, 200 men from the 309th and 316th [German] police battalions were detached to form a special unit, called Kommando Białystok, under the command of Wolfgang Birkner, who was seconded from the Warsaw Gestapo. On 10 July, this unit arrived in Jedwabne by truck. Both the gendarmerie and the auxiliary police were engaged in the operation carried out against the Jews. The auxiliary police were involved only in leading the victims to the square and escorting them out of town. There, the Nazis committed unspeakable cruelty, driving some 900 people into a barn that they next closed, and the walls of which they splashed with gasoline and set alight, causing the martyr's deaths of the men, women, and children inside. Two days later, these same perpetrators murdered almost all the Jews in Radziłów. [According to most sources, the massacre in Radziłów occurred on 7 July, and thus earlier than the one in Jedwabne.] There they burned approximately 650 people in a barn. In both Jedwabne and Radziłów, the Nazis attempted to drag some auxiliary policemen of Polish nationality into the pogrom. Those among them against whom any sort of involvement was proven—and this was most frequently in acts of subsidiary importance—received severe punishment."

Three years earlier, during an oration at ceremonies marking the 250th anniversary of Jedwabne's municipal charter, Prosecutor Monkiewicz stated that 150 German police came to Jedwabne by motor vehicle on the day of destruction in Jedwabne, estimated the number of dead Jewish victims at "about 900, and in any case not fewer than 600," and admitted that he had managed to establish the names of only a few families who perished then. He added that he "would omit for understandable reasons" mentioning the names of the Polish auxiliary police who had anything to do with the crime.

Twenty-two Poles were tried in Łomża in 1949 for cooperating with the Germans in the murder of the Jews of Jedwabne. A death sentence was pronounced against a *Volksdeutsch* from Cieszyn. The others were sentenced to eight to fifteen years' imprisonment. None of them admitted his guilt. Unfortunately, the records of the trial are at present unavailable since the archives of the Main Commission for the Investigation of Crimes against the Polish Nation, where they are preserved, are being moved to new premises.

Prosecutor Waldemar Monkiewicz also asserts that Nazi state functionaries have been tried in Germany for the Jedwabne crime.

To Clarify, Not to Justify

Discussing "anti-Jewish outbreaks and pogroms in occupied Europe" in an article in the book *Holocaust z perspektywy półwiecza* [The Holocaust from the perspective of half a century], published by the Jewish Historical Institute, Prof. Tomasz Szarota writes that "each time it was probably a provocation prepared by the Sipo and SD, and in the east by the *Einsatzgruppen*. The primary purpose was one of propaganda. The world was thus shown that the Germans were not the only ones who felt the need to eliminate the Jews, and that the strength of hatred of the Jews was even greater in countries other than Germany. As a by-product, there was a demonstration of the alleged approval of the occupied countries for the way in which Nazi ideology brandished antisemitic slogans. By intervening at a certain moment as a factor for law and order, the Germans achieved yet another aim—they suddenly appeared as the defenders of the Jews against an assault by the Poles." This scenario fits the events in Jedwabne perfectly.

In 1992 Andrzej Żbikowski of the Jewish Historical Institute stated in the *Bulletin* of the JHI that in the western regions of the Soviet Union (the former Polish eastern borderlands), "after 22 June 1941, the Jewish population became the protagonists of two simultaneous tragedies. One of these, incomprehensible to the majority of the Jews, was the German desire to physically exterminate the Jewish people. The second was the explosion of long-suppressed hatred, founded on an economic and emotional-ideological basis, among the native local population." He added, "The aggression of the local community was not exclusively a result of German manipulation."

During the nearly two years of the Soviet occupation, the relationship between Poles and Jews in the eastern territories became drastically worse. "The Jews have supported us, and only they have always been visible. It has become fashionable for the director of every institution to boast that he no longer has even a single Pole working for him," said the head of the Łomża NKVD at a meeting with activists in 1941. He said that, from the point of view of the Soviet state, this was a highly unfavorable situation.

Someone heard a farmer from the vicinity of Łomża complaining during the war: "Now we have a Jewish empire. They are chosen everywhere, and the Pole is like a horse: he only hauls, and they strike him with a whip. Bad times have come for the Poles." Historians, and not only Polish ones, cite these and similar statements in order to show the reasons for the deepening of the conflict between Jews and Poles between 1939 and 1941.

In a collection of accounts by Poles who joined the army of General Władysław Anders (published as *W czterdziestym nas matko na Sybir zesłali* [In 1940, Mother, they sent us to Siberia] by Irena and Jan Tomasz Gross), there is a report by a member of a clandestine Polish military group from around Jedwabne. In it he blames his imprisonment and deportation on, among other things, a denunciation by a Jew who collaborated with the NKVD.

In Jedwabne in 1940, the NKVD smashed two underground resistance groups: the "Partisans," numbering about thirty-five members, and the Armed Combat Union, whose eighty soldiers came from the Białystok region and the Jedwabne area. After their organization was penetrated by NKVD agents, about a hundred members of the Polish underground gave themselves up in December 1940. Documents unearthed in Soviet archives and published recently in *Studia Łomżyńskie* [Łomża studies] indicate that the NKVD recruited eighteen of these former non-Jewish partisans as agents, a fact that was not known at a time when public opinion placed most of the blame for denunciations on the Jews. In June 1941, the NKVD began arrests in Jedwabne of the partisans who had turned themselves in, along with their relatives and those who had helped them, including one priest. Some were deported eastward just before the German-Soviet war broke out. Others avoided that fate only because of the panicky flight of the Soviet authorities.

"After what happened here during the Soviet occupation, you shouldn't be surprised at the Polish rage that was directed against the Jews," one Jedwabne resident told me.

There are two war memorials in this small town. One commemorates the 180 people murdered between 1939 and 1956 by the Soviet, German, and Polish communist authorities. The other commemorates the 1,600 Jews who were burned alive on 10 July 10 1941.

The Wyrzykowski family of Janczewko saved the lives of seven Jews from Jedwabne by hiding them on their farm. The Yad Vashem Institute awarded Antonina Wyrzykowska a Righteous Among the Nations award, but by then she no longer lived in her native village. She feared that she might pay for saving Jews with her own life. "They beat her black and blue," recalls her son.

Memory

The memorial to the murdered Jews of Jedwabne was erected in 1962 or 1963 by the Łomża branch of ZBoWiD, recalls Eugeniusz Adamczyk, who tended the memorial. The inscription bears the signs of attempts to destroy it. Adamczyk was the first commander of the Citizen's Militia post in Jedwabne. He lucked out twice when he happened to be away from his post during an attack by the underground—and also had the bad luck to lose his job for that reason. "The UB suspected me, although it was a pure coincidence," he explains. He also remembers arresting three men for the massacre of the Jews, and delivering the suspects to Łomża. "The other accused were arrested by 'the security,' " he adds. Adamczyk hails from the Kraków region, but his wife, Henryka, remembers the day of the massacre even though she was only twelve at the time. "My parents ordered me to hide but I can still hear the screaming of the Jews being led to their death, and I can smell the stench of the burning."

No one has ever verified the figures on the memorial plaque. All that is known is that about that number of Jedwabne Jews were never seen again. The remains of those who were burned were never exhumed after the war. None of the residents of Jedwabne can point out to me the place where they were buried.

The institute in Jerusalem for research and commemoration of the Holocaust is called Yad Vashem. These two Hebrew words mean "a name and a place"—the minimum of remembering that the living owe to the victims of the Holocaust or, to put it differently, to those who were sacrificed as a burnt offering. The Jedwabne Jews, who died just such a cruel, holocaustal death, have not been granted even that minimum of memory.

Yet something has started to change: In Wąsosz, a Jewish-Polish committee has erected a monument in memory of the town's Holocaust victims. In Jedwabne, the bishop of Łomża recently held an expiation service at the site where the Jews were executed. After Pope John Paul II spoke in Rome and Jerusalem about the guilt of Christians toward the Jewish people, the Łomża diocese began to reflect on how parishes in which Poles were involved in any way in the persecution and extermination of the Jews should examine their consciences and perform an act of repentance.

·   ·   ·   ·   ·

Andrzej Kaczyński was born in 1948 and is a journalist on the newspaper *Rzeczpospolita*. He was the editor in 1981 of *Tygodnik Solidarność*, and, after the proclamation of martial law, of several underground periodicals. He specializes in reportage describing the relations between different denominational and ethnic communities living in Poland. He lives in Warsaw.

Translation taken from *Thou Shalt Not Kill: Poles on Jedwabne* (Warsaw, 2001).

Gabriela Szczęsna

THE BLOOD OF JEDWABNE

KONTAKTY, 7 MAY 2000

POLES FROM JEDWABNE burned alive 1,600 Jews from the town and its environs in a barn near the cemetery. The Germans didn't have to do anything apart from taking pictures and thus documenting the barbarity of the Poles. Official propaganda as promulgated by Communist Poland subsequently presented the line that the Gestapo and Nazi gendarmerie had burned the Jews.

I

A letter from Montevideo in broken Polish: "Dear Mayor, I, Ester Migdal, born in Jedwabne, Łomża district, Białystok voivodeship, journeyed to Uruguay in 1937—me, my sisters, brothers, and mother. My grandmother, Chana Yenta Wasersztajn, stayed behind. I know that Poles killed all of the Jews, I know who killed my grandmother, her daughters—her entire family. He appropriated her home and now lives in this house. Forgive me, as I don't remember much Polish now, I haven't spoken the language for sixty-two years. I know no Jews remain in Jedwabne because the Poles killed them all and took everything, and now there are no Jews. What a bunch of bandits and thieves you are. You will get your just deserts before God. Not a single Jew is left. You bandits, the marks of what you have done are visible on your hands. You have worked the destruction of a whole town—you bandits, you bandits. What does your priest have to say about this? Your people live better now? Kill the whole town. How do you commit such evil? Now that you have homes that didn't cost you anything, you can dance. Your God will repay you for this. Bandits, bandits. What evil did my grandmother ever do? You didn't leave even a single Jew. Can you sleep at night? Write me and tell me how it is now in Jedwabne. I can throw out these bandits, these bandits from my house. Sir, write me telling me how you killed all of the Jews in the town. Can you sleep at night? Killed the whole town? Is life better now? Bandits, bandits! God will punish you. Write me, I want to know who lives there still."

Someone still lives there.

"How did you feel, to have lived for so many years among people who murdered your loved ones?"

"May God forgive them."

"Have you never felt hatred?"

"May God forgive them."

"Are you afraid of anyone?"

"May God forgive them."

II

"Since that 10 July 1941, the names of the murderers have remained an open secret," says Jerzy Ramotowski, a secondary-school teacher from Jedwabne. "According to documents of the Jewish Historical Institute in Warsaw and Yad Vashem, Jerusalem, the instigators of the crime were the Germans. Shortly after entering Jedwabne, the Germans began to search for a place to hold the executions, and for executioners to carry out 'the sentence.' Then a session of the local town council was held in their presence. The Germans proposed sparing one Jew from each profession. But in the end things turned out the way they turned out. This brings shame onto the people of Jedwabne, but you can't pick and choose with history. The Jews were joint creators of the history of the town from the eighteenth century on, and they and the Poles formed a common social organism."

All these bonds were suddenly severed.

In broad daylight, the Poles of Jedwabne hauled Jews from their homes. They beat them with sticks, spades, clubs spiked with nails, pitchforks, and fists. First of all they were herded into the town square. Then, from a six-meter-high plinth, they removed a bust of Lenin that was left in the wake of the "Russkies," and were ordered to carry it, while repeating the words "This war was caused by us, this war was caused by us." They were herded down Sadowa and Cmentarna Streets, then along a country road, where a barn with open doors awaited them. The barn was made available by a resident, a member of the town council. The Germans walked alongside and did nothing. They took photographs, which served as evidence of the Poles' crime.

"A few Jews were able to escape from the column of death," says Krystyna Raszczyk. "I know this from my grandfather. Five of them hid in his orchard. Among them were Hańcia and Szmujeł; he could see who was murdering his son. Szmujeł also told Grandfather that before herding them into the barn, the Poles ordered the Jews to remove their shoes, good clothes, and jewelry."

The barn doors were closed; a moment later it burst into flames.

This torturous death rose into one great cry, heard in the neighboring villages. The stench of charred bodies hung over the town for several days.

"I was just returning that way from my parents' place," recalls Jadwiga Michałowska. "I cried as I walked along, over this tragedy and the war. My husband was in Auschwitz. Today there's a gravestone for Jews in the field; this is also Auschwitz for me."

Hańcia and Szmujeł hid in Krystyna Raszczyk's grandfather's orchard only a week. They did not want to endanger the life of their benefactor or that of his family any longer. All of a sudden they announced to him that they were going to Łomża, to the ghetto; whatever will happen will happen—and off they went.

It is known that the Jedwabne murderers were no more than a dozen or so people, all of them so-called respectable types. They were joined by Poles from neighboring villages. It started with Wizna. They got worked up about "beating a Jew" and were joined by others from the outskirts of Radziłów and the outskirts of Stawiski.

"There was no ideology behind it. For me it was an ordinary thuggish murder, from envy and for profit. A saying came out of it: "He who in Jedwabne wears a signet ring . . . ," says an old man. "The Jews, however, bore their share of the blame. From the start of the war they sided with the Russkies and informed them as to who the wealthiest Poles were, and together with the Russkies they drew up lists of Poles to be deported. It was difficult to forget about this all of a sudden. I won't give my name. From the newspaper it will get on the Internet and then Jews from around the world will make me out as a defender of Polish thugs and an antisemite from Jedwabne. My family had nothing to do with the slaughter, but as far as the Jews are concerned, every Pole who was of age then played some part in their extermination. Today the Holocaust is also a business for them."

III

The town square, Przytulska Street, Przestrzelska Street. The Polish homeland of Fajgele, Sara, and Rebeka; Moryc, Icek, and Aron. The synagogue, the House of Culture. Honek Gerber's grain purchase center, Zimny's mill, Hania Stryjakowska's haberdashery shop, Hania Kanowicz's dry goods store. It was from her that Antonina Narewska, after passing her seamstress exam, received a present for her profession in life: a fine pair of scissors.

"My family always had acquaintances and good friends among the Jews," she recalls. "My best friend at school was Dwercia Łojewska.

Just before the war she left for Palestine. I missed her. And then when 'this' happened, I thanked God that he had spared her life."

When only bricks remained of the Jedwabne synagogue after the war, the authorities sold them to home builders. There was no shortage of takers.

"I refused: it's not right from a house of God," says Antonina Narewska. "Those bricks would always remind me of the people . . ."

Not long after that, those with lesser scruples occupied Jewish homesteads and drew up notarized deeds of ownership.

IV

In the 1950s, the criminals of Jedwabne came before a court. A few served sentences. The remainder immediately left town with their entire families. "But the memory of them was constantly kept alive for us by Marianna Gosiewska, a prewar teacher," recalls Krzysztof Godlewski, the mayor of Jedwabne. "For her, life always had clear laws: black is black and white is white."

V

A fenced-in stone sits in an open field. An inscription is engraved on it: "SITE OF THE SUFFERING OF THE JEWISH POPULATION. THE GESTAPO AND THE NAZI GENDARMERIE BURNED 1,600 PEOPLE ALIVE 10 JULY 1941."

"The truth is sacred. It's obvious that the inscription must be changed," says the mayor. "However, I'm not in favor of simply naming the perpetrators of the crime. The assassins from Jedwabne were a handful, so the word 'Poles' would be hurtful to all the residents. Each nation is made up of people; it isn't exclusively good or evil. I think the inscription 'Victims of the Second World War' would be the most fitting. As a warning to all about what hatred is."

"And what will you write back to Ester Migdal?"

"That wounds should be left to heal and not be opened anew."

·   ·   ·   ·   ·

Gabriela Szczęsna was born in 1955 in Łomża. She graduated from the University of Warsaw and has been a journalist on *Kontakty* since 1983 dealing with local social and historical issues, as well as nature topics. She lives in Łomża.

Translation taken from *Thou Shalt Not Kill*.

Maria Kaczyńska

IN MEMORY AND ADMONITION

GAZETA WSPÓŁCZESNA, 11 JULY 2000

YESTERDAY, 10 JULY, was the fifty-ninth anniversary of the extermination of the Jews of Jedwabne. Many visited the site of the mass murder and burial of about 1,600 people, although no one officially announced the commemoration. This case represents one of the blackest pages in the contemporary history not only of the region but also of Poland.

The Jewish community of Jedwabne, consisting of some 1,600 people, was ruthlessly exterminated on 10 July 1941. A commemorative marker was placed at the site of the killing and mass burial of the victims in the 1960s. It states that the Gestapo carried out the murder.

Burned in the Barn

In the past several months, various publications have stated unequivocally that the German occupation forces were only observers, and that the then mayor of Jedwabne and his aides initiated the pogrom, with perpetrators coming from the ranks of those living in the town or nearby.

An account by one of the Jewish survivors was published recently, along with documents from the trial of the Jedwabne murderers in Łomża in 1949. From these sources, it transpires that in July 1941, men, women, and even children were dragged from their homes and killed with clubs, axes, and knives. Most of them—more than a thousand— were herded into a barn outside of town and burned alive.

Yesterday, some twenty people from Jedwabne and nearby villages came to the site of the massacre and the grave. Some brought memorial candles.

Here Lie My Friends

"We've been coming here for three years now and we light small candles," says an elderly woman from Jedwabne who was eight years old on 10 July 1941. "The girls I played with as a child and their parents are buried here. They all died in the barn."

The woman states that she knows how the tragedy occurred because she was standing about twenty meters from the blazing barn. Earlier, she had seen how people were dragged out of their homes in town. She also saw the murderers but will not say who they were. She refuses to give her own name or to agree to meet a reporter for an interview. "Let the truth be discovered by those whose duty it is. I'm scared," she says, breaking off and wiping her eyes.

"There are no words for this," says seventy-four-year-old Leon Dziedzic from Przestrzele. Several days after the crime, he was selected by the Germans to gather up the remains of the murdered Jews. "We used rakes to push the piles of corpses into a great ditch dug along the north wall of the barn. I recognized people I knew," he says.

Jedwabne mayor Krzysztof Godlewski and the town and district council chairman Stanisław Michałowski came to the monument yesterday before noon. They brought a mourning wreath with a ribbon decorated with the words "For the murdered Jedwabne residents of Jewish nationality, in memory and admonition—Society." They placed it at the foot of the monument. "If it is confirmed that the truth is different from what is inscribed on the plaque, then it should be changed," said Godlewski, surprised by the presence of the group of local residents, journalists, and a crew from Polish national television.

The Truth above All

In the mayor's opinion, recent publications on the murder have had a sensational tone and should not be given full credence. "An investigation should be conducted and the truth should be established, one to which all will adhere," said Godlewski. "We cannot allow the new monument to divide people. This monument should unify and not divide. It should be a warning for the future."

"We've been stuck with the reputation of a criminal town," added council chairman Michałowski. "This is unfair. As in every community, different kinds of people lived here. We must differentiate the criminals from the normal people. This was just as much a tragedy for the latter as for those murdered."

Will There Be an Investigation?

As Łomża regional prosecutor Krystyna Michalczyk-Kondratowicz informed us yesterday, the case has aroused the interest of the Main Commission for the Investigation of Crimes against the Polish Nation, which is now being transformed into the Institute of National Memory.

"The former head of the commission, Prof. Kulesza, has asked us to question one of the witnesses. Two weeks ago, one of my prosecutors questioned that person," Kondratowicz said. "I don't know what stage the present case is at, however. Most likely, the investigation hasn't started because of the reorganization of the Institute."

Yesterday we were unable to contact the Institute of National Memory.

.　.　.　.　.

Maria Kaczyńska was born in 1954 and graduated from the University of Warsaw in journalism and Polish philology. She has worked for the Łomża *Gazeta Współczesna* since 1991, specializing in local social and historical issues as well as current affairs. She lives in Łomża.

Translation taken from *Thou Shalt Not Kill*.

PART II

THE MORAL DEBATE

INTRODUCTION

The demoralization and bestialization that the slaughter of
the Jews is introducing among us has become a burning
question. For it is not only the Lithuanian auxiliaries, the
Volksdeutsch, or the Ukrainians who have been used for
monstrous executions. In many localities (Kolno, Stawiski,
Jagodne,[1] Szumów, Dęblin), the local population has
participated voluntarily in the massacre.
—Zofia Kossak-Szczucka, *Prawda*, May 1942

P OLAND'S INTELLECTUALS have a long tradition of making
pronouncements on the state of the nation and its moral predic-
aments, dating back to the nineteenth century, when the Polish
intelligentsia took over from the nobility (the *szlachta*) the belief that it
was the embodiment of the Polish nation, its conscience and guiding
force. This tradition was strengthened in the 1880s and after, when
writers bore the main responsibility for the preservation of the Polish
language in the face of Germanization and Russification. As Zygmunt
Wasilewski put it, "The intelligentsia was the guard that kindled the
national spirit from a spark among ashes and carried its flame to Poland, reborn as a state."[2] The consciousness of a special responsibility
persisted in independent Poland, when it was stressed by the influential sociologist Florian Znaniecki, through the Second World War and
into the struggle against the Communist regime. Although the special
position of the intelligentsia has been somewhat eroded by the development of a market economy, with its new social hierarchies, the belief
that intellectuals constitute an elite that has special duties has persisted, and the intelligentsia still sees itself as crucial in shaping public
opinion on important moral issues.

We reproduce here a number of characteristic statements on the
problems posed by the Jedwabne massacre, illustrating the variety of
responses it evoked. They are written by academics, journalists, and
members of the political elite, but all share the belief in the need for the
intelligentsia to shape the views of Polish society on this as on other
important questions. Joanna Tokarska-Bakir is a cultural anthropolo-
gist in the Department of Ethnology of the University of Warsaw and

---

[1] Probably a garbled form of "Jedwabne."
[2] Z. Wasilewski, "Na widowni," *Myśl Narodowa*, no. 16 (15 April 1934).

has made several contributions to the controversy. In her article "Nasz
Człowiek w Pieczarach. Jedwabne: pamięć nieodzyskana" (Our man
in Pieczary. Jedwabne: Unregained memory) she describes other Polish
acts of violence against Jews and their rescuers during the war and
deals with the issue of the repressed memory of the dark past. In her
article "Pułapki wczesnego przebaczania" (The traps of premature forgiveness) she looks closely at the forms of anti-Jewish prejudice that
have persisted in society up to the contemporary period. Moreover,
she takes a critical position on those (like Stefan Chwin) who called for
closing the debate on the Jedwabne massacre and raised the issue of
the need for forgiveness on the part of Jews. Tokarska opposes what
she calls "premature forgiveness" on the grounds that forgiveness cannot be forced upon a group representing the victims. In her opinion
such forgiveness cannot lead to real reconciliation.[3] Hanna Świda-
Ziemba, a professor at the Institute of Applied Social Sciences at the
University of Warsaw, has written extensively on Polish-Jewish relations. In June 2000, in a debate on Zbigniew Kransodębski's article
"Przywracanie pamięci," she called upon the cultural elite to face the
dark past of Polish-Jewish relations and not to leave the task of coming
to terms with it to future generations.[4] Also included is the response
of a leading member of the populist League of Polish Families, Antoni
Macierewicz,[5] as well as one by a leading Polish-American now resident in Poland, Jan Nowak-Jeziorański, the former head of Radio Free
Europe, which is interesting both for its strong expression of contrition
and its nervousness about the American Jewish response to the revelations about Jedwabne.

The final piece is by Jerzy Sławomir Mac, who was, until recently,
one of the leading columnists of the weekly *Wprost*.[6] He has written

[3] She is also the author of the important article "Ganz Andere? Żyd jako czarownica i
czarownica jako Żyd w polskich i obcych źródłach etnograficznych, czyli jak czytać pro-
tokoły przesłuchań," *Res Publica Nowa*, no. 8 (August 2001): 3–32.

[4] Hanna Świda-Ziemba "Rozbrajać własne mity," *Znak*, no. 6 (2000): 41–48.

[5] Macierewicz has written a number of similar pieces, including "Mordowali
Niemcy—sensacyjne zeznania naocznego świadka z Jedwabnego" (The Germans did the
murdering—sensational revelations of an eyewitness from Jedwabne), *Głos*, 24 March
2001; "Niewygodna prawda" (An inconvenient truth), *Głos*, 31 March 2001; and "Oskarżam Aleksandra Kwaśniewskiego" (I accuse Aleksander Kwaśniewski), *Głos*, 14 April
2001.

[6] *Wprost* is the biggest opinion-forming liberal and free-market weekly in Poland and
is comparable to *Time* magazine and *Der Spiegel*. The first issue was published in December 1982, and in 1994 the weekly reached a circulation of 350,000. Among its permanent
contributors are Leszek Balcerowicz, the chief architect of the economic transformations
after 1989, the sociologist Jacek Kurczewski, and the former president of Poland, Lech
Wałęsa. Its editor-in-chief is Marek Król. The magazine has received many prestigious
awards, including the Award for Promotion of Polish Private Business.

extensively on Jewish issues—on which he holds passionate views. On 23 March 2001, in a piece cowritten with Stanisław Janecki entitled "Let Us Apologize to the Jews and Ask for Forgiveness," he enumerated the wrongs done by Poles to Jews. They include silent indifference and cowardice in the face of the mass murder of the Jews, greed in the spoliation of Jewish property, failure to assess appropriately what the Jews had contributed to Polish life, rejection of the Jews, particularly in the last years before the Second World War, and the support of official antisemitism in those years. He describes both a widespread desire to have a Poland free of Jews and a widespread antisemitism, concluding that the failure to come to terms with these facts meant that Poles could not look at the past with a clear conscience. After the unveiling of the new monument in Jedwabne, he expressed his bitterness at the general Polish reaction in a characteristic piece, "*Homo Jedvabicus,*" reprinted below.

This section is prefaced with an article published in May 1942 in *Prawda*, the underground organ of the Front Odrodzenia Polski (Front for the Rebirth of Poland), a Catholic organization some of whose members were involved in the rescue of Jews during the war. This was almost certainly written by Zofia Kossak-Szczucka, since it expresses the same position as her August 1942 pamphlet *Protest*, which Jan Błoński has analyzed, and which, he asserts, enables us "to penetrate the thoughts and feelings of a significant (dominant?) section of Polish society at that time."[7] It is the first reference to the massacre in Jedwabne, here referred to as Jagodne. This voice in some ways is unique. It cannot be seen as belonging to the self-critical liberal tradition we have discussed above, since it contains expressions of anti-Jewish prejudice, typical of Catholic thinking prior to Vatican II. However, it confirms that in some towns the local Polish population took part in the massacres of Polish Jews, and it strongly and unambiguously condemns such acts of murder, which it explains in terms of the demoralization and bestialization of society under conditions of war.

---

[7] Jan Błoński, *Biedni Polacy patrzą na ghetto* (Kraków, 1994), 40. *Protest* is reprinted in full in this volume, which also contains the most penetrating discussion of the issues raised by the document. For an English version, see "Polish-Catholics and Catholic Poles: The Gospel, National Interest, Civic Solidarity and the Destruction of the Warsaw Ghetto," *Yad Vashem Studies* 25 (1996): 184.

Zofia Kossak-Szczucka

PROPHECIES ARE BEING FULFILLED

PRAWDA: PISMO FRONTU

ODRODZENIA POLSKI

May 1942

I T HAS FALLEN upon us to be passive witnesses of a horrible tragedy: the planned mass murder of the Jews by the Germans on the
territory of the Republic. Every day news pours in that is startling
in its ghastliness. Every day, thousands of people die—men, women,
girls, children, infants, old people—because they were born Jews.
Some are buried alive, others are beaten to death with rifle butts, machine guns are aimed at others, and recently there has been poisoning
by gas. The executioners smash the heads of children against walls or
against roadside trees. In a similar way the Jews of Lublin, Chełm, Mie-
lec, Kock, Ryki, Baranów, and a host of other villages and towns are
liquidated, and recently the extermination of the Warsaw ghetto has
begun.[1] The reports of witnesses confirm that in all of the locations
mentioned, the executions were carried out with unparalleled sadism
and cruelty.

". . . Daughters of Jerusalem, do not cry for me, but for yourselves
and for your sons.[2] For the days are coming, when they will say: happy
are they who are barren and the wombs that have not given birth and
the breasts that have not suckled. Then will they begin to say to the
mountains: fall upon us, and to the hills: cover us . . ."[3]

". . . There was heard in Rama the lament of Rachel weeping over
her lost sons, and there was no one to comfort her . . ."[4] The prophecies

---

[1] In the spring of 1942 the situation in the Warsaw ghetto drastically deteriorated: the
size of the ghetto was reduced; new groups of Jews from outside Warsaw were brought
in; and a new wave of German shootings of large groups of Jews, particularly smugglers,
began.

[2] Throughout this selection, the ellipses are in the original.

[3] Jesus' words on the road to his crucifixion, Luke 23:28–31. The last sentence is from
Hos. 10:8.

[4] Jer. 31:16, repeated in Matt. 2:18.

are being fulfilled; the curse they voluntarily took upon themselves has taken on a form ... "His blood be upon us and upon our children ..."[5] —the blood of the Righteous ... —Daughters of Jerusalem, do not cry for me ... —With terrible logic all of the Jews' deeds are wreaking vengeance upon them. No one has hindered Christianity in conquering the world as they have, and it is they who are perishing first as a result of the fact that Europe is not Christian. Driven by Talmudic hate, they accepted no one outside their race as close to them, and they are now being wiped out because there is a nation that took their slogans to heart and did not accept them as close ...

We look on passively, witnesses overcome with terror. We cannot intervene. There have been heroes who tried to stand up for and protect the condemned and paid for it with their lives. Every impulse to compassion, every effort to help, is punished by immediate death.

Forced to be passive, we must nevertheless appreciate the significance of the tragedy being enacted, and take a position on it as Catholics and as Poles.

As Catholics

It is not enough to pray for the victims of murder and pity them; we must at the same time examine our consciences. The fate that Israel is meeting is justly deserved, for God does not admit injustices. But to what degree is it our fault as Christians that the Jews have remained as they are and deserved such a terrible punishment? ... In what measure does it fall upon us to answer for the neglect of the mission among the Jews, the mission that is the obligation of every Catholic, the mission directed by nothing other than sincere Christian brotherly love? Who among us has approached the Jews with a feeling similar to that with which the missionary approaches the pagans? ... In the range of feelings that we have for the Jews, was there room for honest, disinterested desire that they should become different? ... —It seems that the answer to all of these questions is negative, and for this reason the hecatombs of Jewish children who surely are guilty of nothing are troubling to the heart. And if there is a person capable of saying of this ill fortune, of the "weeping of Rachel" foretold some two thousand years ago, that the Jews got what was coming to them, and that the Germans murdering them are rendering the Poles a service, then such a person would be unworthy of the name of Catholic.

[5] Matt. 27:25.

As Poles

There is no point in discussing the errors in our Jewish policy when the subject of that policy is ceasing to exist and the problem has taken on a different face. We all know that these errors were glaring, and our attitude toward the Jews was unplanned, chaotic, and inconsistent; it wavered between two extremes: slavish submission to the Jews or thuggishness. We should suppose that such errors will not reappear, and that in relation to the remaining Jews in Poland society will find honest and proper norms that are in accord with both the interests of the nation and Christian ethics. This is a question of the future, however ... But the demoralization and bestialization that the slaughter of the Jews is introducing among us has become a burning question. For it is not only the Lithuanian auxiliaries, the *Volksdeutsch*, or the Ukrainians who have been used for monstrous executions. In many localities (Kolno, Stawiski, Jagodne, Szumów, Dęblin), the local population has participated voluntarily in the massacre. We must oppose such disgraceful behavior with all available means. We must inform people that they are becoming Herod's hired assassins, stigmatize them in the underground press, call for a boycott of the executioners, threaten, pronounce harsh judgments on the murderers in the free Republic. For now no one is raising this issue; the press timidly passes over it, but the evil is spreading like an epidemic, and crime is turning into an addiction. On no account may we allow this plague of bestiality and sadism to infect us. God justly does what he does, but it would be better if those who of their own free will become the instruments of His punishment had not been born.

.   .   .   .   .

Zofia Kossak-Szczucka (1890–1968) was well known before the war as a right-wing and antisemitic Catholic novelist and publicist. During the war, she was active in the Catholic underground organization Front Odrodzenia Polski (The Front for the Rebirth of Poland) and while not abandoning her anti-Jewish opinions became involved in the rescue of Jews. In September 1942 she was one of the founders of the Tymczasowy Komitet Pomocy Żydom (Temporary Committee for Aid to the Jews), which in December of that year changed its name to Rada Pomocy Żydom (The Council for Aid to the Jews). She was arrested in September 1943 and was in Auschwitz concentration camp until July 1944. After the war she moved to London, returning to Poland in 1956.

Joanna Tokarska-Bakir

OBSESSED WITH INNOCENCE

GAZETA WYBORCZA, 13–14 JANUARY 2001

L AST SUMMER three Nobel Prize laureates met in Vilnius to discuss the meaning of memory. From the many words spoken then, I best remember what Günter Grass said about the strange vicissitudes of German memory. Referring to the recent public discourse in his native land (Ernst Nolte and the historians' dispute in the 1980s and the Wasler-Bubis debate in 1998–1999), Grass described the rituals of collective memory that cause some trouble for his countrymen, especially the older generation. Germans would not be Germans if they did not create a special neologism: "memory work" (a concept that Grass nevertheless mocks—memory is involuntary, unintentional, or, he says, does not exist). Germans are required to work on their memory "as a confession of guilt, it is rejected as an insinuation, and they carefully cultivate it, because for decades, as long as history finds us again and again, it is reworked . . . by younger generations—presumably those without its burden. And it is as if the children and the grandchildren remember in substitution for their silent fathers and grandfathers." What's more, "it seems as if the crimes . . . acquire more importance the greater the distance from the crime."[1]

The Authority of Historians

This portentous epigraph from a Nobel Prize laureate makes a good introduction to the two cents I would like to contribute to the far margin of the discussion of Jan Tomasz Gross's book about Jedwabne. I am following this discussion from Germany, and I think that if it were not for this foreign perspective, which weakens the influence of self-censorship, I would not be able to notice certain elements in this discussion at all. I cannot resist the thought that Gross would not have written this book if he had not worked abroad.

[1] G. Grass, "Milczenie pamięci" (The silence of memory) *Gazeta Wyborcza*, 11 October 2000.

I am referring not to the censorship of academic circles but to a more optical phenomenon. From up close, and especially from inside, it is impossible to see certain things. The Polish obsession with innocence is impossible to notice. It is also impossible to see that the rules that govern Polish public and private debate are controlled by this pressure of innocence. Above all, one cannot see that what Thomas Merton called the "pitiable refusal of insight" is seen by everyone but ourselves.

It appears that one sees only what one knows. How does what Poles know about themselves and about the Holocaust translate into Polish innocence? The question "What do Poles know?" is directed first to historians. Rightly so, because historians are the ones who construct school curricula. And not rightly so, because as the German example shows, even the most certain knowledge about historical guilt translates into national awareness of this guilt indirectly and with difficulty.

If we can talk at all about the responsibility of Polish historians for what Poles *do not know* about the Holocaust, we can do it only in terms of the sin of relinquishment. This is often the result of the innate caution of historians, which drives them away from certain subjects. The aspiring young historian knows of the price that can be paid in Poland for a "premature" publication. Is it necessary to recall here the name of Michał Cichy and the list of historians who replied to his article?[2] A historian, like any other academic, wants first of all to be "serious." "Serious" in Poland means "uncontroversial." An uncontroversial Polish historian strokes his beard, watches with forbearance those who are in a hurry.

What we are to do with this leisurely manner of the historians in a country in which the last witnesses to the war and the Holocaust are dying out is not really known. The quotation from Günter Grass cited above gives us further perspective. It seems that Polish children and grandchildren will also remember in lieu of their silent fathers and grandfathers. Undisturbed by historians, those witnesses will take with them to the grave everything that still should be told about *szmalcownictwo* [blackmailing] and the Blue Police, about the Baudienst formation in which Polish youth served,[3] and about the pogrom in Warsaw during Holy Week in 1940,[4] about priests informing on Jews on

[2] Michał Cichy, "Polacy-Żydzi. Czarne karty powstania" (Poles-Jews: Black pages of the uprising), *Gazeta Wyborcza*, 29 January 1994.

[3] M. Hochberg-Mariańska, "List do redakcji," in *Wizja Polski na łamach Kultury*, ed. Grażyna Pomian (Lublin, 1999), 296.

[4] Marek Edelman, interviewed in A. Grupińska, *Po kole. Rozmowy z żołnierzami getta warszawskiego* (In the circle: Conversations with the soldiers of the Warsaw ghetto) (Warsaw, 2000), 324.

the basis of information received in confessions,[5] about Jedwabne, Radziłów, and about the innocent ritual of "the burning of Judas" practiced during the war,[6] about the glasses of water sold for gold coins to the Jews packed in "death trains."[7] And about the "railroad action" in 1945, in which the partisans of Narodowe Siły Zbrojne dragged some two hundred Jews repatriated from the East out of the trains and shot them,[8] about the murder of Jews returning from exile, about pogroms in Kielce, Kraków, and hundreds of other unknown denunciations during and following the war. Surely this will happen unless, leaving the historians to their own reputations, we do what Jan Tomasz Gross has done and start talking about it.

What the Holocaust Has to Say

Zygmunt Bauman wrote in his book *Nowoczesność i zagłada* [Modernity and the Holocaust] that sociology in its current shape has less to say about the Holocaust than the Holocaust has to say about sociology.[9] I do not know whether Bauman's provocation has influenced the writings of Jan Tomasz Gross, but it seems that what Gross's critics have most held against him is his intentional or unintentional approach to it.

What disgusts historians and even provokes Jacek Żakowski[10] to evoke the phantom of postmodernism, is, for me, most important in Gross's book. I have in mind that scandalous "new approach to the sources." Gross writes about it in the following way: "Our initial attitude toward every report by would-be victims of the Holocaust should be changed from one of doubt to one of affirmation."[11] I am not concerned with whether this sentence would be useful to someone verifying sources. While not taking away the importance of source verifi-

[5] Marek Edelman, in ibid.

[6] Interviews from the archives of the Department of Ethnology at the University of Warsaw.

[7] K. Jeleński, "Od endeków do stalinistów" (From the "Endeks" to the Stalinists), in *Wizja Polski na łamach Kultury*, 101.

[8] A. Cała, H. Węgrzynek, and G. Zalewska, *Historia i kultura Żydów polskich*, s.v. "pogrom."

[9] Z. Bauman, *Nowoczesność i zagłada* (Warsaw, 1992), 22.

[10] A reference to Jacek Żakowski's article "Każdy sąsiad ma imię" (Every neighbor has a name), which was printed in *Gazeta Wyborcza*, 18–19 November 2000. For an English version of this article, see "Every Neighbor Has a Name" in *Thou Shalt Not Kill: Poles on Jedwabne* (Warsaw, 2001), 76–90.

[11] J. T. Gross, *Sąsiedzi. Historia zagłady żydowskiego miasteczka* (Sejny, 2000), 94.

cation, I would like to suggest that something much more important is at stake here.

At this point, in order not to call a spade a spade too soon, I would like to tell two stories. On Chłodna Street in Warsaw, there is a pastry shop that I often visit with my family. From its windows, the view of Chłodna, crowned with the silhouette of the Church of Saint Karol Boromeusz, has always seemed strangely familiar to me. Those cobblestones, the last ones in Warsaw, with the traces of tramway tracks . . . It was only when I saw Wajda's movie *Korczak* that I realized how ignorant I was.[12] I understood that here, over Chłodna, was the famous wooden footbridge that connected the large and small parts of the ghetto. I understood why tourist buses come here. From the café one could see young foreigners in skullcaps, standing on the street in the rain as they listened to the guide. Perhaps they also prayed.

One day the neglected square on Chłodna Street was torn up. Soon a cross appeared and a plaque bearing the inscription "Jerzy Popiełuszko Square."[13] I do not think that those who gave the square at Chłodna the name of a martyred Polish priest had bad intentions (probably the fact that Popiełuszko had an apartment on Chłodna Street was a factor), but there are many squares in Warsaw and the bridge over Chłodna Street was the only one. Neither I nor any of the Warsaw bureaucrats remembered this bridge. Our memory is a place without Jews. Jan Tomasz Gross's idea is a way to remedy this situation. All of us need a "new approach to the sources."

If there is anyone who, despite everything, still does not understand why we need this "new approach to the sources," I can tell one more true story. A few years ago, students from my department organized a field trip to the Yakutsk region. They did not find any especially interesting shamanism there, but they noted a very particular local memory of recent history. The village stood on the permafrost, on the exact location of a former labor camp. On the graves, or rather over the human bodies thrown into the crevasses, life proved to be impossible. The children were dying. The ethnographers were asked to stop being ethnographers and to say their Catholic prayers for the dead. The point

[12] Andrzej Wajda (1926–) is the leading film director in Polish postwar cinema. His film *Korczak* (1990) was highly praised in 1990 at the Cannes Film Festival but later received critical reviews for portraying a "Christian vision of the Holocaust." Betty Jean Lifton, one of the leading experts on Janusz Korczak, defended it in the *New York Times* in May 1991.

[13] Jerzy Popiełuszko (1947–1984) was an outspoken chaplain of the Solidarity movement. During the period of martial law he delivered special sermons for the Homeland in the Church of Stanisław Kostka in Warsaw. The communist Special Forces murdered him in October 1984.

was, probably, to assuage the conscience of the natives, who more than once had been rewarded for catching and delivering escapees from the camp—it was enough to bring only a severed white hand.

This is a naive but educational story. It is sad because it shows the disintegration of native culture (the shamans' prayers do not work anymore). But it is uplifting, because it shows the reality of the spiritual world—among Yakuts, of course.

Mole of Conscience

The "new approach to the sources" proposed by Gross has one fault. It can convince only someone who is already convinced. Influenced by Plato and Socrates, Stanisław Vincenz said once that what decides the worth of a man is his ability to be persuaded.[14] This idea is long out of fashion. Times have changed, and now one who can be easily persuaded is considered not a philosopher or saint but, unfortunately, a fool. It is a mystery how people change their minds at all today.

The person who is persuaded by Gross's postulate of a "new approach to the sources" is probably the same person with whose voice Czesław Miłosz once spoke about the mole-guardian with the red lamp on his forehead;[15] the same to whom Nicola Chiaromonte wrote about the worm of conscience[16] and Jan Błoński addressed his book *Biedni Polacy patrzą na getto* [The Poor Poles look at the ghetto];[17] the same one to whom Tadeusz Mazowiecki spoke in his *Antysemityzm ludzi łagodnych i dobrych* [The antisemitism of the kind and the good][18] and to whom Jan Józef Lipski spoke in *Dwie Polski, dwa patriotyzmy*

[14] Stanisław Vincenz (1888–1971) was a Polish philosopher and writer. One of his best-known works is *On the High Uplands: Sagas, Songs, Tales and Legends of the Carpathians*.

[15] The metaphor of the "mole-guardian with the red lamp on his forehead" comes from the well-known poem of Czesław Miłosz "A Poor Christian Looks at the Ghetto." Although Miłosz himself declined to offer any specific interpretation of the metaphor, it is accepted that the mole represents the guardian of the dead.

[16] Nicola Chiaromonte (1905–1972) was an Italian philosopher and literary critic known for his liberal and antifascist position. The worm of conscience comes from his collection of essays entitled, in English, *The Worm of Consciousness and Other Essays*. ("Conscience" would be a better translation of the original.)

[17] In his collection of essays *Biedni Polacy patrzą na getto* (Kraków, 1994), the distinguished literary critic Jan Błoński analyzes in depth the metaphor of the mole-guardian with the red lamp (16–17).

[18] Tadeusz Mazowiecki (1927–) is a politician and writer representing the liberal Catholic intelligentsia. He was the first noncommunist prime minister (1989–1990). His essay "Antysemityzm ludzi łagodnych i dobrych," published in *Więź*, May 1960, is a classical text about the problem of antisemitism in postwar Poland.

[Two Polands, two patriotisms].[19] All of them are memorable texts completely forgotten. We read little and badly and remember even less. "Remembrance cannot be ordered," argues German writer Martin Walser, who started the German debate about memory.[20] It is worth asking why our memory is so capricious and stubbornly uncooperative in relation to issues so morally clear and right.

Collective memory scorns facts and appeals. Even if those facts are abundantly clear to historians, they place no obligations on human memory. Again the Germans are a good example. German society deserves high praise for the work it started on itself after the war, but observing the reaction of the crowd at certain moments in German history is enough to raise doubts about the extensive resocialization process that has lasted for more than fifty years. In 1998, in the church of Saint Paul in Frankfurt, when Martin Walser ended his speech protesting the masochistic practice of the "constant presentation of German shame" and "the instrumentalization of the memory about Auschwitz," everyone present—nearly all of the local political and intellectual elite—honored the speaker with a lengthy standing ovation.[21] They knew the facts too well. They were protesting against them, demanding a break from the truth, "the right to look the other way." The only person not standing and applauding Walser was the gray-headed Ignatz Bubis, the head of the General Council of Jews in Germany.

Confessing Someone Else's Sins

My discipline, ethnography, is interested not in facts but in what people say about them. What people say about facts is "unimportant" for historians, so it is no surprise that a historian facing the chimera of collective memory is usually helpless. Gross deserves praise because in his book about Jedwabne and in his other works, he discusses not only facts but also what people say about them.

---

[19] Jan Józef Lipski (1926–1991) was a writer and literary critic. In 1987 he became a leader of the newly reestablished Polish Socialist Party (PPS). His essay *Dwie Polski, dwa patriotyzmy* is a historical discourse written from the perspective of the PPS on two models of Poland—one right-wing, nationalistic, and antisemitic, and the other democratic and pluralistic.

[20] " 'Erinnerung kann man nicht befehlen' Martin Walser und Rudolf Augstein über ihre deutsche Vergangenheit," *Der Spiegel*, no. 45 (2 November 1998): 48–72.

[21] Wojciech Piściak writes in detail about Walser's speech and his debate with Ignatz Buber, the head of the General Council of Jews in Germany, in "Ostatnia bitwa o pamięć?" *ResPublica Nowa*, no. 10 (1999): 8–27.

When a discussion of Polish-Jewish relations begins in the context of the Holocaust, Poles say the same things over and over again. In the beginning, when the historians are repeating their time-honored "too early,"[22] the conversation does not go easily. Soon, though, it achieves a certain maturity, turning into something that Stańczyk in *Wesele* called "confessing someone else's sins."[23] Many examples of this "confession of someone else's sins" can be found in the letters to the editor that have flooded *Tygodnik Powszechny*, *Gazeta Wyborcza*, or the Paris-based *Kultura* after they published texts that offended this dogma of Polish innocence in relation to the Jews. Dear editor, are you getting such letters now?

The truly Polish discourse on antisemitism includes a list of topics at the ready—particularly Polish "living images." The subject "Holocaust" automatically starts the projector. But anyone expecting to find the horrors of extermination here would be mistaken. The show would begin with a few old church clichés like "His blood is on our heads and on the heads of our children . . . ," or "Let us pray for the faithless Jews . . ."[24] That those images have lived so long is hardly surprising since they are recalled every year during the Good Friday service. Next comes the image from before the war of the Jew in his dark coat lolling on the bench next to the fountain in the Saski Garden, as if he had already started to fulfill his promise that "the streets will be yours, the tenement-houses ours."[25] In the next picture, other dark-coated Jews welcome first the Russians, then the Germans, and then the Russians again with bread and salt. In the next, Jewish Pole-haters, who were brought by the Soviets, show off their communism and Jewishness in the postwar UB [Security Police]. In the next image Jews—this time hiding behind Polish names—suck the blood from the Poland of Gomułka and Gierek, and, with their characteristic chutzpah, occupy the highest positions in the financial mafia after 1989.[26]

The Polish "confession of someone else's sins" must end with penance, which of course will also be "someone else's." A penitent is obli-

---

[22] "Too early" was also a repeated answer to the survey by *Kultura* in 1957. See Adam Uziembło's letter: "*Kultura* is doing a survey with the goal of doing research on antisemitism. I am not sure it is time for it." In *Wizja Polski na łamach Kultury*, 117.

[23] Stańczyk is the jester in *Wesele* (The wedding), an important national drama written in 1901 by Stanisław Wyspiański (1869–1907). Modeled on a possibly historic figure of the sixteenth century, he is a bitter critic of Polish society and its elite.

[24] *Wizja Polski na łamach Kultury*, 123.

[25] See the illustration to the text "Chałaty w Saskim Ogrodzie," in *Mały Dziennik*, no. 210 (31 June 1939).

[26] Władysław Gomułka (1905–1982) was a communist politician. Between 1956 and 1970 he was the first secretary of PZPR. Edward Gierek (1913–2001) replaced him as the

gated not to say silly things about imaginary Polish antisemitism. "The editors know perfectly well how much damage Polish antisemitism has done to the Polish cause abroad. Is artificially fanning it supposed to repair this damage?" asks Aleksander Grobicki, a correspondent for *Kultura* in 1957.[27]

"Comrades!" Paweł Jasienica cried dramatically during an assembly of the Association of Polish Writers in 1968, "For reasons known only to himself, someone is trying to stigmatize our nation by putting the label of antisemites on us . . . Nothing can do more damage to us than the creation of an opinion in the world that we are a nation of antisemites."[28] The minutes go on: "The applause and cheering continue without pause for a long time."[29]

The applause and the cheering continue today. The list of names, initiatives, and organizations is long. Following the publication of Jacek Żakowski's text we hear again that the only result of all this will be a defeat in the New York court case concerning the return of Jewish property.

The Psychoanalysis of Polish Antisemitism

Maria Janion once formulated the thesis that nothing can cure "cursed Polish problems" but true and thorough psychoanalysis. Konstanty Jeleński advanced an identical thesis in the context of Polish-Jewish problems.[30] He noticed that every time the problem of antisemitism was addressed in the Paris magazine *Kultura*, the editorial office was flooded with letters of protest defending Polish honor. In 1957, *Kultura* sent a survey on Polish-Jewish relations to its readers. The first section was entitled in a provocative way: "The Psychoanalysis of Polish Antisemitism." The replies were few. Those that did arrive were so typical

---

Party's first secretary in 1970, a position that he held for one decade until the workers' strikes of summer 1980.

[27] *Wizja Polski na łamach Kultury,* 109.

[28] Paweł Jasienica (1909 —1970), pen name of Leon L. Beynar, was a writer and popular historian. He is an author of the highly acclaimed *Piast Poland* and *Jagiellonian Poland.*

[29] K. Jeleński, "Hańba czy wstyd?" in *Wizja Polski na łamach Kultury,* 137.

[30] Konstanty A. Jeleński (1922–1987) was a leading intellectual among postwar Polish émigrés in Paris. He was one of the founders of *Kultura* and worked for the French monthly *Preuves.* The survey on Polish-Jewish relations was published in *Kultura,* nos. 1–2 (1957).

that they prompted Jeleński to conclude with a question: "Could it be that Rafał Malczewski[31] is right in saying that Polish antisemitism is a mass neurosis? Neurosis manifests itself in the same way in individual patients: escape from the problem, strong denial of the mere fact of psychosis, cruelty to oneself after admitting the neurosis."[32]

Anyone who is persuaded by the Jeleński-Malczewski diagnosis can easily see all the symptoms of the described illness in Polish private and public discourse about antisemitism and in the debate about Jedwabne. Indeed, what is this persistent impulse to blame the pogroms on the "scum of the society" if not a denial or an escape from the problem? (What is the ratio of scum to not-scum in a society in which, in the region of Małopolska alone, the Home Army listed the names of sixty thousand *szmalcownicy*?)[33] What is this empathic assumption of the damage that the brothers Laudański, the ones most active in the pogrom, had had to suffer at the hands of Jews? What are these attempts to enter into the spirit of Jedwabne ("a tiny town, going mad from the pain," in which "not even one Aryan store could survive" before the war) and these speculations about how hard it was to stand up to the murderous instincts of fellow citizens who had just made up their minds to murder their neighbors?

If we are talking about empathy, why not direct it to the Jews of Jedwabne? (Gross does this, but Tomasz Szarota and Jacek Żakowski hold it against him.) Why are Jewish faces so blurred? Why, indeed, shouldn't we listen as Jews speak their own "language of tragedy," as Jacek Żakowski calls it? As a result of fighting off this language, don't we coincidentally defend our "right to look the other way"?

The Innocence of the Expelled

Psychoanalysis in Poland is something suspicious, unpopular, and not cheap. Luckily Poland is also a country of inconsistent people: they praise some but read others. Another Polish peculiarity fosters psychoanalysis: the *Vater-kompleks*. Because of it Poles accept anything from certain people, even the bitter medicine of the couch. One of them is

[31] Rafał Malczewski (1892–1965) was the son of the distinguished painter Jacek Malczewski. Like his father he was also a painter and after 1945 lived outside Poland in France, Brazil, and Canada.

[32] K. Jeleński, "Problem anytsemityzmu. Ankieta Kultury," in *Wizja Polski na łamach Kultury*, 107–8.

[33] Letter by Jacek Myczka to the editors of *Gazeta Wyborcza*, 10 September 2000.

the Trappist monk Thomas Merton. The other, quite unexpectedly, is a declared enemy of psychoanalysis: Father Józef Tischner.[34]

Amazingly, a passage in Merton's *Conjectures of a Guilty Bystander* can be applied to the problem of Polish antisemitism, and to the even larger problem of its supposed nonexistence. The parallel is hidden because at first glance Merton is talking only about the white American South. Until the Civil War, life in the South was supposed to have resembled paradise—gentle blacks sang on plantations while noble whites looked after them. The outbreak of war annihilated this paradise. Merton writes: "Since the Civil War, the whole nation participated in sin, and the sin has become inescapable. The pioneer child, or the child of plantation-owners, was cruelly awakened. And he has faced in himself the cruelty that he did not realize was there: the meanness, the injustice, the greed, the hypocrisy, the inhumanity! He knows there is a mark on his forehead and is afraid to recognize it—it might turn out to be the mark of Cain!"[35]

Stubborn Southerners did not reconcile themselves to their expulsion from paradise. They coped "justly and scientifically" with this uncomfortable knowledge by projecting it on blacks: "The white racist's hate of the Negro . . . is made acceptable to him when he represents it as a Negro hatred of the whites." Blaming blacks, the white man from the South can safely say that "he is what he always dreamed he was—gentle, kind, fair, noble, courteous, yet simple."[36]

Does the antisemitism of good and gentle people, merciless and touchy, one that preempts a discussion about the Holocaust before it even begins, one that exaggerates every unjust Jewish voice, and is silent about each just voice, come from a similar traumatic experience?

Isn't the Holocaust, from the perspective of many old Poles, just a perfidious Jewish-German dirty trick, which forever cuts off the return to Soplicowo,[37] this paradise in which Jankiel played dulcimers under Gerwazy's eyes as the lion lay next to the lamb?[38]

---

[34] Father Józef Tischner (1931–2000) was a philosopher, representing the liberal wing of the Polish Roman Catholic Church. He is the author of many works, such as *The Ethics of Solidarity* (*Etyka Solidarności*) (1981) and *The Polish Shape of Dialogue* (*Polski Kształt dialogu*) (1981).

[35] T. Merton, *Conjectures of a Guilty Bystander* (New York, 1989), 36.

[36] Ibid. 33, 37.

[37] Soplicowo is a noble Polish estate depicted in *Pan Tadeusz* (1834), the national epic of Adam Mickiewicz (1798–1855). It is a place where Polish culture and traditions are preserved. Jankiel is the Jewish character in *Pan Tadeusz*, representing commitment to Polish culture and the struggle for freedom from the Russian yoke. The character of Jankiel came to symbolize Polish-Jewish cooperation and has been referred to by other artists and writers. Gerwazy (Rembajło) is another character of the epic.

[38] See Simon Schama, "Krajobraz i pamięć," *Krasnogruda*, no. 11 (2000): 16–17.

Soplicowo's paradisiacal myth played an important role in the period of the struggle for independence. Now that we are home again, this myth has become a dangerous illusion. Merton writes: "When a myth becomes a daydream it is judged, found wanting, and must be discarded. To cling to it when it has lost its creative function is to condemn oneself to mental illness."[39]

The Stigma of Innocence

In the book *Jak żyć* [How to live] by Józef Tischner, Jacek Żakowski found a soothing quotation about the limits of human responsibility: "The responsibility of man does not reach beyond the limits of the possibility of effective action." Beyond "Tischner's barrier," as he calls it, Żakowski feels safe. From my point of view, incorrectly so.

I do not think that this is what Father Tischner had in mind. Although Tischner was not a radical in the style of Elias Canetti[40] ("Only he who worries himself to death treats himself seriously"), he knew the human conscience as no one else. He defended the superiority of the conscience even in situations in which it was in conflict with the voice of the Church. He knew that individual conscience—like collective memory, which, it seems, has a lot in common with conscience—cannot be forced into anything. It relies on its own sense of hearing. "Do not be afraid," says Tischner only to those who have the courage to have this hearing, who want to have conscience. "The man who discovers the truth, even if it is a cruel truth, attains dignity. He takes pride in the fact that he can admit the truth. It does not destroy him. On the contrary, it says to him: you are *Homo sapiens*." Those who are innocent do not need these words.

Tischner also knew the traps of conscience. He warned that because of man's innate inclination to self-praise, his voice, often equated with the voice of God, is easy to confuse with other voices; "The nation, for example, or another collectivity then becomes the absolute." Is this not the religious problem of many Polish patriots?

The most common method of self-deception, continued Tischner, consists in giving oneself absolution and blaming others. In the nature of conscience, however, lies a paradox: to be sure, conscience is the moral voice that calls us to remain innocent, but at the same time it is

[39] Merton, *Conjectures of a Guilty Bystander*, 33.

[40] The writer and playwright who won the Nobel Prize in Literature in 1981. He was born in 1905 in Bulgaria.

the religious voice that teaches us something quite the opposite: "The saintliest saint feels that he is the greatest sinner." And finally, this conclusion: "If Poles were truly religious, they would not try so forcefully to convince themselves and others of their innocence."[41] Amen.

· · · · ·

Joanna Tokarska-Bakir was born in 1958 and is associate Professor in the Department of Ethnology and Cultural Anthropology at the University of Warsaw. She has held Alexander von Humboldt and Andrew W. Mellon Fellowships.

Translation by Ewa Dzurak with Carla Lillvik.

[41] *Przekonać Pana Boga. Z ks. Józefem Tischnerem rozmawiają Dorota Zalko i Jarosław Gowin* (Kraków, 2000), 104.

Jan Nowak-Jeziorański

A NEED FOR COMPENSATION

RZECZPOSPOLITA, 26 JANUARY 2001

T HE DISCUSSION AROUND Jan Tomasz Gross's book *Neighbors* goes on. Sixty years after the fact, the book casts a shaft of light on the bestial murder of the Jews of the small village of Jedwabne during the war, rescuing the incident from oblivion. Unfortunately, the debate is beginning to move in the wrong direction.

It is not easy for any nation to acknowledge acts that cover it with shame. It is human nature that we are inclined to remember the wrongs done to us, and that we do not want to remember the wrongs that we have done unto others. Instinctive self-defense compels us to call into question even indisputably proven facts, to seek mitigating circumstances, to clear our own conscience while blaming others.

Pride and Shame

The question is not whether 1,500 or 900 Jews were murdered in Jedwabne. The most essential thing is not whether the motive for the murderers was greed or revenge for the collaboration of Jews with the Soviet occupation regime. And whether Prof. Jan T. Gross overlooked an important source, omitted a sentence in a document he cited, or failed to consider the testimony of a particular witness is not the most important issue.

In the light of not one or two but several testimonies and accounts, not only of witnesses and victims but also of the perpetrators, it is an undeniable fact that old people and children, men and women, were murdered in Jedwabne in an unbelievably brutal manner at the hands of Poles. Attempts to undermine this fundamental assertion are, in the light of the evidence presented, nothing but a denial of the truth. From the documentation presented by the author, it is clear that the Germans were the instigators of the pogrom. In the introduction itself we find out from Gross that on that fatal day German cameras and film crews were waiting, and that there was a meeting of the Gestapo with the village authorities. The pogrom was therefore not spontaneous.

It is also clear from Gross that, without German encouragement, permission, and support, the massacre would not have been possible. This does not in the least change the fact that, acting of their own free, unforced will, Poles tortured and killed their victims. None of the Polish murderers was in uniform, and no one can hide behind the argument that he had to obey orders or perish himself. Nor is it possible to explain the mass murder as revenge for the collaboration of Jews with the Soviet occupation regime and for their participation in the persecution of Poles. Gross cites the written accounts of the ringleaders of the massacre who, before communist Polish judicial authorities, referred to their cooperation with the NKVD during the Soviet occupation as a mitigating circumstance.

Even if it were true that not a single Pole embraced the protective red banner during the Soviet occupation, and that all Jews without exception collaborated with the Soviets, nothing can justify the killing of people like animals—the stoning, the butchering with knives, the decapitation, the stabbing with sharpened stakes, the wholesale murder of women and men, of the old and the young herded to the Jewish cemetery, the burying alive of still-breathing victims, the drowning of women with their children in the pond, and, at the end, the forcing of the remaining victims into the barn in which they were burned alive.

Since we share a national pride in our victories, in our laudable actions, and in the contributions made by Polish artists to the common treasury of human values, we must also bring ourselves to feel national shame for shameful actions. As a nation nearly entirely Christian, we must beat our breasts, acknowledging the sins and transgressions of each Polish Cain who violated the commandment "Thou shalt not kill!" If we expect redress from others for crimes committed against Poland and against Poles, we must also demonstrate the will to redress the evil committed by us against our neighbors.

In the Footsteps of the Germans

No one ever performed a greater service for the Germans than Chancellor Willy Brandt when he fell to his knees before the monument to the heroes of the Warsaw ghetto before the eyes of the entire world.[1]

[1] Willy Brandt (1913–1992) was a German politician and statesman, known for uttering the statement "No people can escape from their history." In December 1970 Brandt as chancellor of the Federal Republic of Germany knelt before the monument to the heroes of the Warsaw ghetto and in 1971 was awarded the Nobel Peace Prize.

This was a symbolic act of atonement for the German crime of genocide, and it was performed by a person who had nothing to do with that genocide. The strong sense of collective guilt shown even now by the majority of Germans has caused the world, not excluding Poland, to more easily pardon them their terrible crimes, and to place the onus on "the Nazis," rather than on the German people.

For many years, we protested against the mendacity of the Russian inscription in the Katyn forest, an inscription stating that German fascists had murdered Polish prisoners of war there in 1941. In Jedwabne, similar falsehoods are inscribed on two monuments. On the one erected during the Polish Communist period, the inscription speaks of the execution of Jewish people burned by the German Gestapo and gendarmerie. Not a word about the Poles. The other monument was erected recently, after 1989, "to honor the memory of 180 persons, including two priests, who were murdered in the territory of the Jedwabne district by the NKVD, the Nazis, and the UB [Security Police]." This marker is signed, "Society." Not a word about the Jews. As I write these words, both monuments are still standing.

Rabbi Baker's Appeal

The effacement of this shameful blot demands at least a symbolic act acknowledging guilt and atonement. This could be the fulfillment of the plea by a rabbi from Jedwabne, Jacob Baker.[2] Invoking John Paul II's request to Jews for forgiveness for the suffering that they have endured at the hands of Christians, Rabbi Baker asks for the dignified burial of the bones of the murdered, their interment in a Jewish cemetery, and the commemoration of the place where the synagogue stood.

A ceremonial commemoration of the victims of the bloody pogrom at Jedwabne, with the motto "Thou shalt not kill," and with the participation of the primate of Poland, the bishops, and representatives of the highest state and civil authorities and of Jewish organizations, could be the symbolic act of atonement that is so necessary. Only in this way can we cure the nation of the ethnic or class hatred that led in the past to the most terrible crimes in human history. Kosovo is a contemporary example.

[2] Rabbi Jacob Baker was born in 1914 in Jedwabne, which he left in 1937. He is a coauthor of *Yedwabne: History and Memorial Book* (English and Hebrew editions). In March 2002 he received—together with Krzysztof Godlewski, former mayor of Jedwabne—the prestigious Jan Karski Prize.

A Common Examination of Conscience

The six centuries of the presence of the Jews in Poland are today a closed book. To close the book with dignity, a mutual and straightforward accounting is necessary. Not everything in the mutual relationship between Poles and Jews was bad. In the centuries before the rebirth of Israel, Poland was a refuge for Jews persecuted and expelled from both the East and the West. The realization of an idea raised in the press—the publication of a great book by Polish and Jewish historians—would be a dignified final accord. It would consist of two parts: the first would present what was good in the life they shared. The second would be a straightforward accounting of the wrongs committed.

This joint and mutual examination of conscience would certainly be rejected with fury by the extremist elements on both sides, but it would have great significance for all those who feel an attachment to the common values based on the Ten Commandments and the Gospels. The question of the mass murder in Jedwabne has a moral dimension that is not just an internal Polish affair, however. It could also strike a fatal blow to the good name of the Poland that belongs to the civilized world. Jan Gross's book will be published in English in New York on 1 April. Simultaneously, the influential *New York Times* will publish excerpts in its book review section, which is widely read by the Western intellectual elite. Since we demanded that the Russians acknowledge the Katyn atrocities and reveal the instigators and the circumstances of the murder of unarmed Polish prisoners of war in the Katyn forest and elsewhere, we cannot feel resentful of the author of *Neighbors* for revealing and documenting, sixty years after the fact, the mass murder committed by Poles in Jedwabne—a murder that we would prefer not to know about and not to remember.

Preventive Action

Historians have the right to carefully verify the documents and accounts provided by Gross. Some of his journalistic conclusions provoked far-reaching reservations in me as well. However, we do not have time to wait for the moment when each item has been placed under the researcher's microscope, tested, corrected, or filled in. Fundamental Polish interests demand the initiation of immediate preventive action to limit the damage caused to Poland by the world reaction to the news of the massacre in Jedwabne.

Within the Jewish Diaspora, especially in America, there are extremist, chauvinistic elements—just as there are in Polish society—as well as others who believe that the cultivation of hatred and demands for revenge can have a dangerous boomerang effect. On the basis of my own personal experience, I am convinced that we have both friends and relentless enemies among the American Jews. The oldest and most influential Jewish organization in the United States, the American Jewish Committee headed by David Harris, supported the efforts to bring Poland into NATO in the most effective of ways.

At the other extreme, there are the Jewish counterparts of belligerent Polish antisemites. They see in Poles—all Poles—the most antisemitic nation in the world. They seem not to perceive the symptoms of this social disease in Russia, Germany, or other countries of our region. The danger exists that Gross's book will be exploited in ways not intended by the author to promote the thesis that "every Pole sucked antisemitism with his mother's milk."[3] I took these words of Shamir's as an insult to the memory of my mother, who was deeply religious and who taught her sons from childhood that displaying contempt for another person because of his origin, religion, or race is a mortal sin that violates the injunction to love one's neighbor. These words must be taken the same way by all those who have fought racial prejudices their entire lives.

Accusing the Polish nation of collaboration with the Nazis and participation in the Holocaust is the same type of slander as the "Auschwitz lie," which denies the existence of extermination camps and gas chambers.

Against Defamation

I spent the war in Poland, and I wandered all over the country. In the first year of the occupation, I met not only with friends and acquaintances from among the Jewish intelligentsia. Supporting myself as a salesman, I often visited the small town of Konstantynów in Podlasie, where Hasidic Jews constituted the majority of the population. They lived in deathly fear of the Germans, but they did not fear the Poles. In the first year of the occupation, relations with the Polish population enabled Jews to avoid hunger and to survive. Only later did *szmalcownicy* [blackmailers] become a terror for Jews who were trying to conceal their origins. From documents in the Jewish Historical Institute in Warsaw, it appears that the pogrom in Jedwabne was not an isolated inci-

---

[3] Yitzhak Shamir (1915–) is a Polish-born Israeli politician and statesman whose father was murdered by his former Polish acquaintances during World War II. In September 1989 Shamir as prime minister made a strongly controversial statement about Poles' "sucking antisemitism with their mother's milk," which caused a wave of protest in the Polish media.

dent. There were others. It is worth noting, however, that they occurred in Lithuania, in the Białystok region, and in eastern Galicia immediately after the flight of the Soviet occupier. Jedwabne was not a common phenomenon throughout Poland.

To conclude from the 1941 pogroms that the Holocaust was the common work of Poles and Germans is a libel. All who feel themselves to be Polish have the responsibility to defend themselves against such slander. The majority of Polish society might be charged with having an attitude of indifference to the extermination of the Jews—if not for the fact that the entire civilized world displayed indifference and passivity in the face of the crime of genocide. The difference is that Poles were eyewitnesses, defenseless witnesses living in constant fear for their lives and the lives of their families.

Adam Michnik correctly, and in my presence, warned Jews gathered at a New York synagogue that the defamation of Poland could provoke a secondary wave of antisemitism among people who had spent their entire lives fighting racial prejudices.

It is worth adding that any eruption of neo-antisemitism in Poland would cause terrible harm not to Jews—there are barely a few thousand of them in Poland—but to the position and the good name of Poland in the world. Certainly this was not Gross's intention when he revealed the crimes committed by the Poles of Jedwabne. In order to avert this secondary antisemitism, it is necessary to place the tragedy of the Jews of Jedwabne on the agenda of the Polish-Jewish dialogue now, especially in the United States. Jan T. Gross ought to be involved on the Polish side, for a great deal depends on how he himself presents *Neighbors* to Western readers.

. . . . .

Jan Nowak-Jeziorański was born in 1913. During the Second World War he was a courier and emissary of the command of the underground Polish Home Army (Armia Krajowa). After the war, he was an editor of the European service of BBC Radio in London and director of the Polish Service of Radio Free Europe from 1951 to 1976. From 1978 to 1993, he was consultant to the U.S. National Security Council and the national director of the Polish-American Congress. He has written a number of articles for magazines, periodicals, and newspapers, and books including *Kurier z Warszawy* (A courier from Warsaw) (London, 1978), *Wojna w eterze* (War on the airways) (London, 1985), and *Polski wczoraj, dziś i jutro* (Poland, yesterday, today, and tomorrow) (Warsaw, 1999).

Translation from *Thou Shalt Not Kill*.

Antoni Macierewicz

THE REVOLUTION OF NIHILISM

GŁOS, 3 FEBRUARY 2001

I T IS DIFFICULT TODAY to pinpoint with complete certainty
when this all began. Perhaps it was when the Jews from Jedwabne
published *Yedwabne: History and Memorial Book*, containing a description of the tragedy of their hometown, or perhaps it was when
Prof. Jan T. Gross received a grant to study the 1939—1941 Bolshevik
occupation of Poland's eastern territories and was given access to materials kept at the Hoover Institution.

For Gross himself, the important date was 1998, when Agnieszka
Arnold, who was at work on a documentary film, showed him footage
from Jedwabne. Prof. Andrzej Paczkowski also played an essential role
by giving Gross access to documents from the Main Commission for
the Investigation of Crimes against the Polish Nation, although they
were off-limits to other researchers at the time, for which Gross especially thanks him.

The Campaign

It is certain, however, that the beginning was not the court case of 1949,
when fifteen men were indicted for the murder of the Jews of Jedwabne (seven other suspects could not be located). The basis of the
trial was the account (or rather the accounts) by Szmul Wasersztajn.
Twelve Poles were sentenced in a pseudotrial that lasted barely a day
(there are obvious parallels with the procedure followed in Kielce in
1946), but it did not occur to anyone back then to accuse the Polish
nation of playing a part in the Holocaust. This comes as no surprise
considering that Wasersztajn's account clearly stated that the slaughter
was carried out on orders issued by the German Gestapo on 10 July
1941 and under German supervision. The indictment also confirms
this: "At the behest of the German state authorities, they took part in
the apprehension of about 1,200 people of Jewish nationality, who were
then burned to death en masse by the Germans."

It would be difficult to assume that the authorities of the UB and the
Stalinist courts consciously aimed to whitewash the Poles and to

falsely place the responsibility on the Germans. Rather, antisemitism was being sniffed out everywhere at the time and was used eagerly as a pretext for repression. In this case, however, the evidence pointed primarily in the direction of the Germans. Gross initially treated Wasersztajn's report similarly. Only later, he writes, "watching Agnieszka Arnold's film footage, . . . I understood what had happened." That was in 1998.

Two years later, Jewish and liberal circles were swept by a hysterical urge to prove that the Poles were responsible for the crime of genocide committed against the Jews by the Germans—for the Holocaust. This campaign was accompanied by lies that would have been difficult to imagine just a short time ago, such as the following statements by Gross: "No one was forced to kill the Jews . . . The so-called local population involved in killings of Jews did so of its own free will"; or "It was in no one's interest in Stalinist Poland to show that Jewish suffering during the war was somehow unique or that it was at the hands of the Poles"; or that strikes in Łódź in 1946 after the "Kielce pogrom" are "perfectly understandable as a protest against the fact that in postwar Poland one could no longer settle accounts with murderers of Polish children."[1] Poles who had harbored Jews "continued to hide this fact from their neighbors in terror; they were inconvenient witnesses to crimes, the fruits of which were still being enjoyed." Gross is thus undertaking a campaign of hatred directed at Poles and Poland, declaring a journalistic and propaganda war against us. Why?

Jedwabne for Kielce?

Perhaps a better reference point for understanding Gross's book is the political mechanism connected with the Kielce affair. For years, the so-called Kielce pogrom, which was later called the "Kielce provocation," served as a key argument against Poland and Poles. In recent years it was proved beyond a shadow of a doubt that the so-called Kielce pogrom was in essence a crime against Poles, committed by the NKVD and the UB [Security Administration]. An essential though still incompletely explained role was played by Jewish communists, especially Luna Bristigerowa, who was then in charge of a department of the UB. She was the superior of the UB officer Sobczyński who supervised the unfolding of the "pogrom." Jewish refugees suffered then, and their

[1] Strikes in various factories in Łódź were organized in protest against the sentences of the first Kielce pogrom trial of July 1946. The strikes were a manifestation of anti-Jewish prejudice.

deaths served as a pretext for unleashing a hysteria that induced Jews to emigrate to Palestine, and for persecuting Poles who were fighting for independence. These goals were achieved. In the 1990s, however, knowledge of this crime committed by the Bolshevik occupation authorities began to penetrate public awareness, despite the resistance of the Commission for the Investigation of Crimes against the Polish Nation and of judicial bodies which, calculating that the truth would never surface, canceled legal proceedings in the matter.

When the myth of Polish antisemitism—previously fueled by stories about the "Kielce pogrom"—ceased to be useful, a decision was made to find a replacement. Is the tragedy of the Jews of Jedwabne to become such a tool? Is the hubbub surrounding Jedwabne intended to eclipse the responsibility of Jews for communism and the Soviet occupation of Poland? The creation of the Institute of National Memory and access to previously unknown sources could soon reveal the horrifying scale of anti-Polish activities. Perhaps, then, this is all about blocking that process or giving it an "ideologically correct" form. And perhaps the goals are even more prosaic. Perhaps it is simply a matter of creating the necessary conditions for the recovery of property that belonged to the Jewish community, murdered by the Germans on Polish soil?

Poles Are Guilty of the Holocaust and the Communist Occupation!

The first publication on this subject appeared in the newspaper *Rzeczpospolita* in May 2000. In that article, on the basis of the memorial book and the Wasersztajn account, Andrzej Kaczyński laid the responsibility for the murder of nearly 1,500 Jews at the feet of the Poles of Jedwabne, accusing them of participation in the Holocaust. Protests from the Catholic right wing had no effect, and the community of professional historians remained silent, so the hate campaign spread even further. To this day, the position of the Polish government is unclear. In any case, at the initiative of the Ministry of Foreign Affairs, several historians met on 19 May 2000, in the ministry's palace on Foksal Street in Warsaw. Their task was to formulate an official position on this issue. As the newspaper *Nasz Dziennik* wrote, "from the statements that were quoted in the press after that meeting, one could arrive at the conclusion that the worst possible reaction on the part of the Polish authorities and public opinion in this matter would be any possible attempt to fundamentally undermine the credibility of the accounts presented in Gross's book or to steer the discussion toward a search for the alleged instigators and beneficiaries of an 'anti-Polish campaign.' "

The results of this position were not long in coming. First Jewish circles, and then liberal ones, began calling loudly for the punishment of the Polish nation for its crimes against the Jews. On behalf of the Jewish community in Poland, Stanisław Krajewski demanded that the president, the prime minister, and the Roman Catholic primate publicly admit the "truth" about responsibility for the slaughter in Jedwabne. Jan Nowak-Jeziorański advanced a similar view in the pages of *Rzeczpospolita*, demanding that the episcopate, the primate, and the prime minister perform an act of repentance in the name of the entire nation—just as Chancellor Brandt had done before the ghetto monument in Warsaw in the name of the German nation. Nowak equated the responsibility of Poles for Jedwabne to the responsibility of the Russians for Katyn, thus adding the identification of the Poles with the Bolshevik NKVD to their identification with the Nazis. This wasn't anything particularly new, because Jan Tomasz Gross, the author of the anti-Polish accusation, himself closed his book with a hypothesis that the true origin of communism in Poland should be sought in the activities of Polish antisemites, who collectively supported the Soviet occupation after 1945!

The Propaganda of Lies

Such a profusion of libelous accusations and absurdities would seem impossible in a country that regained independence after fifty years of occupation directed by communists of Jewish origin supporting Russian Bolshevism. It turns out not only that it is possible, but even that these libelous accusations and absurdities are being propagated by most of the media and, at a minimum, tolerated by the country's authorities. The only exception turned out to be Prof. Radoń, head of the Historical Department of the Institute of National Memory, who voiced a timid reminder that Prof. Gross's book is more of a political newspaper column than a historical work, if only because Gross disavowed in advance any search for sources that could undermine his thesis about the principal responsibility of the Poles.[2]

Gross relies exclusively on reports of the Jedwabne Jews who were saved from the Holocaust (thanks to Poles, after all) while omitting or downplaying any information about the presence and decisive role of German military units. He performs similar contortions in trying to convince his readers that the Jewish population in eastern Poland was

[2] Sławomir Radoń, "Pochopne sądy Grossa," *Gazeta Wyborcza*, 20–21 January 2001.

not involved in any particular way in support for the Soviet occupation authorities in 1939–1941.

The third fundamental instance of Gross's dishonesty as a researcher is his thesis that the origins of communism on Polish soil after 1944 should be sought in the antisemitism of the Poles. It is obvious to any historian that Prof. Gross's book does not hold up to criticism in terms of methodology. Even Prof. Tomasz Szarota alluded to this in *Gazeta Wyborcza*, but that has not hindered these circles in the continuation of their anti-Polish campaign.

A Revolution in Historical Sources

In order to prop up his accusation, Gross proposes a true revolution in the historical sciences. Until now, historians were bound by strict rules regarding evaluation of sources. There was an obligation to take a critical approach to each account and to mutually corroborate the information obtained, and, first and foremost, there was a requirement to take into account all known sources. This means that an author cannot freely pick and choose from among existing accounts those that suit his thesis best, but rather he has an obligation to take into consideration all the information that is known to exist at the time. Failure to exhaust the available sources disqualifies a study as a work of history and demotes it to the rank of historical or political journalism. That is precisely the case here. Gross may not be aware of this, since he is a physicist and sociologist by training and took up history thanks to the grants he received from the Guggenheim and Rockefeller Foundations. Just to be on the safe side, Gross announces in his book the need for a "new approach to sources": "Our initial attitude toward every report coming from would-be victims of the Holocaust," he writes, "should change from one of doubt to one of affirmation." In short, when studying the history of the Holocaust, the point of departure in analysis of reports by surviving witnesses should be to trust their accounts, and not to seek to corroborate their description of events. Given such a premise, in fact, the entire existing historical oeuvre becomes useless and the events of the recent past can be written anew. And then it won't be difficult to prove the theses that Gross's book puts forward: the Poles are responsible for the Holocaust; the operation of the Nazi genocidal machine was underpinned by traditional Polish backward, atavistic antisemitism; the Jews were in no special way helpful to the Soviet occupation either in 1939 or in 1945 and, quite the contrary, were its main victims; and the Soviet army and communist regime were supported by peasant and small-town antisemitic masses who collaborated with every occupying authority—the Germans, the Russians, the communists; in short, THE POLES ARE GUILTY.

Despite appearances, Gross is not the originator either of this "methodology" or of these theses. They have long been spread on a large scale by political commentaries in *Gazeta Wyborcza* and by the circle of historians connected with the paper. Among these historians we must name Andrzej Paczkowski, thanks to whose kindness Gross had access to materials revealing, for example, the names of communist agents, many of them still alive to this day. Paczkowski has long spread precisely such a vision of communism: "Not everything—rather, very little—can be explained by statements about 'outsiders,' 'the Jews,' 'NKVD agents,' 'mercenaries' or 'traitors.' Poles appeared in the role of victim and in the role of persecutor . . . And it is truly difficult today to say with full certainty on which side there were more of them." Krystyna Kersten and Jerzy Holzer write similar articles. This is precisely what the "Polish historical school" looks like today. Part of it willingly erects the edifice of anti-Polish "historiosophy," while the rest remain timorously silent.

What Was It Really Like?

Only recently, in the pages of *Rzeczpospolita*, there appeared a lengthy article by Prof. Tomasz Strzembosz, a distinguished researcher of recent Polish history and especially of the period 1939—1954. Strzembosz's article demonstrates the actual role of the Jewish population in eastern Poland in the years of the first Soviet occupation. The discussion to date, declares Strzembosz, "overlooks the most important fact: what happened in Jedwabne after the German army entered the area, i.e., who carried out the mass murder of the Jewish population of Jedwabne, and when, and under what circumstances." Strzembosz analyzes in depth the behavior of the Polish and Jewish populations in the years 1939—1941, especially in the initial and final periods of the first Soviet occupation. "The Jewish population," writes Strzembosz, "especially the young and the urban poor, participated en masse in greeting the entering [Soviet] army and in introducing the new order, even with guns in their hands. There are also thousands of testimonies to this—Polish, Jewish, and Soviet; there are the reports of the commander-in-chief of the ZWZ [Union for Armed Combat], Gen. Stefan Grot-Rowiecki; there is the report of courier Jan Karski; there are accounts recorded during the war and in the postwar years. Moreover, the 'guards' and 'militias' springing up like mushrooms right after the Soviet attack were in large part made up of Jews. Nor is this all. Jews committed acts of revolt against the Polish state, taking over towns and setting up revolutionary committees there, arresting and shooting representatives of the Polish state authorities, attacking smaller or even fairly large units of the Polish Army (as in Grodno) . . . It was armed collaboration, taking the side of the enemy, betrayal in the days of defeat."

Organizers of the Red Terror

So it was in the first period, when the Polish state was still defending itself, when our army units were fighting and it seemed that not all was lost. The Jews then played the role of a "fifth column." Later, things became much worse. Strzembosz cites Dr. Marek Wierzbicki's conclusions about who implemented the Bolshevik terror: the NKVD and, before that, the Red Army, of course, but on an everyday basis the miscellaneous guard formations and militias played a decisive role. And their ranks were primarily filled with Jews: "Polish Jews in civilian clothes, with red bands on their arms and armed with guns, also played a large part in arrests and deportations. This was the most drastic, but for the Polish community another glaring fact was the large number of Jews in all the Soviet agencies and institutions . . . In the period September–December 1939, there were numerous arrests of those representatives of the Polish population who before the war had fulfilled high functions in the administrative and political structures of the Polish state or who were very involved in community work. The local Jews, members of the temporary administration or militia, provided extensive assistance to the Soviet authorities in tracking them down and arresting them."

Why did this happen? What were the roots of this terrible hatred toward Poland and the cruel revenge on Poles? "It is true," writes Strzembosz, "that things were not going very well for the Jews in Poland. But still, Jews were not being deported to Siberia, shot, sent to concentration camps, or killed by hunger and slave labor. Even if they did not consider Poland their homeland, they did not have to treat it as an invader and join its mortal enemy in killing Polish soldiers and murdering Polish civilians fleeing to the East. Nor did they have to take part in designating their neighbors for deportation."

Torture in Jedwabne

Strzembosz proves beyond a shadow of a doubt that events took precisely the same course in Jedwabne itself. Here is one account from a resident of Jedwabne, Józef Rybicki, summing up what happened in the town after it fell to the Soviets: "Jews had put up an archway and greeted the Red Army. They replaced the old town government and proposed a new one drawn from the local population (Jews and communists). They arrested the police, the teachers . . . They led the NKVD to apartments and houses and denounced Polish patriots."

The description of the tortures inflicted upon Polish conspirators by the NKVD in Jedwabne is shocking. The following is an account by Corporal Antoni B., a member of the anti-Soviet underground who was turned in to the NKVD by Jews:

They took me for interrogation. The investigating judge and the NKVD commander and one torturer came, and they sat me on a stool next to a brick wall. Then I look over and one in civilian clothes takes a stick from behind the stove like the kind in the walls of our tents, that long and thick, and suddenly they threw me on the floor and stuffed my cap in my mouth and started to beat me. I couldn't cry out because the judge sat on my legs and the second one held me by the head and held the cap in my mouth, and I fought back until I tore the cap to bits, and the third torturer beat me the whole time. I got that stick more or less thirty times, and they stopped beating me and sat me on the stool by the wall. I had long hair, and the senior lieutenant grabbed me by the hair and started to beat my head against the wall. I thought that nothing would be left of my head. He tore a whole clump of hair from my head. They threw me on the ground and started to beat me with a hazel stick. They turned me from side to side and beat me, and in addition two of them were still sitting on me and suffocating me and said that they would finish me off. They kept beating me until they probably knew that I couldn't take anymore, so at last they let me go. They beat me like a cat in a sack, and at the end they sat me on the stool and beat me with the stick on the arms. (From *W czterdziestym nas matko na Sybir zesłali* [In 1940, Mother, they sent us to Siberia], published by the Solidarity Interfactory Structure, 82)

I took this text from a collection of accounts prepared for print years ago by Prof. Jan T. Gross.[3] In writing his book about Jedwabne, Gross skips over the description of Antoni B.'s arrest and torture, although he quotes other fragments of this account. Why?

The facts leave no room for doubt: the Jews of Jedwabne, as in the entire territory occupied by the Soviets, constituted the nuts and bolts of the machinery of repression. Up to the last moment, they were deliv-

[3] And also by Irena Grudzińska-Gross.

ering Polish patriots into the hands of the NKVD and preparing the next deportation transports to Siberia.

The Responsibility of Historians

Does this mean that Poles burned 1,500 Jedwabne Jews in the barn as revenge? Certain accounts by surviving Jews indicate precisely this. At the same time, however, we know that the German *Einsatzgruppe* B was active in this area, carrying out murderous raids on Jews in the surrounding towns. We also know that some sort of formation, called "the Gestapo" by Wasersztajn, was in Jedwabne that fateful day, that the Germans had at their disposal the kerosene used to set the barn ablaze, that German sentries were on duty around the town the whole time, and, to top it off, that a German newsreel team was brought in to document the crime and that the German gendarmerie supervised the burial of the corpses. There even exists a description of the course of events, which Gross arbitrarily deems false: "On the critical day the German gendarmerie, with the mayor and Secretary Wasilewski at their head, went around driving men out of their houses to guard the Jews, who had already been herded onto the town square. They came into my house, too, and found my husband and, with strict orders and threats, guns in hand, they drove my husband out onto the square."

The estimates of the numbers of Germans vary. Gross speaks of a dozen or so gendarmes and a few dozen members of the Gestapo. Testifying at the trial, the cook for the gendarmerie, a woman named Sokołowska, recalled, "On the critical day there were sixty Gestapo men, because I cooked dinner for them, and there were a lot of gendarmes because they came from other outposts." It was probably on the basis of this account that Prosecutor Monkiewicz ascertained that the slaughter was supervised by 232 German gendarmes who came to Jedwabne in a column of trucks.[4]

Nevertheless, there has never been a serious inquiry into the identity of the Germans who planned the atrocity, gave the orders, supervised their execution, and filmed it. The involvement of Poles, although shocking, is definitely not equivalent to the involvement of Jewish police who murdered their fellow Jews in the ghettos, delivered them into the hands of their executioners, and drove them onto the Umschlag-

[4] Prosecutor Waldemar Monkiewicz took over the legal investigation into the Jedwabne crime in 1971. His thesis about the group of Germans committing the crime was groundless and ignored the available evidence of the time, such as the statements of eyewitnesses.

platz. Those who, instead of establishing facts, join in the campaign against the Polish nation by trying to burden Poles with blame for the Holocaust under German occupation while "forgetting" that the real perpetrators were the Germans bring shame upon the historian's profession. Prof. Strzembosz's article restores honor to Polish historians, who previously maintained a cowardly silence in the face of the campaign against Poland and the Poles. I would like to believe that there are also Righteous Ones among the Jews, who have not succumbed to the pressure of the pervasive hatred of Poland.

·   ·   ·   ·   ·

Antoni Macierewicz was born 1948 and is a historian and politician. He was an activist in the democratic opposition movement under the communist regime, cofounder of the Committee for the Defense of Workers (KOR) in 1976, and later a Solidarność trade union activist. From 1991 to 1993, he was Sejm (parliament) deputy for the Zjednoczenie Chrześcijańsko-Narodowe (Christian-National Union). From 1995 to 1997, he served as deputy leader of the Ruch Odbudowy Polski (Movement for the Reconstruction of Poland). At present he is an independent Sejm deputy, publisher of *Głos* weekly, and since 1998 chairman of the Ruch Katolicko-Narodowy (Catholic-National Movement). He lives in Warsaw.

Translation taken from *Thou Shalt Not Kill.*

Hanna Świda-Ziemba

THE SHORTSIGHTEDNESS OF
THE "CULTURED"

GAZETA WYBORCZA, 6 APRIL 2001

WITH THE REVELATION of the crime in Jedwabne, I now know that only a thin layer of ice, which can break at any moment, separates "innocent" prejudices from crime.

Before I present my reflections on the crime committed in Jedwabne, I will declare my position on questions that have been at the center of the debate. Above all, I acknowledge only individual subjectivity and responsibility. At the same time, I believe that we are responsible for the social resonance and the social effects of our actions. The responsible person is thus obligated to know and understand social mechanisms and the world in which he makes his choices. He may not falsify reality that is inconvenient for him or turn his back on it. From these assumptions, it follows that the responsible person must know and understand the history of his nation. First of all, history reveals the universal social mechanisms that are the basis for understanding the present and sometimes serve as an ominous warning. Second, there is the phenomenon of the social legacy of attitudes. History is an ongoing process, and the present contains the past within it. Thus it is essential to know which aspects of the history of a nation deserve to be continued, and which should be decisively condemned and resisted.

People with a well-developed sense of individual responsibility should thus not only take note of the crime in Jedwabne but, further, subject the fact of it to deep reflection that will also serve as the basis for evaluation of the present day and the scope of their own responsibility. For such reflection to be possible, we must agree that our knowledge of the crime in Jedwabne is already sufficient for an evaluation of the events. Regardless of whether there were more or fewer Germans in Jedwabne, whether 1,632 people, or significantly fewer (say, for example, 933) were burned in the barn, how many Poles took part in it, and whether the Germans played the role of acquiescent observers or active provocateurs, nothing will change the simple truth, cruel for us today, that all the Jewish residents of Jedwabne were burned alive, and that the crime was committed by the local population.

Before Crime There Are Prejudices

It is difficult not to associate this crime with prewar antisemitism. Until now I had not appreciated its criminal potential. After reading Jan Tomasz Gross's book, I had to agree with the thought that in Polish society, mass murder committed by a mob of ordinary people was possible. I can no longer consider the Kielce crime[1] an isolated case, as I did before. In two distant places, at different times and under different circumstances, crimes were committed that in many respects were analogous. If we add the information about Radziłow, we get a sequence of events indicating that the criminal impulses of Polish society toward the Jews were not incidental occurrences; that at their roots must be widely held attitudes.

Historians who are critical of Gross's book focus on experiences connected with the Soviet occupation. Similarly, in analyzing the crime in Kielce they point to the participation of Jews in the apparatus of force. Let us remember, however, that the partisan unit operating near Jedwabne was in fact crushed as a result of betrayal, though the informers were not Jews. If suspicion fell on the Jews, it was because such suspicion was in keeping with earlier attitudes. It was these attitudes that led the population of Jedwabne during the Soviet occupation to take note of the Jews who welcomed the occupying army, but not to take note of the Poles who behaved the same way. Nor did the local population take note of the Jews who did not take part in the manifestations of joy but were often the victims of Soviet oppression. And because of these attitudes, the pro-occupation behavior of a few Jews was ultimately ascribed to the entire Jewish population of Jedwabne.

My first reflection is therefore of a historical-moral nature. Since we already know that prewar antisemitic attitudes in Poland resulted in crimes during and immediately after the war, then we should examine them closely. But little is said today about that antisemitism. Until now the conviction has dominated that it belonged to the remote past, and was washed away by the war and the horror of the Holocaust.

Jacek Kurczewski wrote in *Wprost* about the fact that prewar antisemitism has only a weak presence in our memory today: "One is tempted to say that it was the backward countryside, but the cities were not free of antisemitism . . . Moreover, the intelligentsia was also infected. This, too, we pass over in silence. When we take a look inside

---

[1] The Kielce pogrom of 4 July 1946 was the worst outbreak of anti-Jewish violence in early postwar Poland. It resulted in the murder of forty Jews and two non-Jews and injuries to more than one hundred Jews.

the Historical Museum of the University of Warsaw, we read about the association Respublica, which did not accept students of Jewish heritage 'regardless of their faith,' . . . and we see the portrait of Czarnowski, who spoke out against antisemitism, but we find nothing about the racist decisions of the academic authorities or about the disgraceful stamping of the letter 'J' for 'Jewish' in students' records."

One could say more: certain parties today make reference to the National Democratic tradition, but only rarely and enigmatically do they mention that this group openly espoused antisemitic slogans; the twenty years of independence are honored, but nothing is said of the antisemitic excesses organized by the youth of the National-Radical Camp. The antisemitic teachings of the Catholic Church at the time are also spoken of only rarely. In writing about antisemitism in prewar Poland, I do not assert that all Poles were antisemites. As a child (when the war ended I was almost fifteen years old), I moved in a number of circles in Vilna, but I almost never encountered such attitudes. People like Stefan Czarnowski,[2] Tadeusz Kotarbiński, and many others who protested publicly against antisemitism are well known. In other words, we cannot say that Poles (in the sense of the entire society) were antisemites at the time, but it is true that antisemitism was widespread in prewar Poland and that the social authorities supported it. In the light of Gross's book these facts take on a new meaning.

The Guilt of Those Who Were Not Present

What we know about Jedwabne prompts not only a revision of Polish history but above all a revision of the general stereotypes that until now I, too, believed to be true. According to a rather general conviction, there is a gulf between antisemitism, even in the drastic form it took in prewar Poland, and crime. After reading Gross's book, I now know that this is not so, and for this I am grateful to the author.

It is mainly for this reason that the information about Jedwabne and Radziłow (particularly in light of our knowledge about Kielce) was a shock for me. I understood that prejudice is separated from crime only by a thin layer of ice that can break at any moment. The explosive charge for crime is rooted in hateful prejudices. It may never detonate, if the circumstances are favorable. But this depends on additional factors, which may differ in each case. Therefore I also believe that de-

---

[2] Stefan Czarnowski (1879–1937) was a sociologist and historian of literature. In the 1920s he radically transformed his political views—he ceased to be a supporter of the National Democrats and in 1929 became a member of the Polish Socialist Party.

tailed historical research can resolve doubts about Gross's book in the quiet of academic offices. Such research may allow us to define the conditions (or "additional factors") that led to the commission of a crime in this particular case. It will not change the fact that this terrible crime occurred and that antisemitic attitudes made it possible.

Characteristic of our public life are the frequently expressed hopes that precisely these historical findings can soften that truth to the point that it will no longer be painful. The subtitle of the report "The Institute [of National Memory] Interrogates New Witnesses" in Życie expresses this attitude well. It says, "Did Poles Murder the Jews in Jedwabne or Was It a German Provocation?" As if provocation could free those who commit murder of responsibility. Provocation is only one of the factors calling forth a readiness to commit murder. There must first be a psychic foundation to which the provocateur appeals. Provocation erases neither the crime itself nor the foundation from which it grew.

So we must reconsider our evaluation of prewar Polish antisemitism, although its manifestations were not always brutal. Often, it led only to commentaries on the "the loathsome Jewish character" and "the Jewish menace," recited at elegant gatherings.

It would seem that between such innocent remarks and the terrible crime in Jedwabne there stretches an insurmountable chasm; the more so as the participants in such conversations sometimes rescued Jews during the war. Prewar Polish antisemites were often too cultured and refined to go as far as committing a crime. But I believe that even such people as these can see themselves in the events of Jedwabne as in a terrible mirror. Though they themselves may have taken no actions that were wrong, they nevertheless created an atmosphere, a way of communicating, that covered the entire expanse of the country. Statements on "the loathsome Jewish character" and "the Jewish menace" lead to various results, depending on the personalities of the people and on the circumstances. But circumstances are unpredictable, personalities varied, and statements spread by word of mouth become disengaged from their authors. On this I agree with Krystyna Skarzyńska (*Gazeta Wyborcza*, 25 November 2001): the Jedwabne murderers were not acting in a social vacuum. In committing murder, they were in harmony—in their understanding—with "cultured society," with people who were not there, but whose voices were "audible" to them in that moment. The views of the murderers were authenticated by what they were taught in church, and by the remarks and assertions of various political and social authorities. In keeping with what they heard, they "were not murdering people" but simply "burning out pestilence."

In this way the circle of those responsible for the crime in Jedwabne and for other crimes against Jews is broadened to include all bearers of antisemitic views in Poland, and—indirectly—to those who were indifferent, who did not oppose them. These may be people for whom all crime is repugnant, who would never have foreseen that they could stoop to it. But as a result of the particular course of historical circumstances, this crime is upon them too.

The third circle of reflection, closely connected to the first two, is the most important, for it concerns the present day. If the crime has its roots in all types of hateful ethnic prejudices, then Gross's book naturally provokes reflection on antisemitism in today's Poland.

According to the widespread conviction of today, it is true that antisemitic attitudes do appear in Poland, but they constitute the narrow margins. Sociological observations cast doubt on this view. On the basis of their findings I can assert that such views are widespread today, although—except for a few cases—they do not take on a drastic character. If we take into account the minuscule number of Jews, we can conclude that these attitudes must be the inheritance of the past. Clearly, during the postwar period the older generation transmitted to the younger generation its beliefs about "the loathsome Jewish character" and "the Jewish menace." The Holocaust did not change the views of many Poles (the majority?) and did not make a mark on Polish consciousness. Attitudes toward the Jews survived unaltered.

On the other hand, a certain form of political correctness took shape after the Holocaust, according to which spectacular, drastic attacks on Jews are evil, but at the same time even authentic antisemites treat the designation "antisemite" as an affront. This is why Poles are offended when Poland is called an antisemitic country, and why even the most antisemitic statement is prefaced by the declaration: "I'm not an antisemite, but . . ." And this is why antisemitism is not always visible in Poland.

It manifested itself more clearly after 1989. Then I, too, who until then had been convinced that it was of a marginal nature in Poland, suddenly observed that among many people antisemitism is deeply rooted. Since then, in observing Polish society, I have seen how antisemitism (negative, generalized stereotypes of the Jew) appears in daily life: in uncontrolled, involuntary proclamations and conversations—at the hairdresser's, while walking the dogs, at the bus stop, on the train, at parties. I believe that such remarks tell us more about social moods than declarations made in surveys.

I will try, for the sake of authenticating my unpopular thesis, to present some manifestations of today's antisemitism. Most painful is when they concern Poles with Jewish roots. There are varying degrees of rootedness in the Jewish people. Having a Jewish great-grandparent is often enough to be qualified as "racially" Jewish. I sometimes hear this sentence at parties: "You know, I found out that X is a Jew." The withdrawal of friendship or respect for X does not always go with this "discovery," but a shadow falls over the person in question. For Poles of Jewish ancestry, this is painful. Such a person feels himself marked as an alien, as unworthy of trust, as one who has to be watched. It is worth noting that only the Jewish "drop of blood" takes on such significance. Belarusian, Lithuanian, Russian, and German extraction arouses no emotion. Only the Jewish "drop of blood" is of such significance that all other personal qualifications, even familial, are pushed into the shadows. Such is the most universal manifestation of Polish antisemitism. We should not be surprised that some Poles hide their Jewish ancestry. In other Western countries, after the war, this phenomenon is not present. Among us it passes as natural. This antisemitism is so deeply rooted under the skin that it is not subject to external control.

What You Know, and I Understand

Antisemitism in Poland does not end here, however. At social gatherings as well as in chance conversations one encounters blatantly antisemitic attitudes. People express them as a rule in a less open manner than was common before the war, but the substance of their remarks is still "the Jewish menace." One finds this much more rarely than one encounters the hunt for Jewish ancestors. But this type of antisemitism appears often enough in Poland that it can be classified as a social problem.

It is expressed, for example, in the conviction that positions occupied by Jews or Poles with Jewish roots—loyal citizens of the Polish state—have been taken over by "aliens." Their presence is seen as evidence of the threat to Poland from an "alien excrescence." As a rule this is not stated openly. Rather, people will tell horrible stories about various specific people, noting in passing that the person of whom they are speaking is a Jew. It goes something like this: "That Paweł—he's a Jew, after all—well, he . . ."

Fantastic tales are also woven around the subject of the perfidious acts and intentions of Jews living both inside Poland and beyond its borders. I encountered a typical example of this during the reconstruction of the monuments on Theater Square, not far from where I live. Before we were informed about what would be housed in the reconstructed buildings, I often heard while walking my dog that there would be a hotel for Jews there, with a synagogue next to it, "so that the Jews wouldn't have far to go." Moreover, the synagogue was to be built on the site of a prewar Catholic church. Neighbors also informed me as they walked their dogs that the co-op building where I lived had long ago been sold secretly to Jews. I could therefore expect to be evicted at any moment.

As a rule, information about "the Jewish menace" is transmitted in code: "What you know, and I understand." People take it as a given that their conversation partner shares their view of reality. If they encounter resistance or polemics, they immediately clam up. The code is clearly reserved for "our people." The reaction of a boy I talked with on the train is very typical. When I reacted negatively to his antisemitic arguments, he looked at me with fear, distrustfully, and said, "I shouldn't have been so candid, because maybe you're one of 'them' or maybe they've bought you off." He fell silent and did not speak again the rest of the way.

Another manifestation of Polish antisemitism is the suspicion that everyone who arouses dislike or distrust is of Jewish ancestry, or the labeling of such people as Jews—for example, government officials, members of the Sejm, certain priests. In Łódź, members of opposing soccer teams are called Jews. Defendants of the thesis that antisemitism is a marginal phenomenon in Poland will say that such behavior cannot be considered antisemitism because it is not directed at real Jews. But that is precisely what we are talking about: the fact that accusing a politician of having Jewish roots is an effective way of defeating him, and that the word "Jew" is an insult.

Finally there is the sensitive issue of *żydokomuna* [Judeo-communism]. This problem requires a separate discussion; I will merely draw attention to it here. First of all, only a few Jews became Communists. And in becoming Communists, they broke with Judaism, with their community, so that for themselves and for Jews they ceased to be Jews. The Soviet government repressed whole masses of Jews, and the majority of them accepted neither the Soviet ideology nor the Soviet system. The Jewish children I knew in Vilna were as anti-Soviet as the Polish children. Thus I ask the readers to reflect on why Polish *szmalcownictwo* [the blackmailing of Jews] or other criminal behavior during the occupation is ascribed to the "dregs of society" or (rationally) to "a few" Poles, while communism is ascribed simply to Jews? And why is it that, as Israel Gutman astutely observed, the Jew who cooperated with Soviet authorities is viewed by Poles differently from "various Piaseckis."[3] There were Polish Communists as well as Jewish Communists, after all. There were also in our former territories Belarusian, Lithuanian, and even Ukrainian Communists. So where did the myth of *żydokomuna* come from?

Second, in comparing the criminality of the Hitlerite and Soviet systems, we generally do not take into consideration differences in their ideological assumptions. But this is essential in the evaluation of the people who espoused them. Communist ideological principles were humanitarian; it was the practice, first revolutionary and then state-bureaucratic, that turned out to be criminal. Thus the acceptance of communist ideology does not debase a person as much as the acceptance of fascist principles does. Knowing the assumptions of communist ideology, it is possible to understand not only why it was attractive to many people, and particularly those of the so-called social avant-garde, but also to understand in human terms why it was particularly attractive for young people of Jewish descent. These people were aware, after all, that in many countries, as in prewar Poland, they were treated as a foreign body, as superfluous, and that at any moment they could expect pogroms and abuse. After the war, the terrible awareness of the Holocaust added to this. For them, a vision of the world in which nationality would have no importance, in which the stigma would once and for all be removed (a utopian and false vision, as would later become apparent), must have had an especially powerful appeal.

Communism is a thing of the past. If we had no anti-Jewish prejudices, there would be a tendency to understand why communism was so unpopular among Poles (as opposed to Czechs or Bulgarians, for example) and more popular among Jews, and to understand the role that Polish behavior toward Jews before the war played in that popularity. But there is hardly any reflection on these matters. Stubbornly repeated stereotypes about *żydokomuna* remain alive, however.

Finally, antisemitism is evident in the reaction of the Catholic Church and the state authorities to spectacular manifestations of social antisemitism. It is true that representatives of these institutions make gestures in support of Polish-Jewish reconciliation. At the same time they behave as though antisemitism were absolutely insignificant in comparison to other factors. For example, they honor the Narodowe Siły Zbrojne [National Armed Forces] as the unit that fought against the Communist government the longest. The fact that these units irre-

---

[3] "Piaseckis" is the plural form of the name Boleslaw Piasecki (1915–1979). In 1936 Piasecki became the leader of National Radical Camp-Falanga—a radical nationalistic organization with strong fascist tendencies. After World War II he was a leader of Pax—a Catholic organization that was fully supported by the communist regime.

futably slaughtered Jews (as Jews) is either ignored or, contrary to the facts, denied. I hear nothing about in-depth historical research, the results of which could be announced in the national press. The reaction to the placement of crosses in Auschwitz came very late, and the "Papal Cross" stands there still, despite the fact that many Jews find its presence there disruptive to their prayers.[4] Offensive and blatantly criminal graffiti on the walls are not removed by city authorities in a timely fashion. In the cathedral in Sandomierz there hangs a painting depicting Jews engaged in the ritual murder of children, and in the name of respect for its historical value, no one speaks of its removal.[5] Father Jankowski,[6] who preached from antisemitic texts in his sermons, bestowing on them the force of "sacred truth," was not decisively condemned and barred for all time from the possibility of preaching to the faithful. Quite the opposite—it is often emphasized that this is a distinguished person who made great contributions to Solidarity.

Through the Prism of Jedwabne

In sum, the government authorities and the Church, despite the destruction of the Jews that was carried out before our eyes and on our land, despite the fact that some of our compatriots participated in the Holocaust, despite postwar pogroms, fail to decisively condemn our antisemites. This absence of unequivocal gestures on the part of the institutions that represent Poland globally (the political authorities and the Polish Catholic Church) has an effect on social moods and on the free dissemination of antisemitic opinions, for these can therefore appear to public opinion as ethically neutral—as an individual matter, an innocent choice of views.

[4] The controversy over crosses in Auschwitz was one of the most difficult conflicts in Polish-Jewish relations of the late 1990s and lasted almost a year. It ended in May 1999 when the Polish police and military troops removed 303 crosses planted outside the former Nazi death camp by radical Catholics. The only cross that was left was the Papal Cross erected in 1979 to commemorate a mass celebrated by Pope John II at the nearby site of the former concentration camp Birkenau.

[5] The painting depicting a ritual murder in Sandomierz, a town in southeastern Poland, in the town's cathedral, belongs to a series of early modern paintings of Christian martyrs. In recent years voices such as those of Father Stanisław Musiał and Świda-Ziemba herself have called for taking the painting down or for providing a critical description of it in the church.

[6] Father Henryk Jankowski emerged in the 1980s as the close confidante of Lech Wałęsa and as chaplain of the Solidarity movement. He is a pastor of the Saint Brygida Church in Gdańsk. In the 1990s, on many occasions including the debate about Jed-

It is true that Polish antisemitism today generally does not take a drastic or threatening form. Jews or people of Jewish descent hold various positions; they are not pushed to the margins, as they were before the war. They socialize with and marry Poles. But I believe that today's Polish antisemites, as well as those who tolerate antisemitism and those who declare it a marginal phenomenon, should evaluate their attitude in light of the crime in Jedwabne. For every hateful ethnic prejudice, regardless of the form it takes, contains within it the trigger for criminal acts.

The events in Yugoslavia have shown this to be true. Students from that country studying in Poland report that before, there may have been some dislike between different nations or between people of different faiths, but it was not flagrantly manifested. Quite the opposite: people of different nationalities became friends, and there were mixed marriages there as well. But the war in Yugoslavia demonstrated that the antagonisms that lay beneath the skin exploded (in some conditions precisely) like a volcano. So the "mildness" of manifestations of ethnic prejudices means nothing. We cannot know the future, so we do not know when and whether that Polish explosive potential of ethnic prejudice against the Jews may detonate.

In sum, I believe that we have a moral obligation not just to accept the truth about Jedwabne into our consciousness and make a series of symbolic gestures that will put an end to the matter. This shock to the consciousness should serve above all as a source for reflection, thanks to which all that was hitherto minimized will now take on new significance. Polish antisemitism, usually mild in its forms, will from now on be viewed through the prism of Jedwabne and will be treated as a real trigger for criminal acts. Jedwabne serves as a warning for the people of today. A new political and social policy should arise from it, governing even the Church, and opening with a strong symbolic gesture. This gesture could be the fulfillment of Dr. Zalman's appeal on behalf of the Israeli Association of Compatriots of Northern Mazowsze, published in *Rzeczpospolita*: "In the name of all political groups, the present Sejm of the free and democratic Republic of Poland should clearly and unequivocally . . . condemn clearly and in the most severe manner that small, radical group within the Polish nation for its genocidal acts. This would be an act of extraordinary human and historical significance, relaxing the atmosphere and cleansing the consciences of our generation and future generations." Such a resolution by the Sejm, like other necessary symbolic gestures, should be only

---

wabne, he has made various antisemitic statements. These have led to several not very successful attempts by the hierarchy to silence him.

the beginning of the revision and fundamental transformation of Poles' current views on the "Jewish problem" in our country. The shock that resulted from the information about Jedwabne should open for us a new chapter in our self-knowledge.

· · · · ·

Hanna Świda-Ziemba is professor at the Institute of Applied Social Sciences at the University of Warsaw. Among her books are *Człowiek wewnętrznie zniewolony* (The internally unfree person) (Warsaw, 1998), *Wartości egzystencjalne młodzieży lat 90* (Existential values of youth in the 1990s) (Warsaw 1995), and *Stalinizm i społeczeństwo polskie* (Stalinism and Polish society) (Warsaw, 1991). Between 1991 and 1993 she was a judge on the State Tribunal.

Jerzy Sławomir Mac

HOMO JEDVABICUS

WPROST, 22 JULY 2001

T HE THIRD MILLENNIUM began with a year-long vivisection of Polish souls.

Jan Gross's book came out last May, and *Rzeczpospolita* brought it into the public eye the following July; a full year of collective shock reached its culmination a week ago on the sixtieth anniversary of the crime. During the course of the year, loud cries arose from the froth of national emotions, and louder still was the silence . . . of *Homo Jedvabicus*.

He is the direct descendant of those who, in July 1941, would not have lifted a hand to persecute the Jews—except under duress—but who would not have objected if others were to do so; who for entire generations had raised their children on the myth of ritual murder; who just before the outbreak of the war would have welcomed the exodus of the Jews from Poland to Madagascar;[1] who during the war viewed the burning ghetto with a feeling of schadenfreude and later protested the trials of the perpetrators of the Kielce pogrom; and who looked on the antisemitic events of March 1968 with enthusiasm. For forty-five years they worked diligently to erase all traces of the presence of Jews in Polish history, tradition, and culture by digging up gravestones from Jewish cemeteries to use as paving stones, demolishing synagogues that had survived, and falsifying textbooks. He is a new mutation of a genetic code formed hundreds of years ago in the Vistula river basin.

The Majority of Majorities

The subspecies *Homo Jedvabicus* comprises some 60 percent of all Poles, according to public opinion surveys conducted right up to 10 July.

---

[1] The Madagascar Plan was a plan for removing the Jewish population and resettling it on the island of Madagascar. Before the outbreak of World War II it was discussed, but not implemented, by politicians in Poland and also other countries of east-central Europe.

That's how many opposed any apologies for the crime in Jedwabne because they were not, after all, its perpetrators; because it was not entirely clear whether the Poles themselves committed the crime, whether they did so under duress, or even whether the Jews themselves were not in fact to blame. This type is united with the true Pole only by language—more or less correct Polish. What divides them is almost everything else: sensibility, knowledge, the format of the psyche, attitude toward the history of the state and the nation. *Homo Jedvabicus* is characterized by spinelessness, hypocrisy, an ostrichlike inclination to stick one's head in the sand, a hysterical fear of unpleasant truths, and an inability to cope with the challenge of shattering the myth of Poles as suffering and heroic during the Second World War. His key features are procrastination, cowardliness, prevarication, a false conception of national solidarity, and an absence of the survival instinct. And above all stupidity. The tragedy of Jedwabne, which sixty years after the fact could have become a national catharsis and an occasion for correcting Poland's record in the international marketplace of the conscience, has become merely the latest display of Polish failure.

Homo Jedvabicus appears in several variants: common, educated, and decision-making. The common, popular *Homo Jedvabicus* organized a collection on the Internet for another, larger barn in which "the rest would fit"; told jokes about how Czesław Niemen would sing at the memorial ceremony;[2] sent obscene letters to Leon Kieres, the president of the Institute of National Memory (who took seriously his mission of searching out the truth about Jedwabne); rejoiced over the results of the exhumations, which unearthed "barely" three hundred victims; and during the ceremony blasted the Bratanków' record "because he's in his own home and can do as he likes."[3]

The educated *Homo Jedvabicus* put every word of *Neighbors* under a magnifying glass, searching out errors; wrote stacks of "anti-Gross" tracts dictated by the national interest; proposed an apology to the Indians of Texas (aroused by a suddenly acquired deep knowledge of the subject) in the columns of the serious right-wing press; brought charges against Gross in the name of the Polish nation; supported the movement for the defense of the Good Name of Jedwabne; constructed Nativity scenes and Easter displays "on the theme";[4] and persuaded

[2] Czesław Niemen (1939–) is one of the most popular singers of jazz and pop music in postwar Poland. His career and popularity can be compared to that of the British group the Beatles.

[3] The Bratanków are a Polish pop group.

[4] In April 2001 Father Henryk Jankowski, in his parish church of Saint Brygida in Gdańsk, constructed a special Easter display, which was a replica of the charred barn of Jedwabne decorated with the slogans "Jews killed Jesus, the prophets, and also perse-

workers from Łomża to block the road to the village on the day of the ceremony.

Homo Jedvabicus with the power to make decisions started a heated argument over the wording of the memorial plaque and lied about the consultations with the Jewish side; as a result the new version was unacceptable to Yad Vashem, which therefore did not send representatives to the memorial service. He tried to divert attention from Jedwabne with the hasty construction of a plaque memorializing Poles who rescued Jews, which he had not managed to accomplish during the previous fifty-five years,[5] and he did not see anything inappropriate in the fact that the mass for the victims was held in a church that housed an antisemitic bookstore.[6] He managed the schedules of government representatives and local authorities so that the president of the Podlasie regional *sejmik*, who was obligated to attend a convention of heads of regional government, could not participate even if he had wanted to; nor could any of the ministers (foreign minister Władysław Bartoszewski represented not the government but the Council for the Preservation of Monuments of Struggle and Martyrdom). He did not even send a wreath from the prime minister or the Council of Ministers of the Polish Republic. Last but not least, he lost the seven-part documentary film *Polanyah*, on the thousand-year history of the Jews in Poland, in "interdepartmental coordination." Israel gave the film to Poland in May as part of a governmental agreement. It was to have been broadcast on Polish television before 10 July.

Our Inferno

On the question of Jedwabne, the failures and cardinal tactical errors of the ruling variety of *Homo Jedvabicus* will be the most politically sensitive for Poland, both in the international arena and for the right-wing camp. The influential Wiesenthal Center is spreading its criticism of the Polish government's "evasive refusal to name the perpetrators of

---

cuted us" and "Poles save Poland." He was ordered by his superior, Bishop Tadeusz Gocłowski, to dismantle the display.

[5] The plaque memorializing Poles who rescued Jews was erected in the Church of All Saints in Warsaw, which is the new main forum of the Committee to Remember Polish Rescuers of Jews (Komitet dla Upamiętnienia Polaków ratujących Żydow). Prof. Tomasz Strzembosz is the chairman of the Historical Commission of the Committee.

[6] The mass for the victims was held on 27 May 2001 in the Church of All Saints in Warsaw. Until the summer of 2001 the bookstore of the church had on sale various kinds of antisemitic literature, a situation that was condemned by members of the liberal clergy and by journalists.

the murder by their names" around the world. The residents of Jedwabne are as far as they can possibly be from feeling gratitude for the big money they received for the plots that were expropriated around the site of the memorial, for the resurfaced roads and the park in the marketplace, which they received as a present on the occasion of the construction of the memorial. They see the stepped-up police presence not as an improvement in their security but as the pacification of Jedwabne. They were captivated, however, by President Kwaśniewski's handshakes and his "Come to me," directed to the people whose path to the podium was blocked by the BOR and the UOP.[7] Politicians of the right had no chance to make such endearing gestures because they were not in Jedwabne. Their position was represented by one Bubel.[8]

Back in January, Stanisław Krajewski, a prominent figure in the Polish Jewish community, made this appeal in *Wprost*: "We must support the residents of Jedwabne, prepare them for the burden of the tragedy. The truth must be solemnly acknowledged and the victims must be honored. Let this be done in such a way that they will write about it in newspapers around the world and show it on CNN, with the president, the primate, and the prime minister in attendance." Only half—the worse half—of this call was fulfilled. No one prepared the residents of Jedwabne to measure up to the burden of history, and only those on the margins of the Polish political scene supported them—with irritating smugness. The full acknowledgment of the truth—the inscription on the plaque—was not accomplished, and few on the Polish and Christian side paid homage to the victims of the Jedwabne slaughter: a dozen or so delegates of the UW and the SLD,[9] superiors of the evangelical church, a couple of nuns, and a few hundred private citizens. The memorial service was shown on CNN and several other stations, including Czech television, and hundreds of newspapers and news agencies around the world reported on it, but neither the primate nor the prime minister joined the president, which some in the world media interpreted as a boycott. The Polish episcopate had earlier organized a separate service, the prime minister took part in a related con-

[7] BOR is an acronym for Biuro Ochrony Rządu (The Security Office of Government), and UOP, which has ceased to exist (it was replaced by the Agency of Internal Security [Agencja Bezpieczeństwa Wewnętrznego]), is an acronym for Urząd Ochrony Państwa (The Office of State Security).

[8] Leszek Bubel is a marginal politician representing the extreme right-wing nationalistic position. He is one of the leading members of the Committee to Defend the Good Name of Jedwabne and the author of antisemitic brochures.

[9] UW—Unia Wolnósi (Union of Freedom), the main liberal party in Poland. SLD—Sojusz Lewicy Demokratycznej (Alliance of the Democratic Left), the postcommunist grouping, which since 2002 has formed the majority of the government.

cert, and the Jewish congregation in Warsaw organized a ceremony in the synagogue four days before that. The Jewish and Polish tragedy of sixty years ago could not bring people together. The Jedwabne barn burned a second time in the flames of the Polish inferno, and *Homo Jedvabicus* looked on with no pangs of conscience.

. . . . .

Jerzy Slawomir Mac is a journalist who formerly wrote for *Wprost*. He is well known for his writings about a variety of challenging social and political issues, such as Polish-Jewish relations and the mafia in postcommunist Poland.

PART III

OFFICIAL STATEMENTS

INTRODUCTION

> I do not fear the return of communism, but there is a
> danger of new conflicts between chauvinism and
> nationalist extremism on the one hand and tolerance,
> liberalism, and Christian values on the other.
> —Władysław Bartoszewski on being awarded the
> Heinrich Heine prize, December 1996

> We express our pain and shame, we give expression to our
> determination in seeking to learn the truth, our courage in
> overcoming an evil past, our unbending will for under-
> standing and harmony. Because of this crime we should
> beg the shadows of the dead and their families for forgive-
> ness. Therefore, today, as a citizen and as the president
> of the Polish Republic, I apologize. I apologize in the name
> of those Poles whose conscience is moved by that crime.
> In the name of those who believe that we cannot be proud
> of the magnificence of Polish history without at the same
> time feeling pain and shame for the wrongs that
> Poles have done to others.
> —Aleksander Kwaśniewski, 10 July 2001

I N THE YEARS FOLLOWING the collapse of the Communist political system, Poland appeared to have achieved a degree of political stability based on the emergence of two camps: one derived
from the Solidarity movement, sometimes called the post-Solidarity
camp, and the other derived from the former Polish United Workers'
Party, now transformed more or less convincingly into a Social Democratic Party of the Western European type. Commentators have
stressed the ideological differences between these two. Thus, according
to Hubert Tworzecki, "Poland is achieving political stabilization rooted
in the development of general political 'tendencies' among the mass
public. The Left is partly economic, partly ideological, combining those
longing for the security of the old system with those who once served
it. The Right is almost entirely ideological in character, united by anti-
Communism and traditionalism."[1] Janusz Reykowski has argued that
two concepts of democracy have developed in post-Communist Poland. One sees the democratic system as primarily concerned with en-

[1] *Parties and Politics in Post-1989 Poland*, (London, 1996).

suring its citizens the greatest amount of freedom; the other sees democracy as primarily concerned with providing them the greatest possible security. Those who favor the first concept see the present social-economic situation above all in terms of the opportunities it affords, while those who favor the second are preoccupied with the dangers inherent in it.

In fact, the two "camps" that have held power in post-Communist Poland have had as much in common as they had dividing them.[2] The post-Communists have upheld the pro-capitalist reforms initiated in 1989 and have basically followed the policies of their predecessors, who were ostensibly more ideologically committed to these reforms. Both groups are committed to maintaining a pluralistic and democratic political system and to Polish integration into NATO and the European Union.

The real division in post-Communist Poland, as Jerzy Szacki, professor of sociology at the University of Warsaw, has pointed out, has been between "liberals" and "populists."[3] The liberals have taken the capitalist West as a model, support "Europeanization," and favor the free market and free competition. The "populists" highlight the negative consequences of unfettered free markets and Europeanization. They tend to oversimplified and demagogic solutions and make use of concepts such as "the people," "the majority," "ordinary people," and "working people," whose interests are clearly at odds with those of the elite (in Polish, *góra*). They mistrust career politicians and existing political institutions and are inclined to believe in conspiracy theories of history. This polarization was evident in the parliamentary elections of September 2001, when two "populist" parties, the Liga Polskich Rodzin (League of Polish Families) and Przymierze Samoobrona (Self-Defense Alliance) together gained nearly 25 percent of the seats in the lower house.

This division was also evident in the reactions of different parts of the political spectrum to the Jedwabne debate. The "liberal" sections of both the post-Solidarity and post-Communist camps reacted strongly to the revelations, calling for a full investigation and an apology. This was the position, for instance, of President Alexander Kwaśniewski, of Foreign Minister Władysław Bartoszewski, of Jacek Kuroń, a key figure in the Unia Wolności, and, with some qualifications, of Prime Minister Jerzy Buzek. Their responses differ somewhat in tone,

[2] The post-Solidarity camp was in power from 1989 to 1993 and again between 1997 and 2001; the post-Communist camp was thus in power between 1993 and 1997 and returned to office in September 2001.

[3] *Polityka*, 14 December 1996.

from Bartoszewski's explanation to an American audience of the steps that will be taken to investigate the massacre in Jedwabne and commemorate it, to Kwaśniewski's moving attempt to come to terms with the difficult truth. We reproduce their views in this section.

A detailed study of the views of twenty leading politicians, representing all opinions except those of the extreme right and left, has been undertaken by Janina Frentzel-Zagórska of the Polish Academy of Sciences. Her conclusions are rather optimistic:

> Compared with rank-and-file Poles, the leading politicians were much more willing to admit the Poles' role in the crime and completely unwilling to put all the blame on the Germans (as did more than one-third of the sample polled by CBOS [The Social Opinion Research Center]).[4] Neither did thay reject the idea of an apology outright (only two did compared with half of the representative national sample) although they had indirectly and delicately expressed reservations. The defensive apologetic attitude so often attributed to the Poles was absent.[5]

It may be that on this issue, the political elite is rather more enlightened than the population as a whole. Some, like the historian Tomasz Szarota, have even claimed that the publication of *Neighbors* and the subsequent controversy was, at least in part, responsible for the successes of populism in recent months in Poland. Asked in an interview, reprinted in part 6 of this volume, with *Tygodnik Powszechny* what effect the debate has had on Polish consciousness, he replied:

> In connection with the debate about Jedwabne, *Wprost* laid out all our sins vis-à-vis the Ukrainians, the Germans, the Jews. It was all true, but our society is not yet ready for this truth, even if the intellectual elite is of a different opinion. For to stand face-to-face with this truth, we need to have a healthy, levelheaded consciousness of our virtues and vices, of the heroic pages in our history and of our offenses and even crimes. But we are too deeply entrenched in our complexes.

When asked what complexes he was referring to, he replied:

> Our national megalomania is, in its essence, the result of a negative stereotype of ourselves, of our lack of national pride. This has been confirmed by sociological research. In our opinion, Jews and Germans possess characteristics that we lack. We wish to be enter-

[4] CBOS Report, 6 April 2001.
[5] Janina Frentzel-Zagórska, "Leading Politicians on Jedwabne," *Polish Sociological Review* 1, 137 (2002): 135.

prising, tidy, and so on. Unless we are able to free ourselves of these complexes, our nation will continue to be xenophobic. To live in harmony with others, one must believe in one's own worth. Yet the debate about Jedwabne has had the consequence that Poles have confirmed in themselves what they already felt—a sense of shame. I am not certain whether the support for the League of Polish Families in the last election was not at some level a perverse reaction to the debate, during which—at least this was how it was understood by a section of society—there was an attempt to persuade us that we "are in the same wagon of shame as the Germans."

Let us hope that this is too pessimistic a judgment. One reason for a more tempered optimism is the impressive way the Institute of National Memory—the body set up by the government to investigate all cases of the abuse of human and national rights in Poland since 1939— has functioned. It has been largely impervious to political pressures, and its leadership has been both statesmanlike and courageous. The results of its investigation were published at the end of October 2002. This was a large document of two volumes (around 1,500 pages). It is fully documented and contains selections from the proceedings of the court cases concerning the massacres in Radziłów and Jedwabne, as well as several hundred comprising testimony concerning the events. It should place the investigation of the massacre in Jedwabne on a more fruitful path. It is also to be hoped that it will shortly be available in English. A brief preliminary report, included among the selections below, was issued on 9 July. Also included in this section is an account by University of Warsaw professor Andrzej Rzepliński of the investigation of the court cases of 1949 and 1954 that he has undertaken on behalf of the IPN.

Living in Truth: Special Statement by Prime Minister Jerzy Buzek regarding the Slaughter of Jews in Jedwabne in 1941, April 2001

T HE SLAUGHTER sixty years ago in Jedwabne of Polish Jews, our fellow citizens, is terrifying in its savagery. Our duty is to honor the victims in a dignified way and to establish the truth. The investigation that is being conducted by the Institute of National Memory will establish the particular circumstance of the crime and identify its perpetrators. As a nation we can live only in truth. The participation of Poles in the crime in Jedwabne is indisputable; it isn't questioned by any respectable historian.

The slaughter in Jedwabne was not committed in the name of the nation, or in the name of the Polish state. Poland was at the time an occupied country. Yet if as a nation we have the right to be proud of those Poles who sheltered Jews at the risk of their own lives, then we must also acknowledge the guilt of those who took part in their slaughter.

We are ready to confront even the darkest facts of our history, but in the spirit of truth—without seeking presumed justifications. We will not, however, agree to have the Jedwabne event serve to popularize false theses about Poland's complicity in the Holocaust or about inborn Polish antisemitism.

I want to say that the crime committed in Jedwabne sixty years ago cannot inculpate all of the town's current inhabitants. I believe that we will find these people to be our allies in our quest for truth and reconciliation.

．　．　．　．　．

Jerzy Buzek was prime minister of Poland from 1997 to 2001. He was born in 1940 to a Lutheran family. During the 1980s he was one of the cofounders of the underground Solidarity movement in Silesia and in the 1990s was one of the coauthors of the economic program of the right-wing bloc Akcja Wyborcza Solidarność (Electoral Action Solidarity, AWS).

Address Delivered by Władysław Bartoszewski,
Polish Minister of Foreign Affairs,
Holocaust Memorial Museum
in Washington, D.C., 5 April 2001

Mr. Chairman,
Ladies and Gentlemen,
Dear Friends,
I am starting in this way because I see only friendly people in this hall.
I think the unfriendly ones have simply stayed home. The authors of
the anonymous letters I often receive regard me as a Jew. They think
that that is a way to offend me, but it isn't. I wonder why they do it.
Do they want to show that there are some vigilant individuals who
classify the views of others according to origin? Apparently that's how
things must be—not only in totalitarian systems.

Those who know me realize that I regard all people as friends regardless of their origin or religion. That does not mean that in practice
I equally love all Jews or all Poles. But I do equally love all decent
people. If I am convinced someone is decent, then the genealogy of his
grandmother or great-grandmother is something of secondary importance to me.

Ladies and Gentlemen, when the program of my official visit to the
United States, whose main points were to be meetings with Mr. Powell
and Ms. Rice, was being arranged, I made a special effort to have the
opportunity for at least a short meeting at the Holocaust Memorial
Museum. I attach tremendous importance to this meeting. More than
one long lecture could be delivered on the problems of common interest to us. Unfortunately, this is not possible at present. A book in English (*Thou Shalt Not Kill: Poles on Jedwabne*, published by Więź) has
recently come out in Poland. It has been laid out in the lobby and everyone is welcome to help themselves to a copy. It contains a cross-
section of voices and views on topics that greatly interest us, and which
pertain to the events revealed at Jedwabne. The texts contained in this
book run only as far as early April, but the discussion in Poland continues. We simply did not want to delay publishing the book. I wish to
call your attention to the fact that it contains the words of professional
historians, journalists, and random individuals, as well as a Catholic

archbishop and Jewish activists. It is prefaced by one of the most distinguished of Warsaw Jews—Prof. Israel Gutman of Jerusalem.

In a moment, Mr. Andrzej Przewoźnik, secretary-general of the Council for the Protection of Monuments to Struggle and Martyrdom, will acquaint you with the investigation now being conducted by the proper judicial and historical authorities. He will also present a project to commemorate the tragedy of Jedwabne that has already been approved. Before he takes the floor, however, I should like to say the following.

First of all, on 26 February I had the opportunity to converse privately with the pope for forty-five minutes. I raised the issue of Jedwabne because I regard it as very important. He listened to my remarks and opinions with interest. He indicated that he was anxious for the commemoration to be timeless in nature, so that it would still be relevant fifty and a hundred years from now. The supreme pontiff conceives of fratricide, crime, and suffering in universal biblical terms. The pope's closest associates told me on that day that of all his trips, his visit to Jerusalem had made the biggest impression upon him. And that impression has remained with him.

The Catholic world now numbers a billion people worldwide. It is important to have such an ally, even though not everyone listens to him with equal attentiveness.

Secondly, I wish to allude to a matter of a completely different kind. I should not like it to be forgotten that it was Poland that put on trial and justly executed such criminals as Hoess, the commandant of Auschwitz; Greiser, the Gauleiter of western Poland, whose territorial jurisdiction included the Łódź ghetto; Biebow, the executioner of the Łódź ghetto; Goeth, the executioner of the Kraków ghetto; and Stroop, the executioner of the Warsaw ghetto. Crimes did get prosecuted and a great many collaborators ended up in jail. But that wasn't sufficiently written up or publicized. The principle then in force was that one could write only about Nazi Germany but not about other perpetrators. That was the prevailing principle in the Poland of that period—a Poland which was not of our making!

But one should take into account the fact that in 1949, those who had committed crimes in certain localities, including Jedwabne, and had fallen into the hands of the police, did go on trial. Public opinion was not informed of that fact, however. Newspapers did not write about it on their front or even second pages. That is not to say, however, that no one was interested. But the moral and educational lessons were not drawn therefrom and everything got put away in archives. Only once we were free could a true discussion get under way.

Ladies and Gentlemen, those of us Poles who helped Jews under Nazi occupation were afraid at that time of certain Poles. What we were doing was certainly not written on our faces. A uniformed German walking down the street could not know it, but a Polish neighbor could. That neighbor could have been a normal, decent person, but he might also have been a traitor. That does not mean that Poles are evil. There have always been honest and dishonest people. Is it not strange that for entire decades in Poland the attitudes of those who had acted decently were not fully appreciated? Only recently did Poland's parliament extend World War II veterans' privileges to those who had rescued others at the risk of their own lives. Earlier, that had been the case only in Jerusalem. It was there, not in Warsaw or Kraków, that righteous Poles were honored. It was therefore not surprising that nothing was said about postwar court trials, when certain matters were not to be raised in public at all.

The truth can come out only under the conditions of freedom and democracy. The truth cannot be discussed under the conditions of a totalitarian system. It is striking that only recently have hundreds of names of people from Ukraine, Russia, and Belarus been added to the list of Righteous Among the Nations. Only now can such people be located and their honest and brave deeds be identified. That was not possible when the Soviet Union was in existence. And yet those people had lived and been among us all along. On 28 October 1963, when I planted my tree in Jerusalem, there were only some thirty Polish trees there. Now there are about six thousand, and each tree often symbolizes a family of three or four. Thus at least ten thousand people were involved.

Ladies and Gentlemen, I believe in God, our common God. That God once said that Sodom would be saved if ten righteous people could be found. They could not be found there and then. But thousands of righteous individuals have been found in other infernal situations—and that is no small number. But, on the other hand, just ten unrighteous people are enough to deface the picture of beautiful, noble deeds. Today we must therefore consider how to transform that terrible evil, that crime, into good, how to bring home to people that they have choices no matter what confronts them.

Ladies and Gentlemen, let us follow the example of Americans who have grappled for years on end with the problem of wartime abuses in Vietnam. They have made films and written books about the crimes; they themselves have written about it, about their young soldiers. They have torn open their wounds for the sake of their nation's health. That is the proper attitude to have. That is why America is regarded as a great country. If America had denied, negated, and lied, nobody would have considered it a great country.

I wish my own small country such moral greatness!

. . . . .

Władysław Bartoszewski was born in 1922 and is a writer, historian, and diplomat. He has twice been foreign minister of Poland (in 1995 and between 2000 and 2001). He is president of the Polish-Israel Society and president of the Polish PEN Club. He has been awarded honorary doctorates by Baltimore Hebrew College (1984), the University of Wrocław (1996), and the University of Marburg (2001). He was granted the medal and title of the Righteous Among the Nations by Yad Vashem in Jerusalem in 1963 and is an honorary citizen of the state of Israel. Among his many books are *Warszawski pierścień śmierci* (Warsaw death ring 1939–1944), 2d ed. (Warsaw, 1970); (with Z. Lewin), *The Blood Shed Unites Us: Pages from the History of Help to the Jews in Occupied Poland* (Warsaw, 1970); *Los Żydów Warszawy 1939–1943* (The fate of the Jews of Warsaw, 1939–1943) (Warsaw, 1983); and *Warto być przyzwoitem: szkic do pamiętnika* (It is worthwhile being decent: A sketch for a memoir) (Paris, 1986).

Address by President of Poland
Aleksander Kwaśniewski at the Ceremonies
in Jedwabne Marking the Sixtieth Anniversary
of the Jedwabne Tragedy on 10 July 2001

S IXTY YEARS AGO, on 10 July 1941, on this land, then conquered and occupied by the Hitlerite Germans, a crime was committed against the Jews. It was a terrible day. A day of hatred and brutality. We know much about this crime, though still not everything. It may be that we shall never know the whole truth. That, however, has not stopped us from being here today. To speak with full voice. We know enough to be able to stand in truth—in the face of the pain, the screams, and the suffering of those who were murdered here, before the families of the victims present here today, before the judgment of our own conscience. It was a criminal act. Nothing justifies it. Among the victims, among those burned, there were women, there were children. The terrifying screams of the people locked in the barn and burned alive continue to haunt the memory of those who were witnesses to the crime. The victims were powerless and defenseless. The criminals had a feeling of immunity because the German occupiers encouraged such actions. We know with certainty that among the persecutors and perpetrators there were Poles. We cannot have any doubt that here in Jedwabne, citizens of the Polish Republic perished at the hands of other citizens of the Republic. People prepared this fate for people, neighbors for neighbors.

Back then, sixty years ago, they wanted to wipe Poland off the map of Europe. There were no Polish authorities in Jedwabne. The Polish ' state was not in a position to safeguard its citizens against a slaughter that was carried out with the consent of the Hitlerites and inspired by them. But the Polish Republic should endure in Polish hearts and minds. And its citizens were constrained, should have been constrained, by the norms of a civilized state—a state with centuries-long traditions of tolerance and the peaceful coexistence of various nations and religions. Those who took part in the roundup, who beat and killed people, who kindled the flames, thus committed a crime not only with respect to their Jewish neighbors; they are also guilty vis-à-vis the Republic, vis-à-vis its great history and splendid traditions.

We stand on tormented land. The name of Jedwabne, tragic to its current inhabitants, by a decree of fate has become a byword summoning the demons of fratricide in human memory. It is not only in Jedwabne that superstitious prejudices were fanned into a murderous flame of hatred in the "epoch of the ovens." Responsibility for the death, the harm, and the suffering visited upon the Jews of Jedwabne, as well as upon those of Radziłów and other localities, rests with the perpetrators and their inspirers. It is impermissible to speak of collective guilt, burdening the inhabitants of any town or nation with guilt. Every individual is accountable only for his own actions. Sons do not inherit the guilt of their fathers. But are we permitted to say: that was long ago, these were other people? A nation is a community. A community of individuals, a community of generations. And therefore we must look truth in the eye. Every truth. Say it was thus, it happened. Our consciences will be clean if, when remembering those days, we always retain in our hearts a horror and moral outrage. We are here to perform a collective examination of conscience. We honor the victims, and we say: never again. Today let us all be inhabitants of Jedwabne. Let us feel as they do. Let us remain with them in the feeling of grief, despair, shame, and solidarity. Cain, after all, could have killed Abel anywhere. Every community could have been subjected to a similar test. A test of evil but also of goodness. Of baseness but also of nobility. He who is able to show compassion in the face of human suffering is righteous. How many Poles—also inhabitants of the surrounding area, also from Jedwabne—merit the name of righteous. Let us remember them all today with the greatest gratitude and highest regard.

Thanks to the great national debate around this crime of the year 1941, much has changed in our lives in this year 2001, the first of the new millennium. Today's Poland has the courage to look in the eye the truth about the nightmare that darkened one of the chapters of her history. We have come to realize that we are responsible for our attitude toward the black pages of history. We have understood that those who counsel the nation to deny this past serve the nation ill. Such an attitude leads to moral self-destruction. We are gathered here, together with all the people of our country who have sensitive consciences, together with the secular and religious moral authorities that strengthen our attachment to basic values, revering the memory of the murdered and expressing our deepest sympathy because of the baseness of the perpetrators of this murder. We express our pain and shame; we give expression to our determination in seeking to learn the truth, our courage in overcoming an evil past, our unbending will for understanding and harmony. Because of this crime we should beg the shadows of the dead and their families for forgiveness. Therefore, today, as a citizen and as the president of the Polish Republic, I apologize. I apologize in the name of those Poles whose conscience is moved by that crime. In the name of those who believe that we cannot be proud of the magnificence of Polish history without at the same time feeling pain and shame for the wrongs that Poles have done to others.

I desire with all my heart that the name of this town should not only remind us of the crime, but that it should also become a sign of a great examination of conscience, that it should become a place of reconciliation. The Polish bishops prayed on 27 May "for all those harboring aversion and rancor toward the Jewish people, that they might accept the grace of a change of heart." Those words express well the feelings of the vast majority of Poles. Let that change take place! Let us seek it out! The tragedy that unfolded here cannot be undone. The evil cannot be wiped away, the suffering forgotten. The truth about what happened cannot fix what happened. The truth does not possess that power. But only the truth—even the most burning, painful truth—will allow the cleansing of memory's wound. That is our hope. That is why we are here. Today we offer words of grief and bitterness not only because that is what simple human decency requires. And not because others expect it of us, not because it will bring satisfaction to the victims, not because the world is listening. We utter these words because that's exactly how we feel. Because it is we ourselves who need them most. We do this in order to be better, stronger in a moral sense, free of aversions, anger, and hatred. To respect mankind and love people. To turn evil into goodness.

· · · · ·

Aleksander Kwaśniewski is president of Poland. He was born in 1954 and began his political career in 1977 as a member of Polish United Workers' Party (PZPR). Between 1991 and 1995 he served as a chairman of the reformed communist party Sojusz Lewicy Demokratycznej (Democratic Left Alliance, SLD). He was first elected president of Poland in 1995 and was reelected in 2000.

Findings of Investigation S 1/00/Zn into the Murder of Polish Citizens of Jewish Origin in the Town of Jedwabne on 10 July 1941, pursuant to Article 1 Point 1 of the Decree of 31 August 1944

I N THE ANALYSIS of the body of evidence collected in the course of investigation S 1/00/Zn, the probable course of events on 10 July 1941 in Jedwabne has been established.

On that day, a Thursday morning, the inhabitants of nearby villages began to arrive in Jedwabne with the intention of participating in the premeditated murder of the Jewish inhabitants of that town. On the evening preceding the events, some Jewish residents were warned by Polish acquaintances that a collective action was being prepared against the Jews.

In the morning hours of 10 July 1941, the Jewish population began to be forced out of their homes and gathered at the market square. They were ordered to pluck grass from between the cobblestones that paved the square. Acts of violence were committed against those who were gathered. Residents of Jedwabne and its environs, of Polish nationality, committed these acts.

Numerous witnesses who have been questioned state that uniformed Germans arrived at Jedwabne on that day. Those Germans, who were probably a small group, assisted in driving the victims to the marketplace, and their active role was limited to this. It is unclear, in the light of the evidence collected, whether the Germans took part in escorting the victims to the place of mass murder, and whether they were present at the barn. Witness testimonies vary considerably on this question.

A group of the Jewish men gathered at the marketplace were forced to break apart the Lenin monument that stood outside the marketplace at a small square on the road leading to Wizna. Next, at about noon, this group was ordered to carry a fragment of the broken bust to the marketplace and then to carry it to the barn, using a wooden stretcher. The group may have consisted of forty to fifty people. It included the local rabbi and the kosher butcher. The manner in which the victims belonging to that group were slain has not been established, but their bodies were thrown into the grave dug inside the barn. Parts of the shattered Lenin bust were thrown onto the corpses in the grave.

The other, larger group of Jewish people was led out of the market after one or one and a half hours, as one witness stated. Other witnesses indicated that it was in the late afternoon. This group included several hundred people, probably about three hundred. This is confirmed by the number of victims in the two graves, according to the estimate of the archaeological and anthropological team participating in the exhumation.

This group consisted of victims of both sexes of various ages, including children and infants. These people were led into a wooden, thatched barn owned by Bronisław Śleszyński. After the building had been closed, it was doused, probably with kerosene from the former Soviet warehouse.

It should be noted that individual murders had been committed before the people were led out from the market. These killings were mentioned by, among others, the victim Awigdor Kochaw, who was at the market square at the time.

The incomplete scope of the exhumations, and the impossibility of verifying the hypothesis that a grave or collective graves exist at the Jewish cemetery, prevent us from determining conclusively the total number of individuals murdered on the day of the events in Jedwabne.

The number of victims established in the course of the investigation may be substantiated only upon receipt of the expected record of the interrogation of witnesses and the data from the archives in Israel.

The figure of 1,600 victims or so seems highly unlikely and was not confirmed in the course of the investigation. On the day of the crime, people of Jewish origin from Wizna and Kolno, among other places, were certainly in Jedwabne seeking shelter. Nevertheless, a certain group of Jewish people survived. It may be assumed that there were at least several dozen people who lived in the town and its vicinity after the date of the crime until the end of 1942. At that time Germans liquidated the small ghettos by removing their inhabitants to larger groupings.

Several witnesses assert in their testimony that Germans took photographs of the events in Jedwabne. In addition, it has been speculated that the crime was documented on film. This hypothesis, however, has not been sufficiently substantiated.

As to the participation of the Polish population in the crime, we should accept that it played a decisive role in the execution of the criminal plan.

It may be assumed that the massacre in Jedwabne was inspired by the Germans. The presence of German military policemen from the police station at Jedwabne and other uniformed Germans (assuming that they were present at the place of the events), though passive, was tantamount to consent to and tolerance of the crime against the Jewish inhabitants of the town. Therefore it should be stated that, in terms of criminal law, it is justifiable to ascribe responsibility *sensu largo* for that crime to the Germans.

The perpetrators of the crime *sensu stricto* were Polish inhabitants of Jedwabne and its environs—at least forty men. On the basis of archival materials from the criminal trials in 1949 and 1953 and other evidence verified in the course of the current investigation, it should be assumed that these men actively participated in committing the murder and were armed with sticks, crowbars, and other tools. The acts ascribed to them as a result of the current investigation have the characteristics of the crime with no statutory limitation described in Article 1 point 1 of the Decree of 31 August 1944, which provides that "he who, assisting the authorities of the German State . . . , participated in committing murders" is subject to a life sentence. Some of the forty people named as perpetrators in the case files were adjudged, and the judgments are final and binding. In the course of the present investigation, sufficient evidence to identify and charge those perpetrators who are still alive has not been found.

On the basis of the evidence gathered in the investigation, it is not possible to determine the reasons for the passive behavior of the majority of the town's population in the face of the crime. In particular, it cannot be determined whether this passivity resulted from acceptance of the crime or from intimidation caused by the brutality of the perpetrators' acts.

Following the commission of the crime, the victims' property was looted. The extent of the pillage and the number of people involved could not be precisely determined.

The utter passivity of part of Jedwabne's population in relation to the crime committed on 10 July 1941 cannot be qualified in terms of criminal law, and therefore cannot be evaluated in terms of ascribing responsibility.

At present, all the activities scheduled to be carried out in this proceeding have been completed. The formal completion of the proceeding will be possible immediately after a reply is received to the request to the State of Israel for legal assistance. The expected data, although relevant for the determination of the minimum number and the identities of the victims of the Jedwabne crime, are not likely to change the findings presented here.

Upon receipt of the expected materials, we plan to issue a resolution to discontinue the investigation as a result of the failure to find perpetrators of the crime other than those already adjudged.

After the investigation has been completed, a decision will be made concerning the pieces of evidence held. They will be donated as museum exhibits.

Radosław J. Ignatiew

PUBLIC PROSECUTOR

DEPARTMENT CHIEF, COMMISSION FOR THE PROSECUTION OF CRIMES AGAINST THE POLISH NATION IN BIAŁYSTOK

9 July 2002

Jedwabne—Let Us Be Silent in the Face of This Crime: Piotr Lipiński Talks with Professor Andrzej Rzepliński

GAZETA WYBORCZA, 22 JULY 2002

PIOTR LIPIŃSKI: At the request of the Institute of National Memory, you have investigated the records of the court cases in which after the war people responsible for the murder of the Jews of Jedwabne were convicted. What emerges from these records?

ANDRZEJ RZEPLIŃSKI: Reading them, one has a feeling of powerlessness in the face of the enormity and apocalyptic character of the crime committed by ordinary unorganized people, and not by the German industrial system for killing the Jews. In my life, I have examined more than fifteen hundred criminal cases and none has made as powerful an impression on me as those connected with Jedwabne.

PL: How did the trial come about?

AL: On 27 December 1947, Całka Migdał, a Jew from Jedwabne, sent from Montevideo a letter to the Central Committee of Jews in Poland [Centralny Komitet Żydów w Polsce, CKŻP][1]—he had emigrated from the town before the war, leaving his family there. He wrote: "We have information that they [the Jews of Jedwabne] died, not at the hands of Germans, but at the hands of Poles. We also know that Poles have not so far been prosecuted for this crime. They live on in the same small town . . . One person from our town, who is today living in Palestine, wrote to us about this matter."

The letter reached the minister of justice. In February 1948, it ordered the prosecutor in the District Court of Łomża to take up the matter. For three weeks nothing was done. In the following three months, nothing occurred of a procedural nature—although probably confidential consultations did occur. The accused were arrested only in January 1949.

---

[1] The Central Committee of Jews in Poland (CKŻP) was a secular Jewish umbrella organization set up in late November 1944. It consisted of Bundist and Communist representatives, and all the factions of the Zionist movement, except for the revisionists. It was recognized as the official representative body of Polish Jewry.

PL: The proceedings were organized by the local security office (UB) in Łomża—those who were convicted in the trial later claimed that they had been beaten. Were their confessions forced?

AR: They were examined by eight UB officials in Łomża. They were very young (the oldest was thirty-one; two were only twenty-one). Most of the accused and the witnesses were examined by a UB cadet, Grzegorz Matujewicz, a Belarusian. These people lacked the requisite qualifications—hardly any of them had completed secondary school. What they knew about was how to beat people up. Ten of the accused complained during the trial that they had been beaten. I do not exclude the possibility that some of the secret policemen—after all, they were members of a criminal organization—struck the accused when they said "hello" or "goodbye." But they didn't do this to extort detailed confessions. The goal of these secret police functionaries was to limit the matter as severely as possible. For instance, when a witness said that in the murder of Jews the following persons took part . . . , the official would write down only one name. When other names were mentioned, he changed the subject.

The largest amount of information was furnished by Bolesław Ramotowski. He gave a list of forty-eight people as alleged perpetrators of the massacre. But he was the first to be examined—afterward the secret policemen clearly discussed the matter among themselves and worked with a smaller list of twenty-three accused. The following day matters were presented in a different way. In addition, most likely those detained discussed among themselves on the first night how they should conduct their defense.

In the investigation, witnesses accused in all more than ninety named individuals of participation in the crime. Most of them were no longer living in Jedwabne or were no longer alive. None of those living was examined, even in the character of a witness.

In accordance with the procedure then in operation, it was not required that the interrogation should commence with providing the accused with an indication of the specific accusation against him. On some occasions, the interrogator himself did not seem to know why a person had been detained. Stefan Kulik, an official of the UB, asked Stanisław Zejer, "Tell me by whom, where and when and why you were arrested." He replied: "I was arrested by an official of the UB on 8 January 1949 in my own home in Jedwabne. I was arrested because I took part, on the orders of Mayor Karolak, in the driving of the Jews into the town square. He was also asked, "In what year did you drive the Jews into the barn?"

Nazi crimes were then subject to criminal prosecution—at most a month was to elapse between the beginning of the accusation and the formulation of a charge. This article of the law of August 1944 allowed accused persons to be brought before a court quickly and had considerable justification. But in this matter, the judge, aware of how little material the prosecution had accumulated after thirteen months of investigation, should have returned the matter to the prosecutor's office with the instruction that in this case the investigation should be extended. (As of the middle of the seventies, 63 cases had been heard in the Białystok District Court in which 95 individuals were sentenced for the murder of Jews.)

PL: The main trial began on 16 May 1949 before the District Court in Łomża. Within two days a verdict was returned. How could a verdict in such a major crime be given in such a short time?

AR: To be frank, I cannot imagine. The court examined in the course of two days (altogether sixteen hours) 22 accused and 56 witnesses: 78 people! In other words, six minutes per person, if one takes into account court procedure, including reading the act of accusation and other documents and the concluding speeches. The judge had a conscious policy of allowing the witnesses to say as little as possible. This was agreed to by the prosecutors, while the defense took the view that this would be in the interest of their clients. The assessors, the prosecutor, and the defense attorneys did not ask any questions. The defense attorneys seem to have believed that if they remained silent, the trial would end more quickly and their clients would probably receive a lenient sentence.

The witnesses as a rule repeated: I know practically nothing. Yet during the investigation, they had made extensive depositions. The large majority of those interrogated in the court were witnesses for the defense—they usually testified that they had seen a particular accused individual away from the scene of the crime. One woman, who had recounted how the accused Jerzy Laudański boasted that he had killed two or three Jews, in the court withdrew this testimony, since, as a resident of Jedwabne, she clearly feared the Laudański family more than the UB.

The first to give his testimony in court was the accused Bolesław Ramotowski. His was one of the longest examinations in the course of the trial—in the court record, it occupies sixteen lines. The whole examination of the remaining accused took the following form: "Gościcki, Wincenty, declared himself not guilty and explained that he had taken no part in the roundup. The court took note of the declaration of the accused."

PL: The witnesses came from Jedwabne?

AR: For the most part. Two Jews from outside the town were called as witnesses—Eliasz Grądowski and Abram Boruszczak—both of whom had found a comfortable niche for themselves after the war. In partnership with some local UB officials and local judges, they "arranged" to provide legal title to those who had acquired property from Jews who had been murdered or who had disappeared. Neither appeared at the hearing, since they had decamped from Białystok to Wałbrzych. The local priest was not cross-examined. He should have been asked at the trial why he had not appeared during the massacre with a crucifix and sprinkler with holy water. He had a good idea how to call a mob to order and then persuade its members to disperse. Poles who saved Jews, like Antonina Wyrzykowska, also did not testify.

The court had a predetermined view in the case of at least three individuals—on the day before the verdict, it ordered two people, who were later found not guilty, to be released, and wrote an opinion on the question of clemency for Karol Bardoń, something that was obligatory in the case of a death sentence. But he was sentenced to death only on the following day. His exculpatory remarks were summarized in three lines. He stated, "On the critical day, I was working in the locksmith's workshop." When his testimony was read out, he added, "I saw only smoke; the driving [to the barn] and burning I did not see."

PL: So what was actually decided in this strange trial?

AR: Marginal matters. The prosecutor hit upon the date of 25 June. But the barn was burned on 10 July; 25 June was the date of the first lynchings and killings—for instance, on that day, the communist Eliasz Krawiecki, known as Elun, a bootmaker, was beaten to death. This date appears in the verdict.

None of those responsible for the prosecution had any idea of the topography of the town. There was no visit to the site of the crime. Apart from arresting the suspects, the officials of the UB, the prosecutors, and the judges could not be bothered to go to Jedwabne. At the trial there was talk of the town square, of certain streets, of driving the Jews, but none of those responsible for investigating the matter bothered to find out what a witness could observe from his or her location. This was exploited by the accused and by witnesses for the defense, who made free with the facts on the question of distance. Thus it was that a distance one could traverse in five minutes would require between twenty and thirty minutes.

There was no exhumation. In this trial, quite simply, there were no victims. The crime consisted in the fact that the inhabitants of Jedwabne and the surrounding areas drove the Jews to the town square and there, for a certain time, kept guard over them. The crime in the trial was limited to this. In the verdict, there is no mention of burning Jews.

PL: Why was so little decided in this trial?

AR: The verdict and its justification are desperately awkward. This was the result not of a lack of competence on the part of the judge but because of his decision to limit the scope of the trial, the number of accused, and the nature of the charges. The chairman of the judges, Antoni Malecki, came from a peasant family in the area and certainly shared the resentments of local people. He is particularly blameworthy. The prosecutors were very young, barely qualified, and typical of those who were responsible for the Stalinist practice of law. But Malecki was a prewar judge, with twenty years' experience. He should have known what to do.

PL: Although death sentences were most frequent in postwar Poland during the Stalinist period, in this case there was only one such verdict.

AR: In the end, ten people were sentenced and twelve found not guilty—of this second group the innocence of several seems extremely doubtful. The sentences ranged from eight years to death. The one capital sentence was imposed on Bardoń, but when he was pardoned by Bierut, this was reduced not to life but to fifteen years. He was sentenced, not for his role in the burning of the Jews, but because he played an active role at the town square—in other words, as an accomplice in a murder. This was in accordance with the law but did not finally amount to the truth. All of those who surrounded the Jews in the town square were accomplices. But what of the individual role, of responsibility? Who drove the Jews to the barn? Who took part in the burning? This was not mentioned in the verdict.

Immediately below the signatures endorsing the verdict, there is a characteristic postscript: ". . . one is obliged to reflect that on the critical day, before the main massacre occurred, there were cases of individual murders of the Jewish population fleeing or trying to escape the roundup, which took place under the eyes of the accused . . . One has to underline that what took place was a mass crime, rarely encountered in human history, in which the victims were defenseless people, numbering 1,500." There follows the signatures of the entire bench of judges. Undoubtedly, this emotional postscript was demanded by one of the assessors, whose conscience and knowledge did not allow him to "settle" [zalatwić] the crime in the lapidary manner of Judge Malecki.

PL: Not every trial in Stalinist Poland diverged from judicial norms. Was the Jedwabne trial a criminal or a political trial?

AR: It was political in the sense that an attempt was made to diminish the significance of the whole matter—some people killed some others, but in the end it is not clear who killed whom and why.

PL: This is the opposite of what we usually think of as a political trial. This trial did not serve to exaggerate the guilt of the accused?

AR: I believe that the decision to limit the scope of the trial was probably taken in the provincial headquarters of the Polish United Workers' Party. Perhaps they feared that if too many people were accused, this would increase their difficulties in retaining control of this area. And the communists certainly had great difficulties. As late as 1948, a unit of the National Military Union [Narodowy Związek Wojskowy] took control of Jedwabne.

A large trial would have no political benefits. There was no way to show that the Germans had killed the Jews in Jedwabne. To accuse a large group of Poles of murdering Jews might result in an international scandal. For in my judgment considerably more than a hundred [*sto kilkadziesiąt*] people should have sat in the dock. In accordance with prewar legislation, all those who were at the town square were accomplices in this crime. It was enough if they stood in the second row as onlookers. Their mere presence meant that the Jews had less chance of escaping and felt more terrorized.

The authorities were certainly not interested in the British or Americans finding the head of the German gendarmerie in Jedwabne in 1941 or the Gestapo official, Schaper, who was roaming around the area with his force. Certainly had they done so, it would have shown that the Germans had inspired the crime and given immunity to those who carried it out, but that they took no physical part themselves. Indeed, the course of events was not what they had wanted, since there were orders to spare Jews whose artisan skills might be necessary for the needs of the front.

PL: Does anything suggest that the decision was taken at a higher level?

AR: The Institute of National Memory investigated the former archive of the Central Committee of the PZPR but did not find anything. No evidence was found either that the investigation department of the Ministry of Public Security concerned itself with the matter—although given the scale of the crime, this ought to have been the case.

PL: We still do not know how many Jews died in Jedwabne. What number was estimated at that time by the court?

AR: It is not at all clear what the position of the court was on this matter. The numbers of 1,200 and of 1,500 murdered Jews appear. But the victims do not appear at all in the trial; their names and surnames are not mentioned. Even when the court had a victim present at the hearing, he was not treated as a victim. Józef (Izrael) Grądowski survived the pogrom with his wife and child. He hid in a pigpen, under a dungheap, for the whole war. His family was murdered by the Germans. Grądowski had a panic fear of revealing who had saved him—in this way he showed his gratitude, taking the view that his silence would protect his rescuer. It is possible it was the local priest, for it seems probable that he and his family were baptized on the day of the pogrom.

This Jew should have been heard first by the court as a victim. In order to give him courage, the accused and the audience should have been removed from the court, to make it easier for him to testify on these terrible matters. But he was pushed into the middle of a crowd of other witnesses, and his testimony was heard in the middle of the trial. Grądowski did not appear in the trial in 1949 as a witness for the prosecution but was used by some of the accused as a witness in their defense. This same Grądowski during the subsequent trial of Józef Sobuta said in 1954 in the course of his evidence: "During the burning of the Jews, a Jewish child escaped from the barn [*szopa*]; a certain Pole saw the child and threw it into the flames . . . I, for my part, have raised a Polish orphan, even though I cannot overlook the wrongs that have been inflicted on me by Poles . . . I heard about the incident of the child from people; I did not see it myself." He constantly changed his testimony, but no one was concerned to find where the truth lay—although his testimony should have been the most important. He also stated that he saw children peering through the legs of the Poles guarding the Jews, who saw everything—these children are certainly alive today and are about sixty-five years old.

PL: What relation does this trial then have with reality?

AR: If I had been a judge of the Supreme Court in September 1949, when the question of an appeal was heard, I would have overturned the verdict and called for the case to be tried again. And today? If one is to go by the strict letter of the law, the procurator general should put forward a motion for the overturning of the case. But in my opinion, this would also be completely unjust, because my deepest conviction is that those ten Poles were rightly convicted, and that for only a small part of what they in fact did. This was after a shockingly mishandled trial—mishandled not because of the lack of technical knowledge, but because of an unwillingness, resulting from antisemitic prejudices, to investigate all aspects of the crime.

. . . . .

Andrzej Rzepliński is a professor of law at the University of Warsaw and a member of the Helsinki Committee. He is an adviser to the president of the Institute of National Memory.

PART IV

THE DEBATE IN THE CATHOLIC CHURCH

INTRODUCTION

We wonder whether Jews should not acknowledge that
they have a burden of responsibility in regard to Poles, in
particular for the period of close cooperation with the Bolsheviks, for complicity in deportations to Siberia, for sending Poles to jails, for the degradation of many of their fellow citizens, etc. The fact that Poles also took part in these
repressions does not exclude the fact that the leading role
was played by officers of the UB [Security Police] of Jewish
descent. This terror lasted until 1956 and a great number of
Poles to this day remain buried under nameless headstones. These victims also need to be considered, as long as
we are speaking about Jews victimized by Poles.
—Cardinal Józef Glemp, 15 May 2001

The case of Jedwabne has become for Poles what one hundred years ago the Dreyfus case was for Frenchmen. Today
the Catholic bishops of Poland spoke out on this case in a
decisive way. It was the voice of the Poland of decent people—above political and religious divisions. A free, democratic, and independent Poland speaking through the
mouths of the bishops.
The bishops declared, "We are deeply grieved by the
actions of those who throughout history, especially in
Jedwabne and other places, caused suffering to
Jews, and caused their deaths." We join the Polish
bishops in this grief.
—*Gazeta Wyborcza*, 27 May 2001

ON THE ISSUE of how to respond to the revelation of the massacre at Jedwabne, the Polish Catholic Church has been
deeply divided. The main position of the Church on Jewish
issues was articulated in the bishops' letter of November 1990, which
is described in the main introduction to this volume, and which was
essentially derived from the 1962 papal encyclical *Nostra Aetate*. Within
the Church, there is a small progressive group, much more strongly
committed to Christian-Jewish reconciliation, that is linked with the
liberal Catholic periodicals *Tygodnik Powszechny*, *Znak*, and *Więź* and
includes people like Father Michał Czajkowski and Father Stanisław
Musiał. At the same time, there is also within the Church a group that

has been described as supporters of the "closed" Church, and that on Polish-Jewish issues tends to adopt a "radical-apologetic" position sometimes tinged with antisemitism. Among its main adherents are Lech Wałęsa's former chaplain, Father Henryk Jankowski; Father Rydzyk, the founder of the conservative Catholic radio station Radio Maryja; and Father Edward Orłowski, the parish priest of Jedwabne. These two groups are sometimes referred to as the "Open" and "Closed" Churches, following the formulation in 1985 of Tadeusz Mazowiecki, then a leading figure of the Solidarity movement and of the Catholic progressive intelligentsia, who was to be the first non-Communist Polish prime minister after 1989. In his view, a major problem was

> ... the question of whether the rendezvous of Polishness and Christianity will be shaped into a kind of Polish-Catholic triumphalism and narrowness or whether it will be a meeting of open Polishness with open Catholicism.[1]

Since the publication of *Neighbors* and the ensuing controversy, the hierarchy has attempted to hold fast to the positions articulated in *Nostra Aetate* and the bishops' letter, while endeavoring, not very successfully, to keep the more anti-Jewish elements under control. It clearly regards as unhelpful the strong attacks mounted on the latter group by the liberals in the Church, which go back at least to Father Musiał's criticism of the hierarchy's halfhearted attempt to discipline Father Jankowski for his antisemitic statements in 1999.

Within the hierarchy, there are also significant differences between the more liberal elements—like Archbishop Życiński, the metropolitan of Lublin, and Archbishop Muszyński, the metropolitan of Gniezno, who have some sympathy for the views of people like Fathers Czajkowski and Musiał—and the primate, Cardinal Glemp, whose views often approximate to those of the "apologists." Archbishop Życiński set out his position in an article characteristically entitled "The Banalization of Barbarity."[2] In it, he argued that the massacre of Jedwabne demonstrated that the barbarism of Nazism could infect those who were not German:

> The drama of Jedwabne bears a bitter lesson of truth about mankind. It is particularly bitter for those who consider the barbarity of Nazism as nothing other than a local variety of genocide, horrifyingly alien to the commendable remainder of humanity. It tran-

[1] On this question, see Janusz Gowin, *Kościół w czasach wolności* (Kraków, 1999), and Joanna Michlic, "The 'Open Church' and the 'Closed Church' and the Discourse on Jews in Poland between 1989 and 2000" (forthcoming).
[2] *Więź*, March 2001.

spires that the truth about human nature is much more complex. The victims of barbarous aggression can easily grow accustomed to it, and end up applying new aggression against the innocent. The spiral of evil knows no ethnic restrictions, and we cannot consider any environment to be immune to the radiation of primitivism. This bitter truth affords protection against ideological delusions whereby some people attempt to extol blood ties or cultural affinities. These values cannot be worshiped as contemporary deities because human susceptibility to evil transcends all the borders of the categories we hold dear.

He concluded by stressing the need for an act of expiation:

Today, we need to pray for the victims of that massacre, displaying the spiritual solidarity that was missing at the hour when they left the land of their fathers. In the name of those who looked upon their death with indifference, we need to repeat David's words, "I have sinned against the Lord,"[3] regardless of whether any protest from the onlookers might have been efficacious in that situation.

Similar views were expressed by Archbishop Muszyński in his interview with *Tygodnik Powszechny* of 25 March 2001, reprinted below. In it, he admitted that "some Polish residents of Jedwabne" were "direct perpetrators of the crime" (the words of the interviewer) and went on to say,

For any crime, it is the direct perpetrator who is answerable; but those who are connected to him by religious or national ties— though they bear no personal guilt—cannot feel themselves to be free of moral responsibility for the victims of this murder.

He referred to the removal of the old monument in Jedwabne as "symbolic of the beginning of the end of the era of falsification, instrumentalization, and the ideologizing of the truth." For this process to continue, Poles, like the pope, would have to ask for forgiveness for "wrongdoing and sins against the Jews." This should take the form of joint participation with Jews in a "community of prayer." Asked by an interviewer about the statement of Rabbi Baker of Jedwabne that the "almost idyllic contacts with his Polish neighbors" were "disturbed primarily around Easter, when the image of the Jew as Christ-killer was evoked in Church teachings," he replied, "I do not question particular facts, but one cannot draw any general conclusions from them . . . as for anti-Judaism: the Church, in the person of the pope,

---

[3] A reference to David's responsibility for the death of Uriah.

has recognized its responsibility for the sins of the past. Since the Council, many excellent documents on the subject of Jews and teachings about Jews have been produced—many of which are still awaiting full recognition."

He concluded:

I express my belief that with such far-reaching spiritual partnership and mutual understanding [between the Polish episcopate the religious representatives of the Jewish community], a proper and dignified way of memorializing this shameful slaughter will be found—as will some form of redress for the evil that was done.

Both Archbishop Życiński and Archbishop Muszyński were much influenced by Michael Schudrich, the American-born rabbi to the Jewish communities of Warsaw and Łódź who played a major role in keeping down the emotional temperature, and who went out of his way to be mindful of Polish sensitivities. In an interview with Bogumił Łoziński and Alina Petrowa-Wasilewicz of the Catholic Information Agency, published in *Rzeczpospolita* on 14 March 2001, he explicitly rejected the concept of collective guilt:

The guilty party in a murder is the person who committed the murder. It is he who should be judged, if not in this world, then certainly in the next, and it would be better for him if it were in this world than the next, for there it will be worse. But there is the Jewish concept of *Eglah Arufa*. Why should the elder of the nearest town pray for the man who perished at the hand of an unknown assailant? It wasn't even in his jurisdiction, and yet, though not guilty, he takes on the responsibility for what has happened. There is a shadow and it falls on everyone. The person who committed murder is individually responsible for the act. However, another person can seek forgiveness and this does not mean he bears the same guilt as the perpetrator.

He stressed the primary responsibility of the Germans for the Holocaust, asserting that "the Holocaust was planned and carried out from beginning to end by the Germans, and representatives of other nations participated," and further argued that Polish antisemitism was neither as strong as Jews sometimes believed nor as marginal a phenomenon as was believed by many in Poland. Asked by his interviewers, "Do you believe that Jews should apologize to the Poles for the sins of their Jewish ancestors?" he responded:

Humans must apologize for every committed wrong. That is also the duty of Jews. We must recognize that we were not only victims, but that we had among us people who wronged others. The

Jews currently must open their eyes wider regarding their own history in the last few decades . . .

We Jews must admit that there were Jews who actively worked for the Communists and even the Hitlerites and who committed crimes against Poles, and also against Jews. They never claimed, however, that they were acting in the name of the Jewish nation. Nonetheless the time has come that if we Jews want the Poles to feel and understand our pain, then we must understand and feel the pain of the Poles.

He also made a number of suggestions as to how the memorial service on the sixtieth anniversary of the massacre could be conducted, calling for joint prayers that would commemorate the victims and lead to a request for their forgiveness.

The primate, Cardinal Glemp, did not rise to the occasion. From the start he ruled out a commemorative service in Jedwabne on the sixtieth anniversary of the massacre. In an interview on Warsaw's Radio Józef on 4 March 2001, in a section entitled, "Politicians Will Not Dictate to the Church," he remarked sarcastically that "toward the end of February, in the course of several days, a number of high-ranking politicians contacted me with virtually identical programs: on such and such day, the Catholic Church should undertake massive prayers in Jedwabne in repentance for the crimes and ask for forgiveness for the genocide, lest we incur anger." (These politicians included Jan Nowak-Jeziorański, Stanisław Krajewski, a prominent figure in Christian-Jewish dialogue in Poland, and presumably the president and the prime minister.) He initially proposed a joint service in Warsaw with representatives of the Jewish community, as had also been suggested by Rabbi Schudrich.

However, the provocative stance he took in his interview on 15 May with the representatives of the Catholic Information Agency, included in this section, made this impossible. In this interview he denied, in contrast to Archbishop Muszyński, that the situation of Jews often worsened during Easter week:

This statement strikes me as improbable. The first time I ever heard about this rise in anti-Jewish feeling was in Mr. Gross's book. Clearly, the book was written "on commission" from someone.

He then went on to make a number of observations on Jews that bordered on antisemitism:

Before the war I had no contact with Jews, because there were very few where I lived. Polish-Jewish conflicts did occur in those times, but they had an economic basis. Jews were cleverer, and they knew how to take advantage of Poles. That, in any case, was the perception. Another cause of dislike for Jews was their pro-Bolshevik attitude. This was a very basic resentment, but it did not stem from religious motives. In Poland before the war, matters of religion did not play any significant role as far as dislike for Jews was concerned. Jews were not liked because of their odd "folk customs." The same sort of dislike based on folk customs can be found today, for example, among fans of different soccer teams in the city of Łódź.[4] Is there any point in looking for religious motives in this?

He then stressed (one might say overstressed) the amount of aid given to Jews during the war, claiming that "we also need to remember that two thousand Poles were executed by German occupying forces precisely because they helped Jews." In fact, according to Israel Gutman's estimate, this number is probably in the "hundreds."[5]

Glemp proceeded to observe:

> I also cannot understand why Poles are unceasingly slandered, especially in the American press, and why we are constantly accused of antisemitism, as though it were somehow different in form from what it is in other countries. In all this Jews continually exhibit their dislike toward Poles. I cannot really understand why they do so. For—in comparison with Europe—Jews had relatively the best situation with us, here in Poland. They felt at home here. Why therefore are there so many unjust accusations today? Think how this hurts Jews who genuinely love Poland and who live in friendship with Poles!

The primate concluded by accusing "Jews" of causing harm to Poles by closely cooperating with the Bolsheviks and by their allegedly prominent role in the Communist secret police. His interview provoked a characteristically sharp response from Father Musiał (reprinted below) in *Gazeta Wyborcza*, which concluded:

> I write these words on Thursday evening, 17 May, and reflect on the feverish preparations for the prayer service in All Saints' Church in Warsaw. About the efforts of "experts in liturgy and subject specialists"—in the words of the primate. And I am beset

---

[4] A reference to the fact that the fans of one of the town's soccer teams refer to those of the other as "kikes" (żydy).

[5] Yisrael Gutman and Shmuel Krakowski, *Unequal Victims: Poles and Jews during World War Two* (New York, 1986), 196. Others have given much higher figures, but these do not seem believable.

by the nagging questions: What did it avail Pius XII that he was surrounded by dozens of subject specialists, nuncios, secretaries, and theologians, if he could not bring himself to utter a few simple words from the heart to condemn the extermination of the Jews and to shout out loud: "This cannot be!" This relativizes the role of experts, though no one would deny that "experts in liturgy and subject specialists" are needed.

It seems to me that the case of Jedwabne, and the moral responsibility that Catholics have incurred toward Jews in history, can be fully stated on half a page of a schoolchild's notebook. One can say simply: "This is the way we were. There is nothing we can say to justify it. We apologize to you and to God for all of this with all our hearts and all our souls. We want to change. We ask you: help us to be better."

That's all. And a large number of penitential psalms.

Although the prayer service took place on 27 May 2001 without Jewish participation (the diplomatic excuse was that it was on the first day of Shavuot), and in the Church of All Saints in central Warsaw, where antisemitic literature was prominently displayed, it turned out much better than could have been anticipated. The church was packed with worshipers, and most of Poland's bishops were also present. Speaking on behalf of the Church, Bishop Stanisław Gądecki said that the Jews were victims of a crime, and that there had been "Poles and Catholics" among the perpetrators. "We are deeply disturbed by the actions of those who caused Jews to suffer and even murdered them in Jedwabne and in other places over the ages." Among the biblical readings were the story of Cain and Abel and the parable of the Good Samaritan. The bishops also prayed for peace in the Middle East. The service concluded with the primate's prayer for the Jewish nation (naród):

God of Abraham, God of the Prophets, God of Jesus Christ, all is contained in You, all is directed toward You, You are the limit of everything. Hear our prayers on behalf of the Jewish nation, which—because of its forefathers—is still very dear to You.

Arouse in this nation unceasingly an ever more lively desire to deepen Your truth and Your love. Aid it, so that in achieving truth and justice, it may reveal to the world the power of Your blessing.

Support it that it may receive the respect and love of all those who do not yet understand the great sufferings that it has undergone, so that they may feel in solidarity a sense of common concern and feel together the wounds that it has suffered. Remember its new generations of young people and children so that they may remain unchangingly true to You, upholding the particular secret of their mission. Strengthen all generations so that thanks to their testimony, humanity will understand that Your redeeming intention encompasses all people and that You, O God, are for all nations the beginning and final goal.[6]

[6] This mass was variously assessed. In an article in *Gazeta Wyborcza* on 9–10 June 2001, Roman Graczyk criticized the hierarchy for failing to rise to the occasion, while in the same issue, Jan Turnau praised the service as an important event in the history of the Polish Catholic Church. Since only the Catholic Church has been discussed in this section, it is perhaps worth mentioning that representatives of the small Protestant denominations in Poland, both Lutheran and Calvinist, took part in various commemorative ceremonies beginning with the mass dedicated to the reconciliation of Christians and Jews that took place in Saint Marcin's Church in Warsaw on 29 March 2001. Neither the Greek Catholic nor the Orthodox Church in Poland has taken part in such acts of reconciliation.

A Poor Christian Looks at Jedwabne:

Adam Boniecki and Michał Okoński Talk

with Archbishop Henryk Muszyński

Tygodnik Powszechny, 25 March 2001

TYGODNIK *POWSZECHNY*: In a letter published by the episcopate eleven years ago on the anniversary of the announcement of the conciliar declaration *Nostra Aetate*, we read: "Unfortunately that same land [Poland] has become in our century a grave for several million Jews. This was neither by our will nor by our hand." After the publication of Jan Tomasz Gross's book about Jedwabne, does this last sentence remain current?

ARCHBISHOP HENRYK MUSZYŃSKI: The Holocaust really was not carried out by our hand, nor was it by our will. This sentence has been questioned, unfortunately, by many Jews. But in the same letter this is also clearly stated: "If even one Christian was able to help, but did not extend a helping hand to a Jew in a time of danger, or caused his death, we are required to ask our sister and brother Jews for forgiveness." The discussion around Gross's book is the consequence of those words. I am not a historian, so it is difficult for me to assess the extent to which *Neighbors* is one-sided, tendentious, or incomplete. The sources are fragmentary, which certainly makes it difficult to reconstruct precisely what happened in Jedwabne on that tragic day of 10 July 1941. But the fact is that thanks to Gross's book, an important debate has begun, and it can have far-reaching consequences for Polish-Jewish relations. It is also good that the Institute of National Memory is continuing its investigation, which will help us—of this I have no doubt—to arrive at the full historical truth. But regardless of whether it turns out that 1,600 or 160 Jews were burned, a crime is still a crime. Someone said, and this pained me greatly, that it's enough to cross out one zero from the number of victims Gross gives in his book. We cannot talk like this because—I repeat—a crime is a crime regardless of the number of victims. Before God every person is unique and irreplaceable.

For any crime, it is the direct perpetrator who is answerable; but those who are connected to him by religious or national ties—though they bear no personal guilt—cannot feel themselves to be free of moral responsibility for the victims of this murder.

TYGODNIK POWSZECHNY: The direct perpetrators of the crime were the Polish residents of Jedwabne . . .

ARCHBISHOP HENRYK MUSZYŃSKI: I would make that statement more precise: some Polish residents of Jedwabne. I think that the current residents of the village feel rightly sensitive about such general statements.

Instigators and Perpetrators

No honest historian can examine that tragedy in terms of Polish-Jewish relations alone. The manner in which the crime was carried out—burning people alive—is analogous to similar crimes perpetrated by the Germans against Jews and Poles. And that indicates that the inspiration came from somewhere else.

TYGODNIK POWSZECHNY: Szmuel Wasersztajn, the main witness cited by Gross, speaks openly of an order given by the Germans, though he adds, "Even though it was the Germans who gave this order, Polish hooligans took it and carried it out in the cruelest possible way."

ARCHBISHOP HENRYK MUSZYŃSKI: Both the indirect perpetrators and the instigators bear moral responsibility for the crime. As a Bible scholar I want to refer to a scene from the second book of Samuel. David sends Uriah to the center of the most furious fighting so that he will be killed. David is not the direct murderer, but it is to him that the prophet Nathan comes to announce: "You have put Uriah the Hittite to the sword. You murdered him by the sword of the Ammonites." David's intention was to kill Uriah, but he used someone else to do it.

Of course, this is not a justification for the indirect perpetrators, but you have to think about this in the process of reaching the full truth. In the moral sense those who mandated and instigated the crime can, like David, be called murderers. It took the voice of the prophet, though, for David to hear: You are a murderer. David, ignoble in sin, became great in acknowledging his guilt with the words "I have sinned before God." Only when he stood before God and man in the full truth did he hear the anticipated "The Lord has remitted your sin." Every crime produces guilt before man but also concerns God Himself, for it represents a violation of the laws He established.

TYGODNIK POWSZECHNY: One could say that the Germans have reckoned with their own past, that they have taken responsibility for the Holocaust. For Poles, information about the participation of their compatriots in the murder of Jews comes as a shock . . .

ARCHBISHOP HENRYK MUSZYŃSKI: Poles cannot take responsibility for the Holocaust, because it was not their doing. But when it comes to the participation of our compatriots in the murder of Jews, the drama lies in the fact that the historical truth that was falsified by Nazi ideology was falsified a second time by Communist ideology. Something similar happened with Katyn, when the Soviet crime was ascribed to the Germans, and also with Auschwitz, where the number of Jewish victims was reduced. We were ordered to pray at some monuments and forbidden to pray at others. That's why, when I saw on television that the old monument in Jedwabne had been taken down, I saw it as symbolic of the beginning of the end of the era of falsification, instrumentalization, and the ideologizing of the truth. Because the truth has been instrumentalized. The truth was that which served Communist ideology.

Antagonism of Suffering

TYGODNIK POWSZECHNY: That is one aspect. Another is the psychologically understandable resistance to the recognition that Poles—victims of Nazism—could also be culprits. We are indignant and outraged when we are reminded that we looked on the tragedy of the ghetto with indifference, not to mention upon reading Gross.

ARCHBISHOP HENRYK MUSZYŃSKI: In the consciousness of Poles, as in the consciousness of Jews, the idea that we were the victims of Hitler's Nazism was and is deeply rooted. I can speak for the generation that survived the war. During the period of German occupation two basic categories were distinguished: perpetrators and victims. And we and the Jews were victims. But one must say here right away: not in the same way and not to the same degree. The Jew was under sentence of death and was supposed to die; the Pole could survive as an *Untermensch*. Nevertheless, when Jews emphasize the exceptional nature, or the uniqueness of the Holocaust, Poles are offended. It is difficult for them to accept that Jews suffered more than anyone else or to understand how, for example, the murder of an entire Jewish family differs from the murder of a Polish family for hiding Jews, when both were carried out by the same people as an integral part of the same criminal plan. Thus is born the antagonism of suffering.

However, the discussion around the Jedwabne incident can serve as a turning point and blunt the antagonism. In his interview with KAI [the Catholic Information Agency], Rabbi Schudrich[1] said that Jews were not just victims, but that there were among them "bad people who harmed others"—acting in the service of the Communists or even the Nazis. This is said by a person who is innocent himself. This is for us a great challenge: to be capable of acknowledging and saying exactly the same thing about the joint responsibility or even the shared guilt of those Poles who in point of fact took part in the crimes. Without this recognition, the cleansing of memory that we have talked about so often lately cannot happen. And we have an additional reason. The Golden Rule, which summarizes the Gospels, says, "Everything that you would have others do to you, do to them." We have the moral right to expect others to apologize only when we ourselves do what Christ expects of us.

We Must Ask Forgiveness

TYGODNIK POWSZECHNY: We recall the expectation that the German bishops would apologize to us, although they were not SS men.

ARCHBISHOP HENRYK MUSZYŃSKI: The analogy is very far removed. Nazism was, to a great degree, the work of the German people and was the state ideology. The murder in Jedwabne was committed by Poles, but not in the name of the Polish people. We cannot confuse these two situations or apply collective responsibility in any way other than moral, appealing to solidarity and community of nation and faith. We are proud that so many Poles were among the "Righteous Among the Nations." But this is not the whole truth about Polish behavior during the war.

And another question. The Polish bishops said to the Germans, "We forgive you and ask forgiveness." We cannot say this to the Jews, because this would mean putting them on equal footing with the Nazis. Here we can only say, "We ask forgiveness." We say to God every day, "Forgive us our sins as we forgive those who sin against us." This does not mean that the Lord God forgives to the extent that man does. Quite the opposite: we take part in God's forgiveness, the Lord God forgives us, and this obligates us to forgive. In some sense Rabbi Schudrich has met us halfway, pointing out the absolute necessity for us to make a

---

[1] Michael Schudrich (1956–), born in New York, is at present chief rabbi of Warsaw and Łódź.

request for forgiveness. This need is urgent as long as a few of the victims of this crime, or relatives of the victims, are still living.

To receive God's forgiveness, everyone who has committed a crime or a sin against another must stand in the full truth before mankind as well. There is no other way to achieve forgiveness. Such gestures have enormous significance. I remember the consecration in the 1980s of a Jewish cemetery in Kielce where there were *matsevah*s [gravestones] that the Nazis had not managed to destroy. As the chairman of the Subcommittee on the Dialogue with Judaism, I made my way to Kielce in the full consciousness that I would stand in a place where a crime had been committed by many Poles. The Jews interpreted my presence not only as an expression of my sharing in their pain, but also as some form of redress. An American woman came up to me and said: "Thank you Bishop. You are the first person on Communist ground to call what happened here a pogrom." Because it had been referred to officially as "the incidents" or as "the Kielce events."

Repentance and Shame

TYGODNIK POWSZECHNY: Archbishop, you have spoken about falsification by Communist ideology, but it was the Communist security agency that conducted an investigation into the Jedwabne case, and a Communist court passed sentence on the participants in the crime. We ascribe the fact that no one spoke about this for half a century to the rather natural tendency to keep silent about shameful things . . .

ARCHBISHOP HENRYK MUSZYŃSKI: After reading *Neighbors*, I had the impression that the trial in the Jedwabne case was rather a farce. How can you fairly judge twenty people in one day? In any case this was not the ruling of an autonomous and independent court—rather, it was truth in the service of ideology. Of course, it is not easy to admit to participation in such a monstrous crime. Perhaps the shame and the pain that we feel today as Poles is a form of self-cleansing and redress. Of course, this takes courage.

TYGODNIK POWSZECHNY: The indictment from that trial reads "that on 25 June 1941 [the error in the date is itself compromising] in Jedwabne in the Łomża district, obliging the authorities of the German state, they took part in the seizure of about 1,200 persons of the Jewish nationality, these persons then being burned as a group in the barn of Bronisław Śleszyński." So the court declared that it was the Germans who burned them . . .

ARCHBISHOP HENRYK MUSZYŃSKI: On the one hand it was "truth in the service of ideology," and on the other hand it was the self-defense reflex on the part of those who were conscious of themselves as victims. The entire wartime generation experienced persecution at the hands of the Germans. Only a handful acted as persecutors.

TYGODNIK POWSZECHNY: Nevertheless, in many reports from the occupation period, the Pole appears to the Jew as a threat. Michał Głowiński recalls a scene in which two ladies in a café are wondering aloud whether the boy at the next table is a Jew. Not to mention the expressions of satisfaction everywhere in the underground press of the time that the Germans were settling matters with the Jews. Simply put, those who hid Jews were hiding them not just from the Germans but also from Poles . . .

ARCHBISHOP HENRYK MUSZYŃSKI: You have to take into account the reigning atmosphere of terror at the time. Rescuing a Jew in Poland and, for example, in Holland did not have the same consequences. Here, hiding a Jew carried a sentence of death for one's entire family. They often forget about this in discussions abroad, but this too is a piece of the historical truth. Of course, from the point of view of morality not only every crime but every act of indifference or harm in relation to Jews or anyone else requires sincere sorrow, repentance, and pleas for forgiveness. However, without questioning the facts, I could point to cases in which some residents of a village knew who was hiding Jews, but did not give them up. All generalizations are inappropriate here.

Cleansing through Truth

TYGODNIK POWSZECHNY: What can the Church do in the matter of Jedwabne?

ARCHBISHOP HENRYK MUSZYŃSKI: First we have to say what it has done so far for the "cleansing of memory." It is enough to point to the attitude of the pope, who apologized for wrongdoing and sins against the Jews in the name of the whole Church. Back in 1990 the Polish episcopate stated that if even one Pole committed murder, that is cause for us to ask for forgiveness. Was it too cautiously formulated? In those days it often happened that Poles and Germans were put on the same plane. Much was said also about the exceptional nature of Polish antisemitism. If we had apologized then for antisemitism, it would have been taken as a recognition of guilt for the so-called Polish antisemitism, which for many Jews is a synonym for the worst possible form of antisemitism. But ten years later, in his penitential introduction to the Jubilee Mass, the primate apologized for the loss of love for people, which led some in the priesthood to "tolerate manifestations of antisemitism."

I have often repeated that Polish-Jewish reconciliation has not yet begun; that we are still in the stage of blaming each other. After Rabbi Schudrich's statement I am ready to change my opinion. The rabbi said that "the Holocaust was planned and realized from beginning to end by the Germans," and that "accusing Poles of participation in the Holocaust is a sin." He also said something that is worthy of the name of Jewish wisdom: "Polish antisemitism is not as bad as the Jews say it is, and not as good as what the Poles think of themselves." To me this signifies a readiness to search for a joint plane of understanding and to arrive at the full truth through dialogue. And I understand this dialogue not as a desire to persuade the other side but as an attempt to understand our partner in dialogue as he understands himself.

Rabbi Schudrich's statement can serve as a turning point in reaching the full moral and even historical truth, and thus in the process of cleansing through truth. A cleansing of the attitude of mutual accusation, of prejudice on both sides, of falsification, can be the beginning of the road to reconciliation. The first and indispensable step along this road, though, is to ask for forgiveness. Although this is a moral, internal act, it has great practical significance in contacts between Poles and Jews. The crime in Jedwabne—like any other crime—divides people. No one can bring the innocent victims back to life, but the moral act of repentance can bring us closer together and can be a decisive step on the road to reconciliation. We Christians believe that in Christ, God reconciled us with ourselves. But reconciliation with God is always achieved through reconciliation with another person. "First go and reconcile with your brother." God wants the reconciliation of people with clean hands. He does not want sacrifices; He speaks of this through the prophets: I do not want your sacrifices, because your hands are bloody.

This is the essence of our Christian faith, and at the same time our obligation. The same is true of forgiveness. Because God has forgiven me numerous times, I am obligated to forgive. Of course, to forgive does not mean to forget.

What Poles Will Say to God

TYGODNIK POWSZECHNY: When we hear praise for Rabbi Schudrich from the mouths of bishops because he counters opinions harmful to Poles, because he recognizes that there was no lack of bad people on the Jewish side as well, we feel a certain discomfort. You have said, Archbishop, that the true dialogue can now begin. As though we need someone to articulate some formulation justifying us, in some way absolve us, and then we will be able to acknowledge our guilt.

ARCHBISHOP HENRYK MUSZYŃSKI: Here I see an analogy with Polish-German reconciliation. There, too, the initiative came from those who were the victims. It is worth adding, though, that although the rabbi took the first step, the primate's answer to his letter was also important. It creates the proper spiritual atmosphere for uniting with the victims through common prayer in mourning for the innocent people murdered. Deeper reflection on the moral dimension of crime and sin also constitutes an appropriate response to the pope's call to "*duc in altum!*"—"sail out into the depths."

Rabbi Schudrich said: "More important for Poles than what people will say about this tragedy in the U.S.A. should be what Poles will say to God." I would say that what is important is how Poles will stand in truth before God, our common God. What they will say interests me less—it is well known that they are talkative . . . But how will they stand in the truth? The commandment we share with the Jews says, "Thou shalt not kill." We must admit that we did not keep this commandment. But the rabbi's statement helps to overcome generalizations and unfair judgments.

Bishop Stefanek said that Jedwabne will be a sanctuary of suffering. I think that it will be something greater: a first step on the road to reconciliation among the victims of Nazism. Here I would like to express sincere spiritual community with today's residents of that town. The vast majority of them are innocent, are Christians, and in Christianity the suffering of innocents has a cleansing, even redeeming character. We must thank them for bearing the suffering with dignity and say a word of hope: that Jedwabne will have a greater part in the process of reconciliation than any other town.

Not long ago I read a story in *Tygodnik Powszechny* about the postwar murder of Germans in Nieszawa. This village is in my metropolitanate, in my diocese. I know some of the people mentioned in it by name, so I read it with feeling. And I found in it an appropriate atmosphere: focus, relation to God, an honest reckoning of conscience, settling with the past, and reformation. I had occasion to speak with a very high representative of the German government, who said that there would be no external interference in this matter, for whatever would be said from outside would only do harm. This is important: any pressure from the outside can have the opposite consequence. From a distance of many kilometers, or miles, everything surely looks different.

TYGODNIK POWSZECHNY: But the Church was silent on these matters for a very long time . . .

ARCHBISHOP HENRYK MUSZYŃSKI: And thank God that it was silent and did not speak, for example, in the pattern imposed by the Communist authorities and did not use the terminology in which "Zionists" constituted the greatest threat to Poles. From the moment when we could speak freely of these matters, the voice of the Church has not been lacking even in the most sensitive of questions.

There Will Be Symbolic Gestures

TYGODNIK POWSZECHNY: So let's repeat the question: what can the Church do today in the case of Jedwabne?

ARCHBISHOP HENRYK MUSZYŃSKI: With this measure of mutual understanding and going out to meet our Jewish brothers, undoubtedly there will be some symbolic gestures on our part. We have common psalms, common prayers that we can use. It is too early to talk about concrete details. The Holy Father demonstrated the significance of symbolic gestures at the Wailing Wall. Without him there would not have been the *Dabru emet*, the declaration of the American rabbis published in the *New York Times*, which calls for a reconsideration of the relationship of the Jews to Jesus of Nazareth, to the essence of the Christian faith and the roots of antisemitism.[2]

I remember the time I went to Rome to meet with Mr. Joseph Lichten, the representative of B'nai Brith at the Vatican. I called his place, and Mrs. Lichten told me that he had just died. Cardinal Mejia, Father Fumagalli, and I took part in the funeral ceremony. All three of us know Hebrew, and the question arose as to whether Catholic clergy could take an active part in a Jewish funeral and recite the psalm *De profundis* in Hebrew. The rabbis were divided in their opinion, but in the end we set a historical precedent and joined in the prayer. I was so moved that I could hardly speak.

It is worth noting that the pope's eloquent gestures at the Wailing Wall and at Yad Vashem had a clearly prophetic aspect to them. There, where words of lamentation are spoken, the great prophets of Israel

---

[2] *Dabru emet* (Speak the truth) is a Jewish statement of September 2000 on Christians and Christianity, which stressed the common roots of Judaism and Christianity. It was signed by more than two hundred mostly American rabbis representing different streams of contemporary Judaism and was positively received in various Christian circles.

used symbols that can never be forgotten. In doing what he did, the pope placed no conditions on the Jews. His inspiration was the gospel: "Everything that you would have others to do unto you, do unto them." Among us, unfortunately, the saying "Do not do to others what is unpleasant to you" has taken root. But that is not yet Christianity. The calling of the Christian is to do good and follow the example of Christ, who went through life doing good and not just avoiding evil.

Tygodnik Powszechny: The Church is virtually absent from historical arguments on the subject of Jedwabne. There are some marginal arguments, like whether Bishop Łukomski did or did not receive candlesticks in exchange for protecting Jews. But everyone is waiting to hear the voice of the Church . . .

ARCHBISHOP HENRYK MUSZYŃSKI: I think it's understandable, because we are talking about the ethical, or religioethical, dimension of the truth. People expect of the Church—and have the right to expect—that it would take a stand on such questions. But the best indicator is the faithful testimony of the gospel.

Tygodnik Powszechny: One could also speak of the responsibility of the Church, at least for the years of teaching anti-Judaism. Rabbi Baker, who left Jedwabne before the war, recalls almost idyllic contacts with his Polish neighbors. The idyll was disturbed primarily around Easter, when the image of the Jew as Christ-killer was evoked in Church teachings.

ARCHBISHOP HENRYK MUSZYŃSKI: I will say yet again: I do not question particular facts, but one cannot draw any general conclusions from them. Rabbi Baker himself asks that one moment, even such a tragic one, should not conceal the centuries of common history. And as for anti-Judaism: the Church, in the person of the pope, has recognized its responsibility for the sins of the past. Since the Council, many excellent documents on the subject of Jews and teachings about Jews have been produced—many of which are still awaiting full recognition.

Tygodnik Powszechny: The primate has said that the Church's participation in the ceremony marking the sixtieth anniversary of the slaughter guarantees that it will be not "hasty and vociferous penance" but, rather, "introspection in humility and truth." In modern politics, apologies have become extremely banal, have become captive to public opinion . . .

ARCHBISHOP HENRYK MUSZYŃSKI: Any posturing in the face of such a terrible tragedy would be a desecration of the memory of the victims. So it must be done in an extremely dignified manner, in an attitude of

compassion, joint participation, and community of prayer. The plat-
form for this has been created; if we do not take advantage of it, we
will be guilty of the sin of neglect. As the primate reminds us, what
we need now is genuinely deep, calm, religious reflection, and not a
multiplication of successive noisy pronouncements.

TYGODNIK POWSZECHNY: But we expected to hear the voice of the episcopate, if only so that the statements of various bishops should not
become a cacophony. What Bishop Stefanek said in Jedwabne was different, after all, from what the primate has said . . .

ARCHBISHOP HENRYK MUSZYŃSKI: Unfortunately I am not familiar with
the full content of Bishop Stefanek's statement. The version put out by
KAI differs rather fundamentally from what I could read in the papers.
Only Bishop Stefanek himself could speak authoritatively in this matter. According to the hierarchical structure of the Church, the statement
of the local bishop is always of the highest significance . . .

It is difficult to expect a reaction from the entire Episcopal Conference in each individual matter. And if matters of this kind arise in the
future? Must the episcopate react each time? On the occasion of the
anniversary of *Nostra Aetate*[3] the Episcopal Conference issued a special
letter that was read in every church in Poland. What was said in it
about asking for forgiveness remains current. So it is not true that the
Church has no voice.

Both the primate, as the chairman of the Episcopal Conference, and
Rabbi Schudrich, in the name of the Jewish community in Poland, have
expressed their readiness to pray together on the occasion of the up-
coming sixtieth anniversary of the tragic events in Jedwabne. Once
again I express my belief that with such far-reaching spiritual partnership and mutual understanding, a proper and dignified way of memorializing this shameful slaughter will be found—as will some form of
redress for the evil that was done.

．　．　．　．　．

Archbishop Henryk Muszyński was born in 1933 and appointed archbishop of Gniezno in 1992. He was the first president of the Polish episcopate's Commission for Interreligious Dialogue.

Translation by Andrzej Tymowski.

---

[3] *Nostra Aetate* is the Declaration on the Relation of the Roman Catholic Church to
Non-Christian Religions, proclaimed by Pope Paul VI on 28 October 1965. This document marked the beginning of a new era in Christian-Jewish relations.

Interview with the Primate of Poland, Cardinal Józef Glemp, on the Murder of Jews in Jedwabne, 15 May 2001

THE CATHOLIC INFORMATION AGENCY (KAI): On 27 May the Polish episcopate will ask God's forgiveness for wrongs committed by Poles. For what specific acts will the bishops apologize? Will it be primarily for the crime committed by Poles against Polish citizens of the Mosaic faith in Jedwabne, or will the context be much broader?

CARDINAL JÓZEF GLEMP: I do not know yet what the specifics of our prayer service will be, but it is clear that it cannot be limited only to Jedwabne. Jedwabne will remain a certain kind of symbol. In my view, ideology or politics motivates the suggestions that have been made that we apologize exclusively for Jedwabne. We realize that this needs to be broadened, because Poles took part in the destruction of Jews in other localities as well, acting as mobs without conscience.

We are well aware in this regard that every crime and every sin has its context. For that reason, in confessing sin we cannot dissociate ourselves from the circumstances or the very complicated context of these tragic events. In speaking of the complexity of this murder, we should note that in some way, Germans, Poles, Jews, and Russians were all entangled in it. We will not be confessing these sins "blindly"; we want to see them precisely in this broad context. That is, to abide in truth.

Another consideration is the fact that we are witnessing a campaign of harassment against the Church to apologize for Jedwabne as quickly as possible. The pressure to have the Church make apologies for crimes against Jews has been underway for a long time. The Polish episcopate has already apologized to Jews, both orally and in a separate letter dated 30 November 1990 on the occasion of the twenty-fifth anniversary of the publication of the conciliar statement *Nostra Aetate*. I am puzzled, moreover, about why no faiths other than the Roman Catholic Church are mentioned in this regard.

KAI: Will the confession of sins extend to all of Polish-Jewish history, or only to the period of World War II?

CARDINAL GLEMP: Yes, we will be mindful of the entire history, although—as far as the gathering of specific facts is concerned—this would require extensive study. But I think that we can take a stand vis-à-vis the entire past, at least in a general way, although it would be difficult to cover everything in one prayer. For that reason, naturally, the war and postwar periods will be most prominent.

KAI: Will this apology be directed only to God, or also to those who suffered—for example, to the still-living relatives of the victims murdered in Jedwabne and in other localities?

CARDINAL GLEMP: We want to ask God for His forgiveness first of all, but we also want to ask forgiveness of everyone who suffered, and to do so on behalf of those Polish citizens who committed evil acts against citizens of the Mosaic faith. We are still gathering suggestions as to how to do this. The content of the prayer service is not yet set; liturgical experts and subject specialists will continue to work on this. However, we want this prayer to be profound, and to contain a genuine apology to God and to people.

KAI: In his book *Neighbors*, Jan Tomasz Gross states, among other things, that in prewar Poland anti-Jewish feelings intensified during Holy Week, when priests in their pulpits evoked the image of the Jewish people as God-killers. Is this statement justified? If it is, the Church would indeed have very serious sins on its conscience.

CARDINAL GLEMP: This statement strikes me as improbable. The first time I ever heard about this rise in anti-Jewish feeling was in Mr. Gross's book. Clearly, the book was written "on commission" from someone. Before the war I had no contact with Jews, because there were very few where I lived. Polish-Jewish conflicts did occur in those times, but they had an economic basis. Jews were cleverer, and they knew how to take advantage of Poles. That, in any case, was the perception. Another cause of dislike for Jews was their pro-Bolshevik attitude. This was a very basic resentment, but it did not stem from religious motives. In Poland before the war, matters of religion did not play any significant role as far as dislike for Jews was concerned. Jews were not liked because of their odd "folk customs." The same sort of dislike based on folk customs can be found today, for example, among fans of different soccer teams in the city of Łódź. Is there any point in looking for religious motives in this?

KAI: What, then, was the relationship of the Church to the Jewish minority in the time just prior to the crime in Jedwabne?

CARDINAL GLEMP: In my opinion the Church hierarchy in prewar Poland was more politically engaged than it is today, with some bishops directly supporting right-wing parties that did not like Jews because of their political allegiances. One example among others of such an attitude was the pastor of All Saints' Church in Warsaw, Monsignor Marceli Godlewski. Before the war he was a determined political opponent of the Jews, but during the occupation he took a very active role in rescuing and defending them. It is necessary to distinguish between two different things: political allegiance and Christian charity. Father Godlewski heroically rescued Jews from destruction. He was well aware of their intended fate, because his church bordered on the walls of the ghetto.

We also need to remember that two thousand Poles were executed by German occupying forces precisely because they helped Jews.

KAI: Is it because of Father Godlewski that All Saints' Church was chosen as the site of the apology that is to take place on 27 May?

CARDINAL GLEMP: Yes, because the ghetto wall ran very close by and a great deal of food was transferred to the ghetto right at that point. Children came across there as well. Rev. Godlewski rescued them himself, hiding them and then passing them on to other hiding places.

KAI: Reverend Primate, why was 27 May chosen as the date, and not, as was suggested by Jewish groups (including the rabbi of Warsaw and Łódź, Michael Schudrich)—10 July, the anniversary of the mass murder?

CARDINAL GLEMP: The rabbi suggested that we meet on 10 July in the synagogue in Warsaw, if we could not meet in Jedwabne. However, July is not the most suitable month for such a ceremony, and many bishops would not be able to be present. On the other hand, all the bishops will gather in Warsaw on 27 May, the day before the anniversary of the death of Cardinal Stefan Wyszyński, in order to honor this great primate. This is a good occasion to reflect in a deeply Christian way on today's situation, including our relations with our Jewish brothers.

KAI: In our faith the act of apology is tied to the sacrament of reconciliation, in particular with the act of expressing sorrow, which is the most important element in doing penance. If our asking God's forgiveness is to have profound meaning, we must acknowledge that we have offended Him and that we want to repair the evil done. But surveys show that more than half of the Polish population believes that we should not apologize for Jedwabne. Should not this act of apology be preceded by some sort of national retreat, some examination of conscience?

CARDINAL GLEMP: Yes, the greatest offense has been suffered by God Himself. His image was sullied by the crimes committed by representatives of those four nations, entangled as they were by tragic events. Of course, as a nation and a community of faith we should prepare ourselves in a properly spiritual way. We should above all understand that it is God who suffered the most harm through the iniquity of His creatures. The plea for God's forgiveness proceeds from a moral imperative that is not contingent on the results of sociological surveys.

KAI: However, some people suggest that it would be better to wait with apologies until all the circumstances of the mass murder in Jedwabne are cleared up, for the results of the detailed investigation being conducted by the Institute of National Memory. Is the Church, then, not acting too hastily?

CARDINAL GLEMP: From the moral point of view, the issue should not be decided based on whether the results of the investigation will be more or less advantageous for us, whether they will show Poles in a better or worse light. For there remains the basic issue: there were people in Jedwabne who caused the death of their fellow citizens. But whether this was done to follow orders, or out of fear, or out of a desire to avenge harm suffered, or as a result of German instigation, or perhaps out of a desire for material gain—these are matters that need to be determined.

As far as the investigation itself is concerned, I believe that the collective grave that exists near the barn burned in Jedwabne should be exhumed, in order to establish how many people were murdered. We have every right to do this, consistent with the Polish law on cemeteries. I do not regard this as tactless, because we are acting within the applicable laws. This action was suspended, however, on requests from Jews, although Jewish law is not binding in Poland. It is certainly possible to treat human remains with dignity, moving them and then replacing them with honor. That has happened in many places, and in such a procedure there should be no question of profanation.

The same sort of issue arose with the Carmelite convent in Auschwitz. In the light of Polish law and our sense of things, they could continue to live there, but yet we retreated, because we acknowledged that this could hurt Jewish feelings.

But I want to emphasize that from the point of view of the law, Poland may conduct an exhumation and determine the number of victims, because it is important to know how many victims there were.

KAI: Reverend Primate, you spoke a moment ago about the campaign of harassment against the Church in Poland. What are the underlying reasons for these attacks, formerly associated with the Carmelite convent in Auschwitz and currently with Jedwabne? Many people find them hard to understand.

CARDINAL GLEMP: I also cannot understand why Poles are unceasingly slandered, especially in the American press, and why we are constantly accused of antisemitism, as though it were somehow different in form from what it is in other countries. In all this Jews continually exhibit their dislike toward Poles. I cannot really understand why they do so. For—in comparison with Europe—Jews had relatively the best situation with us, here in Poland. They felt at home here. Why therefore are there so many unjust accusations today? Think how this hurts Jews who genuinely love Poland and who live in friendship with Poles!

We wonder whether Jews should not acknowledge that they have a burden of responsibility in regard to Poles, in particular for the period of close cooperation with the Bolsheviks, for complicity in deportations to Siberia, for sending Poles to jails, for the degradation of many of their fellow citizens, etc. The fact that Poles also took part in these repressions does not exclude the fact that the leading role was played by officers of the UB [Security Police] of Jewish descent. This terror lasted until 1956 and a great number of Poles to this day remain buried under nameless headstones. These victims also need to be considered, as long as we are speaking about Jews victimized by Poles.

KAI: In your opinion, is antisemitism in Poland only history, or can it still be observed today?

CARDINAL GLEMP: I think that Father Michał Czajkowski has made things much worse in this discussion by his constant imputation of antisemitism to the Church and to the hierarchy, which supposedly arises from dislike toward Jews based on religious beliefs. I have not noted any dislike for the Jewish faith nor have I ever noticed any such phenomenon as anti-Judaism. That is all in the past. On the other hand, anti-Polonism is worth mentioning. Here are a few clippings from newspapers, in particular American papers. These caricatures have been circulated all over the world in thousands of copies, misrepresenting the image of the Church and of Poland. And no one has apologized for that.

KAI: President Kwaśniewski has already apologized for the events in Jedwabne and has announced a great commemorative ceremony on 10

July in that town. At the same time, there are people working in his office who were responsible for the campaign of harassment against Jews in 1968. Are you not concerned, Reverend Primate, that politicians will want to take advantage of the Church's cleansing of its memory and the apology for the murders and the suffering inflicted on the Jews for political purposes and their own opportunistic ends?

CARDINAL GLEMP: That is the politicians' business. I do not want to make judgments on them. I think that President Kwaśniewski does not have the formal authority to apologize in the name of the nation, but I would rather not comment on that.

KAI: Rabbi Schudrich was invited to attend the religious service in All Saints' Church, which is perfectly understandable. Wouldn't it also be possible to at least invite Germans? For you mentioned a moment ago, Your Eminence, that Germans, Poles, Russians, Bolsheviks, and Jews were entangled in hatred by Satan. Would you, Reverend Primate, want also to invite representatives of these faiths to join in a common prayer?

CARDINAL GLEMP: I think that if we did that, some of them might think that we are trying to pull them into our apology and to extend our admission of sins to cover them as well. This is a very delicate matter. The prayer we are planning will be a prayer of the episcopate. Naturally, we will invite the rabbi. But if others come, it will be because they decided to do so on their own.

KAI: At the Jasna Góra Monastery you said, Reverend Primate, that the "I'm sorry" addressed to God and to the Jews must have "such resonance in the scale of Providence that it would reach all the way to the Holy Land and would say to people living there as neighbors: 'Tell each other you are sorry, say to one another: "I apologize." Stop fighting!' " What relation does our Polish plea to God for forgiveness have to the evil being committed in other regions of the world?

CARDINAL GLEMP: It emphasizes the fact that we are part of the human family, and that there is no nation so special that it would be free from crime, from sin. And that we acknowledge this. But because we acknowledge our faults, and the faults of those four aforementioned nations, we say that this is a deformation of human beings as creatures of God in general. These universal truths apply also to the most volatile locales in today's world. We might mention Chechnya or Rwanda, or the Holy Land that is so soaked with blood, for it is there that religious conflicts are greatest. That is why Mr. Gross, if he is a good writer and writes about neighbors in the future, might now write about contemporary neighbors.

. . . . .

Cardinal Archbishop Józef Glemp has been primate of Poland since July 1981. He was born in 1929 and studied at the Theological Seminary in Gniezno and in Rome. From 1964 to 1967 he was secretary of the Primate's Theological Seminary and notary of the Metropolitan Court in Gniezno. Between 1967 and 1979 he worked in the secretariat of Primate Wyszyński and as a lecturer at the Academy of Catholic Theology in Warsaw. From 1979 to 1981 he was bishop of Warmia.

Translation by Andrzej Tymowski.

Rev. Stanisław Musiał

WE ASK YOU TO HELP US BE BETTER

GAZETA WYBORCZA, 23 MAY 2001

I T IS TOO BAD THAT we will not meet together on 10 July in Jedwabne, where sixty years ago Polish citizens committed a horrible crime against Polish citizens—Poles against Jews. It is too bad because both the Polish State and the Catholic Church in Poland are joined in a sorrowful confraternity of guilt against Jews—in Jedwabne as well as over the entire extent of our history. The fact that on 10 July the Polish episcopate will be absent in Jedwabne must not mean that we should leave the president of the Polish Republic there alone—at the gravesite of the murder victims. Quite the opposite. It would also be good if on that evening we were to light candles in the windows of our homes to honor the memory of those who were murdered. As the saying goes, it is better to light a small candle than to curse great darkness.

It is also a great shame that the solution proposed by Rabbi Michael Schudrich was not accepted—he invited the Polish episcopate on 10 July to his synagogue in Warsaw. This meeting could have become a breakthrough event in Polish-Jewish, and Christian-Jewish, relations in our country, on the scale of the Holy Father's visit to the synagogue in Rome. In his interview with KAI [The Catholic Information Agency] a few days ago [printed in *Gazeta Wyborcza* on 15 May (*GW* eds.)] the primate indicated the reason why the July date was not acceptable: "July is not the best month for such a ceremony, and many bishops would not be able to be present." It can be surmised that the 10 July date would conflict with the vacations of some of the reverend bishops. If that were truly the case, it would be a sad instance of minor matters trumping those of great moment.

The 27 May date was prompted by purely pragmatic considerations, to take advantage of an occasion: on 28 May the Polish episcopate comes together in Warsaw on the anniversary of the death of Stefan Cardinal Wyszyński. So there appeared an outstanding opportunity to squeeze the penitential prayer service for Jedwabne into a niche of time on the day before the ceremony honoring the deceased primate. It is obvious that these two matters are not connected with each other in any way, nor do they share any sort of symbolic meaning. With all the praiseworthy deeds, great as they are, that Cardinal Wyszyński has to his credit in service to Poland, he cannot be made into the patron of Polish-Jewish or Jewish-Christian dialogue. But the choice of the place where the episcopate will gather for prayer on 27 May—in All Saints' Church in Warsaw, next to which passed the wall of the ghetto—should be acknowledged as apt.

Offenses against One's Fellow Human Beings, and against God

The interview with the primate did not convey much information about the form that the prayer service would take on 27 May. Not because the primate did not want to share what he knew, but because at that moment final decisions had not yet been made. He said that "liturgical experts and subject specialists" are working on the program of the prayer service. However, among the specialists is surely not to be found Prof. and Rev. Michał Czajkowski, and this is unfortunate. His engagement in Jewish-Christian dialogue was judged by the primate, in this same interview, as having "made things much worse in this discussion."

The apologies, according to the interview, should cover more than Jedwabne. The bishops will be "mindful of the entire history" and, at least "in a general way," will be able to "take a stand vis-à-vis the entire past," the primate explained. Very properly so. It is only too bad that the examination of conscience for our trespasses against the Jews that was made a year ago during the penitential ceremony on Theater Square in Warsaw on the occasion of the Great Jubilee, two thousand years after the birth of Christ, turned out to be so meager. It is only today that we are making up for that shortfall—and only because forced to do so by Prof. Jan Gross's book. This does not bring us Catholics any particular glory, since we should be the first to confess our sins.

From what the primate said it appears that the act of apology will take the form of a prayer that will be put together ad hoc. I will admit that the organizers of the prayer service have set the bar very high for themselves. It would have been easier to articulate the sins for which we are asking forgiveness and then to look to the words of the psalms for the prayers themselves. The organizers are surely aware that a prayer composed for this occasion has to be crystalline-sincere and pure, because it is addressed to God. It should be completely free of all ambivalences, subtexts, searches for extenuating circumstances, and blaming "the other side." I believe that the Holy Spirit will sustain by His light the authors as they compose this prayer. Otherwise we will have pulled down upon ourselves a new sin—profanation of the name of God.

In his interview the primate drew a profound theological connection between an offense against human beings and an offense against God: "the greatest offense has been suffered by God Himself. His image was sullied by the crimes." And quite properly so. An insult directed at one's fellow human being is an insult directed against God Himself. But drawing such a connection between these two kinds of offenses should in no way be understood to lessen or indeed to minimize the enormity of the wrong done by one human being to another. What is more, human suffering becomes much more expressive thereby. There is also no chance that we can secure God's forgiveness while avoiding the human being we wronged. Reconciliation with God for our trespasses against a fellow human being is not possible behind the back of the one who suffered the wrong, as some sort of shortcut. For every person, the path to God must lead through other human beings.

The Church's Trespasses

No apology for trespasses is genuine unless it fulfills at least three conditions. The first is an examination of conscience. It would be too bad if the Church limited itself to an apology for the sins of its sons and daughters. The Church in Poland should also apologize—in a distinctive way—for its own sins, for the sins of the institution that it itself is. For it is not that the sins of the sons and daughters of the Church stemmed only from their disobedience to the teachings of the Church. Many of those sins, which we group under the name "antisemitism," came about from faithfulness to the teaching of the Church at that time and to the generally accepted norms of behavior against which the Church did not protest, despite the fact that some of them were highly immoral.

I will mention a few specific examples of what I mean, in order not to be making unsubstantiated charges. For at least three centuries the Church in Poland tolerated, supported, and usually initiated court proceedings for so-called ritual murder—doing so against explicit papal teachings. As a result of more than one hundred such cases many hundreds of people were put to death, preceded by cruel torture. Not to mention the constant fear pervading Jewish communities, owing to the fact that any randomly discovered child's corpse could be used against them.

The Church tolerated the humiliation of Jews, especially on Christian holidays, and did nothing to stop such practices. An example of this is the following quotation from a work entitled *The Looking Glass of the Polish Crown: The Serious Injuries and Great Afflictions It Suffers from the Jews*, dated 1618 and authored by Father Sebastian Miczyński. The author wrote, among other things, "No one can be found to teach a lesson to the Jew; and that old holy and honorable custom has been lost, wherein boys and child innocents, having sighted a Jew in the town on a holy day, to avenge the Divine suffering, rebuked the Jew for this with stones, mud, and pulling of the beard."

The Church in Poland did not defend the good name of the Jews and did not take up any effort against the tide of vulgar antisemitic writings—beginning with the famous book *Jewish Anger*, authored by Father K. Pikulski in middle of the eighteenth century, which was a collection of improbable calumnies against Jews, and culminating in the graphomaniacal pamphleteering practiced by priests in the interwar period. These are some of the institutional sins of the Church in Poland, for which it would now be appropriate to apologize to Jews.

As far as the 1941 tragedy in Jedwabne is concerned, it made manifest the utter fiasco of the Church's pastoral mission. Not just because Catholics at that time acted the way they did, but because the clergy—at the level both of the parish and of the diocese—failed completely. After the murders committed in Radziłów it was of course obvious what was brewing in Jedwabne. Nothing was done to avert the tragedy. Would it not have been possible, for example, for the priest in Jedwabne to at least arrange a twenty-four-hour special prayer vigil, perhaps an adoration of the Blessed Sacrament? If only he had been there alone in the church praying, that would have been a sign of protest against the crime. The fact that pages have been torn out of the parish chronicle for those days is the best evidence that we have nothing to be proud of concerning the stance we Catholics took during that time in Jedwabne.

This Is the Way We Were

The second condition of a genuine apology for trespasses committed is the disinterestedness of that apology. It cannot take the form of bargaining: "I am ready to forgive you, if you also forgive me." Such huckstering of moral acts should be completely alien to Christianity, which is founded on the salvation freely given by God—on Divine grace that is prior to our pleas that our trespasses be forgiven. That sort of *do ut des* (I give so you will give) is also alien to a secular ethics. It is with genuine pleasure that I cite a short excerpt from a statement by Prof. Hanna Świda-Ziemba on the subject of her own agnosticism (this statement will be published in the summer issue of *Życie Duchowne* published in Kraków: "Making one's own moral action (which is regarded as the proper one) contingent on the behavior of others (that is, its relativization), and using the occasion to declare what one expects of the other side, violates the ethical value of disinterestedness and of internal honesty. It thus violates the fundamental ethical values that in my experience constitute ethical truth."

Let us be very specific—What would we have said if German bishops had issued a statement just after the war that they were ready to apologize to us for all the wrongs that German Catholics wreaked upon Poles during the occupation, but only on condition that we also apologize for the wrongs done to Germans? We certainly would have rejected such a convoluted trade in moral values.

Finally, in order that an apology not be empty words, and that it be effective—that is, that it successfully reach God as well as the injured parties—it must be closely accompanied by a firm purpose of amendment. That purpose needs to be evident not only in theological-moral discussions but above all in the prose of everyday life. For example, why could not the Church in Poland, as an institution, take decisive steps against those who sell antisemitic literature on the premises of churches and other religious grounds? For example, could not the Church as an institution encourage parishes to have all antisemitic graffiti removed eagerly and quickly? This could be an additional sphere of activity for Catholic youth organizations. Could not the Church as an institution make it a point to have all expressions of anti-Judaism removed from catechisms used in schools?

These are only a few examples of specific actions, including in teaching, that could be undertaken in the spirit of genuine apology for wrongs done to Jews in the past.

The national community would be grateful to the Polish bishops if during prayers on 27 May they also addressed those people who, during the war and afterward, burdened their consciences with heavy guilt toward Jews. I am talking about the *szmalcownicy* [who extorted money from Jews (AT)] or those who turned Jews in to the occupying authorities, about people who murdered Jews with their own hands, about people who illegally took possession of Jewish or formerly Jewish property, about members of the Blue Police,[1] etc. The Church after the war did not help these people find peace with themselves, with others, and with God. There were no "national retreats." It is high time

---

[1] Polish police that operated in the occupied zone.

to make up for this moral debt from the past, if only for the handful of still-living people weighed down with heavy responsibility for transgressions against Jews.

I write these words on Thursday evening, 17 May, and reflect on the feverish preparations for the prayer service in All Saints' Church in Warsaw. About the efforts of "experts in liturgy and subject specialists"—in the words of the primate. And I am beset by the nagging questions: What did it avail Pius XII that he was surrounded by dozens of subject specialists, nuncios, secretaries, and theologians, if he could not bring himself to utter a few simple words from the heart to condemn the extermination of the Jews and to shout out loud: "This cannot be!" This relativizes the role of experts, though no one would deny that "experts in liturgy and subject specialists" are needed.

It seems to me that the case of Jedwabne, and the moral responsibility that Catholics have incurred toward Jews in history, can be fully stated on half a page of schoolchild's notebook. One can say simply: "This is the way we were. There is nothing we can say to justify it. We apologize to you and to God for all of this with all our hearts and all our souls. We want to change. We ask you: help us to be better."

That's all. And a large number of penitential psalms.

·   ·   ·   ·   ·

Father Stanisław Musiał, S.J., was born in 1938. He is an essayist and a former editor of *Tygodnik Powszechny*. He studied philosophy and theology in Kraków and Warsaw, as well as in Italy, Germany, and France. From 1986 to 1995 he was secretary of the Commission of the Polish Episcopate for Dialogue with Judaism. He participated in the Geneva meetings in 1986 and 1987 on the Carmelite convent at Auschwitz.

Translation by Andrzej Tymowski.

PART V

VOICES OF THE INHABITANTS OF JEDWABNE

INTRODUCTION

> The public debate is dominated by a search for the truth
> about the murder. If I were to give my view, I do not know
> the truth. I know only what people have been saying for
> the last sixty years. I know only the essence of the long
> collective and individual memory. It is what I learned
> in childhood: "Poles burned Jews alive in a barn.
> And robbed them."
> —Marta Kurkowska
>
> Satan came to this town.
> —Stanisław Przechodzki, interview
> with Anna Bikont, 4 April 2001

ONE OF THE SADDEST aspects of the whole controversy has
been the reaction of the people of Jedwabne. In his interview
of 25 March 2001, Archbishop Muszyński expressed the hope
that the town would be the scene of the "first step on the road to reconciliation among the victims of Nazism." He went on:

> Here I would like to express sincere spiritual community with to-
> day's residents of that town. The vast majority of them are inno-
> cent, are Christians, and in Christianity the suffering of innocents
> has a cleansing, even redeeming character. We must thank them
> for bearing the suffering with dignity and say a word of hope: that
> Jedwabne will have a greater part in the process of reconciliation
> than any other town.

This has not been the case. Already in a film made by Agnieszka Arnold and in the roundtable discussion organized in the town by the
Catholic monthly *Więź*, different points of view were evident. The
position that the town would need to come to terms with its tragic past
was most strongly represented by Stanisław Przechodzki, head of a
branch of the Public Health Center for Podlasie in Łomża. Born in
1955, he was not a direct observer of events in Jedwabne in June and
July 1941 but was fully informed of them by his parents. He argued
that there could be no collective responsibility for the massacre, but
continued:

> There can be only one truth in a fundamental issue. The murder
> was carried out by some neighbors. That was the main murder—

the burning in the barn—but there were also many, very many, individual murders. There is no doubt that they were committed with the approval of the Germans. But to talk of dozens or hundreds of armed gendarmes in Jedwabne is a mockery of the victims. There was no cordon of Germans around Jedwabne.

In his view, the people of the town faced a difficult task:

> They will have to accept the truth of the events that, though they happened in the distant past, are nevertheless a tragedy that is very close to them today. But before that, they will have to prepare themselves by undergoing an internal mental change ... If the people of Jedwabne do nothing but entrench themselves and defend themselves against attacks, if they shut themselves up in their own hell, their defense of the good name of their town will be nothing but a mockery of a defense. On the part of the people of Jedwabne themselves, there should be more sensible, premeditated actions. We should show that we have already understood something and that we have changed.

The position of the parish priest, Father Edward Orłowski, was very different. He asserted provocatively: "Let us tell the whole truth: change must occur on both sides, and not just one. For dialogue applies to both sides. By blaming only one side, we will always be biased." Polish-Jewish relations had been harmonious until the outbreak of the war, he argued, but after 1939 "the Soviets used the Jews against Poland." He went on:

> Later, when the Germans came, they tried to use the Poles against the Jewish community. One cannot say that the crime was committed by the Poles. What happened in Jedwabne also happened all over Europe. However, it cannot be excluded that some Poles were compelled to take part in this crime, others felt like exacting revenge on the Jews, and some may have been ordinary criminals. It is also difficult to accept that Polish society as a whole treated the Jews so cruelly. If it is only individuals who did so, then they did it as part of German operations.

Asked whether as an act of reconciliation the community of Jedwabne might clean up the devastated Jewish cemetery, he replied, "True, the Jewish cemetery is overgrown, but we have so many unemployed people here. If the Jewish community provides the money and employs them, they will tidy up the cemetery." As regards a "community gesture" (the words of one interviewer): "At this moment, that is perhaps impossible."

The mayor, Krzysztof Godlewski, took on himself the thankless task of mediating between these two positions. He realized how difficult this task was to be, admitting, "Whatever I say on this subject, I offend someone's sense of what is sacred." He was unable to persuade the townspeople to undertake even so anodyne a gesture as naming the local school after Antonina Wyrzykowska, who rescued seven Jews during the massacre. "The school is not yet ready for it," he admitted.[1]

The situation soon became more inflamed as local right-wing politicians and the bishop of Łomża, Stanisław Stefanek, encouraged those in the town who wished to adopt a strongly defensive "apologetic" position. In March 2001, a Social Committee for the Defense of Jedwabne's Good Name was set up. In a sermon he gave on 11 March 2001, Bishop Stefanek spoke of an organized campaign to "extract money" from the Poles (*zabrać im pieniądze*).

This "atmosphere of intimidation," as he described it, which "only testifies to the scale of the crime," provoked Stanisław Przechodzki to give an interview to Anna Bikont on 4 April 2001. He pointed out that the argument over the number of dead fails to take into account that most of those murdered were not burned in the barn but killed in random acts of individual violence. He also showed how a number of people had recently been "induced" to change their testimonies to stress German responsibility. Asked directly why in Jedwabne "Polish citizens murdered other Polish citizens of Jewish origin in such a cruel manner," he replied:

First of all, they had received permission to do so from the Germans. The Poles knew that the Germans were murdering Jews and that they would have nothing against the Poles' liquidating them themselves.

Second, before the war, Endek influences were strong here and many anti-Jewish excesses took place.

Third, there was an active group of people, with the mayor at its head, prepared to carry out a pogrom. This group conceived the plan and incited the rest of the residents with the words "Look, in Radziłów it worked out, and now they're rid of the problem." They had to have come to an understanding with the Germans.

---

[1] In June 2001, the school was renamed after Cardinal Stefan Wyszyński. At the ceremony, the guest of honor, Tomasz Strzembosz, compared the dispute over what had happened in Jedwabne to the Battle of Westerplatte in Danzig (Gdańsk), when the city was heroically defended by Polish forces at the beginning of World War II. Perhaps the saddest outcome of the Jedwabne massacre is the fact that Mrs. Wyrzykowska, whose bravery and compassion were so striking, has been ostracized by her fellow Poles, both in Jedwabne and in the United States.

Maybe that group needed three days to convince themselves that the other residents were ready for it.

Fourth, Satan came to this town. Human nature is such that when a person sees around him so much blood, so much pain, so much suffering, he himself is corrupted.

The deterioration of Polish-Jewish relations to which Przechodzki referred was confirmed by Rabbi Baker, who lived in the town until February 1938. In an interview with *Rzeczpospolita* on 10 March 2001, he asserted that "Jews and Poles lived peaceably in Jedwabne," but that

> from the mid-1930s, the hostility of the Poles toward the Jews grew. The picketing of Jewish stores began; restrictions were introduced in regard to ritual slaughter; the "ghetto benches" were established. Also in Jedwabne, gangs of National Democratic youths stood by the Jewish shops with metal spikes, so that Poles could not shop there. Assaults on Jews started and it came to murders. I remember at least two funerals of Jews murdered by Polish hooligans. We lived in increasing fear.

Nevertheless, the "apologetic" majority in the town was by now firmly entrenched. Given the growing atmosphere of intimidation, it is not surprising that the bulk of the town's inhabitants boycotted the ceremony on 10 July 2001, and that after this event Bishop Stefanek repeated in a statement for Radio Maryja that the whole affair was an attempt to extort money from Poles. Father Orłowski, in an interview with the local newspaper *Gazeta Współczesna* on 17 July 2001, described the commemoration as "a sheer lie." Further, he said that he was in possession of secret documents that proved that Poles were not responsible for the killings. Under these circumstances, it is not surprising that Krzysztof Godlewski, who did take part, should have been forced to resign as mayor, and that people like Mrs. Wyrzykowska and the Dziedzic family, who saved Jews in the town, have been compelled by social pressure to seek refuge in the United States.

One cannot help agreeing with Stanisław Przechodzki about the negative influence of Father Orłowski. He concluded his interview with Anna Bikont:

> Let there be no pretense—there's still a lot of antisemitism here. I would imagine that the role of the priest in a place like Jedwabne would be to say to people: "It was not you who did this, but your forefathers' generation. They did not reckon with it, and therefore it falls upon you. If you lie, then how will you stand before the countenance of God?"

There is, however, another Jedwabne. One of its representatives is Leszek Dziedzic, who in Agnieszka Arnold's film observed:

> One has to speak the truth even if it is painful and unpleasant. Still one has to speak the truth in order that the new generations will remember what has happened. Only if the truth is spoken can there be peace in the world.

Another is Marta Kurkowska, a native of the town who received her Ph.D. from the Jagiellonian University in 2001. She provides a moving and convincing account of the atmosphere in the town, which concludes this section. It should also be pointed out that the Polish authorities have attempted to change that atmosphere by providing educational programs for its young people and trying to instill respect in them for the values of civil society and mutual tolerance.

WE ARE DIFFERENT PEOPLE: A DISCUSSION ABOUT JEDWABNE IN JEDWABNE

WIĘŹ, APRIL 2001

P ARTICIPANTS IN THE DISCUSSION held at the Municipal Offices in Jedwabne on February 22, 2001:

    Krzysztof Godlewski, mayor
Stanisław Michałowski, chairman of the town council
Father Edward Orłowski, parish priest
Stanisław Przechodzki, director of the Łomża branch of the
    Podlasie Public Health Center
Senator Stanisław Marczuk, chairman of the Białystok chapter
    of Solidarność from 1981 to 1991
Więź editors Jacek Borkowicz, Father Michał Czajkowski
    (cochairman of the Polish Council of Christians and Jews),
    and Zbigniew Nosowski

ZBIGNIEW NOSOWSKI: We have come together to talk about how to deal with memories of the tragic events that took place here sixty years ago.

KRZYSZTOF GODLEWSKI: In broad terms, the whole "Jedwabne case" has two aspects: a moral one and a political one. These aspects constantly permeate each other and mingle in discussions on this subject. For several months, we have been playing host to a series of journalists. Some of them have come to us in order to learn the truth, while others have come in order to write a sensationalist article. Articles like that cast a very unfavorable light on the entire debate surrounding Jedwabne. First come the questions: How many perished and where, and is that possible? Only at the end do the murdered people themselves appear. A game of numbers begins: Did 500 people die, or 1,600? The tragedy is becoming a game in the hands of the media and politicians.

STANISŁAW PRZECHODZKI: Some people are trying to profit from this tragedy. Somewhere in the rush of words the human being is lost—the tragedy of those who died then, the tragedy of those who were guilty, and the tragedy of those who are still alive today. Jedwabne is a small

---

The transcript of this discussion has been edited by Jacek Borkowicz.

place. Everyone here knows everyone else, and the tragedy concerns everyone. Arguments are revived, and both antisemitic voices and voices accusing the Poles are being heard again. No one should be written off. Those who might think in an untruthful way today, but who follow their own consciences and believe what they are saying, might change someday.

There is no antisemitism in Jedwabne. I say so with full deliberation. I have encountered symptoms of antisemitism in larger towns. But simple people live here. Nevertheless, certain anti-Jewish elements remain inside them, shaped by the history of the interwar period or the war itself. But this is not the aggressive antisemitism that can be found among certain political groups or in some newspapers.

JACEK BORKOWICZ: How did the people here remember the events of July 1941 before May of last year—in other words before the appearance of Andrzej Kaczyński's article "Burnt Offering," which sparked a series of publications about the massacre?

STANISŁAW PRZECHODZKI: I am, and I feel myself to be, a Jedwabne man, though I have been living in Łomża for a dozen years or so. My forebears settled here. My family lived right on the town square. My parents told me about the events when I was still a boy. I didn't find them all that interesting. For most young people here, they were so remote that they seemed to have occurred hundreds of years ago. They were in the past, and that was that. In any case, our parents didn't want to tell us everything; they didn't want to damage us emotionally. We used to go to the so-called tombs, that is, the Jewish cemetery, and our parents shouted at us whenever we gathered nuts there. We didn't realize what we were doing, though we knew that beside the cemetery there was a barn in which the Jews were burned.

Only later, when I visited Jedwabne as a student, did the time come to read up on the subject and reflect upon it. That was when I discovered a few more details. Toward the end of my mother's life I knew much more, but I still didn't know all the details that I read about in Gross's book. However, I know a lot of details that do not appear there. But they make no difference to the letter and spirit of that book.

STANISŁAW MICHAŁOWSKI: I, too, was born here. My family has lived in Jedwabne for three generations. When I was eight, I witnessed a conversation between people who had taken direct part in the massacre. Names were mentioned, details given. I didn't identify myself with the events. I didn't comprehend them. Years later, a very clear memory of what I had once heard came back to me. The words I heard have a completely different dimension today.

STANISŁAW PRZECHODZKI: Those who live here and come from here will never be the same people that they were a year ago. Even at home, among my family, I feel different from how I felt last year, even though I am not to blame for what happened sixty years ago. The Jedwabne that existed before May 2000 is gone.

The people of Jedwabne are facing a difficult task. They will have to accept the truth of the events that, though they happened in the distant past, are nevertheless a tragedy that is very close to them today. But before that, they will have to prepare themselves by undergoing an internal mental change.

One must remember that the overwhelming majority of the population here consists of ordinary people. They are no better and no worse than the inhabitants of many Polish towns. It is a downright lie to portray them in some publications as simple peasant folk who don't read and who live in a village dominated by the all-encompassing weight of the Church.

ZBIGNIEW NOSOWSKI: When you said, "We will never be the same again," everyone nodded in agreement. What has changed?

STANISŁAW PRZECHODZKI: Most of all, Jedwabne is no longer just another Polish town, one of thousands. One can say without exaggeration that we are now on the lips of the world. That creates a very onerous psychological burden. The people of Jedwabne now have to consider how much they are capable of changing and what sort of truth they should accept. Can we stand up to the things that will surely happen over the next few months? In some people, knowledge of the tragedy, even though it happened so long ago, still rouses misgivings. They try to interpret it in their own way—not always in accordance with the truth—with the intention of protecting their families. These people will find it difficult to change and to accept the fact that certain events are irreversible. One always tries to seek an excuse.

But there is no excuse for what happened on 10 July 1941, never mind how difficult the period of Soviet occupation was. My parents and sister were on the deportation list, but at the very last moment, on 20 June 1941, they were warned about this and hid in the forest. Specific individuals and the entire Soviet system are responsible for the tragedy of the people who were deported from this area and mistreated. We know that in those areas where Russians were not the dominant ethnic group, the Bolsheviks systematically recruited, first of all, members of ethnic minorities for the NKVD. The reason was clear. Should it be necessary to disclose the crime, the minority could always be blamed. For instance, in the days of Dzierzyński,[1] the second largest ethnic group among the Chekhists—after the Russians—was the Poles. A similar mechanism was applied to the Jews. I do not know how many Jewish Soviet militiamen there were in Jedwabne, and how many Jewish informers. Perhaps a few, perhaps over a dozen. But all the rest of the Jews were poor, simple people. We do not suspect that a list of Poles to be deported was prepared in every Jewish household, just as we do not suspect that every Polish household thought about how to liquidate the Jews.

After reading some articles, one might get the impression that eastern Poland in the period 1939—1941 was under Jewish occupation, and not Soviet occupation. I did not think it possible to alter history so much in the space of a few months.

STANISŁAW MICHAŁOWSKI: My parents were deported. These days, people say that the Jews handed Poles over to the NKVD, but my family, unfortunately, was handed over by a neighbor, a Pole. What's more, after my father had been deported (he was taken at night, one of the first to go), the Russians came the next morning, threw everything out, drove us out of the house, and ordered us not to enter the property. They were accompanied by another neighbor, also a Pole.

STANISŁAW PRZECHODZKI: One cannot blame the entire Jewish community of Jedwabne for the deeds of a few Jews during the Soviet terror. Yet the same applies to those who took part in the crime of 10 July. This was a not an entire "society," as Jan T. Gross says in *Neighbors*.[2] They were just individuals, perhaps several dozen of them, perhaps more, perhaps fewer. Of course, in a certain sense, the remainder are also responsible. Perhaps they didn't quite manage to prevent it, didn't use all available means, didn't provide shelter.

But generally, after sixty years, it's difficult to judge the acts of our parents and grandparents. The situation was different then. One occupation had passed and another was beginning. No one knew what Nazism would bring, so the German forces received a warm welcome in many places. They were treated as liberators from Soviet occupation.

STANISŁAW MICHAŁOWSKI: What happened in July 1941 is a painful but undeniable fact. In a certain sense, it also concerns me, and I too bear moral responsibility, even though I am in a "comfortable" situation

[1] Feliks Dzierżyński, the Polish first head of the Cheka, the secret police established after the Bolshevik revolution.

[2] Gross writes in the Polish edition that the crime was committed by "society," and in the American edition that it was committed by the "neighbors" of the Jedwabne Jews (trans.).

arising from the fact that my family was neither directly nor indirectly involved in those events. I feel very sorry to say this, but I think the Poles played a certain part in the atrocity. But on the other hand, I do not agree that the involvement of the Germans was marginal, or even nonexistent. Even Prof. Gross has written in his book that were it not for Hitler and the war, the atrocity would never have happened. The Germans organized everything. There was a group of people, ninety-two of them, whose names and addresses are known, who came out onto the square to guard the Jews who were under escort. Most of these people were acting under pressure. They were in the pillory. One wonders what would have happened to them if they had refused to come. Could they have helped? I suspect not. The element of fear that paralyzed the Jews also affected the Poles in a certain sense. There was a group of some thirty people whose participation in the crime is irrefutable and was—to be honest—ruthless. They included people known for an inclination to hooliganism and banditry before the war.

I grieve over what happened—and in our own town at that. But I have never agreed, and still do not agree, with attempts to implicate the whole town in this business. One should not apply collective responsibility. Over 95 percent of Jedwabne's present population came here after the war. These people have no connection with the events of the summer of 1941.

FATHER EDWARD ORŁOWSKI: At this point I would like to correct a certain distortion in Gross's book. He writes that, when they sensed danger, the Jews of Jedwabne asked the bishop in Łomża to shelter them. They were supposed to have offered him silver candlesticks in return for this help. The bishop supposedly kept his word, but only "for a while." His appeal to the Germans proved to be of no avail, and he did not prevent the massacre.

Well, nothing of the sort happened. When the occupation came and Poland was divided up, the bishops went their separate ways. The auxiliary bishop went to live in Ostrów Mazowiecki, under German occupation, while Bishop Stanisław Łukomski hid from the Soviets in Kulesze Kościelne. He returned to Łomża on 8 or 9 July, just before the Jedwabne murders, but he did not actually take up office until August, because the vicarage and bishop's palace had been commandeered by German troops. It would have been practically impossible for Jedwabne Jews, under conditions of wartime isolation, to have contacted the bishop before 10 July.

FATHER MICHAŁ CZAJKOWSKI: Mr. Przechodzki said, "Accept the truth." Jesus said that the truth shall set us free. The more quickly we accept the truth, the sooner we will be liberated from this nightmare.

You will be different, but the important thing is, how? Does change mean an apologetic attitude, a closing of your eyes to the truth—or does it mean liberation, which brings with it the courage of acceptance? The good must be given a chance, so that the world does not associate Jedwabne solely with the evil that happened here.

KRZYSZTOF GODLEWSKI: We could accept the truth if only we knew it in full. For instance, if the exact number of Jews were established. But that unfortunate number of 1,600 Jews has been pulled out of a hat!

We want to bring this issue to a close, because it has gotten too big for me at least, and probably for some others among us. Whatever I say on this subject, I offend someone's sense of what is sacred. Are we still the "royal Piast tribe" that we are proud of being?[3] I was brought up on Mickiewicz[4], on the song of the Pierwsza Brygada [First Brigade].[5] My father was in the Home Army and did time in the Wronki prison.[6] When I ask such questions, I enter unwillingly into a conflict with my own father.

ZBIGNIEW NOSOWSKI: The pope speaks of an examination of conscience by the Church, for in the Church there is a link between present and past generations. We bear all the good, and also all the evil, previously done in the name of the Church. I think one can view the nation in a similar way—after all, this concept also possesses a spiritual dimension.

FATHER EDWARD ORŁOWSKI: Let us tell the whole truth: change must occur on both sides, and not just one. For dialogue applies to both sides. By blaming only one side, we will always be biased. When the two totalitarian states divided Poland between themselves, they took advantage of ethnic minorities in order to set them at odds with each other. Here, the Jews and the Poles coexisted well. Things began to deteriorate only after the outbreak of the war, and the conflict reached its peak when the Germans attacked the Soviet Union. We must admit the whole truth. Young Jews supported communism, and the Soviets used the Jews against Poland. Later, when the Germans came, they

[3] Piast tribe: a legendary tribe of ancestors of Prince Mieszko I, the first ruler of the medieval Polish state. The name Piast became associated with the entire medieval dynasty, which originated with Mieszko. The phrase "royal Piast tribe" comes from the poem "Rota" by Maria Konopnicka, a popular patriotic song.

[4] Adam Mickiewicz (1798–1855), the great Polish romantic poet.

[5] The First Brigade of the Polish Legions (Pierwsza Brygada) was a military formation created by the later ruler of Poland Józef Piłsudski to fight alongside the Central Powers, but as an independent body in order to establish a fully sovereign Poland.

[6] Wronki: a town in central Poland. During the Stalinist period, many Armia Krajowa (Home Army) soldiers and freedom fighters found themselves in the local prison there.

tried to use the Poles against the Jewish community. One cannot say that the crime was committed by the Poles. What happened in Jedwabne also happened all over Europe. However, it cannot be excluded that some Poles were compelled to take part in this crime, others felt like exacting revenge on the Jews, and some may have been ordinary criminals. It is also difficult to accept that Polish society as a whole treated the Jews so cruelly. If it is only individuals who did so, then they did it as part of German operations.

I worked with Father Józef Kembliński, who was the priest here throughout the occupation, when I was vicar in Lipsk on the Biebrza River. We went to Jedwabne then, looked at the monument at the site of the burned barn, and talked. He always said that the murder was carried out by the Germans. I know from his account that the Jews asked him for protection from destruction. They were prepared to give him gold and other valuables. Father Kembliński talked to the gendarmes because he spoke German well, and asked if anything could be done. They replied that it was impossible. They had been given orders—the Jews must die! Father Kembliński did not accept the gold.

FATHER MICHAŁ CZAJKOWSKI: And what did he say about the murder itself? Where was he at the time?

FATHER EDWARD ORŁOWSKI: For three days, the Jews were rounded up to weed the grass and clean the park. No one in town knew how it would end because on the critical day they, too, were herded onto the square. On the day when that unfortunate barn burned, the parish priest stood at the gateway leading to the church and watched. The town square was almost empty. People were only peeking out the windows or around corners. The fear was pervasive.

FATHER MICHAŁ CZAJKOWSKI: Couldn't he have intervened?

FATHER EDWARD ORŁOWSKI: I know that, before the burning of the barn, he went up to an officer who had arrived in Jedwabne that day and said: "What harm have the women and children done to you? Spare them at least!" to which the officer replied: "Maybe you don't know who's in charge here. Clear off, if you want to keep your head on your shoulders!"

ZBIGNIEW NOSOWSKI: The factual plane and the moral plane keep getting entangled here. What exactly happened and what can be done now? Father, you are speaking about motives that can explain the events. But can they justify them?

FATHER EDWARD ORŁOWSKI: Nothing can justify murder, absolutely nothing.

ZBIGNIEW NOSOWSKI: I've heard that Rabbi Baker, who was born in Jedwabne under the name Piekarz and is today elderly and living in New York, has indicated that he could come here and talk to people, young people, but that he would like to be accompanied by the local priest.

FATHER EDWARD ORŁOWSKI: The rabbi has never asked me, but if he wants, then I am ready to meet him. Human fellowship is built not only on the basis of religion but also on the basis of culture and a general sense of humanity. He is invited to the rectory!

JACEK BORKOWICZ: The afterword of Gross's book contains a message from Rabbi Baker in which he asks the people of Jedwabne to tend the Jewish graves and commemorate the site of the synagogue.[7] Would this be possible—not so much in the financial as in the psychological dimension?

FATHER EDWARD ORŁOWSKI: I realize that, as parish priest, I am responsible not just for the Roman Catholic cemetery here but also for the cemeteries of other communities within the parish. We have a German cemetery here, and I never permit the old graves to be destroyed by having people buried there. In 1991, when there were plans to set up a market square close to the Jewish cemetery, I protested from the pulpit and said that it would be a sacrilege. I suggested that the marketplace be moved elsewhere, and I offered 1.1 hectares of parish land in exchange. Thanks to the exchange, neither the Catholic nor the Jewish cemeteries have been trampled. True, the Jewish cemetery is overgrown, but we have so many unemployed people here. If the Jewish community provides the money and employs them, they will tidy up the cemetery.

FATHER MICHAŁ CZAJKOWSKI: But here we are talking about a community gesture.

FATHER EDWARD ORŁOWSKI: At this moment, that is perhaps impossible.

KRZYSZTOF GODLEWSKI: As for looking after the Jewish graves, there might still be some psychological barriers in the minds of the people of Jedwabne, but I see no such danger in the minds of young people. They already think in different terms. For them there are neither Jews, nor Romans, nor Greeks. That initiative could launch the building of not just one but several small memorials in the hearts of these young people, much more durable than stone.

---

[7] The reference here is to the Polish edition. The American edition does not contain Rabbi Baker's comments.

However, there is a polarization of views. On the one hand, we are defending ourselves against historical accusations, and on the other hand the government is preparing major ceremonies on 10 July. What would happen if it turned out that we here are in opposition to all this? Something important is due to happen on 10 July, so let world opinion see us as open-minded and responsible Catholics. But there is no sense in our doing anything that runs contrary to our convictions.

JACEK BORKOWICZ: The people of Jedwabne should be aware that a gesture on their part does not mean that they are confessing to the crime; it's merely an expression of responsibility for the place where they live.

KRZYSZTOF GODLEWSKI: I remember how the government's proposed version of the inscription on the monument ended: "Forgive us, as we have forgiven others!" But if we don't think we share any guilt, then what is the sense of that sort of "forgiveness"? If the 10 July ceremonies are meant to be simply a general reminder of the death of Jews, after which we all go home, then it would be better not to have any ceremonies at all.

On the basis of what Father Orłowski says, we bear practically no guilt at all. Father Orłowski has his information, and we have ours. How are we to tell who is right? I am convinced that the Poles played a considerable part in this crime. But if this participation was only sporadic, then it would be a grave mistake to say that the whole town was involved. We would only be wronging the residents.

No one is criticizing the people of Jedwabne for being forced to leave their homes and guard the Jews. The complaints are about the ones who were overzealous. They should be named, and they alone should be tried. Except that no one is able to do this.

FATHER EDWARD ORŁOWSKI: They are either dead or old.

KRZYSZTOF GODLEWSKI: The question remains: Do we, the Jedwabne community, accept the legacy of those thirty people? Do we distance ourselves from it? Do we apologize for those thirty people?

STANISŁAW MARCZUK: I agree with the mayor. There are no good or bad nations, only good and bad people.

JACEK BORKOWICZ: In the same way that there are no good or bad towns.

STANISŁAW MARCZUK: The pope stresses that one cannot blame the entire Jewish people for the death of Christ. I think the same principle ought to be applied to Jedwabne—individual Poles were guilty, yet there were people with various mentalities among the general Polish population of the town. Their attitudes to the murder of the Jews could not have been identical.

ZBIGNIEW NOSOWSKI: How do children and young people ask their parents today about what happened in 1941?

STANISŁAW MICHAŁOWSKI: I witnessed a five-year-old child listening to a conversation among adults, and then asking, "Listen, Grandfather, was it you who murdered those Jews, or your dad, or my dad?" When you hear such questions, you cannot brush them aside, unless you are totally thick-skinned. Most of us are experiencing this matter profoundly, each in his own way.

KRZYSZTOF GODLEWSKI: Before today's talk, I didn't sleep all night. Whenever I think seriously about this crime, I lose my equilibrium, and emotions get the upper hand. This is not something about which one can speak coolly, calculating and jotting down figures. On 10 July last year, as we were laying a wreath at the memorial, two elderly ladies were talking about what happened sixty years ago. At one point, both of them burst into tears. No one who has the tiniest bit of sensitivity can talk about this normally. We cannot lose sight of this in our discussion.

We in Jedwabne don't need either psychologists or sociologists. Anyone who is incapable of reacting to these horrors on his own is beyond integration with society. For others, it is enough if, when they walk past the monument, they think about things—and then go back in their thoughts, and more than once, to the entire episode and digest it. Their consciences will be enough to remind them to do so.

ZBIGNIEW NOSOWSKI: Mr. Mayor, I understand you wanted to name the local school after Antonina Wyrzykowska, who rescued seven Jews during the German occupation. Has this proposal been considered in the school?

KRZYSZTOF GODLEWSKI: To my surprise, I found that for children this subject was entirely abstract. Should we therefore "make them happy" by digging up old matters?

FATHER MICHAŁ CZAJKOWSKI: The children will find out anyhow. I do not think this can be kept hidden from them. Besides, they probably know a lot already. They must, or else a five-year-old would not have asked who carried out the murders. One should not hide the dark side of local history from children, but one should also show them the beautiful parts of that history.

KRZYSZTOF GODLEWSKI: The suggestion of naming the school after Mrs. Wyrzykowska was just an idea I tossed off the top of my head. The school is not yet ready for it. Remember that the school is an organism consisting of the Teachers' Council, the Parents' Committee, and the pupils. The new name cannot be imposed by an administrative decision. Internal changes have to occur first. And that is a long educational process in which the family and the home must also play their part.

JACEK BORKOWICZ: Gross writes about the Wyrzykowski family in a footnote to *Neighbors*, describing them as wonderful people, and I hope a book will also be written about them one day. But at the same time I do not think anyone will ever write such a book. That is how the logic of the media works, unfortunately. Evil is more attractive than good. That is why commemorating Mrs. Wyrzykowska by naming the school after her would somehow fill this gap.

KRZYSZTOF GODLEWSKI: Let me tell you one thing: I consider it my duty to mediate. Wherever I encounter racial or religious hatred, or other kinds of hatred, I will try to overcome it within the limits of my modest abilities. In this way I want to repay the debt that is owed to those who were murdered. This shall be my absolution and—I don't have a good word here—some kind of redress for the death of those people. What I mean to say is that the death of those people should somehow bear interest. If we all make sure that such events as in 1941 never happen again, those deaths will not have been in vain.

ZBIGNIEW NOSOWSKI: Do you pray for the murdered Jews, Father?

FATHER EDWARD ORŁOWSKI: I feel responsible for the entire history of my parish. Ever since I became parish priest, I have been praying for all its residents living and dead, regardless of their creed. Yes, I do pray for the Jews, but I also pray for the Germans, for the Russians, for all those whose bodies lie in our parish soil. That is my duty. War set these people against each other, and they resorted to atrocities, to death. But that death has reconciled them. They have stood, deeply shamed, before the same God.

FATHER MICHAŁ CZAJKOWSKI: It's a shame that they were reconciled only after their deaths.

FATHER EDWARD ORŁOWSKI: If necessary, I will take up a collection in my parish for a monument to the murdered Jews, then I will take part in a procession with my parishioners and sing the Angelus, and then we will pray at the stone where those who were burned in the barn are buried.

KRZYSZTOF GODLEWSKI: The Church is imbued with the wisdom of two thousand years, but these are times of change. I have three children, whose religious attitudes are different from mine, and completely different from my father's. Certain steps and gestures can only do us good. You, Father, are the highest authority in Jedwabne and have the greatest opportunity to work a gradual change in people's hearts.

FATHER MICHAŁ CZAJKOWSKI: The acts of contrition proclaimed by the pope do the Church good, because they make it credible in the eyes of others. Perhaps there is no such thing as collective guilt, but every community needs a kind of collective responsibility, felt by everyone who considers himself a part of this community. Can anyone say that the pope does not love the Church because he discusses its sins? He discusses the Inquisition, the pogroms, and the expulsion of the Jews from Spain precisely because he feels such a strong attachment to this Church. It is the same when we talk about our own sins. We do so not because we are bad Poles but because we love Poland so much. Gentlemen, you feel so closely linked to this place and experience its history so deeply because it is your town, your life.

KRZYSZTOF GODLEWSKI: Resolving this issue and explaining it in full, even if it is painful to do so, will bring us more benefit than keeping it a secret.

STANISŁAW PRZECHODZKI: Of course. There can be only one truth in a fundamental issue. The murder was carried out by some neighbors. That was the main murder—the burning in the barn—but there were also many, very many, individual murders. There is no doubt that they were committed with the approval of the Germans. But to talk of dozens or hundreds of armed gendarmes in Jedwabne is a mockery of the victims. There was no cordon of Germans around Jedwabne. Just before the barn was burned, my mother, with a baby in her arms, walked through the entire town and left it unhindered. Nowhere did she see any Germans. One kilometer away from Jedwabne, she heard the screams of the burning victims. It was so piercing that she remembers it to this day.

STANISŁAW MARCZUK: Thirty-five years ago, Polish bishops addressed these famous words to the Germans: "We forgive and we ask for forgiveness." There was a heated reaction to these words at the time. People said, why should we apologize to the Germans? And yet as a result of this message, the attitudes of Germans toward the Poles changed, and this was confirmed by surveys. Sometimes we apologize not because we owe someone a debt of guilt, but because we require purification. He who utters these words first is the wiser. We apologize not because we are guilty. We apologize simply in the name of love.

FATHER MICHAŁ CZAJKOWSKI: No one expects the parishioners here to go to the confessionals and confess to the evil of 1941 as their own personal sin. There is a kind of solidarity; not just a surface layer, but one that reaches deep down. In the name of this solidarity we ourselves should commemorate the victims and not just follow instructions from foreign journalists.

STANISŁAW MICHAŁOWSKI: These instructions sometimes smack of blackmail. Being continually lectured to arouses a feeling of being under threat in the local community. And a person who is being attacked naturally begins to defend himself.

JACEK BORKOWICZ: Jedwabne is becoming a symbol, whether we like it or not. An important element of this symbol is that which we Poles find the most difficult to say. Irrespective of the number of perpetrators, irrespective of the degree of German inspiration, and irrespective of whether there was any coercion and how strong it was, we cannot deny that the massacre was committed by Polish hands. The murderers were Poles. I do not agree with the reverend Father that the same thing happened all over Europe. Jedwabne is not typical. If it were, it would never have become the symbol that it now is. Of course, Jedwabne is no exception either—similar events occurred along the entire front, in Lithuania, the Ukraine, and Moldavia, not to mention in the neighboring towns of Wąsosz and Radziłów. But a characteristic feature of a symbol is that it "falls" on one place, in this case Jedwabne, and we have to come to terms with that, because what is done will not be undone. But now we can exercise some influence, albeit restricted, on the form of this symbol. Soon it will be too late to do so.

STANISŁAW MICHAŁOWSKI: But such reflection cannot be introduced by external laws and decisions, even if they are wise. It must start inside people.

STANISŁAW PRZECHODZKI: The atrocity occurred sixty years ago, but a rejection of the truth of it, and, even more, an acceptance of this truth, will change the people here. It will also determine the way in which the outside world looks at Jedwabne. Let us leave it to historians to discover the causes of those conflicts. They had but one outcome—a tragic one. If the people of Jedwabne do nothing but entrench themselves and defend themselves against attacks, if they shut themselves up in their own hell, their defense of the good name of their town will be nothing but a mockery of a defense. On the part of the people of

Jedwabne themselves, there should be more sensible, premeditated actions. We should show that we have already understood something
and that we have changed.

At the same time, we should be courageous. A single courageous
thought, a single courageous act causes the wave of criticism to disinte-
grate. And very often a small gesture suffices, one that does not cost
much but is a Christian gesture and very necessary. Finally, we should
bear in mind that we have children and grandchildren. Our parents
did not deal with this issue. True, the conditions for doing so did not
exist, but these conditions have existed now for eleven years. If we do
not deal with this issue, it will pass to the next generation. And why
should our descendants have to be tormented? It is enough that we
ourselves are tormented . . .

Translation taken from *Thou Shalt Not Kill*.

Marta Kurkowska-Budzan

MY JEDWABNE

I WAS BORN and grew up in Jedwabne; I lived there for almost thirteen years. Now I live in Kraków, where I am a social historian at the Jagiellonian University interested in the past, the present, and the future. In June 2000, when I learned of the conference to be held in London entitled "The Shtetl," I intended to present at it the results of my social-anthropological research on Jedwabne. It was a local study based on oral evidence. Then, perhaps two weeks later, I read Prof. Gross's book on the massacre in Jedwabne. It did not shock me. I had been aware of this tragedy while I was planning my research project, and I knew the facts he described. I refer to his book only because it radically changed the conditions under which research could be undertaken in Jedwabne. Since the opening by the Instytut Pamięci Narodowej (Institute of National Memory) in autumn 2000 of an official inquiry into the massacre, people have been reluctant to talk to anyone.

Fortunately, I had managed to interview some people in the town before the inquiry, and before the media became interested in the Jedwabne affair. I hope to be able to continue my research, although I am aware that nothing will be the same again. I conceive of my project on three levels. The first is to "reconstruct" the Jedwabne of prewar times, with its Jewish, Polish, and German inhabitants, and their houses, shops, crafts, markets, and everyday life. The second is to investigate the memories of the oldest living generation of Polish Catholics: How do they remember the shtetl, their neighbors, their common daily life? How has their individual memory been shaped by prejudices? Do they see their "world before the war" as an arena of conflict or of coexistence?

The third aim is to deal with the tragedy of July 1941: How did it affect the sociocultural memory of the three generations of Polish Catholics living in Jedwabne now? How is it expressed in myths, superstitions, omissions, and fables? Why and how do witnesses choose between testimony and silence? Finally, how does the publicity on the matter influence people's memory?

Lecture delivered at the conference "The Shtetl" held at the Institute for Jewish Studies, University College London, 19–21 June 2001.

Let me recount a personal story: when I was seven or eight years old, my best friend, older than me, told me a "big secret." I vividly recall that sentence: "You know . . . Once Poles burned Jews alive in a barn . . . Here, in Jedwabne." I did not admit to my friend that I had no idea of who those Jews could have been. However, what she had said sounded terrible. Equally terrible was the second part of her story—about people searching for gold jewelry and gold teeth in the smoldering ruins of the barn. Frankly, I did not believe her, although I tried to find out who the Jews were. I told my mother the story and asked for an explanation. She said, "You are too young for that kind of story."

When I was old enough for "that kind of story," I began to make efforts to comprehend what had happened. It seemed to me, as a social historian, that there had to be some aspects of the pogrom that could be subjected to sociopolitical analysis, and I approached the tragedy like any other subject of historical investigation. In my mind I was preserving the distance of a researcher who had been born in Jedwabne and had the exceptional status of an insider in the community, but who had left the town in 1984 so that I had the perspective of an outsider.

Then I read the Jedwabne *Yizkerbukh*. Among the stories and memoirs contained there was the report of Itzchak Yacov (Janek) Neumark, of which a few sentences struck me forcibly:

> In these terrible moments I noticed that my sister and her little daughter became totally gray. In the darkness of the night I took my sister Esther-Lea and her daughter Reizale to the priest of the village of Pshitul, and I myself hid at the house of Dr. Kowalczuk. After the war I was told that they killed my sister Esther-Lea just two weeks before the war ended. Someone recognized her as a Jew. Of her daughter Reizale I never found a trace.

Reading the name of Dr. Kowalczuk, who had brought me into the world—the same person who had helped Janek Neumark—I felt something I would describe as an "illumination." I felt I had touched the past itself, and I felt bound to these people about whom I had read. And then I read once again the *Yizkerbukh*, carefully scanning the list of victims' names. Later on I found out that the old rug I had inherited from my great-grandmother must have been dyed by Mr. Pravda, the only dyer in Jedwabne, whose name, with those of his entire family, is on the list of those murdered.

I was traumatized in a way a historian should not be if she wants to be more or less objective, and as a result I abandoned my methodology of comprehension and adopted Franklin Ankersmit's theory of "experience of history" (which differs from "historical experience"—the experience of those who have witnessed past events).[1] According to this approach, the one and only moment in which the past exposes itself to us is in the moment of trauma, which causes surprise and pain. Trauma causes our convictions, categories, and expectations to shatter. History is created as a result of traumatic collective experiences. History, according to Frederic Jameson, is what hurts. Trauma does not register events from the past but records the power of experiences that cannot be assimilated, cannot be accepted. That is the paradox of trauma: it cannot be forgotten and cannot be remembered. "Normal" history can be acquired, adopted, domesticated; traumatic history cannot. In this way the traumatic past, whether private or national, exists in ourselves like a foreign body that we cannot get rid of. Ankersmit says that the only way of coping with it is to point out that there is a conflict between memory and history that requires the discourse of the historian to be replaced by that of memory. This merely refers to the past but does not try to explore or penetrate it. As an alternative to the coupling of history and text, Ankersmit proposes the coupling of memory and monument (as a relic of the past).

For contemporary inhabitants of Jedwabne (Jedwabniaks), but also for Poles in general, the murder of the Jews there is just this kind of traumatic, undomesticated history. The public debate is painful but inescapable. Surveys in March 2001 show that 50 percent of the population of Poland know the name of Jedwabne and 48 percent connect it with the pogrom.[2]

On the other hand, the prewar history of Jews, Catholics, and German Protestants in Jedwabne and their relationship appear to Jedwabniaks to be "normal" history. Let me give some examples of this "normal" history, based on thirty hours of tape-recorded interviews that I conducted. I should like to emphasize that all interviews took place before Jedwabne had attracted any media attention. These people were not even aware of Prof. Gross's book. While I was interviewing them, I showed them old photos of buildings in Jedwabne and asked for their recollections. Half of these buildings used to belong to Jews. As regards facts, dates, and names, the most valuable interview is that with Stanisław O., who was born in 1920. He was a butcher's apprentice in the late 1930s. According to him—and somewhat surprisingly to me— his employer, a Catholic butcher, cooperated with his neighbor, a Jewish butcher. For example, they shared a large freezer that had been dug

[1] F. Ankersmit, "Remembering the Holocaust: Mourning and Melancholia," in *Reclaiming Memory: American Representations of thee Holocaust*, ed. P. Ahokas and M. Chard-Hutchinson (Turku, 1997).

[2] *Rzeczpospolita* 67 (20 March 2001).

into the ground and filled with ice blocks. Stanisław O. usually assisted in ritual slaughter and still remembers many Yiddish words, since he used to speak Yiddish. He also socialized with the family of the Jewish butcher and attended their parties and wedding receptions. At the same time he was a member of Związek Młodzieży Katolickiej (the Catholic Youth Association), which was hostile to the Jews. When I asked him what activities he took part in within that association, he replied, "Well . . . we were taught how to march nicely in fours."

Another interviewee was Zofia N., born in 1918, who had been head of the women's section of Związek Młodzieży Katolickiej. She remembers taking part in amateur theatricals. She also liked to go to social meetings in the Catholic Community House, but at the same time she went to meetings in the Jewish club room. She said she became fond of Jewish dancing (*pląsy*), and after the war, as part of her job as a community household adviser, she taught Jewish dances to children in the neighborhood village schools.

Apart from the main market square, in which traditional Wednesday markets took place, there was an old market square. With its old wooden buildings it was a center of Jewish crafts, producing for the surrounding countryside. There were eight bakeries in Jedwabne, of which only two were run by Polish Catholics, and many small shops—Jewish and also Polish, and some of them open only on market day. The market was famous for horse-trading, and the town was a lively one. Many remember their Jewish neighbors: Michał Kuropatwa, a coachman who provided transport to Łomża once a day; Lasko, a traveling salesman; Pravda, the dyer; the Cacko family, who were cattle-traders; and the Pecynowitz family, who were millers. They were willing to talk about *that* past. As Zofia N. told me, no one had ever asked her about that; no one had wanted to listen.

Another interviewee, Natalia G., who was born in 1926, grew up in the old market square, virtually together with the seven children of her Jewish neighbor Sholimova. They played together and went to school together. She still recalls the names of all seven. I spent three days interviewing her. On the first day I asked her whether she remembered any Yiddish words; she said, "No, I never understood them when they were speaking their language." The following day I asked if she had ever been to a Jewish party, and she began to recall the wedding day of Sholimova's eldest daughter. The vivid memory of this event made her break into Yiddish song. She was deeply moved, and I had the impression she was transported into the past. I mention this because that was the moment when I realized that my interviewees had in a sense lost a part of their lives. This lost world used to be their world too, in the broad meaning of this notion—their reality. They told me, without needing to be asked, that they missed "something" . . . The willingness of witnesses to the past to share their memories of prewar times proves that this is a domesticated history just waiting to be written down.

I then started to question my interviewees about the Second World War, about the Soviet occupation and the first and second Nazi occupations.[3] And then—the murder. My question was "What happened to the Jews?" Silence. Then women at first shed tears; men, after a while, answered reluctantly, "They were all killed . . . burned alive."

"Who did it?" I asked. The answer was always: "Poles" or "Ours . . . But, you know . . . Germans also" or "Poles and Germans." In personal memories Poles are always in the foreground. The Nazis are the obvious context. "That was wartime," people said.

My interviewees were plagued by emotional recollections. Out of curiosity two of them, the day after the pogrom, went to the scene of murder. Recounting this to me, Natalia seemed to see it just in front of her. Cruelly I asked her, "Did you see Sholimova and her children there? Did you recognize them?" She did. They were lying in a pile of bodies in the corner of the barn. "They were not burned," she said. "They looked suffocated." Afterward, she said, when she went home, she could not speak for several days.

When I talk to people from Jedwabne now, with the media interest upon them, and when I talk to the generation born after the war, they usually begin with denials of Polish participation in the murder of Jews. But it is not long before they say: "Yes. There were Poles involved," and then "The worst thing is, they did it willingly and they did it for Jewish money." Obviously, the media have been educating ordinary people in political and historical language. People now freely use expressions such as "Jewish collaboration with the Soviets" or "Special SS Commando" and so on. This is the language of official, public discourse.

However, for the last sixty years the murder has been well known but still "a big secret" in Jedwabne. It has been the subject of private discussion only. And the subject of local myths, gossip, and even tales. Let me give some examples: Israel-Joseph Grondowski was one of the three Jews remaining in Jedwabne after the war. According to local gossip, he survived the pogrom and converted. He left behind his wife and children, who were then killed. Israel-Joseph went back home after the war and remarried. Polish Catholics apparently accepted him, but he did not completely change his way of life. According to one of my

---

[3] The first one lasted about a month, until the second Nazi-Soviet border treaty. At the end of September 1939, Jedwabne was occupied by the Soviets.

interviewees, he kept kosher and had a Jewish calendar pinned to the wall. People gossip about his drinking problem, claiming that the reason for it must be the betrayal of his family and religion. He did not have children with his second wife: "that was God's punishment," according to local gossip. Then he adopted a baby boy, who, when he grew up, drank so heavily that he eventually died of alcoholism. "That is God's punishment!" But, at the same time, they feel sympathy for him and socialize with him.

God's punishment is at the core of all Jedwabne stories. Most of the murderers, of whom many left the town just after the war, avoided punishment. Some moved to Łomża, just twenty kilometers from Jedwabne, so they were, in a sense, still present in the conscience, memory, and gossip of the local community. Local gossip about them refers to any sudden death or sickness in their families. People talk about "God's punishment," "God's curse," or the "Jewish curse" put on those who have "Jewish blood on their hands." This notion extends to the whole Jedwabne community. People say, "Evil has settled in this town."

This is the usual comment on every crime committed there. One of the most shocking occurred in 1998, when a few drunken young people burned alive a homeless man. People were devastated, and such sentiments as "There must be something wrong with this place. God cursed this land for what happened to the Jews" are heard.

Nowadays they speak about "land," not particular individuals. I should stress that 75 percent of the population of contemporary Jedwabne consists of newcomers, who migrated there in the mid-1950s and 1960s. All of them quickly learned about the murder, and they now share a collective memory, but it refers to the place of Jedwabne rather than to the people who lived there in 1941.

Another story is relatively new. About 1981 women workers from the Public Works Department refused to weed grass growing in gaps in the pavement. The grass had formed in the shape of cross in a place where, it was said, a young Jewish woman and her baby had been killed. People claimed that it was a miracle—God's sign to the sinners of Jedwabne—and gathered there to pray.

Another story has arisen that takes the form of a traditional folktale in three parts. In the first, "Pogromchiks caught a very, very rich Jew, dressed in a fur coat, with a fur hat on his head, gold rings on his fingers, and shiny shoes. They threatened him, telling him to dive into a pond. He resisted, but they threatened again saying, 'You Jew! Jump into the water; otherwise we will drown you!' " The story then relates the three stages of the Jew's entry into the water. The victim stops when the water reaches his knees. The pogromchiks threaten him again. He stops when the water reaches his waist, and again when it reaches his neck, and when he realizes there is no hope, "he puts his hands together and, with all his strength, calls out: 'Jesus! Mary! Saint Joseph! Stand by me!' and plunges into the water."

In the second part of the story the pogromchiks decide to pull the dead man out of the water to rob him. When they find the body, "a true miracle occurs: the Jew is as naked as when God created him."

The moral is contained in the third part: "Since then, everyone tempted to search for lost jewelry still remaining at the bottom of the pond will inevitably be drowned." (There have been a number of drownings, but those who died were drunk while swimming.)

These are examples of a collective memory but are the unofficial discourse. The public discourse is quite different and is defensive, as can be seen in the Jedwabniaks' fierce reaction to Gross's book and to virtually every publication alleging Polish involvement in the murder. In my opinion, these reactions are examples of the people's attempts to domesticate a traumatic past. A past of this sort cannot be remembered in a "normal" way, as is usual in historical works that seek to provide rational explanation.

Prof. Gross broke the taboo. What is most painful to Jedwabniaks is that what occurred in their town became widely known and debated, having never been discussed in public before. Jedwabne today, with its approximately two thousand inhabitants, is a very small community. People are related to each other, and they depend on one other. This is not a community of the size of Oświęcim or Kielce. The public debate, so important to Poles in general, in Jedwabne causes immense distress, in part because of the appearance in newspapers of surnames that are very common in the area.

The public debate is dominated by a search for the truth about the murder. If I were to give my view, I do not know the truth. I know only what people have been saying for the last sixty years. I know only the essence of the long collective and individual memory. It is what I learned in childhood: "Poles burned Jews alive in a barn. And robbed them."

· · · · ·

Marta Kurkowska-Budzan received her Ph.D. in history from the Jagiellonian University in 2001 with a dissertation entitled "The History of the People: English Social Historiography 1945–1997." Her main fields of interest are the philosophy and methodology of history, the social history of ethnic and cultural minorities in Poland, and the social history of medicine.

PART VI

MEMORIES AND METHODOLOGIES:

THE HISTORICAL DEBATE

INTRODUCTION

But facts are chiels that winna ding
And downa be disputed.[1]
—Robert Burns

THE DEBATE AMONG historians has so far been rather unfruitful. Partly this is because of the previously close personal ties between some of the key controversialists, notably Tomasz Strzembosz, Tomasz Szarota, and Jan Gross himself. It will not have escaped the attentive reader that Gross's first discussion of the testimony of Szmul Wasersztajn appeared in the festschrift for Strzembosz. Strzembosz also seems to feel very defensive about the fact that although he had worked for more than thirty years in the area immediately surrounding Jedwabne, he had never, prior to the publication of *Neighbors*, found it necessary to mention the massacres in that town or elsewhere in the region. In the controversy over the Cichy article in 1994, he adopted a strongly "apologetic" stance with little sympathy or understanding for the dilemmas of Jews hiding on the Aryan side.

Partly it is in the nature of such fundamental historical controversies to be extremely acrimonious in their initial stages. This was certainly the case in the dispute aroused by the publication of Fritz Fischer's *Griff nach der Weltmacht*. In the course of a particularly bitter interchange about the "rise of the gentry" in Elizabethan England, the eminent English historian R. H. Tawney commented that "an erring colleague is not an Amalekite to be smitten hip and thigh." But that level of hostility seems generally to prevail. Perhaps it could be argued that the form *Neighbors* took was the result of Gross's own traumatic response to his discovery of the massacre, and his own trauma was expressed in a way that compelled other historians to respond and create their own new approach to memory. It may be, too, that this was a necessary stage before there could be a return to the dispassionate discourse of historical investigation.[2]

The actual historical disputes can be summed up under three headings. First, there are the disagreements about what actually happened in Jedwabne between the collapse of Soviet rule in late June and the

[1] But facts are like young men that cannot be pushed around / They cannot be disputed.

[2] See the discussion of Franklin Ankersmit's views of traumatic history in the introduction to this volume.

final massacre of 10 July 1941. Second, there are differing views about the context of the massacre. Finally, there are arguments over its larger significance. The controversies about what happened in Jedwabne revolve around a number of questions. How many Jews were murdered? How many Poles took part? How much German incitement and involvement was there? These issues have arisen constantly throughout this volume, and one of the main problems in resolving them is the difficulty of reconstructing an event more than sixty years later when there are only imperfect records—and when, in addition, given the criminal character of what occurred, there are great incentives to dissemble. Certainly Gross was compelled in his work to rely on a narrow range of sources, and, in spite of great efforts, the source base for reconstructing the events in Jedwabne has not been greatly enlarged since the publication of the Polish edition of *Neighbors*. Disputes over the interpretation of the sources form the core of the exchange below between Bogdan Musiał, a young historian at the German Historical Institute in Warsaw, and Jan Gross.

The problem of how to reconstruct what actually occurred in Jedwabne is well dealt with in the review article, at the section's end, by Dariusz Stola. He argues that the massacre has to be understood in the context of the collaborationist authority established by the Germans in Jedwabne. The initiative for the massacre clearly came from the Germans, but they were probably not present in large numbers and do not seem to have participated actively. The existence of a collaborationist town council made the implementation of the massacre easier and meant that it could be carried out by a core of what Stola, following Goldhagen, describes as "willing executioners." They had the tacit support of the bulk of the townspeople, and very few had the civic courage to oppose them. The number of Jewish victims, in his estimate, is closer to 600 than 1,500. (Although this does not affect the moral issue, it is important to try to reach as accurate an assessment of this figure as possible. In this context it is unfortunate that the exhumation carried out was so brief and unsatisfactory.)

In the controversy about the context of the massacre, two key points are in dispute: how strong was antisemitism in interwar Poland, and how significant was the effect of Soviet occupation in inflaming Polish-Jewish relations? The intensity of anti-Jewish feeling in interwar Poland remains a matter of controversy, and the different positions adopted in the Jedwabne controversy echo the observations of Ezra Mendelsohn's provocatively titled article "Interwar Poland: Good for the Jews or Bad for the Jews?"[3] Mendelsohn notes that in the historiog-

---

[3] In *The Jews in Poland*, ed. C. Abramsky, M. Jachimczyk, and A. Polonsky (Oxford, 1986), 130–39.

raphy of interwar Polish Jewry two basic positions—one "optimistic," the other "pessimistic"—can be observed. He continues:

> The attitude of most Jewish scholars has been, and continues to be, that interwar Poland was an extremely anti-semitic country, perhaps even uniquely anti-semitic. They claim that Polish Jewry during the 1920s and 1930s was in a state of constant and alarming decline, and that by the 1930s both the Polish regime and Polish society were waging a bitter and increasingly successful war against the Jewish population.[4]

The "pessimistic" point of view has been most clearly expressed by Celia Heller in her book *On the Edge of Destruction* (New York, 1977). Her thesis is clearly encapsulated in the title. In her view, the period between the two world wars was a rehearsal for the Holocaust. Polish actions had by 1939 pushed the Jews to "the edge of destruction," and it only remained for the Nazis to complete what the Poles had begun.

This "pessimistic" view of the situation of Jews in interwar Poland has not gone unchallenged. The most eloquent of the Jewish "optimists" is Joseph Marcus. Marcus reserves his greatest condemnation for what he refers to as the "reformers" of Jewish life in Poland. Blinded by their Zionist and socialist obsessions, they had a great deal to do with the economic decline of Polish Jewry. According to Marcus, Jews in Poland were able to hold their own economically and were, in fact, better off than the majority of the population. They were more than capable of withstanding the assaults to which they were subjected in the 1930s. The real problem, in Marcus's view, was Polish poverty and Jewish overpopulation. "The Jews in Poland were poor because they lived in a poor, undeveloped country. Discrimination added only marginally to their poverty."[5]

These views have been echoed by many Polish scholars, most recently by Marek Wierzbicki in his *Polacy i Żydzi w zaborze sowieckim* (Warsaw, 2001). Their position has been best articulated by the British historian of Poland Norman Davies. Like Marcus, he argues that the intractable nature of the Jewish question was the result of the poverty of the reborn Polish state and "an unprecedented demographic explosion" among Jews that "countermanded all attempts to alleviate social conditions." The Jews were only one of many ethnic groups in conflict in Poland, and they were not singled out for special treatment by Polish chauvinists, who were equally hostile to Germans and Ukrainians.

---

[4] Ibid., 130.

[5] Joseph Marcus, *Social and Political History of the Jews in Poland, 1919–1939* (Berlin, 1983).

He cites the cultural creativity of the Polish-Jewish community as evidence that its situation was not as desperate as has sometimes been claimed, and explicitly rejects Heller's claim that the oppression which the Jews experienced in the last years before the outbreak of the war paved the way for the successful implementation by the Nazis of their policies of mass murder. "[T]he destruction of Polish Jewry during the Second World War," he asserts, "was . . . in no way connected to their earlier tribulations."[6]

It should be stated at the outset that the main feature of Jewish life on the Polish lands is that the attempt to transform the Jews, on the western European model, from a religious and cultural community to citizens—Englishmen, Frenchmen, or Germans—of the Jewish faith did not by and large succeed. By the beginning of the twentieth century, most Jews regarded themselves as members of an ethnic or national group and were so regarded by the surrounding population. This made an accommodation between Jews and the Polish state much more difficult, since what they were now demanding were national as well as individual rights. What is also clear is that the situation of the Jews deteriorated seriously after 1935, a phenomenon that is analyzed in this volume by Jerzy Jedlicki. Antisemitism was intensified by the persistence of the Great Depression; the dangerous example to antisemites of the ease with which the Nazis were able to disenfranchise and expropriate the assets of one of the best integrated Jewish communities in Europe; and the divisions within the Polish government, which led one group within it to seek a rapprochement with the antisemitic right. The period was marked by considerable anti-Jewish violence and by campaigns to exclude the Jews from the universities and the professions. The only specific anti-Jewish legislation actually enacted was a restriction on the use of Jewish methods of animal slaughter (*shekhita*), but other more far-reaching laws were proposed in parliament.

Some qualifications of this gloomy picture should be made. The interwar period saw a considerable growth in the use of the Polish language by Jews, particularly in central Poland, a phenomenon that would have had significant implications had the independence of Poland not been destroyed. In fact, something of a "Polish-Jewish honeymoon" developed in the face of the threat from Nazi Germany on the eve of the war's outbreak, and it continued for a period after the German invasion because of Jewish participation in the defense of Warsaw in September 1939. In addition, Jewish attempts to resist the boycott of

---

[6] Norman Davies, *God's Playground: A History of Poland in Two Volumes*, vol. 2, *1795 to the Present* (Oxford, 1981), chap. 9, "Żydzi: The Jewish Community," 240–66.

Jewish trade, with the help of the Joint Distribution Committee and the Cekabe, a system of low-interest credit unions, were achieving a degree of success.

Yet the conclusion has to be pessimistic. As Jedlicki puts it:

Poland was unquestionably one of the countries most affected by this [antisemitic] obsession. Its ideological leaders never stopped developing ideas for depriving millions of Polish citizens of their rights and property and banishing them from the country. The only groups to actively oppose such ideas were the Socialists and the Communists and the liberal faction of the intelligentsia; the fact that these circles did not treat them with aggression and contempt explains the inclination of assimilating Jews to seek refuge and support in them.

These developments inevitably affected the situation in Jedwabne, as has been pointed out by Anna Bikont in her article this section and in her interview with Stanisław Przechodzki in *Gazeta Wyborcza*, 4 April 2001. It has also been confirmed by recent research, such as that of Jan Milewski.[7]

Jan Błoński, in his article "The Poor Poles Look at the Ghetto" wrote:

[W]hen one reads what was written about Jews before the war, when one discovers how much hatred there was in Polish society, one can only be surprised that words were not followed by deeds. But they were not (or very rarely).[8]

Jedwabne turned out to be one of these exceptions.

The impact of the twenty-two months of Soviet occupation of former eastern Poland in exacerbating Polish-Jewish relations and creating the climate in which the massacre was possible has been stressed by many participants. Certainly the Soviet occupation created divergent interests between Poles and Jews. The Poles saw themselves as confronted by two enemies, the Nazis and the Soviets, and Polish diplomacy and underground strategy were dominated from the time of the Polish defeat in September 1939 by the aim of ensuring the reemergence of Poland as an independent state within its prewar frontiers. The Poles totally rejected the incorporation into the Soviet Union of what were described as Western Belarus and Western Ukraine, and attempted to

[7] Jan Jerzy Milewski, "Polacy-Żydzi w Jedwabnem i okolicy do 22 czerwca 1941 roku" (unpublished).

[8] Jan Błoński, "The Poor Poles Look at the Ghetto," in *'My Brother's Keeper?' Recent Polish Debates on the Holocaust*, ed. A. Polonsky (London, 1990), 47. For the Polish version of this article, see *Tygodnik Powszechny*, 11 January 1987.

organize resistance to the brutal methods adopted by the Soviets to ensure the permanence of their control of their new territorial acquisitions. For the Jews, the Soviets were a lesser evil than the Nazis, whose anti-Jewish policies were all too well known. They did not, by and large, accept Polish strategic thinking and were prepared to accept as permanent the new territorial arrangements in the multiethnic eastern Kresy, a stance that obviously had a seriously adverse effect on Polish-Jewish relations in the area.

In addition, Jewish "collaboration" with the new Soviet authorities aroused widespread Polish resentment. It is undeniable that a fair number of Jews (like the overwhelming majority of Belarusians, a considerable number of Ukrainians, and even some Poles) welcomed the establishment of Soviet rule. In the Jewish case, this welcome was natural, based on a desire to see an end to the insecurity caused by the collapse of Polish rule in these areas and the belief that the Soviets were less hostile than the Nazis, and on resentment at Polish anti-Jewish policies in the interwar period. There was in addition some support for the communist system, although this was very much a minority position within the Jewish community. While the Soviets did offer new opportunities to individual Jews, they acted to suppress organized Jewish life, both religious and political, dissolving *kehillot* (Jewish communal bodies), banning virtually all Jewish parties, and arresting their leaders. Jews made up nearly a third of the more than half a million people deported (and in many cases thereby saved) by the Soviets from these areas. Under these conditions, the overwhelming majority of the Jewish population here very quickly lost whatever illusions they had about the Soviet system.

This was not how most Poles saw the situation. They were affronted by Jewish behavior in 1939, probably exaggerated Jewish participation in the new system because a Jewish presence in the apparatus of government was so unprecedented in Poland, and accused the Jews of disloyalty and treason in a moment of national crisis. This position has also been espoused by some historians, most notably Tomasz Strzembosz. An example of his views is the article that is reproduced in this volume.

It is clear that more research needs to be done on the impact of Soviet rule in the Jedwabne area. Yet what is obvious is that the widespread acceptance of the stereotype of the pro-Soviet and anti-Polish Jew greatly widened the gulf between the two communities. This stereotype, embodied in the Polish concept of Żydokomuna (Judeo-communism), had a long history on the Polish lands, going back to Julian Ursyn Niemcewicz's 1817 dystopia, *The Year 3333*, which described a

Warsaw of the future—renamed Moszkopolis, after its Jewish ruler—
that had been taken over by a mafia of superficially Europeanized
Jews. It was given a new lease on life by the Bolshevik revolution.
Many Poles felt directly threatened both by the prospect of revolution
and by Russian imperialism in a new guise, which they saw embodied
in the Soviet regime. The fact that Jews played a significant part both
in the government of the USSR and in the illegal Polish Communist
Party further strengthened the hold of this form of political paranoia,
which was clearly apparent during the Polish-Soviet War of 1919–1920
and became a basic feature of the political discourse of the radical right
in the 1930s. It now seemed to have been confirmed by the events of
1939.

The problem of how to assess the implications of the Soviet occupation of Jedwabne on Polish-Jewish relations there is well summed up
by Bencion Pinchuk, whose views on this topic were favorably contrasted with those of Gross by Bogdan Musiał.[9] Pinchuk observed:

> The subject of "Jewish-Soviet 'collaboration' " is as old as the Red
> Army's invasion of the eastern provinces of the Second Polish Re-
> public on September 17, 1939. The sights and sounds of jubilant
> Jewish masses that met the advancing troops, expressing publicly
> their sense of relief and joy; the role played by Jewish communists
> and sympathizers in establishing the Soviet regime as well as tak-
> ing up positions formerly held only by the ruling Poles—these
> were difficult to digest. It went contrary to what might be called
> the "natural order" of things as perceived by the ordinary Pole.
> For twenty-two months the traditional roles were at least partially
> reversed. Moreover, it occurred under Russian rule, the powerful
> historical enemy of the Poles. In the minds of Polish patriots there
> had to be some sinister plot behind it. Equality of the Jew under
> the Soviet rulers was perceived as "collaboration" if not actual
> treason on their part. In Polish memory this period of "unnatural"
> relations with their Jewish neighbors remained an open sore. It
> was a score to be settled in due time.[10]

The term "collaboration" is a loaded one and is of questionable use in
analyzing the complex question of the impact of Soviet occupation on
the ethnically mixed area of former eastern Poland. As Pinchuk has
further written:

---

[9] Interview with Paweł Paliwoda, *Życie*, 2 February 2001.

[10] "Facing Hitler and Stalin: On the Subject of Jewish-Soviet 'Collaboration' in the
Occupied Territories," in *Contested Memories: Poles and Jews during the Second World War*,
ed. J. Zimmerman (New Brunswick, N.J., and London, 2003).

Between September 1939 and June 1941, the Soviet Union ruled the eastern provinces of Poland. The multi-ethnic population of the region had to adapt to the new rulers, to learn to live and survive under Soviet rule. In one way or another, when active fighting against the invaders ceased, the vast majority of the population accepted the new regime and in varying degrees "collaborated" with the Soviet rulers. However, the use of the term "Collaboration" in research is problematic at best and misleading at its worst. By its very use, it implies negative moral judgment, and comes pretty close to meaning actual treason. Its use in research means a priori the assumption of an unwarranted moral superiority of the investigator and prejudgment of the subjects of his research. It is misleading rather than enlightening.[11]

Finally, as Strzembosz himself admits, to use the alleged Jewish responsibility for the crimes of the Soviet Union to explain the massacre of women and children comes close to attempting to excuse murder.

The arguments over the larger significance of the massacre are concerned with three issues. First, there is the question of collective guilt. No sentence in *Neighbors* has aroused more controversy than the statement with which the book concludes: "[T]he 1,600 Jedwabne Jews were killed neither by the Nazis, nor by the NKVD, nor by the UB . . . but by society."[12] This was widely taken as a statement of collective guilt. Thus Bogdan Musiał has observed:

> If Gross had written that X or Y was responsible for these crimes, that would be acceptable. However, he makes the society of Jedwabne, Polish society, responsible for this crime.[13]

However, this is an interpretation that cannot be sustained by a careful reading of the whole of the final paragraph of the Polish edition. Gross explained his intentions in an article in *Gazeta Wyborcza* on 25–26 November 2000. He points out that he led up to this paragraph by observing that Poland was no exception in Europe: "And like several other nations, in order to reclaim its own past, Poland will have to tell its past to itself anew." He continues, "After this assertion that the truth about our history in the period of the Second World War still remains to be written comes the paragraph that reads thus:

---

[11] Ibid.

[12] This is taken from the Polish version, 114–15. In the English version the final sentences read: "For, indeed, the 1,600 Jedwabne Jews were killed neither by the NKVD, nor by the Nazis, nor by the Stalinist secret police. Instead, as we now know beyond reasonable doubt, it was their neighbors who killed them."

[13] Interview with Paweł Paliwoda, *Życie*, 2 February 2001.

An appropriate memento is, of course, to be found in Jedwabne, where there are two monuments with inscriptions carved into the stone that will have to be chipped away in order to liberate the historical truth in them. One says simply that the Germans killed the Jews: "THE PLACE OF THE SUFFERING OF THE JEWISH POPULATION. THE GESTAPO AND THE NAZI GENDARMERIE BURNED 1,600 PEOPLE ALIVE 10 JULY 1941." The other one, erected in a Poland that was already free, either implies that there were no Jews at all in Jedwabne—or else it bears witness, in spite of itself, to the crime that was committed: "TO THE MEMORY OF APPROXIMATELY 180 PERSONS INCLUDING TWO PRIESTS MURDERED IN THE TERRITORY OF JEDWABNE DISTRICT IN THE YEARS 1939–1956 BY THE NKVD, THE NAZIS, AND THE UB [signed:] SOCIETY." For, in fact, the 1,600 Jedwabne Jews who are omitted here (even though they were "murdered in the community of Jedwabne in the years 1939–1956") were not murdered by any Nazis or NKVD or UB, but rather by society.

The issue is thus the falsification of memory perpetrated by those who erected the two monuments, or, in Gross's words, "My point is that it is necessary to write the truth, because the truth will always out." He added, perhaps aware that his subtle observations risked being misunderstood:

> On reflection, I nevertheless feel that the final word in the book, "society," should have been put in quotation marks, to make it immediately plain that it unconsciously reveals the truth hidden in the lies inscribed on the Jedwabne monuments.[14]

The difficult question of the overall attitude of Polish society toward the Jewish genocide remains to be addressed. On this issue, while rejecting the concept of collective guilt, Gross takes a rather strong line, highlighting the widespread antisemitism and the "general debasement of morality during the occupation."[15] Others have stressed, rather, the Poles' widespread fear and indifference, and also examples of Polish aid to the Jews. We still lack a broad and nuanced picture of this important subject.

Gross also makes a number of challenging assertions. For example, he claims that

> it is manifest that the local non-Jewish population enthusiastically greeted entering Wehrmacht units in 1941 and broadly engaged in

[14] *Gazeta Wyborcza*, 25–26 November 2000.
[15] "Poduszka pani Marx," *Tygodnik Powszechny*, 11 February 2001.

collaboration with the Germans, up to and including participation in the exterminatory war against the Jews.[16]

This is an important assertion and seems, at least partially, to be borne out by the findings of Martin Dean on Polish participation in German-organized police forces east of the Curzon line. He has shown that about half of those persons punished in Poland after the war for war crimes in the former eastern Polish territories served as local policemen in the *Schutzmannschaft* (several hundred individuals, especially from the territory of modern Belarus). It is also partly confirmed by Shimon Redlich's work on Berezhany and by Sarunas Liekis's investigation of the three-way civil war in southern Lithuania among Poles, Lithuanians, and Soviets.[17] But only further research will demonstrate how far it can be justified.

The same applies to Gross's observation that

in the process of Communist takeover in Poland after the war, the natural allies of the Communist Party, on the local level, were people who had been compromised during the German occupation.[18]

This is an attempt to counteract the widespread view in Poland that the post-1944 regime was dominated by Jews. The participation of former Nazi sympathizers and collaborators in the new communist government does seem to be borne out by some of the work of Padraic Kenney and Andrzej Paczkowski.[19] But at present it is still no more than an interesting hypothesis.

More recently, the temperature of the debate seems to have cooled. This was evident in the discussion organized by *Rzeczpospolita* on 3 March 2001, reprinted below. It was marked by a much greater willingness to exchange opinions and contrasted strongly with the earlier debate in November 2001, at the Historical Institute of the Polish Academy of Sciences, which Szarota describes as "one of the most unpleasant experiences of my life."[20]

One reason for the more sober nature of the discussion is the large mass of information that has been collected by investigative journal-

---

[16] *Neighbors* (English edition), 155.

[17] Martin Dean, "Die Armija Krajowa und die Beteiligung von Polen bei der einheimischen Hilfspolizei in den von den Deutschen besetzten ostpolnischen Gebieten" (unpublished); Shimon Redlich, *Together and Apart in Brzezany: Poles, Jews, Ukrainians 1919–1945* (Bloomington, 2002); Sarunas Liekis, "Soviet Resistance in East-Southern Lithuania and the Jews" (unpublished).

[18] *Neighbors* (English edition), 164.

[19] Padraic Kenney, *Rebuilding Poland: Workers and Communists 1945–1950* (Ithaca, 1997); Andrzej Paczkowski, ed., "Raporty o Pogromie," *Puls* 50, 3 (1991).

[20] *Gazeta Wyborcza*, 2–3 December 2001.

ists. Perhaps the most skilled of these is Anna Bikont, a veteran Solidarity journalist and one of the founders of *Gazeta Wyborcza*.[21] An experienced investigator, she has conducted many interviews in Jedwabne and has also unearthed much important background material. Her reports are essential reading for an understanding of the massacre and demonstrate what can be achieved by patient probing even today, more than sixty years after the event. These reports should be read together with the material in part 5, "Voices of the Inhabitants of Jedwabne." Ms. Bikont is at present writing a book on what happened in Jedwabne and Radziłów. In December 2001 she was awarded the Polish "Press" prize for her reports in *Gazeta Wyborcza*, one of which is "We of Jedwabne," reprinted below.

The new tone is also reflected in Dariusz Stola's reflective review, which concludes this part of the volume. Another hopeful sign is the widespread trust in the Instytut Pamięci Narodowej and in particular in its head, Prof. Leon Kieres. The various more detailed investigations being undertaken by Marek Wierzbicki, Anna Bikont, and Andrzej Żbikowski, among others, as well as the publication of documentary materials—such as the collection from the Ringelblum archive of Jewish reports from the eastern Kresy—should also produce important results. It is to be hoped that these developments will make possible an investigation of the difficult and painful issues raised by the Jedwabne massacre in a calmer and more dispassionate atmosphere than has thus far prevailed.

---

[21] *Gazeta Wyborcza* was founded in May 1989. It is one of the biggest Polish dailies, with an average circulation of 559,000. Its chief editor from the beginning has been Adam Michnik—historian, well-known leader of political opposition of the 1980s, and propagator of ideas of freedom, democracy, and civil society. Its political orientation is left-liberal. *Gazeta* and its team of journalists have received many prestigious national awards for coverage of a variety of political, social, and ecological issues. In 2001 Anna Bikont received the Grand Prix Award for articles dedicated to the massacres of the Jewish populations in Jedwabne and Radziłów.

Tomasz Strzembosz

COLLABORATION PASSED OVER IN SILENCE

Rzeczpospolita, 27 January 2001

I HAD NOT intended to lend my voice to the discussion that followed the publication of Prof. Jan T. Gross's book *Neighbors*, about the murder of Jews carried out in July 1941 in the little town of Jedwabne in the Podlasie region.[1] Above all, because the discussion to date, while raising many essential themes, had ignored the most crucial fact: what happened in Jedwabne after the German army entered the area—that is, who committed the mass murder of the Jewish population of Jedwabne, when, and under what circumstances.

That is what should be written about first and foremost, the more so since Gross's theses, in the light of certain sources, do not appear to be entirely true. On the other hand, the documentation in my possession still does not authorize me to speak out publicly on precisely that key issue.

Nevertheless, both Gross's book and Andrzej Żbikowski's recent article in *Rzeczpospolita* (4 January 2001) contain statements so shocking that they cannot be passed over in silence. They concern the attitudes of the Polish and Jewish populations in the lands first occupied and subsequently annexed by the Soviet Union, as well as the evaluation of those attitudes.

Before I address the subject proper, I must make several basic assertions. Murders carried out on any group of civilians cannot be justified. Nothing justifies the killing of men, women, or children simply because they represent some social class, nation, or religion, because justice must be meted out on an individual basis. Neither one's own convictions, nor the orders of one's superior, nor "historical necessity," nor the welfare of some other nation, class, religion, or social group, nor the good of any organization, military or civilian, overt or clandestine, can justify such crimes.

I would like those who read this text to be aware of the fact that this is my basic position. I am also fundamentally opposed to the murder

---

[1] By Podlasie, I understand the territory of the eastern part of historical Mazovia, the inhabitants of which include the Mazovian minor gentry and Belarusians and Jews, far less numerous here.

of the soldiers of any military or police formation simply because they serve in it, especially when they are unarmed or have surrendered. Whoever carries out such a murder, regardless of whom he represents, is to me nothing more than a murderer.

General Horror

Before engaging in an evaluation of the attitudes and behavior of various social and national groups in the lands occupied by the Worker-Peasant Red Army, one should recall some basic facts, for without an awareness of the realities of that period it would be impossible to understand the people living there and those swept in by the storm of war.

The German incursion into Podlasie horrified the general population, which received the German forces with easily discernible hostility. The locals supported units of the Polish Army that were being driven to the East. Many unmobilized reservists and young people of preconscription age traveled eastward in search of units willing to accept them and give them arms. Hence a number of men from that region (including unmobilized ones) ended up taking part in the defense of Grodno and the Sopoćkinie region against the Red Army.

Especially after the Battle of Andrzejów, which was fought by the Eighteenth Polish Infantry Division, the population of Podlasie supported the small partisan detachments emerging in the area of Czerwony Bór and the Biebrza Marshes. These units saved them from destruction. The anti-German attitudes of the locals were uniform and resolute.

The period following the incursion of the Red Army into the eastern regions of the Republic of Poland may be broken down into three subperiods. The first, referred to by Prof. Ryszard Szawłowski (and not only by him!) as the Polish-Soviet war, lasted two weeks, until the beginning of October 1939, when organized resistance by larger combat units of the Polish Army ceased—although individual subunits continued partisan-type actions. The second involved the conquest of the area, combined with a sociopolitical and economic "revolution," pre-planned and carried out with the aid of Soviet troops and special services. Therefore I call it "the marionette revolution." It was during this period that the first arrests took place. The period ended in November 1939 with the incorporation of the northeastern lands of the Republic of Poland into the Belarusian Soviet Socialist Republic, and of the southeastern lands into the Ukrainian Soviet Socialist Republic.

In actuality, that period lasted another two months, as the Soviet administrative system (republic, *oblast'*, *raion*) was finally introduced in the annexed areas.[2] The third subperiod, early 1940 to June 1941, was marked on the one hand by unification with the USSR's socioeconomic system (forced collectivization of agriculture, strengthening of state farms,[3] completion of the nationalization of industry, trade, and the banking system, and so on). On the other hand, it witnessed a violent increase in reprisals, especially in the first half of 1940, in the form of mass arrests and deportations. In the area of so-called Western Belarus deportations continued until the end and involved some 150,000 people. I wish to dwell a bit on this because, though few people are aware of it, these actions were carried out in accordance with the principle of collective responsibility.

The Time of Deportations

The first deportation, on 9–10 February 1940, encompassed military and civilian settlers and foresters together with their families. The second, on 13 April 1940, involved those whose family members (heads of households, brothers, sons) had been captured as Polish soldiers, policemen, and the like, or had fled abroad, gone into hiding, or been arrested as conspirators or "enemies of the people"—that is, as socially dangerous elements. The third, carried out on 29 June 1940, mainly involved people living in the towns. It encompassed the so-called *bezhentsy* [refugees], including many Jews,[4] notably those who had registered to return to the part of Poland under German occupation. This fact partially explodes the myth of Polish Jews joyfully welcoming the Red Army solely owing to their fear of the Germans. The last deportation began on 14 June 1941 in the Wilno region (taken over when the Republic of Lithuania was liquidated in June 1940), and in the lands of the Belarusian Republic on 20 June. It was interrupted by the German attack.

[2] The formal incorporation of the Polish eastern lands into the Soviet Union occurred at the beginning of November 1939, but the division into *oblast'* and *raion* was not completed until January 1940.

[3] The collective farm or *kolkhoz* was an agrarian production cooperative, and the state farm, the *sovkhoz*, was set up as soon as the Red Army entered, when vast landed estates immediately became state property and others were parceled up.

[4] According to Soviet documents, there were 72,896 refugees in the area known as Western Belarus at the beginning of 1940. Only 25,621 had jobs; the rest shared the miserable lot of the unemployed. In ethnic terms, there were 4,290 Poles, 65,786 Jews, 1,703 Belarusians, 577 Russians, and 169 Ukrainians. On 29 June 1940, a total of 18,650 people were deported; according to Albin Głowacki, 84 percent of them were Jewish.

As we can see, all these acts of violence were undertaken on the basis of the principle of collective responsibility. An entire family was held responsible for a father who had been a soldier or for a brother who had fled. All those who had lived in a forester's house were considered guilty. Blows were struck at the "nest." In Warsaw, for instance, the Germans retaliated for armed street attacks by shooting all the inhabitants of the nearest building, even though they had no links to the resistance fighters, or by killing prisoners in Pawiak prison, or the people of a village near which a military train had been blown up. That collective responsibility encompassed children, women, and the elderly. It was the weakest who paid with their lives during transport or exile, in Siberia or on "the starvation steppes" of Kazakhstan.

Betrayal during the Days of Defeat

Who carried out the terror? The NKVD did, and in the early period so did the Red Army, which had under its command Chekist operational groups that followed the army "to clear the area," just as *Einsatzgruppen* had followed the *Wehrmacht*. What about the militia (police)? Few people know that, from 1939 to 1941, there were three different kinds of militia.

The first were the various emerging "red guards" and "red militias," consisting of locals armed with clubs, sawed-off shotguns, axes and revolvers, though sometimes also machine guns, who backed up the Red Army in its "liberation march" and implemented the "class anger" of social groups oppressed by "feudal Poland." They generally appeared shortly after 17 September 1939 (or on that very day—a rather telling fact) and most often acted with bloodthirsty savagery, not only behind the lines of the Polish Army but also after the incursion of the Red Army, which gave local "revolutionary elements" several days of grace to settle past scores and exact class revenge.

Later, these "militias" were replaced by the Workers' Guard, which were set up in the occupied territories in accordance with an order issued by the commander of the Belarusian Front on 16 September 1939, and by the Citizens' Militia, which was established on the strength of a similar order of 21 September 1939. After Western Belarus had been incorporated into the Belarusian Soviet Socialist Republic, they were replaced by the NKVD-linked Worker-Peasant Militia, which initially comprised only newcomers (so-called easterners) [i.e., from the Soviet Union proper (ed.)], and later were supplemented by locals.

Apart from a small number of Communists in the towns and an even smaller number in the countryside, the Polish population responded to the USSR's aggression and the Soviet system being created there the same way it had reacted to the German aggression. There are thousands of diverse testimonies attesting to this. Participation by Polish peasants in what were called *selsovets* (rural communal soviets) was no indication of anything, because these bodies were of a decorative nature. The executive committees and—even more importantly, the party and police apparatuses controlling them—were what mattered. It was the latter that were frequently involved in the looting of the gentry manor houses and palaces left behind by their owners.[5]

By contrast, the Jewish population, especially young people and the town-dwelling poor, staged a mass welcome for the invading army and took part in introducing the new order—some with weapons in hand. This, too, has been attested to in thousands of Polish, Jewish, and Soviet testimonies. There were also the reports of the chief commander of the Union for Armed Combat, Gen. Stefan Grot-Rowecki, the report of the emissary Jan Karski,[6] and accounts recorded both during the war and years later. This has also been reported in the works of Gross himself. Primarily on the basis of Polish accounts, of which there are thousands in the archives of the Hoover Institution in the United States, he arrived at conclusions that he expressed clearly and unequivocally.

The Soviet army was enthusiastically welcomed not only in areas formerly occupied by the *Wehrmacht*, but also in border areas that the Germans had never entered. Moreover, the "guards" and "militias" that sprouted like mushrooms after a rainfall in the wake of the Soviet aggression consisted largely of Jews. And not only that. Jews engaged in acts of rebellion against the Polish state by occupying localities, setting up revolutionary committees there, arresting and executing representatives of the Polish state authorities, and attacking smaller and even quite large units of the Polish Army (as in Grodno).

Dr. Marek Wierzbicki, who has been researching Polish-Belarusian relations in what was called Western Belarus in 1939–1941 for several

[5] It is significant that we find no reports of Polish peasants looting the manor houses in "Western Belarus," while such attacks were committed frequently by Belarusian peasants.

[6] It may be worth quoting a fragment of this report, which is omitted by Gross in his *Upiorna dekada*. It reads: "Things are worse when [the Jews] inform on Poles, students of Polish nationality, and Polish political figures, and when they sit at desks and direct the work of Bolshevik police or are members of this police, or when they untruthfully slander the way things were in former Poland. It must unfortunately be stated that these incidents are quite widespread, far more frequent than cases indicating their loyalty to the Poles or their sympathy for Poland." Artur Eisenbach, "Raport Jana Karskiego o sy-

years, has also taken note of Polish-Jewish relations. In a lengthy, as-yet-unpublished article, he writes about the three-day battle between Jewish rebels and the Polish Army and police in Grodno (18 September, before the arrival of Red Army units), the two-day clash over nearby Skidel, and Jewish revolts in Jeziory, Łunna, Wiercieliszki, Wielka Brzostowica, Ostryń, Dubno, Dereczyn, Zelwa, Motol, Wołpa, Janów Poleski, Wołkowysk, Horodec, and Drohiczyn Poleski. Not a single German had been seen in any of these localities. The revolts were directed against the Polish state.

This was armed collaboration, siding with the enemy, treason committed during days of defeat. How large was the group of people who took part in it? In all probability, we will never be able to present any figures. At any rate, this phenomenon encompassed the entire area in which the Belarusian Front of the Red Army was deployed.

New Arrangements in Public Offices

A second question concerns cooperation with organs of repression—above all, the NKVD. The "militias," "red guards," and revolutionary committees were the first to cooperate, and the workers' guards and citizens' militias began later. In towns, they consisted mainly of Polish Jews. Subsequently, when the Worker-Peasant Militias took control of the situation, Jews—as Soviet documents have indicated—were considerably overrepresented in them. Polish Jews in civilian dress, wearing red armbands and armed with rifles, participated in the arrests and deportations in large numbers. This was the most extreme example, but for Polish society the most glaring fact was the large number of Jews in Soviet public offices and institutions—the more so since Poles had been the dominant group before the war!

On 20 September 1940, at a conference in Minsk, the capital of the Belarusian Soviet Socialist Republic, the head of the municipal NKVD office in Łomża stated: "Such a practice has taken root here. The Jews have supported us and only they were always visible. It has become fashionable for the director of every institution to boast that he no longer has even a single Pole working for him. Many of us were simply afraid of the Poles." At the same time, at Party meetings in the Białystok oblast', there were numerous "complaints" that one heard only Russian and Yiddish spoken in Soviet offices, that Poles felt discrimi-

---

tuacji Żydów na okupowanych ziemach polskich na początku 1940r.," *Dzieje Najnowsze* 2 (1989): 179.

226 MEMORIES AND METHODOLOGIES

nated against, and that a cleaning woman in one Białystok office was harshly rebuked for singing Polish songs while she worked. This was in accordance with the truth and the current "party line," for a "new policy" regarding Poles had been agreed upon in the Soviet leadership at that time.

In his article, Wierzbicki summarizes the situation of that period as follows:

> The bloated Soviet administrative structures gave masses of un-employed Jews the opportunity to find jobs. That was of no mean importance to them, since the industrially impoverished towns of the eastern borderlands had provided few job opportunities. Being considerably better educated than the Belarusian commu-nity, the Jewish population provided numerous clerks, teachers, and functionaries of the security apparatus. That undoubtedly in-fluenced Polish-Jewish relations, since Jews most frequently took the place of previous clerks and teachers of Polish nationality . . . Moreover, between September and December 1939, many repre-sentatives of the Polish community who had held senior posts in the administration and political authorities of the Polish state be-fore the war, or who had been engaged in public affairs, were ar-rested. Local Jews—members of the interim administration or mi-litia—were very helpful to the Soviet authorities in tracking down and detaining them.

He continued, this time citing none other than Jan T. Gross: "It also occurred that representatives of the Jewish population ridiculed Poles, emphasizing the sudden change of fate that had befallen both commu-nities. Often directed to Poles were such malicious remarks as 'You wanted a Poland without Jews, now you have Jews without Poland' or 'Your time is over.' "[7]

Thus the participation of Jews in the Soviet apparatus, including the militia, is documented in Polish accounts (especially in those on which Gross has been basing his books and articles for a quarter of a century), in accounts recorded during the war and preserved at the Hoover Insti-tution in the U.S.A., in documents of the Soviet and Party authorities of the former USSR that are now being analyzed, and in reports of the (Polish) Union for Armed Combat published long ago in the work *Armia Krajowa w dokumentach* (The Home Army in documents) (vol. 1 [London, 1970]).

---

[7] J. T. Gross, introduction to *W czterdziestym nas matko na Sybir zesłali* (Warsaw, 1989), 29.

Prof. Gross therefore lacks justification when he states in *Neighbors* that, "[t]o put it simply, enthusiastic Jewish response to entering Red Army units was not a widespread phenomenon at all, and it is impossible to identify some innate, unique characteristics of Jewish collaboration with the Soviets during the period 1939–1941."[8]

A False Equation

The second part of that statement, this time pertaining to Poles, runs as follows: "On the other hand, it is manifest that the local non-Jewish population enthusiastically greeted entering *Wehrmacht* units in 1941 and broadly engaged in collaboration with the Germans, up to and including participation in the extermination campaign against the Jews. The testimony by Finkelsztajn concerning how Radziłów's local Polish population received the Germans reads like a mirror image of widely circulating stories about Galician Jews receiving the Bolsheviks in 1939."[9]

Without going into the merits of the issue, I should first like to call attention to the methods. The hundreds of surviving accounts, the reports of Underground Poland, including that of Jan Karski, who was favorably disposed toward the Jews, do not justify such generalizations. And perhaps rightly so. One must study the situation in various localities rather than relying on even the most widespread general opinions. And yet Finkelsztajn's account and several accounts by peasants from surrounding villages have justified passing judgment not on the attitude of individual people but on the entire local population (with the exception of Jews). The same is the case with the thesis that the Polish population of the several-thousand-strong town of Jedwabne murdered their Jewish neighbors, based on the testimony of Jews who had escaped and managed to survive, as well as on UB materials, obtained as a result of (undoubtedly cruel) interrogations in 1949 and 1953, at a time when Polish bishops were being sentenced for betraying the Polish nation and spying for "the imperialists."

[8] One question begs to be asked: Why is it that accounts in the archives of the Hoover Institution, which were reliable enough to serve as the basis for the description of the most complicated issues connected with the Soviet occupation, become unreliable and cease to be "sources" wherever they have anything to do with the Polish Jews? We should add that each of these accounts is corroborated by dozens of others published in free Poland since 1990, as well as by documents to be found in the archives of Belarus, Ukraine, and Russia.

[9] *Sąsiedzi*, 155.

I shall now move on to what has been referred to as Polish collaboration. Andrzej Żbikowski has presented it more extensively than has Prof. Gross. It supposedly involved the murder of Jews by Polish "gangs" composed primarily of people recently released by the Germans from Soviet jails, as well as attacks on "retreating smaller Soviet army groups," also carried out by such gangs. A plain and simple equation: 1939 equals 1941.

But, by God, joyfully greeting Germans who arrive right in the middle of a horrible deportation and thereby make it possible for hundreds of people to leave their grim places of torture—the jails of places like Brześć, Łomża, Białystok, and Jedwabne—is one thing, attacking Red Army soldiers who had been occupation troops only the day before is another, and killing soldiers of the Polish Army is something else again. Indeed, Jews may not have had things too good in prewar Poland, and there was undoubtedly "a balance sheet of wrongs," to quote Broniewski's poem. However, they were not deported to Siberia; they were not shot or sent to concentration camps; they were not killed through starvation and hard labor. If they did not regard Poland as their homeland, they did not have to treat it as an occupation regime and join its mortal enemy in killing Polish soldiers and murdering Polish civilians fleeing to the East. They also did not have to take part in fingering their neighbors for deportations, those heinous acts of collective responsibility.

Only Three Houses Did Not Display Red Flags

Let us now move from general matters to the situation in the town of Jedwabne and the surrounding rural community. Gross is right in saying there are not many testimonies regarding the town itself, but there are more than a few. In fact, there are considerably more than those on which he based his account of the burning of the Jews on 10 July 1941. The "new approach to sources" that he is promoting with regard to Jewish accounts could be applied in this particular case. These, after all, were accounts provided by persecuted individuals who were saved from annihilation only thanks to the Sikorski-Maisky agreement of July 1941. These are the voices of eyewitness survivors of a crime. In their accounts, they touch on "the Jewish problem" spontaneously and "from the heart," even though no one encouraged them to do so.

Did Jedwabne Jews, like others, cordially welcome the Red Army incursion? The accounts recorded during the war, as well as those I obtained in the early 1990s, indicate that this was indeed the case.

First, accounts submitted to the army of Gen. Anders and archived in the Hoover Institution, and now also available at the Eastern Archives in Warsaw.

Account No. 8356, recorded by cartwright Józef Rybicki from the town of Jedwabne: "The Red Army was received by Jews who built arches. They removed the old authorities and introduced new ones from among the local population (Jews and Communists). The police and teachers were arrested . . ."

Account No. 10708, recorded by Tadeusz Kiełczewski, a municipal government employee in Jedwabne: "Right after the encroachment by the Soviet Army, a municipal committee was spontaneously set up, composed of Polish Communists (the chairman was the Pole, Czesław Krystowczyk, and the members were Jews). The militia also consisted of Jewish Communists. At first there were no reprisals, because they did not know the population. The arrests started only after local Communists had provided the necessary information. Local militiamen searched the homes of people they felt were concealing weapons. The main arrests by the Soviet authorities started only after the first elections."

Account No. 8455, recorded by Marian Łojewski, a locksmith-mechanic from Jedwabne: "Following the incursion of the Red Army, first an order was issued for all the weapons owned by the local population to be turned in. Anyone who held back would face the death penalty. Next, searches were conducted in various houses as a result of the accusation by Jewish shopkeepers that Poles had stolen various goods from them in their absence.[10] Numerous arrests were made of the people against whom the local Jewish Communists held a grudge for their own persecution by the Polish authorities."

Account No. 2675, recorded by wood-sorter Aleksander Kotowski of Jedwabne: "I was not present when the Red Army entered. Jewish and Polish Communists who had done time in prison for Communist activities were admitted into the administration. They led the NKVD to apartments and houses and they denounced patriotic Polish citizens."

And finally, the account of Łucja Chojnowska, née Chołowińska, on 9 May 1991. Mrs. Chołowińska, the sister of Jadwiga, whose married name was Laudańska, found herself in the spring of 1940 in a partisan camp at the Kobielno forest range, situated amid the Biebrza Marshes. During a battle between Polish partisans and the Soviet army on 23 June 1940, she was captured. Our conversation, which took place in Jedwabne, pertained to that battle, not to the situation in the town both

[10] As can be imagined, Jews left their homes and went into hiding during the short-lived German occupation of Podlasie in September 1939, and this may have led to theft.

women had formerly lived in. Nevertheless, in the course of the conversation, Łucja Chołowińska-Chojnowska said: "In Jedwabne, which was inhabited mainly by Jews, there were only three houses that had not displayed red flags when the Russians marched in. Our house was among them. Before the first deportation, a Jewish woman, a neighbor (we got along with the Jews very well), ran over and warned us we were on the deportation list. Then my sister Jadwiga, her child (a four-year-old girl), and I fled to Orlików, taking only some clothing." Let us note that the Jewish neighbor lady knew who was on the deportation list, even though that was the most closely guarded of secrets. So much for beginnings.

The Arrests Begin

And now further questions: Who made up the militia in Jedwabne, and what was their attitude toward townsfolk regarded as being too closely linked to the Polish state, as unfavorably disposed toward the new system, or as enemies? Did terror also take place in Jedwabne? If so, how did it come about, and was it implemented only through the agency of the Soviet citizens known as "easterners"? Or was it bolstered by "former" Polish citizens, inhabitants of Jedwabne and the surrounding countryside? Let us look for the answers in what historians call "personal documents" created during the war and after.

Account No. 1559 was given by Kazimierz Sokołowski, a worker from Jedwabne: "Soviet authorities set up a militia, consisting mainly of Jewish Communists, and the arrests of farmers and workers on whom the militia had informed began. They imposed heavy taxes on the population. They imposed taxes on the churches and arrested a priest. There began mass searches of the homes of unfavorably disposed people, enemies of the people . . . The local populace in the main avoided voting [on 22 October 1939]. All day, the militia led them by force and at gunpoint to the polling station. Shortly after the vote, they staged a nighttime raid, arrested entire families, and deported them to the USSR."

Account No. 1394, recorded by Jedwabne worker Stanisław Gruba: "Homes were raided in search of weapons, anti-Communist literature, etc. Suspects were immediately arrested, as were the families of priests, and put in prison so that an investigation could be conducted."

Account No. 2589, recorded by Józef Karwowski, a farmer from the rural Jedwabne area: "In October 1939, the NKVD ordered preelection meetings and rallies. People were forcibly herded to them by the

NKVD and militia. Whoever resisted was immediately arrested and never heard from again."

Account No. 2545 was provided by Józef Makowski, a farmer from the rural Jedwabne area: "They arrested people, tied their hands, threw them into cellars and pigsties, starved them, didn't give them any water to drink, and brutally beat them to force them to confess to belonging to Polish organizations. I myself was beaten unconscious during NKVD interrogations in Jedwabne, Łomża, and Minsk."

Account No. 8356 was recorded by Józef Rybicki of Jedwabne (whom we have already met): "Searches were conducted in the homes of better-off farmers, whose furniture, clothing, and valuables they took away. A few days later, they came at night and arrested them. They took people to meetings by force. Anyone who resisted was called a *vreditel'* [wrecker] and arrested. The mayor of the village drew up lists, going from house to house and writing down the names of many people and the year they were born. The commission comprised soldiers and Jews and local Communists.[11] Candidates to the assembly were imposed from above. They were Jews who had come from the USSR and local Communists."

They Donned Red Armbands

Let us now move on to the postwar accounts I received while preparing a story on the battle of the Kobielno forest range. Jerzy Tarnacki, a partisan from Kobielno, wrote in a letter of 24 October 1991: "A patrol comprising a Pole named Kurpiewski and a Jew called Czapnik came for me and my brother Antek. During the arrests we managed to flee from our own backyard. I went into hiding in the village of Kajtanowo [Kajetanowo] at the home of a friend, Wacław Mierzejewski. From him I learned of the existence of a Polish partisan unit on the other side of the River Biebrza. I was in hiding from January to mid-April 1940."

Stefan Boczkowski of Jedwabne wrote in his letter of 14 January 1995, "The local Jews in Jedwabne donned red armbands and helped the militia arrest 'enemies of the people,' 'spies,' etc."

Dr. Kazimierz Odyniec, a physician, the son of Sgt. Antoni Odyniec, who was killed in action at Kobielno on 23 June 1940, wrote in his letter of 20 June 1991: "Toward the end of April 1940, a local Jew came to our home in the uniform of a Russian militiaman and told my father to report to the NKVD . . . My father told us good-bye but first had my

---

[11] The conscription commission. Young men were drafted into the Red Army in September 1940.

mother follow that militiaman and see where else he would go, because he had a dozen or so names on his list. As it later turned out, my father did not go to the NKVD. The next day the NKVD arrested my mother, demanding that she tell them where my father had hidden." In a letter I received after Gross's book came out, Dr. Odyniec noted: "Gross emphasizes the cruelty of the Polish side without saying a word about the behavior of a sizable group of Jews who openly cooperated with the Soviets and were the people who showed the Soviets who should be arrested or deported. I can give you an example close to home." Here he repeated the above account. "I also remember that the corpses of Polish partisans killed in the fighting in Kobielno were transported by the Jew Całko, my Uncle Władek Łojewski's neighbor" (letter of 25 October 2000).

Roman Sadowski, a Home Army officer and the husband of Kazimierz Odyniec's sister Halina, was deported into the depths of the USSR on 20 June 1941. He wrote to me on 10 November 2000: "During the Soviet occupation Jews were the 'masters' of this region. They entirely cooperated with the Soviet authorities. According to the accounts of my wife's cousins, it was Jews together with the NKVD who compiled lists of those to be interned (deported)."

Although I did not conduct a systematic or sufficiently early search of the documents pertaining to the attitudes of Jews from Jedwabne and its environs, we can see that a considerable number of spontaneous and unsolicited testimonies have accumulated. I cannot say, as Gross has, that "I found only one statement providing specific information about the kind of reception that the entering Soviet army received from the population of Jedwabne in September 1939—as we know, this was the moment when the memory of Jewish disloyalty was fixed for many Poles—and it is none too reliable, for it was written more than fifty years after the events it describes."[12] Gross then goes on to discuss the information obtained by Agnieszka Arnold during her work on a film on the burning of Jews in Jedwabne.

Not being a specialist in these questions, I have cited the five accounts above, which were mainly recorded before 1945 and concerned the attitudes of Jedwabne Jews toward the Soviets who were in the process of establishing their authority. I have also quoted nine accounts of the activities of the militia, which was composed mainly of Jedwabne Jews—although their commandant was the well-known prewar Polish Communist Czesław Kurpiewski.

[12] [Strzembosz is quoting here from the Polish edition of *Neighbors*; the corresponding passage in the American edition breaks off after "in September 1939" (ed.).]

To that should be added an extremely characteristic piece of information, independently repeated in two separate accounts: apart from Jewish militiamen, Jews in civilian clothing, wearing red armbands and armed with rifles, also took part in the arrests.

Trzcianne: A Characteristic Incident

The same documents from the archives of the Hoover Institution, which, after all, Jan Gross was quite familiar with, provide a list of towns and smaller localities in which Jews enthusiastically welcomed the Red Army and later manned militia posts. The towns of Zambrów, Łomża, and Stawiski are on the list, as are the villages of Wizna, Szumowo (the militia commander there was a Jew named Jabłonka), Rakowo-Boginie, Bredki, Zabiele, Wądołki Stare, and Drozdowo.

We also know of the characteristic incident that occurred in the Jewish town of Trzcianne, situated opposite Jedwabne across the River Biebrza. According to the account (recorded on 16 August 1987) of Czesław Borowski, who lived in the village of Zubole adjacent to Trzcianne, the course of events was as follows: "Somewhere toward the end of September, or perhaps at the beginning of October 1939, the Germans had withdrawn from the area but the Russians still hadn't arrived, so a kind of neutral zone arose. Fighting was still going on in Czerwony Bór. In Trzcianne, Jews were preparing to welcome the encroaching Red Army. Jewish militia patrols went out ahead as far as Okrągłe (a bend in the road and a bus stop) in the direction of Mońki. Seeing a cloud of dust in the distance and believing it to be the Red Army, they moved back to the welcome arch built at the head of the village [town (TS)]. But it was not Soviet soldiers, but rather ten to fifteen Polish *uhlans* [cavalrymen] moving through the neutral zone. They came upon the arch of welcome and the rabbi with bread and salt. The *uhlans* charged the crowd, destroyed the triumphal arch, struck out with the flat of their sabers, smashed up a few Jewish shops, and wanted to burn down the town, but that did not occur. The rabbi's daughter died of a heart attack. The *uhlans* rode off. The Jews of Trzcianne had weapons . . ."

That account, which I recorded nearly fifty years after the event, has been verified by Russian sources. According to these sources, at the end of September 1939, "a band of Polish soldiers" commanded by two landowners, Henryk Klimaszewski and Józef Nieczecki, attacked the town, where they engaged in "plunder and a pogrom of the Jewish population." During that action, Henryk Klimaszewski was said to have called for a settling of scores with the Bolsheviks and the Jews, saying: "Beat the Jews for Grodno and Skidel. The time to settle accounts has come. Down with Communists. We'll butcher every last Jew."

The Germans Saved Hundreds of Inhabitants

Apart from the Hoover Institution collection, with which Prof. Gross is familiar, and aside from the accounts I have obtained, there are other testimonies to the behavior of Jews from Jedwabne in the period 1939–1941. In their article "To Survive" (*Kontakty*, 19 July 1988), Danuta and Aleksander Wroniszewski noted the account of a Jedwabne inhabitant: "I remember how the Russians loaded the Poles onto carriages to be taken to Siberia. On top of each carriage was a Jew armed with a rifle. Mothers, wives, and children knelt before the carriages, begging for mercy and help. The last time this happened was 20 June 1941."

Did the Polish inhabitants of Jedwabne and the surrounding villages enthusiastically welcome the Germans as saviors? Yes, they did! If someone pulls me out of a blazing house in which I could burn to a crisp in seconds, I will embrace and thank that person. Even if the next day I regard him as yet another mortal enemy. At that time, the Germans rescued hundreds of local villagers (perhaps also Jedwabne residents?) who had for days been hiding in the fields or the brush-covered slopes of the Biebrza. They saved them from being sent to their death in the wastelands of Kazakhstan or the Siberian taiga. By then everyone knew what such exile meant: letters and other signals from the *spetsposelek*s (special emissaries) had been getting through. The deportations were accompanied by a simultaneous wave of arrests, often overlooked by historians, of suspects who ended up in the camps or in prisons for long sentences that they often failed to survive.

Let us not wonder therefore at their joy or at the fact that those "bands," as Andrzej Żbikowski calls them, attacked groups of Soviet soldiers leaving the area—these soldiers who until the day before had been their persecutors, representatives of one of the cruelest systems known to mankind.

A Horrible Day for Poles

Not long ago, a very specific and very credible source was published: *The Chronicle of the Benedictine Sisters of Holy Trinity Abbey in Łomża (1939–1954)*. Published in Łomża in 1995, it was compiled by Sister

Alojza Piesiewiczówna. Let us quote the fragments dealing with 20–22 June 1941:

> 20 June. The Feast of the Sacred Heart of Jesus. A horrible day for Poles under Soviet subjugation. Massive deportations to Russia. From early morning carts full of Polish families rolled through town to the railway station. Wealthier Polish families, the families of nationalists, Polish patriots, the intelligentsia, and the families of people in Soviet prisons were taken away. It was difficult even to comprehend what categories of people were being deported. In Polish souls there was weeping, moaning, and terrible despair. But the Jews and the Soviets, on the other hand, were triumphant. It is impossible to describe what Poles are going through. A hopeless situation. But the Jews and Soviets are demonstratively overjoyed, threatening soon to deport every last Pole. And that could well have been expected because on 20 June and on the following day, the 21st, they carted people to the station without interruption . . . And God truly saw our tears and blood.
>
> 22 June. In the early morning there was the droning sound of airplanes and every so often the blast of bombs exploding over the town . . . Several German bombs fell on the more important Soviet outposts. An incredible panic broke out among the Soviets. They began fleeing in disarray. Poles were very happy. The sound of each exploding bomb filled their souls with inexpressible joy. Within a few hours there wasn't a single Soviet left in town, and the Jews were hiding somewhere in basements and cellars. Before noon, prisoners left their jail cells. People on the streets embraced one another and wept for joy. The Soviets had withdrawn without their weapons, and they had not fired a single shot in response to the approaching Germans.
>
> That evening there wasn't a single Soviet in Łomża. But the situation remained unclear. The Soviets had fled, but the Germans had not entered. The next day, 23 June, the town was just as empty. The civilian population began looting. All Soviet stores, bases, and shops were smashed and robbed. On the evening of 23 June, several Germans entered the town. The people breathed a sigh of relief.

In those days there could have been no other reaction. Several weeks later the Union of Armed Combat hastily rebuilt the underground network broken up by the Soviets. Weapons left by the fleeing Russians were gathered up everywhere, and the "interregnum" was used to prepare for a struggle against the next occupation regime. There are as many testimonies to that as there are to such facts as robberies, retaliation, and pogroms. As usual, the reality is far more complex than we are able to imagine.

.   .   .   .   .

Tomasz Strzembosz was born in 1930 and is a professor at the Institute of Political Studies at the Polish Academy of Sciences and at the Catholic University of Lublin. He is the author of *Akcje zbrojne podziemnej Warszawy 1939–1945* (Military actions of the underground in Warsaw, 1939–1945) (Warsaw, 1978), *Odbijanie i uwalnianie więźniów w Warszawie 1939–1944* (The rescue and freeing of prisoners in Warsaw, 1939–1944) (Warsaw, 1972), and *Rzeczpospolita Podziemna* (The underground republic of Poland) (Warsaw, 2000). He also deals with the history of the Polish resistance movement in northeastern Polish territories under the Soviet occupation between 1939 and 1941.

Translation taken from *Thou Shalt Not Kill*.

Jerzy Jedlicki

HOW TO GRAPPLE WITH THE
PERPLEXING LEGACY

POLITYKA, 10 FEBRUARY 2001

I

THE BOOK *Neighbors* by Jan T. Gross has inspired heated debates and disputes. Its publisher, Fundacja Pogranicze, planned its circulation poorly: the book sold out just as sales were peaking. No wonder: it speaks of an event that is quite incredible. It speaks about how, on one summer day in 1941, supervised by German occupation troops, the Polish residents of a certain little town outside of Łomża murdered over a thousand of their Jewish neighbors, showing unusual cruelty and not sparing a soul. It also speaks of how reports of the event were silenced for over sixty years.

It would be rather strange if the book aroused no emotions. This, however, is not the first time we have seen such excitement. One need only recall the agitation spurred by the publication of the article "The Poor Poles Look at the Ghetto" by Jan Błoński in *Tygodnik Powszechny* in 1987, the publication of an article by Michał Cichy on the killings of Jews during the Warsaw Uprising published in *Gazeta Wyborcza* several years later, or the film *Shoah* by Claude Lanzmann. Every time someone presents the public with texts or images casting a shadow on the Polish treatment of Jews under the German occupation, a wide range of emotions is stirred up. Some people experience pangs of conscience and shame, while others claim fabrication or even libel. Still others cite mitigating circumstances that reduce the guilt, or portray the incidents as only marginally significant. Despite the time that has elapsed, there is perhaps no other historical issue in Poland that plays so powerfully on hidden sensitivities and resentments. Magazine editors know what huge volumes of emotionally charged mail they receive after publishing such articles. Why is this so? The responses certainly go beyond disputes over facts. It is noteworthy that some information, including the history of pogroms in the Łomża province, has remained hidden in archives for a long time (this in itself is something to think about), yet there is little that can surprise the professional historians of the period. The volume of scholarly writing on the German occupation in

Poland has been growing exponentially. The only differences in opinion among historians concern minor details. The real barrier is being erected between the body of well-evidenced historical knowledge and popular beliefs formed when available information is passed through a thick filter of preconceived notions, prejudices, and personal recollections. Some items of information never make it through the filter, while many of those that do are rejected as contradicting generally accepted opinions.

Bookstores have offered many titles that should shatter public opinion or at least inspire serious reflection. The first was *Stosunki polsko-żydowskie w czasie drugiej wojny światowej* [Polish-Jewish relations during World War II] by Emanuel Ringelblum, a leading Jewish historian and founder of the Warsaw Ghetto Archive. Ringelblum managed to complete the book in a Grójecka Street shelter in 1944 before he died, along with all the other inhabitants of the shelter, when someone informed on them. Marked by an admirable concern for fairness, the book took many years to pass through the barbed wire entanglements of censorship. Prof. Artur Eisenbach finally published it in 1988, but it did not make much of a splash. A 1992 collection of articles by Krystyna Kersten entitled *Polacy—Żydzi—Komunizm: Anatomia półprawd 1939–68* [Poles—Jews—communism: An anatomy of half-truths 1939–1968] attracted more attention. The collection did not touch directly on the Holocaust but rather confronted documented knowledge with deeply rooted stereotypes on both sides. Then came a series of publications analyzing images of the Holocaust and accompanying events retained in the memories of survivors and external witnesses, as well as how such memories turned into the collective "recollections" of entire communities, or coagulated into those communities' versions of history. *Zagłada i pamięć* [The Holocaust and memory] by Barbara Engelking (1994) and *Pamięć żydowska—Pamięć polska* [Jewish memory—Polish memory], the proceedings of a colloquium, published by the French Institute of Kraków (1996), are two examples of publications that went practically unnoticed by the press and the public. We are still waiting for the release of [a Polish version of] the serious and unbiased book *Bondage to the Dead: Poland and the Memory of the Holocaust* by Michael Steinlauf. Meanwhile, the collection of articles by Feliks Tych, *Długi cień Zagłady* [The long shadow of the Holocaust], published in 1999 by the Jewish Historical Institute and exploring the same regions of Polish memory—historical consciousness and educational stereotypes—has also failed to stir interest so far. The thin volume *Upiorna dekada: trzy eseje o stereotypach na temat Żydów, Polaków, Niemców i komunistów 1939–1948* [The monstrous decade: Three essays on stereotypes concerning the Jews, the Poles, and the Communists 1939–1948] by Jan Tomasz Gross, which preceded *Neighbors* by two years, fared better. It was noticed by *Gazeta Wyborcza*, while *Więź*, invaluable in its sensitivity to such issues, discussed it at some length. Nevertheless, the reception of this book gave no indication of the way that *Neighbors* would be talked about. I refer to these books because the volume of source and interpretive materials contained in these and other titles is sufficient to make us ask whether the time has come for a reassessment of the received views on the wartime deeds of certain Polish circles. No such reassessment, however, has been performed. It took a blow as powerful as the news of what had happened in Jedwabne to break through our defensive walls and stir the garrison of the Polish stronghold. It is still too early to predict how successful this breach of the wall will be (for it was not the first such breach to be opened). Not to be ruled out is a scenario in which, after an exchange of arguments, each side sticks to its own version of the truth—the well-entrenched convictions in which it has invested so much faith and emotion that it cannot now call them into doubt.

II

As it is, we have several thousand people who have been declared "Righteous Among the Nations," and probably several times as many who deserved that title, if only they had lived long enough or someone had remembered them. Considering that the punishment for hiding a Jew in Poland was death, the merits of those who took the risk are all the greater and more praiseworthy. It is fortunate that their valor has been commemorated in collections of reports compiled by Władysław Bartoszewski and Zofia Lewinówna (theirs were the first to be published), Szymon Datner, and more recently Elżbieta Isakiewicz in *Ustna harmonijka: relacje Żydów, których uratowali od Zagłady Polacy* [The harmonica: Reports of Jews saved from the Holocaust by Poles], not to mention the great many diaries that convey testimony of gratitude.

The question is: Who is entitled to take pride in the rescuers' acts after all these years? After all, diaries and reports show that, as is remembered well by those who lived in the General Government, it was not only the Jews in hiding but also their benefactors who trembled under the prying eyes of neighbors, the inquisitive gaze of janitors, storekeepers, and passersby ... If there had been only the Gestapo, how much easier it would have been to survive in hiding and count on a network of human solidarity; how much less need there would have been to constantly move from hideout to hideout. What, then, counts in the general, nationwide balance sheet? Heroism or baseness?

Compassion or a lack of mercy? Both count. There is no way to subtract one from the other or offset one with the other. There will always be two separate ledgers.

However, though we are happy to preserve the former in our memories, we would rather forget the latter, or consider it marginal in terms of numbers and social significance. But the problem was not marginal, and, even if it had been, it would still cast a dark shadow over all of Polish life under the occupation. It is also difficult to forget 1968, when a new generation of *szmalcownicy* [blackmailers] and police agents staged a national antisemitic campaign that filled us and the rest of the world with the worst associations. They had the nerve to protest against the "anti-Polish" response that they provoked, and to appeal to the merits of the Righteous—and this also happens today. Inconveniently for us, the things we would rather ignore or forget are known and remembered by others. We cannot have the one ledger without the other. Psychological comfort is no more available to us than it is to other nations that were conquered at the time. If we are the heirs of previous generations, then there is no way around it: upon us fall both their greatness and their baseness, their honor and their disgrace.

Nevertheless, the two ledgers—that of the rescuers and that of people who denounced hidden Jews to the Nazis—represent two small sections of society: the opposite extremes. Which one you ended up in depended more on your character than on your social background. The people who put their lives and their families' lives on the line to save friends and strangers because they strongly believed that it was the right thing to do came from all walks of life. So did people for whom the Nazi invasion and the sea of human suffering provided an excellent opportunity to do business. Both groups lived in a social environment that, as has been said repeatedly with a mix of sorrow and reproach, was indifferent to the fate of their Jewish neighbors. Yet this is exactly the place where a question mark needs to be placed.

III

Poles were indifferent to the Jews—pleasantly or contemptuously indifferent—as long as it was clear that the social status of the Jews was beneath that of the gentry, the Christian bourgeoisie, and the intelligentsia. The indifference disappeared when the Jews, at different times in the different partitions, began to claim equal legal, and sometimes civil, rights, and then the equal treatment of their language and culture as well. The more collective dignity they achieved, the more they became a nation (as opposed to just followers of the Old Testament), and the tenser their relations grew with Polish circles that turned out to be reluctant and, in their view, unable to support such aspirations. Added to these developments was a wave of racist antisemitism from the West that sought to block all paths to assimilation (in the sense of integration in terms of customs or, in some cases, of consciousness, to the point that any distinguishing features, often including religious denomination, vanished). The zealous champion of antisemitism in Poland, as is well known, was the Endecja (the National Democrats). However, dislike and even animosity toward the Jews spread to other political groups—except for those on the left—and to the Catholic Church. Shortly before World War I, the struggle against the Jews became an obsession, garnering more coverage in the Warsaw press and stirring up more emotions than any other issue.

So it has been ever since, with fluctuating intensity. This is not the place to describe the history of this turbulent stream or its most dramatic episodes, including the assassination of a president, the exclusion of Jews from Polish professional institutions, "ghetto benches" at the universities, and finally bloody pogroms. Nor is there any reason to idealize the Jews of Poland or anywhere else: they were as diverse as any nation, representing all possible classes and political views. They were deeply religious or completely secularized, nationalistic or totally Polonized, immensely wealthy or starving to death, brilliant and primitive, full of virtues and vices. However, regardless of who they were, what they did, or why they earned merit or condemnation, all were targets of demeaning accusations and insults from all sides simply because they had been born Jewish. The recent book *W jednym stali domu . . . Koncepcje rozwiązania kwestii żydowskiej w publicystyce polskiej lat 1933–1939* [In one house . . . Concepts for solving the Jewish question in Polish publications from 1933 to 1939], by Anna Landau-Czajka, provides extensive documentation of a phenomenon that today, in hindsight, seems to have been a madness that spread to a large section of the intelligentsia, the Church, and public opinion.

Needless to say, none of the above was unique to Poland. To varying degrees, nearly all of Europe fell victim to the psychological and mental pathology that was used in Germany even before the war (and in Austria after its annexation) to justify the totalitarian order. This, however, is little consolation. Poland was unquestionably one of the countries most affected by this obsession. Its ideological leaders never stopped developing ideas for depriving millions of Polish citizens of their rights and property and banishing them from the country. The only groups to actively oppose such ideas were the Socialists and the Communists and the liberal faction of the intelligentsia; the fact that these circles did not treat them with aggression and contempt explains the inclination of assimilating Jews to seek refuge and support in them.

This, in a nutshell, was the state of Polish-Jewish relations at the time of the Nazi and the Soviet invasions. It would be extremely idealistic to imagine that Polish attitudes toward the Jews changed overnight just because both ended up under the oppression of the same invader. In the Soviet zone, some Jews, especially those who had suffered severely and sympathized with the left wing, had their hopes for safety and decent treatment revived. It soon turned out that the expropriations, the closing of places of worship, and the deportations to the East proceeded without regard to nationality. Under German rule, no one would feel safe in the face of the terror of the occupation regime from the very beginning, but it soon turned out that there were many circles in this hell, and the denizens of the better circle saw no reason at all to renounce their long-established biases against the even more severely persecuted *Untermenschen*.

In his recently published book *U progu Zagłady* [On the threshold of destruction], which has been reviewed in *Polityka*, Tomasz Szarota presents a vast and meticulously documented panorama of "antisemitic incidents and pogroms in occupied Europe" in the years 1940 and 1941, from Paris to Antwerp, from The Hague and Amsterdam to Warsaw and Kaunas. The book is no less moving than Gross's. It offers copious evidence of the fact that wherever the German occupation forces attempted to instigate unrest against the Jews and to demonstrate that the invaded populations were ready to volunteer for a settling of scores, they found people eager, or even overly eager, to comply. Warsaw was no exception. Such attitudes could be found both among ideologists who (mistakenly) saw their advancement by the Germans as encouragement to collaborate, and among Polish civilian "squads" for whom the opportunity to humiliate, beat, and rob Jews with total impunity was a pleasure in itself.

The situation deteriorated drastically from the day the Germans invaded the Soviet Union. Szarota presents serious evidence for the view that the decision to exterminate the Jews must have been made in Hitler's leadership clique on the eve of the invasion. At any rate, the first act of the "Final Solution" was played out in the East. The entire operation was assigned to special task forces called *Einsatzgruppen*. At least in the first days of the invasion, these units were to encourage local volunteers to stage "self-cleansing" operations. Wherever they succeeded (e.g., in Kaunas), the pogroms of the summer of 1941 were extremely bloody and cruel. By all indications, Jedwabne became a part of that plan.

Regardless of how many of them were present at the scene of the crime, there is no doubt that the Germans played the role of instigators of the massacre. Historians are still arguing about how many Germans were there. The occupying forces encouraged such acts, guaranteed impunity, and, most likely, provided rewards. Evidently, they found eager accomplices in the Łomża district who, having tasted blood once, proved impossible to restrain from an orgy of mass murder. Nor do any known reports speak of anyone in the town endeavoring to stop them.

IV

The extermination of the Jews led to a fragmentation of Polish opinion that did not always correspond to previous divisions. For many people, the plan carried out by the Nazi occupation regime was monstrous in its inhumanity. The reaction of moral protest and compassion for the victims inspired attempts to provide shelter and assistance to the extent that this was possible. In addition to thousands of individual acts, such sentiments also took the form of pleas for help voiced by some of the underground publications, and in particular by *Biuletyn Informacyjny*. They also led to the establishment in 1942 of the Council for Aid to the Jews, known by its code name, Żegota. However, a large portion of society did not share such sentiments. While the occupation forces were, of course, held to be the enemies of Poland, what they did to the Jews did not necessarily meet with objections. If only it had been mere indifference. Unfortunately, when the Warsaw ghetto was burning, sneers at the dying or laughter and relief at the sight of this uncommon spectacle were heard in the streets of Warsaw, on trams, in stores and schools, rather than compassion or horror. I am not talking about solidarity, for solidarity could not be expressed out loud. I am talking about responses expressed among acquaintances and legitimized by a large part of the underground press, in those many clandestine newsletters whose chief editors were concerned mainly with how to cleanse Poland of Jews who might manage to survive the extermination once the war was over. As we know, this desire was to a great degree fulfilled, in part shortly after the war, and in part only in 1968.

The Holocaust therefore failed to bring about any dramatic transformation of Polish attitudes, although it did exacerbate existing divisions. What for some was the most dreadful event of the twentieth century remained for others an episode devoid of any great significance. Still, even in the souls of people whose racial and religious biases are so deeply engrafted in their brain tissue that no experience will ever root them out, the Holocaust has left a certain dissonance: namely, that admitting to antisemitism has become highly indecent anywhere in the world. Moreover, even the slightest suspicion of having supported the Nazi plan for eradicating the European Jews had to be shunned as a calumny. Thus there arose a language of camouflage in which feelings and beliefs were communicated no longer directly but in a roundabout way.

On the other hand, some people began to worry, justifiably, that Poles would be remembered in the world not for the noble courage of the Righteous but rather for the snickers of the onlookers at Krasiński Square [near the Warsaw ghetto][1] and for the howling of the Kielce mob on 4 July 1946. It was also thought that it would take time to get over feelings and attitudes, and that such work could not be completed when society was in the pillory. After all, who has the right to make accusations? And whom can they accuse? In a word, it is better not to stir things up but rather to wait until a new generation, with no bad memories, takes over.

Such fears are not groundless; they are familiar to any nation bearing the stigma of having participated even in part in acts that, years later, turn out to be shameful—even if they did not look that way to their perpetrators. All those defense mechanisms, those half-conscious concealments and lapses of memory, are comprehensible in psychological terms, even if they defer the moment of facing up to the dark episodes in one's history. Such episodes always come to light in the end and often catch us off guard. Could such things happen? Were Poles really capable of throwing infants into the flames? While others watched? Germans, certainly. Lithuanians, of course. Ukrainians—who would expect anything different from them? But Poles? It is far from easy to find out half a century later that no one earned a certificate of collective innocence. This is precisely the basis for infection of hatred and contempt.

We do not have to do penance for murderers and collaborators who, incited by invaders, volunteered sixty years ago to perform a task that would horrify any normal human being. What must be noted, however, is that along with its many noble elements, the baggage of historical tradition handed down to us also includes a moral culture that made such crimes possible and helped us to justify them or pass over

---

[1] During the Easter festival of 1943 that coincided with the Warsaw Ghetto Uprising, the public rode a merry-go-round at Krasiński Square located near the ghetto. The poet Czesław Miłosz, at that time living in Warsaw, made the merry-go-round a subject of his wartime poem "Campo di Fiori." The revelers on the merry-go-round were made into a symbol of the widespread Polish indifference to the fate of the Jews.

them in silence. We will bear responsibility for what we make of our past, for how we reconcile its glory and its shame, for the way we relate it to ourselves, and for the conclusions we draw.

We are not the first in Europe and certainly not the last to go through a process of reexamining our own legends. The process is difficult for any nation, just as it is difficult and painful to review one's life story when, in the light of new experiences and values, it becomes necessary to change the way one looks at deeds from the past. It is always difficult to admit that we have failed to pass honorably some tests in our lives, and that some of our most cherished convictions have turned out to be illusions or frauds. The same is true for national history. The case of Jedwabne gives us an opportunity to undertake such work in a significant way in at least one respect. We may, of course, continue to sidestep the issue. We may say it is too early, that reports are unclear, that there is no exact count of the murderers or the victims, that one set of archives or another still needs to be investigated. Investigation is always worthwhile; it should have been done many years ago. But it will not change a thing. The truth will not become any more pleasant than it is now, and sooner or later we are going to have to deal with it.

However, I hear yet other doubts. I hear fears that the whole controversy stirred up by Gross's book will only elicit an antisemitic response, and that in general dragging such bad memories into the light of day will not do anyone any good, especially if imprudent generalizations are made. I do not wish to underestimate such fears. They were expressed recently by Jacek Żakowski, a journalist who can hardly be accused of bias. As it turns out, however, sleep therapy is also ineffective. The virus of antisemitism has crept in to infect the young generation, which has no knowledge or experience of the topic, but whose members respond to the appropriate signals and slogans. Let them at least know what they are talking about and what they think they believe in. It is time to start calling a spade a spade.

Then there are also, they say, assaults from abroad meant to defame Poland's good name and its history, and Jews are playing no small role in this. That is true. Statements that do not steer clear of fabrication and slander can be read in American newspapers or heard in the Israeli Knesset. Nor are we surprised any longer by the lawyerly practice of exploiting the Holocaust to fulfill the entirely earthly interests of the heirs. Everyone knows that those who are accused, whether individually or collectively, think first of a defense rather than of their moral responsibility to the past.

It should be noted, however, that it is not without reason that bitter disenchantment has accumulated on the Jewish side over the years. Our own settling of accounts with our history and with our narrow-minded mentality is not what fuels Jewish complaints and stereotypes. On the contrary, if anything fuels them, it is the obstinate denial of Polish guilt, the refusal to admit the unpleasant parts of the Polish legacy. And finally, this is not about foreign countries; it is about being able at long last to speak openly among ourselves. This is the only way to break free of fears and complexes.

. . . . .

Jerzy Jedlicki was born in 1930 and is professor emeritus at the Institute of History, Polish Academy of Sciences, in Warsaw. His main field has been Polish and European social and intellectual history of the eighteenth–twentieth centuries. Among his many books are *Jakiej cywilizacji Polacy potrzebują* (Warsaw, 1988) (English edition: *A Suburb of Europe: Nineteenth-Century Polish Approaches to Western Civilization* [Budapest, 1999]), *Źle urodzeni, czyli o doświadczeniu historycznym* (Badly born, or about historical experience) (London, 1993), and *Świat zwyrodniały. Lęki i wyroki krytyków nowoczesności* (A depraved world: Fears and judgments of critics of modernity) (Warsaw, 2000). He has also published many historical articles and political essays in various European and American journals and contributed volumes. He serves as the chairman of the Council of the Polish Association against Antisemitism and Xenophobia (Otwarta Rzeczpospolita).

Translation taken from *Thou Shalt Not Kill*.

A ROUNDTABLE DISCUSSION:
JEDWABNE—CRIME AND MEMORY

RZECZPOSPOLITA, 3 MARCH 2001

R *ZECZPOSPOLITA*: The subject of our discussion is the events in Jedwabne in 1941, with all their surrounding circumstances and consequences. As a newspaper, we consider this matter very important, and we have been taking part in the public debate in Poland on this subject ever since the first publications by Prof. Gross appeared. We would like to start with a straightforward question that probably has still not received a definitive answer. What really happened in Jedwabne on 10 July 1941?

JAN TOMASZ GROSS: I have described this matter, and I think most of the historians who have spoken out on this topic do not question my basic findings. What happened in Jedwabne was genocide. It cannot be called a pogrom because it involved more than just a small group of riffraff. In fact, an enormous part of the local population took part. All day long, the Jewish population was cruelly murdered and tormented relentlessly, and at the end of the day all those who had not been murdered were burned alive. We cannot say exactly how many people died. The number given on the monument and in many reports is 1,600, but that is just an approximate number of victims of this terrible killing. This crime was the work of the local Polish population.

TOMASZ STRZEMBOSZ: I am in a weaker position than Prof. Gross because my only sources are his article, his information on the reports on which he based his book, and a group of reports I gathered from people who were in Jedwabne at the time. I am not acquainted with the records of the 1949 and 1953 court cases, and I am not acquainted with the materials of Prosecutor Monkiewicz.

As we know, eyewitness accounts are often varied and may be questioned. I do not have many of them—five—but as someone who has been collecting them for forty-odd years, I believe that they are genuine. Each of those people saw Germans in Jedwabne. One German took a young girl of twelve, living near the town square, for a Jew and dragged her to the square. She was saved by her mother and an ac-

---

The discussion was chaired by Jan Skórzyński and Paweł Lisicki.

quaintance. Germans were also seen on other streets. People say that they surrounded the Jews who were working on the square. They were seen clearing Śleszyński's barn of its contents. They were also seen later, during the burning. One account even says that they acted as the perpetrators.

By Polish Hands

RZECZPOSPOLITA: Let us therefore ask: Was the massacre of the Jewish population an independent action by Poles, in which the Germans played only a passive role, or was it stage-managed by the Germans themselves, who used the Poles for the actual dirty work?

ANDRZEJ ŻBIKOWSKI: Prof. Strzembosz is dealing with reports obtained today, fifty years after the event. I am using mostly Jewish reports that were submitted immediately after the war in 1945 and 1946. It is worth giving some thought to their reliability. This is a fundamental issue because, for instance, if Wasersztajn had not submitted his report, the Jedwabne atrocity might never have come to light. I took the trouble to count the number of Jewish accounts we have. The archives of the Jewish Historical Institute contain thirty-six reports from the area of Radziłów, Jedwabne, and Łomża, concerning nineteen localities and written during the first two years after the war. Mass murders and the burning of Jews in barns occurred in only two places—Radziłów and Jedwabne. True, we do not know much about the authors of these accounts, but there is no evidence that these people were dishonest or politically involved in any way. They were ordinary, average people. All the reports were collected and written down in Yiddish. As far as Radziłów and Jedwabne are concerned, neither of the two main witnesses—Wasersztajn and Finkelsztajn—was in the barn itself or anywhere near it, and could not have been there. The person nearest the barn in Radziłów was Finkelsztajn's wife, Chana, some one hundred meters away. From that distance, she saw exactly what was happening. A dozen or so Jews survived the pogroms of Jedwabne and Radziłów. They lived together for two years afterward. The reports of Wasersztajn and Finkelsztajn are a generalized record of these people's recollections, the result of their collective memory. This is, in any case, shown by the language of these accounts. Wherever they recall individual murders that they witnessed, the style of writing is sharper and more detailed. In those parts where they describe what happened in the barn, they present more generalized views. One can see that this is no eyewitness account. The same applies to the reports by Hersz

Piekarz and Rywka Fogel in *Yedwabne: History and Memorial Book*. These are important accounts, despite the fact that neither of the authors was an eyewitness and they did not see the burning barn.

RZECZPOSPOLITA: Do the Germans appear in these reports?

ANDRZEJ ŻBIKOWSKI: No, these accounts mention no Germans. As for Radziłów, Finkelsztajn implies that the Germans herded the Jews onto the town square and then left. It seems to me that the situation was as follows: In the Białystok area, in Tykocin, Wizna, and other places, the Jews were murdered mainly by Germans. There is a lot of evidence for this. Only in Jedwabne and Radziłów was the situation different. There is no doubt that the Germans were there earlier, but they left before the massacre itself.

PAWEŁ MACHCEWICZ: I would like to return to the general question of what we know about the events in Jedwabne and what facts we can all agree on. I also want to stress, like Prof. Strzembosz, that I, too, have never done any research on the matter. Such an investigation has now been taken up by the Institute of National Memory. Perhaps they will confirm Prof. Gross's claims and permit a few corrections to be made; perhaps they will reveal new facts. In my analysis, I can base what I say on Prof. Gross's book and on articles about this book by historians.

It seems obvious that the Jewish population in Jedwabne was massacred, and that they died at the hands of Poles. However, what needs to be clarified is the role of the Germans. Did the Germans merely approve the deed, did they inspire it, or did they indeed participate? We know that these were not spontaneous events, because there was a film crew in Jedwabne, or perhaps just a few Germans with cameras. There are many different currents that deserve our attention, even in the materials cited by Prof. Gross. Wasersztajn himself says at one point that what happened was on orders from the Germans.

Various reports contain conflicting information about the presence of Germans in Jedwabne. One of the people interrogated says that there were sixty Germans there. Others also mention that the Germans helped or even drove the Poles onto the town square to make them carry out the atrocity. I think this issue must be clarified. German archives should be searched. And that is what the Institute of National Memory plans to do. It has submitted queries to these archives, asking if there is any material on the Jedwabne atrocity. We have also commenced talks with German historians, who have provided us with valuable advice, so that we might be able to say more about this topic in a few months' time.

Another issue not fully clarified is who actually did the murdering. Even if we agree that it was the Poles, the question remains: Was it a group of ruffians, social outcasts consisting of, perhaps, several dozen murderers, or was it the entire Polish community, or society, as Prof. Gross claims? The 1949 trial raises a lot of doubts. We know that evidence in that trial was forced out of the witnesses, which Gross admits.

My question is: To what extent can we rely on these materials and believe that the trial singled out the people who were actually responsible, and that these people actually carried out the murders? Prof. Gross writes that the municipal authorities planned and coordinated the massacre with the Germans. I think the terms "municipal authorities" and "town councillors" are misleading to an extent. The truth is that when the Soviets pulled out, a certain group of people came together on their own and took over authority in Jedwabne. But I do not think that they had any right to act as municipal authorities.

And one more thing. There are accusations that delving into details is an attempt to conceal the truth and shift the blame from the Poles. I disagree with this most strongly. As a historian, it is my duty to investigate the truth, and the truth consists of a lot of details that are essential in order to present a full picture of events. Such details do not relativize Polish responsibility at all. As researchers, it is our duty to discover what part the Germans played in these events. But our delving into details is not intended in any way to diminish the responsibility of the Poles for this massacre.

RADOSŁAW IGNATIEW: I have been listening carefully to what you are saying. I can say only this without infringing upon the confidentiality of the investigation: I understand what a painful issue this is for Polish-Jewish relations. However, I view the matter solely from the investigative point of view, and as an investigator I remove the matter from its historical context because for me this is a question of victims and criminals. The nationality of the victims or the perpetrators is not the most important thing in my work. I question everything. So if there are reports by victims, I doubt their credibility because victims were naturally shaken up by what happened. If I listen to the testimony of witnesses, I doubt the authenticity of what they are saying because witnesses reconstruct observations after a period of time has passed. So it is possible that some details are made up while others are forgotten. The witnesses may also be telling lies. Everything has to be checked.

I interviewed one eyewitness three times. His final account diverged from his first. I think I discovered why he changed his testimony. As for the report of Jan Neumark, I came across a witness who says that Neumark was not in Jedwabne at the time. In June 1941, a German tried to shoot him, so he fled and hid with his sister. All these accounts have to be checked.

As for the 1949 trial, I would say this: I do not have enough data to prove conclusively that the law was broken, and that unacceptable methods of obtaining testimony were applied. What I can say is that the trial was conducted in a slipshod manner. My task is to establish what material from the trial can be used to arrive at the truth. I have already contacted people who took part in the trial, both as defendants and as witnesses.

I interview witnesses very carefully, asking them for all sorts of details. I do not limit myself to July 1941; there is a hypothesis that the outbursts might have come about because of collaboration between one of the victims and the Soviet authorities, so I also ask about the entire period of the Soviet occupation. I also try to get hold of documents from that period in order to verify this issue. And I can tell you this: the work is such that, having clarified one matter, I immediately come across two or three others that also need clarification.

RZECZPOSPOLITA: Does what you have learned so far challenge the way events are portrayed in Prof. Gross's book and in articles in *Rzeczpospolita* in any fundamental way?

RADOSŁAW IGNATIEW: Of course I can present some thesis, but as a prosecutor I will not defend such a thesis. I can formulate a thesis and defend it against all attacks if I first establish the evidence precisely, back it up by more evidence, and state why that evidence is credible and cannot be refuted. For example, there is an account that someone saw a column of German vehicles in Jedwabne. That is a piece of information that must be verified, because I cannot immediately tell whether the witness who saw the German vehicles is telling the truth, is mistaken, or is in a position that forces him to defend the Poles. In any case, here, too, I am following in your footsteps, gentlemen. I have made a very careful analysis of Prof. Gross's book, and it will be helpful in the investigation, together with all other publications, including those of the gentlemen present here.

RZECZPOSPOLITA: Prof. Gross, what kind of role do you assume the Germans played in the Jedwabne massacre? Do you think the reports mentioned by Prof. Strzembosz alter the picture?

JAN TOMASZ GROSS: To be honest, I am surprised that Prof. Strzembosz considers modern reports to be a serious counterweight to the evidence gathered in 1945, 1949, and 1953. Accounts provided fifty years after the event are not worth much. You come from a family of lawyers, Tomasz, so ask your brother [a former president of the Supreme Court] if this sort of formulation after fifty years has any weight, and whether it can stand up to fifty accounts. My book was not based on the reports of victims and would-be victims. It was based on the reports of those who committed the atrocity and of witnesses—Poles—who gave evidence in 1949. Of course I realize that that was the Stalinist period, so since we are dealing with a trial that took place then, we have to look at these materials with a critical eye. And my book says a lot on this subject. The first thing I considered was whether this was a political trial. As the prosecutor said a minute ago, the trial was held in a hopelessly shoddy manner. But there is no doubt that it was not a political trial. Back then, no one cared about whether the Jews were murdered by the Poles or by anyone else. That was 1949, when Stalin was already fiercely antisemitic. What did the Auschwitz museum look like in those days? Anyone who did not know what had happened in Auschwitz would never have guessed from a visit that Jews had died there. That is how the Stalinists portrayed the history of the German occupation. So this was not a political trial.

RZECZPOSPOLITA: I repeat my question to Mr. Gross. What role do you ascribe to the Germans?

JAN TOMASZ GROSS: The role of the Germans has been described by several dozen witnesses. Apart from a gendarmerie where ten or twelve men were stationed, there were no Germans in Jedwabne that day. We know this from Poles who worked at the gendarmerie. Witnesses say the Poles did it, and that there were no Germans around, apart from a dozen or so gendarmes. Moreover, if we examine the manner in which the Germans murdered Jews during that period, Jedwabne is qualitatively different. Up to the middle of August 1941, the Germans did not kill women, children, and old people en masse. They killed only men. That is what happened in Wizna, among other places, where they shot several dozen men. The victims there were also rounded up by the local Poles, because Jews in that area were physically indistinguishable and could not be identified, since they were not a Hasidic community.

If the murders in Jedwabne had really been carried out by the Germans, we would have had evidence of this in the reports on the operations of the *Einsatzkommandos*. These reports are very detailed. No German *Einsatzkommando* commander would have missed the opportunity to boast that he had murdered 1,600 Jews in a single day.

ANDRZEJ ŻBIKOWSKI: I agree with Prof. Gross. In my work as a historian, I try not to use modern accounts. If one does, one is dealing not with history but with sociology, a completely different subject. The

Jewish Historical Commission's 1945 instructions on the method of gathering memoirs contain the following point: "All phenomena in this sphere must be noted: both positive ones—for example, about help given to Jews; and negative ones—for example, about the participation of certain sectors of society in anti-Jewish actions." In 1945, the commission was led by people who left Poland soon afterward, except for Szymon Datner. These were not anonymous figures. They are well known, with great moral stature.

As far as the Germans are concerned, I am not saying that they played no part in all of this. The following record of events in Radziłów exists: After some sort of meeting between the Poles and Germans, numerous groups moved off to the town, each consisting of one German and one member of the town council or some other trusted person. The Germans were present in both places for a while, but certainly not during the actual massacre. Finkelsztajn clearly writes that in Radziłów, the Gestapo handed out weapons to their supporters among the local population, left a man in Polish uniform, got into their cars, and said, and I quote, "You have three days to take care of the Jews." Afterward, there were only Poles present. The Jews were lined up and driven into the barn, and murdered. That is the story, and no one has refuted it yet because there is no evidence against it. Of course the Germans murdered Jews, but not in that way. They tried to do everything in an organized manner, just as in subsequent years. In other words, they rounded the people up, preferably on the town square, and then transported them outside town, shot them, and buried them. That is how they did it in Tykocin, for example. From the middle of August, the Germans also started to murder women and children. They gathered all the Jews, took them away, and murdered them.

Historians have written a lot about two orders issued by Heydrich to the *Einsatzgruppen* on 29 June and 1 July 1941, in which he said that if a pogrom could be arranged, so much the better. I found no confirmation in Jewish reports from that time that the Germans managed to arrange such pogroms frequently. Of course they did arrange them, but rarely.

The Credibility of the Sources

ANDRZEJ KACZYŃSKI: I am rather surprised by the dispute about which accounts are more important, the older or the more recent ones. Every source deserves criticism. Of course, reports gathered recently have to be subjected to particularly severe criticism. During the months when I visited Jedwabne, Radziłów, and Łomża and gathered various accounts, I noticed that later ones already bore the hallmark of newspaper articles.

Accounts from 1945 should also be corroborated. For instance, Finkelsztajn talks about a delegation of Jews from Radziłów who went to the bishop of Łomża to ask him for protection, taking valuables and silver with them. Well, they couldn't have reached the bishop because he wasn't in Łomża at the time; he was in hiding. In any case, in that situation it is unlikely that the bishop would have been able to accept the proposition that he might ensure the security of the Jews.

PAWEŁ MACHCEWICZ: I would like to return to the question of the credibility of the accounts and investigative materials from the trial of 1949. Prof. Gross writes in his book that, during the trial, each defendant claimed he had been beaten during interrogation and, in this way, forced to give evidence. A few pages later, the author nevertheless concludes that the investigative materials can be used to reconstruct the truth. This surprises me. The materials on which Prof. Gross bases his findings contain various threads, and some reports contradict each other. This is not unequivocal material. There are many threads that require investigation: for example, the statement that the Germans— that is, the Gestapo or gendarmerie—took part in driving the Jews to the town square.

One more remark. Of course, Prof. Gross is the only historian to have used this material, and that is your advantage, Professor. But I wish to remind everyone that for the past few years, historians have not had access to these materials, because, first of all, the Main Commission for the Investigation of Crimes against the Polish Nation was being dismantled following the passage of the law to set up the Institute of National Memory, and you were the only one who had access to them. Later, the materials were also used by Prosecutor Ignatiew. I have only now received permission to release the materials to historians. Our task at the Institute of National Memory is to publish these materials. Then we will have a debate about the material stemming from these investigations.

As far as the presence of Germans is concerned, I think that for the time being we are simply not fully acquainted with the documentation, and the statements of Prof. Gross seem too categorical.

The Silence of the Historians

JAN TOMASZ GROSS: I have one question, which can serve as a reply to Mr. Machcewicz's remarks. How is it that for fifty years, not a single historian dealing with the German occupation and Polish-Jewish relations has uttered so much as one word on the dramatic fate of the Jews of Jedwabne? This question is addressed to you in particular, Tomasz, because as a historian you cover not just that period, but that very region. Why have you never written about it? Didn't you know anything about it? In 1966, Mr. Datner published a long article on the massacre of Jews in the Białystok area in the *Bulletin of the Jewish Historical Institute*. That article says in no uncertain terms that in Wąsosz, Radziłów, and Jedwabne, the murders were carried out by Poles. Mr. Machcewicz says that no one has had access to records for the past eighteen months because everything is under wraps. Fine, but for fifty years everything was accessible, yet no one tackled the subject. That is a great question with which Polish historiography will have to struggle.

TOMASZ STRZEMBOSZ: There are two things I would like to discuss. A report from 1945 need not necessarily be accurate, and a report from fifty years later need not necessarily be inaccurate. I am capable of describing my wedding day forty-four years ago in perfect detail, because that was an important day for me. And for many people, the murder in Jedwabne was also a very important event. The fact that today, after sixty years, the prosecutor is investigating these matters and talking to people confirms the view that later reports possess importance. I am not saying they are of decisive importance; merely that they possess some importance. It is not true that the Germans did not burn Jews. If one reads Jewish reports contained in the Eastern Archive, describing the situation of Jews in the Lublin region and in eastern parts of Warsaw province, one comes across descriptions of the mass burnings of synagogues, and on many occasions of people dying in these synagogues. There is also the case of the burning of fifty Jews beneath the bridge at Pułtusk, repeated in many reports. And that was in 1939. Not only men were murdered. Jewish accounts speak of children being shot, of mass murders, of people being shot with machine guns while trying to cross the San River (though the Soviet Union did not want to admit them on the other side). The same thing happened in the Augustów area. So it is not true that up to a certain point the Germans killed only adults, and children later.

JAN TOMASZ GROSS: Why didn't you write anything about this for fifty years?

TOMASZ STRZEMBOSZ: Because I was out on a limb. Between 1982 and 1990, I wrote no letters and made no phone calls. I was engaged in matters that the system viewed as treason against the Polish state. In other words, I was examining the Polish resistance to and armed struggle against the Soviet occupation regime between 1939 and 1941, before the Jedwabne massacre. If I had gone any further, I might have been found dead in the mud. That was made clear to me. And aside from that, I am not a historian of Polish-Jewish relations.

RZECZPOSPOLITA: The question of the silence of Polish historiography does not concern only, or even chiefly, Prof. Strzembosz. It is perhaps more appropriate to Dr. Żbikowski.

ANDRZEJ ŻBIKOWSKI: In 1990 I got to know Prof. Gross, and he talked me into specializing in eastern Poland and in Polish-Jewish relations during the Soviet occupation. In 1990 and 1991, I wrote my first and, for a long time, my only sentence in which I said that apart from the pogroms in the Ukraine, in June and July 1941, pogroms also occurred in Podlasie, Wizna, Wąsosz, and Jedwabne. I provided references to the reports at the Jewish Historical Institute, but, to be honest, I did not really believe that such things could have happened on such a scale. I was completely unprepared for it.

I think that we will be discussing for a long time to come whether Jedwabne was the most important episode in Polish-Jewish relations during the occupation. I do not think that it was, though of course the case has to be examined very closely. The wave of murders in June and July 1941 occurred during a transitional period, when the Russians had left and the Germans were only just arriving. And that is when the murders occurred, along the entire belt of land previously held by the Soviets.

These crimes had a certain context. On the one hand there were, let us say, economic reasons—the envy of possessions and the desire to get hold of them. I think that was the strongest motive. But on the other hand, there was an ideological motive, a tendency to blame the Jewish people for the Soviet occupation. The Jews became a scapegoat.

PAWEŁ MACHCEWICZ: Until 1989, there was no freedom to engage in research, and the Communist authorities wanted to hush up sensitive issues. But I agree with Prof. Gross that, first, historians committed flagrant negligence by failing to write about this topic after 1989, and, second, that even if they did write about it, as Andrzej Żbikowski did, they were unable to get through to public opinion. The Jedwabne memorial book was published in the United States in 1980. Before that, there was a memorial book for Grajewo, published in the early 1950s. But knowledge of the murders did not penetrate to Jewish historians, either.

In an interview for *Gazeta Wyborcza*, Prof. Gutman said that when he learned about Jedwabne, he felt as if he had been hit over the head with a hammer. It seems that none of us was prepared for such facts, which have altered our picture of Polish-Jewish relations during the occupation. If society is incapable of accepting certain controversial ideas, there will be no discussion about them. To come to a reckoning with one's own past, and not just in Poland, one has to follow a very tortuous route. In Germany, the great debate on the subject of Nazi atrocities did not start until the 1960s, and in France the debate on the Vichy regime started even later—in the 1980s. Therefore, in their attitudes toward their own past, the Poles are no exception.

RADOSŁAW IGNATIEW: I would like to refer to two matters—the accounts from 1945, and those gathered sixty years later. I treat both with the same degree of seriousness, regardless of how sensational they sound, because, as Prof. Strzembosz has said, one can remember certain traumatic events sixty years later even if they did not affect one directly. However, after a short time one also remembers such events.

Szmul Wasersztajn's report is a typical example of how collective memory works. This man and six others were themselves saved by hiding beneath a barn for twenty-six months. Janek Neumark writes that the Poles drowned two unfortunate women with their children. But Rywka Fogel claims that the women had attempted to commit suicide, and that the Poles dragged them out. This shows how a recollection of events can be distorted by the subjective point of view of the observer.

As for traces of Germans, which I am also investigating, we can forget about *Einsatzkommandos* from Group B. At that time, they were already in the East, somewhere near Minsk. In Białystok, there were only rearguard units. In his 1966 article, Szymon Datner also suggests that Wolfgang Birkner and his Kommando Białystok were engaged in the extermination of Jews between June and 10 August 1941. Datner even says that that Kommando was responsible for the Jedwabne massacre. All of this has to be checked.

One cannot say that July 1941 was a period of anarchy. I have materials which show that there was a German gendarmerie in Jedwabne even before 10 July. They arrested and killed people there. There were already some Germans in Jedwabne during that period. The question is, just how many Germans were there and what was their role? Were they passive observers of the crime or active coperpetrators?

Let me get back to the 1949 trial. I have reliable knowledge on this because I have read the court materials many times. None of the twenty-two perpetrators was charged with the murder of Jews. They were charged merely with aiding and abetting, broadly understood. Aiding and abetting whom? The Germans. In escorting the Jews onto the square and guarding them there, and leading them to the barn. One cannot ignore the fact that the same court materials contained the names of persons who had committed acts of violence or murder against persons of Jewish nationality. But the trial did not deal with this fact at all.

ANDRZEJ KACZYŃSKI: Let me tell you how I learned about Jedwabne. I first read about it in Prof. Gross's article contained in a book dedicated to Prof. Strzembosz to mark the forty-fifth anniversary of his scholarly debut. The article cited Wasersztajn's entire, shocking report, which Gross amplified with a rather general commentary and reflections. The things I expected from a historian and sociologist—that is, criticism and verification of the sources—were absent. I was disturbed by the fact that he had not compared this account with others. I thought to myself, well, if Gross has not done so, then I will. So I went to Jedwabne. In the space of several hours I succeeded in obtaining quite convincing accounts that confirm a major part of Wasersztajn's narrative. In the end, people said, with pain, "It was not the Germans who did this, it was our people . . ."

The Germans were already in Jedwabne before the massacre. There was a police outpost there. Some uniformed Germans arrived from outside. That happened more than two weeks after the front line had passed through. But the residents said that the massacre was perpetrated by Poles. Some people remembered individual uniformed and armed people, but rather as spectators—onlookers rather than perpetrators and leaders. This information usually came from the lips of people who were too young to have taken part in the atrocity or even to have been present on the square. No, they witnessed some fragments—for instance, they watched from behind the curtains, or from behind the fence, as the Jews were herded to the site of the massacre near the Jewish cemetery, for as soon as the parents learned what was going on that day, they shooed their children into their houses and locked the doors. Later I met people who had seen more. Besides direct testimony like this, the truth of the crime has been passed down in oral tradition. It is a paradox that as long as the circumstances of the massacre of the Jews in Jedwabne were not generally known, it was a public secret. The townspeople kept the truth to themselves and repeated it among themselves, but as soon as the truth came out into the open, many people became determined to deny it.

As for the negligence of historians, the *Bulletin of the Jewish Historical Institute* containing Szymon Datner's essay on the massacre of Jews in the Białystok area is dated 1966, but that particular volume was not published until 1969. That may explain why the fragments that concern Jedwabne and Radziłów are ambiguous. He wrote that in both those places, and in several others, the Germans managed to draw a certain number of local Polish hooligans, riffraff, and criminals into committing crimes. This is formulated in such a way that a reader not prepared to take in such information may understand that here, like everywhere else, the perpetrators were mostly armed Germans, assisted by a small number of Poles.

ANDRZEJ ŻBIKOWSKI: The situation with the Datner report is complicated. Most of the books were published in order to rescue the Jewish Historical Institute and the entire community in 1968. That was a difficult situation, and the point was to rescue Jewish institutions. It wasn't so much a matter of committing falsification as of reaching certain compromises.

JAN TOMASZ GROSS: There is one thing I cannot understand. In our assessment of the Jedwabne events, what difference does it make whether the Germans were, let's say, twenty kilometers from Jedwabne, or had only just arrived, or had only just left? We know they were there. We know they wanted to terrorize the population and perhaps involve it in the massacre, and we also know that they themselves murdered Jews en masse. That is a fact. But at the crucial moment, they were absent from Jedwabne. They never issued any order that, if disobeyed, might have put anyone in danger. It's not true; there is no evidence of such an order.

PAWEŁ MACHCEWICZ: We are not discussing a moral assessment of the atrocity; we are wondering whether it was perpetrated by the Poles independently, or under German influence. If we want to investigate everything, it is important to know whether the Germans were thirty kilometers or five hundred meters from the events. I think we have to pay attention to details.

Collaboration with the Soviets

RZECZPOSPOLITA: Let us consider the origins of this crime. Mr. Żbikowski said that the chief motive of the perpetrators was greed. Prof. Strzembosz said that one of the motives could have been revenge for the fact that some Jews had collaborated with the Soviet authorities.

TOMASZ STRZEMBOSZ: I never said that. I do not link the burning of the Jews in Jedwabne to what happened there before 22 June 1941. The killings that occurred earlier might have been acts of revenge, but the burning of everyone in the barn exceeds any measure of vengeance for the actions of the militias, etc.

RZECZPOSPOLITA: The dispute is that Mr. Strzembosz claims that during the Soviet occupation, many Jews in this area, in cooperation with the Soviet authorities, took an active part in persecuting the Poles. However, Mr. Gross basically denies this.

PAWEŁ MACHCEWICZ: Even accounts now to be found in the Eastern Archives of the Karta Center contain opinions that in various places, including Jedwabne, the Jews were the most visible group collaborating with the Soviets and the NKVD. An examination of the very events of 10 July shows that elements of vengeance existed there. The Jews were forced to dismantle Lenin's statue, carry the red flag, sing "This war is because of us," etc. So the problem seems to exist.

JAN TOMASZ GROSS: You are absolutely right. This problem exists in many different guises. It was revealed recently in an interview with Maria Janion in *Gazeta Wyborcza*. She cites Konstanty Jeleński from 1956: "A favorite argument of Polish antisemites is that the Jews joyfully welcomed the Red Army entering eastern Poland in 1939. In any case, it seems absurd to level accusations against those citizens whose collaboration can be explained by self-preservation. Jews would have been less attracted to communism if Poland had not shunned them for so many years."

So the population generally believed that the Jews had collaborated with the Soviets. This is just another way of saying that the Polish population was antisemitic. For this is an antisemitic stereotype that is firmly rooted, and of course one has to pay attention to it. One cannot talk about the events in Jedwabne and gloss over the fact that there was antisemitism and that the National Democracy was the leading ideological force penetrating the minds and moods of the local population. It is not without reason that they murdered Jews rather than, say, old people.

In your article, Tomasz, published in *Rzeczpospolita* under the title "Collaboration Covered Up," you say a lot of things that are obviously untrue. First of all, from beginning to end you use large-scale quantifiers such as: The Jews persecuted the Poles; the Jews sent Poles into banishment; the Jews shot at the Polish Army. This is the mirror image of Shamir's famous remark about the Poles drinking in antisemitism with their mothers' milk. Your image of Jews is that they are Pole-haters. I wonder what kind of sensitivity enables us to reverse stereotypes in that way.

Second, when you say the Jews sent the Poles to Siberia, it's an outright lie. There were proportionately more Jewish victims of these deportations than Polish victims. Between one-fourth and one-third of the deported civilians were Jews. Your article says: The Poles are persecuted by the Jews; the Jews send them to God knows where. Well, it was not like that. The Jews suffered just as much as everyone else under the Soviet occupation, if not more. The whole stereotype of Jews supporting the Bolsheviks and Communists is nonsense. They supported them to such an extent that they engaged in anti-Soviet behavior on a mass scale, for which they were punished terribly.

TOMASZ STRZEMBOSZ: These are two completely different issues—someone's attitude toward the USSR and the Communist system on the one hand, and the attitudes of the Soviets to that person on the other. This problem arises when the Jews flee from the Lublin region across the San River but are greeted with machine gun fire. They choose the Soviet Union, but the Soviet Union does not want them. These are two totally different matters. If the Jews collaborate with the Soviets, and I know of several such cases, and are subsequently deported into the depths of the USSR, it does not mean that they are merely victims and never executioners. Besides, Yezhov, the head of the NKVD, was also shot. What does that make him, an executioner or a victim? He was an executioner and he was a victim. Polish Gulag inmates met NKVD officers there, and these were sometimes murdered later by their fellow prisoners. Many Jewish Communists also abandoned their Communist ideology once they were in prison or exile. But that does not mean that all Polish Jews were Communists. That's like saying that no Poles were Communists.

However, it is a fact that a lot of Jews worked in the militia, both uniformed and plainclothes, and not just in Podlasie. In accounts gathered in Palestine in 1944—in other words, at a very early stage—Jews who had survived the USSR themselves say how many of them had joined the militia in the Lublin area, which was taken over by the Red Army in late September and October 1939, even though the Red Army ruled over them for only a few weeks. This confirms Polish reports, by the way. But what troubles me is not triumphal arches, but the fact that in sixteen places in so-called Western Belarus, Jews opened fire on Poles.

That is why information about 30, 40, or 5 percent of the Jews being deported is no answer to the question about the extent of their collaboration with the occupation regime. Why? Because that was a system that devoured its own children.

JAN TOMASZ GROSS: Do you think Wanda Wasilewska, one of the main collaborators, attended synagogue? And what about Felix Edmundovich Dzierżyński, who founded the KGB?

TOMASZ STRZEMBOSZ: One can cite other cases, this time Jewish ones. There was something that, in my opinion, equaled the phenomenon of *szmalcownicy*: representatives of Jewish circles collaborated with the Soviet authorities and handed Poles over to them.

JAN TOMASZ GROSS: In Jedwabne, the Poles delivered fellow Poles into the hands of the Soviets. Mr. Laudański was an NKVD agent. He said so himself.

TOMASZ STRZEMBOSZ: You are mistaken. The case of Laudański and others is linked to Kobielno. The Jews of Jedwabne are not guilty of betraying the partisan base in Kobielno. But they are blamed for the arrests that occurred in Jedwabne from 1939 onward, including the great arrest on the night of 16–17 June preceding the Kobielno operation, and for involvement in the deportations on 13 April 1940 and 20 June 1941. In any case, revenge for collaborating with the NKVD did not apply only to the Jews of Podlasie. It also applied to Polish peasants throughout the Jedwabne area. We know of many cases.

ANDRZEJ ŻBIKOWSKI: As far as the Soviet occupation and the collaboration of Jews is concerned, it is necessary to clarify a few matters. What is collaboration? It is cooperation. So if it is cooperation, it has many shades, and various groups of people cooperate in various ways. If we are talking about cooperation with the apparatus of repression, then of course a group of Jews collaborated, but a group of Poles, Belarusians, and Ukrainians collaborated as well. I think one can speak about the overrepresentation of Jews in the sense that in Jedwabne there were more or less as many Jewish agents as Polish ones. The Soviets needed only a dozen or so agents. I know of many reports submitted, while the war was still on, by Jewish *bezhentsy* [refugees from German-occupied territories], and these reports mention groups consisting of one NKVD agent, one Jew, and one Pole. Such groups went around together arresting people. But in small towns, groups of several or a dozen or so Jewish agents were organized, as were identical ones consisting of Poles and other nationalities residing in the area.

As to the number of Jews deported, the Soviets deported Jewish *bezhentsy* not because they were Jews but because they were *bezhentsy*. And they wanted to solve the problem of these *bezhentsy* in their own way. First, they wanted to send them for "voluntary labor" in Belarus and Ukraine. Several thousand Jews went there. Some of them returned, so that did not work. Then they were given a choice: either return to the General Government or take Soviet citizenship. Most of them, some 80 percent, refused Soviet citizenship. Why? Because they were scared that if they took it, they would never leave Russia again.

So they were punished by being deported under the same terms as the Poles, Ukrainians, or Belarusians before them.

JAN TOMASZ GROSS: What I meant was that the Jews under Soviet occupation were treated the same as everyone else. Before that they had been discriminated against, like all other minorities in these areas, because the Polish government between the wars practiced discrimination. But communism discriminated against people on a class basis, not on a religious or ethnic basis. The Jews under Soviet occupation were attacked in various ways for being Jews. Zionists were persecuted, and members of the Bund were locked up. Religious life, so important to the Jews, was completely destroyed, and so on.

ANDRZEJ ŻBIKOWSKI: Concerning Polish-Jewish relations under Soviet occupation, the welcoming of the Red Army is not the most important matter. The Red Army was welcomed by a handful of people, mainly Jews, but not many. The problem was a shift in the situation of people during the occupation. Poles suffered the greatest persecution because they were citizens of a defeated country. They were removed from positions of authority. The Jews reaped certain benefits from the situation. Social space does not tolerate a vacuum. If experts are required, and no Poles are employed, and there are no Belarusians or Ukrainians with the right qualifications, then the jobs go, for instance, to Jewish doctors. From the sources, one can also discern a rather visible schadenfreude on the part of the Jewish population.

PAWEŁ MACHCEWICZ: The question of Jewish relations with the Soviets goes beyond just the number of NKVD agents of Jewish origin on the one hand, and the number of Jewish deportees on the other. But it is true that numerous accounts—for example, many reports by the Polish Underground State or Karski's report—keep repeating that the Jews built triumphal arches welcoming the Soviets. We also know that in September 1939, in eastern Poland, the Jewish population took part in many acts against the Polish authorities. We know of various kinds of militias that collaborated with the Soviets, and in which the Jews took an active part. I wish to ask Prof. Gross, are all these the accounts of antisemites?

JAN TOMASZ GROSS: I have read practically every single report at the Hoover Institution on this subject. I have been dealing with this subject for twenty years. When did the collection of these accounts begin? Very early. The head of the institute has written the following memorandum: The antisemitism of the remarks we have gathered is so all-embracing that before the texts are published, we should seriously consider editing them. As far as the antisemitism of the people in General

Anders's Army is concerned, we do not have to reach for the archives. You can read about it in plenty of works on the subject of Anders's Army. Anders even issued a special order on this matter—antisemitism was that widespread.

The Exception or the Rule?

RZECZPOSPOLITA: To what extent does the history of the atrocities in Jedwabne and Radziłów compel us to take a completely different look at the history of the occupation in Poland, especially the history of Polish-Jewish relations? To what extent were the things that happened in Jedwabne and Radziłów an exception?

ANDRZEJ ŻBIKOWSKI: I have read many thousands of Jewish accounts in various languages, and in none of them did I find a single mention of burning people alive in barns. This must be the tip of some pyramid. At the bottom of the pyramid, Polish-Jewish relations spread out on other levels. Usually, these relations are vexed. In my opinion the matter of that one month in 1941 is not the biggest problem. The problem is the attitudes connected with the concealment of the Jewish population, with the lack of assistance, and with widespread indifference. This indifference forms the base of the pyramid whose apex is Jedwabne. Very few organizations or political forces were involved in helping the Jews. The heroism of the Żegota activists and of all those righteous people who already have or should have a tree planted in their honor is, of course, commendable, but these were just a drop in the ocean. Most of the population was indifferent. Acts of hostility, envy, blackmail, and betrayal were much more numerous than we had previously thought.

PAWEŁ MACHCEWICZ: For me, the most controversial part of Prof. Gross's book was his remarks toward the end. I felt he was metaphorically extrapolating his specific analysis of the events in the two towns to the whole of Polish-Jewish relations and to the general attitudes of Poles toward the Holocaust. He said the following, and I quote: "In collective Jewish memory this phenomenon is ingrained—that local Polish people killed the Jews because they wanted to, not because they had to . . . After all, Jedwabne—though perhaps one of the most excessive (the most excessive, it must be hoped) of all murderous assaults by Poles against the Jews—was not an isolated episode." In light of what Andrzej Żbikowski said just now, I think this is wrong. Jedwabne and Radziłów were exceptions. The opinions of Prof. Gross are expressed in a way I find unacceptable.

ANDRZEJ KACZYŃSKI: It seems to me that the question of whether we should adopt a new approach toward history, different from what has previously been regarded as canonical, because of Jedwabne and Radziłów, is badly posed. History never ends. It is always being written anew. Numerous new facts and phenomena that no one has ever investigated before—and not just on Polish-Jewish relations—are now coming to light. I consider this a challenge. They must be described and explained. It is necessary to continue to investigate the events in Jedwabne and Radziłów—not just with the help of the prosecutor and the Institute of National Memory, but also with the help of journalists. Many of the assessments that have been plentiful in the media on the present debate are, in my opinion, premature.

TOMASZ STRZEMBOSZ: After this discussion, I still do not know what happened in Jedwabne. I have encountered reports that seemed to me much more credible than Wasersztajn's. And these reports all told me something different. I cannot ignore them completely. Also, like other Warsaw historians, I do not have the UB documentation.

JAN TOMASZ GROSS: Jedwabne and Radziłów are a phenomenon that goes far beyond anything else that happened in this area. This is because of the pure tragedy of a situation in which the Jewish population of those towns was slaughtered by their Polish neighbors in such a cruel and final way. This is an event that, to my mind, creates a completely new way of recording the history of the occupation.

As far as Polish-Jewish relations are concerned, we have a great deal to do. The Poles, themselves the victims of the German occupation, behaved with indifference toward the Jews and displayed no sympathy for their suffering. The Jews were in a lower circle of hell, and this fact was exploited. I am very pleased that Mr. Machcewicz, who will be engaged in education and is responsible for this at the Institute of National Memory, promises that these matters will be investigated and that we will learn everything. I hope he is right. Because we have never properly mourned the fate of our Jewish fellow citizens. We have not suffered through and lamented the Jewish disaster during the war. I would like to believe that the Jedwabne case will represent an opening in that direction, because it is so exceedingly dramatic.

·   ·   ·   ·   ·

Tomasz Strzembosz is a professor of history and for many years has studied the history of the Polish underground in the northeast territories of the republic under the Soviet occupation.

Radosław Ignatiew is a prosecutor and is conducting the Institute of National Memory's investigation of the Jedwabne events.

Jan Tomasz Gross is a professor of political science, a historian, and a sociologist. He is the author of the book *Neighbors*.

Andrzej Żbikowski has a doctorate in history and works at the Jewish Historical Institute.

Paweł Machcewicz has a doctorate in history and is the director of the Office of Public Education at the Institute of National Memory.

Andrzej Kaczyński is a reporter for *Rzeczpospolita*. His article "Całopalenie" (Burnt offering) was the first attempt in the Polish press to clarify the course of events in Jedwabne in July 1941.

Translation taken from *Thou Shalt Not Kill*.

Anna Bikont

WE OF JEDWABNE

GAZETA WYBORCZA, 23 MARCH 2001

A YELLOWED FORM from half a century ago, filled out by some unskilled hand. The title above it reads, "Dossier on Individuals Suspected of Criminal Acts against the State." Prepared by: the Łomża District Security Administration.

Name and surname: Zygmunt Laudański
Birth date: 12 January 1919
Declared nationality: ———
Actual nationality: Polish
Religion according to birth certificate: ———
Actual religion: Roman Catholic
Relatives employed in state institutions: brother Kazimierz Laudański, district council secretary in the district administration in Pisz
Profession: bricklayer
Education and languages spoken: five grades of elementary school
Properties owned: none
Habits and addictions: nonsmoker
Known to: the whole town of Biała, Pisz district
Suspected of: murdering Jews in the town of Jedwabne, Łomża district
Political affiliations: member of the PZPR [Polish United Workers' Party] in Pisz
Date of arrest: 15 January 1949
Posture: straight
Eyes: blue
Teeth: all healthy
Speech: pure Polish

The files of the 1949 case, in which twelve people were sentenced for having taken part in the murder of the Jews of Jedwabne on 10 July 1941, also include the dossier on Zygmunt's brother Jerzy. He was born three years later, so he was just nineteen years old at the time. He had finished seven grades of elementary school. "Cobbler" is written in the

Initials of those who did not want their names to be made public have been changed.

space for "profession"; in the space for "contacts of particular importance" are the words "the German gendarmerie in the town of Jedwabne"; in the space for "language"—"loud, pure Polish."

Zygmunt Laudański was sentenced to twelve years in prison, of which he served six; Jerzy was sentenced to fifteen and served eight. Despite their age, the two brothers have kept their straight posture and loud speech.

Such Was a Pole's Lot

Zygmunt, eighty-two years old, and Jerzy, seventy-nine, both living in Pisz, are the only two of all those convicted still living. When the papers began mentioning the Laudańskis' name in the context of Jedwabne, their elder brother Kazimierz, who also lives in Pisz, wrote a letter to Adam Michnik protesting the slander of their good name: "Officers of that name used to serve under Marshal Piłsudski.[1] President Mościcki[2] recommended me personally to the *starosta* [chief administrator] of Łomża for employment in the local government administration." Of himself and his brothers he wrote, "Like the whole nation, we suffered under the Germans, the Soviets, and the People's Republic of Poland."

"We come from a family of real Polish patriots. Many of us were killed and tortured," says Kazimierz Laudański. "Pity you didn't meet our great-grandfather. It is no accident that all three of us are still alive. It's because we don't smoke; we don't drink. How can anyone say my brothers are hooligans? Whatever we did, we did out of patriotism; none of us has ever allied with the enemy against the nation."

He doesn't hide the fact that in the difficult struggle to get by, the family would sometimes write letters: to Stalin and the NKVD during the Soviet occupation, and then, after the war, to the security minister and to the Central Committee of the PZPR.

Commenting on his letter praising Stalin, written under the Soviets, Zygmunt Laudański says: "Had things turned out otherwise, I would have written to Hitler and praised Hitler. But that's obvious."

"It's not that I want to defend my brothers," Kazimierz continues; "Justly or unjustly, they have already been tried and cannot be sen-

---

[1] Józef Klemens Piłsudski (1867–1935) was a statesman, politician, and founder and leader of the Polish Socialist Party (PPS). Between the coup of May 1926 and his death in May 1935, he was the de facto ruler of Poland.

[2] Ignacy Mościcki (1867–1946) was a politician and professor of chemistry. In 1926 Józef Piłsudski supported his candidacy for the presidency, a position that Mościcki held until the outbreak of World War II. He died an émigré in Switzerland.

tenced again for the same thing. I am meeting with you *pro publico bono*, so you can tell Michnik one mustn't scratch those old wounds unnecessarily. Presenting Poles as criminals is not a wise thing to do. And now is not the time, when Jewish financial circles are attacking Poland, to start a campaign teaching Poles what's right. It's so vile and low to accuse Poles of such things. What were the Jews doing in the UB [Security Administration] after the war? We could say a lot about that, but what's the use. We have nothing against the Jews. We have forgiven the Gestapo and the NKVD; why is it that now, in this small quarrel between the Poles and the Jews, no one's going to forgive anything?"

When I came to Pisz again, it was Kazimierz who organized a meeting for me with his brothers in his well-kept house in the center of the city. His opening words were: "Those Jews in Jedwabne—whether they were burned then or not, their fate was sealed. The Germans would have killed them sooner or later. It's such a small thing, and someone is trying to stick it on Poles; my brothers, what's more. We feel hurt." There is elegant china on the table and an excellent homemade gingerbread cake. Kazimierz Laudański is well known in the area as a beekeeper; together with his brothers he keeps three apiaries, and people come all the way from Germany to buy his honey.

"It's a lie," Zygmunt Laudański adds, "that my brother and I killed over a thousand Jews. We are an honest family and always have been. This tragedy cannot overshadow our honesty."

The host interrupts him: "I'm speaking now, Zygmunt; you stay quiet. You'll speak when I let you."

Kazimierz is the unquestioned leader of the family. He wasn't in Jedwabne at the time but came home three days later to see what was happening with the brothers. He moved them out of the town and later found them jobs and places to live. "They are always with me," he says. "I give them advice and they always listen to me."

He was in Ostrów Mazowiecki when the war broke out between Germany and the Soviet Union. "When the Germans came," he says, "they set the Jewish quarter on fire; then they caught all the Jews, drove them along the road, made them dig a big hole in the ground, and then killed them. A friend of mine was there; he had to watch as they shot. He came back pale and trembling. Such was a Pole's lot."

It Looked Spontaneous

Szmul Wasersztajn, who was rescued from the pogrom in Jedwabne, testified before the Jewish Historical Committee on 5 April 1945 (five years later, his report would become the basis for starting the investigation): "The order [to annihilate all the Jews] was given by the Germans, but it was Polish hooligans who took it up and carried it out in the most horrible ways; after all kinds of persecutions and tortures, they burned all the Jews in a barn. During the first pogroms and in the slaughter itself, the following scum distinguished themselves by their cruelty: . . ."

Among the fourteen names mentioned is that of Jerzy Laudański.

"When I came to Jedwabne, there was still the hideous stench of burnt corpses. Right away I found out in conversations what had happened. The Germans had found a barn right across the bridge, on the Łomża side. They wanted to confiscate it from Józef Chrzanowski, but he had served in the German army and begged them in German not to take it. So they found another one by the Jewish cemetery. They said, 'We'll burn it down and build a new one.' "

A little later the Laudański brothers told me that when the Jews were being led to the barn, no one in town expected that they would be burned there. "Didn't you know that three days earlier the Jews of Radziłów had been burned alive in a barn?" I ask Jerzy Laudański.

"I didn't hear about any such thing."

Kazimierz Mocarski, who left the region right after the war and is now a retired school principal in Stegny in the Pomorze region, says: "We lived in a village called Niedbory in the municipality of Jedwabne. A day or two before the slaughter, a dozen or so Jews came to our house. My mother was baking rye bread, and she gave them two loaves, saying, 'You must run away, quickly.' Because it was already known what had happened in Radziłów."

A few other people, too, have told me that the news about what had happened in the village eighteen kilometers from Jedwabne immediately spread around the region.

Kazimierz Laudański: "The trial took place seven and a half years after the crime. There were beatings in the Security Administration, but the Yids, small children thrown into a barn, it wasn't spoken of then. And now after sixty years such things are said. When we're all dead, they'll write of eyes being ripped out."

Zygmunt Laudański: "There were no horrible things like that. It's all made up now out of vengeance."

From Szmul Wasersztajn's report, made fifty-six years ago: "The bandits went around to search Jewish homes, looking for the sick and the children left behind. They carried the sick people that they found to the barn one by one, but they tied the small children together by their legs a few at a time and carried them on their backs. Then they put them on pitchforks and threw them onto the smoldering coals."

Sławomir S., a retired lawyer who left Jedwabne in the 1950s, says: "Please don't mention my name. The Laudańskis are still alive, I do my shopping in Pisz; I met one of them once on the street, and it sent shivers down my spine; I don't want any trouble. Maybe this fear has been in me since that time, but even now friends warn me about talking with you and say, 'You're better off staying out of it.' I was ten years old in 1941. Some mothers wouldn't let their children out on that day, but I was the kind that would put his nose everywhere. And so I found myself in front of that barn. There was no big crowd, maybe fifty people, all men. Me and my buddies were standing a little to the side. There was some fear that they would take us for Jewish kids and throw us in. There was Józef Kobrzyniecki, who had led the crowd when the Jews were made to carry the statue of Lenin, who'd beaten them the hardest, and who was going around all the houses to find the ones still trying to hide, to finish them off with a bayonet. He was throwing children into the burning barn. I saw it with my own eyes. A horrible crime was committed by Polish hands. When I grew up, I left Jedwabne immediately, and since then I haven't wanted to have anything to do with that place."

"Our people organized the gathering of the Jews but took no part in the burning," says Kazimierz Laudański, who came to Jedwabne after it was all over. "Their attitude was normal and peaceful. There was fear, pity, and a terrible stench for three hundred meters around the site. The shocked Poles would say, 'A punishment from God.' It was a devilish trick organized by the Germans. They directed the whole thing, and the Poles served as actors in a theater. But that the Poles wanted to burn the Jews—it was nothing like that."

He doesn't deny, however, that between 22 June 1941, when the Soviet occupation ended, and 10 July Jews were murdered.

"There were many acts of revenge," he says. "But who were the victims? Only the spies and the Communists would get lynched. They did get what they deserved, indeed. But the Jewish community and a gang of Communists were two different things. Our people acted in self-defense, as in all those uprisings that we are not ashamed of. Where there is fire, there is smoke. Many of them were uneducated, so there may have been a lot of innocent victims. But the Communists, Polish and Jewish, shouldn't have been collaborating with the NKVD. Treason is punishable by death."

Zygmunt Laudański: "We must get to the crucial day, because that's what the whole affair is about. I was at home and this little girl comes with a note: 'Laudański, report to the mayor at once.' Karolak was the mayor at the time. So I took the note and went. On the way I met Karolak with a German, and they were dragging a Jew out of his house, a tailor with a pair of trousers. The trousers were mine: a Russian gave them to me, but they were too big, so I took them for alterations. So I say, 'Guten morgen.' The German asks 'Jude?' and Karolak answers no. They took us, me and that Jew. We walked through the market square and saw Jews weeding it with spoons. The grass was overgrown. They were working calmly, as if nothing was happening. The Poles were just staring. Karolak, who was living in the middle of the square, told me to go repair his stove. His wife says, 'Mr. Laudański, I'm sorry to call you on such a day'—because that was the day when they gathered all the Jews; maybe she knew what was going to happen to them, and she was a decent woman—'but some Germans will be visiting my husband and I can't even make tea, because the stove is broken.' She gave me a hammer; I took a bucketful of trash out of the oven, then covered it over with clay. When I was done, I went to Przytulska Street, but there was a German on guard there, and he says 'Zurück.' So I go out on the Łomża side of town, but there's a German there, too, who says the same. I go toward Wizna—another German. So I cut through people's gardens toward 11 Listopada Street. A friend of mine, Borawski, was living there. We talked a bit. No one thought of such horror. So I walked on, then I hid in the rye for a while, and when I got back to my yard, I saw the smoke."

That is the version Zygmunt Laudański presented in 1949, when he was already in prison and appealing the sentence. He mentioned one detail, however, which showed that someone had been thinking of the horror, after all: "The mayor and the Gestapo officer were taking away that Jewish tailor I'd given my trousers to a few days before, when we were still under Soviet rule, and when he saw me he called to me and gave me the trousers back, still unfinished, saying he didn't know whether he would return."

Jerzy Laudański: "The mayor was giving orders, but the initiative was the Germans'. I was standing by the bakery and mixed into the crowd."

"How did you come to be there?"

"Curiosity. Hit someone's car and see how many people gather. There was something going on; the Germans were driving out the Jews. There was a huge Lenin statue—it must have weighed a ton and a half, and the Jews were carrying it. No one was crying over Lenin being taken away, except maybe some followers of his; after all, thousands of people had been sent to Siberia.

"Were the Jews beaten at that point?"

"There were Poles in the market square, but I saw nothing like that. There may have been five hundred Jews where I was standing, but I didn't see a single one beaten. The Jews were calmly talking and weeding the soil between the cobblestones. The Germans like to have things in order, so the marketplace had to be weeded. And then everything took its own course and seemed spontaneous."

"What do you mean, spontaneous?"

"The Jews spontaneously went obediently, the Poles spontaneously followed them, because nobody was expecting that kind of tragedy. When they say that the Poles committed the murders—it would be a disgrace for Poland, and it's not true."

"How did the Poles react?"

"Some were happy, some not, but there was curiosity. People were laughing that just a little while ago, under the Soviets, the Jews wouldn't have been cleaning the marketplace."

"What about you?"

"I was standing in front of the barn, at a distance of thirty meters, and there were many people in front of me."

"What were you doing there?"

"I was talking to my friends."

"Wasn't anyone trying to help the Jews?"

"Who could help? There was this one great hero, Father Kolbe,[3] but he knew he had tuberculosis and wouldn't survive the camp, anyway. He was a hero, though, because there aren't many who would give their lives for another, even if they know they're already done for."

"And what about the Germans?"

"They say the Germans were standing behind and taking photographs."

In the following hours of the conversation I would hear from that very same Jerzy that everybody went along spontaneously: first the Jews, then the Poles, and finally the Germans.

"What kind of uniforms did they have?" I asked.

"That I couldn't say."

Only after many more conversations in Jedwabne did I notice the following pattern: Those who now accuse the Jews of collaborating with the NKVD during the Soviet occupation and with the UB after the war saw lots of Germans on the scene. Those who feel pity for their murdered neighbors did not see a single German participate in driving the Jews to the barn on 10 July 1941. They do not question the fact that the murder took place with the Germans' permission or by their

[3] Father Maksymilian Kolbe (1894–1941) was a Franciscan who as a prisoner in Auschwitz volunteered to die in the place of of another Polish prisoner. He was canonized by Pope John Paul II, an act that raised controversy owing to Kolbe's prewar position as a founder of the strongly nationalistic and antisemitic Catholic papers *Rycerz Niepokalany* and *Mały Dziennik*.

inspiration. They just say that the Germans did not participate directly in the crime, and that one or two of them were taking photographs of the market square.

"The Germans did it purposefully with Polish hands," says Zygmunt Laudański.

"But what did those Polish hands do?"

"Many Poles ran away. Many Jews, too. Then they ended up in the Łomża ghetto. I went there to buy things. My wife stood on those ruins and tried on shoes until she found a pair that fit."

Some people from Jedwabne did, indeed, "run away"—those who didn't want to take part stayed home on that day or else went to visit relatives or friends among the farmers in the region. I didn't hear of anyone's being punished by the Germans for this. (Except that the Poles who were known to have been friendly with the Jews, like one of my interlocutors, Leon Dziedzic, were told to clear away the bodies the day after the pogrom. That, however, was probably at the initiative of Karolak the mayor.) All the same, not one hair fell from the head of Józef Chrzanowski, a relative of the Laudańskis', who hadn't wanted to give up his barn.

There were also some Jews who ran away. We don't know how many, but on the day of the massacre groups of young men would search the nearby fields, so it was difficult to save oneself. Seven are known to have survived. They were hidden until the end of the war by Antonina Wyrzykowska, a resident of the nearby village of Janczewsk.

Kazimierz Mocarski remembers the stories told by his mother about how some people left town on that day because they didn't want to get involved, while others from the area harnessed up horses and carts and came to Jedwabne because they knew there would be houses, workshops, and stores to be plundered. I ask Zygmunt Laudański what he knows about the plunder, and on what grounds Jewish houses and flats were taken over.

"People took them over because many had been living in basements. They would enter spontaneously and the town authorities didn't throw them out. People say that things were plundered. The gendarmerie didn't manage to grab everything, so maybe someone took something, maybe some sheets or some clothes. But it was the Germans who would take things and then put them up for auction, hold rags up and say, this many rubles. Because at the beginning of the war there were still no German marks."

"A German would sell Jewish clothes?"

"To earn money for a few extra beers."

They Shouldn't Have Thrown That Snow

"Why," I ask the Laudańskis, "were the Jews of Jedwabne burned in the barn?"

"It was the Germans' revenge," the brothers repeat in turn.

They say that before the war there were some fifteen German families living in Jedwabne, and most of them left for the Reich in accordance with the Ribbentrop-Molotov pact. During the Soviet occupation in 1940, a small committee came from Germany to estimate the value of the property they had left behind. Officers in shiny coats came out of two black cars, and some Jews surrounded the cars and started throwing wet snow and insulting them to such a degree that the Germans had to ask the Soviet militiamen for help.

Jerzy Laudański learned about this from Karol Bardoń in the prison's walking yard. Bardoń worked in the gendarmerie throughout the German occupation. In the Jedwabne trial he was sentenced to death, but later the sentence was changed to fifteen years in prison. Bardoń supposedly told Laudański that one of the Germans who came to Jedwabne in July 1941 had been on that committee and was now saying, "They gave us a hard time then; now they deserve a lesson."

"That's probably why," Zygmunt Laudański comments; "the Jews made a mistake—they shouldn't have thrown that snow."

The brothers suggested that I meet Alina Łukowianka in Jedwabne. Zygmunt Laudański spent the evening with her on 10 July 1941. She was chopping wood in the woodshed when I met her. She lives alone in a communal flat and has to keep the stove going. We talked for two hours, and she never took a break from her work.

"Did Zygmunt tell you then that he had escaped into the fields because he didn't want to take part in the rounding up of the Jews into the barn?"

"He didn't tell me anything of the sort. I have already testified before the prosecutor [Radosław Ignatiew, the prosecutor from the Institute of National Memory, who was running the investigation], haven't I? He's never contacted me before, so what does he want from me now? I was in Pisz last year; I saw Jurek [Laudański]; the papers were already beginning to write about Jedwabne. I asked him, 'Have you read the papers?' and he said no. He was lying. One filthy Jew in that book by Gross is lying, too: he says he ran away from the barn, when he wasn't even there. Back on that evening, when the Jews had already been burned, I ran into Gienek Kalinowski, a neighbor of the Laudańskis. He told me there was an order from the mayor to stay up and watch over the households because the Jews might take revenge. So I sat with Laudański in front of our shacks. The Laudańskis are big guys now, their pictures are in *Rzeczpospolita*, and they want to clear themselves, show they're so pure. What were they tried for, then? I didn't see them do it. But the screams could be heard two kilometers away."

Both in eyewitnesses' reports and secondhand reports—for it is common knowledge in the older generations in Jedwabne who murdered and who got rich off the Jews—certain names recur persistently: Eugeniusz Kalinowski, Józef Kobrzyniecki, Czesław Mierzejewski, Stanisław Sielawa, Józef Sobuta, Michał Trzaska. And then the Laudański brothers. But even now, sixty years later, those who witnessed the crime are afraid to testify under their own names.

Marianna K. from Jedwabne: "They had clubs and rubber bars. They must have cut up the rubber the night before, when they decided on the murder. My father had said they were hoping to kill Jews two days in advance. He'd worked for the Jews and helped them to buy grain. When they drove the Jews out into the market square, I saw twelve-year-olds chasing them, and many seventeen- or nineteen-year-olds. Sometimes they had been schoolmates. How could they look them in the eyes when they were killing them? The Jews were defenseless, so sad, and they [the Poles] were so enraged. We were afraid to come closer to the barn, afraid of getting dragged in there, too."

Kazimierz Mocarski: "A few days later one of my friends invited me to his place; he wanted to show me the Jewish flat he'd taken over. He told me how the Jews were beaten before the burning, how they were pushed around and forced to say Polish prayers."

Jan Cytrynowicz [Jewish by birth], a harness maker, lived in Wizna before the war and had been baptized there as a child. He lived in Jedwabne after the war and now lives in Łomża: "I came to Jedwabne after the war and lived with my Polish stepmother. My drinking buddies didn't know about my origins, so after a few drinks they'd start their stories: 'I chased that one,' 'I stabbed that one hard.' They were proud if they had killed two or three Jews."

Janusz Lech Dziedzic, a farmer from Przestrzel, a settlement two kilometers from the town, whose grandparents kept Szmul Wasersztajn hidden for some time before he ended up in Antonina Wyrzykowska's place: "I can't even imagine it, I mean the burning alone is so painful, and then the suffocating . . . And these people had never done them any harm. My father, Leon Dziedzic, had been a friend of Samuel Wasersztajn's before the war. He would visit the synagogue with him, although my father's friends said that when you go in there, you have to trample a cross first. One day, some time in the 1970s, a man came to our yard when my parents were gone, and I knew it had to be Samuel, because I remembered my grandmother's stories about his big protruding ears. He had come from Costa Rica. I showed him Grandma's picture in the family album; he kissed it, and he cried like I'd never heard even a child cry before. He said, 'My mother gave me my life, but she couldn't help me keep it, and this woman risked the lives of her own eight children to save my lousy Jewish life.' "

No Antisemitism, Just Advertising

In 1660 a group of Jews moved from Tykocin to Jedwabne. In 1770 they built a beautiful wooden synagogue, which can be seen in the well-known album of Polish synagogues by Kazimierz and Maria Piechotka. It burned down in September 1913. In the *yizkerbukh* [memorial book] of the Jews of Jedwabne we read that for the next two generations the burning of the synagogue was remembered as the worst, almost unimaginable disaster to befall the community.

Jerzy Laudański: "We lived together for a couple hundred years and there were no differences between us."

"Did you ever visit a Jewish home?"

"Well, no, that far I didn't go."

Kazimierz Laudański: "The Jews would lease orchards from the peasants in the summer, so I decided to put a stick in their wheel and to do the same thing. Michał Jałoszewski, the local pharmacist [and National Party activist], gave me five hundred zlotys to start the business.

"What did you invest it in?"

"Apples and textiles. You could go around towns and put up tables. Poles always bought from the Jews, because a Jew would sell cheaper. Why? Because the Jews had the means. They owned the mines, the warehouses, they controlled everything. And I had no job and was getting more and more angry. I wrote a letter to President Mościcki. It started with: 'You are the father and the steward of the Polish nation . . .' and then I wrote, 'Even though we are nationalists and our great-grandfathers have been dying for Poland in uprisings, we are now in a disadvantaged position.' The president told the local magistrate in Łomża to hire me. So I left the business to my parents and my brothers and became the assistant to the head of a department. When the war broke out, I was earning 176 zlotys, more than a schoolteacher. I've always been lucky, but you've got to help your luck along."

"He was a fervent National Democrat," Kazimierz Laudański tells me about his father, the bricklayer. He was active in the Church Building Committee and on good terms with the priests, which earned him the hatred of the local Communist unit.

Sławomir S.: "Not long before the war they already wouldn't let the Jews do any business in Jedwabne. They would stand in front of Jewish shops with crowbars. On Wednesdays, when there was a market day, the *narodówka* [nationalists] would usually come from Łomża, and some locals would join them."

Kazimierz Mocarski: "The *narodówka* would smash Jewish stands so that the police had to intervene. And the Jews were so polite; they'd say, 'Good morning, what a beautiful boy,' and give me a piece of candy. When my mother said, 'Listen, Jew, the other Jew sells this fabric for 2.10 zlotys and you want 2.20?' he'd bow down and say, 'We can reach an agreement, Mrs. Mocarska; I can contribute and sell it for 2.05.' "

Zygmunt Laudański: "Of course, I heard the slogan 'Don't buy from Jews' in church. There was another one: 'Buy from your own kind.' But can't you have a slogan like that when you want to open a business in your own country? How can you call that antisemitism? It was just advertising."

"It was the mob that killed the Jews on 10 July 1941," Janusz Lech Dziedzic says. "But had the priest stood in their way and said, 'You'll go to hell for this and you'll have to reckon with the devil,' they would have listened to him, maybe except for a couple of bandits who were already drunk at that point."

Rise, O White Eagle, Strike the Jews

The father of Zygmunt and Jerzy, Czesław Laudański, was indeed active in the National Party, known in the area as the *narodówka*. Old press clippings attest to how strong it must have been in Jedwabne back in those days.

"On 3 May 1936, after the mass, there was a parade in the town of Jedwabne, attended by members and sympathizers of the National Party, about 1,500 people, accompanied by a band and escorted by a group on bicycles. During the parade, people shouted, 'Long live great national Poland,' 'Long live Polish national trade,' 'Down with Jewish Communism.' The parade was a success and made a deep impression on the people of Jedwabne and the wider area."

The nationalists had their own repertoire. Józef "Kmicić" Stankiewicz, a partisan of the Narodowe Siły Zbrojne [National Armed

Forces], recalled one song that was often heard in the villages of the
Białystok region (in an interview with Jerzy Kułak, published by the
journal *Karta*):

> Poland beloved,
> You have millions of people,
> But your land
> Is still full of Jews.
> Rise, O White Eagle,
> Strike the Jews,
> Let them no longer
> Be our lords.

The energetic and active National Party was shaping the consciousness
of most Poles in Jedwabne and other towns and villages in the area.
Its influence spread through the local church papers, which were the
chief source of news and opinion. The bishop, Stanisław Kostka
Łukomski, was known for his antisemitism, and he was a personal
friend and collaborator of Roman Dmowski's.[4] There was a farmers'
weekly, *Life and Work: A Weekly Magazine for Catholic and Social Affairs
in the Łomża Diocese* (renamed in 1935 *The Catholic Cause*), published by
Father Antoni Roszkowski; apart from advice on how to fight weeds
and household pests, it contained information on the activities of the
National Party and the Akcja Katolicka [Catholic Action Movement],[5]
which was under that party's ideological influence.

Reading this magazine gives one an idea of how powerful and how
deep antisemitism must have been in the region. The main theme, as
one of the authors put it, is "the ceaseless enlightening of our compatriots about the Jewish danger."

On the front page there was always an editorial, presumably written
by the priest who was the editor-in-chief. Here are some of the titles:
"The Jews Are Taking Liberties," "The Land Must Be Taken Away from
Jewish Hands," "Polish Youth Suffers for Jewish Sins," "How Poland
Has Become Infested with Jews."

"The Polish nation has matured and understood that all relations
with the Jews must be broken off, not in a year or two, but today," we
read in an editorial entitled "Breaking with the Jews." "No other nation
would suffer what we have borne for years because of the Jews. They

[4] Roman Dmowski (1864–1939) was a politician, statesman, and the founder of the
modern Polish nationalist movement Narodowa Demokracja (National Democracy),
known as Endecja.

[5] Akcja Katolicka (the Catholic Action Movement) is a conservative Catholic lay social
organization set up to oppose secularization. Akcja Katolicka was first set up in Poland
in 1930 and by 1937 numbered 615,000 members. It was reestablished in Poland in 1997.

have taken over all our trade and handicrafts. We are facing the nightmarish vision of a Jewish Poland. We don't want to pay back evil with evil; our response must be worthy of a civilized Christian nation. We are breaking all relations with the Jews. Polish youths cannot have Jewish friends; social relations with Jews are not befitting for a Christian and must be broken off. We have to sound the alarm. The Jews stand in the way of Poland's greatness. Breaking off all relations with them is called for by both our common sense and our conscience."

The Germans, who "know how to handle the problem of Jewish overpopulation," were referred to as a model. Apparently their life in Poland is too easy, if they dare to criticize the Poles, as we read under the title "A Warning to the Jews": "Things in Poland are the way they are, but it's all our internal affair and none of the Jews' business!" The phrase "No country can tolerate or digest such a mass of Jews" is repeated in the following issues.

An appeal is made: "A little child buying a roll or a piece of candy, a pencil or a notebook; a farmer doing his shopping—they should only know the way to the Polish shop; Poles must buy from Poles!" A vision of "Jewish Poland" was presented in which "the kikes, driven out of business," start buying land, and "the Polish people, the longtime masters of this land, would have to go wander homeless among strangers." That's why "every Jewish farm is a splinter in the Polish farmer's flesh." "One would think the Jews would have realized by now that Poland belongs to the Poles. The Jews either cannot understand it or refuse to understand it, but this can't work out well for them."

The journal was a window on the world for the local people. As I look through issues from the 1930s, in the "National News" section, I find: "Jewish Usury," "Cleansing Łódź of Jews," "Two Jews from Lwów Were Buying Gold Stolen from Churches." In the "World News" section: "Rumors of Ritual Murder," "Jews Whipped for Opening Shops on Sundays" (the latter in Tripoli). Among the books recommended for the parishioners there is *The Life and Teaching of Jesus Christ: An Outline* by Father J. Unszlicht, a book that "gives us a clear presentation of the Jews' perversity in their dealing with Jesus Christ."

One can, of course, wonder how strong the influence of the press could have been, when over one-third of the people in the voivodeship of Białystok were illiterate and another third had completed only two grades of elementary school. However, the journals were read by the town elites, including Czesław Szumowski, the vicar of Jedwabne. The contents of the diocesan press were made known and propagated in the parish by the Catholic Action Movement. In Jedwabne, as in the surrounding regions, the movement had its agencies, beginning with kindergartens. Little children were members of the Eucharistic Crusade, also known as the Knights of Jesus; the older ones would belong to the Female and Male Polish Youth groups. The adults would perform plays—it's not difficult to guess the contents of *The Jewish Match-maker*. They attended lectures and rallies with titles like "On the Need for and Methods of Battling *żydokomuna* [Judeo-Communism]."

The words would then turn into deeds. The same scenario was repeated in one town after another, as reported by the Białystok daily newspaper: "On market day several Jewish merchants were beaten up and stabbed with knives; many ran away, leaving their stands unguarded, and all their goods were stolen."

The Polish state was trying to protect its Jewish citizens. There were police interventions, arrests, and trials. The diocesan journal, on the other hand, was openly sympathetic to the organized boycotts. While trials were under way, it would report on the beautiful speeches of the defense attorneys and the noble attitude of the neighbors who plowed the arrestee's field. It would also provide information about the effectiveness of the boycott. Thus, for example, "in Zaręby Kościelne the Jewish market stands were so tightly guarded that no farmer dared approach them, and now 250 Jewish families are facing starvation."

Among the many places where Jewish shops and stands were attacked and demolished I find familiar names: Radziłów, Stawiska, Tykocin, Zaręby Kościelne. According to the stories recorded by the Jewish Historical Committee immediately after the war, the Poles in those towns were murdering their Jewish co-citizens and looting their properties in 1941. In a report from Tykocin, written in 1946 by the survivor Menachem Turek, we read: "[In June 1941] a crowd of Poles, led by a group of nationalists, veterans of the prewar boycott, stormed Jewish houses and emptied them completely. With wild cries of vengeance, threats, and curses, the drunken mob robbed the Jewish shops, taking whatever they could get their hands on."

Don't You Know What the Jews Had Been Doing?

Some people in Jedwabne, when they see a journalist, start telling me how powerful and bossy the Jews became under the Soviet occupation.

Jadwiga Biedrzycka, the daughter of Bronisław Śleszyński, who made his barn available for the burning of the Jews, welcomes me with the words "Don't you know what the Jews had been doing here?" In Agnieszka Arnold's film *Where Is My Elder Brother Cain?* which was broadcast on Polish TV, she said that the Jews enthusiastically welcomed the Red Army troops as they entered the town. Asked for specifics, she answered that there was a table on the main street, covered with red cloth, and that two Polish families and one Jewish family were sitting behind it (a year later, though, when Agnieszka Arnold was preparing her next film, *Neighbors*, soon to appear on Polish TV, Biedrzycka changed the proportions to one Polish family and four Jewish ones).

Sławomir S.: "When the Soviets came in, there was joy among the Jews. Some of the young people put on red armbands and joined the police. That didn't last too long. The Soviets soon got rid of them; they preferred to do everything by themselves. The poorer Jews were a bit bossy. From their point of view the Soviets meant liberation. The ones just a bit richer were as likely to be deported east as the Poles.

The Soviet occupiers were welcomed by the Communists—both Polish and Jewish—with enthusiasm, and by very many Jews with hope. It was obvious to them that anything was better than the German occupation; besides, there was hope that a country preaching internationalism might also bring an end to the wave of antisemitic persecutions by their Polish neighbors. For most Poles, it was from the beginning a time of constant threat and uncertainty about tomorrow, a time of deportations and arrests.

The beginning of the occupation was described by Jan Karski in his report for the Polish government-in-exile. He also wrote about Polish-Jewish relations under both occupations. Writing of the friendly or often even enthusiastic attitude of the Jews welcoming the Soviet troops, he commented, "It is hardly surprising in their situation." He was anxious about the mood among the Poles: "In general, however, the Jews as a mass have created a situation in which the Poles think of them as loyal to the Soviets, and there can be hardly any doubt that they are waiting for the moment when they can pay the Jews back . . . A great majority (mainly the young people, of course) are, quite literally, looking forward to a bloody revenge."

And Now Patriotism

Kazimierz Laudański: "The Soviets came and took our father to prison. They put him in the *czerwoniak* [the red house] in Łomża. Everybody knew who was behind his deportation."

"Who?"

"Well, the Jews were never deported, were they? The NKVD didn't know us, and the Jews were neighbors. Those Communist Jews would give them the names of the Polish families to be deported."

Kazimierz Laudański: "When they came at night to take away whole families, there was always one NKVD officer, one Polish Communist, and two Jews."

I ask Zygmunt Laudański who came to take his father.

"I wasn't home that night, but my grandmother said there were two Russians and one Pole, probably Chrystowczyk [there was a Chrystowczyk family living in Jedwabne, and some of the brothers were Communists]."

"If you want proof that it was the Jewish Communists who did it," Kazimierz Laudański says, "I can tell you that there were many rich Jews in Jedwabne and none of them was deported or lost his shop. They deported only one rich Jew, Jakub Cytrynowicz, because he was baptized."

"You mean other Jews denounced him because he was baptized?"

"Right."

Jakub's son, Jan Cytrynowicz, tells me, however, that his father was deported because they caught him smuggling flour from Ostrołęka. He also remembers that the rich Jews were deported, too.

"And now patriotism . . . The very existence of the partisan movement, our father's sister who died in combat, fighting against the Soviets, the deaths of many other Poles in the area—all this speaks for itself," wrote Kazimierz Laudański in his letter to Adam Michnik.

Jadwiga Laudańska, together with several hundred other people from Jedwabne and its environs, belonged to a partisan group that hid in the forests near Kobielno. They were surrounded by the NKVD, many were killed (Jadwiga Laudańska among them), and many were deported.

This family tragedy is meant to explain that the Laudańskis had reason to take revenge on the Jews. Many other statements in the Polish press make the same suggestion, including those of Prof. Tomasz Strzembosz and Sławomir Radoń, the chairman of collegium of the Institute of National Memory.[6] In the context of Jewish collaboration with the Soviets, the latter has mentioned the Laudańskis' sister who was killed by the NKVD (she was, in fact, their uncle's wife, not their sister), and another one (not mentioned by the Laudański brothers) who was deported to the USSR.

The assumption behind it all, which is taken as obvious, is that it was the Jews who denounced people to the Soviet authorities. In fact, what happened has been determined by historians and even described by Prof. Tomasz Strzembosz: the partisan group that consisted largely of people from Jedwabne was located by the NKVD thanks to information from Polish informers.

Leszek Dziedzic: "I know that here, in Przestrzel, it was a Polish woman who was collaborating with the Russians and denouncing

---

[6] Sławomir Radoń is also director of the state archives in Kraków.

people. In the neighboring village the informer was also a Pole. There must have been a Jewish one somewhere, too; every nation has its scoundrels."

Sławomir S.: "I very much doubt that it was the Jews who did the informing. What I know for sure is that it was the Soviets who came for my uncle; there were no local people."

Many documents I have looked through confirm what Sławomir S. has told me. After the first burst of enthusiasm and hope for a safer and more decent life, most of the local Jews were brought back to their senses. This was partly because the Russians themselves had brought their own people (this is confirmed by the Soviet sources that served as a basis for a number of works by Prof. Michał Gnatowski of the University of Białystok) and did not need any self-appointed police; besides, when they needed any help, they preferred to seek it from Polish Communists.

A time of poverty and fear was upon the Jews. Private property, mills, and shops were confiscated; religious activities were forbidden; the synagogues were requisitioned and turned into warehouses.

When I read the reports belonging to General Anders's Army and archived in the Hoover Institution (accessible in Warsaw's Eastern Archives, "Karta" section; sixteen of the reports refer to the municipality of Jedwabne), the picture I got was very different from that of Prof. Tomasz Strzembosz. Referring to the same materials in his article in *Rzeczpospolita*, he writes of Jewish treason and uses it to explain the Jedwabne murders.

The greatest numbers of eager Jewish collaborators can be found in the generalized statements and in the reports from the beginning of the occupation. When they get down to specifics, and names are mentioned, the same reports that had just spoken of Jewish omnipotence under the Soviets tell us that the people in the election committees were Russians, and that the candidates selected by the authorities were usually Communists, either Soviet or Polish. In Jedwabne, for instance, it was Czesław Krystowczyk. In the numerous reports of property confiscations, deportations, and house searches, there is no mention of those theoretically omnipresent Jews.

Why, then, are there so many general statements about the dominant role played by the Jews? It seems to me that those reports were not made with the conscious intention of giving false evidence. On the contrary, they reflect the subjective reality of the local people.

In the thirties, whenever a Jewish teacher appeared in one of the schools, the Catholic Action Movement would announce a boycott, the children would stop going to school, and the parish would collect letters of protest. "No Christian family will put its child into Jewish hands," the local church paper would say; "protesting against the Jewish presence in Polish schools, we Catholics are only doing what our faith demands. Our Catholic conscience and our national pride demand that we get rid of Jewish teachers."

Whenever a Polish citizen of Jewish nationality was installed in a state administrative position, the local church press would raise the alarm. Every such case was reported under the title "Jew Replaces Pole." Thus "The Jew Pinkus Rajgrodzki has been appointed tax collector in the town hall"; "The rumor we mentioned some time ago has turned out to be true: a Jewish doctor has been appointed head of the health service in Łomża. The appointment of people who are racially alien to us to high posts in Poland is painful for the Polish majority"; and further, "Incredible, but true: the representative of the Class Union of Rural Workers is a Jew named Turek. Isn't it an anomaly that a man so alien to the Polish spirit in terms of his race, religion, and nationality is now to determine the fate of a purely Polish organization?"

Even the aforementioned Mrs. Mocarska, who was basically friendly to the Jews, would naturally address the shopkeeper by saying "Listen, Jew . . ." And he would bow down before her. Encountering Jews in schools, in offices, or in the police must have been a traumatic shock for the majority of the residents of Jedwabne and its environs, magnifying their sense of threat.

It is worth noting that the Soviet occupation forced almost everyone—except for those who chose to go into hiding and fight—to collaborate. According to one Jedwabne official (Hoover Institution report no. 10708): "This is how the propaganda before the elections was run: each agitator was in charge of ten houses. People from those houses would gather every day, have the constitution read to them, and be told about the rights of Soviet citizens. The election meetings were held every evening."

The people of Jedwabne had to attend those meetings if they wanted to avoid arrest or deportation. They decorated their barns with red flags and portraits of Lenin and Stalin. They participated in the electoral farce and accepted Soviet citizenship. It must have been a humiliating experience, the kind one prefers to push deep into oblivion. How much easier it is to do it when the reality is replaced with a stereotype like "It was the Jews who collaborated."

An Appeal to the Generalissimus

Kazimierz Laudański says, "My mother went into hiding in the forest with my two brothers."

I ask Zygmunt Laudański about their hiding under the Soviets. "We spent five months wandering around. I was a bricklayer, so I slept wherever I was working. I had a girlfriend in one of the villages where I worked, and another acquaintance elsewhere. A few cousins, an uncle. The uncle had a big wooden house with a double attic. My mother and my brother were there and sometimes I slept there, too. But it wasn't much of a hideout. The uncle believed in dreams, and sometimes he'd wake me up at midnight, saying, 'Get the bike and run away; I saw a black dog run over by a car in my dream.' What a miserable life. I finally decided to write a letter to Stalin."

Zygmunt Laudański wrote about that letter to Stalin in July 1949, while he was awaiting trial in the Ostrołęka prison:

"To the Ministry of Justice and the Public Security Office in Warsaw: I was in hiding from the Soviet authorities for about six months. While hiding to avoid deportation, I did not join any of the bands that were operating in the area at the time but wrote a letter of appeal to Generalissimus Stalin. The letter was read by the public prosecutor's office in Moscow, 15 Pushkinskaia St., and sent to the NKVD in Jedwabne for further examination. After an interrogation and investigation it turned out I had been unjustly harassed and so I was spared the necessity of hiding and was compensated. After examining my views, the NKVD in Jedwabne summoned me to cooperate in fighting anti-Soviet evils. Then I started contacting the NKVD regularly [he does not give his pseudonym]. During my contacts, in order to make my work effective and to avoid being spotted by the reactionaries, my supervisors told me to assume an anti-Soviet position, since I was already known to the authorities at the time."

Zygmunt Laudański today: "While I was still in hiding, I heard about those meetings, and the Russians telling the people they had come to liberate them, and handing out the Stalinist constitution. So I borrowed a copy of it and analyzed it and in section 4 I read that in the Sovetskii Soiuz [Soviet Union] no one answers for anyone else— neither a father for a son, nor a son for a father. So I visited the priest that night to get some office paper, and I wrote a letter to Stalin. I was very straightforward; I wrote that he had liberated us from the capitalists and the fascists and that I was not fighting with a gun, but with a pen, on the basis of the constitution. I started with 'The Polish nation is very grateful for the liberation from the capitalists and the fascists and for making property communal . . .' Look, you don't write things like that with holy chalk, goddammit. And then I wrote that I was forced to hide because of my father. I had the guts to tell him that if things went on like that, half of the population would go into the forests."

"They sent my letter from Moscow to the NKVD in Jedwabne. A month passed and then they called me; my cousin sent me the message, because I was still in hiding. They told me that if I reported, I would be *opravdannyi*, or acquitted. They didn't show that letter to anyone—neither Poles nor Jews. So I translated it for them, because I had learned some Russian by that time. I wrote a similar letter to Kalinin, the minister of the interior. I went to a Russian course for recruits and then wrote another letter to Stalin, in the name of my father, in Russian. The *komandir* was stationed in our house, so he corrected it for me.

From Kazimierz Laudański's letter to Adam Michnik: "Just as the Poles killed Kutschera in Warsaw, they killed a similar oppressor, Shevelev, in Jedwabne."

Zygmunt Laudański tells me: "In May 1941 I reported to the NKVD, to give them my letter to Stalin for my father to sign. I came and the chief officer says: 'Some bandits have killed one of our good men.' It was Shevelev, the deputy chief of the NKVD in Jedwabne, who had been killed. So I say, '*Zhalko* [Pity].' And he says, 'You could help us find the murderer if you wanted.' I say, 'How?' and he says: 'You know the people. You'll see if there are any new faces around and let us know.' I say, 'How?' and he says: 'There is a mailbox on our post. Put a note in there and sign it, but don't use your name—just write Popov.' I say, '*Khorosho* [Fine], I'll contact you for sure.' He was just asking; it was no obligation. That trick was a real success. I got replies both from Kalinin and from Stalin that my father should either be sentenced or let out, that the investigation was going on too long indeed, and that they would let me know. But then the war broke out. The partisans came and destroyed the wooden monument with a red star that had been built on Shevelev's grave. I think they even dug up the body."

There Was Euphoria

"You say the Jews welcomed the Soviet Army joyfully. And when the Germans came, didn't it happen that local people went out to greet them?" I ask Kazimierz Laudański.

"They say that near Zambrowo the Jews welcomed the Germans with bread and salt, but the Germans rebuffed them."

"I'm not asking about the Jews; I'm asking about the Poles."

"The Poles had been in a terrible situation before the German-Soviet war: arrests and deportations to Siberia all the time. People would pray, 'Let Lucifer come, if only this devil would go away.' "

"So people were happy when the Germans came?"

"The Germans struck the Russkies and the prisons opened. There was euphoria. Thousands of people who had been hiding in the forests now came home. Everybody was happy to see the school principal back, to see a neighbor back, to see a son back from the forest. How could my brothers not be happy to see their father back from prison and their mother back from the forest?"

Jerzy Laudański started to work in the German gendarmerie right away. During the trial he said it was his brother who told him to do it, so that he could get the NKVD papers in which he had promised to cooperate. At that time, Kazimierz Laudański was working in the municipality office in Poręba nad Bugiem, which was part of the German protectorate. It was from there that he managed to get to his brothers in Jedwabne in July; he took Jerzy back with him.

"I wrote myself a pass in German," he says, "because I was an official: 'Kazimierz Laudański is crossing the border; please present no obstacles.' And I stamped it. I came to find my brother Jerzy and to tell him to escape."

"Why escape?"

"Because Karolak wanted to hire him as a janitor. The Germans needed youngsters like that for the police. We had escaped the Russkies once; now we had to escape the Germans."

Kazimierz Laudański: "In Poręba I was working for the Information and Propaganda Office of the Home Army, which was still known back then as the Union for Armed Combat. I was distributing the underground press."

Jerzy Laudański: "I belonged to the Polish Partisan Union, and then I was in the Home Army. They made me distribute underground papers. There was *Rzeczpospolita* [The republic] and the other one, I think, was *Żołnierz Polski* [Polish soldier]. I made a pledge to a prewar officer in the presence of my brother. In the forest there was a special place to pick up mail, in the moss under a tree. You weren't supposed to stop there, just pass by on a bicycle and pick it up, so that no one would notice. Then there was a major roundup in Ostrów, and a dozen or so of us were caught in the forest. I spent four months in Pawiak prison during the investigation. Twice they took me to the Gestapo headquarters at Szucha Street. I was in a number of concentration camps: Auschwitz, Gross-Rosen, Oranienburg."

"I consider my brother Jerzy a hero," Kazimierz Laudański says. "He spent three years in German camps and never informed on anybody. Here's a photo of him from the camp. Come on, Jurek, show it to the lady."

Kazimierz Laudański himself worked in the German administration. He admits that after the war he was interrogated in the case of the Jews of Poręba nad Bugiem. "They were driven here from throughout the district. On 10 February 1942 they were all ordered to go to Treblinka [probably the work camp Treblinka 1, which was opened before the concentration camp]. Thirty-three remained. I was told to write down their names and fine them: I was supposed to take fifty zlotys from each of them and put it in a bank account. And then in May another order came that they must go to Treblinka. They did, but not all of them. One survived and later became head of the Security Office in Ostrów."

Safe from the Reactionary Bands

Jedwabne is mentioned every now and again in the *Situation Reports of the Regional Command in Łomża on the State of Security 1944–1948.*

April 1945: "Attack on the station commander, who was disarmed."

October 1945: "A group of militiamen was attacked by bandits as they were driving back to town on the Jedwabne-Przytuły road. There were shots and four militiamen from the Łomża District Post and two from the District Security Office were killed, and two were slightly wounded. The commander of the Jedwabne post, Zygmunt Jakubowski, was killed on the same day."

The most spectacular operation in the area was the one on 23 September 1948, when a NZW [National Military Union] troop took control of the town. The NZW was based on the NSZ [National Armed Forces], and was created after the war and commanded by a partisan known in the area as "Crazy Stasiek." His real name was Stanisław Grabowski, and his partisan nickname was "Wiarus"; he was arrested in 1949 and sentenced to fifteen years, of which he served seven.

"They captured a car from some butchers going from Jedwabne to the market in Wizna," Jan Cytrynowicz says. "They drove into the market square, announced that the British army was in Poland, that there was a revolution in Warsaw, and that the Communist government had already fallen. They put a machine gun and a couple of flags in the middle of the square. There were twelve of them, all in British uniforms, and then the people started plundering the cooperative shops, looking mainly for vodka."

Zygmunt Laudański: "In Jedwabne there were two partisan groups: the AK [Home Army] and the NSZ. Some people thought I was in the AK, some thought I was in the NSZ, but I was in neither. The two groups would shoot at each other at night; one group would go steal someone's cow; then the other one would come and shoot them. After the war they were all tried, and we were told to come and see the trial. There I heard one farmer tell how they had taken his last cow and beaten him up so hard that one of his ears was still deaf and festering. I wanted to stay away from all that mess, so in 1947 I left Jedwabne. And after the People's Republic was formed, my brother became secretary of the Biała municipality and found me a job as a shopkeeper. Later I was arrested in that very shop."

Kazimierz Laudański: "After the war I became secretary of the Biała Piska municipality, then the district inspector, then the head of the Farmers' Mutual Aid. I was given the first car in town. I was organizing the first cooperatives, telling the mothers and all the women that there would be no more war, that America was too weak, that the Russkies would stay, and that we had to get to work.

Zygmunt Laudański's letter from Ostrołęka prison, 4 July 1949: "To the Ministry of Justice and the Public Security Office in Warsaw. I left [Jedwabne for Biała] to be safe from the reactionary bands that were ravaging the area, and to work for the country and support my wife and two children. On 24 April 1948 I became a member of the PPR [Polish Workers' Party] in Biała and then, after the unification of the two parties, a PZPR executive member and supervisor of a party unit."

Zygmunt Laudański's letter from Ostrołęka prison to the Supreme Court in Warsaw, 8 November 1949: "As a former PZPR member and supervisor of a party unit, I have always propagated the idea of social justice that has become a fact in the present-day reality. I am looking for that justice now, and you must realize how happy the reactionary circles are in situations like this, when a worker cooperating with the state system ends up in prison."

For Jerzy Laudański, Kazimierz found a job as the municipality's controller of payments in kind. "The farmers were supposed to deliver grain, and we would go around and check how much each municipality had given. We made sure they delivered the required amounts, because they didn't want to. There were rumors that Russian airplanes were transporting our grain to Russia.

In the files it says that in 1947 Jerzy Laudański was sentenced by the Special Committee to nine months of work camp in Mylęcin.

"What happened?" he answers. "Well, it was, how should I put it, a legal cash shortage. There was a rule that such and such percent of the money could be missing in a shop, and I did take that permitted percent. Later I worked in the State Agricultural Properties office, then in a collective farm in Kaliszki, as a storekeeper. I was fired from that job."

... Which We Did

Kazimierz Laudański: "The people who were tried were normal people who had been maneuvered into the whole thing. Well, maybe one of them once hit a Jewish Communist or spat at him or something like that. There's nothing to justify it, but on the other hand, it's a normal thing, too."

Jerzy and Zygmunt Laudański were arrested on 15 January 1949.

From Zygmunt Laudański's reports on 17 January: "Yes, I participated in the murder of the Jews. I was watching and making sure they wouldn't run away. The Jews were carrying the statue of Lenin on the market square. Then we drove all the Jews carrying the statue out of town, to the barn. I want to stress that when I came back home, the Jews were 250 meters from the barn."

From Jerzy Laudański's reports, also on 17 January: "I was working in the gendarmerie as a janitor. I had been told to go work there by my brother Zygmunt Laudański, who is now in custody. Four or five Gestapo officers came by taxi, and they started talking in the town hall. After some time Marian Karolak told us Poles to go round up the Jews to work, which the people did. I was also taking part in the rounding up of the Jews in the market square, together with Eugeniusz Kalinowski. Where he is today I don't know; I know only that in 1945 he was in a unit in the forest. I saw him myself. That Kalinowski and I rounded up about eight persons of Jewish nationality, and when we got back, the Jews were already carrying the statue of Lenin around the square and singing, "This war is because of us." I don't know who ordered them to sing. We Poles were only making sure they wouldn't run away. I must stress that there were Germans around, too. Then Marian Karolak, the mayor, gave us the order to gather all the Jews by Bronisław Śleszyński's barn, which we did. We rounded them up, told the Jews to go in, which they were forced to do; then the barn was set on fire. I didn't see who did it. After that I went home, and the Jews were burned in that barn, more than a thousand people altogether."

Apart from the Laudańskis' own reports and those of other defendants, there were also witnesses that spoke against them.

Bronisława Kalinowska: "The local people started murdering the Jews. It was an unbearable sight how they were torturing them. I was standing on Przytulska Street and saw Jerzy Laudański from Jedwabne running down the street; he was very nervous, said he had already killed two or three Jews, and then ran on."

Eljasz Grędowski: "Jerzy, Czesław, and Zygmunt Laudański were forcing the Jews to carry the statue of Lenin."

Stanisława Sielawa: "The local people, together with the Germans, started murdering the Jews. I saw the following people: (1) Czesław Laudański [father of Zygmunt and Jerzy] standing on Przytulska Street with one German. I said I wanted to buy some beer for my husband and he said, Go home, or you'll end up like the Jews. I saw Jerzy Laudański and Jurek Kalinowski and one Russkie beat a Jew. They threw him down from above, beat him with clubs, and when I asked them to stop, they said, You're gonna get yours like the Jews."

Abram Boruszczak: "The following took part in the murder of the Jews: Jerzy Laudański, Zygmunt Laudański, and their father Czesław. They led the whole action against the Jews. They rounded them up in the market square, beat them with clubs, beat them at the cemetery, and forced the Jews into the barn, where they were burned. After the massacre, they plundered Jewish possessions."

At the trial on 16 and 17 May, one defendant after another withdrew what they had reported during the interrogations. They complained they had been beaten. A number of witnesses, too, withdrew what they had previously said, Bronisława Kalinowska among them: "I didn't see the Laudańskis, and I heard nothing. The man who was interrogating me told me what to say; he screamed and shouted at me, scared me, and I don't know what was written down. I don't know how to read or write."

There is no doubt that the Laudańskis were beaten during the interrogations. They spoke about it during the trial and wrote about it from prison, as they were appealing their sentence. Zygmunt Laudański (letter from November 1949): "I was interrogated in an inhuman manner, made to bend down and held by the head; I was beaten with fists and rubber clubs on the face and ears, until I lost my balance. The investigator forced a report out of me and added names of people I hadn't seen; he had them written down on a separate sheet." Jerzy Laudański (letter from August 1956): "During the investigation I was told that my origin was German. One of the investigating officers said I had a Nazi name. I was treated like a regular war criminal and had to respond 'yes' to everything."

Reports by people who were beaten and threatened cannot serve as evidence in a case. This is obvious, but the seven-hundred-page record of the trial still makes one think.

The investigation was careless and superficial; most people were interrogated quickly and only once, with a standard set of questions. Everything that goes beyond that standard set seems, therefore, to be a personal contribution of the interrogated. Especially since those reports, either by witnesses or by defendants, that expose some new thread in the case (new names of participants, for instance) were not investigated further.

The majority of those reports were made by illiterate people, signing three crosses for their names. This meant that the court clerk could write anything he wished to, even without beatings. I did not, however, find any specific stories that appeared to be added to the illiterate people's reports.

It is interesting that Czesław Laudański pleaded innocent and was acquitted in the trial. In addition, eleven other defendants were acquitted.

"Why was your father set free?" I ask Jerzy Laudański.

"No evidence was found."

"Why were you and your brother sentenced, then?"

"We weren't kosher, because we had been in hiding under the Soviet occupation."

If that had been a factor, though, they would probably have been set free, too, because of Zygmunt Laudański's offer to collaborate with the NKVD.

As for the witnesses, the pressure of their peers may have been a lot stronger than that of the court. The people of Jedwabne showed a lot of solidarity with the defendants; they wrote collective letters to the authorities in their defense (though not in the Laudańskis' defense): "I want to testify loyally that citizen Roman Górski has always been a good man and a good citizen of the Polish state." The Laudańskis' testimony may be a result of the beatings. But wasn't the withdrawal of witness testimony—for instance, by Bronisława Kalinowska—the result of pressure from the neighbors?

Victim of the *Sanacja* Regime's Legacy

The arrests of his brothers did not hinder Kazimierz Laudański's professional and political career. He kept his post as the municipality secretary and remained politically active.

"On the anniversary of Stalin's death, a number of people were gathered in Biała," he tells me. "So I got up and started praising the great Stalin."

Laudański stands up; his voice sounds more energetic and youthful, as he recollects his own speech from years ago.

" 'The great Stalin was a leader. The victorious Polish nation shall never forget that. He did not die without progeny. He always told us to be critical and self-critical. If he were to ask you today what you are doing for the Polish people, could you look him in the eyes?' And I would mention and point out all those cases where things were messed up. I raised my fist. I got applause from the party and the Security Administration agents, but the audience was with me, too, because they knew I was doing a parody. I've always had courage."

Zygmunt Laudański: "Once in Strzelce Opolskie the prosecutor from the public prosecutor's office came to me and advised me to appeal to the [PZPR's] Central Committee. I got six sheets of paper. On 4 April 1955, I was conditionally released."

"How did the people treat you after you left prison?"

"Very well. The director of the dairy in Biała came and said, 'Come work with us.' They knew I was someone they could rely on."

In 1956 Jerzy Laudański was diagnosed with tuberculosis. The four pages of neat handwriting are his letter of appeal to the minister of justice, sent from the Sieradz prison:

"At that early age I was not only a victim of the war but also of the *Sanacja* regime and its legacy, because back then youth was educated only in the nationalist spirit. All the more since the period when I was growing up and being molded as a future citizen of my Fatherland was a time of intensive anti-Jewish struggle. The people and the youth were fed all kinds of anti-Jewish slogans. We were taught to hate the Jews on the pretext that they were guilty of all evils, etc. Now we can read in the press about those times and know who was behind those boycotts and for whom the Jews were an obstacle in Poland under the *Sanacja* regime . . . After the Soviet Army liberated us in 1945, I did not follow those who abandoned their devastated homeland and chose the life of luxury in the West, to come back later as spies or saboteurs. Without any hesitation I returned to my ravaged country, for which I had been sacrificing my twenty-year-old life to fight the occupiers . . . Since my return, I had been working in state institutions until I was arrested . . . I am a worker from a family of workers and never experienced any good in my godforsaken life. With all the lessons I have been given in life, I know well enough by now why I've had to endure such sufferings: I have been a victim of fascism, of capitalism, of the *Sanacja* regime with its legacy, and that is why I ended up in prison for so long."

The last report on "the conduct of the prisoner Jerzy Laudański" was made in Sieradz prison in 1956: "No hostility toward the People's Republic of Poland has been detected in general observation and conversations with the prisoner. He considers the sentence just, but too harsh."

He left prison in February 1957.

Jedwabne 2001

Janusz Lech Dziedzic: "This is a certain kind of community: whatever bad thing happens, it always turns out to be the Jews. I've been hearing this since I was born—whether about bad government, bad weather, or a dying cow, it was always the Jews' fault. My father had money because he was a good farmer and a prudent manager. My mom used to get up at night to pick strawberries and carry them to the market in the morning. And the people would say we had Jewish money for helping the Jews. Now I keep hearing that the Jews got what they deserved, because they had been denouncing Poles to the NKVD. I no longer have the energy to tell them that the Poles did that, too. I just ask, 'And what were those children guilty of?' When journalists started coming and my father talked with them, people would ask me, 'How much money did the Jews pay your father for that interview?' I asked one of them, 'And how much was *your* father paid for murdering the Jews?' and he turned beet red. It hurts to know that your father has raped a Jewish woman, cut her head off. One of my friends visited me three times to reread Prof. Gross's book and see whether anyone from his family was mentioned there. He said, 'I have to know whether any of my forebears has blood on his hands.' "

Everybody in Jedwabne knew about what happened on 10 July 1941. They talked about who had gotten rich on "Jewish gold." But all those conversations took place in private, at home, or with friends in a bar. Four years ago Agnieszka Arnold started coming to Jedwabne with a camera crew; her film about Polish-Jewish relations entitled *Gdzie Jest Mój Starszy Brat Kain?* [Where is my elder brother Cain?], which was shown on Polish TV in April 2000, speaks plainly of the murder of Jedwabne's Jews as committed by Poles. In May 2000 the book *Neighbors* by Jan Gross was published. Then there was a series of newspaper reports. The murder had to become conversation topic number one.

The local "negationists" have consolidated around Father Edward Orłowski, the local priest.

The prosecutor Radosław Ignatiew asked Father Orłowski to announce to his parishioners that he would like to meet the people who might contribute to the investigation. He wanted to tell them about the principles of its conduct and to guarantee the confidentiality of the conversations.

7 February 2000. In the former cinema of a devastated mansion it's hard to find an empty seat. The majority of the people are men between thirty and fifty years old. The atmosphere is that of a rally. It is difficult for the prosecutor to run the meeting. There are angry murmurs in the audience. People who say that the Jews used to denounce Poles to the NKVD win applause.

"They're writing lies. If they had stuffed them all like herrings in a barrel, there still wouldn't have been enough space for 1,600 Jews. We protest."

"And why does that Jew call himself Wasersztajn, if his name here was Caśka? Can someone explain why he doesn't give his real name?

I have my name and I'm not changing it. Who is accusing the people of Jedwabne? That is what we want to know. But we know one thing: if you have the money, you rule."

"We're not antisemites. I used to play with Jewish kids. But you have to remember that whenever a Pole was taken from his house to be deported to Siberia, there would be two Jews keeping guard at the door."

"Prof. Strzembosz has written how it was. Why don't the others write about how much the Poles suffered in Siberia because of the Jews?"

"The Institute of National Memory ought to sue Mr. Gross for all those lies."

The vicar Czesław Orłowski had the final word: "All this is intended to present us as murderers. The Jews used to live on very good terms with the Poles. Those good relations were destroyed by the Jews during the Soviet occupation. And what's going on now? This is a continuation. When Poland was conquered in 1939, Jedwabne was probably the first town to organize a resistance movement. The Poles were getting killed in Auschwitz. Why are they talking now about Jedwabne and not about those sufferings? It's not just Jedwabne that's being slandered but the Polish nation as a whole. We have to defend ourselves."

As I walk out, Wojciech K. (one of my interlocutors from Jedwabne, a man who feels responsible for the murder, although he didn't take part in it) tells me: "The one on the right, who shouted so loud about Polish patriots deported to Siberia because of Jews, knows all too well that his father denounced mine. And that it was his father who joined the NKVD when they came to arrest him. When my father came back to Jedwabne after the war, his father begged him on his knees to keep it secret."

I met the vicar at the parish office.

"Many parishioners came to the meeting with the prosecutor," I begin.

"They came because I asked them. The Jews joined the NKVD and the Komsomol on a mass scale. They denounced Poles. Kobielno was surrounded by the NKVD, and there's a suspicion that there was a Jewish denunciation, because the Jews had been closely following the partisans. We should take a closer look at Gross. Jedwabne is just a tip of the iceberg."

"What do you mean?"

"If this Jedwabne thing is settled the way Gross wants it, it will be like piercing a hole in a ship and waiting for it to sink. The truth is, it was the Germans who committed the murders, not the Poles. And then it turns out that this Mr. Wasersztajn was called Caśka here. This is the way the Jews act."

"What do you mean by that?"

"When we studied the Bible, our priest used to tell us: 'A Jew will put a hat on a stick and say, "Watch out, now we're two." ' That's the Jewish soul. I met a Jewish multimillionaire in New York, and he was boasting about how he had sold his huge factory to the Germans when the war was already on. 'They gave us a lot of gold and drove us to Hamburg by cars, and from there we went to America by boat,' he was telling me. Here their whole nation was being killed, and see what they did; nothing but swindle. Those are the facts."

"Do you ever come across antisemitic statements in your parish?"

"There is no problem of antisemitism here. In our parish most people voted for Mr. Krzaklewski; he was a definite winner here. I made my opinion clear. Was I supposed to vote for a Jew, or what? Because Kwaśniewski is a Jew—the SLD [Democratic Left Alliance] has as many of them as the Freedom Union."

"What should the sign say at the site where the Jews were killed?"

"I have thought a lot about that. It should say that the Jews were murdered by the Nazis. And that's it. This is the correct way of putting it, a compromise that should satisfy both the Jews and the Poles. We don't have the feeling that we murdered them. The town will have to defend itself."

"How do you imagine this happening?"

"You saw how much bitterness there was. We may have to organize ourselves. There are many patriots here. I'm considering a committee for the defense of the town's good name."

The tone of my interlocutors in the town hall was very different. The mayor, Krzysztof Godlewski, and the head of the city council, Stanisław Michałowski, were wondering what the town ought to do for the sixtieth anniversary of the massacre. They said that the sign saying that the Jews were killed by the Nazis should be changed as soon as possible.

"The Jewish citizens of Jedwabne were cruelly murdered," the mayor says. "I think it's beneath human dignity to calculate things like that and argue that maybe there were 1,328 victims and not 1,600. What difference would that make? We have to acknowledge the fact of this crime with Christian humility."

The mayor was just telling me how at first the town council refused even to discuss changing the sign on the monument, but that now it was at least possible to discuss it, when one of the council's members entered the room. I asked him what the sign should say in his opinion.

"When it came out that they were talking about 1,600 people, I counted exactly how many people could squeeze into the church, and it could be only 800, if they stood really close to each other . . . ," the alderman begins—although the sign speaking of 1,600 victims had stood in Jedwabne for a couple of decades, and as long as it said they were murdered by the gendarmerie and the Gestapo, nobody questioned their number. "Even if you'd cut them in quarters beforehand, they wouldn't have fit. I was born in 1950, but I know from my parents and neighbors that they were destroyed by Hitler. A Pole couldn't do much when a German was holding a gun to his head. One-tenth or so of our townsmen were acting at gunpoint; it is not their fault."

"But eyewitnesses tell me it was Poles who committed the murders."

"Well, maybe somebody was paid to say so. I don't know whether they did it with joy or under pressure, but I know there were armed Germans around. At that meeting with the prosecutor, I liked it when people started reminding him how many had been deported to Siberia because of Jewish denunciations."

"But what should the sign say?"

"It should clearly say, '1,600 Jewish persons were not burned.' That lie must be done away with."

The mayor's reaction to the alderman's words was calm. "The people have been put in a terribly difficult situation," he said later. "They need some time to digest it all. I suppose it's a natural reaction that when you have the choice, you choose the version that's easier to take."

When President Kwaśniewski said in public that the crime had been committed by Poles, and that we ought to apologize for it, the Jedwabne committee for the defense of the town's good name was in the process of being constituted. Voices were heard: "One Jew is going to apologize to another." Michał Kamiński, a ZChN [National-Christian Union] deputy, came to Jedwabne and suggested writing an open letter ("What we find particularly outrageous is that certain state officials pass their own sentences while the investigation of the Institute of National Memory is still on, and 'apologize' for the Jedwabne crime in the name of the whole nation").

It was obvious that there would be politicians eager to utilize the moods of that part of Jedwabne's population. I was not surprised that the committee emerged; what surprised me was that it was led not by the vicar but by the mayor.

The meeting with Deputy Kamiński was attended by about a hundred people. "Let's give the mayor a chance to rehabilitate himself," the audience said, and there was a threatening tone in their voices. "Let's make him the head of our committee."

The mayor agreed.

"The committee was established so that the community would have representatives and in order to resist attempts to ascribe collective re-sponsibility for the crime," he told me then. And he distanced himself decisively from Kamiński's letter.

But Józef Goszczyński, one of the committee's initiators, spoke in a very different tone. He said that the honor of Poles must be defended, that those lies about the 1,600 Jews murdered were unacceptable, and so on. I had heard of Goszczyński before from one of his neighbors: "I met him in church—we sing in the choir together," the neighbor said. "We walked out, and he gave me a leaflet saying the Holocaust had been caused by the Jews themselves. And he says, 'We have to pass this on.' And to think that his father was a decent man; he was in the Home Army and took no part in the massacre."

A day after the committee was founded, Primate Józef Glemp said that "the murder of the Jewish people, rounded up by Poles in a barn and burned alive, is unquestionable," and that "this is connected with an acknowledgment of generational responsibility, which consists of asking God's forgiveness for our forebears' sins."

The mayor felt relieved.

"Now it's clear that the committee's letter must be completely differ-ent from what Deputy Kamiński has suggested—that it should be in accord with the primate's speech," he said optimistically. "I say to them, 'Don't run a political campaign for Kamiński; wait and listen to what the primate and the bishop say.' I've proposed a different version of the letter, which is in agreement with the primate's statement. Either they accept it or I resign."

The mayor remained the head of the committee for two days. His idea for calming things down was a failure. Meanwhile, Senators Jad-wiga Stokarska and Jan Chojnowski of the AWS [Solidarity Electoral Action], and Deputy Witold Tomczak of Polskie Porozumienie [Polish Agreement] came to support the committee.

After resigning, the mayor told me: "I was afraid that if I didn't join the committee, they would be collecting signatures under Kamiński's letter the next day, and that they would even sharpen its tone, because I'd already had a phone call from a committee member who said that the letter was too moderate. So I joined to try to temper those who would defend the town's bad name rather than pour ashes on their heads during Lent. Jedwabne needs to present its good side the way a fish needs water. One of my colleagues said, 'You're right—apologiz-ing is nothing to be ashamed of,' and that warmed my heart. But gen-erally I don't hear comments like that. We ought to accept the truth, even the most painful truth. We can defend the town's good name by acknowledging our guilt."

I ask him whether it wouldn't be better for him to start and lead a committee in support of commemorating the sixtieth anniversary of the murders.

"For now, I don't see any volunteers," he says. "The only hope is that the bishop will come and give a good, unambiguous sermon."

That's probably what the committee's members expect from the bishop, too. A good and unambiguous sermon, only a completely different one. The bishop of Łomża, Stanisław Stefanek, is coming on Sunday, 11 March, to conduct a holy mass in Jedwabne.

I ask the mayor whether he has ever envisioned in his worst dreams that the 10 July celebrations may go undisturbed simply because the participants will be cordoned off by the police. He says he does imagine a boycott of the celebration as a black scenario, but he can also imagine an optimistic one.

"I imagine the child of Rabbi Baker and a child of one of the murderers embracing. Or at least Stanisław Michałowski and I embracing Rabbi Baker. I don't want any pompous welcomes, just something that would stir a tear in someone's eye, something so moving that it would make people kneel down spontaneously. I would like to be able to say, 'Dear Jews, our brothers who were born here, please be our guests.' "

At the moment, however, those inhabitants of Jedwabne who shout about everything's being the fault of the Jews dominate the town— even though they're in the minority. They feel strong. Their vicar supports them. They have their own scientific authority: I have heard the name of Prof. Strzembosz mentioned by even the most intoxicated of my interlocutors—someone I wouldn't suspect of reading any historians. The other residents are intimidated by them.

And the Laudańskis keep writing their letters. The letter to Adam Michnik quoted above has been sent by Kazimierz Laudański to other papers, too, and also to Adam Cyra of the Auschwitz-Birkenau State Museum, who distributed it further with comments of his own. Cyra's article, "For a Fair Judgment of History," was published by several papers, including *Rzeczpospolita* and *Nasz Dziennik*. Both have printed it with large photographs of Jerzy Laudański from the concentration camp. Cyra writes, "With determination, Jerzy Laudański's elder brother, Kazimierz, speaks in his defense, refusing to give up his faith in the fair judgment of history." All that Dr. Cyra has to say about the Jedwabne matter is that Jerzy Laudański was tortured and sentenced in a Stalinist trial because of it.

Kazimierz Laudański, pleased with the success of his own version of history, kept writing in an ever sharper tone. *Gazeta Wyborcza* received two more letters from him. "The Poles are accused of antisemitism," he wrote on 12 February, "but one cannot expect us to love

neighbors who are traitors. The very fact that Prof. Gross has the courage to say all this rubbish in public is proof of our tolerance. He
wouldn't dare do this in Iran, would he? Mr. Gross wants the Poles to
build a monument commemorating the victims in Jedwabne, to acknowledge their own guilt in the epitaph, and to bring all the elite,
including the Church, to the opening ceremony. Who should then
build those hundreds of thousands of monuments along the Ural Kolyma trail for the Poles deported to Siberia? Maybe Mr. Gross would
be so kind as to help us find the graves of our heroes in prisons all
over Poland and around Barrack 10 in Warsaw in particular? Mr. Gross
knows all too well who was the torturer there. All kinds of things happen between neighbors. Isn't it better to keep silent? Must the Egyp-
tian, Spanish, or German exoduses still be the fate of Israel? The solution is easy: a change in attitude toward neighbors and towards . . .
money."

And here is what he wrote in a 24 February letter about one of the
few survivors and witnesses of the Jedwabne murders, a man who lost
his whole family that day: "Mr. Gross based his accusations on the 'reports' of Szmul Wasersztajn, who had been everywhere, seen and
heard everything. He's a regular Sherlock Holmes with a hat to make
him invisible. He saw the Jewess Ibram raped and killed, he saw
beards burned, infants killed at their mothers' breasts, he heard the
band play . . . Isn't that too much for one kid to see and hear?"

And They Went Quiet till the End of Time

Nowadays the three brothers, all retired, meet a lot, talk about politics,
and have the same views. "All three of us are nationalists, right-wing-
ers, but we vote for Kwaśniewski," Kazimierz Laudański tells me. "I
listen to lectures on Radio Maryja, and when they say the president is
a drunkard, murderer, and pornographer, everything rebels inside me,
because, as they say, there has to be order, *Ordnung muss sein*."

"Do you remember that cry?" I ask Jerzy Laudański.

"When they were being shut in that barn, they did shout something
in Yiddish; I don't know what. It was a spontaneous scream, maybe to
let them out; maybe they were praying that way. And then they suffocated from the smoke right away. When they went quiet, it was till the
end of time."

Zygmunt Laudański says he couldn't hear anything, because he was
standing more than two hundred meters from the barn.

Another interlocutor of mine who did not hear the scream is Janina
Biedrzycka, the barn owner's daughter (their house was about two
hundred meters from the barn).

"I went home from the barn," she says, "so I didn't see or hear the incident."

Sławomir S.: "When they were going around houses and rounding up people in the market square, there was shouting and crying everywhere, because they were dragging children and old people, making them stand in rows, and they were armed with clubs. I remember those screams till now. It was something horrible. When they set the barn on fire, the screams went on till the roof collapsed, causing death by suffocation."

Kazimierz Mocarski: "I was mowing hay on the banks of the Biebrza, a few kilometers in a straight line from Jedwabne. The sun was going down, so it must have been afternoon, when I heard a frightening cry from a large group of people, and the high voices dominated, so it must have been women screaming. It was getting more and more desperate, and when it stopped, there was a thick black smoke rising into the sky. When I came home, my mother told me, 'They've burned the Jews.' "

Marianna K.: "That terrible scream couldn't have gone on for more than two minutes, but it is still in me. Today I woke up at four in the morning and remembered it again. Why I went there, a little girl, I myself don't know; maybe so that I could tell the truth today. I always go there without letting anybody see me, to light a candle on the anniversary of the murders and on All Saints' Day."

"Didn't that scream ever wake you up at night?" I ask Zygmunt Laudański.

"A young organism doesn't react that way, I never woke up at night."

"What did you think about the whole thing?"

"What was I supposed to think? It happened and it's over."

"Is there anything you regret in your life?"

"Ask anybody and you'll see I have no enemies and no one's ever complained about my work, either."

"I understand that you have always been dutiful, but my question is: Don't you regret anything you have done?"

"Certainly not."

.   .   .   .   .

Anna Bikont was born in 1954 and worked in the Department of Psychology at the University of Warsaw from 1980. She became involved with the democratic opposition from the late 1970s and was responsible for the printing in the independent publishing house, NOWA. She was one of the editors of *Tygodnik Mazowsze* during the period of martial law and one of the founders of *Gazeta Wyborcza*, for which she has worked since 1989. She was the editor of the collection *"I ciągle widzę ich twarze". Fotografie Żydów polskich* ("And I still see their faces": Photographs of Polish Jews) (Warsaw, 1996). She is at present writing a book about the events in Jedwabne and Radziłów. In December 2001, she received the Polish "Press" award for her reportage from Jedwabne and Radziłów.

Bogdan Musiał

THE POGROM IN JEDWABNE: CRITICAL REMARKS ABOUT JAN T. GROSS'S *NEIGHBORS*

RECENTLY, Poland's young democracy has been experiencing the most animated public controversy in its short history. The controversy was triggered by the book *Neighbors* by Jan T. Gross, which examines the mass murder of Polish Jews on 10 July 1941, in the small town of Jedwabne near Łomża, where—according to Gross—1,600 Jews were herded into a barn and burned alive.[1] The alleged perpetrators were the Polish inhabitants of Jedwabne, who were motivated simply by greed and traditional antisemitism. Gross's depiction of this event has deeply shocked Polish public opinion, and the ensuing polemic has become politically charged and highly emotional.

Neighbors immediately became an international sensation. Even before it was translated into any foreign language, reviews had appeared, as they continue to do, in many countries of the world. Positive opinions prevail; critical reactions are scarce. The latter have been more frequent in Poland where, from the very beginning, Gross's neglect of the historical context and his cavalier treatment of sources have been regularly pointed out and commented upon. Nevertheless, no serious Polish historian has ever expressed any doubts about the Polish participation in this crime.[2] Unfortunately, the crucial documentary evidence

---

The opinions expressed in this paper are those of the author alone and do not represent the official position of the German Historical Institute in Warsaw.

[1] Jan Tomasz Gross, *Sąsiedzi: Historia zagłady żydowskiego miasteczka* (Sejny, 2000), hereafter, *Sąsiedzi*. An expanded English-language version has been published as *Neighbors: The Destruction of the Jewish Community in Jedwabne, Poland* (Princeton, 2001), hereafter, *Neighbors*. The German version has been published as *Nachbarn: Der Mord an den Juden von Jedwabne* (Munich, 2001).

[2] See Tomasza Szarota, "Czy na pewno wszystko już wiemy?" *Gazeta Wyborcza* (hereafter, *GW*), 2–3 December 2000; Krzysztof Jasiewicz, "Sąsiedzi niezbadani," *GW*, 9–10 December 2000; Marek Chodakiewicz, "Kłopoty z kuracją szokową," *Rzeczpospolita*, 5 January 2001; Tomasz Strzembosz, "Przemilczana kolaboracja," *Rzeczpospolita*, 27–28 January 2001; Bogdan Musiał, "Historiografia mityczna," *Rzeczpospolita*, 24–25 February 2001; Piotr Gontarczyk, "Gross kontra fakty," *Życie*, 31 January 2001. Some of these articles are published in English in *Thou Shalt Not Kill: Poles on Jedwabne* (Warsaw, 2001).

could not be investigated firsthand before the beginning of 2001, since the sources explored by Gross had remained inaccessible to anyone else until then.[3]

I will focus primarily on the analysis of Gross's methodology and on his approach to the sources. A reconstruction of the actual course of events in Jedwabne is not one my goals here.

According to Gross, the murder of 10 July 1941 in Jedwabne was planned and executed by Poles and by Poles alone. The Germans allegedly gave the Poles free rein, while they themselves engaged only in photographing and filming the massacre. However, a systematic and critical analysis of the very same sources used by the author of *Neighbors* clearly indicates that this scenario does not reflect accurately the actual contents of those archival materials.

Gross's book is based on a scant selection of sources that consists of a few accounts by Jewish survivors and the court records from the 1949 trial of twenty-two men accused of active participation in the crime. (At that time, the Łomża District Court delivered one death sentence, later commuted to fifteen years in prison; eleven other accused defendants received twelve to fifteen years in prison, while the remaining ten were acquitted.) Even more disturbing than the glaring narrowness of such a source base is the unprofessional way in which it has been interpreted by Gross.

The 1949 Trial Records as a Historical Source and Their Use by Gross

Gross states unambiguously that he wrote his book on the basis of the aforementioned trial records: "The bulk of documentation for this study comes ... from the perpetrators and was produced during a court trial" (26).

The importance of court documents for a historian needs no explanation. However, we must keep in mind that such documents have particular characteristics that necessitate not only a substantial dose of criticism but also a specific methodology in their interpretation. This is especially true in the case of records produced by the Stalinist justice system in Poland and often based on materials provided by the Com-

---

[3] These documents were located in the archives of the Main Commission for the Investigation of Crimes against the Polish Nation, which were taken over by the Institute of National Memory (Instytut Pamięci Narodowej—IPN) in the summer of 2000. Until March 2001 they were not accessible to researchers. Gross received special permission to research these documents (*Sąsiedzi*, 10 n. 4.).

munist Security Office. Gross duly notes this fact himself: "The judi-
ciary as well as the investigative authorities (the so-called Security Office, *Urząd Bezpieczeństwa* [UB]) acquired in those years [1949–1953
(BM)] a well-deserved notoriety. Furthermore, in the courtroom, defendants revealed that they were beaten during interrogation and thus
compelled to make depositions—a very plausible complaint, given the
methods that were employed at the time by the UB" (28). Just the same,
he surprisingly declares that "materials produced during the investigation can serve us well in our reconstruction of what actually took place,
though we must not lose sight of the fact that the accused are likely to
have tried to *minimize* both the events themselves and the extent of
their own involvement" (32, emphasis added).

Radosław Ignatiew, a prosecutor from the Institute of National
Memory (IPN), who has been investigating the Jedwabne crime since
the summer of 2000, responds skeptically to such a conclusion. In a
press interview he explained his reservations:

> We need to ask whether the proceedings were just sloppy, or
> whether they were illegal. The trial records contain a hint, in the
> depositions of the principal defendants, at the use of unlawful in-
> terrogation methods. I have personally reached several people
> who had participated in that trial as either defendants or wit-
> nesses. They all maintain that illegal interrogation methods were
> employed and that the testimonies were not recorded in the form
> given by witnesses.[4]

Internal memoranda of the security apparatus from that era confirm
in full Ignatiew's insights. Stanisław Radkiewicz, the minister of public
security, criticized the investigation methods commonly used at that
time as follows:

> All forms of "fixing" an investigation are harmful and intolerable.
> Meanwhile, even this sin is not unknown to some of our opera-
> tives, especially in the investigative sector. On the basis of its own
> practice, the office of the public prosecutor reports in a document
> submitted to the Party leadership that "a phenomenon that is
> often seen is the lack of objectivity in an investigation, the com-
> plete omission of the circumstances and evidence given by the sus-
> pects, the phrasing of witnesses' testimonies in a way that favors
> the prosecution but does not reflect reality . . . Unfortunately, this
> practice is undoubtedly still followed in some parts of our appara-
> tus." . . . And, finally, the question of using illegal methods of in-

[4] *Biuletyn Instytutu Pamięci Narodowej* (hereafter, *BIPN*), no. 3 (April 2001): 56.

terrogation, which is still unresolved despite numerous orders to the contrary and the disciplinary and court actions taken against the perpetrators ... They cause irreparable political harm, and, as shown by our entire operative experience, they never help in uncovering the objective truth; on the contrary, they complicate the case and make it easy for the real culprits to escape justice.[5]

Gross himself does not hold similar objections to the quality of the Security Office's investigative skills. His very selective attitude toward the aforementioned trial records must also give rise to mistrust in a historian's mind. On the one hand, Gross expresses doubts about the veracity of those statements which tend to exculpate the defendants, or to contradict the main theses of *Neighbors*. He consistently presents them as untrustworthy, or—much more often—he simply ignores them. On the other hand, Gross accepts at face value those testimonies which, after a careful analysis, must be rejected as false.

A good example of the latter is the deposition of Eljasz Grądowski. This man was interrogated twice, on 19 and 26 January 1949, in Łomża. He testified that, on 10 July 1941, he had been present in Jedwabne, and that he saved himself by escaping, at the very last moment, from the barn. He also stated for the record that the Poles had been the sole initiators and executors of the Jedwabne murder: "I declare that Germans did not take part in the murder of Jews in the town of Jedwabne, and that they even hid a few [Jews] from the murderous Poles; they stayed on the side and kept photographing it all, how the Poles were tormenting the Jews."[6] Eljasz Grądowski named thirty-five men who allegedly participated in the crime. He also related the tragic events (violence, robbery, etc.) that had supposedly taken place at that time. Gross quotes, or refers to, Grądowski's account many times in his book and bases his main premises on this particular testimony. (I will return to this subject later.)

However, Eljasz Grądowski was not an eyewitness to the Jedwabne crime. According to several other witnesses, in 1940 he was tried for stealing a gramophone and deported to Siberia.[7] This has been partly confirmed by Grądowski himself who, on 24 May 1948 (i.e., eight

[5] A speech by Minister Stanisław Radkiewicz on the tasks of the public security apparatus in light of the resolutions of the Sixth Plenary of the Central Committee of the Polish United Workers Party, in *Aparat Bezpieczeństwa w Polsce w latach 1950–1952: Taktyka, strategia, metody*, ed. Antoni Dudek and Andrzej Paczkowski (Warsaw, 2000), 75–77.

[6] Witness interrogation record, 19 January 1949, IPN, SOŁ 123, 674–77.

[7] Letter to the prosecutor of the Regional Court in Łomża of 29 March 1949, IPN, SOŁ 123, 755; deposition of the witness Piotr F. of 29 March 1949, ibid., 748; deposition of the witness Józef Grądowski of 29 March 1949, ibid., 749, and before the court 16 May 1949, ibid., 212v.

months before the Jedwabne trial), testified before the Municipal Court in Łomża. He stated at that time that in July 1941, he resided in the Russian interior; he also related completely different circumstances of the murder in Jedwabne. Now it was the Germans, and not the Poles, who were to blame for it: "My mother, Bluma Grondowska [*sic*] was murdered by Germans in Jedwabne on 10 July 1941 by being burned alive in a barn along with other Jews from that town. At that time I lived in Russia."[8] In yet another testimony, from 25 February 1947, Eljasz Grądowski declared that Fejga Zajdensztat had been "murdered on 10 July 1941 by the Germans by being herded along with other Jews into a barn in Jedwabne and burned alive. I know that because I was then hiding in the vicinity of Jedwabne."[9]

In spite of these mutually exclusive—albeit sworn—depositions, Eljasz Grądowski received Gross's full endorsement as a trustworthy witness. When these contradictions were pointed out to him,[10] Gross explained: "Two Grądowskis appear in the documents of this action, one of whom was in Jedwabne during the war, the other in Russia. But the fact that Eljasz Grądowski repeats in court information circulating in Jedwabne doesn't change anything. It may even strengthen the significance of that information."[11]

It is quite improbable that Gross could have confused Eljasz Grądowski with Józef Grądowski (the name of the other man) through a simple "oversight." Only Józef Grądowski testified before the Łomża tribunal; contrary to Gross's assertion, Eljasz Grądowski did not appear in court. It is also important to note that it was precisely Józef Grądowski's deposition that undermined Eljasz Grądowski's credibility and helped to exculpate some of the defendants. He was a genuine participant in the Jedwabne tragedy, and—in his own words—he had been "saved out of German hands" by the Polish citizens of Jedwabne.[12] Nevertheless, none of these facts were mentioned in Gross's *Neighbors*.

Another purported witness to the Jedwabne murder on whose testimony Gross has built his case is one Abram Boruszczak. He was interviewed in Łomża by the local authorities on 20 and 22 January 1949.

---

[8] Record of 24 May 1948, Archiwum Państwowe w Łomży (hereafter, APŁ), records of the Sąd Grodzki in Łomża (hereafter, GSŁ), Zg 130/48. Eljasz Grądowski made that declaration under oath when he applied for confirmation of his mother's death in order to regulate inheritance matters, about which more later.

[9] Record of 25 February 1947, APŁ, SGŁ Co 13/47.

[10] Piotr Gontarczyk, "Gross przemilczeń," *Życie*, 31 March–1 April 2001.

[11] Jan Tomasz Gross, "A jednak sąsiedzi," *Rzeczpospolita*, 11 April 2001.

[12] Deposition of Józef Grądowski of 29 March 1949 and his testimony before the court of 16 May 1949, IPN, SOŁ 123, 221v, 749.

At that time he stated that he had seen the massacre with his own eyes, and that he also had managed to escape from it at the very last moment. He stressed that the entire responsibility for the crime had rested with the Polish inhabitants of Jedwabne. According to him, the role of the Germans was limited to taking photographs of the events. Boruszczak named seventeen men and women from Jedwabne who allegedly participated in murdering the Jews and stealing their property.[13]

The credibility of this witness also raises justified doubts. Józef Grądowski, along with several Polish residents of Jedwabne, stated categorically that Abram Boruszczak had never lived in their town. Also, it appears that the testimonies of Eljasz Grądowski and Abram Boruszczak—in their factual contents and even verbal expressions—are in many places identical. These two had known one another for some time, so that these parallels are very likely not accidental.

There exists yet another suggestive indication of collusion between Eljasz Grądowski and Abram Boruszczak with regard to the content of their depositions. In his testimony of 19 January 1949 in Łomża, Eljasz Grądowski mentioned Boruszczak as an eyewitness to the events who could also testify about them. On the very next day the Łomża office of the UB conducted Boruszczak's hearing. We must keep in mind, however, that both Grądowski and Boruszczak—as they clearly declared in their statements—lived in the city of Wałbrzych, about 550 kilometers southwest of Łomża, where they worked as locksmiths.[14] Interestingly enough, neither of them reappeared before the court at a later date, because when the summonses were sent to their alleged place of residence, the two men were unreachable at that address.[15]

Another witness of importance to Gross is Henryk Krystowczyk. He testified against several defendants both during the investigation and in the course of the trial. The author of *Neighbors*, however, keeps silent about the fact that, after finding Krystowczyk's testimony full of inconsistencies, the court rejected it as spurious. Krystowczyk stated that, during the massacre of the Jedwabne Jews, he had been hiding in a garret from which he was able to observe the events. After scrutinizing the entire bulk of his depositions, the court reached the conclusion that this was not possible. The judges also remarked that Henryk Krystowczyk's actions were motivated by personal revenge toward several defendants with whom he had had old scores to settle.[16]

---

[13] Deposition of Abram Boruszczak of 20 and 22 January 1949, IPN SOŁ 123, 681–83.

[14] Interrogation record of the witness Eljasz Grądowski of 19 January 1949, ibid., 674; Deposition of Abram Boruszczak of 20 January 1949, ibid., 681–83.

[15] Record of the main proceedings, 17 May 1949, IPN, SOŁ 123, 221v.

[16] Justification of the verdict, IPN, SOŁ 123, 227–29; deposition of Wacław Krystowczyk (Henryk Krystowczyk hid in his home), ibid., Bl. 218v; Henryk Krystowczyk was

An important link in Gross's chain of evidence is formed by those fragments of the defendants' testimonies in which they inculpated themselves and other townspeople. These testimonies had been made during the UB interrogation and then incorporated into the court evidence by the state prosecutor. Later on, the majority of those defendants retracted their statements before the court and stated that their "confessions" had been coerced by violence. Thus, for example, Czesław Lipiński stated, "During the interrogation I said whatever they wanted to hear; they kept beating me very hard." Władysław Dąbrowski declared in court: "I said those things during the interrogation because I had been beaten and I was scared of more beating . . . I was beaten horribly."[17]

Not only the defendants but also the witnesses retracted their earlier testimonies during the trial. Stanisława Sielawa stated, "I did not say what's written there." Bronisława Kalinowska stated: "During the examination that officer who was asking questions, he told me what to say; he yelled at me so I got scared, and I don't know what they have taken down . . . I can't read or write, so they have written whatever they felt like, but it is not true."[18] Twice Gross quotes with approval the testimony subsequently withdrawn by Kalinowska (70, 230). He does the same with the retracted statements of Julia Sokołowska who, on 11 January 1949, named sixteen alleged participants in the massacre.[19]

The author of Neighbors considers it quite probable that the defendants had been beaten during the interrogation. His following conclusion is revealing: "In any case, there is no trace in this trial of efforts to elicit from the accused any specific information . . ." (28). But the court documents that have served as the basis of the narrative of Neighbors do contain such "specific information," which clearly contradicts Gross's conclusion. Bronisław Ramotowski stated: "During the examination I was forced to accuse other people as well because I was beaten, very hard. I accused Jan Zawadzki, the Żyluks, and others." Similarly, Zygmunt Laudański stated, "I did not see Józef Żyluk in the market square, and I testified against him under pressure."[20]

---

one of the few Communists of Polish origin in Jedwabne who collaborated with the Soviets. That was one of the reasons why he had to hide after the entry of the Germans.

[17] Similar testimonies were given by Roman Górski, Władysław Mieciura, Jerzy Laudański, Zygmunt Laudański, and Bolesław Ramotowski. Record of the main proceedings, 17 May 1949, IPN, SOŁ 123, 203–7.

[18] Ibid., 210, 211v.

[19] Interrogation of the witness Julia Sokołowska of 11 January 1949, IPN, SOŁ 123, 630–32; interrogation of Julia Sokołowska of 28 March 1949, ibid., 744.

[20] Record of the main proceedings of 17 May 1949, IPN, SOŁ 123, Bl. 203–7. These statements demonstrate that force was used to elicit incriminating statements.

Gross argues next that the authorities at that time did not have any interest in extracting false confessions because, in this specific case, the trial was not political. He thus assumes that UB agents used force to obtain desired testimonies only in political cases. The speech of Minister Radkiewicz cited above undermines such speculation:

> Very often the direct cause of the use of force against the suspect by our officers is the faulty operational work. Arresting people without sufficient grounds, without double-checking the reports and denunciations, without any sense of responsibility, with unnecessary and incomprehensible haste—all this in a way pushes an agent to look for the proof, because, on the one hand, he tends to think that he is, after all, dealing with a real criminal, and, on the other hand, he tries hard to find such proof through a forced confession in order to justify his incorrect (as it turns out) decision to arrest the suspect.[21]

Gross confirms the fact that the court proceedings in the Jedwabne case were prepared and conducted in a rash and superficial fashion (31). Nevertheless, he interprets this as an indication that the trial had not been "fixed" beforehand. His conclusion is thus exactly the opposite of that of the chief of the Security Office, Minister Radkiewicz. Furthermore, Gross lists other arguments against the possibility of "fixing the case": "The late forties and early fifties, after all, were a time when Stalin's anti-Jewish phobia was at its peak and already serving as a driving force for political persecution throughout the entire camp of the so-called people's democracies" (31). Gross adds in an endnote, "I have in mind not only the Kremlin's so-called Doctors' Plot, or the antisemitic context of the Slánský trial in Czechoslovakia, but the general ideological trend that by then was emanating from Moscow" (217).

However, Gross's arguments run contrary to the actual course of historical events. The affair of the Kremlin doctors occurred shortly before the death of Stalin in March 1953, four years after the Jedwabne trial. In 1949, Rudolf Slánský was still first secretary of the Czechoslovak Communist Party and thus an architect of the Communist terror himself. He was arrested only in November 1951 and condemned to death one year later.[22] In Poland, the year 1949 was spent on a campaign to eliminate "the forces of reaction" and to fight against "the rightist-nationalist deviation" within the Polish United Workers' Party (PZPR). The reasons for these particular persecutions cannot by any means be attributed to antisemitism. Apart from Bolesław Bierut, an ethnic Pole, the two other members of the triad ruling Poland at that time were

[21] Dudek and Paczkowski, *Aparat Bezpieczeństwa*, 77.
[22] *Brockhaus Enzyklopädie*, Siebzehnter Band (Wiesbaden, 1973), 500.

312 MEMORIES AND METHODOLOGIES

Jakub Berman (the political overseer of the security apparatus) and Hilary Minc, both of Jewish origin. Jan Tomasz Gross has obviously confused two different periods of the Communist terror in Poland.

The case of Czesław Laudański stands out in Gross's book. The author of *Neighbors* turned him into one of the most active "perpetrators" of the Jedwabne crime, twice "quoting" words that were supposedly his own to this effect: " 'A lot of people were there, whose names I do not remember now,' we are told by Laudański *père*, who with his two sons was among the busiest on this day, 'I'll tell them as soon as I recall' " (86). And on page 99: " 'We chased jews under the barn,' Czesław Laudański would later report, 'and we ordered them to enter inside, and the jews had to enter inside." '

According to Gross, Laudański's self-incrimination is to be found on pages 666 and 668 of the trial transcripts. I checked the pages in question without finding the indicated material there. The court records contain three depositions by Czesław Laudański, on pages 207, 669, and 680, respectively. None of them contains the statements attributed to Laudański by Gross. During an interrogation on 17 January 1949, Laudański declared, "I did not take part in the murder of the Jews in the town of Jedwabne, because at that time I was bedridden after returning two weeks earlier from Soviet prison; I don't know who participated in murdering those Jews because I was not present there."[23] During the follow-up interview with the prosecutor on 18 January 1949, he repeated verbatim his testimony from the day before. In the court transcripts we read, "Czesław Laudański pleads not guilty and explains: on the day in question I was sick in bed after returning from prison, I was blind and swollen all over."[24]

When we take into account the terrible conditions in Soviet jails, these testimonies become coherent and plausible.[25] They were also con-

[23] Interrogation record of the accused, 17 January 1949, IPN, SOŁ 123, 669v.

[24] Record of the main proceedings of 17 May 1949, IPN, SOŁ 123, 207.

[25] According to his eldest son, Kazimierz, Czesław Laudański was arrested toward the end of September or the beginning of October 1939 and was held without trial until June 1941. At that time he was confined to a bed in the prison hospital in Łomża. After the escape of the Soviets but before the entry of the German army, all of the prisoners were freed. (Interview with Kazimierz Laudański, 22 May 2001.) This is confirmed by, among other things, the entry in *Kronika Panien Benedyktynek Opactwa Świętej Trójcy w Łomży 1939–1954: Czas wojny. Czas okupacji sowieckiej i niemieckiej. Łomża w strefie frontowej. Czas zniewolenia*, prepared by Sister Alojza Piesiewiczówna (Łomża, 1995), 77, which reads, "Before noon [on 22 June 1941] the prisoners left their cells." For more about conditions in Soviet prisons see Bogdan Musiał, *"Kontrrevolutionäre Elemente sind zu erschießen": Die Brutalisierung des deutsch-sowjetischen Krieges im Sommer 1941* (Berlin, 2000), 86–97. In actual fact the Soviets did not have time to evacuate the prison in Łomża. Ibid., 99.

firmed during the trial by numerous witnesses, while the depositions to the contrary—by Eljasz Grądowski, Abram Boruszczak, and Henryk Krystowczyk—were deemed false and rejected by the court.[26] The name of Czesław Laudański as that of an alleged perpetrator is also mentioned in the digest of Szmul Wasersztajn's testimony (see below), which is found among the trial records. Characteristically, in the original, full text of a copy of Wasersztajn's deposition, there is no mention of Czesław Laudański.[27] This is only one among many indications pointing to the fact that, at some point during the investigation, a portion of the incriminating evidence had been fabricated, and the "corrected" version of Wasersztajn's account was presented to the court as additional proof of Laudański's guilt. Nevertheless, the District Court in Łomża acquitted him completely.

It has recently been pointed out to Gross that the trial records do not contain the statements ascribed by him to Czesław Laudański.[28] At first he tried to maintain his version by stating that there was nothing wrong with his quotations.[29] It was only after Czesław Laudański's eldest son took Gross to court for defaming his father's name that Gross finally conceded that the "admission of guilt" had not come from Czesław Laudański's deposition. He explained that the quotations had been extracted from two different testimonies, namely, those of Jerzy Laudański and Zygmunt Laudański. In short, he treated the entire matter as just another "oversight."[30]

The analysis of the court transcripts outlined above clearly proves that the 1949 inquiry into the Jedwabne massacre is a classic example of the "fix" so typical of Stalinist Poland: false accusations (by Eljasz Grądowski, Abram Boruszczak, and Henryk Krystowczyk, all of whom are still considered trustworthy by Gross), unlawful methods of interrogation, forced extraction of self-incriminating confessions, doctoring of the depositions, and fabrication of evidence (in the case of

[26] Record of the main proceedings of 6 May 1949, IPN, SOŁ 123, 201–23, ibid.; depositions of Stanislaw S. (210), Józef M. (212), Alina Z. (212), Natalia R.(214), Teofil Ch. (218), Zygmunt W. (218v), Henryk Krystowczyk (213v); deposition of Eljasz Grądowski of 19 January 1949, ibid., 674; deposition of Abram Boruszczak of 20 January 1949, ibid., 681.

[27] An excerpt from the account of Szmul Wasersztajn located in the archives of the Jewish Historical Institute (Żydowski Instytut Historyczny—ŻIH), no. 152, ibid., 600; a complete transcript of this account is also found in the trial documentation, but there is no mention of Czesław Laudański (IPN, SOL, 123, 700).

[28] Piotr Gontarczyk, "Gross przemilczeń," *Życie*, 31 March–1 April 2001.

[29] Jan Tomasz Gross, "A jednak sąsiedzi," *Rzeczpospolita*, 11 April 2001.

[30] "Profesor pozwany," *Życie*, 15 June 2001; interview with J. T. Gross, *Życie*, 16–17 June 2001; "Teraz książkę zajmują się prawnicy," *Rzeczpospolita*, 15 June 2001; "Autor *Sąsiadów* przyznaje się do pomyłki," *Rzeczpospolita*, 23–24 June 2001.

Czesław Laudański). In light of all this, the arguments on which Jan Tomasz Gross has constructed his thesis about the unimpeachable character of the Jedwabne investigation are both completely unhistorical and incoherent.

Reminiscences of Holocaust Survivors: An Affirmative and Selective Choice

Accounts of the Jewish Holocaust in Europe can be found in hundreds of Jewish publications, memorial books (*yizkor bukher*), collections of reminiscences, and scholarly works. In addition, we are confronted with an ever-growing number of Holocaust memoirs. Even though such testimonies are undoubtedly important for the proper understanding of the Shoah, their scholarly interpretation—like the interpretation of any other historical source—presents numerous problems. Dr. Samuel Gringauz, himself a Holocaust survivor, described them in his 1950 article as follows:

> The difficulties in studying the great Jewish catastrophe are manifold. There is the vast geographical area of the disaster and the enormity of personal suffering and of social and emotional upheavals brought about by the events of the catastrophe ... Last but not least, there is what perhaps may be termed the hyperhistorical complex of the survivors. Never before was the event so deeply sensed by its participants as being part of an epoch-shaping history in the making, never before was a personal experience felt to be so historically relevant. The result of this hyperhistorical complex has been that the brief post-war years have seen a flood of 'historical materials'—rather "contrived" than "collected"—so that today one of the most delicate aspects of research is the evaluation of the so-called "research material." The hyperhistorical complex may be described as *judeocentric, lococentric*, and *egocentric* [emphasis in the original]. It concentrates historical relevance on Jewish problems or local events under the aspect of personal experience. This is the reason why most of the memoirs and reports are full of preposterous verbosity, graphomanic exaggeration, dramatic effects, overestimated self-inflation, dilettante philosophizing, would-be lyricism, unchecked rumors, bias, partisan attacks, and apologies. The question thus arises whether participants of such a world-shaking epoch can at all be its historians and whether the time has already come when valid historic

judgment, free of partisanship, vindictiveness, and ulterior motives is possible.[31]

Today, half a century after these words were written, the observations of Dr. Gringauz are more valid than ever. Jan Tomasz Gross, however, disregards such warnings and calls for a diametrically opposed course of action: "I suggest that we should modify our approach to sources for this period. When considering survivors' testimonies, we would be well advised to change the starting premise in appraisal of their evidentiary contribution from a priori critical to in principle affirmative" (139).

With his "affirmative" approach to the sources Gross would like to create new standards for Holocaust research. In fact, this perspective—now raised to the level of a scholarly norm—has been tacitly observed for years among Holocaust scholars who pay special attention (and deference) to survivors' testimonies. Peter Novick comments thus on this phenomenon: "In recent years 'Holocaust survivor' has become an honorific term, evoking not just sympathy but admiration, and even awe. Survivors are thought of and customarily described as exemplars of courage, fortitude, and wisdom derived from their suffering."[32]

In such an atmosphere a critical evaluation of these sources seems to many writers and researchers simply improper. Some scholars watch this development with justified misgivings. István Deák is one of them: "An accurate record of the Holocaust has been endangered, in my opinion, by the uncritical endorsement, often by well-known Jewish writers or public figures, of virtually any survivor's account or related writings."[33]

Not so for Gross. He also maintains that there is no reason to suspect Jewish survivors of concocting false accusations against Poles (28). This would mean that Holocaust survivors have either managed to completely rid themselves of any negative emotions, such as prejudice or desire for revenge, or that they never harbored them in the first place. However, scholars agree that the experience of the Holocaust must have caused in the survivors very severe emotional crises, with which some of the survivors have come to terms in various ways, while the others are still trying to do so.[34] A different reaction to such

[31] Samuel Gringauz, "Some Methodological Problems in the Study of the Ghetto," *Jewish Social Studies: A Quarterly Journal Devoted to the Historical Aspects of the Jewish Life*, no. 12 (1950): 65–66.

[32] Peter Novick, *The Holocaust in American Life* (Boston, 1999), 68.

[33] István Deák, "Memories of Hell," *New York Review of Books*, 26 June 1997, 38.

[34] After 1945, it was clear in Jewish circles that the Holocaust had had a demoralizing effect on survivors. (Compare Novick, *The Holocaust*, 68–69). A desire for revenge had

a catastrophe would have been very strange indeed. One of the survivors, Joseph L. Lichten, wrote in 1966:

> They [diaries, memoirs, accounts, etc.] were written in the main during or immediately after a grave emotional crisis, when the observing eye was blinded with tears. Even in those composed several years later, the commentator, including the present writer, finds himself again overwhelmed by grief at the recollection of the ghastly period. The result frequently is a document of pain, born out of the tragedy which both the writer and the people he is writing about lived through.[35]

The starting point for Gross's research on the Jedwabne case was the aforementioned account of Szmul Wasersztajn. The author of *Neighbors* quotes it in extenso (16–20), arranging his entire narrative around it. This document also happens to be the source of Gross's central contentions (about the respective roles of the Germans and Poles, the chronology of events, the scale of the violence, etc.), while the remaining sources—dissected and utilized in a peculiar way—serve only as the complementary material.

Wasersztajn's account is supposed to have been recorded in Yiddish on 5 April 1945, and subsequently translated into Polish, but its original version has been never found. Szmul Wasersztajn hailed from Jedwabne, and, at the time of the events in question, he was eighteen years old. There exist two versions of his testimony, and they display substantial differences. The one quoted extensively by Gross is the more detailed of the two; it was translated by M. Kwater and is held at the Jewish Historical Institute (Żydowski Instytut Historyczny—ŻIH) in Warsaw (reference no. 301/152). The other version, also held at ŻIH (reference no. 301/613) is considerably shorter. These two documents are supplemented by the aforementioned digest prepared for the Łomża trial in 1949.

The longer version of Wasersztajn's testimony quoted in *Neighbors* contains numerous shocking episodes and basically constitutes one large and dramatic accusation against the Polish inhabitants of Jedwabne, who murdered their Jewish neighbors with mind-numbing

---

become for many a driving force. John Sack, for example, argued that many Jews had joined the security apparatus in Poland after the war for that reason. John Sack, *An Eye for an Eye* (New York, 1993), 110–11; see also Marek Jan Chodakiewicz, *Żydzi i Polacy 1918–1955: Współistnienie, Zagłada, komunizm* (Warsaw, 2000), 408–9.

[35] Joseph L. Lichten, "Some Aspects of Polish-Jewish Relations during the Nazi Occupation," in *Studies in Polish Civilization: Selected Papers Presented at the First Congress of the Polish Institute of Arts and Sciences in America, November 25, 26, 27, 1966 in New York*, ed. Damian S. Wandycz (New York, 1970), 156.

cruelty. Wasersztajn speaks of eyes gouged out, tongues cut off, infants slaughtered at their mothers' breasts, toddlers tied together in bundles and thrown with pitchforks into the hot embers of the burned-down barn. After the killing the Poles supposedly started extracting gold teeth from the bodies. Gross takes these descriptions at face value, quoting them without reservations.[36]

However, in studying both versions of Wasersztajn's testimony, we cannot help but notice their contradictions, which surface not only in the act of comparing the two texts but even during a careful reading of any one of them. Thus, in the longer version, we read that the order to kill the Jedwabne Jews was given by the Germans on 10 July 1941, but two sentences later we discover the following (quoted in *Neighbors*, 18–19):

> On the morning of July 10, 1941, eight gestapo men came to town and had a meeting with representatives of the town authorities. When the gestapo asked what their plans were with respect to the Jews, they said, unanimously, that all Jews must be killed. When the Germans proposed to leave one Jewish family from each profession, local carpenter Bronisław Szleziński [Śleszyński], who was present, answered: We have enough of our own craftsmen, we have to destroy all the Jews, none should stay alive. Mayor Karolak and everybody else agreed with his words. For this purpose Szleziński gave his own barn, which stood nearby. After this meeting the bloodbath began.

It is clear, then, that the account in question contains two mutually exclusive statements in regard to who was responsible for the massacre. Similar contradictions abound. One version mentions a picture of Lenin that the Jews were forced to carry in a procession while singing Soviet songs. The other version speaks of a statue of Lenin that the Jews were made to destroy (seventy-five men supposedly participated in this act), and then to carry to the nearby Jewish cemetery and throw into a ditch already dug for this purpose. The men carrying the statue were allegedly butchered on the spot by "local hooligans," and their bodies were buried with the statue. Gross, quite arbitrarily, accepts the second version of the events (19).

There are many indications that both versions are imprecise reflections of what actually occurred. During the exhumation in Jedwabne in May 2001, within the foundations of the burned-down barn, a grave containing human remains was found and the aforementioned statue of Lenin uncovered. The concrete bust of the Soviet leader was seri-

---

[36] He quotes them, for example, in the interview in the *New Yorker*, 6 March 2001.

ously damaged and charred.[37] One should conclude from this that the sculpture was buried after the barn was burned down. This fact undermines the credibility of the information contained in both versions of Szmul Wasersztajn's account, as well as the stories about the burial of Lenin's statue at the Jewish cemetery and about the killing of seventy-five Jews there by "Polish hooligans."

It is characteristic that Gross quotes the following testimony of a Polish witness: "While carrying the statue all the Jews were chased toward the barn, and the barn was doused with gasoline and lit, and in this manner fifteen hundred Jewish people perished" (99). Zygmunt Laudański's account (regarded by Gross as reliable) is very similar: "The Jews carried the statue of Lenin around the market square; then we herded all the Jews with the statue out of the town to Bronisław Śleszyński's barn ... where they were burned."[38] The author of *Neighbors* does not see these contradictions between the sources he cites.

Interestingly enough, the two versions of Wasersztajn's testimony give different numbers of victims. The shorter version speaks of 1,200 killed and only three survivors. In the longer version we read that, before the outbreak of the war, Jedwabne was inhabited by 1,600 Jews, of whom seven survived.

We discover still more contradictions by comparing Wasersztajn's account with the depositions of other Jews from Jedwabne. Gross quotes the following episode from Wasersztajn's account:

On the same day I observed a horrible scene. Chaja Kubrzańska, twenty-eight years old, and Basia Binsztajn, twenty-six years old, both holding newborn babies, when they saw what was going on [the mistreatment of Jews by Polish "bandits" (BM)], they ran to a pond in order to drown themselves with the children rather than fall into the hands of bandits. They put their children in the water and drowned them with their own hands: then Baśka Binsztajn jumped in and immediately went to the bottom, while Chaja Kubrzańska suffered for a couple of hours. Assembled hooligans made a spectacle of this. They advised her to lie face down in the water, so that she would drown faster. Finally, seeing that the children were already dead, she threw herself more energetically into the water and found her death too. (17)

[37] "Nowa mogiła ofiar w Jedwabnem," *Rzeczpospolita*, 1 June 2001; "Tragedia w dwóch aktach," *GW*, 1 June 2001; "Drugi grób w stodole," *Życie*, 1 June 2001.
[38] Record of the interrogation of Zygmunt Laudański of 16 January 1949, IPN, SOŁ; 123, 667–68.

Rivka Fogel, a Jewish woman who survived the Jedwabne massacre, describes the same scene as follows:

> The sisters, the wife of Avraham Kubzanski and the wife of Saul Binshtein, whose husbands left with the Russians after enduring horrible punishment at the hands of the Germans, decided to end their own lives and that of their children. They exchanged the children between themselves and together they jumped into deep water. Gentiles standing nearby pulled them out, but they managed to jump in again and were drowned.[39]

In her description Polish witnesses behave in a completely different way than in Wasersztajn's and Gross's version; that is, they tried to save the women. Their suicides were brought about not by Polish "bandits," as alleged by Wasersztajn and Gross, but by German persecution. The following example is similar: Wasersztajn (quoted on page 16), states, "I saw with my own eyes how those murderers [two Polish inhabitants of Jedwabne, Wacek Borowski and his brother Mietek (BM)] killed Chajcia Wasersztajn, Jakub Kac, seventy-three years old, and Eliasz Krawiecki" (16). Rivka Fogel, however, writes, "On the very first day that the Germans entered the city of Yedwabne, they murdered the harness maker Yakov Katz [Jakub Kac], the stitcher Eli Krawiecki [Eliasz Krawiecki], the blacksmith Shmuel Weinstein, the businessmen Moshe Fishman, Choneh Goldberg and his son."[40]

The author of *Neighbors* is certainly familiar with the testimony of Rivka Fogel (he quotes it on pages 91–92 of *Neighbors*); nevertheless, he does not point out the vital discrepancies between her account and Wasersztajn's. The following observation by Fogel, one of approximately 125 Jews who survived the ordeal and were kept in a ghetto created in Jedwabne, was also ignored by Gross:

> There was one Jew whose name was Israel Grondowski.[41] He was a carpenter and a well-known citizen, who during that time of distress profaned G-d's name. He and his family ran to the Catholic Church, fell to the feet of the priest and asked him to convert them to Christianity, thereby saving their lives. This same man turned against his own people. About one hundred and twenty-five Jews had been lucky enough to hide out and escaped being burned alive. The new Christian told the goyim where the hideout was

[39] *Yedwabne: History and Memorial Book*, ed. Julius L. Baker and Jacob L. Baker (Jerusalem, 1980), 101 (hereafter, *Memorial Book*).
[40] Ibid.
[41] Grądowski's name is frequently given in documents as Grondowski.

located. However, after that terrible day of horror, the anger of the goyim against our people had subsided.[42]

Fogel speaks here about one Józef Grądowski, who, according to his own testimony, on 10 July 1941 saved himself, his wife, and their two sons only thanks to the help of Poles.[43] His sister and her family were murdered that same day.[44] It is true that Józef Grądowski converted to Catholicism (he did so alone because his wife and children had, in the meantime, lost their lives), but not on 10 July 1941, as stated by Fogel. This occurred much later when he married a local Polish woman, as we learn from the following entry in the records of the Jedwabne parish: "This took place on 19 August 1945. One Izrael Grondowski, of the Mosaic faith, an artisan from Jedwabne, fifty years old . . . has come and declared that, owing to his inner conviction and without any external persuasion, he wants to convert from the Mosaic faith into the fold of the Catholic Church. The said Izrael Grondowski has been baptized today at the local church, receiving the name of Józef."[45]

Further comparisons between the accounts of Jewish survivors and other available sources bring to light even more contradictions. On page 71 of *Neighbors* Gross relates the following event, based on the testimony of Wiktor Niełacki (a.k.a. Avigdor Kochav and Victor Kohav), which he obtained in February 2000:

> Leaders of the Jewish community [in Jedwabne] delivered silver candlesticks to the Catholic bishop of Łomża and sought assurance that he would not permit a pogrom in Jedwabne and would intervene with the Germans on behalf of the Jewish community. "Yes, the Bishop kept his word for a while. But the Jews placed too much confidence in his promise and refused to listen to the constant warnings that came from friendly Gentile neighbors. My uncle and his rich brother Eliyahu did not believe me when I told them what had happened in Wizno [Wizna, a nearby village (BM)]. 'And if it had happened there,' they said, 'we here in Yedwabne are safe because the Bishop promised to protect us.' "

However, a substantially different account by Niełacki was published in the Jedwabne memorial book in 1980, where this particular

---

[42] *Memorial Book*, 103.

[43] Record of the main proceedings, Appeals Court in Białystok, 15 June 1950, IPN, SOŁ; 123, [page number illegible].

[44] Deposition of Józef Grądowski of 29 March 1949, IPN, SOŁ 123, 749; record of the interrogation before the Town Court in Łomża, 8 July 1947, APŁ, SGŁ; Co 52/47.

[45] Baptismal certificate of Józef Grądowski of 19 August 1945. A copy of this certificate is in the author's possession.

event is described as follows: "The leaders of the Jewish community [in Jedwabne] collected a large sum of money and delivered it to the Catholic Bishop of Łomża, who promised that he would not permit a pogrom in Yedwabne. Yes, the Bishop kept his word for a while."[46]

To sum up, one testimony mentions "silver candlesticks," while the other speaks of "a large sum of money" supposedly given to the bishop as a "ransom." Furthermore, the earlier 1980 version does not contain any mention of Nieławicki's uncle going in person to see the bishop. These discrepancies are explained by Gross in the Polish version of *Neighbors*: "In his conversation Nieławicki clarified some inaccuracies in the English-language version of his testimony published in the memorial book" (49 n. 41). This "clarification" was supposedly made in the year 2000.

However, there are many indications that both the original version of Nieławicki's recollections and the "clarified" one are far from the truth. Stanisław Łukomski, the bishop of the Łomża diocese (who allegedly took the "ransom" and then broke his word), had to leave his residence in the autumn of 1939 to hide from the Soviets in the countryside. According to the memoirs he wrote after the war, he returned to Łomża on 9 July 1941, after obtaining permission from the Germans to do so. However, he reclaimed his residence only a month later, because the palace had been requisitioned by the *Wehrmacht*.[47] This is confirmed by an entry of 8 July 1941 in the chronicle of the Benedictine sisters' convent in Łomża: "His Excellency Bishop Stanisław Kostka Łukomski has returned to Łomża." Three days later, on 11 July, the bishop received in audience two Benedictine sisters.[48]

If we take into account these established facts, Nieławicki's information about a delegation of Jews from Jedwabne being received by the bishop and taking a "ransom" to him several days before the tragic events of 10 July 1941 becomes rather implausible.[49] It is also worth adding that Polish bishops had very limited ability to intervene in the policies and actions of the German occupation authorities. Suffice it to say that, under the circumstances, Bishop Łukomski could not even prevent the execution by the Germans of a priest in one of the parishes of his diocese.[50] Notably, the earliest known account by Nieławicki,

[46] *Memorial Book*, 100.
[47] See *Rozporządzenia Urzędowe Łomżyńskiej Kurii Diecezjalnej* 36, 5–7 (May–July 1974): 61.
[48] *Kronika Panien Benedyktynek*, 79.
[49] W. Nieławicki writes that the bishop "kept his word for a while." I interpret "a while" in this context to mean several days.
[50] *Rozporządzenia Urzędowe Łomżyńskiej Kurii Diecezjalnej*, 62.

from 11 June 1945, speaks about the massacre of Jews in Jedwabne but does not mention at all the bishop, the ransom, and the treachery.[51]

There are other problems with the witnesses. According to a description in *Neighbors*, Stanisław Sielawa was one of the most active and brutal murderers in Jedwabne on 10 July 1941. Wasersztajn (quoted by Gross on page 97) wrote that on that day "Stanisław Szelawa [Sielawa] was murdering [Jews (BM)] with an iron hook, [stabbing] in the stomach." But on page 100 Gross presents a different description of Sielawa's actions based on the testimony of Janek Neumark: "At the last moment Janek Neumark managed to tear himself away from this hell. A surge of hot air must have blown the barn door open. He was standing right next to it with his sister and her five-year-old daughter. Staszek Sielawa barred their exit, wielding an ax. But Neumark wrestled it away from him and they managed to run away and hide in the cemetery." In this version, Sielawa is supposed to have been using an ax as an instrument during the crime.

Stanisław Sielawa was among the accused in the 1949 trial. He stated for the record: "I plead not guilty . . . I am a cripple, I did not go anywhere, and I don't know anything . . . I have had a crippled leg since I was three years old." The court acquitted him.[52]

---

[51] Account of Avigdor (Wiktor) NiełAwicki of 11 June 1945, ŻIH 301/384. In total the author of this article is aware of six versions of the tragic events in Jedwabne presented by W. Nieławicki: the account of 11 June 1945; the account in the *Memorial Book* from 1980; the "clarified account" found in Gross's book; an interview that appeared in the *Guardian* on 14 March 2001 (Kate Connolly, "A Holocaust Tale Is Finally Told"); an interview in *Der Spiegel* of 28 May 2001; and a conversation in *Gazeta Wyborcza* of 10 June 2001. These accounts are contradictory. For example, in the account of 11 June 1945 and in the *Guardian*, Nieławicki elaborates that his parents and other family members were murdered in the barn in Jedwabne. The *Memorial Book* (100) says the opposite: his parents and family had returned to their village of Wizna a few days before the massacre. Nor do their names appear in the list of victims published in the *Memorial Book*. In 1945 Nieławicki claimed he had joined the NSZ (National Armed Forces), whereas in the *Der Spiegel* interview he mentions the Armia Krajowa (Home Army) and talks about the antisemitic attitude of its soldiers, without mentioning the unit in which he allegedly fought. In is worth noting that in his most recent statements he does not mention the bishop of Łomża and his betrayal. Since January 2001 that claim has been regarded as untrustworthy (cf. Marek Jan Chodakiewicz, "Kłopoty z kuracją szokową," *Rzeczpospolita*, 5 January 2001). Nieławicki has been monitoring the discussion about Jedwabne that is taking place in Poland on the Internet (see the *Guardian*). He told *Der Spiegel* that his account from 1945, which was recorded in Yiddish by the Jewish Historical Commission in Białystok (as was Wasersztajn's), was falsified.

[52] Transcript of the main proceedings, 16 May 1949, IPN, SOŁ 123, 208v; reasons for the verdict, ibid., 228v. Jan Sokołowski, who lived in Jedwabne until 1947, testified that Stanisław Sielawa had a straight wooden prosthesis from the knee down that he had whittled for himself. (The author is in possession of a drawing of the prosthesis and the written declaration of Jan Sokołowski, Białystok, 28 May 2001.)

The author of *Neighbors* has also committed other errors. On page 209 (endnote 5), he reproduces a fragment of a report from the Security Office (UB): "A letter was sent to the Ministry of Justice by the Jewess Calka Migdał, who escaped when the jews [*sic*] were being murdered in Jedwabne, and who saw everything and also who took part in the murder of jews [*sic*] in 1941 in Jedwabne." According to the author of this memo, quoted uncritically by Gross, the person in question is a Jewish female survivor of the July 1941 tragedy. In fact, "Calka Migdał" is a man, "Calka" being a popular male name, and "Migdał" his surname. Moreover, Migdał could not possibly have witnessed the Jedwabne massacre because in 1937 he had already emigrated from Jedwabne to Uruguay. These facts are easy to establish on the basis of Migdał's original letter, a copy of which is attached to the trial records. Migdał states in it that he learned that the perpetrators of the Jedwabne massacre were Poles, not Germans, and that they remained unpunished.[53]

Our analysis has revealed numerous contradictions in Jewish testimonies that were either overlooked or ignored by Gross. These Jewish accounts render it difficult to separate the truth from gossip or exaggeration, and facts from baseless and false accusations. Considered on their own strength, they certainly cannot serve as a sufficient basis for a detailed and reliable reconstruction of the course of events in the Jedwabne massacre. Polish historians for the most part agree that none of the Jewish witnesses quoted in *Neighbors* had been able to observe firsthand the events that they subsequently described. The common perception in this respect tends to classify these descriptions as products of their collective memory.[54]

Although it goes without saying that not all Holocaust survivors' testimonies are useless in the reconstruction of historical events, we

[53] IPN, SOŁ 123, 599.

[54] "Jedwabne, 10 lipca 1941—zbrodnia i pamięć," *Rzeczpospolita*, 3–4 March 2001; "Ustałam wszystkie okoliczności" (an interview with Radosław Ignatiew), *BIPN*, no. 3 (April 2001): 10. At least one hundred Jews who had survived the massacre continued to live in Jedwabne until November 1942, when they were transferred by the Germans to the ghetto in Łomża. Many other Jews from Jedwabne made their way to nearby localities such as Łomża, Wizna, Goniądz, Choroszcz, Przytuły, Szczuczyn, Stawiski, Kolno, Białystok, and Zambrów, as confirmed in the *Memorial Book*, 88, 94, 103, 107, 113, and the necrology, and in Zdzisław Sędziak, " 'Napiętnowani znakiem śmierci,' " in *Ziemia Łomżyńska* 2 (1986): 190, 193–96. The Wyrzykowski family sheltered seven Jews from the fall of 1941 until the entry of the Red Army, among them Szmul Wasersztajn and Józef Grądowski. Several Jews lived in Jedwabne after the end of the Second World War, until most of them emigrated from Poland to Israel, Australia, the U.S.A., and Honduras. They maintained contact with one another, and one may assume that the matter of Jedwabne was often discussed in conversations and correspondence, as evidenced by the undertaking of a *Memorial Book*.

must remember the real dangers inherent in the uncritical and affirmative approach to this source material. The foregoing analysis also reminds us of the importance of following the strict requirements of scholarly methodology when engaging in historical inquiries of any kind.

For some time now, even Gross himself has been trying to minimize the weight and importance of the accounts utilized in *Neighbors*: "My book was not written on the basis of the testimonies of the victims and survivors of the Holocaust."[55] He insists that the foundation of his work is to be found in the 1949 trial records. In reality, however, the testimonies are simply crucial to the message of his book. The most drastic details and scenes (the rapes, the kicking around of the severed head of a Jewish girl, etc.) were taken straight from them, and the entire construction of the narrative is modeled on Wasersztajn's testimony.

The Number of Victims

Every historian should be aware of how problematic—and at the same time how important—an accurate and honest estimate of the number of victims is. Different sources present very different accounts of the extent of the Jedwabne tragedy. The court records and numerous other documents mention numbers ranging from a few hundred to more than 3,000 victims. For reasons not explained in his book, Gross accepted the figure of 1,600, and this number has achieved a symbolic status. As it happens, it is a significant overestimate.

According to Soviet data, in September 1940 in the entire Jedwabne region (*raion*), there were 37,300 ethnic Poles, 185 Belarusians, and 1,400 Jews.[56] Apart from Jedwabne, this particular Soviet administrative region also included, among other places, Wizna, Radziłów, and Przytuły, where many Jews also resided. In yet other Soviet documents we find the information that in 1940, Jedwabne counted 562 Jews, while Wizna counted 476 and Radziłów about 500.[57] The sum total then

[55] "Jedwabne, 10 lipca 1941—zbrodnia i pamięć," *Rzeczpospolita*, 3–4 March 2001.

[56] Information about the economic, social, and political situation in the Jedwabne region from the Regional Section of the NKVD in Jedwabne of 16 September 1940, published in Michał Gnatowski, *W radzieckich okowach: Studium o agresji 17 września 1939 r. i radzieckiej polityce w regionie łomżyńskim w latach 1939–1941* (Łomża, 1997), 256. Gross is aware of this book and cites it.

[57] Characteristics of the towns and regions of the District of Białystok (1940, no day or month given). Gosudarstvennyi arkhiv obshchestvennykh obedinennyi Grodnenskoi oblasti, sygn. 6195/1/132, 37 ff.; Overview of the economic characteristics of the towns,

comes to about 1,540 Jews in the whole *raion*. These figures, as well as the lack of any serious discrepancies between them, allow us to conclude that around 600 Jews lived in the town of Jedwabne during the Soviet occupation.

It is not known, however, how many Jews were present in Jedwabne on 10 July 1941. After the outbreak of the German-Soviet hostilities, many Jews, who either had been collaborating with the Soviet regime or were simply afraid of the Germans, escaped from the border territories.[58] The Soviet sources quoted above, which were ignored by Gross in *Neighbors*, indicate quite clearly that 1,600 Jews could not possibly have perished in Jedwabne on 10 July 1941, since Jedwabne and Wizna (some of whose Jewish residents had taken shelter in Jedwabne) put together did not have more than 1,100 Jewish inhabitants in the period immediately preceding the German invasion. As we have already mentioned, not all of the Jews were murdered on 10 July 1941. Some had escaped earlier, some had been killed before 10 July, and others died after that date. Very few of the Jewish residents, however, survived the war.

In March 2001, the Council for the Preservation of the Memory of Struggle and Martyrdom ordered its experts to investigate the site of the crime. They dug up the foundations of the barn burned in July 1941 and located a mass grave. For religious reasons, a thorough search was not carried out (primarily to respect the wishes of the Jewish community). Nevertheless, in May–June 2001, on the order of the Institute of National Memory (IPN), a partial exhumation took place at the same site. On this occasion a second mass grave was found. The first grave is located very close to the foundations of the barn, and the second is within its foundations. According to media reports, both graves contain the remains of at least 150 victims (250 at the most).[59] Andrzej Kola, an archaeologist who took part in this partial exhumation, estimates the number of victims at 300–400, preferring a "cautious" figure of about 300.[60] There are no indications of the existence of other mass graves holding the bodies of victims from the barn.

---

regions, and village soviets in the District of Białystok (1940), ibid., sygn. 6195/1/129, 153, 160, 166.

[58] See Rivka Fogel and Itzchak Yaacov (Yanek) Neumark, in *Memorial Book*, 101, 112; Musiał, *Kontrrevolutionäre Elemente*, 273–76.

[59] "Archiwa mniej tajne," *Życie*, 29 March 2001; "Wizja lokalna w Jedwabnem," *GW*, 29 March 2001; "Ofiar było mniej?" *GW*, 5 June 2001; Jarosław Kaczyński, "Ofiar było znacznie mniej niż 1600," *Rzeczpospolita*, 5 June 2001; " 'Tylko' kilkaset ofiar?" *Życie*, 5 June 2001.

[60] " 'Ślubne obrączki i nóż rzezaka': Wywiad z Andrzejem Kolą," *Rzeczpospolita*, 10 July 2001. The objects found during the exhumation, such as wedding bands and gold coins, seem to contradict the claim that the victims were robbed after being murdered.

With his uncritical and arbitrary acceptance of the figure of 1,600 victims, the author of *Neighbors* has triggered an inappropriate and none-too-serious discussion about the "capacity" of the barn, that is, whether a barn that size (19m × 7m) could have accommodated 1,600 people.[61] In spite of the publications criticizing his conclusions in *Neighbors*, and contrary to the findings during the partial exhumation, Gross still insists that local Poles murdered 1,600 of their Jewish "neighbors" in Jedwabne on 10 July 1941.[62]

The Establishment of the Town Council in Jedwabne and the Mass Murder

Gross writes on page 72: "In the meantime, Jedwabne's municipal authorities were constituting themselves. Marian Karolak became the mayor, and among his closest collaborators we can identify a certain Wasilewski and Józef Sobuta. What municipal authorities were doing during those days, again, we cannot tell precisely, beyond recognizing that they consulted with the Germans and eventually carried out the mass murder of Jedwabne Jews."

Gross thus holds that the town authorities "constituted themselves" after the entry of the Germans into Jedwabne; he also keeps referring to them as the "town council" and "town council members," thus suggesting that they were freely elected representatives of the Polish community.

Neighbors does not contain any indication of the sources on which Gross bases his assertion about the "constitution" of the "town council"; nor can we find in this book any details of this particular procedure. The possibility of local elections' having taken place in Jedwabne after the entry of the Germans is, in my opinion, remote. It would be completely contrary to the internal logic and reality of the Nazi occupation in Poland. On the other hand, it is possible that, shortly after Jedwabne was seized, the occupiers appointed one of its inhabitants (who could speak German) as acting mayor. His duties were to receive

[61] In a discussion that took place on the Internet on 17 May 2001, Gross was asked how it was possible to have burned to death 1,600 people in a small barn. Gross replied: "It wasn't such a small barn at all. Besides you can pack in as many people you want with the use of scythes, pitchforks, and knives." Posted at http://www.gazeta.pl/alfa/home.jspłdzial=050406.

[62] "Prof. Gross: Źle się stało, że przeprowadzono ekshumację," *GW*, 2 July 2001; "Gross o ekshumacji," *Życie*, 2 July 2001; "Aus Nachbarn wurden über Nacht Mörder" (interview with Jan T. Gross), *Tagespiegel*, 6 July 2001.

and convey German orders. The entire "town council" of Jedwabne probably "constituted itself" in the same manner.[63]

Gross devotes several pages to the alleged negotiations between the "self-constituted town council" and the Germans. To prove the veracity of this fact, he refers to the statements of Henryk Krystowczyk and Eljasz Grądowski (whose testimonies, as demonstrated above, are not trustworthy), and also to the account of Szmul Wasersztajn, who, for previously stated reasons, could not possibly have been a witness to these negotiations.

By employing terms such as "town council" and "town council members," Gross tries to imply that the Poles enjoyed significant autonomy in undertaking fairly independent decisions and actions. According to Gross, they used this autonomy to get rid of their Jewish neighbors. Such speculations do not find any support in the available sources and run contrary to the German modus operandi in the territories they occupied in the summer of 1941. For Gross, however, they form another link in the very important sequence of evidence supporting his thesis of exclusive Polish responsibility for the Jedwabne murder.

Omissions and Distortions of the Historical Context

Another characteristic feature of Gross's narrative is the omission of the historical context together with the simultaneous distortion of facts. This applies to both the genesis (the Soviet occupation of eastern Poland and its consequences) and the actual course of the crime in Jedwabne (the role of the Germans).

The Soviet Occupation of Eastern Poland and Polish-Jewish Relations in 1939–1941

In September 1939 the Red Army occupied eastern Poland, including Jedwabne and the entire area around Łomża and Białystok. The occupiers immediately began to impose the Soviet system there. They applied their typically ruthless methods, including arrests, deportations, relocations, and mass executions. These measures had a different im-

---

[63] This thesis was confirmed by, among others, Kazimierz Laudański, who stated in reply to my question: "After their entry the Germans appointed Karolak as 'mayor' and ordered him to look for collaborators. Karolak spoke German." Laudański was informed of this after the fact because he was not in Jedwabne during that time. Interview with Kazimierz Laudański, 28 April 2001.

328 MEMORIES AND METHODOLOGIES

pact on the various national groups in the Polish borderlands (Poles, Ukrainians, Belarusians, Jews). The Jewish population found itself in a particularly difficult situation. On the one hand, its elites were persecuted and many Jewish refugees from central and western Poland were deported to Siberia. On the other hand, the Soviet system created for other Jews new possibilities and new prospects. For many, especially the youth, Soviet rule meant social advancement. The active pursuit of these opportunities set them on a collision course with the other ethnic groups. In this fashion, anti-Jewish sentiments gained a new dimension during the Soviet occupation. The body of traditional prejudices, economic conflicts, and socioreligious differences was reinforced by a new image of Jews profiting from Sovietization and collaborating with the Soviet enemy.[64] Thus Soviet policy significantly intensified the ethnic antagonism already present in these territories before September 1939.

Despite these facts, Gross writes on page 43, "But there is no reason to single out Jedwabne as a place where relationships between Jews and the rest of the population during those twenty months of Soviet rule were more antagonistic than anywhere else." At the same time he suggests that those relations remained more or less the same as they had been in the pre-1939 period. But the sources used by Gross contain more than enough evidence to the contrary.

Gross states, for example, that at the Hoover Institution on War, Revolution and Peace at Stanford University in California, there are only three testimonies with "three general remarks about Jews from Jedwabne, indicating that they displayed zealous support for the Soviet regime" (43).[65] A simple check of that institution's archives shows that the actual number of such accounts is not merely three but at least seven. Furthermore, they do not just indicate "zealous support" but explicitly describe such instances. Aleksander Kotowski of Jedwabne recalled: "Power was given to Jewish and Polish Communists who had been imprisoned [before the war] for communism. They led the NKVD to people's lodgings and homes, and they denounced Polish patriotic

[64] See Musiał, *Kontrrevolutionäre Elemente*, 273–76.

[65] Several hundred thousand Polish citizens had been deported to the Soviet interior during the Soviet occupation of eastern Poland in 1939–1941. Then, in the aftermath of Hitler's attack on the USSR in June 1941, Polish citizens detained in the USSR were "amnestied" and a Polish army was established. In 1942, about 120,000 people—soldiers of the newly created Free Polish Army and their families—were evacuated to Iran. These people were questioned about their experiences under the Soviet regime. Their testimonies can be found in the archives of the Hoover Institution in Stanford, California, filed in two collections: the Polish Government Collection and the Anders Collection (*Neighbors*, 220–21 n. 2).

citizens."[66] Marian Łojewski from Jedwabne: "Numerous arrests were made of the people against whom the local Jewish Communists held a grudge for their own persecution by the Polish authorities."[67] The remaining accounts are similar.[68] We also have two analogous testimonies about the situation in Wizna.[69]

It appears that Gross did not examine the documents found in the Hoover Institution. In Michał Gnatowski's book, which is quoted by Gross in a different context, there is the following passage: "During a conference in Minsk on 20 September 1940, the head of the NKVD for the [Łomża] municipal district stated: 'Such a practice has taken root here. The Jews have supported us and only they were always visible. It has become fashionable for the director of every institution to boast that he no longer has even a single Pole working for him. Many of us were simply afraid of the Poles.' "[70]

Apart from disregarding these accounts, Gross ignored other similar sources as well as the related literature on the subject—which demonstrates the rapid deterioration of Polish-Jewish relations during the Soviet occupation.[71]

The Soviet terror in eastern Poland, both in Jedwabne and in its environs, continued during the retreat of the Red Army before the victorious German *Wehrmacht*. It is true that in that region, unlike the rest of eastern Poland, mass executions of prisoners did not take place; there

[66] Hoover Institution, Poland, Ministerstwo Informacji i Dokumentacji: Powiat Łomża (Reports of Polish Deportees), no. 2675.

[67] Ibid., no. 8455.

[68] Józef Rybicki (ibid., no. 8356), Tadeusz Kiełczewski, both from Jedwabne (ibid., no. 1078), Tadeusz Wądołowski, village of Bronik, township of Jedwabne (ibid., no. 8493), Antoni Śledziński, village of Makowskie, township of Jedwabne (ibid., no. 9990), Corporal Antoni B. from the village of Witynie, township of Jedwabne, as cited in Jan Tomasz Gross and Irena Grudzińska-Gross, eds., *W czterdziestym nas matko na Sybir zesłali . . . Polska a Rosja* (London, 1983), 332.

[69] Tadeusz Nietkiewicz: "Even before the entry of the Red Army the local Jews formed a revolutionary committee, and, as the Red Army entered, they cheered them as they persecuted our soldiers and people in a horrible fashion. A committee and police were formed that were made up mostly of Jews . . . It was the local Jews, and I have much evidence of this, who above all harassed and denounced our people." (Hoover Institution, Reports of Polish Deportees, no. 1932). Józefa Dobrońska: "The Jews were very favorably disposed toward the Soviets and cooperated with them to our great disadvantage. They became the right hand of the Soviets. The activity of the NKVD was based on depriving the population of its freedom by deporting it to the interior of Russia" (ibid., no. 3377).

[70] Gnatowski, *W radzieckich okowach*, 159–60.

[71] See, for example, the monographs of Ben-Cion Pinchuk, *Shtetl Jews under Soviet Rule: Eastern Poland on the Eve of the Holocaust* (Oxford, 1990), and Dov Levin, *The Lesser of Two Evils: Eastern European Jewry under Soviet Rule, 1939–1941* (Philadelphia and Jerusalem, 1995).

simply was not enough time.[72] But in the region of Łomża, as in the entire Soviet zone, another mass deportation of the local populace commenced on 19–20 June 1941. According to Soviet data from the Łomża and Białystok regions, 22,353 persons were deported at that time (entire families, including women, children, and the elderly), and 2,059 individuals were arrested.[73] Numerous families from Jedwabne and Wizna were included in the deportation.[74] The entry for 20 June 1941 in the diary of the Benedictine sisters reads:

> This is the most terrible day for the Poles under the Soviet occupation. Mass deportations to Russia. From early morning carts carrying Polish families drove through the town toward the railway station . . . Wailing, moaning, and terrible despair ruled in Polish souls. On the other hand, the Jews and the Soviets are jubilant. It is impossible to describe what the Poles are going through. A completely hopeless situation. And the Jews and Soviets loudly rejoice and threaten that soon they will deport all the Poles.[75]

It would be unhistorical to conclude that the Jews were either responsible or coresponsible for the Soviet terror in eastern Poland, since Jews were also victims of the very same terror. The responsibility for the deportations lies squarely with the Soviet regime, which enlisted the aid of local collaborators, including those of Jewish origin, to carry out this deed. However, the association, in popular perception, of the last deportation (and the entire Soviet terror) not only with the Soviets but also with actual and supposed Jewish accomplices bore truly tragic consequences for future relations between the Jewish and non-Jewish populations. A Polish witness from Jedwabne related in 1988: "I remember how Poles were rounded up for the transports to Siberia. On every wagon there sat a Jew with a rifle. Mothers, wives, and children fell on their knees begging for mercy, for help. The last such transport left on 21 June 1941."[76] There exist many similar Polish complaints about the behavior of Jews in Jedwabne during the Soviet rule there; we may also add that, in this respect, Jedwabne does not constitute an exception.[77]

[72] See Musiał, *Konterrevolutionäre Elemente*, 98–171, especially 99 concerning the prison in Łomża.

[73] Gnatowski, *W radzieckich okowach*, 115.

[74] Katolicka Agencja Informacyjna, ISSN 1426-1413, 23 February 2001; and interview with Jadwiga Szymanowska, 23 February 2001, Wizna.

[75] *Kronika Panien Benedyktynek*, 74–75.

[76] Cited in Danuta and Aleksander Wroniszewski, ". . . aby żyć," *Kontakty—Łomżyński Tygodnik Społeczny*, 10 July 1988.

[77] Compare, for example, Krzysztof Rółycki, "Sąsiad twój wróg," *Angora*, 17 September 2000; Tomasz Strzembosz, "Uroczysko Kobielno: Z dziejów konspiracji i partyzantki

The Yad Vashem Institute holds the 1966 testimony of Chaja and Israel Finkelstein from Radziłów. The person who recorded their accounts observed: "The communal worker [i.e., Chaja Finkelstein (BM)] observed how the hatred of the Poles grew against the Jewish activists of the new regime [1939–1941]. She felt in advance that revenge would at some time be taken against all Jews."[78] Dov Levin concludes, "Labeling of the Soviet administration as a 'Jewish regime' became widespread when Jewish militiamen helped NKVD agents send local Poles into exile."[79] Yitzhak Arad writes:

During the night of June 14, 1941, the town [Święciany] was shocked when NKVD and militia members took hundreds of people from their houses and placed them under arrest. Most of those arrested had been officials of the Polish government, landowners, officers in the Polish army, men who had been wealthy or active in political parties (excluding the Communist party). That night similar raids took place throughout Lithuania; close to 30,000 people, entire families among them, were arrested and deported to Siberia and Kazakhstan. Among those were five to six thousand Jews . . . But the expulsions also brought about increased anti-Semitism, because although there were thousands of Jews among the exiles, Jews played a relatively large role in the Communist party apparatus that was behind the action. In this situation, with overall fear of further expulsions and rising hatred of both the Soviet regime and the Jews, the German army invaded the Soviet Union.[80]

Michel Mielnicki from Wasilków near Białystok (born 1927), who at present lives in Canada, recalls how his father, Chaim Mielnicki, collaborated with the NKVD to the detriment of the Poles:

I do remember, however, the NKVD commissars from Moscow, who would most often arrive at our house after dark, sitting in the living room, smoking one cigarette after another until they could barely see each other through the haze, talking in low voices with Father, as they went over their lists of suspected fifth columnists (so-called *Volksdeutscher* Poles), Polish fascists, ultranationalists, and other local "traitors" and "counter-revolutionaries."

---

nad Biebrzą, 1939–1940," *Karta*, no. 5 (May–June 1991): 3–27; and an expanded version in *Ziemia Łomżyńska*, no. 6 (2001): 367–401.

[78] Yad Vashem Archives, File 033033-2636/256.

[79] Levin, *The Lesser of Two Evils*, 63.

[80] Yitzhak Arad, *The Partisan: From the Valley of Death to Mount Zion* (New York, 1979), 26–27.

It was my understanding that he served as advisor to the NKVD
about who among the local Poles was to be sent to Siberia, or otherwise dealt with . . . My mother was terribly upset by my father's
collaboration with the Russian secret service . . . I remember her
begging him not to get involved. He disagreed. "We have to get
rid of the fascists," he told her. "They deserve to go to Siberia.
They are not good for the Jewish people . . ."

Naturally, word of Father's clandestine activities got out . . .
Consequently, when the Germans invaded Russia in June 1941, the
name of Chaim Mielnicki was on the hit lists of both the local anti-
Semites (who proved more numerous than anyone imagined) and
their new-found allies, the *Gestapo*.[81]

Such collaborators constituted a relatively small portion of the Jewish
community, but they were highly visible and very active. The fear and
loathing of them was extended, by association, to the entire Jewish minority, causing a very distinct rise in antisemitic sentiment. For his
part, Gross has completely glossed over these important facts. Nevertheless, it was precisely the Soviet policies and their social perception
that brought about, in the summer of 1941, an increased resentment of
Jews, and this, in its turn, shaped the anti-Jewish mood among the Polish population.[82]

Gross's omission and distortion of this historical context might possibly be explained by his lack of familiarity with the source material
and the literature on the subject. However, such an explanation would
be incorrect, since Gross himself wrote in 1983, "Antisemitism grew
vehemently during the Bolshevik occupation, as soon became apparent in the first days of the Soviet-Hitlerite war in the summer of 1941."
At that time, Gross perceived the reason for this rise in antisemitic feelings to be "Jewish collaboration with the Soviet authorities."[83]

The Role of the Germans

In a similarly selective and self-contradictory way Gross describes the
course of the destruction of the Jews in Jedwabne. He states on page
78 of *Neighbors*: "As to the Germans' direct participation in the mass
murder of Jews in Jedwabne on July 10, 1941, however, one must admit

---

[81] John Munro, *Białystok to Birkenau: The Holocaust Journey of Michel Mielnicki* (Vancou-
ver, 2000), 82–84.

[82] See Musiał, *Konterrevolutionäre Elemente*, 71–81.

[83] Gross and Grudzińska-Gross, *W czterdziestym*, 28–30. The author is not aware of a
publication in which Gross has revised, in a scholarly and substantiated way, the findings he made in 1983.

that it was limited, pretty much, to their taking pictures." The trial records, on the basis of which Gross has constructed his book, as well as the depositions taken during the 1949 investigation and accepted by Gross as trustworthy, explicitly contradict this statement.

A few examples follow. Stanisław Zejer: "They [Stanisław Sokołowski, Józef Kobrzyniecki, and Stanisław Sakowski] took part with me in the herding of the Jews on the order of the mayor and the Gestapo."[84] Stanisław Dąbrowski: "The task was to make sure that not a single Jew would cross the lines, which I did because I had received such an order from Karolak, Sobóta, and a German."[85] Feliks Tarnacki: "On the day when the roundup of the Jews took place, the mayor, Marian Karolak, and the town council secretary, Wasilewski (I do not know his first name), came to my place with a Gestapo man and chased me out to the market square."[86] Roman Górski: "On that day I arrived home at 12 o'clock . . . At that time Marian Karolak, who was the mayor, came over with a German gendarme who kicked me, and they took me to the main square of the town of Jedwabne where they ordered me . . . to guard the Jews so that they wouldn't escape, and I did it."[87] Władysław Minciura: "In July 1941 . . . several cars with Gestapo men arrived and organized a roundup of the Jews, herding them into the market square . . . A gendarme came and told me to go to the market square to guard the Jews so that they wouldn't escape . . . I guarded the Jews until 4 P.M. Afterward I was going back to work, but they told me not to work but to herd the Jews into the barn, which I did, and I stayed there until the barn, which was full of Jews, was set on fire."[88] Bolesław Ramotowski: "Yes, I admit that in the summer of 1941 in Jedwabne . . . , acting under orders from the mayor and the German gendarmerie, I took part in guarding the Jewish population, which had been herded into the market square."[89]

In the certificate of indictment, which was based at least in part on forced confessions, we find the following sentence: "All of the accused justified their actions by stating that they had acted on orders of the

[84] Interrogation record of the accused Stanisław Zejer of 11 January 1949, IPN, SOŁ 123, 605v.
[85] Interrogation record of the accused Stanisław Dąbrowski of 11 January 1949, ibid., 610v.
[86] Interrogation record of the accused Feliks Tarnacki of 11 January 1949, ibid., 612v.
[87] Interrogation record of the accused Roman Górski of 10 January 1949, ibid., 616–616v.
[88] Interrogation record of the accused Władysław Minciura of 10 January 1949, ibid., 619v.
[89] Interrogation record of the accused Bolesław Ramotowski of 10 January 1949, ibid., 646v.

German authorities."[90] This matter is expressed even more emphatically in the verdict: "The local population, including the defendants, were forced to participate [in the crime] by terror, as can be seen from all the testimonies of the defendants, wherever they have been deposed, and from the depositions of witnesses."[91] These findings of the court, which constitute a summary of the findings of the investigation and the court proceedings, have not been considered in Gross's book.

A fundamental prerequisite of a scholarly approach to any subject is the critical analysis of any and all available testimonies, depositions, accounts, and documents. One may ignore only those sources about whose veracity there exist reasonable doubts. However, it is unacceptable to disregard specific documents only because their content does not fit a preconceived thesis.

The State Archives in Łomża contain numerous depositions that point to the exclusively German instigation of the Jedwabne crime. These depositions were collected in 1947–1949 by the Town Court in Łomża to certify the deaths of local Holocaust victims. Some examples follow. Helena Chrzanowska stated, "Abram Kruk [Chrzanowska's grandfather] . . . was murdered by the Germans in a barn, by burning, on 10 July 1941."[92] A similar testimony was given by "Jankiel Bein, 46, of the Mosaic faith . . . 'I was a permanent resident of Jedwabne. On 10 July 1941 I saw how the Germans herded all the Jews into a barn, and then they set it on fire . . . At that time I was hiding from the Germans. On that day I was hiding in the cemetery, and I saw everything.' "[93] Witness Zelik Lewiński testified on 30 July 1949: "I, along with the father of the petitioner, was in a group of people being herded into the barn, but at the last moment I managed to escape and hide by the cemetery wall near the barn. I declare with utmost certainty that I saw with my own eyes how Zelik Zdrojewicz was chased by the Germans into the barn, and how they eventually set the barn on fire with all the Jews inside. Several hundred Jews were burned in that barn."[94]

At least twenty-eight testimonies of this kind, deposed by nineteen witnesses (including nine by the relatives of the victims), have been preserved. Among these nineteen witnesses, nine described them-

---

[90] Certificate of indictment of 31 March 1949, ibid., 3v.

[91] Reasons for the verdict, ibid., 227.

[92] Helena Chrzanowska, application to confirm a death, 25 October 1948. APŁ, SGŁ Zg 334/48.

[93] Record of 2 October 1948, APŁ, SGŁ Zg 308/48.

[94] Record of 30 June 1949, APŁ, SGŁ Zg 105/49.

selves as eyewitnesses, and five of these were Jewish.[95] In all of these documents the Germans are identified as the perpetrators of the crime in Jedwabne.

Of course, the question arises as to how trustworthy these depositions are. It is certain that these documents must be approached with caution because of the circumstances in which the testimonies were collected. The deponents did not strive to discover the culprits and to reconstruct the events of the pogrom precisely. Instead, they aimed simply for the quickest possible issue of death certificates for their relatives. We thus cannot exclude the possibility of the petitioners' exchanging mutual favors and testifying on each other's behalf in order to obtain official documents entitling them to perform numerous legal actions, for example, to receive inheritance. Eljasz Grądowski, for instance, made several such depositions, sometimes presenting himself as an eyewitness and on other occasions stating that, at the time in question, he had lived in the interior of the Soviet Union.[96]

It is also worth mentioning that the deponents might have named the Germans as the culprits in order to avoid any further questioning by the court about the specific circumstances of the deaths of the petitioners' relatives. In this way the procedure of issuing death certificates was accelerated. In the reasons for the confirmation of the death of Bluma Grądowska (Eljasz's mother) there appears the following statement: "On the basis of the witnesses' testimonies it has been ascertained that, on 10 July 1941, the Germans herded all the Jews of Jedwabne, including Bluma Grondowska, into a barn and burned them. The aforementioned witnesses saw the murder with their own eyes. Furthermore, the court states that the fact of the burning of the Jewish population of Jedwabne in a barn is common knowledge; therefore there exists no doubt whatsoever that Bluma Grondowska was burned alive."[97]

It is a certainty that Polish citizens of Jedwabne took an active part in the massacre of 10 July 1941. Their number probably ranged between a dozen or so to several score.[98] We can also safely assume that some of them voluntarily took part in some anti-Jewish excesses. On the other

[95] APŁ, SGŁ Zg. 167/47, 236/47, 129/48, 130/48, 165/48, 234/48, 235/48, 308/48, 334/48, 105/49, 178/49, Co 4/47, 13/47, 52/47.

[96] Record of 25 February 1947, APŁ, SGŁ, Co 13/47; record of 29 May 1948, ibid., Zg 129/48; record of 8 July 1947, ibid., Co 52/47.

[97] Reasons for certifying a death, 24 May 1948, APŁ, SGŁ Zg 130/48.

[98] Gross writes, "Sources at our disposal cite, by my count, ninety-two names (and, often, home addresses to boot) of people who participated in the murders of Jedwabne Jews" (86). This number has no reliable basis in the sources.

hand, there are numerous indications that the Germans used coercion, and even violence, to force the Polish inhabitants to participate in the crime. Moreover, we cannot forget about the instances of Polish assistance to the persecuted Jews. Józef Grądowski testified, "Thanks to the help of a certain man, I managed to escape from the hands of the Germans."[99] The fact that at least one hundred Jews escaped from the Jedwabne massacre is an indication that this was not the only instance of such help.

There is sufficient evidence in the sources used by Gross to indicate that the murder of 10 July 1941 was planned, organized, and conducted by the Germans with some Polish participation. This thesis is also supported by other sources whose existence has been known of for a long time.[100] They include the order of Reinhard Heydrich, the chief of the Security Police and the Security Service, addressed to the *Einsatzgruppen* on 1 July 1941:

> Order Number 2: Poles residing in the newly occupied Polish territories may be expected, *on the basis of their experiences*, to be anti-Communist and also anti-Jewish. It is obvious that the cleansing activities have to extend first of all to the Bolsheviks and the Jews. As for the Polish intelligentsia and others, decisions can be taken later, unless there is a special reason for taking action in individual cases considered to be dangerous. It is therefore obvious that such Poles need not be included in the cleansing action, especially as they are of great importance as elements for initiating pogroms and for obtaining information. (This depends, of course, on local conditions.) (Emphasis in source)[101]

The *Einsatzkommandos* belonging to the *Einsatzgruppe* B, whose area of operations covered the Łomża region (including Jedwabne), were present in the vicinity of Minsk, in Belarus, on 10 July 1941. Gross notes this fact correctly on pages 23–24, but his subsequent conclusion regarding this detail as further proof that the Jedwabne murder was a local Polish initiative is mistaken: at the time, special *Einsatzkommandos* continued to be active in the environs of Łomża and Białystok, as established in the 1960s by the Zentralen Stelle der Landesjustizverwal-

[99] Witness interrogation record of 29 March 1949, IPN, SOŁ 123, 749.

[100] Alexander B. Rossino writes about this matter in detail in his study "Polish 'Neighbors' and German Invaders: Contextualizing Anti-Jewish Violence in the Białystok District during the Opening Weeks of Operation Barbarossa," *Polin: Studies in Polish Jewry* 16 (London, 2003) and posted on the Internet at http://www.pogranicze.sejny.pl/jedwabne/angielskie/rossino.html.

[101] Ereignismeldungen UdSSR, no. 10, 2 July 1941, Bundesarchiv, Berlin, R. 58/214, 52–53.

tungen (Central Bureau) in Ludwigsburg, Germany, which is charged
with the prosecution of Nazi crimes:

> With the beginning of the Russian campaign the *Einsatzkommando*s
> of the Security Police followed the fighting units into the occupied
> territories in the East . . . Since the German units advanced more
> quickly than the *Einsatzkommando*s could carry out their tasks, in
> the hinterland of the front, especially in the Białystok region, in
> the area of operation of *Einsatzgruppe* B (*Einsatzkommando*s 7–9),
> was a zone where there were no police forces. In order to ensure
> the execution of the police tasks in these territories, the Main Secu-
> rity Office of the Reich (RSHA) ordered the creation of special *Ein-*
> *satzkommando*s (abbreviation: EK z b. V). They were to be created
> by the offices of the State Police in territorial units contiguous to
> the occupied territories. They were to take over the tasks of the
> *Einsatzkommando*s that had been there earlier. About these special
> *Einsatzkommando*s the following information, among other infor-
> mation, has been preserved in the "*Ereignismeldungen UdSSR*"
> of the Chief of the Security Police and Security Services . . . :
> "In order to ensure the greatest latitude for the operation of the
> *Einsatzgruppen* and *Einsatzkommando*s permission was given to
> the chief of the Security Police in Kraków as well as to the State
> Police Offices in Tilsit and Allenstein (Olsztyn) to cleanse the bor-
> der territories with the help of additional provisional *Einsatzkom-*
> *mando*s . . . In subsequent *Ereignismeldungen* one can find reports
> of the activities of these additional provisional *Einsatzkommando*s
> of the Offices of the State Police in Tilsit and Allenstein as well as
> of the group of the commandant of the Security Police in Warsaw
> regarding the Białystok region. It is worth noting that the Com-
> mando of the State Police Office in Ciechanów-Płock, which also
> borders on the Białystok region, is not named in the aforemen-
> tioned '*Ereignismeldungen*.' In spite of this, it has been established
> that such an *Einsatzkommando* of the State Police in Ciechanów-
> Płock did operate in the Białystok district, especially in the county
> of Łomża."[102]

One Hermann Schaper has been tentatively identified as the possible
commander of the *Einsatzkommando* of the State Police Office in Ciecha-
nów-Płock. His group has been accused of committing the following
crimes: the shooting of Jews in Tykocin (about 30 km from Jedwabne)
at the beginning of August 1941, the killing of Jews in Radziłów (15

---

[102] Abschlußbericht, 17 March 1964, BA-AL, 205 AR-Z 13/62, 156–57; for details see
Rossino, "Polish 'Neighbors.' "

km from Jedwabne) by burning them alive in a barn, the shooting of Jews in Rutki (about 20 km from Jedwabne) on 4 September 1941, the shooting of Jews in Zambrów (about 35 km from Jedwabne) in the summer of 1941, the shooting of Jews in Łomża (18 km from Jedwabne) in August 1941, and the "liquidation" of Jews in Jedwabne on 10 July 1941 and in Wizna at the end of June 1941. Hermann Schaper was recognized by Jewish witnesses as the person in charge of the operations in Tykocin and Radziłów. After 1945 he lived in West Germany under an assumed identity, returning to his true surname in 1953. The Central Bureau in Ludwigsburg, however, did not have sufficient proof (apart from a few testimonies and some circumstantial evidence) to initiate formal proceedings against Schaper, who continued to deny everything.[103]

Gross did not conduct research in any German archive. On page 211 n. 1 of *Neighbors*, he writes, "Neither David Engel nor Christopher Browning, who both thoroughly know German archives pertaining to the period, was familiar with the name of the town Jedwabne." Indeed, Christopher Browning knows the German archives very well, but the same probably cannot be said about David Engel. Furthermore, a simple query directed to the Central Bureau in Ludwigsburg would have revealed the fact that Jedwabne is listed in their index as a murder site of Jews, and that an investigation of this case had once been opened. Even after perusing the *Ereignismeldungen*, copies of which are available in the United States and Poland, Gross could have learned that provisionally organized *Einsatzkommandos* operated in the area of Białystok.[104]

The results of the investigations undertaken by the Central Bureau in Ludwigsburg do not provide definitive proof of German instigation of the Jedwabne crime. Nevertheless, they establish the presence of special *Einsatzkommandos*, which perpetrated massacres of Jews, in the Łomża region in the summer of 1941. It is also worth keeping in mind that the sources used by Gross contain numerous references to the arrival of just such a commando unit in Jedwabne on the critical day.

Wasersztajn states (quoted in *Neighbors*, 18), "On the morning of July 10, 1941, eight gestapo men came to town." In the testimony of Jerzy Laudański, treated by Gross as reliable, we read: "[On 10 July] 1941 four or five Gestapo men arrived in a car." Karol Bardoń testified, "Before the start of this mass murder . . . I saw in front of the Jedwabne

---

[103] Ibid., 157–66; notation of 8 September 1965, ibid., 195–200; for details see Rossino, "Polish 'Neighbors.' "

[104] Gross states mistakenly (211 n. 1) that these reports are found in the Bundesarchiv in Koblenz. In fact since 1996 they have been located in the Bundesarchiv in Berlin.

town hall a few gestapo men, but I don't remember if it was on the day of the mass murder or the day before."[105] Władysław Minciura said, "In July 1941, I don't remember the exact date, several cars came with Gestapo men inside, and they organized a roundup of Jews, herding them all into the market square."[106] Witness Julia Sokołowska stated in the presence of the court that sixty-eight Gestapo men, as well as many gendarmes from nearby posts, arrived in Jedwabne on 10 July 1941.[107] These numbers seem to be exaggerated; perhaps Sokołowska tried in this way to deflect the charge of collaboration with the Germans from the accused Poles.

A mobile armed unit consisting of several members of the security police, aided by eleven local gendarmes (according to Gross, page 76), was quite sufficient to carry out an operation like the one in Jedwabne. The Germans could also make use of the Polish members of the auxiliary police.[108] Such a commando would then follow specific directives (e.g., Heydrich's order), effectively exploiting the strong anti-Jewish sentiments that were in large measure the product of the Soviet occupation. Moreover, the Germans could freely give orders to both the Polish and the Jewish inhabitants of Jedwabne, which—according to the sources—they did. Such a force was absolutely sufficient to the task of burning several hundred Jews in a barn.

A clear distinction needs to be drawn between the crimes against Jews in Jedwabne or Radziłów and the pogroms that took place after the German entry into the territory of present-day western Ukraine. The latter had occurred immediately after the Soviet retreat from these areas, in a very tense social and nationalistic situation, among eruptions of extreme emotions often caused by the grisly discoveries of atrocities committed by the NKVD.[109] The Jedwabne massacre took place two weeks after the entry of the Germans, making it difficult to speak of a sudden, autonomous explosion of anti-Jewish violence there. There are many indications that this particular action was organized and conducted by the Germans with Polish participation.

Spontaneous eruptions of violence in the Łomża area had taken place earlier, immediately after the arrival of the Germans. At that time, the local population staged regular hunts for the Soviets and for

[105] Cited in Gross, 75.

[106] Witness interrogation record of 10 January 1949, IPN, SOŁ 123, 619v.

[107] Transcript of the main proceedings of 16 May 1949, IPN, SOŁ 123, 209v.

[108] Perhaps among their members were Jerzy Laudański, who admitted to being a messenger for the gendarmes (IPN, SOŁ 123, 665), and Karol Bardoń (reasons for the verdict, ibid., 227), who later was put on the German *Volkslist* (State Archives in Białystok, Der Landrat-Kreiskommisar des Kreis Lomscha, 1:12–15, 23–24).

[109] Musiał, *Konterrevolutionäre Elemente*, 172–99.

their actual and alleged collaborators, and sometimes their families, whether Jewish or Polish. Gross himself comments on this (54–56). The earlier violence had a clearly anti-Soviet overtone. Similar events took place in the summer of 1941 in virtually all of the territories recently conquered by the Germans.[110]

Conclusion

As demonstrated above, Jan T. Gross's *Neighbors* contains numerous contradictions, erroneous interpretations, unhistorical speculations, and false statements. Furthermore, this publication levels serious allegations against specific individuals; as it turns out, however, they are based on unconfirmed sources, false accusations, and "proof" constructed ad hoc by the author himself, which, later on, are explained away as "oversights."

Of course, the examples discussed above do not exhaust the subject; an analysis of all the strictures regarding *Neighbors* would vastly exceed the limits of this article.[111] It is unusual, however, to find so many serious errors and flaws in a small book that is a mere two hundred pages in length after just a partial analysis. Nonetheless, many renowned academics, as well as Gross himself, consider *Neighbors* a work of scholarship.[112] The shortcomings of this book disqualify both its intrinsic value and Gross's "affirmative" approach to the sources.

Neighbors is a model example of the current tendencies toward the "ahistoricizing" of the Holocaust (the extermination of the Jews is removed from the context of the Second World War, while the war itself

[110] Ibid., 192–99.

[111] An example of such strictures is the author's citing of works and sources that do not contain the information that he states they do in his book. For example, after citing Tadeusz Frączek, Gross writes: "After the war various anti-German guerrilla detachments continued their activities, directed now against the Communist Party–sponsored state authorities. Detachments of NSZ (National Armed Forces), NOW (National Military Organization), and NZW (National Military Association) that were active in this region killed numerous Jews, communists, and other people whom they considered undesirable. In Frączek's doctoral dissertation ('Formacje zbrojne obozu narodowego na Białostocczyźnie w latach 1939–1956'), quoted earlier, we find ample information on this aspect of their postwar activities (see pp. 150–51, 187, 194, 254, 297)" (229 n. 8). After examining that manuscript I was able to ascertain that pages 150, 151, and 187 contain no information about any executions.

[112] Gross stated on 17 May 2001 in an Internet discussion on the Web site of *Gazeta Wyborcza*: "*Neighbors* is a scholarly publication written on the basis of the available documentation of the topic and conscientious research. If you take the book into your hands, it is easy to ascertain that it contains notes and references." Posted online at: http://www.gazeta.pl/alfa/home.jespłdzial=050406.

is reduced to the Holocaust) and toward the mythologization and mystification of the historical events (the Holocaust as a rationally inexplicable event). These two trends are conditional upon each other: the lack of a proper contextual analysis makes the events in question incomprehensible. This is complemented by insufficient "quality control" in the realm of Holocaust research, which has been pointed out by, among others, Raul Hilberg.[113]

Neighbors is a textbook case of a selective and manipulative use of sources that serves only to confirm a preconceived thesis and, at the same time, to obscure the historical truth. Even Gross's public pronouncements indicate that he had had a clearly formed opinion about the events in question long before he began his archival research. In an interview published in the *New Yorker* he stated: "I read the testimony of Szmul Wasersztajn, a witness to the Jedwabne pogrom . . . several years ago . . . For me the moment of realization that Wasersztajn had to be taken literally came when I saw, by coincidence, raw footage for a documentary on Polish-Jewish relations that a filmmaker, Agnieszka Arnold, was working on . . . When I saw this woman on the television screen saying something to the effect of 'They took the keys to the barn from my father. What could he do?' I had an epiphany. I realized instantly that this all had happened."[114]

Similarly, he writes in *Neighbors* on pages 21–22: "This is, more or less, the amount of time [four years] that elapsed between my discovery of Wasersztajn's testimony in JHI's [the Jewish Historical Institute's] archives and my grasp of its factuality . . . I watched raw footage for the documentary film *Where Is My Older Brother Cain?* made by Agnieszka Arnold, who, among other interlocutors, spoke with the daughter of Bronisław Śleszyński, and I realized that Wasersztajn has to be taken literally." Thus it becomes quite obvious that Gross took for granted the accuracy of Wasersztajn's account before even looking at the other historical sources.

After stripping the Jedwabne tragedy of its proper historical context, Gross declares that it is impossible to discover a rational explanation for its origins. To a question from the *Kontakty* journalist about the reasons for the massacre he responds: "The only explanation is as follows: the devil descended on the earth. It does happen from time to time. Unless you have a different answer."[115] In the Polish version of *Neighbors* we find the following passage, which does not appear in the En-

[113] "Rücksicht auf die Verbündeten," *Berliner Zeitung*, 4 September 2000.
[114] "Jan Gross on Poland's Shame," *New Yorker*, 12 March 2001; likewise in the interview in the *Badische Zeitung*, 22 March 2001.
[115] "Diabeł zstąpił do Jedwabnego," *Kontakty*, 25 February 2001.

glish version: "[A]n evil spirit was necessary to awaken and activate that monster [that is, according to Gross, the desire to murder on the part of the peasant "rabble"] drowsing in people" (83). At the same time Gross holds that "[e]ver since Khmielnicki's peasant wars (which in Jewish mythologized memory are encoded by the terrifying word *Khurban*, catastrophe, a foreshadowing of the Shoah), Jews had suffered the destructive force inimical to everything different that lay in wait in the countryside of those lands, bursting into the open, occasionally, in paroxysms of violence" (123).

This style of reasoning reminds one of Daniel Jonah Goldhagen's thesis about the "eliminationist anti-Semitism" of the Germans.[116] Meanwhile, Goldhagen's pronouncements are not being treated seriously by the experts, although at first they were hailed as a milestone in Holocaust historiography. The advance publicity for Gross's book sounds disturbingly similar. The dust jacket of the English-language edition of *Neighbors* bears the following statement: "It is the most important study of Polish-Jewish relations to be published in decades and should become a classic of Holocaust literature . . . Gross's new and persuasive answers to vexed questions rewrite the history of twentieth-century Poland."

In the course of his research Gross has taken into account only those sources (or their isolated fragments) that conform with his own preconceived notion of the events. Everything else he has either ignored or deemed unreliable without even so much as attempting a scholarly verification. Gross shuns on principle many important primary and secondary sources—Jewish testimonies, works by Jewish historians, even his own earlier publications—that contradict the thesis of *Neighbors*. Ignoring of inconvenient testimonies of Holocaust survivors in this way is an inescapable consequence of the "affirmative" approach to selected sources. After all, it may happen—and it does happen in the case of Jedwabne, for example in the depositions of Eljasz and Józef Grądowski—that one testimony contradicts another. A factual consideration of the entire available historical material would immediately reveal the absurdity of Gross's "affirmative method."

In the light of all this, it is easy to understand why the author of *Neighbors* avoids any discussion of the merits of his thesis and the results of his research. He either ignores criticisms or attacks their authors *ad personam*.[117]

---

[116] Daniel Jonah Goldhagen, *Hitler's Willing Executioners: Ordinary Germans and the Holocaust* (New York, 1996).

[117] For example, Gross accused his opponent, Tomasz Strzembosz, a highly regarded historian, of "propagating historical falsehoods that demonstrate Strzembosz's antipa-

A solid, scholarly study of the murder in Jedwabne would be very desirable indeed. *Neighbors*, however, is not such a work.

· · · · ·

Bogdan Musiał was born in 1960. A historian, he is an academician at the German Historical Institute in Warsaw. The scientific article in which he proved that the exhibition *Wehrmacht Crimes* comprises materials illustrating NKVD crimes brought him international fame. He is the author of *Deutsche Zivilverwaltung und Judenverfolgung in General-gouvernement. Eine Fallstudie zum Distrikt Lublin* (German civil authorities and persecution of the Jews: The case of the Lublin District) (Wiesbaden, 1999); *"Konterrevolutionäre Elemente sind zu erschießen". Die Brutalisierung des deutsch-sowjetischen Krieges in Sommer 1941* ("Counterrevolutionary elements are to be shot": The brutalization of the German-Soviet war in the summer of 1941) (Berlin, 2000); and *Stosunki polsko-żydowskie na Kresach Wschodnich RP pod okupacją sowiecką 1939–1941* (Polish-Jewish relations in the Polish eastern marches under Soviet occupation 1939–1941) (forthcoming). He lives in Warsaw.

---

thies toward Jews," and asserted that "by writing texts full of biases and distortions in his own defense, Strzembosz sows confusion not only among the drunkards from Jedwabne but also among the sources of influential public opinion." Gross deprecatingly described Piotr Gontarczyk, another adversary of his, as a "juvenile historian" (Gross, "A jednak sąsiedzi," *Rzeczpospolita*, 11 April 2001).

Jan Gross

CRITICAL REMARKS INDEED

BOGDAN MUSIAŁ concludes the opening section of his "Critical Remarks" about *Neighbors* by asserting that I based my research on a "scant selection of sources," and that "[e]ven more disturbing than the glaring narrowness of such a source base is the unprofessional way in which it has been interpreted by Gross." I'll deal with Musiał's observations about the professionalism of my ways in what follows. Here, I simply want to state for the record that I used all the extant sources about the Jedwabne massacre; that no other sources of any significance have been found since; and that those developed after the publication of the book—through the first-rate investigative reporting of several journalists (Anna Bikont, Andrzej Kaczyński, and Adam Wilma in particular) and the brilliant work of documentary filmmaker Agnieszka Arnold—have all amplified and confirmed the findings presented in *Neighbors*.

The reader of Musiał's remarks should also know that on 19 December 2001, the Institute of National Memory (IPN) held a widely advertised and well-covered press conference where several leading officers from the institute unveiled the preliminary conclusions of the Jedwabne murder investigation.[1] The head of the IPN, Prof. Leon Kieres, stated on this occasion "that no proof whatsoever was uncovered during the investigation of any armed German unit coming to Jedwabne on 10 July," while another IPN expert and investigator, Prof. Andrzej Rzepliński, analyzed evidence produced during the 1949 Łomża trial and found it to be a reliable source of information about the July 1941 killing.[2] "Poles were actual executors" of the crime, an-

[1] Musiał's submission of his article came about three months after the press conference was held. The IPN investigation of the Jedwabne murders was opened in September 2000. In October of 2002, a two-volume compilation of Jedwabne-related court and archival documents, as well as expert studies, was published by the Institute of National Memory—*Wokół Jedwabnego*, ed. Paweł Machcewicz and Krzysztof Persak (Warsaw, 2002)—more than 1,500 pages altogether.

[2] The trial, in his assessment, offers "a history of neglect and nonaction, indicating that the judicial authorities were uninterested in shedding light on the circumstances of the crime. Some of the defendants testified during the trial that they were forced during the investigation to give false depositions. Prof. Rzepliński did not exclude the possibility that the defendants were beaten [during investigation], but if so the aim was not to extract their confessions. In other trials of this period defendants who had been tortured

nounces a front-page headline in *Rzeczpospolita* reporting on the IPN's press conference.[3]

Thus whoever reads Musiał's emphatic claims "that there is sufficient evidence in the sources used by Gross to indicate that the murder of 10 July 1941 was planned, organized, and conducted by the Germans with some Polish participation"; that the 1949 Łomża trial of a score of Jedwabne murderers was "a classic example of a 'fix' so typical of Stalinist Poland" and therefore unreliable as a source of information on the actions of perpetrators; whoever reads Musiał's long disquisition on the German police unit under the command of Hermann Schaper and Musiał's carefully weighed opinion that "[a] mobile armed unit consisting of several members of the security police aided by eleven local gendarmes . . . , was quite sufficient to carry out an operation like the one in Jedwabne" should know that these arguments and suggestions did not survive scrutiny by media or historians, except among the right-wing, nationalist, milieus. All of this has now been refuted directly by the findings of the IPN's investigation.

Musiał does not care to mention the results of the IPN's investigation in his "Critical Remarks." He fails to address these findings despite his stated conviction that "[a] fundamental prerequisite of a scholarly approach to any subject is a critical analysis of any and all available testimonies, depositions, accounts, and documents. One may ignore only those sources," he continues, "about whose veracity there exist reasonable doubts. However, it is unacceptable to disregard specific documents only because their content does not fit a preconceived thesis." Musiał articulates the above credo to castigate me for not mentioning documents that came to light some eight months *after* the pub-

---

also made self-incriminating statements in the courtroom. Courts [judging the Jedwabne murder cases] were not interested in finding out who was injured, by whom, and for what reason. Sentences were not unjust for the accused; indeed, some of the perpetrators were found not guilty as a result of the court's sloppiness. The court reconstructed only the course of events on the market square and came up with an absurd image of a *danse macabre* where one German would guard one Pole so that he would guard one Jew, but only until the German turned around" (*Rzeczpospolita*, 20 December 2001).

In the first volume of *Wokół Jedwabnego* Rzepliński published his full study, more than one hundred pages long, in which he documents these points in detail. By the time the volumes went to print, the IPN team of scholars had identified sixty-one postwar trials from the Białystok court district alone, in which Poles were accused after the war of having been involved in killings of their Jewish neighbors in the summer of 1941. It is evident from these court records—many of which are published in the IPN volumes—that mass killings took place all over the area, and that the courts in Poland after the war prosecuted perpetrators of these murders with utmost reluctance, convicting only a handful. Rzepliński makes the same points about the Jedwabne trial—see, for example, *Wokół Jedwabnego*, 1:368, 373, 374, 405, 406, 408–411.

[3] "Bezpośrednimi sprawcami byli Polacy," *Rzeczpospolita*, 20 December 2001.

lication of *Neighbors*, and that are worthless as a source of information about the circumstances of the Jedwabne murders.[4] Endowed with such a degree of self-awareness concerning requisites of sound scholarship, without batting an eye, Musiał ignores the findings of a more than yearlong, intense, and scrupulous investigation by the IPN that renders all his central claims vacuous.

One could at this point desist from any further exegesis of Musiał's text on the grounds that it is simply dishonest and misleading. We're dealing here with a polemicist who engages in major historical controversies in bad faith. Ostensibly engaging with the substance of historical interpretation, he actually diverts his readers' attention to the historiographical marginalia, which he often distorts, the better to draw attention away from the substantive scholarly and moral issues at hand to which he has no contribution to offer. Given the horrible crime that is portrayed in *Neighbors*—a mass murder committed with savage cruelty—the sarcasm and opaqueness of Musiał's text makes it additionally unpalatable. Hence I undertake my task reluctantly and as a public service.[5]

---

[4] On 26 March 2001 newspapers in Poland reported on a press conference held in the State Archives in Warsaw where twenty-eight folders found in the archives of the Łomża Municipal Court were presented. These were files of cases brought by descendants of people who were killed during the war. Petitioners filing these cases needed to obtain official death certificates in order to take possession of family property that they couldn't otherwise inherit. Such cases were handled en masse at the time all over Poland, since Germans, as a rule, did not issue death certificates to families of people whom they killed in mass executions. Hence, after the war, to get a death certificate for a slain family member, one had to make a sworn deposition, confirmed by a witness, that one's relative was killed by the Germans in such and such circumstances, and the matter was settled.

Little wonder that five relatives of murdered Jedwabne Jews made statements following this blueprint and not a word appears in their depositions describing how their family members were killed or asserting that Polish neighbors had anything to do with their death. Needless to say, truthful testimony about the circumstances of Jedwabne murders would have led to the opening of a criminal case and a lengthy investigation instead of prompt issuing by the court of a death certificate. Except for the right-wing nationalist press, which had a field day showing *Neighbors* to be contradicted by Jewish testimonies, the issue promptly died as commentators noted that the content of these testimonies was tailored to obtain a specific document quickly and sheds no light on the actual circumstances of the Jedwabne massacre.

On the unreliability of these depositions and various swindles that were perpetrated by people giving false testimony in such cases in order to claim property that was not theirs, see Krzysztof Persak's introduction to the sixth chapter of the Jedwabne documents, where they are also printed in extenso (*Wokół Jedwabnego*, 2:375–89).

[5] In Robert van Pelt's magisterial study *The Case for Auschwitz*, I came across an observation that resonates with my experience: "In an endnote [to his earlier book *Architectural Principles*] I commented that the hours spent reading those negationist writings

A general, overarching strategy of Musiał's approach is to "pull a switch job" on his readers. The maneuver comes in several variations, but its effect is always meant to be the same—to sideline and avoid the real issues presented in *Neighbors*. At times Musiał sets me up as an advocate of something patently wrong, or plain silly, that I never argued. And then he has a field day ridiculing or correcting, as the case may be, a figment of his own imagination. At other times he will impute to me methods or procedures that I have never used, and scold me for what I did not do.

The other general principle underlying this genre of writing is to pick a detail or a side issue, often unrelated to *Neighbors* and introduced by vague or arbitrary association, and to harp on it in the hope that such "critical remarks" will somehow invalidate the entire story in the mind of a reader.

In the opening segment of his article Musiał meticulously analyzes testimonies of three witnesses named Eljasz Grądowski, Abram Boruszczak, and Henryk Krystowczyk. He points out that Abram Boruszczak was not from Jedwabne, that Grądowski was deported to Russia in 1940 and returned after the German occupation (a fact Grądowski acknowledges), and that Henryk Krystowczyk was found by the court to hold a personal grudge against some of the defendants. Judging by the amount of space and the strength of rhetoric dedicated by Musiał to casting doubt on their trustworthiness, one would be led to believe that these were important witnesses in the trial and sources for the book. Musiał says so directly on several occasions. And yet, as a reader of *Neighbors* will easily realize, nothing, literally *nothing*, turns on their testimony.

Neighbors is filled to the brim with verbatim testimonies of several participants or witnesses, frequently quoted for stretches of half a page or longer—they are Karol Bardoń, Jerzy and Zygmunt Laudański, Boleslaw Ramotowski, Julia Sokołowska, Leon Dziedzic, and others.

'were among the worst I have had in my professional work.' Characterizing this literature as an insult to the intellect I observed that their 'evidence' is doctored and in their attempts to reveal a great 'conspiracy' to blot the reputation of Germany, these 'scholars' . . . ignore half of the evidence, and that part of the evidence they attempt to discredit they butcher and mutilate beyond recognition" (Robert Jan van Pelt, *The Case for Auschwitz: Evidence from the Irving Trial* [Bloomington and Indianapolis, 2002], 69, 70).

Of course the analogy needs to be scaled to proportion—Musiał is not a "negationist," and we are dealing here with attempts to derail efforts to come to grips with a single episode of the Holocaust. But to a reader empathizing with the fate of 1,600 brutally murdered victims it is nonetheless deeply upsetting.

But neither Boruszczak nor Grądowski nor Krystowczyk is among them. One could excise all *four* lines of the text based on Grądowski's testimony (*six*, if we add information derived from Boruszczak's testimony) and the story of the Jedwabne massacre wouldn't be changed one iota.

To state, as Musiał does, that "Gross quotes, or refers to, Grądowski's account many times in his book[6] and bases its main premises on this particular testimony"; that "[a]nother purported witness to the Jedwabne murder on whose testimony Gross has built his case is one Adam Boruszczak"; and that "[a]nother witness of importance to Gross is Henryk Krystowczyk" is an affront to the intelligence of the readers of *Neighbors*.[7] Musiał's claims about the role of Grądowski's, Boruszczak's, and Krystowczyk's testimonies in the book are pure nonsense. And for those who have not read the book they are deliberately misleading.

In the same vein, further exposing weaknesses of my "ways" with documents on which I base the narrative in *Neighbors*, Musiał points out with sarcasm various inconsistencies in two of Wasersztajn's testimonies preserved in the Jewish Historical Institute. Wasersztajn could not have seen with his own eyes everything that he describes in his narrative and therefore is an unreliable witness, and Gross, Musiał admonishes me, is wrong to put faith in his testimony.

The reader should know, as Musiał does, that Wasersztajn does not give testimony in court, and that his deposition has not been made

[6] Musiał confuses Eljasz and Józef Grądowski at one point, but this does not make his claims any less of an exaggeration. I referred to Eljasz Grądowski twice.

[7] Episodic references to looting and killing that Grądowski and Boruszczak provide are used as examples, alongside other testimonies. Tales about wartime Jedwabne families that enriched themselves with Jewish property are part of local folklore to this day ("Why does so-and-so have such a big house ... ?") And that Jews had been murdered amid unspeakable cruelties was attested to by scores of witnesses.

I explain in the book that several testimonies given in the trial assert not what people saw but what they knew about the goings-on from others. Prominent looters of Jewish property, the most drastic episodes of murderous assaults, who killed some specially large number of Jews on that day and how many—these were facts generally known and freely discussed in town. Grądowski's testimony is thus entirely reliable and congruent with the general state of knowledge about the crime.

Many Jews who were in Jedwabne on 10 July fled there to seek shelter from neighboring towns and hamlets, where killings had taken place earlier. That Boruszczak was not a resident of Jedwabne is therefore meaningless. As to Krystowczyk, he is the sole source for one anecdote, where he tells what happened *after the war* to Śleszyński's barn, which was rebuilt for him (after the Jews had been burned in it) by the Germans. For a similar assessment of these witnesses in Rzepliński's study of the Jedwabne trial, see *Wokół Jedwabnego*, 1:379.

part of the legal proceedings. He gave an account of what happened in Jedwabne before the Jewish Historical Commission in April 1945. Naturally, he told the story of the destruction of his hometown community as he saw it *and* as he knew it from what other people had told him. With this caveat in mind my critic is right: I do trust Wasersztajn's story, and for a simple reason—because he is telling the truth. We know this, luckily, thanks to a quilt of narratives by many witnesses who didn't read his deposition before the Jewish Historical Commission in 1945, and who basically tell the same story.

Thus when Wasersztajn says in one interview that Jews in Jedwabne were ordered to carry a portrait of Lenin on their way to death, and in the other that they carried a monument of Lenin, I read into this a spectacle of humiliation to which they were subjected before they were killed, not a contradiction. And when he says in one statement that seventy-five strong young men were killed in the initial stage of the pogrom, and in the other interview he states that there were fifty of them, I read into this testimony not a contradiction but an indication that a brutal mass killing took place.[8]

Musiał concludes: "There are many indications that both versions [of Wasersztajn's testimony] are imprecise reflections of what actually occurred. During the exhumation in Jedwabne in May 2001, within the foundations of the burned-down barn, a grave containing human remains was found and the aforementioned statue of Lenin uncovered. The concrete bust of the Soviet leader was seriously damaged and charred. One should conclude from this that the sculpture was buried after the barn was burned down. This fact undermines the credibility of the information contained in both versions of Szmul Wasersztajn's account, as well as the story about the burial of Lenin's statue at the Jewish cemetery and about the killing of seventy-five Jews there by 'Polish hooligans.' "

The credibility of which information is undermined by the discovery of a "damaged and charred" bust of Lenin in the barn? That a procession of Jews was ordered to carry the broken-up statue of Lenin on their way to death, and that they were buried with it in a common grave? That the entire Jewish community of Jedwabne was killed in a single July day by their neighbors? That scores of people were killed

---

[8] I have analyzed discrepancies between Wasersztajn's testimonies in an essay published several months before *Neighbors* appeared in print: "Lato w Jedwabnem. Przyczynek do badan nad udziałem spoleczności lokalnych w eksterminacji narodu żydowskiego w latach II wojny światowej," in *Europa Nie-prowincjonalna*, ed. Krzysztof Jasiewicz (Warsaw, 1999), 1097–1103. Musiał does not acknowledge that I have done so.

in the cemetery? That they were first assembled on the town square, subjected to humiliations, torture, and killings for the better part of the day, and then herded into a barn and set afire? Such is the gist of Wasersztajn's testimony, and a good dozen witnesses, independently, invoke the same details of this horror story.

Musiał relentlessly strives for precision, however. "There are other problems with the witnesses," he continues. "According to a description in *Neighbors*, Stanisław Sielawa was one of the most active and brutal murderers in Jedwabne on 10 July 1941. Wasersztajn (quoted by Gross on page 97) wrote that on that day 'Stanisław Szelawa [Sielawa] was murdering [Jews (BM)] with an iron hook, [stabbing] in the stomach.' But on page 100 Gross presents a different description of Sielawa's actions based on the testimony of Janek Neumark: 'At the last moment Janek Neumark managed to tear himself away from this hell. A surge of hot air must have blown the barn door open. He was standing right next to it with his sister and her five-year-old daughter. Staszek Sielawa barred their exit, wielding an ax. But Neumark wrestled it away from him and they managed to run away and hide in the cemetery.' In this version, Sielawa is supposed to have been using an ax as an instrument during the crime. Stanisław Sielawa was among the accused in the 1949 trial. He stated for the record: 'I plead not guilty . . . I am a cripple, I did not go anywhere, and I don't know anything . . . I have had a crippled leg since I was three years old.' The court acquitted him." And then Musiał tells us in a footnote that he "is in possession of a drawing of the prosthesis and the written declaration of Jan Sokołowski," who lived in Jedwabne till 1947. Musiał obtained both, declaration and drawing, in Białystok on 28 May 2001.

Good research, undoubtedly, but does it really point to a contradiction? Sielawa's leg problems are not at issue here. After all, he has not been identified by either Wasersztajn or Neumark as a kung fu artist delivering deadly kicks to his hapless victims. On the other hand, could a lame murderer ax his victims, or rip them to death with an iron hook? Could a murderer on the way from the cemetery (where, according to Wasersztajn's testimony, he was operating with a hook) to the barn (where Naumark wrestled an ax from him) drop an awkward instrument of murder and provide himself with one better suited to do the job? But, then, maybe he wielded an ax all along, or a hook, or maybe he used his prosthesis as a deadly weapon—it doesn't really matter.

What is the point of such inquiries, anyway? Could history of the Holocaust ever be written if scholars withheld judgment about what happened because of this sort of "problems with witnesses"?

Were we supposed to doubt what happened in Auschwitz because bona fide estimates of the number of victims killed there differed by several million?[9]

In addition to specific issues concerning individual testimonies, Musiał questions the validity of information derived from the proceedings of the 1949 Łomża trial because it was held during Stalinist times. I've argued in detail in the book why the Łomża trial cannot be viewed as "political." I showed that defendants' testimonies, dissatisfying in all kinds of ways, cannot be portrayed as having been extracted during interrogation with a view to enabling the prosecution to prove a politically predetermined point. But because defendants changed their self-incriminating testimonies during the trial and stated that they were beaten during interrogation, Musiał concludes that they had been intimidated.

From several important interviews published in *Gazeta Wyborcza* we know that an overbearing pressure to change incriminating testimonies was indeed exercised on people involved in the trial at the time, but . . . by their neighbors. Renegade remnants of the wartime nationalist underground, as readers of *Neighbors* well know, tried to kill the Jedwabne Jews saved by Antonia Wyrzykowska. A squad of several men mercilessly beat her when she refused to divulge their whereabouts. Local inhabitants were threatened with death and often killed after the war in all kinds of interpersonal vendettas. Stanisław Przechodzki, from Jedwabne, would later tell Anna Bikont that his parents "mentioned the trial to [him], and how witnesses were intimidated." They were threatened that if they didn't change their testimonies, they

---

[9] Again, a passage from van Pelt elucidates the workings of a mental process behind this kind of argumentation: "As he surveyed the literature, the great debunker found many contradictions in, among other things, statements about the total number of victims who had died in Auschwitz. Shortly after the liberation the Russians had given the number of 4 million victims. Commandant Rudolf Hoess had mentioned at one time 3 million victims, of whom two and half million had been gassed—the rest having died from 'natural causes,' and at another time he had mentioned a number of some 1,130,000 victims. And historians such as Gerald Reitlinger had estimated that 'only' 700,000 Jews had died in Auschwitz. Faurisson discovered other contradictions in the literature: for example, the plan of the crematoria published in the wartime War Refugee Board report, based on the testimony of two escaped prisoners and released in November 1944, showed little relation to the plans of the crematoria published after the war. And of course, many eyewitness testimonies contradicted each other, while some plagiarized other texts. Faurisson concluded that all these contradictions pointed at only one possible conclusion: the story that Auschwitz had been an extermination camp was a hoax" (van Pelt, *The Case for Auschwitz*, 26, 27).

would find their bodies in coffins. The secret police were far away in
Łomża, and the neighbors—right there. They didn't fear anybody as
much as they feared their neighbors. After all, a witness returned home
from making a deposition and wanted to wake up alive in the morning. And what was going on after the war? Many killings, settling
scores between families, sometimes over Jewish property. Even today
there is an atmosphere of intimidation in Jedwabne."[10]

Musiał knows all the relevant press articles and interviews with inhabitants from the area. He knows who exercised pressure, on whom,
and for what purpose. He also knows the preliminary conclusions
reached by IPN investigators, and prominently announced in a well-
covered press conference by the entire leadership of the IPN, in December 2001. He ignores them, as I have already pointed out, and instead
invokes the words of the prosecutor, Radosław Ignatiew, spoken in
April 2001 as allegedly backing his claims that the Łomża trial was
rigged. In fact, Ignatiew merely stated, as he had to at this early stage
of the investigation, that one must proceed prudently and not jump to
conclusions: "We need to ask whether the proceedings [of the Łomża
trial] were just sloppy or whether they were illegal." But even back in
April Ignatiew was already of the opinion—in the very same interview
that Musiał quotes, though conveniently omitting words that don't fit
his claim[11]—that there were no reasons to deem the 1949 Łomża trial
"political."

Musiał's assertion that "[t]he analysis of the court transcripts outlined above clearly proves that the 1949 inquiry into the Jedwabne
massacre is a classic example of the 'fix' so typical of Stalinist Poland"
is but his wishful thinking. His statements concerning my alleged mis-
handling of sources are based on deliberate misrepresentation of the
character and role of Grądowski's, Boruszczak's, and Krystowczyk's

---

[10] "After the war people lived here in fear," said Stanisław Ramotowski from Ras-
ziłów. "On one occasion, about two years after the war, my wife wanted to buy back an
oak family dresser. She could have had a better one, but this was a family heirloom. And
somebody didn't like it. We found a piece of paper stuck to our house door saying that
we were sentenced to death. At that time the NSZ [National Armed Forces] gave out a
lot of such sentences in our area. They stole, they beat people up, they killed. I went to
my own people, because I was a member of the AK [Home Army] . . . And then the AK
made them take the sentence back. And so we survived." ("Nieporządnych było więcej,"
Gazeta Wyborcza, 1 April 2001, interview with Stanisław Ramotowski); "Szatan wstąpił
do Jedwabnego," Gazeta Wyborcza, 4 April 2001, interview with Stanisław Przechodzki;
also see "Przed Jedwabnem. Mord na Żydach w Radziłówie," Gazeta Wyborcza, 15 June
2001, and Rzepliński, Wokół Jedwabnego, 1:381).

[11] "Chociaż w tamtym czasie odbywały się procesy polityczne, w tej sprawie dotąd
nie ma przesłanek, ze byl jakiś nakaz udowodnienia winy," stated Ignatiew (Rzeczpospolita, 27 April 2001).

testimony, utterly irrelevant disquisitions on general points culled from statements by a Stalinist minister of the interior, misleading attribution of views to the IPN prosecutor handling the case, and concealment of conclusions reached by IPN investigators.

In addition to "critical remarks" about methods I employed, Musiał offers a critical aperçu of several substantive points. He devotes pages to what he calls the missing context of my presentation of the Jedwabne murders—the period of Soviet occupation of the eastern half of Poland, from September 1939 through June 1941. As it happens, I have studied this period over the years and stated early in the book what issues I think it raises for the subject matter of *Neighbors*. Since half of Poland's territory was under Soviet occupation and the Jedwabne murder was unique, I pointed out that one needs to ask whether Polish-Jewish relations in this town during Soviet rule had some very special, unique character which provoked that outburst. And then I wrote an entire chapter on this matter in *Neighbors* and showed that they had not.

Here is Musiał's critique of my argument: "The body of traditional prejudices, economic conflicts, and socioreligious differences was reinforced by a new image of Jews profiting from Sovietization and collaborating with the Soviet enemy. Thus Soviet policy significantly intensified the ethnic antagonism already present in these territories before September 1939. Despite these facts Gross writes on page 43, 'But there is no reason to single out Jedwabne as a place where relationships between Jews and the rest of the population during those twenty months of Soviet rule were more antagonistic than anywhere else.' *At the same time he suggests that these relations remained more or less the same as they had been in the pre-1939 period*" (emphasis mine).

Except that I have not "suggested" any such thing anywhere. But inserting this inconspicuous sentence allows Musiał to write several pages admonishing me that Polish-Jewish relations deteriorated under the Soviet occupation, and to conclude this section of his review with a tongue-in-cheek compliment: "Gross's omission and distortion of this historical context might possibly be explained by his lack of familiarity with the source material and the literature on the subject. However, such an explanation would be incorrect, since Gross himself wrote in 1983, 'Antisemitism grew vehemently during the Bolshevik occupation, as soon became apparent in the first days of the Soviet-Hitlerite war in the summer of 1941.' " He footnotes this with the assertion "The author is not aware of a publication in which Gross has revised, in a scholarly and substantiated way, the findings he made in 1983."

As Musiał knows very well, there is nothing for me to revise about these "findings," and, as he states in print, I have not done so. This, however, does not prevent him from writing a disquisition refuting a point that I did not make, while portraying me as an ignoramus who is also untruthful to himself. To spice this soup he also implies that I lie about the sources by allegedly claiming that in the Hoover Institution "there are only three testimonies with 'three general remarks about Jews from Jedwabne, indicating that they displayed zealous support for the Soviet regime.'" A simple check of that institution's archives"—Musiał goes on—"shows that the actual number of such accounts is not merely three but at least seven."

That's serious. But a reader of *Neighbors* who looked up in my book the full sentence referenced by Musiał would notice that I am making claims not about the Hoover Institution Archives in general but rather about "a long memorandum, describing the history of Łomża County under Soviet rule and prepared on the basis of 125 questionnaires filled out by witnesses from the area at the request of the Historical Bureau of the Polish Army in the East (the so-called Anders Army)" held in the Hoover Institution Archives. And there are only three remarks about sycophantic Jews from Jedwabne in this memorandum.

In his article Musiał refers to two original testimonies that were used together with the other 123 depositions as a basis for the memorandum. The questionnaires numbered 2675 and 8455 are quoted in the memorandum, but not with reference to Jewish behavior under the Soviets. Surely, as readers of Musiał's critique can see for themselves, because in the eyes of rapporteurs of the Historical Bureau of the Anders Army they had nothing concrete or illuminating to add on the subject.

Musiał knows that he is referring to a different document from the one I invoke in the book, but pretends otherwise in order to charge me with distorting the content of sources. He thus pulls a switch job on me, which on top of being dishonest is also pointless, since witnesses he quotes only spew general platitudes about Jews "indicating that they displayed zealous support for the Soviet regime."

Or take the following fragment from *Neighbors*: "The late forties and early fifties, after all, were a time when Stalin's anti-Jewish phobia was at its peak and already serving as a driving force for political persecution throughout the entire camp of the so-called people's democracies." I supply the following clarification in an endnote: "I have in mind not only the Kremlin's so-called Doctors' Plot, or the antisemitic context of the Slánský trial in Czechoslovakia, but a general ideological trend that by then was emanating from Moscow," and I go on to quote from a brilliant essay by Nicolas Werth showing that a shift from a class to an ethnic definition of the enemy took place in postwar communism.[12]

The reference to the Slánský trial, as any reader can tell, is a throwaway sentence, a signpost really, to orient readers to the general drift of postwar communism, where the Slánský trial and the plot of the Kremlin doctors serve as shorthand references to Stalin's antisemitic phobia. In "Critical Remarks" these references serve as a takeoff point for Musiał's display of historical erudition: "Gross's arguments run contrary to the actual course of historical events. The affair of the Kremlin doctors occurred shortly before the death of Stalin in March 1953 . . . Jan Tomasz Gross has obviously confused two different periods of the Communist terror in Poland." And he draws on the big gun of the *Brockhaus Encyclopedia* to tell us that the Slánský trial was held in 1952.

Only I am not placing the Jedwabne trial at the same time as Slánský's. I am merely saying that Stalin was already acting on his antisemitic prejudice in 1949, and there was no Communist agenda then to portray Jews as victims (and hence no reason to stage a political trial with contrary intent). The great Jewish actor Salomon Mikhoels was killed by Soviet secret police in January of 1948, thus introducing a murderous stage of Stalin's assault on the Jewish remnants *a good year before* Jedwabne defendants were put on trial. Anyway, this is all immaterial. Slánský's trial has nothing to do with the killing of Jedwabne Jews more than a decade earlier. Try as Musiał may, the ghosts of Jedwabne will not be chased away by reference to the *Brockhaus Encyclopedia*.

Criticizing (indeed, ridiculing) *Neighbors* for naive (indeed, plain silly) arguments that I have never made but that Musiał imputes to me is a consistent strategy. Thus I am also made a laughingstock for having, as Musiał puts it again, "suggested," that Jedwabne town leaders who organized and supervised the murder "were freely elected representatives of the Polish community. . . The possibility of local elections' having taken place in Jedwabne after the entry of the Germans," writes Musiał with understated irony, "is, in my [Musiał's (JG)] opinion, remote." Wrong again, I say it is nonexistent.

As to Musiał's query why I am employing such terms as "town council" and "town council members," the answer is easy to find in *Neighbors*—these are the very terms that deposed witnesses and defendants use in their testimonies. They also identify the main organizer presiding over the mayhem, a certain Karolak, as "the mayor." All of

---

[12] *Neighbors*, 31, 217.

this scorn was piled on me by Musiał for one sentence: "In the mean-time Jedwabne's municipal authorities were constituting themselves."

There is more nonsense of this kind. I write, "[T]here were no rea-sons whatsoever for Jews, in their recollection of Shoah episodes they experienced and witnessed, to attribute to Poles those crimes that were in reality perpetrated by the Germans" (25–26). And Musiał portrays this as "[Gross] also maintains that there is no reason to suspect Jewish survivors of concocting false accusations against Poles . . . This would mean that Holocaust survivors have either managed to completely rid themselves of any negative emotions, such as prejudice or desire for revenge, or that they never harbored them in the first place." The logic of this assertion is completely unfathomable.

I am glad to know that Musiał believes Jews are only human, and I fully share his opinion in this respect. But I do not "maintain" what he claims I do. My claim is narrow: I say there is no reason for the Jewish victims of the Holocaust to deliberately blame the Poles for crimes per-petrated by the Germans.

Or take another matter: Musiał's revelation of the whereabouts of the Łomża diocese bishop, Stanisław Łukomski. One of the few survivors of the death march to the barn in Jedwabne, Wiktor Nieławicki, tells a story about a group of Jedwabne Jews, including his uncle, who took silver candlesticks to the bishop of Łomża in the early days of the Ger-man occupation, together with a plea that he intervene on behalf of the Jedwabne Jewish community with the Germans.

No big deal—Germans were mercenary and could be bribed. This was common practice during the occupation, and the targeted victim who wanted to stave off some impending disaster (various Jewish communities, in particular) needed only to find a proper intermediary. According to Nieławicki's recollection the bishop, or whoever received the Jews in his residence, accepted the valuables and agreed to try in-terceding with the Germans, as any decent person in these circum-stances would. The right-wing nationalist and Catholic press in Po-land, and Musiał belatedly alongside, took this as an attempt to bribe the bishop himself.[13] And what they chose to point out in the bishop's defense was that he was absent from his residence until 9 July, and therefore Nieławicki's story must be false.

[13] As Musiał puts it in his inimitably amplificatory and acerbic style: "However, there are many indications that both the original version of Nieławicki's recollections and the 'clarified' one are far from the truth. Stanisław Łukomski, the bishop of the Łomża dio-cese (who allegedly took the 'ransom' and then broke his word), had to leave his resi-dence in the autumn of 1939 and hide from the Soviets in the countryside." Except that

Perhaps the Catholic right knows best. I won't second-guess them, or Musiał, about why the bishop of Łomża couldn't be bribed at the time. But as long as their pleas for help, along with valuables, were accepted, small-town Jews from Jedwabne had every reason to think that they had the bishop's protection—irrespective of who actually received them in his Łomża residence.

The whole matter, however, raises a very important issue—namely, that of church archives for the period. I have been denied access to the archives at both the Łomża and the Białystok diocese. But if Bishop Łukomski's whereabouts in July 1941 can be tracked with day-by-day accuracy, this bodes well for researchers like Musiał, who, among others with connections to church officials, should probe deeper. To begin with, it would be most important to locate the torn-out pages of the Jedwabne parish book covering the war period. As all of Poland could see on their television screens during last April's broadcast of Agnieszka Arnold's documentary, this is a book wherein the local priest kept a rather detailed record of goings-on in town. We should by all means strive to learn more about the actions of Bishop Łukomski and the Łomża diocese clergy vis-à-vis the Jews during the war years. And Musiał, who has an obvious knack for this sort of research, should be encouraged to explore the issue.

Before we turn to Musiał's style, we must consider one more contested issue of substance, namely, how many Jews were killed in Jedwabne on 10 July 1941?

Let me say up front that I do not fancy depriving of life, even on paper, more people than were actually killed in Jedwabne. If I could have my preference, I would wish for fewer Jewish victims there, not more. Besides, the moral issues at stake, as well as implications for Poles' self-understanding as to the historical significance of their collective experience during the German occupation (I discuss this in *Neighbors* in the chapter entitled "Is It Possible to Be Simultaneously a Victim and a Victimizer?"), remain exactly the same, no matter whether 400 or 1,600 Jews were killed on 10 July.

Irrespective of what my polemicists would like the readers to believe, the number of "1,600" victims is not my invention. This is a number, or rather the order of magnitude, that describes how many Jews were killed in Jedwabne on 10 July 1941. Specifically, "1,600" was given as the number of victims in Wasersztajn's testimony; this very number was carved by the Polish authorities two decades ago into the stone

---

Nieł.wicki never suggests that a "ransom"—yet another of Musiał's insinuations—was paid to the bishop.

monument at the site of the barn; "one and a half thousand" is offered as the tally of victims by Polish witnesses at the trial,[14] and the same number appears in a secret police summary report; "1,460" is given in the memorial book of the Jedwabne Jews; and "1,640" appears currently on the Jedwabne high school Web site. These are all, if you will, identical figures insofar as they convey the truth accepted by all—namely, that by and large the entire Jedwabne Jewish community was murdered on that single day. And 1,600 is, more or less, how many Jews should have been there, judging by the 1921 and 1931 population censuses.[15] Why would all of these sources deliberately inflate the number of Jews in Jedwabne by a multiple of four or five?

So there is a remarkable irony in the broad-mindedness of assorted right-wing nationalist writers who wouldn't normally touch a Communist with a ten-foot pole, and who are suddenly embracing as in-

[14] See, for example, excerpts from Bolesław Ramotowski's, Władysław Dąbrowski's, and Zygmunt Laudański's depositions quoted by Rzepliński, *Wokół Jedwabnego*, 1:390, 393, 395.

[15] The official 1921 census data yield 61.9 percent for the relative size of the Jedwabne Jewish population (*Skorowidz miejscowości Rzeczypospolitej Polskiej . .* , vol. 5—quoted in Marcin Urynowicz, "Ludnosc żydowska w Jedwabnem. Zmiany demograficzne od końca XIX wieku do 1941 roku na tle regionułomżyńskiego," in *Wokół Jedwabnego*, 1:86). The 1931 census data give population totals but do not permit the disaggregation of data by ethnicity to county town level, as original census questionnaires were destroyed during the war. In his historical-demographic study of population changes in Jedwabne, Marcin Urynowicz quotes significantly different population ratios for 1931, following H. Mejer's published lecture delivered at a convention of industrial and social activists on 25 March 1934 in Łomża; there the relative proportion of Jewish and Polish populations in Jedwabne is reversed, with Jews making up 40 percent and Poles 60 percent of the total (ibid., 95). He also quotes another figure from a source published in February 1931, where the percentage of Jews in Jedwabne is set at 48 percent (ibid., 96; see also Jan Milewski, "Polacy i Żydzi w Jedwabnym i okolicy przed 22 czerwca 1941 roku," in *Wokół Jedwabnego*, 1:64). The larger figure for Poles would be obtained if some Jews had identified Polish as their mother tongue to census takers. Thus, according to Urynowicz, the more likely total for the Jedwabne Jews on the eve of the Second World War would be 1,000 (or 1,200 if 48 percent is the correct ratio), rather than 1,600.

It is impossible to settle on a correct figure, given the quality of sources. I think that higher estimates are more plausible, if only because the Jedwabne town council elected in 1928 was made up evenly of Polish and Jewish councilmen (Milewski, 64). Such an election result would be highly unlikely in a predominantly Polish town situated, as Jedwabne was, in a strongly nationalist region.

In any case, whether 1,000 or 1,200 Jews resided in town on the eve of the war, in the days immediately preceding the mass murder of 10 July many Jews flocked into Jedwabne from the surrounding towns, where murderous assaults against them had taken place earlier. One source speaks of 230 Jews from Wizna alone who had fled to Jedwabne and were murdered there (*Wokół Jedwabnego*, 2:366). Thus the number of victims on 10 July 1941 in Jedwabne could easily be in the 1,500–1,600 range, just as the witnesses have repeatedly stated.

controvertible truth some "Soviet data," just to prove me wrong. As-sorted Polish data (as quoted by various witnesses, the court, the secret police; as put on the Jedwabne monument or derived from prewar census figures), or Jewish data (from the Jedwabne memorial book or individual statements), about the approximate numerical size of the Jedwabne Jewish community are not good enough. Apparently Polish inhabitants of Jedwabne had no idea how many Jews lived in their town, nor did Jewish inhabitants of Jedwabne know how many they were altogether. The real light for Musiał and his fellow polemicists comes from the East—Soviet data tell the true story.

But what data? A figure of "1,400" for the total number of Jews in the entire Jedwabne *raion* (i.e., including Wizna, Radziłów, and vicinity) in September of 1940, as quoted in a book by Michał Gnatowski ("Gross is aware of this book and cites it," adds Musiał pointedly in a footnote).

What happened to the remaining couple of thousand Jews, who lived in this area before the war, then? Had they been deported to Siberia by September 1940? Or, in a reversal of the general pattern of population movement at the time (when Jews fled eastward from the advancing German army and inflated by some 10 percent the ranks of their coreligionists in the Soviet occupied territory), did Jedwabne, Radziłów, and Wizna Jews flee en masse from under the Soviet occupation to the General Government? Why did they hate the Soviets so much, then? Or is it that Gnatowski copied something incorrectly, or perhaps that an NKVD typist made a mistake? Perhaps the Soviet data in question referred to something else altogether?[16]

The entire dispute concerning the number of Jewish victims evolved from unfortunate confusion resulting from the purported exhumation that has been carried out in Jedwabne in early June 2001. This is the only aspect of the Jedwabne investigation handled carelessly by the IPN, though its inadequacy was motivated by a well-meant desire to appease the distress of religious Jews.

According to experts an exhumation of the Jedwabne-size mass grave should have taken many months, perhaps as long as a year. What has been called an exhumation in Jedwabne lasted all of five days. Polish authorities consented to such a truncated procedure in order to accommodate Jewish religious sensibilities.[17] Indeed, rabbis

[16] In a footnote Urynowicz comments on another dubious population figure quoted from Soviet sources by Gnatowski as proof of the "thoughtlessness of Soviet functionaries, confirming the low credibility of Soviet sources in matters concerning demographic data for the region" (*Wokół Jedwabnego*, 1:99).

[17] I protested against this decision in an article published by *Gazeta Wyborcza* on 6 June 2001. At the time Rabbi Baker, formerly from Jedwabne and now residing in Brooklyn, suggested to me that it would be a *mitsva* (charitable act) to move the remains of "the

from Warsaw, Israel, and London were present at different times during these few days in Jedwabne to make sure that religious laws concerning proper handling of the remains of the dead were observed, or
violated as little as possible. Only the outer layer of one common grave
was uncovered, and disturbing the bones was prohibited. Forensic
specialists directly identified remains of several dozen victims, including women, children, and elderly people.

And then an archaeologist opined on the spot that 150 to 250 people
altogether were buried near the barn. Prof. Kulesza, the chief of the
IPN's investigative department present at the site, in turn communicated this opinion to the minister of justice, Lech Kaczyński, who
immediately made the announcement, and thus the archaeologist's
instant opinion became "a fact." The leader of the Jedwabne team,
Prof. Kola, deplored the haste of his collaborator and later amended
the count to 300 to 400 bodies. In any case, this was certainly the
fastest exhumation and evaluation of results in the annals of forensic
medicine.[18]

But according to the expert opinion of an international observer
present on the site, Dr. William Haglund, who was there for three days
and even met with Kulesza, the total number of people buried in Jedwabne mass graves simply could not be estimated on the basis of the
work that had been done there. Haglund is currently director of the
International Forensic Program of the organization Physicians for
Human Rights. Previously, for eight years he was chief medical investigator in the King County Medical Examiner's Office in Seattle, and
then for two years he served as senior forensic adviser to the United
Nations International Criminal Tribunal for Rwanda and the Former
Yugoslavia (ICTR and ICTY).

Haglund's experience is vast. He flew to Jedwabne directly from
Cyprus, where he served as director of the Humanitarian Mission to
Nicosia for exhumation and analysis of human remains from the 1974
conflict between Cyprus and Turkey. He has worked on mass graves
and human remains in Sri Lanka, Indonesia, and Somaliland. He was
team leader for forensic investigation involving exhumations and examinations of victims from four mass graves in Bosnia Herzegovina,
and near Vukovar, in Croatia, for ICTY. In the same capacity, as team
leader for forensic investigation, he worked in Kigali and Kibuye in

---

Jedwabne martyrs" to a burial ground in Israel. A well-known Jewish scholar, Rabbi
Pollak from Boston, later published in the journal *Tradition* ("the Cadillac of halakhic
studies," as he told me) a learned treatise demonstrating that according to Jewish law
the remains of Jews in Jedwabne should have been moved to a proper burial ground.

[18] "Ślubne obrączki i nóż rzezaka," *Rzeczpospolita*, 10 July 2001.

Rwanda for ICTR. Earlier, as a consultant for Physicians for Human Rights, he worked at mass grave sites in Honduras and Guatemala. He is, arguably, one of the most experienced forensic specialists in the world. The IPN declined his offer of assistance in the Jedwabne investigation.

But we don't need to set the word of one expert against that of another when considering how many Jews were killed in the barn in Jedwabne. Numbers, including population figures illustrating historical events, do not float in a void, and a historian invoking them has to show that they are consistent with the general narrative about the events in question. Since we know that more or less the entire Jedwabne Jewish community was killed on 10 July 1941, anyone maintaining that 150 or 400 were incinerated in the barn must also be able to tell what happened to all the rest. And since the Jedwabne Jews met their fate in situ,[19] the only plausible alternative explanation of what happened to them would not easily fit into the nationalist paradigm of Poland's wartime history. For if indeed "only" between 150 and 400 Jews were set afire in the barn on 10 July, then all the remaining Jedwabne Jews must have been killed earlier during the day in face-to-face encounters with their murderers. Thus what Musiał and his fellows implicitly tell us is that more than one thousand individual murders took place on that day in Jedwabne!

Even discounting for record-setters, such as a certain Kobrzyniecki who boasted of having killed eighteen people by himself, this would require a good 300 to 350 murderers among the local Poles. If Musiał is right, then quite a few octogenarians residing in the area must be trembling for their lives today, for there is no statute of limitations on genocide, and the IPN has the mandate to prosecute.

In addition to engaging Musiał's vigorous polemics on substantive points, I also want to draw the readers' attention to yet another—I'll call it stylistic for lack of a better word—device used in his presentation. On several occasions Musiał tries *to create an impression* that Germans were responsible for the Jedwabne killing, and that I have mishandled the sources. Of course these are the very same points that he argues as well, but time and again he knowingly draws on materials that have no merit whatever, and does not "argue" much of anything. He just creates an impression.

[19] Otherwise, the *Landsmanschaft* of the Jedwabne Jews—which predates the war, published the memorial book, exists to this day, and occupies itself exclusively with following up on the fate of relatives and fellow Jedwabniaks—would certainly know about it.

Thus, for instance, he quotes extensively from statements made by Jedwabne Jewish survivors seeking to establish their right of inheritance after the war. As we know, survivors all over Poland used boilerplate language to describe the circumstances under which their relatives were killed in order to quickly obtain official death certificates from the courts. Otherwise they weren't able to dispose of their property. In the event, their statements had very little to do with actual circumstances of death of the Jedwabne Jews, and Musiał knows that this is the case.[20] But the reader of "Critical Remarks" will have to plow through a page of Jewish testimonies according to which the Germans killed the Jews of Jedwabne. Not bad for creating the right atmospherics.

The same goes for extensive quotations from the Łomża trial depositions, in which defendants described how German gendarmes ordered them to guard the Jews assembled in the square. Musiał introduces these quotations as a revelation, presumably showing what has been omitted from *Neighbors*. Except that I used these depositions, quoted some fragments directly, and referred to them in the book in the first place.[21] Some readers will recognize that Musiał is dragging in a red herring. But others will be left with the impression that I use sources "selectively," and that Germans indeed played more of a role in Jedwabne than is stated in *Neighbors*. Again, not bad for atmospherics. And these minor sallies accumulate force as readers encounter one after another of them.

---

[20] "Of course," writes Musiał, "the question arises as to how trustworthy these depositions are. It is certain that these documents must be approached with caution because of the circumstances in which the testimonies were collected. The deponents did not strive to discover the culprits and to reconstruct the events of the pogrom precisely. Instead, they aimed simply for the quickest possible issue of death certificates for their relatives. We thus cannot exclude the possibility of the petitioners' exchanging mutual favors and testifying on each other's behalf in order to obtain official documents entitling them to perform numerous legal actions, for example, to receive inheritance." So not only did Musiał raise the question of "how trustworthy these depositions are," but he also answered it. All the same he goes on plying his readers with worthless (as historical evidence) but "atmospherically" correct quotations.

[21] Here is a passage from pages 76 and 77 of *Neighbors*: "In the sources at our disposal the term 'gendarmes' (or, actually, far more frequently 'a gendarme') appears as part of an explanation describing the circumstances that led several of the accused in the Ramotowski trial to appear in the market square or near the barn. Thus, in a rather typical deposition, Czesław Lipiński tells the court how Jurek Laudański, Eugeniusz Kalinowski, 'and one German' came to fetch him, and how he went with them to round up Jews to the square; Feliks Tarnacki was visited by Karolak and Wasilewski, who 'together with a gestapo man chased [me] to the square' and told him to guard the Jews. Miciura, who was employed this day at the gendarmerie outpost doing some carpentry work, was told by a gendarme at some point 'to go to the square to watch the Jews.' "

Yet another—perhaps the most important—attempt to convey the "proper" impression is Musiał's long and convoluted disquisition on German archives that I have ignored, and how I failed as a result to recognize the role of "one Hermann Schaper" in the Jedwabne killing. Again, a reader who does not follow the story or the unfolding IPN investigation would not know that in all of these German archives, which have by now been carefully reviewed by a team of historians and professional investigators from IPN, not a single speck of evidence was found, not *one* word, that would place Schaper in Jedwabne on 10 July 1941! *Nothing*. The closest he came to Jedwabne, according to testimony recorded *in Israel in the 1960s*, was Radziłów. An elderly Jewish woman, Chaja Finkelsztajn, recognized Schaper's photograph twenty years after the event as that of a German who was in Radziłów during that day. But then, in her long and fascinating memoirs deposited in Yad Vashem (her daughter makes the same point in a brief statement held in the Jewish Historical Institute in Warsaw), she states that the Germans *left town before* local residents of Radziłów and vicinity proceeded with their final murderous assault on their Jewish neighbors. And this is the extent of German records on Schaper's role in Jedwabne.[22]

But once you have been treated to several pages of "Schaper this" and "Schaper that"; to a long list of dates and places in the Białystok area where Germans killed Jews in the summer of 1941; to assorted footnotes and helpful pointers (that "[a] mobile armed unit consisting of several members of the security police, aided by eleven local gendarmes . . . , was quite sufficient to carry out an operation like the one in Jedwabne "), you are thoroughly befuddled. From now on "Schaper" will sound familiar. He will become a component of the general atmosphere surrounding the story of the Jedwabne murders.

A special place in the "creating an impression" procedure is occupied by Musiał's presentation of a mistake I made in the attribution of

---

[22] See the final report of councillor Martin Opitz from Ludwigsburg, dated 17 March 1964. It shows clearly that there is no German document of any kind indicating Schaper's presence in Jedwabne. The probability of his having been there is deduced by Opitz from Chaja Finkelsztajn's testimony in Israel, not from some German source. We learn from the next document published in the volume—a decision dated 2 September 1965 by the Hamburg prosecutor Otto—that the investigation of Schaper's alleged participation in the Jedwabne massacre is dismissed for lack of evidence that he was there (*Wokół Jedwabnego*, 2:173, 177). Chaja Finkelsztajn's deposition from Yad Vashem is also published in the Jedwabne documents volume in a Polish translation (ibid., 263–317). For specific reference to Germans' (presumably, a group including Schaper) leaving Radziłów before the Polish population proceeds to murder all the town's Jews, see ibid., 309; for the deposition in the Jewish Historical Institute in Warsaw of Chana Finkelsztajn (Chaja's daughter) stating the same, see ibid., 258.

two quotations. Once the mistake was pointed out to me, and I confirmed the error by consulting my notes, I instructed Princeton University Press as well as Pogranicze, my Polish publisher, to make requisite corrections in all future printings, as well as to make sure that a correct version appears in all the translations. Since I had previously defended my original version in a newspaper discussion,[23] I also published a statement in *Rzeczpospolita* on 23 June 2001 admitting to the mistake and explaining how it was made, and that it was inadvertent. Somehow I confused first names of the three Laudański defendants in the case. On page 86 I attributed to Czesław Laudański a sentence from a deposition of his son Zygmunt, and on page 99 I attributed to Czesław Laudański a sentence from a deposition of his son Jerzy.

The story of the Jedwabne massacre stays the same irrespective of which Laudański says what. I had no incentive to intentionally misattribute a quotation from a son to a father. Quite the opposite—a historian should not make mistakes of this sort as a matter of professional pride. Unfortunately, I let this mistake slip by, and, as a result, I've been sued by the third brother, Kazimierz Laudański, for allegedly defaming their father—paterfamilias of three boys raised as rabid nationalists before the war, who among the three of them managed to include murderers, traitors, NKVD and Nazi collaborators, sycophantic early joiners of the Polish Workers' Party and the postwar Communist administration, and a convicted thief.[24]

Musiał knows everything there is to know about the Laudański brothers, who are alive and well, writing letters to newspapers, and giving interviews to anyone interested. The most revealing has been published in *Gazeta Wyborcza* on 23 March 2001. Incredibly, Polish television audience could meet them in a chilling eye-to-eye during Agnieszka Arnold's film broadcast in April. The hypocrisy of the Laudańskis' lawsuit is their business only and a minor infraction in the context of the family history. But Musiał's presentation of the whole matter is scandalous and deliberately misleading given that he is writing with full knowledge of all the particulars.

[23] I was in Poland at the time and didn't have access to my notes; I took what was written in two separate places in the book to be correct.

[24] Zygmunt and Jerzy Laudański were two of the most active murderers on 10 July; earlier, under Soviet rule, Zygmunt had been an NKVD secret agent; after the German occupation began, Jerzy worked in the gendarmerie; Kazimierz was employed in the Nazi administration and among other duties registered, as he put it, some Jews who were later sent to Treblinka. After the war he became a zealous activist of the Polish Workers' Party and the local Communist administration—he was the first to get an official car in his *gmina*, he boasted in an interview with Anna Bikont. Jerzy Laudański, before being arrested in the Jedwabne case after the war, managed to spend eleven months in jail for theft from a warehouse where he was employed as a manager.

Here is Musiał's take on the issue: "The case of Czesław Laudański stands out in Gross's book. The author of *Neighbors* turned him into one of the most active 'perpetrators' of the Jedwabne crime, twice 'quoting' words that were supposedly his own to this effect ' "A lot of people were there, whose names I do not remember now," ' we are told by Laudański *père*, who with his two sons was among the busiest on this day, ' "I'll tell them as soon as I recall" ' (86). And on page 99: ' "We chased jews under the barn," ' Czesław Laudański would later report, ' "and we ordered them to enter inside, and the jews had to enter inside." ' According to Gross, Laudański's self-incrimination is to be found on pages 666 and 668 of the trial transcripts. *I checked the pages in question without finding the indicated material there. The court records contain three depositions by Czesław Laudański, on pages 207, 669, and 680, respectively. None of them contains the statements attributed to Laudański by Gross"* (emphasis mine).

This is a very crafty passage in which my critic impresses upon readers that I have invented two quotations. For what else is the reader to conclude from the above but that words which I put in a fellow's mouth and referenced to court transcripts *are not* part of the record? In plain English—they have been invented by me; in plainer English yet—I cheated. Except that those very words *are* in the trial transcript and on the very pages—666 and 668—that I indicated! So, is Musiał lying when he states, "I [Musiał (JG)] checked the pages in question without finding the indicated material there"?

Well, here is the switch job he pulls on this occasion: Musiał knows, of course, that I did not invent the words in question, and that they *are* to be found on pages 666 and 668, and anyone who reads these pages will find them there. (Since the publication of *Wokół Jedwabnego* these quotations can be found in any research library holding the volumes. They are referenced to pages 666 and 668 of the original files, and can be found in volume 2, on pages 480 and 482.) And that is why in the sentence insinuating that I cheat about the content of sources he put the word "material." The words that I attribute to Czesław Laudański are there, you see, but not "the material," that is, they had not been spoken by Czesław Laudański (a fact that I do not contest; I publicly admitted and explained it in my 23 June 2001 article in *Rzeczpospolita*).

Thus I've been portrayed as a liar, and he cannot be sued for libel. So the proper impression is conveyed (i.e., Gross is cheating), Musiał is covered, and I am discredited because no one, except a very careful reader of *Neighbors* and of all the polemics surrounding it, will take note of those manipulations. But a careful reader of *Neighbors* will not read beyond the first page of Musiał's "Critical Remarks" anyway.

On top of everything else the reader is also informed that I bad-mouthed a sick man, a victim of Soviet persecution to boot. For Czesław Laudański, by his own admission, was in bed at the time, recovering from beatings—"blind and swollen all over"—inflicted on him by his Soviet captors. This eventuality, Musiał reassures us, is quite plausible "[w]hen we take into account the terrible conditions in Soviet jails," and he footnotes this helpful insight with Bogdan Musiał's *Kontrrevolutionäre Elemente*—his own book published two years ago without any connection or reference to the Jedwabne murders.

Yet despite Musiał's general expertise on the subject, what Czesław Laudański was doing in bed, and when, will have to remain somewhat of a mystery. It turns out that several witnesses saw him in the streets of Jedwabne on 10 July. "Blind and swollen," he apparently found his way out, and his presence in town etched itself in the memory of one Stanisława Szelawa owing to a verbal exchange between the two: "In 1941, when the German occupying army entered Jedwabne, the local population together with the Germans proceeded to murder the jews and killed about one and a half thousand; I saw the following people: 1. Czesław Laudański stood on Przytulska Street with a German, and he spoke to me when I came out in the street asking where I was going, so I said that I wanted to buy beer for my husband, and Czesław Laudański said, Go home or else you will be with the jews, so I went back home."[25]

Musiał knows this testimony—he read it in *Rzeczpospolita*—but he is free to rely instead, as he does, on the content of his 22 May 2001 interview with Czesław Laudański's eldest son, Kazimierz. Undoubtedly, since he is so meticulous about checking the trustworthiness of witnesses, he makes this choice because he finds him more reliable. And why not?—after all, this eldest of the Laudański brothers was the only grown-up male in the family who did not end up in the dock in 1949 accused of murdering the Jedwabne Jews.[26] No matter that he took a job in the Nazi administrative apparatus during the war, that immediately after the war he joined the Communist Party and rose to prominence in its local administration, that he expresses admiration for his younger brother Jerzy (who fetched the second-highest prison term, fifteen years, in the Łomża trial and was universally identified as one of the most brutal killers on 10 July), whom he calls "a national hero"—

[25] The statement may be found on page 690 of the Łomża trial files (*Wokół Jedwabnego*, 2:504) and was quoted in my article published in *Rzeczpospolita* on 23 June 2001, which Musiał also references in his "Critical Remarks." See also Rzepliński, *Wokół Jedwabnego*, 1:382.

[26] On 10 July 1941 Kazimierz Laudański happened to be out of town.

and sues me for defaming his father when I mistakenly attributed a sentence spoken by this hero to the hero's father.

Could Kazimierz, absent on that day from Jedwabne, be an eyewitness to his father's whereabouts on 10 July (vide Musiał's blistering attack on Grądowski's credibility as a witness earlier)? Is a son an unprejudiced, reliable witness in matters concerning his father's reputation (vide Musiał's earlier criticism of Krystowczyk's personal biases)? For Musiał, apparently, Kazimierz Laudański has all the credentials to recommend him as a trustworthy witness in the Jedwabne murder story. Clearly, Musiał has a soft spot for family men—loving brothers and dutiful sons.

There is additionally in "Critical Remarks" an assortment of gratuitous little barbs—that I "avoid discussion" on the subject of Neighbors, that "Polish historians by and large agree" that Neighbors is deeply flawed, that what I have said here and there is baseless, and so forth. I won't engage Musiał on these or numerous other points. Not in order to "avoid discussion," but because it's bunk. But for the sake of interested readers let me just indicate that some of my polemical writings and interventions from the past year can be found in English translation in the Thou Shalt Not Kill volume, published by Więź, and on the Web site of my publisher Pogranicze. Early next year these writings will be assembled and published in Poland in a separate volume.

As to the reception the book received in Poland from the country's intellectual elite, it is worth mentioning that Neighbors was nominated for Poland's most prestigious literary prize, Nike, for the year 2000, as well as the most important media prize—"Twórca w mediach"—established in memory of Rzeczpospolita's founding editor Dariusz Fikus. Sąiedzi has also received the "As [as in 'Ace'] EMPIKu" award in the category "Event of the Year," for a book "that has had the greatest impact and brought a new quality into Polish culture during the past year."[27] Clearly, Neighbors was not as maligned in Poland as Musiał would like us to believe, though apparently his associates didn't like it much. To be honest, I wouldn't have it any other way.

To summarize: the fundamental premise of writings such as Musiał's "Critical Remarks" is that the public they address is illiterate; that it does not read books or much of anything else; and that it certainly has not read Neighbors. And this is not a vacuous premise: a nationwide survey of a thousand Poles at the end of August 2001 (i.e., after the sixtieth-anniversary commemoration of the Jedwabne massacre, car-

[27] EMPiK is a major Polish bookseller.

ried live on national television; after Poland's president's public apology for the crime; after eight months of incessant debate in all the media) found that 28 percent of the respondents believed the sole perpetrators of the Jedwabne killings to have been the Germans (to be fair, a slight improvement over the results of a similar poll in April, when 34 percent of the nationwide sample held this belief).[28]

This state of collective confusion in Poland on the subject of Jedwabne is due largely to the efforts of a whole posse of journalists cum historians who authored dozens of articles and several book-length publications, previously duly serialized in large-circulation newspapers and magazines, with such provocative titles as *One Hundred Lies of Gross*[29] or *Geshefts of Jedwabne*. Bogdan Musiał offers a highbrow product in this genre. He is knowledgeable about the period and has consulted the sources. These are not necessarily extenuating circumstances.

Stretched between Sielawa's prosthesis and the *Brockhaus Encyclopedia*, Musiał's net is widely cast. He oozes scorn about details and methods of *Neighbors* alike. I have never met him, and I don't know of any harm I may have caused him. So what is the point of this strange exercise, the reader might ask?

Musiał made a reputation for himself as a spoiler with a sharp eye for detail. In Germany he castigated the exhibition on *Wehrmacht* war crimes, to the frantic applause of a nationalist segment of German public opinion, by pointing out that 9 out of 1,433 photographs documenting the atrocities were mislabeled.[30] Would he be once again attempting to piggyback ride somebody else's work to notoriety? Maybe so. But I suspect there is more at stake here than personal ambition. Musiał has a very specific notion of what constitutes proper rules of historical research, and he vigorously defends those views. In a recent piece (wherein a distinguished historian of the middle generation, Włodzimierz Borodziej, gets a full treatment and I'm attacked only en passant, merely as an afterthought), he puts out in one breath a call to enforce "respect for basic principles of scientific craftsmanship" and "quality control," and then writes the following reflections: "After fifty years of

---

[28] Centrum Badania Opinii Społecznej, *"Polacy wobec zbrodni w Jedwabnem—przemiany sposecznej świadomosci,"* komunikat z badań (Warsaw, 2001). It is perhaps even more disturbing that 19 percent of those questioned who had a university education believed that Germans were the sole perpetrators of the crime.

[29] "I could have enumerated three hundred," said its author, Jerzy Robert Nowak, choking with laughter, during a program broadcast 26 June 2001 on Radio Maryja, an obscurantist Catholic radio station with a devoted audience of several million.

[30] See his "Bilder einer Ausstellung," *Vierteljahrshefte für Zeitgeschichte* 4 (1999): 589.

our quasi-absence on the international market, Polish aspects of the Second World War are still generally written about in a poor and incompetent manner. Theses of such a degree of absurdity have currency in American and German historiography that a mere publication of documents from Polish or post-Soviet archives will be a real breakthrough ... We can only be glad that Polish scientists are publishing works abroad that pertain to Polish history. Unless we write about our own history, others will do it for us with all the consequences of such a development—a telling example of this is precisely the latest 'opus' by Jan Tomasz Gross."[31]

So not only is Polish history exclusively for the Poles to write about, but, apparently, it is for Musiał to decide who is a Pole. And as he is really committed to the "basic principles," he goes on angrily: "In Poland there is an atmosphere of almost total impunity in this matter. The book by Prof. Borodziej is not the only example after all. Another, much more spectacular example of the lack of 'quality control' is the latest publication by Jan Tomasz Gross, *Neighbors*." What kind of punishment does he have in mind for "others" daring to write about Polish history, one wonders?[32]

"God save us from friends; from enemies we can defend ourselves," goes a well-known proverb. During the yearlong public debate concerning the Jedwabne massacre, Poland's good name has been put to a hard test by assorted defenders from the nationalist spectrum of public opinion. And such deserved respect and admiration as the country has received in the world for boldly confronting its unflattering past was due instead to the unwavering clarity with which Poland's president has always spoken on the issue; to the unflinching determination of Prof. Leon Kieres and the IPN to carry out an honest and thorough investigation of the crime; to first-rate investigative reporting on the issue by the two main daily newspapers in Poland, *Rzeczpospolita* and *Gazeta Wyborcza*; to excellent coverage and commentary in two most important Polish weeklies, *Polityka* and *Wprost*; to profound and grip-

[31] "Casus profesora Borodzieja a stan polskiej historiografii," *Arcana*, nos. 4–5 (2002): 311. The subtext on this occasion is that some people owe their careers to the patronage of old Communist Party hacks.

[32] So far he merely ridicules the trespassers' ignorance and premeditated ill-will: "[Gross] has even officially proclaimed in [*Neighbors*] the need to 'affirmatively' treat some sources, i.e., to abandon scientific criticism. He also mentions a 'revelation' that allowed him to understand the unfolding of the Jedwabne massacre without a proper investigation. The list of 'oversights,' mistakes, ahistorical speculations, and baseless accusations against concrete individuals is, in this rather small publication, so long that it is hard to believe it is just the effect of superficial 'research' and lack of elementary knowledge about the conditions in occupied and postwar Poland, rather than a result of deliberate action." And he references this passage to his "Critical Remarks" (ibid.).

ping reflections on Jedwabne and its implications in the most highly respected venues of the Catholic intelligentsia—the weekly *Tygodnik Powszechny* and the monthly *Więź*; to the funding by Polish public television and broadcasting in prime time of a searing two-hour documentary by Agnieszka Arnold; and to many a program and interview carried by various radio and television stations in Poland. One can say regrettably little in this vein about statements from Poland's Catholic bishops.

But to return to the primary topic, we should give Musiał credit for sitzfleish and taking on difficult subjects. Perhaps future historians will benefit from his dogged persistence to uncover telling details about the Second World War. But so far, as best one can tell, his original contribution to the historiography of the Jedwabne murders has been limited to procuring a sketch of Sielawa's prosthesis.

· · · · ·

Jan Tomasz Gross is professor of politics and European studies at New York University and the author of *Polish Society under German Occupation: The Generalgouvernement, 1939–1944* (Princeton, 1977), *Revolution from Abroad: The Soviet Conquest of Poland's Western Ukraine and Western Belorussia* (Princeton, 1988), *Upiorna dekada: Trzy eseje o stereotypach na temat Żydów, Polaków i komunistów 1939–1948* (Kraków, 1998), and *Sąsiedzi: Historia zagłady żydowskiego miasteczka* (Sejny, 2000)—English translation, *Neighbors: The Destruction of the Jewish Community in Jedwabne, Poland* (Princeton, 2001; paperback, New York and London, 2002). He is the coeditor of *War through Children's Eyes: The Soviet Occupation of Poland the Deportations 1939–1941* (Stanford, 1981)—Polish edition, *W czterdziestym nas Matko na Sybir zesłali* (London, 1983).

JEDWABNE WITHOUT STEREOTYPES:
AGNIESZKA SABOR AND MAREK ZAJĄC
TALK WITH PROFESSOR TOMASZ SZAROTA

TYGODNIK POWSZECHNY, 28 APRIL 2002

YGODNIK POWSZECHNY: Professor, in following the historical discussion of the last ten years, one could come away with the impression that the world looks at the history of the Second World War and even at the entire second half of the twentieth century almost exclusively from the perspective of the Holocaust, treating the destruction of the Jews as the main point of departure both politically and morally.

TOMASZ SZAROTA: For some historians the destruction of the Jews is an event whose scale eclipses everything else. And in reality, no nation can compare its suffering to that of the Jews, because under the Nazis every Jew was, by reason of ancestry, condemned to death. In this sense it is a misnomer to speak, for example, of the Polish Holocaust— though Richard Lukas titled his book about the Poles under German occupation (published in the United States in 1986) *The Forgotten Holocaust*.

Today we can speak of the phenomenon of the "cosmopolitanization" of memory of the Holocaust. The Israeli sociologist Natan Schneider, who participated in the ceremonies in Jedwabne on 10 July of this year, used this term. The term "globalization of memory of the Holocaust" has also appeared.

We must be conscious of the fact that situating all the world's tragedies in the context of the Holocaust alone may lead to the result that the suffering of other nations during World War II will cease to play a role altogether. The reaction of the Germans to our debate about Jedwabne is evidence that this is already happening to some degree. Reading the German commentaries—not all, but many of them—I had the impression that in the consciousness of their authors, the only victims of the Second World War were Jews, and that there are no other victims of Hitlerism or Stalinism at all today other than those who belong to the Jewish people. This form of memory of World War II cannot be accepted.

For People by People

TP: In the debate about the Holocaust, the question of the degree to which the Germans above all were its perpetrators, and what responsibility other nations bear, comes up repeatedly.

TS: The catchphrase of Zofia Nałkowska's *Medallions*, published in 1946, was "People prepared this fate for people."[1] If an institute for the study of public opinion had existed at the time in Poland, and if Poles had been asked whether this statement was true in their opinion, the majority would probably have declared a rather different opinion—the opinion that "the Germans prepared this fate for people."

Today the situation is different. The historiography of the 1990s changed our thinking about the Holocaust. Now it is emphasized that the Germans are not the only ones burdened with responsibility for the destruction of the Jews, because they found assistants in many nations. Moreover, it is no longer the battle against Hitlerism but the attitude toward Jews that is becoming the primary measure of morality during World War II. In modern eyes, not only those who committed murder, but also those who looked upon the destruction with indifference, are guilty. For example, in France, even Jean-Paul Sartre and Simone de Beauvoir are accused of failing to react to the arrest of their Jewish friends. In recent years in almost all of the countries that were occupied by the Germans, historians researching the Holocaust are stressing that their compatriots do not have clean hands.

TP: It is above all the younger generation of historians that wants to know the bitter side of the truth as well. There are many examples. In 1997, Nanda van der Zee's book about the destruction of the Jews in Holland was published there. The Germans . . . are barely discussed in this book, but the Dutch and Jews who collaborated with the Germans are pilloried. In the opinion of the author, Queen Wilhelmina also bears responsibility for the death of the Jews, because instead of emigrating to Great Britain she should have remained with her people and protected the Jews. But this thesis is utter nonsense, because the Belgian king remained in the occupied country and nothing came of it. So on what does the joint responsibility of the Dutch depend?

TS: The Dutch organized the first strike in defense of the persecuted Jews, and for that they deserve credit. But on the other hand the

---

[1] *Medaliony* (Warsaw, 1946), by Zofia Nałkowska (1885–1954), is a collection of short stories about Nazi policies in occupied Poland. An English translation (by Diana Kuprel) appeared under the title *Medallions* (Evanston, Ill., 2000).

percentage of Jews murdered there during the war is close to the percentages in Poland and other countries of Eastern Europe: 75 percent of the Dutch Jews perished, while in collaborationist France 50 percent of the Jewish community was murdered.[2] After the strike was crushed in February 1941, the Germans were able to break the resistance of the Dutch.

An example from Eastern Europe: The Latvian historian Andries Ezergailis published (in Washington and Riga simultaneously) a book about the destruction of the Latvian Jews.[3] The author's findings are appalling: it turns out that a commando unit led by the Latvian Viktor Arajs has half of the murdered Latvian Jews (35,000) on its conscience. And a historian from Iceland has written in a recently completed doctoral dissertation that even the Danes—a nation that seemingly had nothing to do with the Holocaust—have their dark chapters in the history of the Second World War. The time has come to look the historical truth in the eye. This is true not only for the Second World War but also for the postwar period. As for the Poles, the courage to confront the dark chapters of our history is evidence of normalcy. The evasion of such questions was evidence not only of censorship but also of our complexes.

The Testimony of the Witness Schaper

TP: You have cooperated with the IPN [Instytut Pamęci Narodowej—Institute of National Memory] in the preparation of the "White Book," which contains the most important documents and findings in the matter of the slaughter at Jedwabne.[4] What really happened there on 10 July 1941?

TS: It is still too early to answer that question precisely. In writing his book *Neighbors*, Jan Tomasz Gross was convinced that he knew everything there was to know. Today historians know significantly more, but there are still more questions than answers. I'm afraid that we will never know the full truth about that pogrom. It surprises me that Gross has completely ignored the voices that have appeared since the publi-

---

[2] Editorial note [AP; JM]: This is an error. According to Michael Marrus, writing in *Encyclopedia of the Holocaust* (New York, 1990), 1:512, "In all, over 77,000 Jews from France were either killed in concentration camps in Poland or died while in detention . . . about one-fifth of the country's Jews."

[3] Andries Ezergailis, *The Holocaust in Latvia* (Riga, 1996).

[4] Paweł Machcewicz and Krzysztof Persak, eds., *Wokół Jedwabnego*, 2 vols. (Warsaw, 2002).

cation of *Neighbors*. For example, the IPN wanted to provide him with materials that it had been able to collect, but he replied that he was not interested. Nor did Gross make any revisions to the German edition of *Neighbors*, which came out in the fall of 2001, and thus after the exhumation in Jedwabne and the appearance of several important witness accounts of the events. Except for one change: instead of "this was done by society," Gross wrote in the German edition that "neighbors" carried out the slaughter.

TP: The investigation will soon be finished?

TS: Yes, but we must take a critical attitude toward reports collected after several decades. The material collected by prosecutor Radosław Ignatiew, who interviewed the witnesses, does not carry much weight, especially since we are dealing with conflicting reports. The documents discovered in German archives by the historian Edmund Dmitrów are of greater significance. However, even new sources do not completely explain the matter.

TP: But several days ago the media reported on the interview of an important witness: Hermann Schaper, the commander of the unit that was active in Łomża in the summer of 1941. Prosecutor Ignatiew participated in his questioning in Germany.

TS: On the evening of 18 April, Jolanta Pieńkowska interviewed Ignatiew on that subject on Polish television. I was greatly impressed with his calm, straightforward attitude, and it confirmed my previous experiences. On 19 April, *Gazeta Wyborcza* published a commentary quoting the Polish Press Agency. On the same day, Andrzej Kaczyński's article "Witness Hermann Schaper" appeared in *Rzeczpospolita*. My comments concern these three reports.

Gazeta Wyborcza failed to mention that Schaper was the subject of a lengthy text, published simultaneously in *Rzeczpospolita* and *Süddeutsche Zeitung*, by Thomas Urban. After consulting with Dmitrów, who tracked down Schaper in Ludwigsburg, the German journalist tried to investigate his fate. Although he was unable to get to Schaper himself, he collected a lot of material about him. Several months later it turned out that the Germans—inspired by the IPN—had found this person. This is an important correction: it was not the IPN that found the witness, but the Germans, consequent to a letter addressed to them by the IPN. Next, Prosecutor Ignatiew was invited to Germany, where he presented a list of questions and participated in the questioning of the ninety-one-year-old, ailing Schaper. The questioning had to be stopped when the witness became ill. *Gazeta Wyborcza* called this "the Gestapo man's dodge"; but Schaper, although he had been informed that he could refuse to testify, tried to answer all of the questions straightforwardly so long as his health allowed. *Gazeta Wyborcza* reported, in a rather mocking tone, that no one managed to ask him about Jedwabne. However, Schaper gives us to understand that he participated in some kind of execution, but that he had nothing to do with those events; that his command unit was there for other purposes, but that there were some other units in the area as well. And he does not exclude the possibility that in addition to acts of terror on the part of the Polish people, we are dealing with the activities of another German unit.

The questioning of Schaper is a good example of Polish-German cooperation in the search for the truth about those tragic events. German journalists should learn from the example of the German prosecutors.

TP: What is the significance of that interrogation?

TS: One thing has become clear: that other units operated in that territory. This in turn constitutes indirect evidence that these tragic events might not have happened if not for the presence of the Germans, who in one way or another organized the pogrom. Their numbers were significantly smaller than had been thought: a dozen or several dozen soldiers, but not several hundred. A separate issue is the question of whether such a small group is enough, together with the forces of the desperate and bloodthirsty part of the local population, to lead to what happened in Jedwabne.

One other remark: Gross believes it is possible (I quote *Gazeta Wyborcza* here) that photographs and films made by the Germans in Jedwabne will be found. So there really is a chance, however minimal, of finding such photographs, just as the photos of the Łódź ghetto were found by a miracle. But the German crew did not shoot any film in Jedwabne. Of a hundred witnesses interviewed, there is probably not one who would confirm that the Germans filmed anything in Jedwabne.

Germans in Jedwabne?

TP: So what part did the Germans play in the pogrom?

TS: Jedwabne was one of the so-called self-cleansing actions conducted at the time, inspired by the Germans, directed by the Germans, and with the assurance of immunity for the participants in the pogrom. But the pogrom itself was carried out at the hands of the local population— in this case Poles. Such activities had a propagandistic character: they were supposed to prove that hatred of the Jews was universal. The German units of the Special Police and the Security Services (*Einsatzgruppen* and *Einsatzkommandos*) were given an order in 1941 to organize such "self-cleansing actions," leaving no trace of their own role and participation. So it is no surprise that there is little in the German source materials that implicates the Germans.

TP: At the Nuremberg trials there were no charges of organizing pogroms?

TS: War criminals—commanders of *Einsatzgruppen* and *Einsatzkommandos*—were also tried in Nuremberg before the American military tribunal. In April 1948 the indictments were announced in the so-called Case no. 9. One of the sections was titled "Incitement to Pogroms." We read in it that "certain *Einsatzkommandos* committed crimes which, from the point of view of morality, were perhaps greater than the murders they committed. These were incitement of the population to the abuse, mistreatment, and murder of their fellow citizens." It is a shame that this document has not been mentioned in the course of the debate about Jedwabne.

TP: Were the authorities of the Polish underground aware of these German tactics?

TS: On 23 June 1941, the day after the Soviet-German war broke out, Prime Minister Władysław Sikorski and Minister Stanisław Kot signed "National Order No. 2." Two days later it was sent to occupied Poland, to the commander of the Union for Armed Combat, General Stefan Rowecki, and to the government delegate for the homeland, Cyryl Ratajski. Here's a fragment of it: "The government places great emphasis on the necessity of warning the population against succumbing to German instigations to overt acts against the Jews in the territories liberated from Soviet occupation." So the underground was aware of the Germans' intentions.

And one more document, a fragment of a text published in *Prawda*, the underground organ of the Catholic Front for the Rebirth of Poland, which was edited by Zofia Kossak-Szczucka.[5] The journal began to appear in April 1942, and this quotation is from the second issue, from May 1942: "But the demoralization and bestialization that the slaughter of the Jews is introducing among us has become a burning

[5] The Catholic Front for the Rebirth of Poland (FOP) was founded at the end of 1940 by Zofia Kossak-Szczucka and Witold Bieńkowski. This was a social organization based in Warsaw, representing the Polish Roman Catholic elite. The monthly *Prawda* was one of its main papers published between 1942 and 1944.

question. For it is not only the Lithuanian auxiliaries, the *Volksdeutsch*, or the Ukrainians who have been used for monstrous executions. In many localities (Kolno, Stawiski, Jagodne, Szumów, Dęblin), the local population has participated voluntarily in the massacre. We must oppose such disgraceful behavior with all available means. We must inform people that they are becoming Herod's hired assassins, stigmatize them in the underground press, call for a boycott of the executioners, threaten, pronounce harsh judgments on the murderers in the free Republic."

Kolno and Stawiski are well known as sites of pogroms. Jagodne is, in my opinion, a mangled form of Jedwabne. On Szumów and Dęblin I found no information.

TP: Are there other indications that the Germans directed the pogrom in Jedwabne?

TS: Yes, if only the destruction of the monument to Lenin: at the time, Soviet monuments throughout the entire Białystok region were destroyed on German orders. The fact that the Jews were forced to clean the market square is also worthy of attention. I can't imagine that the local Poles were bothered by some grass growing through the stones ... That was a typical Hitlerite mania: the Jew was associated with dirt, and he needed to be taught cleanliness. Right after the Austrian Anschluss, the Jews were herded out to clean the sidewalks of Vienna with toothbrushes.

And another example: We know it is not possible that as many as 1,600 Jews were burned alive in Śleszyński's barn, as Gross asserts. Though in consideration of the rabbis' protest the exhumation was left incomplete, it allowed us to reduce the number of victims to a maximum of 400. From the point of view of morality, though, it's not about the numbers; 42 people perished in the Kielce pogrom, and that event was entered in the encyclopedia. It's unlikely that eight liters of kerosene or oil could have set off such a huge conflagration at the barn (witnesses saw the explosion and the pillar of fire). It had to be gasoline, and the Germans probably supplied it. The so-called Białystok Commando Unit also operated in this area. The figure of Wolfgang Birkner is important here. I came across this name in one of Waldemar Monkiewicz's articles, and I began to track him down. I picked up Władysław Bartoszewski's book *Warszawski pierścień śmierci* [Warsaw ring of death] and R. Domańska's *Pawiak—więzienie gestapo* [Pawiak: Gestapo prison]. And I quickly learned a lot about Birkner. In September 1939 that capable Gestapo officer was in *Einsatzgruppe* IV, which operated in the Białystok region. In October 1939, he was transferred to Warsaw. And most important of all: on 3 July 1941, having become the head of one of the four units created here, he moved from Warsaw to Białystok to reinforce *Einsatzgruppe* B, which was operating in the region. Gross asserts that on 10 July that *Einsatzgruppe* was already in Minsk. But he does not know that Birkner had an order to remain in the Białystok district. I found this information in documentation published in Germany in 1997 on the activities of the *Einsatzgruppen*, of which Gross is unaware. And when an investigation into the crimes of SS-Obersturmführer Hermann Schaper was being conducted in Israel in 1963, a certain Chaja Finkelsztein, a survivor of the pogrom in Radziłów, picked his photograph out of twenty others and indicated that he had been the leader of the action. The pogrom in Radziłów took place on 7 July 1941, and it was exactly the same scenario as in Jedwabne: driving people to the market square, the barn, the burning. A photograph of Birkner, who died at the front on 24 March 1945, was preserved in the Berlin Document Center, but it was never shown to witnesses of the events in Jedwabne.

TP: And what about Polish participation? Did "the community of Jedwabne" take part in the pogrom, as Gross tried to demonstrate, or was it only individuals, the dregs of society, as Szymon Datner wrote in *Biuletyn Żydowskiego Instytutu Historycznego*?[6]

TS: In Gross's opinion, half of the adult residents of the town participated in the slaughter. In reality it was about forty people who, thanks to German influence in my opinion, terrorized the rest. Unfortunately we do not know how many people there were in Jedwabne that day, because many people had come from out of town.

Was it just the rabble? No. Among the participants in the pogrom there were also victims of Soviet persecutions. Some had just gotten out of the NKVD prison in Łomża, others came out of the forest, and still others remembered the Soviet deportations—their final phase, after all, was in July of 1941. These people hated Communists and believed in the label *Żydokomuna* [Judeo-communism]. The fact that the aunt of the Laudański brothers, who appear in the testimonies as the ringleaders, had been murdered by the Soviets several months earlier was also not without significance. If Gross asserts that not a single Jew from Jedwabne collaborated with the local NKVD, then he contradicts himself, for earlier he mentioned a local Jew who gave Poles up to the Soviets. This does not mean that Poles did not collaborate with the

---

[6] In the article "Eksterminacja Żydów Okręgu Białostockiego" published in 1966 (which was also clearly subject to censorship), Datner did in fact describe the massacres in Jedwabne and in other places in the Łomża region as the work of the "local population" (*ludność miejscowa*).

Soviets also. And we cannot be surprised by the attitude of some of the Jews toward the Soviets because in the Second Republic they did not have equal rights as citizens, and they greeted the Soviets as liberators. Later, under the Soviet government, Poles welcomed the Germans the same way. Both sides were soon disappointed!

Let us go further: the events in Jedwabne remind us exactly of what had happened in Radziłów three days earlier. On 5 July there was a similar incident in Wąsosz. In many localities in the Białystok region there were attacks against the Jewish population: beatings, murder, plunder. All of these events took place on territories that had been under Soviet occupation from 1939 to 1941. Did people here know about the horror of German occupation in the General Government? What information from Kraków reached Wilno and Lwów? We know little about this. It is not impossible that people deluded themselves that the Germans were really liberating eastern Poland from the Communists.

However, I emphasize that in no way do I want to justify the barbarism. The enraged mob committed murder against innocent people. Among the victims were women and children. A twelve-year-old girl had her head cut off. But if you leave out the historical context, you get nowhere. A historian must find out "how it was" and understand. But to understand does not mean to approve or justify.

TP: How does the murder in Jedwabne differ from the pogroms of 1940–1941 in occupied Warsaw, Paris, The Hague, Amsterdam, and Antwerp, which you describe in your book *U progu Zagłady* [On the threshold of the Holocaust]?

TS: The debate about when the Germans decided on "the final solution of the Jewish question" is ongoing among historians today. For many years it had been believed that it happened in January 1942 at the villa of Wannsee near Berlin. Today there is no doubt that the decision was made earlier. Christian Gerlach, a German historian of the younger generation, asserts that Hitler made his decision about the *Endlösung* at the moment the American-Japanese war broke out in December 1941. In my book I demonstrate that the decision was reached before the outbreak of war with the USSR. Jedwabne was the first stage in the realization of the Holocaust—carried out in the Białystok region, Lithuania, Latvia, Belarus, Ukraine, and Moldova—also at the hands of the local populations. The German organization entered later: the ghettos arose, particular groups of people were liquidated, and finally gas chambers were built.

But earlier pogroms in Warsaw, Paris, The Hague, Amsterdam, and Antwerp took place before the decision about the "Final Solution" was made, when the Germans were still really thinking about dispatching the Jews to Madagascar. It was like a continuation of *Kristallnacht*, the pogrom against the Jews in Germany in November 1938.

"Germans? Who Cares?"

TP: In the fall of 2000, when the debate about Jedwabne began in Poland, you criticized Gross's work in the pages of *Gazeta Wyborcza*. How do you evaluate the book today?

TS: *Neighbors* shocks the reader. Particularly the photographs of the victims. In Poland we are accustomed to the anonymity of the victims of the Second World War. No names are given on the ubiquitous plaques around Warsaw memorializing Poles who were shot down. Five thousand people perished in Palmiry. We know the names of only 2,500, and we remember only a few: Kusociński, Rataj, Niedziałkowski.[7] Near Paris there is a place of execution similar to Palmiry: Mont-Valérien, where the Germans executed members of the French resistance movement. We know the names of those killed, their dates of birth, their professions. But many Poles and almost all of the Jews murdered have no graves at all.

As for the character of the book: for me *Neighbors* is an important essay, forcing the historian to undertake research. Gross believes that he has written a serious scholarly work, but in my opinion he does not have the professional training to write a historical work that would meet the professional requirements of the discipline. He is a sociologist and never learned the historian's craft: the search for and evaluation of sources. He interprets our (meaning, historians') accusations and critical remarks as a manifestation of deep-rooted Polish antisemitism. Gross cannot understand why no one had studied Jedwabne earlier. After all, he says, it was enough to go there, go into some corner bar, and start talking with people. My answer to that is that history is not written by going into bars. It's a question of craft.

I suppose that *Neighbors* could have passed without a trace, like Gross's earlier book, *Upiorna dekada* [Monstrous decade]. But in May 2000 Andrzej Kaczyński of *Rzeczpospolita* read a text by Gross in the

[7] Palmiry—a small village in Mazovia—was a place of Nazi mass executions of Polish intelligentsia between December 1939 and July 1941. Among the estimated figure of 1,700 individuals who were murdered there were the Polish athlete Janusz Kusociński (1907–1940), former marshal of Polish parliament and writer Maciej Rataj (1884–1940), and theorist and politician of the Polish Socialist Party (PPS) Mieczysław Niedziałkowski (1893–1940).

book *Provincial Europe*, published in honor of Prof. Tomasz Strembosz, and he was so horrified by it that he went to Jedwabne to ask people whether it was true. Unfortunately he received confirmation. And then he wrote the article "Całopalenie" [Burnt offering] in *Rzeczpospolita*. Until November 2000 *Gazeta Wyborcza* had devoted no attention to *Neighbors* other than a brief note. The situation changed when Adam Michnik found out that an American edition of *Neighbors* was ready for publication. And, fearful of a scandal on a worldwide scale (for example the accusation that Poles don't want to discuss the dark chapters of their history), he concluded that *Wyborcza* could not remain silent.

TP: Some participants have asserted that after *Neighbors*, it is necessary to reform Polish historiography, to write differently about the history of Poland.

TS: One chapter of *Neighbors* bears the title "For a New Historiography." Gross comes across there as the teacher of not-too-clever students, to whom he is pointing out the direction they can take so that Polish scholarship can rise to the occasion and finally create an honest historiography. Gross is convinced that he has created a new historiography. To put it mildly, this is megalomania. The demand for further research not only on the Holocaust but on World War II in general— with its many blank pages—is quite enough.

In German commentaries we have read that what is happening in Poland around Jedwabne is a debate among historians. Not at all: we have been dealing with a great journalistic, political, moral, and psychological debate—but certainly not a scholarly debate among historians. After the publication of *Neighbors* in Germany, I read with amazement in the weekly *Der Spiegel* that *Neighbors* is one of the most important historical works written in Europe since the fall of communism.

TP: The German reaction to *Neighbors* and Jedwabne has aroused a lot of emotion in Poland.

TS: Not without reason. The interpretation of the Jedwabne events and the ongoing discussion in Poland by a part of the German press is surprising. Joachim Trenkner drew attention to this in his great and honest article "Komu to przystoi" [For whom is it proper?] (*Tygodnik Powszechny*, 9 December 2001).[8] It seems the slaughter in Jedwabne autho-

---

[8] Joachim Trenkner is a journalist and writer and a former chairman of the public radio and TV station Sender Freies Berlin. He is a regular contributor to *Der Aufbau* and *Tygodnik Powszechny*.

rizes certain German journalists to assert that these events shatter the myth, completely unjustified in their opinion, of Poles as "a nation of victims." And they make of us accomplices in the Holocaust and collaborators, rather than victims of Nazi barbarism and "unbowed" fighters against the Hitlerite occupier. In Germany the consequence of this interpretation of the debate about Jedwabne is the generalization of attitudes: it's not just some neighbors who are guilty, but Polish society, the nation, Poles.

Proportions are important here. For the resident of Melbourne or New York, the name of Jedwabne may mean almost as much today as Auschwitz, Treblinka, or Majdanek. Two American journalists came to me one time to talk about Jedwabne. I asked whether the name Babi Yar meant anything to them.[9] They looked at me with surprise: "What does it have to do with Jedwabne?" they asked. Nothing, I said, except that in the course of two days, 33,000 people were murdered there. "What? Where?" I say: the Germans murdered 33,000 Jews in Babi Yar. Their answer: "Germans? Who cares?"

TP: How, then, should we evaluate the attitude of Poles toward the Jews during the war?

TS: In writing about the Holocaust, Raul Hilberg distinguishes three categories: perpetrators, victims, and witnesses (onlookers). Until now Poles were included in the last group, and *szmalcownicy* [blackmailers] were treated as marginal. The message of Gross's book is this: we cannot stop at Jan Błoński's theses from his 1987 article "Biedni Polacy patrzą na getto" [The poor Poles look at the ghetto], because Poles are not just passive witnesses but also the executioner's helpers. But this was not so. In my book *Okupowanej Warszawy dzień powsiedni* [Daily life in occupied Warsaw] I quote an analysis conducted by the Office of the Government Delegate for the Homeland in mid-1942 and titled "Three Warsaws." Assuming that the attitudes of about a million residents of Warsaw were evaluated, it was estimated at the time that "ignoble Warsaw" constituted 5 percent of its inhabitants, "the Warsaw of the Kowalskis" (passive) constituted 70 percent, and "fighting and heroic Warsaw" constituted 25 percent. *Szmalcownicy* formed a certain portion of the "ignoble," and among the 250,000 who fought against the Germans there were certainly a few who aided Jews. But only some of them received the Righteous Among the Nations medal.

---

[9] Babi Yar, a ravine in the northwestern part of Kiev, was a place of Nazi mass execution of the entire Jewish community of Kiev. The killing began on 29 September 1941. It is estimated that more than 100,000 Jews were killed there. Other social groups murdered at Babi Yar were Soviet prisoners of war and the local Roma population.

TP: What influence has the debate about Jedwabne had on Poles' identity?

TS: Our national identity crisis, which has lasted for decades, has deepened. Not long ago *Rzeczpospolita* published a series of articles with characteristic titles: Andrzej Nowak asked the question "Westerplatte czy Jedwabne?" [Westerplatte or Jedwabne?], and Paweł Machcewicz of the IPN responded: "I Westerplatte i Jedwabne" [Both Westerplatte and Jedwabne]. Finally Tomasz Merta's article "Wspólnota potrzebuje ideałów" [The community needs ideals] was published. In the author's opinion we cannot say endlessly to a nation that its history is a string of shameful acts. And Merta is absolutely right.

In connection with the debate about Jedwabne, *Wprost* laid out all our sins vis-à-vis the Ukrainians, the Germans, the Jews. It was all true, but our society is not yet ready for this truth, even if the intellectual elite is of a different opinion. For to stand face-to-face with this truth, we need to have a healthy, levelheaded consciousness of our virtues and vices, of the heroic pages in our history and of our offenses and even crimes. But we are too deeply entrenched in our complexes.

TP: What complexes?

TS: Our national megalomania is, in its essence, the result of a negative stereotype of ourselves, of our lack of national pride. This has been confirmed by sociological research. In our opinion, Jews and Germans possess characteristics that we lack. We wish to be enterprising, tidy, and so on. Unless we are able to free ourselves of these complexes, our nation will continue to be xenophobic. To live in harmony with others, one must believe in one's own worth. Yet the debate about Jedwabne has had the consequence that Poles have confirmed in themselves what they already felt—a sense of shame. I am not certain whether the support for the League of Polish Families in the last election was not at some level a perverse reaction to the debate, during which—at least this is how it was understood by a section of society—there was an attempt to persuade us that we "are in the same wagon of shame as the Germans."

TP: Are you suggesting that we should have spoken of Jedwabne in some other way?

TS: As a historian I must search for the truth. However, there is a difference between researching the course of history and the manner of speaking about history and about the model of national tradition that is transmitted to society. This national tradition should also teach about mistakes and sins committed—that is clear. But mistakes cannot cover up achievements. We cannot look at Poles only through the prism of Kielce and Jedwabne.

As a historian I have conducted research on stereotypes as well. Today I am afraid that the "Jedwabne matter" has by no means corrected the already none-too-positive image of Poland in the world . . .

TP: So perhaps the mistake lay not in the debate itself but in its form: at times one could have come away with the impression that people cared less about the truth than about demonstrating the correctness of previous assumptions.

TS: Jan Tomasz Gross has sometimes behaved like someone who believes that if he gives even an inch from the line he has taken, it will undermine the credibility of his entire book . . . This was not a serious scholarly debate.

TP: His ever more radical adversaries did not behave any better, however.

TS: Of course not: they assumed in advance that everything written in *Neighbors* was a lie, thought up for the purpose of harming the Polish nation. I hope that after the publication of the IPN's "White Book" about the murders in Jedwabne, we may perhaps begin an honest historical discussion at last.

At the same time we must recognize that our compatriots committed those shameful acts at that time. And that will not change even if someday we find documents confirming that a German commando unit was behind the pogrom of 10 July 1941.[10]

. . . . .

Tomasz Szarota was born in 1940 and is a professor at the Historical Institute of the Polish Academy of Sciences. Among his books are *Oku-*

---

[10] In his reply in *Tygodnik Powszechny* on 5 May 2002, Gross differed with Szarota over his discussion of the role of the Germans in the massacre and over his treatment of the number of victims. He specifically denied Szarota's claim that he had turned down an offer from the Instytut Pamęci Narodowej to provide him with new information. He also argued that there were no significant methodological differences between the way a sociologist and a historian would approach the problem of how to establish what happened in Jedwabne on 10 July 1941. But like Szarota he acknowledged that, up to that point, there had been "no discussion among historians about the whole set of problems raised by the publication of *Neighbors*," which he regarded both as a pity and even more as a matter for shame. He agreed with Szarota that "in the works of historians of the Second World War, the problem of the persecution of the Jews by the local population had been ignored," and conceded that "*Neighbors* is only the first step on the road to unveiling the truth about an epoch that drew the inhabitants of many Polish localities

powanej Warszawy dzień powszedni (Everyday life in Warsaw under the occupation) (Warsaw, 1978), *Życie codzienne w stolicach okupowanej Europy* (Everyday life in European capitals under the occupation) (Warsaw, 1995), and *U progu Zagłady. Zajscia antyżydowskie i pogromy w okupowanej Europie* (On the threshold of destruction: Anti-Jewish riots and pogroms in occupied Europe) (Warsaw, 2000). He lives in Warsaw.

---

into a vortex of crime." Szarota published a response to Gross's reply under the title "Zmarnowana Szansa" (A wasted chance) in *Tygodnik Powszechny* on 12 May 2002.

Dariusz Stola

JEDWABNE: HOW WAS IT POSSIBLE?

W RITING HISTORY is a collective undertaking, which moves forward thanks to the proposal of new narratives of the past and sources previously unknown, followed by criticism, the positing of alternative narratives, critiques of these narratives, and so on. Jan Gross should be credited with setting this process in motion around a case that is not only confounding and difficult but of great significance as well. Thus I appreciate his book *Neighbors*, yet my appreciation does not preclude my criticism. Many objections— some of them warranted—have been raised against *Neighbors*, but none of them can disqualify the book. By the same token, bringing up objections cannot be a reason for disqualification. In the playing field demarcated by good customs and principles of historical methodology, we cooperate and serve the truth even when we debate and argue.

We have some grounds for reflection, which can contribute to the success of the collective effort of historians, as well as to the better understanding of the events by other readers. Because of the most serious nature of the problems under consideration and the debatable quality of sources, the reflections need to be self-critical. Cautious formulations—all those *probablys* and *possiblys*—can be annoying, but they are better than offering the illusion of certitude while the sources leave room for divergent interpretations. Such an illusion may be particularly harmful when it contributes to misjudgments in assigning responsibility for the crime(s).

This article focuses on just a few questions that Jan Gross's book and the ensuing debate have raised. More extensive discussion of additional questions is presented in my other article on the topic.[1] Astonished by the horrifying scenes presented in the book, I have tried to understand *how* it happened. This in turn led to the questions of *what* happened and what the necessary preconditions were.

From the perspective of our knowledge about the murder of nearly six million European Jews, including almost all (i.e., more than 90 percent)

---

[1] D. Stola "A Monument of Words," *Yad Vashem Studies* (Jerusalem, 2003), originally published as "Pomnik ze słów," *Rzeczpospolita*, 1–2 June 2001. I am indebted to *Yad Vashem Studies* for permission to use the translation by Jerzy Michałowicz when preparing this article.

of the Polish Jews, the crime in Jedwabne stands out because of the participation of Poles and the archaic killing methods, not because of its total scale. Most of us are no longer surprised that the extermination embraced almost all the Jewish community. Yet stressing the total nature of the crime is necessary to put it into a correct perspective. Without this emphasis (which we do not find in the book), readers may easily overlook some essential features of the killing and reach inadequate or simply wrong conclusions.

The basic observation, which many sources confirm and none contradicts, is that of all the Jews who were in Jedwabne on the morning of 10 July 1941—reasonable estimates range from five hundred to fifteen hundred—only a handful lived to see the evening.[2] We do not know exactly how many managed to avoid death on that day. Besides the seven who hid with the Wyrzykowski family there likely were others, maybe even up to a hundred people, who found shelter in the town and beyond, at least for the time being. In any case, the number of survivors amounted to a small fraction of those condemned to slaughter. I believe that this fact leads to a few conclusions about the killing. Namely, that it was:

1. intended to be (almost) total;
2. highly effective;
3. organized and systematic (otherwise it would not have been so effective); and
4. unprecedented (in this part of modern Europe).

First, I do not think that the deadly outcome of the events of 10 July can be construed as an unintended effect of an unorganized, largely chaotic social process. I believe that the killing of all, or almost all, the Jews in Jedwabne was the consciously defined goal of at least some of the participants in the crime. Without such intention there would have been some people left alive whom none wanted to kill. The sources make clear that *all* the Jews were to be gathered in the marketplace, that attempts by *any* of them to escape or hide were to be prevented, and that *all* those who were in the market square were to be killed individually or rushed into the barn, where the largest group perished in fire. The murder of (almost) the entire community of several hundred people on a single day cannot happen unintentionally.

[2] The numbers provided by Jan Gross are questionable. It is far from certain that 1,600 Jews were killed on 10 July or that Jews made up 60 percent of the population of Jedwabne before the killing. There are strong arguments for the claim that the number of victims was much lower. The size of the mass grave of the victims, as explored by archaeologists this summer, allows for an estimate of up to 400. The size of the barn where the victims met their death (144 square meters) confirms such an estimate. Soviet regis-

Second, those participants in the murder who shared the genocidal aim proved extremely effective. Their efficiency is demonstrated by the death ratio: because probably only several Jews survived the day, a hundred at most, the death ratio was between 80 and 99 percent, depending on the assumed initial number of the Jews in the town.

Such a high efficiency of collective action requires organization. "Cacophony of violence," as Jan Gross terms chaotic actions of individual wrongdoers in Jedwabne,[3] is not enough to bring about a genocide, even if the cumulative character of the outcome is assumed and the social dynamics of the aggression flows from strong ethnic and religious prejudice, individual greed, and desire for revenge. I do not know of a single case of killing of such a scale and intensity that would have resulted exclusively from the dynamics of uncoordinated aggression of the mob. I do not recall any ethnic disturbances, pogroms, or other attacks by a mob where violence proved so efficient, resulting in such a large number of victims. The limited (self-)organizational capacity of the mob makes it a very unlikely agent for effective genocidal killing. It takes a government, or its substitute, such as a paramilitary organization, to make a genocide.[4] The deductionist argument—that because the killing in Jedwabne was of a total, genocidal character, it therefore had to be organized—is further supported by the available sources that provide limited yet sufficient insight into the organization of the killing on 10 July 1941 (on which more below).

Because of the rich history of interethnic violence in east-central Europe, and anti-Jewish violence in particular, we may place the murder in Jedwabne against a background that will highlight its particular features. The wave of pogroms that swept over Ukraine in 1918–1919 offers a suitable comparison. The factors that seem to have contributed to the crime in Jedwabne—ethnic resentment, the stereotype of "Jewish Bolsheviks," and greed—were not weaker or less widespread in Ukraine in 1919 than in the Podlasie region (where Jedwabne is located) in 1941. The tradition of peasant violence, including anti-Jewish violence, had been in fact much stronger in Ukraine than in Podlasie, and military or paramilitary organizations were often involved in the pogroms in Ukraine. A detailed analysis of the data on some 1,300 po-

---

tration data from 1940 report only 600 Jewish residents in Jedwabne. These three are sources *contemporary* with the crime, which should not be simply ignored.

[3] *Sąsiedzi*, 68.

[4] F. Chalk and K. Jonassohn, eds., *The History and Sociology of Genocide* (New Haven and London, 1990); H. Fein, *Genocide: A Sociological Perspective* (New York, 1993). The killing of (almost) all Jews in only one town does not meet the definition of genocide as set forth by Raphael Lemkin or endorsed by the relevant UN convention. It certainly was a part of the genocide, a *genocide in part*, or a *genocidal killing*.

groms in Ukraine shows that in 36 percent of them fewer than ten persons perished, in 88 percent the death toll was below one hundred, and in no case did the death ratio approximate the ratio in Jedwabne. Eighty percent of Jewish families in the localities affected by the pogroms survived without casualties.[5] As another comparison I offer the first pogroms in Kovno and Lvov, which took place in the aftermath of the Soviet flight in the summer of 1941, that is, almost concurrently with the crime in Jedwabne. Each of them resulted in several thousand deaths, but these figures amounted to a small fraction of the total Jewish population of the cities.

This data shows that the crime in Jedwabne was not an extraordinarily bloody pogrom. Had the excited mob of Jedwabne Poles launched a chaotic attack on Jewish houses and stores, the result would have resembled the pogroms in Ukraine: several people killed, several dozen wounded, and, above all, extensive looting and vandalism. The murder of 10 July was clearly a case of something else and essentially different. To be sure, there was the "cacophony of violence," yet one cannot reduce the events of 10 July to this dimension. Besides the pogromlike violence there was an action of a different order: premeditated, systematic, and disciplined. The "cacophony of violence" was orchestrated; it was one of the means to reach the overall goal.

Here we come to the question of where the idea originated to kill all the Jews of Jedwabne. The Jedwabne killing, together with a similar crime in neighboring Radziłów, about which we know even less, was one of the early instances, if not the earliest, of an almost complete annihilation of an entire Jewish community. As far as I know, such an idea had not appeared in the prewar antisemitic writings in Poland. Although the rhetoric of Polish antisemites was often eliminatory in nature, they saw emigration of a considerable proportion of Polish Jews as their solution to the Jewish question.[6] After all, the path from a dangerous metaphor to the realization of mass murder takes some time, as exemplified by the long road taken by the most devoted Nazi antisemites.

Even the Nazi leaders, whose rhetoric had long since made their audience used to an eliminatory and ruthless approach to the Jews, reached the decision about total killing step-by-step, beginning with the early stages of discrimination, forced emigration, and later ghettoization, destruction through starvation and disease, and various plans

[5] Henry Abramson, *A Prayer for the Government: Ukrainians and Jews in Revolutionary Times* (Cambridge, Mass., 1999), 119.

[6] Anna Landau-Czajka, *W jednym stali domu. Koncepcje rozwizania kwestii żydowskiej w publicystyce polskiej lat 1933–1939* (Warsaw, 1998).

for "reservations" and resettlement, which radicalized as the war went on.[7] Thus it seems implausible that the idea of killing each and every Jew—that is, the idea of the Holocaust—was invented by the Polish mob in Jedwabne. Although this cannot be ruled out (in which case it can be considered their remarkable contribution not only to the town's history but also to the history of the world), circumstantial evidence points to the Germans as those who brought the idea to the town.

It seems more than sheer coincidence that concurrently with the crime in Jedwabne, German authorities conducted or staged genocidal killings of Jews in many other localities, which followed specific orders of German leaders to "intensify . . . efforts at self-cleansing by anticommunist and anti-Jewish activists" and make it appear as spontaneous.[8] Especially as before the killing in Jedwabne a mysterious group of German officers arrived in the town. This author finds it hard to believe that Karolak, the German-appointed mayor of Jedwabne, invented the idea of killing all the Jews in town and then requested that the German authorities agree to the murder and send for this occasion a special group of officers with photographic equipment.

As stressed above, besides the remarkable efficiency of the killers, the primary sources also point to the organized and planned nature of the anti-Jewish action on 10 July. The organization is a marginal topic in the testimonies, but this should not surprise. The witnesses saw a sequence of terrible scenes, especially if they observed them from the victims' perspective. They were shocked by the horrifying events, and their accounts revolve around the two aspects of the crime they evidently found most traumatic: the cruelty and the participation of their neighbors. The participants who were in a position to see the overall picture or could have known the plan had good reasons not to speak about it during the trial.

Nevertheless, the testimonies provide enough information to point to at least a few organizational aspects of the crime. The origins of the murder were in a meeting between the group of Germans who had arrived in the town and the town authorities. During the meeting they prepared or elaborated a plan of action. The fact that some of the survivors had been warned by their Polish friends, and that some peasants from outside Jedwabne showed up in town in the morning, possibly indicates that preparations began before 10 July. Members of the mu-

---

[7] On the debate between "functionalists" and "intentionalists," see Michael R. Marrus, *The Holocaust in History* (Hanover, N.H., 1987).

[8] Reinhard Heydrich's instruction to Security Police of 29 June 1941, quoted by A. B. Rossino, "Polish 'Neighbors' and German Invaders," *POLIN: Studies in Polish Jewry* 16 (2003).

nicipal executive, usually with German gendarmes, visited Polish residents and ordered a number of men to gather at a designated location. Sticks and clubs (which someone must have prepared and stockpiled earlier) were handed out to those assembled. Polish conscripts were given specific assignments, such as to drive the Jews to the market square, keep watch over the assembled Jews, guard the streets leading out of town, and, later on, to escort the Jews from the square to the barn outside the town. These are the instructions that witnesses and defendants in the postwar trial mentioned. It is possible that they had been given other assignments as well, to which they did not want to admit in court. The apparently small scale of looting on that day also attests to organization and discipline of sorts. While we know that in the following days the administration and Polish individuals took over the property of the murdered victims, this topic seems to be absent from the accounts of 10 July, which is most unusual for a pogrom.

Evidently premeditated was the killing of a number of Jewish men at an early stage of the action. They were first forced to "exercise" or parade with the heavy statue of Lenin and to bury it (which exhausted, humiliated, and stigmatized them). Then they were brought out of the town and slaughtered—in small groups, which gave the executioners numerical superiority over the victims on the killing site. Killing ablebodied men first helped decrease the risk of resistance in the next stage, when the crowd of the remaining, beaten and terrorized, Jews (mostly women, elderly, and children) was driven to the barn.

Thus the collective actions on 10 July manifest some order: there were a goal, a division of labor, and a plan of action, although it was modified. Obviously, the pattern of action in Jedwabne differed from that of mass executions carried out by German police units alone. In Jedwabne that was probably a framework, so to speak, which left room for individual initiatives and loosely coordinated actions by individuals and small groups of excited executioners, who gave vent to personal hatreds or settling of scores. At the same time, however, individual initiatives had their limits. For example, no exception could be made for any of the victims; one could not abandon his post; one had to (temporarily) refrain from looting. In some cases these rules were violated, but the violations stand out precisely as exceptions to the rule.

What I believe especially important in the above pattern is the division of labor, which structured the collective action, with various roles marked by different degrees of involvement in killing. At the top, owing to their deadly and shocking deeds, were the direct murderers armed with iron tools or wooden clubs. At the end of the day, one of them allegedly cast a lit match at the barn doused in kerosene. The image of such "willing executioners" (to use Daniel Goldhagen's term), feverishly active and mobile ("Jerzy Laudański was running down the street ... very nervous"),[9] imprinted itself in the memories of the survivors and other witnesses. Their testimonies portray the "willing executioners" with sufficient clarity to leave no doubt as to the existence of this group, even though its size and composition remain unclear. The group also included volunteers who were not conscripted, including arrivals from neighboring localities.

At the other end of the list of roles was "standing on the market square," the only one to which the defendants in the 1949 trial were willing to confess. In contrast to the bloody deeds of the executioners, this role did not require moral savagery or hatred toward the victims. It seems that general obedience to the authorities and fear of punishment were sufficient reasons for those who undertook this task. Between the most direct involvement in killing and the minor, auxiliary roles, there were various tasks of decreasing degrees of violence, such as removing the Jews from their houses, rounding up those trying to escape, and the like. Let us stress that the minor tasks which did not involve use of violence were also necessary for effective realization of the genocidal plan. Even the activities that in a different context would have been perfectly innocent, such as opening the barn and removing unnecessary items from inside, furthered or facilitated the genocide.

It appears that the number of people in the various roles from the above list was in inverse proportion to the savagery needed to perform them and to the degree of involvement in killing. Implementing the genocide did not require a large number of "willing executioners." They could be few in number thanks precisely to the division of labor—specialization of tasks, which relieves the experts from activities that others could perform. Even their cruelty turns out to be instrumental: in spreading terror, they paralyzed the will of the victims, decreased the risk of undesirable behavior, and consequently reduced the resources needed to carry out the action. I do not mean that all these elements were planned in advance; however, without them the course of events could have been different. After all, when launching the action on 10 July, the Germans and Mayor Karolak operated under conditions of considerable uncertainty.

We know that some Poles who were called by the mayor or the Germans refused to accept their assignments and fled the town or hid in their houses. This shows that passive resistance of this kind—refusal to take part in the operation—was (seen by them to be) risky but possible. We also know about people who helped the Jews escape or hide;

[9] *Sąsiedzi*, 70.

in other words, they actively resisted the operation. However, these acts of passive and active resistance were carried out in secrecy. We know of no instance of an open, blatant act of resistance. Obviously, fear was at least one cause for this. It is equally obvious, it seems, that not only the Germans were feared but also, perhaps foremost, some of one's Polish neighbors. The cruelty of the "willing executioners" and Karolak's rule evoked fear not only among the Jewish victims.

Karolak himself or his close associates did not necessarily stain their hands with blood, but within the perspective of this study, their role appears critical. They led other participants in the crime; they managed the anti-Jewish action. Mayor Karolak played the key role, followed by Bardoń and members of the town administration, Sobuta and Wasilewski.

Unfortunately, although witnesses emphasize the significance of these three men in the events, we have little knowledge of how they performed their managerial tasks. This is the question of the leadership. Without leadership, collective actions are easily distracted or run aground. Why did the participants carry out Karolak's instructions? Who was Karolak himself? I don't have satisfactory answers to these questions. I pose them because a good question is half an answer.

When considering the issues of leadership and organization of the murder, we inevitably reach the question of the role of the Germans. Germans make their appearance in Jedwabne not only as members of an ethnic group but also in specific roles. These are important not only in "the higher, historical-metaphysical sense," as Jan Gross believes,[10] but also in the most practical meaning of the term. Polish and Jewish witnesses have relatively little to say about the Germans' specific actions on 10 July; in testimonies they usually appear as faceless and nameless figures in uniforms. We do not even know with any certainty how many of them were present.

The accounts speak about their meeting with the town administration, their participation in conscripting Polish men (including coercion and "threats with firearms"), participation in driving the Jews to the market square, beating them, and chasing them to the barn, and photographing (or filming) the events. In addition, we can presume their involvement in several moments of crucial importance in terms of organization that were hidden from the witnesses' eyes, or simply inconspicuous, especially against the background of the shocking scenes of violence and savagery.

First, as mentioned above, the plan to murder *all* the Jews was most likely not conceived locally but imported. Second, the meeting be-

---

[10] Ibid., 56.

tween the Germans and the municipal administration, which turned out to be critical for the course of events, was a briefing rather than a consultation. After all, the town council was appointed by the occupying forces (though the circumstances surrounding its establishment remain unclear) and remained totally subordinated to them, so that no partnership of any sort between the two sides was possible. The claim that the municipal administration "reached an agreement"[11] with the Germans is grossly misleading. This, however, does not change the fact—attested to in numerous testimonies—that the members of the administration showed a commitment in carrying out the anti-Jewish action that exceeded regular obedience.

Fourth, the high effectiveness of this action testifies to the considerable organizational skills of those who headed it. Again, it cannot be ruled out that the natural skills of Karolak and Bardoń were responsible. However, we do not have any information that they had performed any managerial tasks or had shown any leadership skills before the war. It seems more plausible that the effectiveness resulted from good planning and skillful supervision by the German officers, who were people of higher education and police experience.

The last group of Jedwabne Poles to list here consisted of onlookers watching with curiosity what was happening to the Jews. In all likelihood they made up the largest group of Poles who were present during the crime. At the same time, their silent passivity makes them the most impenetrable of the groups. The wrongdoers, the persons who actively evaded taking part in the operation, those who extended assistance to the Jews or showed compassion with words, or those who expressed satisfaction at Jewish suffering—all of these people revealed themselves at least a bit; they expressed themselves in a way. In contrast, members of the passive group gave the historians nothing but silence. The question of how to interpret passivity is a key problem for explaining reactions to the Holocaust. Bystanders were the largest group not only in Jedwabne but also in Poland at large, as well as in other countries affected by the Holocaust.

Having considered the typology of behaviors, we may turn to the question of the number of Polish participants in the crime. This question is key for the debate on the degree to which they can be said to represent the entire Polish population of Jedwabne. While Jan Gross speaks of at least ninety-two participants from Jedwabne alone, Tomasz Strzembosz gives the number of just twenty-three. Both figures raise my serious doubts. The estimate by Prof. Strzembosz runs counter to testimonies that speak about a "crowd" around the Jews.

[11] Ibid., 51.

On the other hand, Prof. Gross took his number from protocols of inter-rogation by the Security Office in 1949, which have obvious faults as a source. In particular the security officers proceeded routinely—that is, using their regular methods (beating included, which we know from the court protocols), they sought to extract confessions incrimi-nating as many persons as possible. The divergence in the estimates can largely be explained by different approaches to the people who performed auxiliary duties in the crime. Strzembosz clearly leaves such persons out of his account, whereas Gross lumps them together with "the willing executioners."

The higher of the two estimates, approximating nearly half the num-ber of all adult Polish males in the town, allows for extrapolation from their behavior to the population as a whole. But then the question arises: which (or whose) behavior may we generalize? The higher the estimate one accepts, the larger the number of people it includes who performed minor, auxiliary tasks, did so unwillingly and under duress, or even abandoned their posts at the first opportunity (as some wit-nesses testified in the trial). The common denominator of their behav-iors that one could extrapolate is this: they were present and did noth-ing to help the victims. Such a conclusion is not very illuminating.

On the other hand, when we turn to the horrible deeds of the "will-ing executioners," we speak of a group that included volunteers from outside Jedwabne and/or was smaller than Jan Gross suggests; thus the argument erodes that they were a sufficiently large sample of Jedwabne Poles to permit generalization. Furthermore, the group of the "willing executioners" was not a random sample. In all likeli-hood, when carrying out the conscription (which did not sweep all the men in town) and handing out various assignments, Karolak took into account the personality traits of the town residents with whom he was familiar. More important, later on, a self-selection took place: various individuals joined or left the group of executioners by taking on or shirking assignments, by showing particular eagerness in car-rying them out, and so forth. They were not "ordinary men," such as the Germans so insightfully described by Christopher Browning, who were *drafted* into Reserve Police Battalion 101 and murdered the Jews in the town of Józefów.[12] Therefore, focusing on the executioners, we lack the grounds to draw from their behavior any generalized conclusions about the Polish population of the town that would ex-pand our knowledge. The conclusion that this population included

---

[12] Christopher R. Browning, *Ordinary Men: Reserve Police Battalion 101 and the Final Solution in Poland* (New York, 1992). Browning's outstanding book can be recommended to everyone moved by the story of Jedwabne.

people ready to participate in murder seems not more illuminating than the former one.

The above reflections on the crime in Jedwabne lead to a different conclusion from the one proposed by Jan Gross. He wrote, "The [Jedwabne's Polish] society ... and not any Nazis committed the murder."[13] Contrary to some of his critics, I would like to juxtapose, not the Germans with the Poles, but the "society" ("the people") and "rulers" ("the government")—the pair of concepts that dominate our thinking about totalitarian regimes. Jan Gross has long since been advancing a new perspective on the practices of totalitarian regimes. His excellent book *Revolution from Abroad*[14] offers the best example of this approach. His point of view is close to my heart, because within a microhistorical perspective it shows the human face(s) of the regime (which does not make it less frightening). It restores agency to individuals who are usually portrayed just as cogs of bureaucratic machinery or inert particles of the human mass. My impression, however, is that this time Jan Gross went too far in de-etatizing the course of events, or he chose a wrong example.

Apart from "spontaneous reflexes and behavior" of some of Jedwabne Poles, there was an order or framework without which matters would have taken a different course. In the absence of this framework, gruesome and shameful deeds could have taken place, but they would have belonged to a category different from genocide. This framework emanates from the state; this order is the state. There was a grotesque state in Jedwabne on 10 July 1941. It existed by the fiat of the Nazis and was (co)administered by their local collaborators. It cannot be seen as a form of social self-organization, a product of civil society that emerged to fill the void after the Soviet retreat. This was a German administration, a temporary administration set up by the occupier to manage an area in a newly acquired province. Karolak and his followers were simply local collaborators admitted to the lowest level of the administration. Yet the legitimacy of the collaborators rested on more than the military power of Germans. It was also rooted in the feeling of relief at the end of Soviet occupation, thanks to which the new occupier could be seen as a liberator. Some Poles could have found this new administration easier to accept because it was anti-Jewish.

The fact that this was not a Polish state points to the fact that Karolak and his men were not only murderers but also traitors, who collaborated with the enemy to the detriment of their fellow countrymen.

[13] *Sąsiedzi*, 115.

[14] Jan Tomasz Gross, *Revolution from Abroad: The Soviet Conquest of Poland's Western Ukraine and Western Belorussia* (Princeton, 1988).

Their motives for committing treason—ethnic hatred, desire for revenge, or booty—are of secondary importance. By cooperating with the occupier against their Jewish neighbors, they clearly violated the fundamental laws of the Polish Republic and disobeyed calls of the legitimate leaders of the nation. The legitimate leaders were the Polish government-in-exile in London and the underground in Poland. Both the exiles and the underground leaders had warned Poles against any cooperation in the Germans' anti-Jewish actions. Even if the participants in the killing of Jedwabne Jews had not heard of any of these calls, the treacherous character of their collaboration is obvious. This is what they were accused of in the 1949 trial. Notably, because they were accused of cooperation "with the German state . . . against the people persecuted by the [German] authorities for political, ethnic, religious, or racial reasons,"[15] to evade the death penalty they took a peculiar line of defense downplaying the German involvement in the events of 10 July. From this point of view it was of course bad that they participated in killing the Jews, but it was much worse that they did it in collaboration with the Germans.

What is most important is that the Jedwabne administration had the fundamental property of the state: namely, it commanded the means of violence and could designate who might use violence, and on what grounds. On this basis, on 10 July, the administration allowed the use of violence by everyone and without any restrictions, provided the Jews and only the Jews were the targets. Violence against the Jews was not only permitted but also expected and rewarded (by promise of participation in the spoils), whereas attempts to resist or protest could result in punishment. This way the stage was set for acts of savagery, with the "willing executioners" from the local population acting singly or in small groups. In addition, on that day the administration called up a certain number of men into an auxiliary service, to implement the plan of genocide. Some of the conscripts tried to shirk this order; some did what they were told under duress and reluctantly; some willingly applied themselves to even the most ghastly assignments.

The final outcome clearly shows that the essential posts were sufficiently manned, and that it was possible to murder nearly the entire community within one day with relatively little involvement of German forces. Even if we accept higher estimates of German presence (a few dozen men) and low estimates of the number of Jews in the town (about 500), there were not enough Germans to kill the Jews in a short time. In the town of Józefów, mentioned above, an entire battalion—500 armed men—was deployed against 1,800 Jews. In Białystok, on 12–

[15] As defined by the decree of 31 August 1944.

13 July 1941, two battalions conducted the operation of shooting more than 3,000 Jews. Thus without the participation of the local population, the Germans present in Jedwabne would hardly have been able to murder all the Jews on their own on 10 July. Undoubtedly, they could have done it later on, as they did in hundreds of other localities. But they did not have to.

The question arises, however: why did Jedwabne (and Radziłów) remain an exception? Why did the Holocaust take a different course in hundreds of other localities with mixed Polish-Jewish populations under Nazi rule? I believe that the case of Jedwabne and environs was exceptional, which is precisely why the existence of this crime remained hidden from the public and historians—and not only Polish historians. Arguably, had there been many similar incidents, they would have been made public earlier—if not by Poles, then by people for whom facts of this sort would fit well with their image of Polish attitudes to the Jews. I do not claim that in other places Polish attitudes were exemplary. Various sources indicate that in many localities acts of violence and looting took place, that individuals and small groups of local Poles aided the Germans in the persecution of the Jews, but we do not encounter any information about crime and collaboration comparable in their scope to those in Jedwabne. What, therefore, made Jedwabne and its environs so unique?

In brief, the area under consideration had been an ethnically Polish (i.e., Polish-Jewish) part of the Soviet zone of occupation. One can hardly overestimate the influence that the experience of Soviet occupation in 1939–1941 had on the population of eastern Poland. Jedwabne provides an excellent example of the context of the Soviet occupation as an explanatory factor. During the Second World War the Germans entered Jedwabne twice. They were there in September 1939 and left the area to the Soviets, fulfilling the German-Soviet treaty that divided Poland. There is no information on any collaboration of local Poles with the Germans in 1939; to the contrary, they joined the army and fought against the invader. There is also no trace of any anti-Jewish behavior by the Jedwabne Poles, although the Germans quickly made their Jewish policy clear through burning the town's synagogue. Evidently, the preexisting anti-Jewish prejudice and intergroup tensions were not sufficient at that time to spur Polish participation in the German action. Between September 1939 and July 1941 this changed. At the second entry of Germans the attitudes of Jedwabne Poles were clearly different (and the Germans' aims were different too).

It was not just the alleged (actual and imaginary) collaboration of Jews with the Soviets that made some of the Jedwabne Poles prone to collaborate in German anti-Jewish action. The experience of Soviet rule was traumatic, profoundly disturbing psychologically, and most destructive for the social order. Through imposing revolutionary changes and mass terror, and by inciting social and ethnic tensions, the Soviets deliberately unleashed demons. Jan Gross himself presented this in *Revolution from Abroad*. Sociopsychological consequences of totalitarian rule constitute a topic of great importance for an understanding of twentieth-century history, yet in the former Soviet bloc it still awaits comprehensive research. If it is difficult to explore and explain consequences of living under a totalitarian regime, it is more difficult to explore and explain consequences of falling under two totalitarian regimes consecutively, as happened with Jedwabne and a large part of Eastern Europe.

Undoubtedly, the experience of the Soviet occupation made some Poles initially perceive Germans as liberators and made them ready to cooperate with the new occupiers. On a larger scale other groups that had recently fallen under Soviet rule welcomed the Germans and collaborated with them, especially Balts and Ukrainians, who expected that Germans would (re)establish their nation-states. Their significant involvement in the extermination of the Jews cannot be explained by a higher level of anti-Jewish prejudice. The key factor seems to be a political one, namely, their leaderships' decisions to stand on the German side and the German policy to use them. In the ethnically mixed areas of eastern Poland, local Poles watched Ukrainian and Lithuanian nationalists' cooperation with the Germans with great anxiety. They remembered their ex-minorities' anti-Polish sentiments and were afraid that they would be the next targets after the Jews. A particular feature of the Jedwabne area was that it was located in the relatively small western strip of the Soviet zone of occupation, where the ethnic structure was similar to that in central Poland, that is, without a significant presence of minorities other than Jews.

The position of Poles was different from that of Lithuanians or Ukrainians, as Germans had invaded and occupied the western half of Poland since 1939. Nazis had not sought organized Polish collaboration and had treated the Poles so badly as to earn widespread hatred and prevent the Polish leadership from considering any such collaboration. Thus in the former Soviet zone the German invaders could appear as liberators from the Soviet yoke only to some Poles and temporarily, in the first weeks after 22 June 1941. Later on, Germans' behavior and news coming from western Poland left no doubt that they were just another occupier, at least as hostile and ruthless as the Soviets had been.

Therefore, the Jedwabne area in July 1941 was a place and a moment of particularly favorable conditions for organized Polish collaboration with the Germans, as was not the case east or west of the area, earlier or later on. The area was small and the moment was short, but that was enough for the crime in Jedwabne to take place, to bring death to Jedwabne Jews and leave some of their Polish neighbors stained with innocent blood, and to leave us with a past that we cannot change.

. . . . .

Dariusz Stola works at the Institute of History of the Polish Academy of Sciences in Warsaw. His research has concentrated on Polish-Jewish relations during World War II and mass migrations in Central Europe. He is the author of *Nadzieja i zagłada: Ignacy Schwarzbart—żydowski przedstawiciel w Radzie Narodowej RP 1940–1945* (Hope and destruction. Ignacy Schwarzbart: the Jewish representative on the National Council of the Polish Republic 1940–1945) (Warsaw, 1995) and *Kampania antysyjonistyczna w Polsce 1967–1968* (The anti-Zionist campaign in Poland 1967–1968) (Warsaw, 2000). He has published articles in *Więź*, *Mówią Wieki*, *Polityka*, and the *International Migration Review*.

PART VII

THE DISCUSSION OUTSIDE POLAND

INTRODUCTION

The need to heal the wounds stretches from President
Kwaśniewski to the townspeople of Jedwabne and the
surrounding villages and reaches around the world, where
Polish and Jewish descendants seek paths to reconciliation.
—David Harris, executive director,
American Jewish Committee

T HE DEBATE outside Poland did not fulfill the alarmist predic-
tions of those who feared that it would lead to a widespread
assumption in the West that the Poles were as guilty as the Germans in the mass murder of the Jews during the Second World War.[1]
On the contrary, there was considerable understanding in the Jewish
world for the dilemmas created for Polish society by the revelation of
the Jedwabne massacre. The American Jewish Committee organized a
delegation of Polish Americans and American Jews to attend the dedication of the monument in Jedwabne in July 2001. In the introduction
to the pamphlet written by one member of this group (Prof. Alvin Ro-
senfeld of Indiana University), David Harris, executive director of the
American Jewish Committee, wrote:

> Why should we care so deeply about the dedication of a modest
> stone memorial to 1,600 Holocaust victims in a tiny village in the
> Polish countryside? The events surrounding the unveiling of a
> monument to the Jewish martyrs of Jedwabne reverberated
> around the world precisely because this was not the familiar Holo-
> caust atrocity. The Jews of Jedwabne were not murdered by the
> cold, faceless Nazi death apparatus that Hannah Arendt charac-
> terized as the "banality of evil"—but rather were beaten, blud-
> geoned, and burned alive by Gentile neighbors, by people with
> whom they had had a passing acquaintance for most of their lives.
> This was not state-sanctioned killing, but, in essence, fratricide.
>   How the descendants of the perpetrators dealt with their his-
> tory and how the town of Jedwabne acknowledged the deed that
> had stained its soil speaks volumes about the issues of Polish guilt,
> innocence, responsibility, and self-image. The contentious debate

---

[1] Thus Cardinal Glemp, in a radio broadcast on 4 March 2001, expressed the fear that
"divulging the truth to Americans will lead to sharp attacks on Poles by the Jewish
community."

around the memorial revealed how deeply felt the Polish-Jewish wounds still are and how men of courage and honesty, such as Polish President Kwaśniewski, might heal them by speaking the truth about the wartime record. "One cannot be proud of the glory of Polish history without feeling, at the same time, pain and shame for the evil done by Poles to others," he stated unflinchingly at the dedication.

The need to heal the wounds stretches from President Kwaśniewski to the townspeople of Jedwabne and the surrounding villages and reaches around the world, where Polish and Jewish descendants seek paths to reconciliation . . .

Today, while Jedwabne is *judenrein*, remarkably Jewish life in other parts of Poland is beginning to stir. If the ghosts of the past are properly exhumed and courageously confronted—and, fortunately, there are a number of Poles dedicated to this goal, with whom we collaborate closely—who knows if there will not be another glorious chapter in Jewish-Polish history ahead?

There was, it is true, an acrimonious correspondence in the *Times Literary Supplement* following Abraham Brumberg's review of 2 March 2001 that reflects some of the sentiments which the revelations of the Jedwabne massacre and the subsequent debate provoked among surviving Polish Jews. Brumberg summed up his view of the controversy in an article in *Foreign Affairs*, September–October 2002, which considerations of space have made it impossible for us to include. Most Jewish responses were more moderate. In Israel the tone was set by the introductions written by Israel Gutman and David Engel to the Hebrew edition of *Neighbors*. Gutman stressed the importance of coming to terms with the past and that it was not possible to hold all Poles responsible for the massacre. Engel, for his part, compared the debate to that provoked by the "new historians" in Israel.

In America, the responses were similar. Samuel Kassow, writing in *Forwards*, 20 April 2001, asserted:

> In fairness, Jedwabne was more the exception than the rule. Indifference rather than murder best characterized Polish attitudes, and Poland still furnished more "righteous gentiles" than any other occupied country. But the murder of Jews certainly created new and unforeseen opportunities for neighbors who were otherwise decent people.

He further observed:

> The Jedwabne incident was one part of a complex mosaic of Polish Jewish relations. But there were many other stories and themes

deeply embedded in the complicated web of everyday life. During good times and bad, Poles and Jews dealt with each other face to face as neighbors, as business partners, even as friends. On the eve of destruction, more Jews spoke Polish than ever before—and they loved Polish culture no less than the Poles.

The tone of the debate in North America was set by the exchange between Adam Michnik and Leon Wieseltier, here reprinted, which is a model of civilized disagreement on a highly complex and morally charged subject.

Of the scholarly analyses, the most notable so far has been that in the *New York Review of Books* on 31 May 2002, where István Déak, who has written extensively on Holocaust issues, reviewed *Neighbors* along with a book on the Bulgarian rescue and one on the Nazi persecution of the Jehovah's Witnesses. The sections dealing with *Neighbors* are reproduced below. Déak praised Gross's "horrifying and thoughtful" book but criticized it for devoting too little attention to the devastating impact that the two years of Soviet occupation in former eastern Poland had on Polish-Jewish relations. He also felt that Gross's use of the term "willing executioners" to describe the Polish perpetrators of the Jedwabne massacre, derived as it was from Daniel Goldhagen's well-known collective indictment of the German people, was misplaced. He concluded:

> Jan Gross cannot be praised enough for having awakened the Polish public to the need to address the dark episodes in their national history. A sure sign of his success is the sudden and unprecedented soul-searching that has swept Poland ... And yet I believe that had Gross been a little less rigid in some of his generalizations, his argument would have been even more persuasive.
>
> What is needed now is much good will among those trying to interpret history. Not until we understand that every ethnic group harbors its share of potential murderers who can be readily mobilized to commit violence will the cause of peace truly be furthered. Meanwhile, we ought to celebrate, more than ever, such heroes, whether Polish saviors of Jews, Jewish ghetto fighters, Bulgarian bishops and politicians, Jehovah's Witnesses, or Polish guerrillas, who stood up for their beliefs and died fighting the worst tyrannies in modern history.

Within the Polish-American community, cleavages similar to those in Poland may be perceived. The "self-critical" position was well represented by Jarosław Anders in an article in the *New Republic* on 9 April 2001. He described how the "Jewish issue" was never discussed, either publicly or privately, while he was growing up in Poland, and how he first became aware of it during the "anti-Zionist" campaign of 1968, which also revealed that "some of my best friends were, indeed, Jews." Although since that time there had been a major change in "Poland's approach to its Jewish past," there were "still precincts of Polish collective memory in which facts are distorted, hushed up, or simply repressed." Gross's book has broken this taboo and made it obvious that "the whole sphere of Polish-Jewish relations simply did not fit into the established Polish narrative of innocent, heroic suffering."

He concluded:

> But now the time of maturity has truly come. We are three generations away from the war, and the Polish nation really has survived. Political freedom begets the moral obligation of intellectual freedom. Today's Poles have no need to feel that they are guilty of the sins of their grandfathers. And collective apologies, which some have suggested, seem rather meaningless. We know that Polish history was not only about anti-Semitism, and that even the history of Polish-Jewish cohabitation in Poland cannot be reduced to a one-dimensional chronicle of unhappiness. But the obstacle has to be surmounted, somehow.
>
> Gross's book has proved, among other things, that the existence of the silent zone is more troubling to Poles than to anyone else. It is a constant moral and social irritant, a cause of pointless recriminations and irrational fears. As Gross writes at the end of his book, the history of a nation is a biography in which everything connects with everything else.
>
> And if at some point in this collective biography a big lie is situated, then everything that comes afterward will be devoid of authenticity and laced with fear of discovery. And instead of living their own lives, members of such a community will be suspiciously glancing over their shoulders, trying to guess what others think about what they are doing. They will keep diverting attention from shameful episodes buried in the past and go on "defending Poland's good name," no matter what. They will take all setbacks and difficulties to be a consequence of deliberate enemy conspiracies. Poland is not an exception in this respect among European countries. And like several other nations, in order to reclaim its own past, Poland will have to tell its past to itself anew.
>
> With the appearance of this extraordinary book, the telling has finally begun.

Apologetic voices, often of a radical type, were, however, more commonly heard within American Polonia. A good example is the article, below, by Richard Lukas. This is a moderate statement of the position, and far more extreme and antisemitic responses could be cited.

Perhaps the last word should be left to Rabbi Baker, who departed from Jedwabne shortly before the war, and who spoke movingly at the commemoration service of the long history of the Jews in the area. In his interview with Krzysztof Darewicz of *Rzeczpospolita* on 10 March 2001, he remarked:

> The most important thing is that the silence has been interrupted. That you have begun to tell the truth about Jedwabne, for it was not possible to wait any longer. Of those Jews born in Jedwabne only a handful remain. But their families number in the thousands, maybe tens of thousands. They deserve that truth above all. But so do all Jews and all Poles also. For only on its basis is it possible to build anew the friendship between us. The Poles, as a nation, are not of bad character. If it had not been for Hitler, Stalin, and other evil men, there would be no problems between us.

> I grew up with Poles; I had friends; we were as one family. I remember how they respected our rabbi, Avigdor Białostocki, in Jedwabne. The Polish priests were friends with him, would go with him for walks, discussed religion. I believe that . . . we must not forget this friendship of ours. Showing goodwill on both sides, we need to continue it and strengthen it. I am convinced that even with full knowledge of what happened in Jedwabne, this is possible.

David Engel

INTRODUCTION TO THE
HEBREW EDITION OF *NEIGHBORS*

I N A CERTAIN SENSE, Jan Tomasz Gross can be called the leading
figure among Poland's "new historians." Like his Israeli colleagues
who bear the same title, Gross, too, confronts his people's collective memory and subjects it to the test of academic inquiry. Like them,
he strives to hear the voices of individuals and groups whose memories are routinely relegated to the margins of public consciousness, and
to allow those voices to be heard by all. And like the writings of the
new historians in Israel, his research also arouses sharp public disagreements, for the memories and historical episodes they uncover
present a picture of the past in radical conflict with the one that most
are accustomed to regard as indisputable truth.

The Polish edition of this book was published in mid-2000. It painted
a heartrending picture of a horrific event: on 10 July 1941, in the town
of Jedwabne in the district of Łomża, a Polish mob brought together
virtually all of the local Jews, shoved them forcefully into a barn,
poured kerosene on the building, and set it afire. Sixteen hundred Jewish men, women, and children, about half of the town's population,
were burned alive. But for Gross the most shocking feature of the episode was that "it was not the Nazis who murdered those Jews, nor the
NKVD, nor the security services of the Communist regime in Poland,
but the [local Polish] community," the victims' neighbors. Gross himself appears to have recoiled from the magnitude of the shock: as he
testifies in the book, four years passed between the time he first came
upon traces of the event and the moment he understood that in light
of what had happened at Jedwabne, one could no longer conceive of
the relations between Poles and Jews in the terms that Polish historiography has employed to date. Since he came to such an understanding,
however, he has been adamant: "We must throw away the sleeping
pills that the historians, publicists, and journalists have been shoving
down our throats for the past fifty years, [which were supposed to
make us believe] that only the Germans killed the Jews ... Framing
the question of Polish-Jewish relations in this [new] spirit obliges us to
confront anew the enormous problems of Polish wartime and postwar
history."

Reactions were not immediate, but once they came (following extensive coverage in the liberal newspaper *Gazeta Wyborcza*, edited by the former Solidarity activist Adam Michnik), it became clear that the book touched a raw nerve. Prof. Ryszard Bender of the Catholic University of Lublin, one of the country's leading historians, rejected the book out of hand: in an interview with the Catholic-nationalist weekly *Głos* he thundered against "the one-sided testimonies, filled with anti-Polish falsehoods," cited in the book, challenging its "sensationalistic" style and "superficial" research, which, he claimed, were aimed at creating "an emotionalized and tendentious description of the events." Another nationalist weekly also wondered about Gross's intentions in giving publicity to "horror stories" with no basis in fac., after all, the newspaper claimed, "the world is already convinced that the Poles are guilty of everything." But not only ardent defenders of the traditional national narrative were alarmed; more moderate voices, seemingly open to a critical examination of the Polish past, also expressed reservations about the book's findings and conclusions. In *Gazeta Wyborcza* itself, journalist Jacek Żakowski expressed doubt about whether it is possible "indisputably to confirm many details after sixty years." It might be, he warned, that the massacre in Jedwabne—which he termed "a monstrous crime . . . , shocking, nauseating, and shameful," knowledge of which had caused him "to look differently at our neighbors and even at ourselves"—was not carried out in accordance with the desires of the town's entire Polish population; and that at least some of the responsibility for it was borne by the "Hitlerites that were sent" there as part of the German invasion of the Soviet Union, which had begun two weeks earlier. Prof. Tomasz Szarota of Warsaw University, one of the leading scholars of the Nazi occupation of Poland, expressed similar thoughts: on the one hand he welcomed the book's publication as "a sign of our independence, normalization, and liberation from our complexes," but on the other hand he insisted that only after all possible documentary stones had been turned could the transfer of responsibility for the murder from the Germans to the Poles be justified.

The question of the German role in the episode is not a trivial one, if only because it is known that during the initial weeks following the invasion of the USSR German forces perpetrated murderous acts against Jews precisely in the area in question. Gross, however, is well aware of this fact, as well as of testimonies attributing to the Germans some sort of role in the events at Jedwabne. In fact, he discusses the significance of those testimonies at length in the chapter entitled "The Preparations." One can disagree with his conclusions, to be sure, but in light of his methodical analysis of the problem of sources, the complaints of his critics about lack of exhaustive research and an insufficiently critical approach to the interpretation of evidence seem groundless. In the event, it is not scientific precision that appears to be hanging in the balance in the stormy argument that the book has aroused, but the very image of the Polish people, both in its own and in the world's eyes. Ever since the Polish state was erased from the European political map at the end of the eighteenth century, Poles have cultivated a self-image that presents their nation as the eternal innocent victim of the rapacity of their neighbors to the east and west. Against the lustful belligerence that characterized the foreign occupiers throughout the generations, the Polish nation, according to its national myth, inscribed on its banner the loftiest of all human values—liberty, democracy, and brotherhood. Polish children learn from their earliest years that the Second World War represented the supreme expression of this tradition: the Polish nation refused as one to collaborate with the Nazis in any form, establishing instead an exemplary military and civilian underground movement whose contribution to the victory of the forces of goodness and light was substantial. Moreover, Poland's stubborn resistance to German pressure immediately before and during the war is regarded as proof of the nation's constant readiness to offer itself as a sacrifice upon the altar of righteousness for the sake of the freedom of all mankind. Such readiness is actually regarded as an essential part of the Polish nation's historic mission to redeem the world.

Unfortunately, the systematic murder of Polish Jewry during the years 1941–1944, though planned by the German occupier, was executed in the presence of the Polish community, most of which turned its back upon the cry of the victims. For this reason the story of the Holocaust is liable to subvert the national self-image. In 1996, two Polish sociologists, Ireneusz Krzemiński and Ewa Koźmińska-Frejlak, considered the psychosocial implications of this damage:

> "The problem with the Holocaust" stems among other things from the fact that its impression clashes with the strongly rooted image of "Polishness." The events of the Second World War did not confirm the myth of the Polish nation as a chosen people. Although the Poles themselves experienced the cruelty of the occupiers, they were witnesses to the crime, unprecedented in human history, that the Nazi Germans perpetrated upon the Jews. At the same time, the apathetic reaction often displayed toward what was happening to the Jews contradicted the universally accepted ideal of struggle "for our freedom and yours." The fact that historians agree that the Polish community could not have stopped the crime was nonetheless liable to arouse subconscious guilt feelings.

But now, after the findings of Jan Tomasz Gross's study of the incident at Jedwabne have been published, it has become evident that not all historians agree that the Poles were unable directly to affect the fate of entire Jewish communities. On the contrary, a scholar like Gross, of international reputation, who was himself a victim of the Communist regime, and upon whom the free Polish government bestowed a medal for distinguished service, presents the Polish community, at least in one town, not as a powerless bystander but as a willing murderer, active and cruel. No wonder that one of his critics called his book "an atomic bomb with a delayed fuse."

Yet not all of the reactions have been defensive. Columnist Jacek Kurczewski has criticized Gross's critics for "not getting it into their heads that Poles were capable of doing something like this." "Polish intellectuals, like all intellectuals, love myths that portray their nation as exceptional," he warned, "but in truth we are not exceptional." And in response to what he took as Żakowski's attempt to avoid coming to grips with the meaning of the Jedwabne episode, the journalist Konstanty Gebert, who gained fame during the early 1990s for his reporting about interethnic conflicts in post-Communist Europe, wrote that "books like [Gross's] ... are vital for Poland no less than those that document crimes in which the Poles were victimized, for [only through them] will we know where we were treated unjustly and where we did injustice [to others]." Only if we know this, he continued, "will we be able to forgive in the first instance and to ask forgiveness in the second, and in this way finally to achieve a moral order in which it will be impossible to condemn a person for crimes committed half a century ago just because he is a Pole (or a Russian, or a German, or a Ukrainian, etc.)." Calls are going out with ever increasing force for an extensive and uncompromising public discussion both of the facts of the Jedwabne episode and of their practical and moral implications.

Readers of the Hebrew edition will no doubt welcome the prospect that Gross's book will encourage a national Polish effort at soul-searching over Polish treatment of Jews in general and during the Holocaust in particular. In stark contrast to the Polish self-image, Jewish historical consciousness has conjured over the years an image of Poles as a nation consumed by Jew-hatred, whose children "imbibe antisemitism with their mothers' milk." Gross even states explicitly that the story he tells about Jedwabne contains "a partial answer to the question that vexes Polish public opinion: Why do the Jews have such a long-standing brief for the Poles, one more deeply rooted even than the one they carry for the Germans ... ?" But if the appearance of the book in Israel will be greeted sympathetically for this reason, it is difficult to imagine that it will cause even the slightest public uproar. On the contrary, many readers are liable to find in it only confirmation of the traditional image and to wonder what there is in it that requires explanation.

In this context it is important to keep two facts in mind. First, the present state of historical research does not allow for an unambiguous determination of the extent to which the events in Jedwabne were typical or extraordinary. Gross has uncovered traces of similar occurrences in two nearby towns, Radziłów and Wąsosz, and there is evidence of murderous violence against Jews by aroused Polish mobs in other locations around Łomża, such as Stawiski and Szczuczyn. However, such behavior does not appear to have been a general phenomenon, even in the specific region under discussion. It is true that we know of not a few cases in which individual Jews were murdered by Poles, but for the most part these cases involved Jews who were living in hiding outside of the ghettos. Scholars of Polish-Jewish relations during the Second World War have not yet looked into the phenomenon of the destruction of entire Jewish settlements along the lines of Jedwabne and have not tried to estimate its extent. For this reason there are at present no scholarly grounds for viewing the Jedwabne incident as indicative of a general pattern. It can be assumed that, following Gross's lead, other scholars will devote attention to this matter, but in doing so they will automatically put not only Polish but also Jewish historical memory under critical scrutiny. At the present moment it is impossible to predict the outcome of either test.

Moreover, Gross's study does not point unequivocally to a long-standing tradition of Jew-hatred as the principal cause of the murder. Until the Germans came along, no signs of any special tension between Poles and Jews in Jedwabne were apparent; on the contrary, it appears that between the two world wars the relations between the two groups were more or less calm. To be sure, Gross raises the issue of the influence of the blood libel on the town's Polish inhabitants, but, in his words, "an evil spirit had to come along in order to wake the sleeping monster inside the people and move it to action." He finds the source of that evil spirit in personal and local factors—partly in the greed of the local Polish population, which saw an opportunity to take over all of the Jews' property in one fell swoop, and partly in the conformist nature of the leading perpetrators, who assumed the conqueror's brutal behavioral norms, seeking to ingratiate themselves by doing what they presumed to be the occupiers' will before being told to do so. Thus in the final analysis Gross rejects any all-encompassing explanation of the massacre, so that anyone hoping to find in the book scientific validation for the idea that the Polish people is distinguished by an inborn cultural propensity to harm Jews will be sorely disappointed.

On the other hand, a reader prepared to approach the book without prejudice will find in it much food for thought. The author wants to know not only what the particular historical incident under examination teaches about the collective character of the Polish people, but also whether and to what extent it is possible to speak about any people's collective character or to derive conclusions about that character from history. He appears to walk a fine line in discussing these matters. In principle he rejects collective responsibility: "Only the murderer is responsible for the murder." But at the same time he acknowledges the existence of cultural collectivities, constructed out of a sense of participation in a common past, whose existence extends over a period of many generations. According to Gross, it is customary for such communities to take pride in the glorious accomplishments of earlier generations, as if the good deeds of the parents are a favorable omen for the children. But if so, he asks, why should they not also assume part of the stain that attaches from their forebears' crimes and moral failures?

Standing at the center of the book is thus a question of universal significance, especially in an age when intergroup relations are coming to be based more and more upon the liquidation of collective accounts by means of apologies for past sins: Where does one draw the line between a legitimate demand for amends to those who have suffered historical injury as a way to national atonement and catharsis, and an unfair visitation of the sins of the fathers upon the second, third, and fourth generations? Today, as the Jewish population in Israel also wrestles with various aspects of this problem, the appearance of Jan Tomasz Gross's book in Hebrew translation appears most timely.

. . . . .

David Engel is Skirball Professor of Modern Jewish History at New York University and a fellow of the Diaspora Research Center at Tel Aviv University, where he serves as editor of *Gal-Ed: On the History of the Jews in Poland*. He is the author of *In the Shadow of Auschwitz: The Polish Government-in-Exile and the Jews, 1939–1942* (Chapel Hill, 1987) and *Facing a Holocaust: The Polish Government-in-Exile and the Jews, 1943–1945* (Chapel Hill, 1993). His latest book is *Bein shihrur liverihah* (Between liberation and flight: Holocaust survivors in Poland and the struggle for leadership, 1944–1946) (Tel Aviv, 1996).

Israel Gutman

DO THE POOR POLES REALLY LOOK AT THE GHETTO? INTRODUCTION TO THE HEBREW EDITION OF *NEIGHBORS*

T HE PIONEERING ARTICLE by Jan Błoński, a well-known literary scholar in Poland, "The Poor Poles Look at the Ghetto" (after Czesław Miłosz's poem, "A Poor Christian Looks at the Ghetto"), published in the weekly journal *Tygodnik Powszechny* in 1987,[1] ended a lengthy period of silence in Poland on the sensitive topic of Polish-Jewish relations during World War II. The article and the tumultuous debate that it precipitated undermined the dogmatic and befuddled view of the Holocaust and its significance that had been widely held in Communist Poland. This view, which overlooked inconvenient facts and Holocaust research throughout the free world, routinely likened the sufferings and losses of the Poles during the Nazi German occupation to those of the Jews. For this reason, Poland did not fully experience the shock that Western Europe and the United States underwent when the full extent of the Holocaust came to light.

Błoński wrote about the burden of guilt that the European countries and their peoples, the core of Christian civilization, carry, and argued that it should perturb Poland above all, as a country where so many Jews had dwelled for centuries. Although he courageously confronted painful truths, he also expressed relief that Poland had been spared the worst:

> [W]hen one reads what was written about Jews before the war, when one discovers the amount of hatred rife in Poland, one cannot help wondering why words were not followed by deeds. In point of fact, they were not (or only in isolated cases). God restrained our hand. Yes, God, because if we did not take part in that crime it was because we were still Christians, because at the last moment we recognized the Devil's hand in this undertaking.

---

[1] For an English version, see Jan Błoński, "The Poor Poles Look at the Ghetto," in *'My Brother's Keeper?' Recent Polish Debates on the Holocaust*, ed. A. Polonsky (London, 1990), 59–68.

Błoński's thinking in this regard was shared by the Poles and by many friends of Poland. However, in view of the horrific massacre at Jedwabne and additional towns in its vicinity, one can no longer claim that Poles were not complicit in the murder of the Jewish people.

The horrors of the Nazi occupation and the Poles' harsh suffering during it did not cleanse the Poles of antisemitism; in fact, Poles evinced antisemitism both during the Holocaust itself and afterward. The plague of *szmalcownicy*, Poles who denounced and extorted from Jews, threatened every Jew who sought shelter among the Poles and was one of Polish antisemitism's most accursed manifestations. Although denouncers came forth in most Nazi-occupied countries, only in Poland did bands of thugs and zealots make Jew-hunting a "profession." The underground press, especially that published by the ultranationalists, continued to stress its animosity toward the Jews even during the war and the occupation. Here and there, armed groups that operated in the Polish resistance murdered roving Jews and groups of Jews who sought refuge in the forests.

It would also be improper to overlook manifestations of depravity in certain strata of Polish society during the war, as noted by Kazimierz Wika, another literary and social researcher of stature. In the collection *Życie na niby* (Ostensibly living), Wika wrote:

> One may sum up the average Pole's socioeconomic attitude toward the tragedy of the Jews as follows: The Germans did a cruel thing when they murdered those Jews. We would never have done such a thing, and the Germans will be punished for their actions. They stained their conscience, but from our own standpoint we only come out ahead, and so will we in the future. We neither stained our conscience nor defiled our hands with blood. It is hard to find a more repugnant moral example than our way of public thinking ... The methods with which the Germans obliterated the Jews rest on their conscience. But the response to these methods *rests on our conscience* [emphasis in the original]. A gold tooth removed from a corpse will bleed forever, even if everyone forgets its origin.

Such views, however, were uncommon. Good people in Poland and elsewhere argued that Poles had committed terrible misdeeds against the Jews in only sporadic ways, and that the sole perpetrators were bands of incorrigible extremist thugs who, gripped with insanity or mental illness, jettisoned all moral restraint amid an inhuman reality. Most Poles, repressed by the Nazi reign of terror, looked indifferently upon the fate of others because they had been overwhelmed by their own fears and concerns.

The Jedwabne affair and other mass murders that have come to light undoubtedly denote something much broader than horrific indifference. Much of the population seems to have participated in these despicable massacres, which took place in broad daylight for no particular reason other than the advent of the German occupiers. They were acts in which one religious-ethnic faction murdered another. The perpetrators and the victims had lived in close proximity for generations. They knew each other, their children had studied and played together, and they visited each other on festivals and for family events. The massacre, in which defenseless people, children and infants, were murdered and burned alive, attests to a nadir in human conduct that had not been known before. Amazingly, apart from one or two exceptions, no rescue attempts were made. Neighbors did not open their doors to children and friends, and the town and its surroundings became a death trap of ambush and persecution.

Prof. Tomasz Szarota, an expert on daily life during the occupation in Poland, told a journalist in an interview, "The unchallengeable facts [concerning Jedwabne] are so shocking that they force even me, a historian who has read and written extensively about Poles' shameful behavior under the German occupation, to draw totally new conclusions . . . By means of his publications, Gross has forced us to change our views about the attitudes of Poles during World War II." The publication of Gross's book touched off a tempestuous debate in Poland. Several participants in the debate, including Szarota, believe that Poles committed the murders ("There's no denying the fact"), and add that the Germans' influence and role in the slaughter at Jedwabne deserve careful examination. The Institute of National Memory (Instytut Pamięci Narodowej—IPN) in Poland, tasked with determining the facts by fielding a team of expert investigators and jurists, has been working on the matter intensively and still has not formed conclusions. It faces the complex mission of reconstructing an event that occurred sixty years ago, retracing the facts, and reassembling the documentation. Two legal actions were taken against participants in the slaughter in the 1950s, but both were conducted hastily and inadequately prepared, and the accused were allowed to deliver elusive and mendacious testimonies. In the past, historians who attempted to track down the facts encountered many difficulties. Until the late 1980s, the regime in Poland was not interested in investigating the Poles' role in the crime and preferred to hold the Germans fully or, at least, mainly at fault. The townspeople colluded to maintain secrecy, scramble the facts, and impede the identification of the rioters. The relevant documentation was kept behind lock and key for decades. Szymon Datner, a Jewish historian who was well acquainted with the affair and knew both the existing documentation and the situation in the area, chose under the circumstances of the time to report allusions only and not to reveal the full truth. Finally, the testimonies of the few survivors of the slaughter appeared in the community's memorial book, published in the United States, or were mothballed in forgotten archives. In Jedwabne itself, a stone that was set up where the barn had stood in which the victims were burned commemorated 1,600 Jews whom "the Germans" had murdered, as its inscription explained.

Jan Tomasz Gross, the Polish-American researcher, learned about Jedwabne from the Polish scriptwriter Agnieszka Arnold, who had prepared a film about the events in the town. Gross painstakingly analyzed the far-reaching testimony of a survivor of the massacre, Szmuel Wasersztajn, and with the help of other materials that he gathered from trials and archives he blazed a trail through the thicket and produced a portrayal that retells the atrocity step-by-step. In his book *Sąsiedzi* (Neighbors), written in Polish, Gross describes the massacre, its perpetrators, and the horrific devastation in clear, frank, and pointed terms. As one of his readers expressed it, "I could not let the book rest as I read it, and after I read it, it would not let me rest."

Neighbors was greeted with silence at first, but soon afterward Poland was swept by a mighty reverberation and a powerful wave of written and oral responses. Historians and ordinary people, clerics and intellectuals have been carried by the rising tide of the debate. Alongside the soul-searching and breast-beating, some debaters have subjected the author to pungent criticism. They allege that Gross failed to make proper use of documentation in German archives; some say that the book was prompted by a malevolent urge to malign Poland; and a few recognized historians actually hinted that the killings in Jedwabne, perpetrated by the Poles, should be viewed as revenge for Jews' displays of sympathy for the Soviets, who had invaded Poland, and for Jewish-Soviet collaboration.

The Poles fear that the massacre in Jedwabne will destroy the self-image that they have gone to much effort to cultivate—a people and state that had been victimized by aggressor states for years, abandoned and betrayed by others during World War II, and utterly innocent of wrongdoing when in control of their country. Although the stormy debate surrounding Jedwabne has not yet ended, additional mass murders in the area, in which Poles were complicit, are being discovered. In the second half of June, the large-circulation daily newspaper *Gazeta Wyborcza* published a carefully crafted investigative article by the journalist Anna Bikont, "They Had Vodka, Arms, and Hate." The article is based on confirmed information and fragmentary reports from several generations of inhabitants of Radziłów concerning murders that took place there on 7 June 1941. In Radziłów, as in Jedwabne, Poles rounded up the Jews, ran down and shot escapees, and burned several hundred people to death in a barn. "Thus," Bikont wrote, "Menachem Finkelstein [one of the few survivors of the Radziłów massacre] concluded his testimony to the Jewish Historical Commission: the Jewish community of Radziłów, which had existed for five hundred years, vanished from the face of the earth. Along with the Jews, everything that was Jewish in the town—the school, the synagogue, the cemetery—was destroyed."

Did these appalling murders occur only in Poland? Were they a uniquely Polish phenomenon? As it turns out, they were not. When the military forces of the Nazi Third Reich launched an offensive against the Soviet Union in the last week of June 1941 (Operation Barbarossa), they were accompanied by units subordinate to the SS that were tasked with purging the occupied territory of Communist activists, hostile civilian elements, and, above all, Jews. Along the lengthy front, Jews in cities and towns were subjected to a murder campaign with the participation of SD units, subordinate to Heinrich Himmler, and recruits and volunteers from the local population. In a string of locations in the Baltic countries, the Ukraine, and parts of Romania, mass murders, pogroms, and expulsions of Jews were initiated and perpetrated by local populations and military forces. According to testimonies in our possession, Lithuanians unleashed violent riots against Jews in forty locations, all of which were outside Poland; the killers or the participants in the killings were organized in units of national complexion. In Romania, regular Romanian military forces engaged in deportations and participated in killings along with the Germans.

In the Polish territories, the resistance that did the bidding of the government-in-exile and its institutions in Poland was not the agency that ordered or encouraged the killings. Accordingly, one cannot blame the underground institutions of state and the Polish population at large for the crimes in Jedwabne, Radziłów, and other localities. Furthermore, rampant killings by local civilians or police or military units became possible under the patronage of the Nazi ideology and regime and were due to the widely held view that Jewish lives were free for the taking. What is more, the Germans encouraged and facilitated the murder of Jews. The looting and appropriation of Jews' dwellings and property were also a motive force for riots and murders.

How large a role did antisemitism play in these spectacles of pogrom and murder? Plainly, the intensity of antisemitism in these countries (the matter is more complex in the Baltic countries) in the murder initiatives of certain circles is inseparable from the local population's acquiescence in these initiatives. Several participants in the debate in

Poland argue that Jedwabne lacked a core group of legitimate public leaders, clerics, and intellectuals that could restrain the bands and avert the disaster. I consider this argument devoid of substance. Polish antisemitism reached its peak in the second half of the 1930s; the idea that Poland had too many Jews and should rid itself of all or most of them, by means of departure and emigration, was shared by most political forces and commanded sweeping support that was manifested, at its furthest extreme, in a campaign of rioting and physical violence. The vicinity of Jedwabne was under the influence of ultranationalist circles that had the support of much of the student population, the intelligentsia, and even the clergy. Between 1932 and 1939, for example, half of the Jewish-owned shops in Jedwabne were liquidated, and relations between Poles and Jews deteriorated severely. The perception of the Jew as an alien, hostile, and unwanted element in Poland was one of the factors that led to the tragedy. Even today, as the handful of Jews in Poland carry on in one of Europe's smallest Jewish communities, bereft of its great centers, public and personal manifestations of antisemitism—an "antisemitism without Jews"—have not vanished altogether.

Antisemitism is a difficult disease to eradicate. In view of the wretched experience of the twentieth century, as humankind teetered on the verge on self-destruction, all of us are duty-bound to be forever vigilant against all forms of totalitarianism, racism, and antisemitism. In his 1956 study of antisemitism, Leszek Kołakowski, the most important Polish thinker at the present time, wrote: "An essential condition for the blood-drenched pogroms, massacres, and horrors that were inflicted on the Jews was always a social climate of emotional tolerance of antisemitism, even in its most trifling and superficial form. Wherever the horrors took place and the system of discrimination and suspicion was set in motion, a pool of destructive social forces that fueled and gave growth to criminals, ostensibly harmless in appearance, had already been amassed."

Nevertheless, the notion that the Poles are an antisemitic people—an idea that has made some inroads among us—ought to be rejected. Poland had more Righteous Among the Nations, Gentiles who rescued Jews, than any other country. Moreover, rescuing or aiding Jews in Nazi-occupied Poland augured death not only for the Jewish victim but also for the rescuer and his or her family. The rescuers subjected themselves to daily risk, sometimes shared their scanty food at no recompense with Jews who hid in their homes or on their farms, and lived in constant dread of the enemy and, sometimes, of their Polish neighbors as well. Many of them paid for their actions with their lives. The circumstances in Poland were such that only about 1 percent of

Jews were rescued by Poles, but the act of rescue in such an era serves as a ray of light and hope that sustains faith in man in benighted times.

The events in Jedwabne and Radziłów deviate from everything we know about social norms and rules of human conduct. The antisemitic hatred exhibited there, unless we rise up and stamp it out, ignites under circumstances in which a society and the human psyche lose their way, and creates a conflagration that, while claiming Jews as its main victims, threatens to consume all of humankind.

. . . . .

Israel Gutman was born in 1933 in Warsaw and was, until his retirement, Max and Rita Haber Professor of Holocaust Studies at the Institute of Contemporary Jewry at the Hebrew University in Jerusalem and head of the Institute for International Holocaust Research at Yad Vashem. He has also held the position of head of the Institute of Contemporary Jewry. At present he is an academic adviser at Yad Vashem. A member of the Jewish Fighting Organization, he took part in the Warsaw Ghetto Uprising. His books include *Anashim ve'afar* (Men and ashes) (Jerusalem, 1956); *Mered hanotsrim: Mordekhay Anielevich ve'milkhamot getto Varsha* (The revolt of the beseiged: Mordecai Anielewicz and the revolt of the Warsaw ghetto) (Jerusalem, 1963), and *The Jews of Warsaw 1939–1943: Ghetto, Underground, Revolt* (Brighton, 1982). Together with Shmuel Krakowski he wrote *Unequal Victims: Poles and Jews during World War II* (New York, 1986). He was chief editor of the *Encyclopedia of the Holocaust* (New York, 1990).

István Deák

"HEROES AND VICTIMS"
(EXTRACTS)

New York Review of Books,

31 May 2001

I N 1941 POLISH TOWNSPEOPLE and farmers who had been persecuted by the Soviet occupation forces took their revenge on their
innocent Jewish neighbors by torturing them and burning them
alive. In 1943 Bulgarian right-wing politicians saved virtually all the
Jews in their country and were later rewarded for their efforts by execution or imprisonment under the Communist government. Throughout the war German religious zealots refused to say "Heil Hitler," preferring to be guillotined by the Nazis to serving in the war.

Such are the major themes of the three books under review. They
raise questions that defy clear answers. Why did Poles, who had suffered badly under the Soviet occupiers, choose to kill those even more
downtrodden than they were? Do murders committed by semiliterate
Polish farmers, craftsmen, and day laborers belong in the same category as murders committed by educated and trained German policemen, as Jan Gross seems to suggest in *Neighbors*? Does the suffering
freely accepted by German Jehovah's Witnesses belong in the same category as that of the Jews, who were not asked what they thought of
the Führer and were not allowed to recant? Why did the Bulgarians
succeed in saving Jews while the Dutch, who were also not generally
anti-Semitic, failed abysmally, with a nearly 100 percent Jewish survival rate in one country and only about 20 percent in the other? . . .

Jan T. Gross's horrifying and thoughtful book *Neighbors* is about
Poles and Jews, the two major victims of World War II. In his introduction, the author writes that he wants to show how "one day in July
1941, half of the population of a small East European town murdered
the other half—some 1,600 men, women, and children." According
to his account, the members of the Gentile Polish population of
Jedwabne, located in the poverty-stricken Białystok province in northeastern Poland, either took part in the most bestial forms of torture
and killing or cheered on the killers. With the exception of a single

family, no one helped the victims. Although a handful of German gendarmes were present in the region, Gross states, Poles alone committed the crime, with the tacit approval of the Germans but without their participation. No wonder that when Gross published this devastating accusation in Polish and in Poland a year ago, an intense debate took place which, far from being over, seems to be gathering momentum. Fresh evidence and new polemical articles appear in Poland virtually every day.[1]

Jan Gross, who is a professor of politics and European studies at New York University, was born in Poland. He participated in the democratic student movement of the 1960s, for which he was briefly imprisoned. Having witnessed government-inspired anti-Semitism, he left the country in the late 1960s. As an American scholar, he has published fine studies on the Soviet and the German occupation of World War II Poland. Several years ago, while in the Warsaw Jewish archives, he came across a deposition by Szmul Wasersztajn, dated April 1945, which described in detail the horrors inflicted in Jedwabne. Wasersztajn had himself escaped the massacre by hiding. His revelation led Gross to study the records of two court proceedings that took place in 1949 and 1953, respectively, in provincial courts of Communist Poland, against about two dozen Jedwabne defendants charged with carrying out the massacres. During the last few years, other eyewitness accounts by both Jewish and Gentile inhabitants of the town have been found. A memorial book about survivors in Israel was published in 1980 and the Polish filmmaker Agnieszka Arnold conducted interviews in 1998 with those willing to remember what happened in the town on July 10, 1941.

While all this means that the monstrous events at Jedwabne were not completely unknown in Poland after World War II, no one seems to have been interested in investigating them further. Nor had the public taken notice of them. Such lack of awareness might seem inconceivable; yet until recent stories were published, I wonder how many Americans had ever heard of what happened in Tulsa, Oklahoma, at the end of May 1921, when the city's whites, incited by the press and by politicians, massacred several hundred innocent blacks. Although I am a professional historian, I heard of this atrocity only last year, forty-four years after I arrived in the US. The Tulsa massacre, moreover, took

[1] I am indebted to a number of colleagues, friends, and former students for providing me with hundreds of pages of documents and translations on the Jedwabne debate in Poland. Among the most helpful have been Daniela Baszkiewicz-Scott, Marek Chodakiewicz, Jurek Krzystek, John Micgiel, Andrzej Paczkowski, Robert Scott, and Piotr Wandycz.

place when the United States was at peace, whereas Jedwabne occurred during a terrible war, under alternating cruel occupations, and
in the midst of total administrative and political chaos.

According to Wasersztajn and others, the Jewish and non-Jewish inhabitants of Jedwabne lived in relative harmony until the late summer
and fall of 1939, when, following the Hitler-Stalin pact of August 23,
first the Germans and then the Soviet Red Army occupied the town.
There can be no doubt about the horrors of Soviet occupation in the
eastern half of Poland, which had immediately been incorporated into
two of the Soviet Union's western republics. In an excellent earlier
study, *Revolution from Abroad,*[2] Gross describes how the Communist authorities brutally deported 1.25 million people from eastern Poland,
mostly Poles, but also Jews and others, to Siberia; many of them died.
The principal victims were from the Polish social, political, and military elite. Gross also writes that the Soviet NKVD executed about
100,000 people, nearly a tenth of the total male population. As he
writes in *Revolution from Abroad,* "Very conservative estimates show
that [between 1939 and 1941] the Soviets killed or drove to their deaths
three or four times as many people as the Nazis from a population half
the size of that under German jurisdiction."[3]

Farmers were hard hit by Soviet confiscations of land as well as by
anti-Soviet partisan activity and the even more violent retribution by
the Soviet army and police that followed. It is no wonder that, following the German attack on the Soviet Union on June 22, 1941, many
people in the region—Poles, Ukrainians, and Belorussians—received
the Germans as liberators. Similar events took place, one might add,
in the Baltic countries and in Bessarabia (today's independent Moldova), all of which the Soviets had occupied as a result of the Hitler-
Stalin pact.

As Gross explains in *Neighbors,* no sooner did the Germans arrive in
eastern Poland at the end of June 1941 than rumors spread that the
new masters of the land had given permission for Polish Gentiles to
kill the Jews. By then, the German police had been shooting thousands
of Jews in towns not far from Jedwabne. It seemed to many inhabitants
of Jedwabne that the time had come to take revenge for what they perceived to have been Jewish-Communist oppression. Besides, there was
now the prospect of acquiring Jewish riches. Much of *Neighbors* is devoted to a detailed discussion of how the pogrom started a day or two
after the arrival of the German troops, and how it culminated in an

---

[2] Jan T. Gross, *Revolution from Abroad: The Soviet Conquest of Poland's Western Ukraine and Western Belorussia* (Princeton, 1988).
[3] Ibid., 229.

orgy of killing on July 10. Even before then, peasants came from neighboring hamlets driving empty wagons in the hope of taking over some booty from Jews.

On July 10, under orders of the self-appointed new mayor, Marian Karolak, the chief culprit in what followed, young men armed with clubs, knives, and axes burst into Jewish homes, beating, kicking, and driving all the Jews they could find to the town square. One man stabbed eighteen Jews; others cut off heads, gouged out eyes, and slashed open the stomachs of their victims. Others forced young Jews to carry and then to bury a large statue of Lenin before killing them. All this was observed, according to Wasersztajn, by laughing spectators. Finally, all the survivors were driven into a peasant's barn and burned alive. The spectators bludgeoned to death those who tried to escape.

While speculating on the significance of these events, Gross dismisses the argument that the Communist regime in the region included many Jews, or that Communist oppression had a major part in arousing the fury of the villagers. He concludes that they acted both out of sheer greed and because of their age-old hatred for the "killers of Christ" and "the shedders of the blood of Christian children." It seems hard, however, to square this assessment with the scene described above involving the statue of Lenin, or the extreme savagery of the killing. Gross adds that no priest in the region was willing to lift a finger on behalf of the Jews, even though in Catholic Poland local priests would have had sufficient prestige to have stopped the atrocities.

Gross does not claim that all Poles were similar to the inhabitants of Jedwabne, but he points out that spontaneous atrocities occurred elsewhere, that violent anti-Semitism flared up again after World War II, and that the single family that had harbored Jews in Jedwabne was subjected to such hatred and even physical attacks that, after the war, they decided to leave Poland and now live in Chicago. In a clear allusion to Daniel Jonah Goldhagen's famous collective indictment of the German people, Gross uses the term "willing executioners" in reference to the Poles of Jedwabne.[4]

This seems to me an unfortunate choice of words. Not surprisingly, the *New York Times Book Review* entitled its review of Neighbors "Hitler's Willing Executioners." The statement is untrue when applied to the Polish or even to the German people as a whole; in any case it

---

[4] Daniel Jonah Goldhagen, *Hitler's Willing Executioners: Ordinary Germans and the Holocaust* (New York, 1996). Gross uses the term "willing executioners" on 121 in *Neighbors*.

contradicts Goldhagen's controversial argument that the German people were a unique breed of killers.[5]

The reception of Gross's book in Poland has been nothing short of astonishing: it seems to have evoked more favorable responses than negative ones. Here we must remind ourselves that, since the eighteenth century, Poles have tended to see themselves as a martyr nation, occupied, humiliated, and oppressed by aggressive imperial powers. Many times in modern history, whether under Russian or other foreign rule, it was a punishable offense for a Pole to refer to his own country as Poland. While imprisoned or executed at home, Polish patriots fought in many parts of the world "For Your Freedom and Ours," as they liked to put it. During World War II in Europe only Great Britain, the Soviet Union, and Poland never surrendered to the Nazis, even though Poles were simultaneously persecuted by the Soviet Communists. More than a million non-Jewish Poles were killed in German prisons and camps; thousands upon thousands died fighting alongside the British, American, and Soviet armies. During the Warsaw uprising, between August and October 1944, nearly a quarter of a million people perished. At the end of the war, Poland became the subject of a deal in which the Western allies accepted both Soviet domination of Polish territory and the shift of the entire country's borders from East to West at an immense cost in Polish, German, and Ukrainian lives.

Because of the hospitality extended by the old Polish kingdom, Poland historically harbored more Jews than all the other European countries combined. Although there was a tremendous rise of political anti-Semitism in independent Poland during the interwar years, Jewish political and cultural activity also flourished there. Against this background, Gross's accusations have been devastating. The recent revelations of collaboration with the Nazis throughout Europe, and of Europe-wide participation in the Holocaust, seem to have made it more possible for many Polish intellectuals, young people, politicians, and clergymen to accept the notion that their countrymen had not been innocent either. Today the president as well as the government of Poland, and even the Catholic primate, Cardinal Glemp, are apologizing for crimes of which nearly all Poles had been unaware until the publication of Jan Gross's writings. Moreover, not only these people but

---

[5] See Steven Erlanger, "Hitler's Willing Executioners," *New York Times Book Review*, 8 April 2001. The same reviewer drew a parallel between the behavior of the Poles during World War II and that of the Austrians, as if there were no difference between a country in which there were hundreds of thousands of fighters against Nazi Germany and a country that contributed hundreds of thousands of soldiers to the Third Reich, including a vastly disproportionate number of SS men and concentration camp commanders.

even most of Gross's critics praise him for bringing into the open an appalling episode in Polish history.

There are, of course, those who denounce Jan Gross and his book. In their objections one can sometimes detect the old charge of a Jewish "worldwide conspiracy." But these voices are not the loudest today. With some justification, other critics are asking for more evidence and confirmation. Asking questions about a crucial historical event does not make one automatically an anti-Semite, yet this is how some of Gross's Western supporters have chosen to view those raising questions about parts of his work. No book of history should be treated as Holy Writ, especially not a book which is based on a limited number of documents.

Of the published objections to Jan Gross's account, one of the most prominent claims is that he pays too little attention in *Neighbors* to the horrors of the Soviet occupation. In truth, for a more forceful description of why this occupation drove some people to extremes of violence, one must turn to Gross's own *Revolution from Abroad* as well as to other sources. When he discusses the most controversial of all questions in Jewish-Polish relations, namely that of Jewish participation in Soviet rule, Gross presents convincing evidence that Jews in Białystok province were only marginally involved in Soviet oppressive measures, and that the Jews of Jedwabne were entirely innocent. However, Gross's critics in Poland, especially the well-known historian of World War II Polish resistance movements Tomasz Strzembosz, argue that, in eastern Poland as a whole, a disproportionate number of Jews were involved in Communist police actions and police crimes. In *Neighbors* Gross says somewhat less than he says in his *Revolution from Abroad* about the joyful reception many of the Jews gave to the Soviet Red Army in September 1939, or about the large number of Jews in the Polish Communist movement.[6] It was quite natural for many Jews to rejoice over the arrival of the Soviet Red Army in September 1939: if nothing else, it saved them from Nazi rule. It was also predictable, in those circumstances, that many Jews would work for the Soviet regime, some of them as militiamen or political policemen. Gross is correct, of course, in stating that the Soviets deported thousands of Jews to Siberia and that, in desperation, thousands of Jews applied for Soviet permission to move to the Nazi-held zone in Poland. But why deny

---

[6] On Jewish participation in the Polish Communist movement and government, see especially Jaff Schatz, *The Generation: The Rise and Fall of Jewish Communists in Poland* (Berkeley, 1991); Bernard Wasserstein, *Vanishing Diaspora: The Jew in Europe since 1945* (Cambridge, Mass., 1996); and Stefan Korbonski, *The Jews and the Poles in World War II* (New York, 1989).

that any Jews participated in Communist crimes? Jews, like everyone else, behave in a variety of ways.

Some critics argue that Wasersztajn, who was in hiding, could not have seen all the horrors he claims to have witnessed. Others wonder about evidence from the trials in 1949 and 1953 which, according to Gross himself, were perfunctory affairs. (Marian Karolak, who should have been indicted for the major crime of ordering murder, was arrested by the Germans for theft during the war and disappeared.) The trial in 1949 lasted only two days, and in court the defendants complained of having been severely beaten by the police during their interrogation. The trial in 1953 involved a single defendant. Altogether, only one person was sentenced to death, but he was not executed, and within a few years all the accused were set free. Some historians, among them Tomasz Strzembosz, assert that Gross has misread some of the trial documents regarding the participation of Germans in the mass killing. He claims that there are more sources on Jedwabne in other Polish archives that Gross did not consult, and that Gross did no research in the German archives.[7]

The main issue in contention is whether or not there were more than a handful of German soldiers, gendarmes, or Gestapo men on July 10 in Jedwabne. Gross says that there were fewer than a dozen of them and that all they did was take photographs of the massacre (photographs that haven't been found). In response to the debate over Gross's sources, the government-sponsored Institute of National Memory in Poland sent a historian to look into the relevant German archives; so far, he has found no conclusive evidence confirming or denying the presence of German soldiers in Jedwabne.

The question of German presence leads to another difficult issue, namely why the Jews did not defend themselves. As Gross writes, Jews made up two thirds of Jedwabne's population. The Poles had no firearms. When some Polish writers raised this question, Jan Gross answered bitterly, arguing that the Jewish heads of families had to look after their wives and children. Yet is it not precisely in defense of their families that people tend to risk their lives? It is well known that, in extremis, some Polish Jews dared to confront even heavily armed SS soldiers; one can ask why the town's Jewish blacksmiths, for instance, did not grab iron bars to fend off the attackers. They may have been hopelessly outnumbered, but the fact that they did not fight back may

---

[7] Only a short time ago, Jan Gross contributed an essay to a festschrift to honor Tomasz Strzembosz, a historian at the Catholic University at Lublin; Gross also mentions Strzembosz favorably in *Neighbors*. In his more recent writings, Strzembosz, in my view, is quite excessive in his criticism of Jewish behavior under Soviet occupation.

also suggest that there were more than a handful of armed Germans present at that time. In brief, there is good reason for research and debate on the Jedwabne massacre to continue.

Gross is entirely right to point out that many Poles who bravely opposed the Nazis were anti-Semitic, and that many who did so even killed Jews. At least one of the Jedwabne murderers was later sent to Auschwitz. Conversely, the founder of Żegota, the one organization in Poland and in Europe as a whole that had as its sole purpose the saving of Jewish lives, was herself a zealous anti-Semite. She repeatedly expressed her wish that the Jews she was protecting would disappear from Poland after the war.

None of this explains the horrifying behavior of the one hundred–odd Jedwabne farmers and artisans who did the killing; nor does it explain the abominable behavior of the onlookers. Gross himself finds no satisfactory explanation for what took place. What is clear is that many, many Eastern Europeans participated in German-initiated killings in those years. Even more Europeans rejoiced over what was happening to the Jews, or at least turned their backs on them. Pogroms similar to that in Jedwabne occurred elsewhere in Poland as well as in Austria, Lithuania, Ukraine, and Romania. In my native Hungary, the authorities generally protected the Jews until 1944; but when the Germans occupied the country, the same officials zealously arrested and dispatched half a million Hungarian Jews to die in Auschwitz. Because in Hungary the authorities took charge of the persecution, there was little opportunity for popular participation in it. But after the war, anti-Jewish feelings flared up, and some mothers would not let their children out of their houses for fear that Jews would snatch them in order to drink their blood. There was also concern that the Jews would come home and claim their stolen property.

Jan Gross cannot be praised enough for having awakened the Polish public to the need to address the dark episodes in their national history. A sure sign of his success is the sudden and unprecedented soul-searching that has swept Poland. Some of the most important articles on the subject are now available in English, published by *Więź*, a progressive Catholic monthly, under the title *Thou Shalt Not Kill: Poles on Jedwabne*.[8] The introduction is by the well-known Polish-Jewish historian Israel Gutman, and the authors include Jan Gross, his main opponent, Tomasz Strzembosz, and more than thirty others. And yet I believe that had Gross been a little less rigid in some of his generalizations, his argument would have been even more persuasive . . .

---

[8] Edited and partly translated by William Brand (Warsaw, 2001).

What is needed now is much good will among those trying to interpret history. Not until we understand that every ethnic group harbors its share of potential murderers who can be readily mobilized to commit violence will the cause of peace truly be furthered. Meanwhile, we ought to celebrate, more than ever, such heroes, whether Polish saviors of Jews, Jewish ghetto fighters, Bulgarian bishops and politicians, Jehovah's Witnesses, or Polish guerrillas, who stood up for their beliefs and died fighting the worst tyrannies in modern history.

. . . . .

István Deák is Seth Low Professor of History at Columbia University. Among his many works are *Weimar Germany's Left-Wing Intellectuals: A Political History of the Weltbuhne and Its Circle* (Berkeley, 1968); *The Lawful Revolution: Louis Kossuth and the Hungarians, 1848–1849* (New York, 1979), and *Beyond Nationalism: A Social and Political History of the Habsburg Officer Corps, 1847–1918* (New York, 1996). His current research interest is in collaboration, resistance, and retribution in Europe during and shortly after World War II.

Richard Lukas

JEDWABNE AND THE SELLING
OF THE HOLOCAUST

POLISH AMERICAN JOURNAL, MAY 2001

S ELLING THE HOLOCAUST is a gigantic enterprise that has
less to do with preserving the memory of Jewish victims than
exploiting the Holocaust for political, ideological and economic
purposes. The consequence is that history has become a major casualty.
In the absence of any quality control on the type of books that are published, Holocaust historiography is subject to a kind of Gresham's Law
where bad history drives out good history, making it difficult for even
professional historians to determine where sensationalism, propaganda and martyrology ends and history begins.

To have a book published by a major publisher on the Holocaust,
the author must meet only a few criteria: Does the book depict Jewish
victimization in pristine terms (i.e., nothing negative or compromising
about Jewish behavior)? Even if the book tangentially deals with Christian victims of the Nazis, does the author drown these Christians sufficiently in antisemitism to compromise their victimhood and emphasize their role as victimizers in order to maintain the sovereign wartime
experience of the Jews? Better yet, does the author depict non-Jewish
groups, especially Catholic Poles, as either Nazi collaborators or accomplices or perpetrators of atrocities?

If these criteria are met, then it is extraordinarily easy for an author
to garner notoriety for his book in leading American newspapers and
news magazines, which are notoriously unsympathetic with the Polish
dimension of Polish-Jewish relations.

This is what has happened to Professor Jan T. Gross, a Jew who emigrated to the West from Poland in 1968. His book, *Neighbors*, published
last year under its Polish title, *Sąsiedzi*, was recently released in the
United States by Princeton University Press. Gross is not a professional
historian, but a sociologist, an important point in analyzing the merit
of the book.

Gross's thesis is that Christian Poles were solely responsible for killing 1600 Jews in the village of Jedwabne in northeastern Poland in July
1941. As he puts it, "Half of the population ... murdered the other

half." His explanation for the atrocity is that antisemitism made the Poles do it. Polish-Jewish relations had been good before the war, would the Poles suddenly decide to kill their Jewish neighbors? Gross presents the tableau of hundreds of Poles mindlessly slaughtering Jews because now, quite suddenly, they despised them and lusted after their property. Is this scenario really credible? What had changed in Polish-Jewish relations? Gross dismisses a critical fact—Jewish treason in eastern Poland, where Jedwabne is located, during the Soviet occupation.

Eastern Poland was inhabited by Poles, Jews, Belorussians, Ukrainians, and others who fought, brutalized and betrayed each other in one of the worst places in wartime Europe. In June, 1941, the Nazis broke their non-aggression pact with the Soviets, who had occupied eastern Poland since September, 1939, and invaded the area.

There is a mountain of documentation which shows that in this area, occupied by the Soviets during 1939–1941, a significant number of Jews collaborated with the Soviets in the arrest, deportation and death of thousands of Poles. Jedwabne Jews were no exception. When the Soviets reconquered the area from the Germans in 1944–1945, Jews again were prominently involved in the destruction of the Polish Home Army and the arrest and execution of Poles loyal to the Polish democratic government, then in exile in London. That process of Jewish involvement in the persecution, imprisonment and execution of Poles continued throughout the Stalinist era. Even though in his earlier writings Gross had admitted Jewish complicity with Poland's enemy, he now conspicuously dismisses this aspect of Jewish behavior because to acknowledge it would depict Jews as victimizers of Poles, a contradiction of the prevailing Holocaust image that all Jews were victims.

Cast in the light of Jewish collaboration with the Soviets, it should not be too surprising that some Poles may have sought out Jewish traitors and tried to kill them. It worked the other way too. Several hundred Poles, including women and children, were murdered by a Jewish-Soviet partisan unit in Koniuchy in 1944. One of the members of the unit was even honored by the U.S. Holocaust Museum in Washington, D.C.

As is so often the case with sensationalist accounts of the war, the author raises more questions than he answers. He bases his claims primarily on the allegations of Szmul Wasersztajn, who was not an eyewitness to the events at Jedwabne but was in hiding some distance away, and the testimonies elicited during the Łomża trials in 1949 and 1953, a period when Poles underwent the brutal Stalinization of their country. Regarding German documentation concerning Jedwabne, Gross claims he looked for it but "I was unable to find it." I am not entirely convinced Gross personally investigated German and, for that matter, former Soviet archives during his research on his book. He makes the quaint observation that he asked two scholars, both of whom allegedly familiar with German archives, about Jedwabne and neither of them heard of it. Does asking two colleagues about the subject replace the need to immerse oneself personally in critical documents, which are absolutely essential to prove one's allegations about what happened at Jedwabne?

Even though Gross admits the presence of the Gestapo in Jedwabne and even acknowledges that without the Germans the massacre would not have occurred, he insists that the Germans confined themselves to the role of bystanders and clears them of responsibility. The fact that in other nearby towns in the district of Białystok—Tykocin and Wizna—the Germans were responsible for the massacre of Jews does not make Gross doubt his allegation that the Poles were entirely responsible for the atrocity.

Since the publication of Gross's controversial book, new documentary evidence has come to light which suggests that the Germans, not the Poles, were primarily responsible for the massacre. According to one report, the Polish role was limited to less than 50 people, who were forced to guard Jews in the town square prior to their execution. Even the number of murdered Jews has been called into question. One report pointed out that a scanning of the grave site uncovered German bullets (Poles would not have been allowed to possess guns and rifles) and that approximately 400, not 1600, Jews perished. Whether 400 or 1600 lost their lives is not the point. It was an atrocity that every decent person should deplore. But the fundamental question of who was primarily responsible for the massacre is still unanswered. Was it the Germans? Was it the Poles? If the Poles were involved, what was their precise role in the affair?

Gross's credibility is seriously compromised when he asserts his own bizarre idea of historical methodology. He asserts that the testimonies he read should be accepted as "fact" without first skeptically reviewing the material and seeking independent verification. That's quite a reversal of fundamental historical methodology! It is astonishing that all the Holocaust experts who have given their nihil obstat to this flawed volume completely ignored this strange approach to establishing historical truth. Gross seems more concerned about the alleged lack of Polish national grief over the Jews than about determining precisely and accurately what really happened in Jedwabne. The *Washington Post* quotes him, saying, "I deeply believe that getting to know what happened in Jedwabne will become a breakthrough in our historical myths and will help us clean our conscience." Obviously, he is more concerned about Polish than Jewish historical myths. Poles should honestly face the negative aspects of their behavior toward Jews. But what about Jews candidly facing their collaborationist past with Poland's enemies? Gross is silent on this point.

It is testimony to the power of the "Holocaust Industry," to borrow Professor Norman Finkelstein's apt description, that an obscure event that occurred in eastern Poland sixty years ago should be dredged up in this slim volume that is long on sensationalism and short on acceptable historical evidence and receive the hysterical media acclaim that it has received. We are a long way from the quality control Holocaust historiography desperately requires. Now more than ever we need fair and balanced investigations of the Holocaust and the related genocides of eastern Europeans by the Nazis. The highly sensitive subject of Polish-Jewish relations can no longer be painted with the broad brush of antisemitism. The subject needs trained professional historians to present all the facts and who refuse to apply one standard of moral behavior to Jews and a more severe one to Poles. Let us hope that the research currently underway by the Polish National Institute of Memory will give us the answers to Jedwabne that Professor Gross failed to provide us.

·   ·   ·   ·   ·

Richard Lukas is a retired professor of history at Tennessee Technological University and has also taught at universities in Florida and Ohio. He is the author of *Bitter Legacy: Polish American Relations in the Wake of World War II* (Lexington, Ky., 1982); *Did the Children Cry? Hitler's War against Jewish and Polish Children, 1939–1945* (New York, 1994), which won the Janusz Korczak Literary Award, and *The Forgotten Holocaust: The Poles under German Occupation, 1939–1944* (New York, 1997).

Adam Michnik

POLES AND THE JEWS:
HOW DEEP THE GUILT?

NEW YORK TIMES, 17 MARCH 2001

D O POLES, along with Germans, bear guilt for the Holocaust? It is hard to imagine a more absurd claim. Not a single Polish family was spared by Hitler and Stalin. The two totalitarian dictatorships obliterated three million Poles and three million Polish citizens classified as Jews by the Nazis.

Poland was the first country to oppose Hitler's demands and the first to stand against his aggression. Poland never had a Quisling. No Polish regiment fought on behalf of the Third Reich. Betrayed by the Ribbentrop-Molotov pact, Poles fought alongside the anti-Nazi forces from the first day until the last. And inside Poland armed resistance to the German occupation was widespread.

The British prime minister paid homage to the Poles for their role in the Battle of Britain and the president of the United States called Poles an "inspiration" to the world. Yet that didn't stop them from delivering Poland into Stalin's clutches at Yalta. Heroes of the Polish resistance—enemies of Stalin's Communism—ended up in Soviet gulags and Polish Communist prisons.

All of these truths contribute to Poland's image of itself as an innocent and noble victim of foreign violence and intrigue. After the war, while the West was able to reflect on what had happened, Stalinist terror stymied public discussion in Poland about the war, the Holocaust and anti-Semitism.

At the same time, anti-Semitic traditions were deeply rooted in Poland. In the 19th century, when the Polish state didn't exist, the modern nation that was to emerge was shaped by ethnic and religious ties and by opposing antagonistic neighbors often hostile to the dream of Polish independence. Anti-Semitism was the ideological glue of great political nationalistic formations. And yet it was also used at various points as a tool by Russian occupiers in accordance with the principle "divide et impera."

In the 1920's and 30's, anti-Semitism took hold. It became as fixture of radical right-wing nationalists and it could be detected in the utterances of the hierarchy of the Catholic church. Though historically Poland had been a relatively safe haven for them, Jews began to feel increasingly discriminated against and unsafe—and they were, with noisy anti-Semitic groups, segregated seating at universities and calls for pogroms.

During Hitler's occupation, the Polish nationalistic and anti-Semitic right didn't collaborate with the Nazis, as the right wing did elsewhere in Europe, but actively participated in the anti-Hitler underground. Polish anti-Semites fought against Hitler, and some of them even rescued Jews, though this was punishable by death.

Thus we have a singularly Polish paradox: on occupied Polish soil, a person could be an anti-Semite, a hero of the resistance and a savior of Jews.

Fourteen years ago an essay recalled a well-known appeal to save the Jews that was published by a famous Catholic writer, Zofia Kossak-Szczucka, in August 1942. She wrote of hundreds of thousands of Jews in the Warsaw ghetto awaiting death without hope of rescue and how the entire world—England, America, Jews overseas and Poles—was silent. "The dying Jews are surrounded by Pilates washing their hands," she wrote. "This silence cannot be tolerated any longer. No matter what the reasons for it, this silence is a disgrace."

Speaking of Catholic Poles, she continued: "Our feelings toward the Jews haven't changed. We still consider them the political, economic and ideological enemies of Poland. Furthermore, we are aware that they hate us even more than they hate the Germans, that they hold us responsible for their misfortune ... The knowledge of these feelings doesn't relieve us of the duty of condemning the crime. We don't want to be Pilates. We have no chance to act against the German crimes, we can't help or save anybody, but we protest from the depths of our hearts, filled with compassion, indignation and awe ... The compulsory participation of the Polish nation in this bloody show, which is taking place on Polish soil, can breed indifference to the wrongs, the sadism and above all the sinister conviction that one can kill one's neighbors and go unpunished."

This extraordinary appeal, full of idealism and courage while openly poisoned by anti-Semitic stereotypes, illustrates the paradox of Polish attitudes toward the dying Jews. The anti-Semitic tradition compels the Poles to perceive the Jews as aliens while the Polish heroic tradition compels them to save them.

The same Kossak-Szczucka, in a letter to a friend after the war, described a wartime incident on a Warsaw bridge: "Another time, on the Kierbedz bridge, a German saw a Pole giving alms to a starving Jewish urchin. He pounced and ordered the Pole to throw the child into the river or else he would be shot along with the young beggar. 'There is nothing you can to do help him. I will kill him anyway; he is not allowed to be here. You can go free, if you drown him, or I will kill you, too. Drown him or die. I will count . . . 1, 2 —'

"The Pole could not take it. He broke down and threw the child over the rail into the river. The German gave him a pat on the shoulder. 'Braver Kerl.' They went their separate ways. Two days later, the Pole hanged himself."

The lives of those Poles who felt the guilt of being helpless witnesses to atrocity were marked by a deep trauma, which surfaces with each new debate about anti-Semitism, Polish-Jewish relations and the Holocaust. After all, people in Poland know deep inside that they were the ones who moved into the houses vacated by Jews herded into the ghetto. And there were other reasons for guilt. There were some Poles who turned Jews in and others who hid Jews for money.

Polish public opinion is rarely united, but almost all Poles react very sharply when confronted with the charge that Poles get their anti-Semitism with their mothers' milk and with accusations of their complicity in the Shoah. For the anti-Semites, who are plentiful on the margins of Poland's political life, those attacks are proof of the international anti-Polish Jewish conspiracy. To normal people who came of age in the years of falsifications and silence about the Holocaust, these allegations seem unjust.

To these people, Jan Tomasz Gross's book *Neighbors,* which revealed the story of the murder by Poles of 1,600 Jews in Jedwabne, was a terrible shock. It is difficult to describe the extent of this shock. Mr. Gross's book has generated a heated response comparable to the Jewish community's reaction to the publication of Hannah Arendt's *Eichmann in Jerusalem.* Arendt wrote about the collaboration of some of the Jewish communities with the Nazis: "The Jewish Councils of Elders were informed by Eichmann or his men of how many Jews were needed to fill each train, and they made out the list of deportees. The Jews registered, filled out innumerable forms, answered pages and pages of questionnaires regarding their property so that it could be seized the more easily; they then assembled at the collection points and boarded the trains. The few who tried to hide or to escape were rounded up by a special Jewish police force . . ." We know how the Jewish officials felt when they became instruments of murder—like captains "whose ships were about to sink and who succeeded in bringing them safe to port by casting overboard a great part of their precious cargo." Soon afterward, her Jewish critics said that Hannah Arendt claimed that Jews themselves implemented their Shoah.

Some of the reactions to the book by Mr. Gross were as emotional. An average Polish reader couldn't believe that something like this could have happened. I must admit that I couldn't believe it either, and I thought that my friend Jan Gross had fallen victim to a falsification. But the murder in Jedwabne, preceded by a bestial pogrom, did take place and must weigh on the collective consciousness of the Poles— and on my individual consciousness.

The Polish debate about Jedwabne has been going on for several months. It is a serious debate, full of sadness and sometimes terror— as if the whole society was suddenly forced to carry the weight of this terrible 60-year-old crime; as if all Poles were made to admit their guilt collectively and ask for forgiveness.

I don't believe in collective guilt or collective responsibility or any other responsibility except the moral one. And therefore I ponder what exactly is my individual responsibility and my own guilt. Certainly I cannot be responsible for that crowd of murderers who set the barn in Jedwabne on fire. Similarly, today's citizens of Jedwabne cannot be blamed for that crime. When I hear a call to admit my Polish guilt, I feel hurt the same way the citizens of today's Jedwabne feel when they are interrogated by reporters from around the world.

But when I hear that Mr. Gross's book, which revealed the truth about the crime, is a lie that was concocted by the international Jewish conspiracy against Poland, that is when I feel guilty. Because these false excuses are in fact nothing else but a rationalization of that crime.

As I write this text, I am weighing words carefully and repeating Montesquieu: "I am a man thanks to nature, I am a Frenchman thanks to coincidence." By coincidence I am a Pole with Jewish roots. Almost my whole family was devoured by the Holocaust. My relatives could have perished in Jebwabne. Some of them were Communists or relatives of Communists, some were craftsmen, some merchants, perhaps some rabbis. But all were Jews, according to the Nuremberg laws of the Third Reich. All of them could have been herded into that barn, which was set on fire by Polish criminals.

I do not feel guilty for those murdered, but I do feel responsible. Not that they were murdered—I could not have stopped that. I feel guilty that after they died they were murdered again, denied a decent burial, denied tears, denied truth about this hideous crime, and that for decades a lie was repeated.

This is my fault. For lack of imagination or time, for convenience and spiritual laziness, I did not ask myself certain questions and did not look for answers. Why? After all, I was among those who actively pushed to reveal the truth about the Katyn massacre of Polish soldiers, I worked to tell the truth about the Stalinist trials in Poland, about the victims of the Communist repression. Why then did I not look for the truth about the murdered Jews of Jedwabne? Perhaps because I subconsciously feared the cruel truth about the Jewish fate during that time. After all, the bestial mob in Jedwabne was not unique. In all of the countries conquered by the Soviets after 1939, there were horrible acts of terror against the Jews in the summer and in the autumn of 1941. They died at the hands of their Lithuanian, Latvian, Estonian, Ukrainian, Russian and Belarussian neighbors. I think that the time has come to reveal the truth about these hideous acts. I will try to contribute to this.

Writing these words, I feel a specific schizophrenia: I am a Pole, and my shame about the Jedwabne murder is a Polish shame. At the same time, I know that if I had been there in Jedwabne, I would have been killed as a Jew.

Who then am I, as I write these words? Thanks to nature, I am a man, and I am responsible to other people for what I do and what I do not do. Thanks to my choice, I am a Pole, and I am responsible to the world for the evil inflicted by my countrymen. I do so out of my free will, by my own choice, and by the deep urging of my conscience.

But I am also a Jew who feels a deep brotherhood with those who were murdered as Jews. From this perspective, I assert that whoever tries to remove the crime in Jedwabne from the context of its epoch, whoever uses this example to generalize that this is how only the Poles and all the Poles behaved, is lying. And this lie is as repulsive as the lie that was told for many years about the crime in Jedwabne.

A Polish neighbor might have saved one of my relatives from the hands of the executioners who pushed him into the barn. And indeed, there were many such Polish neighbors—the forest of Polish trees in the Avenue of the Righteous in Yad Vashem, the Holocaust memorial in Jerusalem, is dense.

For these people who lost their lives saving Jews, I feel responsible, too. I feel guilty when I read so often in Polish and foreign newspapers about the murderers who killed Jews, and note the deep silence about those who rescued Jews. Do the murderers deserve more recognition than the righteous?

The Polish primate, the Polish president and the Rabbi of Warsaw said almost in one voice that a tribute to the Jedwabne victims should

serve the cause of reconciling Poles and Jews in the truth. I desire nothing more. If it doesn't happen, it will be also my fault.

.   .   .   .   .

Adam Michnik was born in 1946. He was expelled from the University
of Warsaw for antigovernment activities in 1968 and became one of the
most prominent members of the democratic opposition to the communist regime. A founder of the Committee for the Defense of the Workers (KOR) and of Solidarity, he also played an active role in the roundtable negotiations in 1989 that led to the end of communism in Poland.
Since then he has been an editor of *Gazeta Wyborcza*. Among his books
are *Kościół, lewica, dialog* (The Church, the left, dialogue) (Warsaw,
1977), *Letters from Prison and Other Essays* (Berkeley, 1985), and (with
Jozef Tischner and Jacek Żakowski) *Miedzy Panem a plebanem* (The lord
of the manor and the vicar) (Kraków, 1995).

Leon Wieseltier

WASHINGTON DIARIST: RIGHTEOUS

NEW REPUBLIC, 9 APRIL 2001

I HAVE LEARNED from a friend about the pitfall of moral exquisiteness. By moral exquisiteness, I mean the sort of moral reasoning that has become so refined, so attentive to every aspect of every
case, so sensitive to every standpoint in every situation, that all moral
friction is dispelled, and every moral question is settled, and the individual is left with a pleasing sensation of his own clarity, his own recti-
tude. A diligent conscience can also be complacent; it can be complacent about its diligence. Professors of moral philosophy sometimes
offend me in this way, when they seem like virtuosos of virtue. But the
disappointing friend of whom I am speaking is not a professor of
moral philosophy. He is, in fact, a moral hero. And now he has baffled
me with an exercise in moral casuistry about an evil that requires nothing fancy for its proper understanding, an evil that is so shocking precisely because it is so simple.

The evil to which I refer is the fevered murder of the Jews of Jedwabne by the Poles of Jedwabne on 10 July 1941. With the appearance
of Jan T. Gross's crushing book *Neighbors*, this obscenity has been rescued from oblivion, not least in Poland, where oblivion suited many
people just fine. (See "The Murder of Memory," by Jarosław Anders,
in the *New Republic*, 9 April 2001.) The *New York Times* asked Adam
Michnik for his thoughts about the crime in Jedwabne, and about the
tender subject of Poles and Jews. He obliged, alas. "As I write this
text," he explained in his piece, "I am weighing words carefully." Oh,
how carefully! A howl would have done quite well. Instead my friend
has produced a contorted moral calculation that is more a document
of the problem than a discussion of the problem.

There are the usual Polish apologetics. Michnik begins by reminding
his readers that the Poles were also victims: "Not a single Polish family
was spared by Hitler and Stalin." (Gross efficiently retires this line of
argument in a chapter called "Is It Possible to Be Simultaneously a Victim and a Victimizer?") And Michnik repairs also to the Poles who
rescued Jews during the war. He cites the forest of Polish trees at the
Avenue of the Righteous Gentiles at Yad Vashem in Jerusalem, as if a
stroll along that shattering lane should lighten anybody's load. "Do

the murderers deserve more recognition than the righteous?" Michnik asks. Well, yes, they do, because there were many more of them. (I write this as the grateful son of a Jewish woman who was saved by Poles.) The mention of the righteous is a way of changing the subject, if the subject is the unrighteous. It is designed to leave no guilt uncomplicated, no shame unqualified, no sorrow unalloyed.

Michnik's example of Polish decency toward the Jews in Nazi-occupied Poland is grotesque. He cites an appeal by a well-known Polish writer in August 1942. "The dying Jews are surrounded by Pilates washing their hands," she stirringly wrote. "This silence cannot be tolerated any longer." And she continued: "Our feelings toward the Jews haven't changed. We still consider them the political, economic and ideological enemies of Poland . . . [But] the knowledge of these feelings doesn't relieve us of the duty of condemning the crime. We don't want to be Pilates." This "extraordinary appeal," Michnik explains, "illustrates the paradox of Polish attitudes toward the dying Jews. The anti-Semitic tradition compels the Poles to perceive the Jews as aliens while the Polish heroic tradition compels them to save them." But I do not see a paradox in this writer's language. I see a poison in it, and a piety that lives very comfortably with a poison. The Poles were not Pilates, because the Jews were not Jesus, though they were suffering also from the cross. If these were the philosophical and emotional grounds for "Polish heroism" on behalf of the Jews in Poland, it is no wonder that such heroism was rare.

"I don't believe in collective guilt or collective responsibility or any other responsibility except the moral one," Michnik continues. "And therefore I ponder what exactly is my individual responsibility and my own guilt." This is the voice of an ethically scrupulous man. But then things go awry. "Certainly I cannot be responsible for that crowd of murderers who set the barn in Jedwabne on fire." Certainly; but it is a little demagogic to suggest that anybody is imputing such responsibility to him, or to any other person who was not in Jedwabne on that day of hell. "When I hear a call to admit my Polish guilt, I feel hurt the same way the citizens of today's Jedwabne feel when they are interrogated by reporters from around the world." There is a strange nativist quality to that last phrase; but it is my friend's hurt feelings that disturb me. I think that they require a closer look at the notion of collective responsibility.

It is not true that the moral life is lived only individually, even if acts of good or evil are the work of individuals acting together or alone. Individuals belong to groups, and it is a cost or a benefit of their belonging that they are morally implicated by their groups, which are moral agents, too. One can oppose the misdeeds of one's group, but one cannot secede from it, I mean not neatly after the fact. For this reason, I am not hurt when I am interrogated about the misdeeds of Jews or the misdeeds of Americans, because I have chosen to be known as a Jew and as an American. I understand why they are coming to me with their questions, even with their slanders. I accept that I have some explaining (or refuting or apologizing) to do. To be sure, I am not just a member of my groups, I am also an individual whom they cannot entirely reach or entirely rule; but I cannot hide behind the fact of my individuation, behind the doctrine of individual responsibility, when the going gets rough. Indeed, I could not permit myself to feel pride about the accomplishments of my people and my country if I did not require myself to feel shame about the perfidies of my people and my country. If those perfidies were not the work of my own hands, neither were those accomplishments.

I do not believe that Michnik would disagree with what I have just written. And so I am puzzled by the haggling tone of his reckoning with Jedwabne. He appears to have experienced a contradiction, to have needed to experience a contradiction, where there should be no contradiction. "Writing these words, I feel a specific schizophrenia: I am a Pole, and my shame about the Jedwabne murder is a Polish shame. At the same time, I know that if I had been there in Jedwabne, I would have been killed as a Jew." But this is not a schizophrenia at all. Hybridity, a common fate, is not always morally rending. The multiple identity that Michnik describes means only that he has multiple reasons for anger, for tears, for the repudiation of every excuse and every extenuation. As a Pole and as a Jew, he should have come to the same obvious conclusion: that Poland has many glories, but its history with the Jews is not one of them; and that the interest in innocence always stands in the way of the interest in goodness . . .

. . . . .

Leon Wieseltier was born in New York in 1952 and is the literary editor of the *New Republic* and the author of *Kaddish*.

Reply of Adam Michnik
New Republic, 17 April 2001

Dear Leon,

You are disappointed in me because, in my article in the *New York Times* ("Poles and the Jews: How Deep the Guilt?," March 17), I was weighing words carefully when "a howl would have done quite well." I think that in Polish-Jewish relations there have already been enough howls of pain. I have heard plenty of them from Polish anti-Semites; and the Jewish cry that "the Poles sucked anti-Semitism with their mother's milk" is indelibly imprinted in my memory. This is why I prefer balanced judgment and a willingness to understand one's adversary. The problem for the Poles and the problem for the Jews are similar: Each of these two groups thinks of itself as the innocent victim. This is a stereotype of two peoples who, as Isaac Bashevis Singer put it, have lived alongside each other but not with each other.

The book by Jan Gross describing the murder of Jews in Jedwabne caused moral shock among Poles and a huge public debate that is still going on. It was a murder inspired by Nazi encouragement and acquiescence but committed by Poles. No sensible person in Poland tries to justify this horrible crime. On the contrary: brought face to face with it, Poles now feel a sense of lost innocence.

In my article I described this Polish shock and the temperature of the Polish debate. I knew that I was touching the dark side of the Polish collective memory, but I believed that this is how a Polish writer should react in the face of an exposed crime of this kind. When I picked up a copy of the *New Republic*, I assumed that you would react in a similar way, with a contemplation on the darker aspects of Jewish memory. However, Leon, in your reply ("Righteous," April 9), you chose to use several remarks about the "moral exquisiteness" you perceived in my text. I shall disregard this dimension of our controversy, except to recall Spinoza's opinion that "when Jan speaks about Paul, it reflects on Jan and not on Paul."

I wrote that there is no Polish family that was not wounded by the war. You call it "the usual Polish apologetics." But the truth is, Leon, that is a simple Polish fact. And although such facts should not be used to relativize the crime in Jedwabne, to know them is a prerequisite to understanding Polish-Jewish relations. For many years after the war Poles grieved over their murdered compatriots without acknowledging that the fate of their Jewish neighbors was incomparably more tragic—an utterly exceptional tragedy in the history of humanity.

On the other hand, there has prevailed among Jews—as Rabbi Klenicki put it—a triumphalism of pain, as though Jews decided that only the Jewish tragedy was worthy of preservation in the consciousness. And this is the context of our own polemic here. Polish authors today are trying to transcend the stereotype of Polish innocence and are grappling with the legacy of anti-Semitism. This is difficult and painful. But to read recent Polish articles on the issue is to be deeply moved. The Poles are truly breaking away from the Polish stereotype. I am sorry, Leon, that you have written as though you are still in the comfortable grip of Jewish stereotypes, like someone with neither the will nor the courage to enter into a difficult dialogue with the Poles. Such a dialogue requires a revision of stereotypes. You have to assume that there may be certain aspects of the Polish-Jewish reality that you do not know, and that perhaps, therefore, you may not be able to fully understand.

Poles also have a right to the memory of their own pain. And they have a right to expect that Jews will be aware of it as well. Try to transcend the Jewish stereotype and look at the wartime reality with a Polish eye. I think that every Pole has an obligation to look with a Jewish eye in order to understand the suffering of the Jews. And you should also try to see in your Polish interlocutor a friend who is grappling with a difficult history, not an anti-Semite and prevaricator who wants "to leave no guilt uncomplicated."

The Poles are neither genetically tainted anti-Semites nor trying to avoid looking truth in the eye—even the most difficult truth. But that does not mean succumbing to false generalizations. Were the Poles both victims and victimizers at the same time? I am afraid of such generalizations. Which Poles? Those who were killed in the struggles against the Nazis? Or perhaps those who saved Jews, among them your mother? Do you make those Poles responsible for the crime in Jedwabne? Do you make them responsible for the blackmailers, known in Polish as *szmalcownicy*? Or perhaps it is precisely the *szmalcownik*, and not the hero of the anti-Nazi underground, whom you take as a symbol of the Polish response to the German occupation. Such a judgment, which I would not dare to ascribe to you, could only be the result of ignorance or dishonesty. I see symbols in the heroes of the Ghetto Uprising and not in the Jewish policemen who served the occupiers and were clearly both victims and victimizers.

You write, Leon, that there were many more murderous Poles than there were righteous ones. How did you make your count? Yes, there were Poles during the occupation who committed crimes against Jews. But those crimes were condemned by the Polish government-in-exile in London and were punished by the Polish underground. I will go further and say that, among members of the Polish resistance, there were also many people shaped by anti-Semitic stereotypes; but the overwhelming majority of Poles on the anti-Semitic right—unlike their counterparts in France, for example—took part in the anti-Nazi resistance, and some of those people saved Jews. Among them was Zofia Kossak-Szczucka, author of the moving appeal to save Jews that I quoted in the *Times*.

The appeal issued by Kossak-Szczucka—no doubt anti-Semitic in its qualifying remarks yet heroic in its plea—counters the Jewish stereotype according to which anti-Semitism equals extermination. This is why, Leon, you did not find anything in Kossak-Szczucka except anti-Semitic poison. I, on the other hand, found in her appeal the evidence of a heroism of the highest order. For years, day after day, this Catholic writer and prisoner of Auschwitz risked her life saving Jews—people whom she neither knew nor particularly liked—in a situation where public executions and fear for the safety of one's immediate family paralyzed almost everybody. Such an attitude deserves not contempt but respect. And respect is the basic elementary condition for an honest Polish-Jewish conversation about truth and reconciliation. I would like to be of service to such a conversation, helping to break both Polish and Jewish stereotypes. I feel I have a responsibility to do this.

However, I do not believe in any collective responsibility except a moral one. What I mean is that I can blame myself for the acts of others, but I would not give anyone else the right to blame me for those same acts. This is why I feel guilty neither for the crimes of the murderers of Jedwabne nor for the crimes of Communists of Jewish lineage (although for the latter I feel somewhat more responsible, but for purely personal reasons). My sense of moral responsibility has made me very reluctant to impose collective guilt onto any other community whatsoever. You wrote, Leon: "Individuals belong to groups, and it is a cost or a benefit of their belonging that they are morally implicated by their groups, which are moral agents, too ... I am not hurt when I am interrogated about the misdeeds of Jews or the misdeeds of Americans, because I have chosen to be known as a Jew and as an American ... I could not permit myself to feel pride about the accomplishments of my people and my country if I did not require myself to feel shame about the perfidies of my people and my country ..." And then you add, "I do not believe that Michnik would disagree with what I have just written."

Of course I agree with you, but this agreement does not get us anywhere. Of course I feel pain and shame for the murder in Jedwabne and for other Polish crimes. But for these crimes committed by specific murderers, I will never agree that I, my Polish friends, and the Polish nation should be accused collectively. I understand, Leon, that, as an American, you have a right to be proud of Washington, Jefferson, and Lincoln and a right to feel ashamed of slavery, the extermination of Native Americans, racial segregation, and the betrayal of Poland at the Yalta conference. As a Jew, you have a right to be proud of Moses, Spinoza, and Einstein and a right to be ashamed of the Bolshevik murderers with Jewish names, the massacre of Palestinians in the Sabra and Shatila, and the murder of Prime Minister Yitzhak Rabin. You have a right to be ashamed, but I do not have the right to blame you for these crimes. But, frankly speaking, I do not really know what comes out of this pride or this shame. After all, that kind of understanding leads to utterly absurd questions. Is it because of Lincoln and Spinoza that you feel better than I, having up my sleeve only Copernicus, Mickiewicz, and Chopin? Do you feel any less morally burdened because of the lynchings by Ku Klux Klan bandits than the average Pole because of Jedwabne? Do you feel the need to apologize to Poles for Yalta? Or to Christians for crucifying Jesus?

Let's be serious. Both you and I are responsible for ourselves, for our deeds, for those close to us with whom we identify ourselves. So I eagerly accept responsibility for your sins, because I have chosen you as my friend. But I do not feel any identification with the murderers in Jedwabne, just as you do not feel any bond with the Jewish *szmalcownicy* from the Gestapo who denounced my relatives. Those are the reasons why I am writing "carefully" and "weighing words." Poland is saying the Kaddish over the graves of the murdered. And the Kaddish is said with solemn dignity, and not with howling.

Yours, with warm regards,
Adam

Reply of Leon Wieseltier
New Republic, 24 April 2001

Dear Adam,

When you were confronted with Jan Gross's revelations about the horror at Jedwabne, you were perfectly correct to explore "the dark side of the Polish collective memory"; correct and also intrepid, in the inflamed context of the debate in Poland. But why did you assume that I "would react in a similar way, with a contemplation on the darker aspects of Jewish memory?"

The Jews at Jedwabne in the summer of 1941 did nothing but die. I do not accept that the events at Jedwabne deserve to provoke any special Jewish self-examination. This, I assure you, is not because Jews have nothing in the world with which to reproach themselves. It is not solidarity with my brethren that prevents me from agreeing with you. Quite the contrary. I believe that solidarity is sometimes an impediment to an honest life and a decent life. No, I insist upon the onesidedness of this reckoning because of my general understanding of prejudice and oppression. If you wish to understand anti-Semitism, do not study Jews. Study non-Jews, because the fantasies and the atrocities are theirs. If you wish to understand racism, do not study blacks. Study whites, for the same reason. The notion that in some significant sense there are two sides to such questions, that prejudice has a basis in reality and oppression has a cause in the behavior of the oppressed, is itself a concession to the injustice that we both despise.

Who is against dialogue? But dialogue is a shibboleth of this sensitive age. So let us think a little more strenuously about dialogue. It is not the only form of moral discussion; it is not even the only form of respectful discussion. For dialogue makes the assumption of a perfect symmetry between the individuals who take part in it. Its ethical beauty is owed to the equality that it posits between the interlocutors. But often this equality between individuals is mistakenly promoted into an equivalence between their views. The premise of the summons to dialogue is that there is truth in what you say and there is truth in what I say. This is frequently the case. But what if you are completely right and I am completely wrong? Surely this is possible. Then our "dialogue" must consist of my admission of error, which of course is not an impairment of my dignity. In a discussion between Poles and Jews about Jedwabne, I do not see that there is a dialogical symmetry between the interlocutors. One has suffered at the hands of the other. This absence of symmetry does not mean that one is superior to the other: there is no moral superiority in suffering. It means only that history is asymmetrical. This asymmetry is an empirical matter. It is also a matter of common experience: there are many disparities of power in ordinary life. As a result of those disparities, we injure each other in many ways, and these injuries cannot be comprehended or absolved by fictions of parity. In such situations we must certainly have a conversation, but I am not sure that we must have a dialogue. If ever I do anything to harm you, you will have a right to expect more from me than dialogue. (I am speaking generally: you do not owe me an apology for Jedwabne.)

You call, quite reasonably, for "a willingness to understand one's adversary." This you take to be an essential element of dialogue. Are you saying that the Jews in Poland were Poland's adversary? Your notion of dialogical equivalence would seem to require you to be saying this; but I do not see how you can mean it. I am certain, in fact, that you do not mean it. For it sounds terribly like the statement about the Jews by Zofia Kossak-Szczucka ("We still consider them the political, economic and ideological enemies of Poland") that you cited in your original article with disapproval. Recently I have learned more about her heroism, and also more about her worldview. You are right: good and evil can live together in the same soul. Yet I am still reluctant to accept your view of her contradictions as an adequate basis for Polish-Jewish reconciliation. Respect for the other is infirm and untrustworthy if it is forever an act of self-overcoming. Must we really settle for so little? If you believe that anti-Semitism is an ineradicable feature of Polish life, then you should say so. But I have never known you to be a pessimist in affairs of conscience. When you write that as a consequence of Gross's book "Poles now feel a sense of lost innocence," I am startled. What nation ever had innocence to lose? I find it hard to dignify the disillusion that you describe, because this would obscure or even obliterate the precious distinction between history and memory. Memory nourishes not least because it lies, and collective memory lies most gorgeously of all. But memory is not our only source of knowledge about the past, or our most reliable source. Surely it is the task of the intellectual to rectify memory with history. Historically speaking, there were times when Poles were victims and there were times when Poles were victimizers. (The same is true of Jews, though the times when Jews were victims, when they lacked power to use or to abuse, were desperately long, and included the centuries of the Jewish sojourn in Poland.) And there were times when Poles were both victims and victimizers. But none of this has anything to do with "innocence," which is not so much a collective memory as a collective deception. I see why the generalizations of identity make you uncomfortable. They trip me up, too. They must be made concrete, as you insist. But I do not see how anybody except cosmopolitans can do without them, and even cosmopolitans generalize about themselves. More importantly, these generalizations represent a recognition of the moral agency of groups, which is the subject of our disputation. (The consoling fact is that we fall, all of us, under many generalizations. I am not your friend, I am your friends.) If I am still in the "grip of Jewish stereotypes," I assure you that I am alive to the danger that collective memory poses to intellectual probity. We are certainly morbid. But "a triumphalism of pain"? That, too, is a stereotype about the Jews, Rabbi Klenicki or no Rabbi Klenicki. It is these days the "advanced" stereotype, the pre-ferred stereotype of certain critics of contemporary Jewish culture. I used to entertain it myself. For the salience of the Holocaust in Jewish identity is plain, and it is unfortunate. Yet it is also under-standable: how could a catastrophe of such magnitude not over-whelm a community, not stupefy it, not break its heart, not embit-ter its expectations of life, not fix it for at least a generation in grief and anger and fear? I, too, deplore that Jewish culture has become increasingly a culture of commemoration—but I, too, have what to commemorate. (Remember, I am a son of Drohobycz and Stryj.) I will tell you this: I have never met a Jew who "decided that only the Jewish tragedy was worthy of preservation in the conscious-ness." The suggestion is unworthy of you. (When you were strug-gling to bring the tragedy of communism to an end, did you have difficulty in finding Jewish allies?) In the aftermath of the almost complete annihilation of European Jewry, it is not the specter of triumphalism that Jews have to banish from their midst, it is the specter of defeatism. They must devise a way to honor what they know about the world without being undone by what they know about the world. Should they forget what they know about the world, so as to be acquitted of a "triumphalism of pain"?

There is no sense in which I consider myself "better" than you. Also, I never, not for a moment, regarded you as "an anti-Semite." Also, I was not sarcastic when I imputed moral exquisiteness to you: there are worse vices, and in other circumstances you have made it a virtue. Also, the Jews did not crucify Jesus. As for your accepting responsibility for my sins: I warn you, my friend, it is a terrible responsibility for you to bear.

Yours affectionately,

Leon

CHRONOLOGY

Early September 1939 The German army invades the region. The local synagogue in Jedwabne is burned.

28 September 1939 According to the German-Soviet Boundary and Friendship Treaty, the Podlasie region is placed under Soviet occupation. The Soviet army enters Jedwabne.

23 June 1941 Following the outbreak of the war between Nazi Germany and the Soviet Union on 22 June, the German army reenters Jedwabne. The Germans introduce a new administrative division of the region according to which Jedwabne is placed in "Okręg Białostocki."

25 June 1941 The first anti-Jewish riots in Jedwabne.

5 July 1941 The massacre of the Jewish community of Wąsosz by the local Polish population, the first of such massacres in the region.

7 July 1941 Massacre of the Jewish community of Radziłów by the local Polish population. A small group of survivors hides in Jedwabne.

10 July 1941 Massacre of the Jewish community of Jedwabne.

August 1941 Germans set up a ghetto in Łomża. Jewish survivors of the Jedwabne massacre move into the ghetto.

November 1942 Szmuel Wasersztajn, together with six other Jewish men and women, finds refuge on the farm of Antonina Wyrzykowska in the hamlet of Janczewska near Jedwabne. She takes care of them until the Red Army reenters the region in January 1945.

March 1943 The Germans declare the Okręg Białostocki *judenrein*.

Spring of 1945 Antonina Wyrzykowska is badly beaten by a small group of Poles who suspect that she has provided refuge to Jews and disapprove of her rescue activities. Subsequently her family is forced to leave their farm in Janczewska and relocate to Łomża. As the news of her rescue activities spreads, the family is forced to leave the entire region for Warsaw.

5 April 1945 Szmuel Wasersztajn testifies about the massacre of Jedwabne Jews to members of the newly established Jewish Historical Commission in Białystok. His testimony is later deposited in the Jewish Historical Institute in Warsaw.

29 December 1947 Całka Migdał, a former inhabitant of Jedwabne, sends a letter from Montevideo to the Central Committee of Jews in Poland. The letter claims that "the Jews of Jedwabne were murdered not by the Germans but by the Poles, and that those Poles still live in the town and have not been prosecuted." Całka Migdał left Jedwabne before the outbreak of the Second World War. However, his family remained in Jedwabne and were murdered in the massacre of 10 July 1941.

February 1948 The Ministry of Justice, to which Calka Migdal's letter has been given, orders the chief prosecutor of the district court of Łomża to begin investigation into the Jedwabne massacre.

February 1948–January 1949 The district court of Łomża takes no action against the suspected perpetrators of the Jedwabne massacre.

8 January 1949 The local Public Security Office (UB) arrests fifteen individuals from Jedwabne suspected of having taken an active part in the massacre. They are interviewed between 8 and 22 January.

16–17 May 1949 Court proceedings in the district court of Łomża. On 17 May the court passes sentence: twelve individuals are released; one individual, Karol Bardoń, is sentenced to death; and nine others receive sentences of between eight and fifteen years of imprisonment.

18 February 1957 Jerzy Laudański, the last of those sentenced on 17 May 1949, is freed.

1963 The local section of the Union of Fighters for Freedom and Democracy (Związek Bojowników o Wolność i Demokrację, *ZBOWiD*) in Łomża erects a monument to commemorate the Jedwabne Jews. It attributes the entire responsibility for their murder to the Germans.

December 1966 The first scholarly discussion of the involvement of the local Polish population in the Jedwabne massacre appears in Szymon Datner's article "Eksterminacja Żydów Okręgu Białostockiego," *Biuletyn Żydowskiego Instytutu Historycznego*, no. 60 (October–December 1966): 1–29. Datner describes the event as a massacre committed by the local population (*miejscowa ludność*); the use of such terminology is undoubtedly dictated by communist censorship.

1967 The District Commission to Investigate Nazi Crimes in Białystok reopens the investigation into the Jedwabne massacre. The findings of the investigation are published by Waldemar Monkiewicz, the chief prosecutor, twenty-two years later in the journal of the University of Białystok *Studia Podlaskie*. Monkiewicz attributes the crime to the special German military unit called Kommando Białystok led by Wolfgang Birkner.

March 1968 Polish students protest against limitations of freedom of speech; even before the protests, the authorities, under the guise of "anti-Zionism," began a purge of Jews in Poland. After the suppression of the student protests, the communist authorities forced a wave of Jewish emigration from Poland.

1980 The publication of *Yedwabne: History and Memorial Book* by the former inhabitants of the Jewish community of Jedwabne, members of the Jedwabner Societies in Israel and the United States of America. The book, edited by Julius L. Baker and Jacob L. Baker, appears in Jerusalem and New York.

December 1981 The government of General Wojciech Jaruzelski introduces martial law and bans Solidarity

10 July 1988 *Kontakty,* a weekly published in Łomża, prints the article ". . . aby życ" (. . . to live), written by Danuta and Aleksander Wroniszewscy, in which the massacre in Jedwabne is discussed and the testimony of Szmuel Wasersztajn is cited.

18 July 1999 Agnieszka Arnold's documentary film *Where Is My Elder Brother Cain?* (*Gdzie jest mój starszy brat Kain?*), dedicated to the subject of Polish-Jewish relations, which is shown on Polish television, refers in passing to the massacre of the Jews of Jedwabne.

9 February 2000 Szmuel Wasersztajn dies in his home in Costa Rica.

Spring 2000 The testimony of Szmuel Wasersztajn is cited and discussed by Jan Tomasz Gross in the article "Lato 1941 w Jedwabnem. Przyczynek do badań nad udziałem społeczności lokalnych w eksterminacji narodu żydowskiego w latach II wojny swiatowej" (Summer 1941 in Jedwabne: A contribution to research on the role of local societies in the extermination of the Jewish nation in the years of the Second World War). The article appears in the festschrift dedicated to Tomasz Strzembosz, *Europa nieprowincjonalna*, ed. Krzysztof Jasiewicz (Warsaw: Oficyna Wydawnicza Rytm).

3 April 2000 Jan Tomasz Gross delivers a paper entitled "Jews and Their Polish Neighbors: The Case of Jedwabne during the Soviet Occupation in the Summer of 1941" at the conference "Polish-Jewish Relations during and after the Holocaust–New Approaches" held at Yeshiva University in New York.

5 May 2000 The journalist Andrzej Kaczyński publishes the first of his many articles on Jedwabne, entitled "Całopalenie," in the national Polish daily *Rzeczpospolita*. In the article he refers to Jan Gross's research on Jedwabne massacre. The article appears in English entitled as "Burning Alive" on the Web site of Morlan Ty Rogers, twenty-seven of whose relatives were killed in Jedwabne on 10 July 1941.

8 May 2000 The Town Council of Jedwabne, the Association of Jewish Communities in Poland, and representatives of the prime minister undertake to establish the truth about the massacre of the Jews of Jedwabne and to commemorate its victims.

13–14 May 2000 The right-wing Catholic and nationalistic daily *Nasz Dziennik* accuses Kaczyński and Gross of propagating "lies" about the massacre in Jedwabne. It claims that it was the Germans and not the Poles who killed the Jedwabne Jews, and that Jewish support of the Soviet regime and the Soviet secret police was a major factor in creating anti-Jewish attitudes among the ethnic Polish population.

Late May 2000 The publication of *Sąsiedzi. Historia zagłady żydowskiego miasteczka* by Pogranicze, Sejny. Two thousand copies are printed. However, because of public demand, the publisher makes the book accessible to readers free of charge on the Internet.

August 2000 The Polish government assigns the Institute of National Memory (Instytut Pamięci Narodowej, IPN) the task of investigating the massacre and of issuing an official report. The chairman of IPN, Prof. Leon Kieres (1948–)—professor of law at the University of Wrocław and former senator—appoints Prosecutor Radosław Ignatiew of Białystok the chief investigator.

18 November 2000 *Gazeta Wyborcza* publishes Jacek's Żakowski's article "Każdy sąsiad ma imię" (Every neighbor has a name) and his interview with Tomasz Szarota "Diabelskie szczegóły" (Devilish details). The publication of these articles marks the beginning of the most intensive phase of the debate on Gross's book—the second phase.

4 March 2001 The Committee to Defend the Good Name of Jedwabne (Komitet Obrony Dobrego Imienia Jedwabnego) established. Sejm deputy Michał Kamiński of Łomża, representing Zjednoczenie Chrześcijańsko-Narodowe (ZChN—Christian National Union), and Mayor Krzysztof Godlewski propose different strategies for the committee. Krzysztof Godlewski is appointed chairman. On 6 March Godlewski's strategy is rejected and he resigns as chairman and committee member. He is replaced by Michał Kamiński, who proposes a protest to the government against "the world campaign of slander against Jedwabne and the whole of Poland" and attacks Aleksander Kwaśniewski's promised apology for the crime committed in Jedwabne. Rev. Edward Orłowski is one of the committee's principal members.

5 *March 2001* Primate Józef Glemp makes his first public statement about the Jedwabne massacre. In the interview conducted by journalists of the Catholic Information Agency Glemp suggests that common prayers of Christians and Jews for the victims of the Jedwabne massacre should be held in Warsaw. He rejects the idea of participating in the official commemorative ceremony of the sixtieth anniversary of the crime in Jedwabne on 10 July 2001. While he acknowledges the fact that ethnic Poles participated in the massacre and speaks about "the generational responsibility for the crime," he also makes controversial and anti-Jewish remarks, which he repeats on 15 May.

15 *March 2001* The monument erected in Jedwabne in 1963 is removed in the presence of Andrzej Przewoźnik, general secretary of the Council to Defend the Memory of Fighting and Suffering (Rada Ochrony Pamięci Walki i Meczeństwa).

3 *and 4 April 2001* Agnieszka Arnold's documentary film *Sąsiedzi* (Neighbors) is broadcast on Polish television. The film is followed by a discussion chaired by the journalist Marian Turski, with the participation of Leon Kieres of IPN, Marek Siwiec, spokesman of the presidential office, and Marek Urbański, spokesman of the prime minister's office.

6 *May 2001* Prime Minister Jerzy Buzek states that the participation of Poles in the murder of the Jews in Jedwabne is unquestionable. At the same time he stresses that "the crime was not committed in the name of the Polish nation and state."

27 *May 2001* The Polish episcopate organizes a special repentance mass for the murdered Jews of Jedwabne in All Saints' Church (Warsaw), which during the Second World War was located on the border with the Warsaw ghetto. One-third of the episcopate—fifty bishops—take part in the mass, which is led by Primate Józef Glemp. Among other participants are the pope's representative Archbishop Józef Kowalik; Rev. Janusz Narzyński of the Reformed-Protestant Church; Maciej Płażyński, former speaker of the Polish parliament; Władysław Bartoszewski, minister for foreign affairs; and Barbara Sułek-Kowalska, adviser to the premier. All Saints' Church is also the site of the office of the Committee to Remember Polish Rescuers

of Jews (Komitet dla Upamiętnienia Polaków ratujących Żydów) of whose Historical Committee Tomasz Strzembosz is the chairman.

30 May and 3 June 2001 The IPN conducts a partial exhumation of the Jewish grave located in the place where the barn used to be. Present at the exhumation are representatives of IPN Radosław Ignatiew and Witold Kulesza, Rabbi Menachem Ekstein of Israel, an expert in exhumation, and Michael Schudrich, the rabbi of Warsaw and Łódź, and young members of the Warsaw Jewish community. The director of the International Forensic Program "Physicians for Human Rights," Dr. William Haglund, is also present as an observer. The exhumation lasts only five days owing to pressure from various Jewish Orthodox religious groups. Shortly afterward, one of the Polish archaeologists claims that approximately 150–200 bodies of men, women, and children were found in the grave, and the figure of 200 murdered Jews is widely cited in the right-wing press.

According to Wiktor Kulesza of the IPN, the same grave could have contained between 300 and 400 bodies. Lech Kaczyński, minister of justice, also states that the number of Jews murdered on 10 July 1941 was much lower than the number cited by Jan Tomasz Gross. In the area of the grave pieces of Lenin's monument and 100 German bullets are also uncovered. The latter evidence will lead to premature conclusions that the Germans were responsible for the execution of the massacre.

Early June 2001 Jan T. Gross issues appeal to the IPN not to stop the exhumation. The appeal is published in *Gazeta Wyborcza* on 6 June. Gross, who consulted Dr. Haglund, estimates that the entire exhumation of the remains of Jewish bodies in Jedwabne should last many months, if not a year.

May–June 2001 The publication of anti-Gross books—Jerzy Robert Nowak, *100 kłamst J. T. Grossa o żydowskich sąsiadach w Jedwabnem* (100 lies of J. T. Gross about the Jewish neighbors in Jedwabne); Henryk Pająk, *Jedwabne geszefty* (Jedwabne swindles); and Lech Z. Niekrasz, *Operacja "Jedwabne"—mity i fakty* (Operation "Jedwabne"—myths and facts)—and of the Polish version of Norman G. Finkelstein's *The Holocaust Industry: Reflections on the Exploitation of Jewish Suffering*. The term "Holocaust Industry" is widely cited in the debate on Jedwabne by those advocating the strong self-defensive approach to Polish-Jewish issues.

28 May–June 2001 Controversy over inscription on the planned new monument. Jewish groups are disappointed by the new inscription proposed by Andrzej Przewoźnik, secretary of the Council to Defend the Memory of Fighting and Suffering, since it fails to state clearly that it was Poles who killed their Jewish neighbors. At the end of the two-week discussion, agreement is reached to shorten the inscription, which is to read in Hebrew, Yiddish, and Polish, "In memory of the Jews of Jedwabne and surrounding areas, men, women, and children, fellow dwellers (*współgospodarze*) of this land, murdered and burned alive at this site on 10 July 1941."

10 July 2001 The official commemorative ceremony of the murder of the Jews of Jedwabne on the sixtieth anniversary of the event. The commemoration consists of two parts, the first in the main square and the second at the old Jewish cemetery and a new Jewish cemetery where the two collective graves are situated and where the monument is sited. The president of the Polish Third Republic, Aleksander Kwaśniewski, and the Israeli ambassador to Poland, Szewach Weiss, deliver speeches in the town square, while Rabbi Jacob Baker of New York, who originally came from Jedwabne, and the chief rabbi of Warsaw and Łódź, Michael Schudrich, say prayers at the new memorial.

Approximately one thousand people attend, including Władysław Bartoszewski, Ministry of Foreign Affairs; two vice-parliament speakers, Marek Borowski (SLD) and Jan Krol (UW); Leszek Miller of the Democratic Left Alliance (SLD); and Tadeusz Mazowiecki and Bronislaw Geremek (UW). Representatives of the German episcopate are also present. Members of the Polish episcopate do not take part in the event. Among other participants are members of the Polish Society of the Righteous Among the Nations, families of Jewish victims, and ordinary Poles from different parts of the country. The local population of Jedwabne, together with their priest Father Orłowski, do not participate in the commemoration, describing it as "the Jewish celebration." Krzysztof Godlewski, the mayor of Jedwabne, and Stanisław Michałowski, the chairman of the Jedwabne Town Council, take part in spite of the opposition of the Town Council and Father Orłowski.

19 December 2001 During a press conference Leon Kieres and Andrzej Rzepliński of the IPN state that the latest evidence about the Jedwabne massacre appears to confirm suggestions that German troops were not involved in the massacre of Jedwabne Jews. The investigation into bullets found earlier at the barn reveals that they were not of a type used by the Germans in 1941, but that they came from earlier and later periods. The investigators state that they also have no evidence indicating any significant German presence in the area.

22 February 2002 The antisemitic books of Jerzy R. Nowak and Henryk Pająk about Jedwabne and Gross's *Neighbors* are removed by the police from the bookshop Nasza Księgarnia in Tychy. The antisemitic nationalistic press interprets the event as an attack on freedom of speech in Poland. The Toronto Branch of the Canadian Polish Congress also issues a protest letter against the removal of the books.

25 February 2002 Agnieszka Arnold receives the prestigious Award of Wielkiej Fundacji Kultury (Award of Great Culture Foundation) for her film *Neighbors.*

21 March 2002 Former mayor of Jedwabne Krzysztof Godlewski and Rabbi Jacob Baker are awarded the Jan Karski Prize. Although the decision of the Town Council to dismiss Godlewski was rejected by the provincial authorities as illegal in late August 2001, Godlewski is forced by members of council to leave both his job and the town of Jedwabne.

17 April 2002 Investigator Radosław Ignatiew of IPN states that the brief questioning in Germany of former Obersturmführer Hermann Schaper, the only German witness to be interviewed in the Jedwabne inquiry, has not revealed significant new facts. Schaper, now ninety, was the commander of the Gestapo unit from Ciechanowice, which was present in the Łomża province in the summer of 1941. Some of those who participated in the historical debate had claimed that Schaper took an active part in the Jedwabne massacre of Jews.

8 July 2002 Leon Kieres, chairman of IPN, issues a preliminary report about the findings of the investigation into the crime.

9 July 2002 At a press conference in Białystok, Prosecutor Radosław Ignatiew announces the findings of the investigation. The official report confirms that the local Polish population was responsible for conducting the massacre, and that the Germans allowed the massacre to take place. The report questions the number of 1,600 victims but does not provide an exact figure. The report also announces that the investigation is going to be discontinued, and that no new perpetrators were found who were not charged by the communist authorities in 1949 and 1953.

October 2002 Publication of the two-volume report of the Institute of National Memory *Wokół Jedwabnego.*

EXPLANATORY NOTES

Anders's Army The army established in the Soviet Union in 1941 by General Władysław Anders under the auspices of the Polish **government-in-exile** (q.v.) in London as a result of the **Sikorski-Maisky Agreement** (q.v.). This army left the Soviet Union for Persia and the Middle East in mid-1942 and traveled by way of Iran and Palestine to Italy, where it took part in battles such as the capture of Monte Cassino (1944).

Armia Krajowa Literally "Home Army." The largest resistance movement in Poland during the Second World War, controlled by the Polish **government-in-exile** (q.v.). It carried out numerous acts of sabotage and armed offensives, of which the most important was Warsaw Uprising of 1944. In communist Poland, Home Army soldiers were persecuted, and some joined the secret organization WiN (Freedom and Independence).

Arnold, Agnieszka Agnieszka Arnold was born to a Lutheran family in Łowicz in central Poland. She has made thirty documentary films, the majority of which are dedicated to Polish-Jewish relations or to the theme of Lutheran minority in Poland. (In 1994 she received a prestigious award from the Fundacja Kultury for her film about an evangelical village near Cieszyn *Kto ziarno w nadziei siał?*) She began her work on *Neighbors* in 1998 and completed it in early 2001. The first of her films in which she dealt with the Jedwabne massacre, *Gdzie jest mój starszy brat Kain?*, was made in 1999.

Barbarossa Code name for the 1941 German offensive against the Soviet Union.

Berman, Adolf A key figure in Poland during the Stalinist period who, between 1949 and 1954, was a member of the Commission of Security Matters of the Central Committee of the Polish United Workers' Party. His Jewish origin was often commented on.

bezhentsy Russian term used after the 1939 campaign for refugees, mostly Jewish, who fled from the German to the Russian portion of occupied Poland.

Biuletyn Informacyjny The information bulletin, the main press organ of the **Polish Underground State** (q.v.).

Blue Police (Policja granatowa—also sometimes referred to as "Navyblue Police")—A popular name, taken from the color of their uniforms, for the prewar Polish police retained in existence by the Nazi-occupation authorities in the **General Government** (q.v.).

Bund General Jewish Workers' Alliance. A Jewish Socialist Party, founded in 1897. It joined the Russian Social-Democratic Labour Party but seceded from it when its program of national autonomy was not accepted. In independent Poland, it adopted a leftist anti-communist posture and from the 1930s cooperated increasingly closely with the Polish Socialist Party (PPS).

Chadecja The Christian Democratic Party (Partia Chrześcijańsko-De-mokratyczna). In interwar Poland its main area of support was Upper Silesia. Its adherents were referred to as "Chadecy" (sing. "Chadek").

Cheka Special Commission against Counterrevolution and Sabotage, the political police in the first years of the Soviet state's existence (predecessor to the **NKVD** [q.v.] and KGB).

Commonwealth (Polish: *Rzeczpospolita*)—The term *Rzeczpospolita* is derived from the Latin *res publica*. It is sometimes translated as "Commonwealth" and sometimes as "Republic," often in the form "Noblemen's Republic" (*Rzeczpospolita szlachecka*). After the union of Lublin in 1569, it was used officially in the form *Rzeczpospolita Obojga Narodów* (Commonwealth of Two Nations) to designate the new form of state that had arisen. In historical literature, this term is often rendered as "The Polish-Lithuanian Commonwealth."

Congress Kingdom (Otherwise Kingdom of Poland or Congress Poland)—A constitutional kingdom created at the Congress of Vienna (1814–1815), with the tsar of Russia as hereditary monarch. After 1831, it declined to an administrative unit of the Russian Empire in all but name. After 1864, it lost the remaining vestiges of the autonomy it had been granted at Vienna and was now officially referred to as "Privislansky kray" (Vistula territory).

Edelman, Marek One of the leaders of ŻOB, the Jewish Fighting Organization, during the Warsaw Ghetto Uprising in 1943; a member of the democratic opposition during the 1970s and 1980s.

Einsatzgruppe, Einsatzkommandos Special Nazi police units charged with the extermination of Jews in newly occupied territories beginning in 1941.

Endecja Popular name for the Polish National Democratic Party, a right-wing party that had its origins in the 1890s. Its principal ideologue was Roman Dmowski, who advocated a Polish version of the integral nationalism that became popular in Europe at the turn of the nineteenth century. The Endecja advanced the slogan "Poland for the Poles" and called for the exclusion of Jews from Polish political and economic life. Its adherents were called "Endeks."

first partition The first of the **partitions** (q.v.) of the Polish-Lithuanian Commonwealth, which led to its disappearance as a state at the end of the eighteenth century. The first partition, which was carried out by Russia, Prussia, and Austria, took place in 1772.

General Government An administrative-territorial unit created in Poland during the Nazi occupation from some of the territory seized by Germany after the Polish defeat. The GG was established on 26 October 1939 and first comprised four districts: Kraków, Lublin, Warsaw, and Radom. Its capital was the town of Kraków, and its administration was headed by Hans Frank. After the Nazi invasion of the Soviet Union, an additional province, Galicia, made up of parts of the prewar Polish provinces of Lwów, Stanisławów, and Tarnopol, was added to the GG. In the territory of the GG, the Germans pursued a policy of mass murder of the Jewish population and reduced the Christian Poles to disenfranchised slaves, who were to provide a reservoir of labor for the Third Reich.

Główna Komisja Badania Zbrodni Hitlerowskich Main Commission for the Investigation of Nazi Crimes in Poland. This was formed in 1945 under the original name of Główna Komisja Badania Zbrodni Niemieckich w Polsce and was the official organ in communist Poland dealing with research on and investigation (including criminal prosecutions) of crimes committed by Germans occupying Poland during World War II. After the fall of communism, it was transformed into the **Główna Komisja dla zbadań zbrodni przeciwko Narodowi Polskiemu** (Main Commission for the Investigation of Crimes against the Polish Nation) (q.v.).

Główna Komisja dla zbadań zbrodni przeciwko Narodowi Polskiemu Main Commission for the Investigation of Crimes against the Polish Nation—formed after the fall of communism as the official organ dealing with research on and investigation (including criminal prosecutions) of crimes committed by Germans occupying Poland, as well as—in contrast to its predecessor the **Główna Komisja Badania Zbrodni Hitlerowskich** (Main Commission for the Investigation of Nazi Crimes in Poland) (q.v.)—those committed by the communist authorities during the period 1939–1956. At present, its mission is carried out by the **Instytut Pamięci Narodowej** (q.v.). One part of the IPN, the Komisja Ścigania Zbrodni przeciwko Narodowi Polskiemu, deals with criminal investigations.

government-in-exile After the German defeat of Poland in 1939, a government was established made up of the less-compromised elements of the **Sanacja** (q.v.) regime and representatives of the democratic opposition, and headed by General Sikorski. This government made its headquarters in Angers, and after the fall of France it moved to London. It attempted to represent the Polish cause but was abandoned by the Western powers at the Yalta Conference in February 1945. There it was decided that the pro-communist government established in Poland by Stalin should be recognized on condition that it broaden its ranks by the addition of democratic politicians from Poland and the West, and that it hold free elections. In practice, neither condition was fulfilled in any meaningful way.

Great Emigration (Polish: Wielka Emigracja)—After the failure of the Polish Insurrection of 1830–1831, between eight and nine thousand of those who had participated in it emigrated; because of its political and cultural significance, this group became known as the "Great Emigration." It was composed of those who were not included in the amnesty proclaimed by Tsar Nicholas I on 1 November 1831 and those who were unwilling to acquiesce in the new political order in Russian Poland. Its members were mostly officers and civil servants who had worked for the insurrectionary government, and they were predominantly noble in social origin. The largest part of them settled in France, mostly in the provinces because of the restrictions imposed by the French government. They were deeply divided politically between the more conservative followers of Prince Adam Jerzy Czartoryski (the Hotel Lambert group) and the more radical supporters of the Polish Democratic Society. Among leading Polish writers and artists who were associated with the Great Emigration were Frederic Chopin, Zygmunt Krasiński, Adam Mickiewicz, Cyprian Kamil Norwid, and Juliusz Słowacki.

Haller's Army A Polish military formation during the First World War, popularly named for its leader, General Józef Haller; incorporated into the Polish army after the recovery of independence. Notorious for the antisemitic excesses of its troops. See also **Second Polish Republic**.

Hasidism A mystically inclined movement of religious revival consisting of distinct groups with charismatic leadership. It arose in the borderlands of the Polish-Lithuanian Commonwealth in the second half of the eighteenth century and quickly spread through eastern

Europe. The Hasidim emphasized joy in the service of God, whose presence they sought everywhere. Though their opponents pronounced a series of bans against them beginning in 1772 (*misnagdim*, lit. opponents, i.e., of Hasidism), the movement soon became identified with religious orthodoxy.

Instytut Pamięci Narodowej Institute of National Memory—the official organ that took over the archives of the communist secret police. Its task is to make these files available to victims of persecution as well as to journalists and researchers investigating crimes committed by the totalitarian Nazi and Communist states against Polish citizens and others of Polish nationality; also charged with conducting research and educational programs on the subject.

January Insurrection The ill-fated insurrection against the tsarist monarchy, which began in January 1863. After its defeat, the Russian government embarked on a determined effort to Russify not only the **kresy** (q.v.) but also the **Congress Kingdom** (q.v.).

Jewish Agency The international, nongovernmental body, with its headquarters in Jerusalem, that was set up in accordance with the League of Nations Mandate for Palestine, to assist and encourage Jews to help in the development and settlement of "Erets Yisrael." After 1948, it relinquished many of its functions to the government of Israel but continued to be responsible for immigration, land settlement, youth work, and other activities financed by voluntary Jewish contributions from the Diaspora.

Judenrat (pl. Judenräte) The Jewish administrative councils established by the German authorities in the Jewish communities of occupied Europe. Judenräte were first established in occupied Poland according to the guidelines laid down by Reinhard Heydrich on 21 September 1939 and through an order promulgated by Hans Frank, head of the **General Government** (q.v.), on 18 November 1939. They were subsequently created in many other countries occupied by the Germans. They did not have a uniform structure—some held authority in one town only, while others administered all the Jewish communities in a district or even in a country. Their role has been bitterly disputed. Some, like Raul Hilberg and Hannah Arendt, have argued that they considerably facilitated the anti-Jewish genocide; others, like Isaiah Trunk, that their role was much more positive, and that they were able on many occasions to mitigate the harsh effects of Nazi rule and to strengthen the Jews' ability to withstand the deadly onslaught to which they were being subjected.

Karski, Jan Polish political envoy for the underground authorities in Nazi-occupied Poland who brought information about the extermination of the Jews to the West in 1942.

Katyn A town in Russia where, in 1940, the **NKVD** (q.v.) murdered several thousand imprisoned Polish reserve officers; a symbol of Soviet crimes against the Poles. The communist authorities banned the truth about this crime, maintaining the Soviet version that blamed the mass murder on the Germans.

Kielce pogrom The Kielce pogrom of 4 July 1946 is regarded as the most horrifying outbreak of anti-Jewish violence in early postwar Poland. It resulted in the murder of forty Jews and two non-Jews and injuries to more than one hundred Jews.

Kolyma A river in eastern Siberia near which the harshest penal camps in Stalin's Russia were concentrated.

Korczak, Janusz (Pen name of Henryk Goldszmit)—Polish physician, educator, and press and radio commentator of Jewish ethnic origins, a pioneer of contemporary educational practices; he voluntarily accompanied "his" children when they were deported during the liquidation of the Warsaw ghetto and died with them in August 1942 in the gas chamber at the Nazi death camp in Treblinka.

kresy (Lit. borderlands)—The eastern provinces of Poland between the two world wars. Today they form part of Lithuania, Belarus. and Ukraine.

Kultura (Paris) The most important postwar Polish émigré monthly, which published texts that could not be printed in communist Poland because of censorship. Published through 2000.

Milicja Obywatelska Citizen's Militia—the police in communist Poland.

Miracle on the Vistula The popular name given to the battle outside Warsaw in 1920.

Narodowe Siły Zbrojne (National Armed Forces—NSZ)—An underground armed formation created in November 1942 by the union of the Reptile Alliance (Związek Jaszczurczy), which was linked with one faction of the National Radical Camp (ONR-ABC) and that section of the Narodowa Organizacja Wojskowa (National Armed Forces—NOW), a force linked with the **Endecja** (q.v.), which had been unwilling to subordinate itself to the Home Army (**Armia Krajowa**, q.v.) command. By October 1943, the NSZ had approximately

70,000 members. In March 1944, a section of the NSZ agreed to subordinate itself to the Home Army command, but the former ONR members refused to do so. This latter group criticized what it regarded as the excessively conciliatory stance of the Home Army toward the Soviet Union and the Red Army, proclaiming openly the doctrine of "two enemies"—Nazi Germany and the USSR. In the later stages of the war, the NSZ command took the view that the Nazis were less of a danger than the Soviets and supported a strategy of not confronting the Germans and withdrawing their forces westward to keep them in being. A section of these, the Brygada Świętokrzyska, was eventually able to reach the U.S. zone in Germany. Another section fought in the Warsaw Uprising of 1944. The NSZ continued anti-Soviet partisan operations after the liberation of Poland. In 1945–1946, there were about ninety groups linked with the NSZ, numbering around 4,300 soldiers. Some of these were referred to as the **Narodowe Związek Wojskowy** (National Military Union—NZW) (q.v.). They attacked the militia and security forces, murdering communists and Jews and undertaking armed raids on cooperatives and state organizations to finance their activities. Their activities were finally suppressed in early 1947.

Narodowy Związek Wojskowy (National Military Union—NZW)— This was an underground military organization of the National Democrats (**Endecja**, q.v.). It was set up in late 1944 out of military units of the NSZ (National Armed Forces) and NOW (the National Military Organization).

NKVD The People's Bureau for Internal Affairs, the political police in Stalin's USSR.

November Insurrection The unsuccessful Polish insurrection against Tsar Nicholas, which began in November 1830 and was followed by the **Great Emigration** (q.v.).

Obóz Narodowo-Radykalny (National Radical Camp—ONR)—An extreme right-wing and fascist organization created in April 1934 as a result of a secession of young radicals from the National Party (**Endecja**, q.v.). Its armed squads attacked Jewish shops and socialist and trade union meetings, and it achieved a certain amount of influence among university students. It was declared illegal in July 1934 but continued to function, splitting in 1935 into ONR-ABC (known for the periodical of that name it issued) and what came to be known as the Ruch Narodowo-Radykalny (National Radical Movement— RNR), which was led by Bolesław Piasecki, and which attempted to come to terms with the Obóz Zjednoczenia Narodowego (Camp of

National Unity—OZON), the pro-government movement created in 1936. After the Nazi occupation, both groups continued to operate, the ONR-ABC creating a military force called the Reptile Alliance (Związek Jaszczurczy), and the RNR taking from 1941 onward the name Konfederacji Narodu (The Confederation of the Nation).

Obóz Wielkiej Polskiej The Camp for a Greater Poland. Extreme right-wing and pro-fascist organization founded in December 1926 by Roman Dmowski because of his dissatisfaction at the weak reaction of the National Democratic Party (**Endecja**, q.v.) to the coup of May 1926 that brought Józef Piłsudski back to power.

pan Polish for "lord," "master," or "noble." Also used today as the polite form of the second person singular.

partitions Between 1772 and 1795, Russia, Prussia, and Austria divided among themselves the territory of the Polish State (First Republic); "partitions" also refers to the parts of Poland under the control of each of these "partitioning powers" until the recovery of Polish independence in 1918.

Poles from Kazakhstan In the 1930s several tens of thousands of Poles, as a "national minority," were deported from the Soviet Ukraine to Kazakhstan; an even greater number were deported during 1939–1941 from the occupied eastern Polish territories.

Polish Commonwealth See **Commonwealth**.

Polish Underground State The common name during the Second World War for the clandestine army and civilian structures in Nazi-occupied Poland; the Underground State recognized the authority of the London **government-in-exile** (q.v.).

Polska Zjednoczona Partia Robotnicza PZPR—Polish United Workers Party, the ruling party (practically the only one) in communist Poland.

Recovered Territories The official propaganda term for former eastern territories of Germany that were given to Poland in 1945 on the strength of the agreement in Potsdam. The term referred to the fact that these territories had belonged to the Polish state in the Middle Ages. The majority German population there was resettled, mainly to West Germany, and its place taken by Polish settlers. Many of these settlers had themselves been expelled from the formerly Polish lands in the East that were awarded to the Soviet Union as part of the same postwar settlement, which was drawn up by the leaders of the USSR, U.S.A., and Great Britain without Polish participation.

Revisionist Zionists Followers of Vladimir Jabotinsky, who split off from the main international Zionist organization in the 1930s and wished to pursue a more aggressive strategy to establish a Jewish state in Palestine.

Rzeczpospolita See **Commonwealth**.

Sanacja From the Latin *sanatio*—healing, restoration. The popular name taken by the regime established by Józef Piłsudski after the coup of May 1926. It referred to Piłsudki's aim of restoring health to the political, social, and moral life of Poland.

SD Sicherheitsdienst, "security service" (political intelligence) of the Nazi Party (NSDAP—National Socialist German Workers' Party).

Second Polish Republic The Polish state from 1918 to 1939, reborn after the period of partitions.

selsoviet (Russian: "village council")—The lowest organ of facade local government in the Soviet state.

shtetl (Yiddish: "small town")—The characteristic small town of central and eastern Poland, Ukraine, Belarus, and Lithuania, with a substantial Jewish population that sometimes amounted to the majority of the inhabitants. These were originally "private" towns under the control of the **szlachta** (q.v.).

Sikorski-Maisky Agreement In September 1939, the Soviet Union, in an understanding with the Germans (the Ribbentrop-Molotov Pact), using the pretext of the disintegration of the Polish state, took over eastern Poland. After Hitler's attack on the USSR in 1941, the Polish supreme commander and prime minister in exile, General Władysław Sikorski, signed an agreement renewing diplomatic relations with the Soviet Union (signed by Ivan Maisky, the Soviet ambassador in England). In 1943, Stalin broke off relations with Poland after the **Katyn** (q.v.) massacre was revealed.

Sipo—Sicherheitspolizei Security Police, one of the political police formations of the Third Reich.

sledovatel (Russian: "investigator")—In the Soviet state, *sledovatele* carried out investigations and interrogations in political cases and regularly subjected the "suspects" to psychological and physical torture.

Sonderkommandos Special units of Jews who were forced by the Nazis to work in the death camps.

spetsposolek Russian term for a settlement of deportees sentenced by the Stalinist system to banishment in desolate places such as Kazakhstan and Siberia.

szlachta The Polish nobility. A very broad social stratum making up nearly 8 percent of the population in the eighteenth century. Its members ranged from the great magnates, like the Czartoryskis, Potockis, and Radziwiłłs, who dominated political and social life in the last century of the Polish-Lithuanian Commonwealth, to small landowners (the *szlachta zagrodowa*), and even to landless retainers of the great houses. What distinguished members of this group from the remainder of the population was their noble status and their right to participate in political life in the dietines, the Sejm, and the election of the king.

szmalcownicy Common, contemptuous term for persons who blackmailed Jews in hiding outside the ghetto in German-occupied Poland, using the threat of informing on them to the German authorities.

Umschlagplatz The place where, in the summer of 1942, the Warsaw Jews were assembled before deportation by rail to the Treblinka death camp.

Urząd Bezpieczeństwa UB—Security Office, the political police during the Stalinist epoch in Poland.

Volksdeutsch Popular term, derived from German, for a Polish inhabitant of the **General Government** (q.v.) who declared himself or herself to be ethnically German by signing the so-called German nationality list (*Deutsche Volksliste*).

Żegota Council for Aid to the Jews, a voluntary community organization in existence from 1942 to 1945 as part of the structure of the **Polish Underground State** (q.v.), concerned mainly with the material support and protection of Jews in hiding outside the ghettos.

Zomowcy Derived from the acronym ZOMO (Zmotoryzowana Obywatelska Milicja Obwodowa—Motorized Citizen's Militia Reserves), a riot police formation used to suppress popular demonstrations, especially during the martial law period; see also **1981**.

Związek Bojowników o Wolność i Demokracji ZBoWiD—Union of Fighters for Freedom and Democracy, the official and only permitted organization for World War II veterans in communist Poland.

Związek Walki Zbrojnej (Armed Combat Union)—A nationwide anti-Nazi underground organization set up in occupied Poland, in

November 1939, under the command of the Polish **government-in-exile** (q.v.) in London and transformed into the **Armia Krajowa** (q.v.) in February 1942.

żydek (pl. żydki) (Lit. little Jew)—A mildly derogatory word used by Poles of Jews.

Żydokomuna "Judeo-communism"—a long-standing antisemitic stereotype blaming the Jews for advocating, introducing, and running the communist system.

Żydowski Instytut Historyczny (Jewish Historical Institute)—a Warsaw-based organization, successor to a Jewish educational and research organization that held university-level official status before the war, conducting research on the history of the Jews in Poland.

INDEX